THE ECON SOLUTION

Special Note To Students

It is important to begin reading this text with one thing in mind: *This business course does not have to be difficult*. We have done everything possible to eliminate the problems that students encounter in a typical class. All the features in each chapter have been evaluated and recommended by instructors with years of teaching experience. In addition, business students were asked to critique each chapter component. Based on this feedback, the text includes the following features:

- *Learning objectives* appear at the beginning of each chapter.
- *Inside Business* is a chapter-opening case that highlights how successful companies do business on a day-to-day basis.
- *Margin notes* are used throughout the text to reinforce both learning objectives and key terms.
- *Boxed features* highlight how both employees and entrepreneurs can be successful.
- *Spotlight* features highlight interesting facts about business and society and other provide a real-world example of an important concept within a chapter.

Visually Engaging Textbook

Online Study Tools

Tear-Out Review Cards

Interactive Ebook

STUDENT RESOURCES:

- Math and Graphing Tutorial
- Flashcards
- Concept Videos
- Interactive Quizzing
- Additional Case Studies
- Aplia Problem Sets

INSTRUCTOR RESOURCES:

- NETA Testbank
- NETA PowerPoint Slides
- Image Library
- Instructor's Guide
- Instructor Prep Cards
- Aplia Assignments

Students sign in at **nelson.com/student**

Instructors sign in at **nelson.com/instructor**

"The online learning is great and the review cards in the back make test review easy!"

– Kyle McConnell, Student

NELSON

NELSON

ECON Macro, Canadian Edition

by William A. McEachern, Morris Altman, Mustapha Ibn-Boamah, Rob Moir, and Bridget O'Shaughnessy

VP, Product and Partnership Solutions:
Anne Williams

Publisher, Digital and Print Content:
Amie Plourde

Senior Marketing Manager:
Alexis Hood

Technical Reviewer:
Ross Meacher

Content Development Manager:
Maria Chu

Photo Researcher and Permissions Coordinator:
MRM Associates

Senior Production Project Manager:
Natalia Denesiuk Harris

Production Service:
MPS Limited

Copy Editor:
Wendy Thomas

Proofreader:
Nayyer Shamsi

Indexer:
Chris Banta

Design Director:
Ken Phipps

Managing Designer:
Franca Amore

Interior Design:
Peter Papayanakis

Cover Design:
Courtney Hellam, Trinh Truong

Cover Image:
LEONELLO CALVETTI/Science Photo Library/Getty Royalty Free

Compositor:
MPS Limited

Library and Archives Canada Cataloguing in Publication Data

McEachern, William A., author
  ECON macro / William A. McEachern, Morris Altman, Mustapha Ibn-Boamah, Rob Moir, Bridget O'Shaughnessy.

Includes index.
ISBN 978-0-17-650279-9 (paperback)

  1. Macroeconomics—Textbooks.
I. Altman, Morris, author
II. Ibn-Boamah, Mustapha, author III. Moir, Rob, author
IV. O'Shaughnessy, Bridget, author V. Title. VI. Title: ECON macroeconomics.

HB172.5.M3975 2015   339
C2015-906447-3

ISBN-13: 978-0-17-650279-9
ISBN-10: 0-17-650279-3

Brief Contents

To access online chapter, appendixes, and case studies, go to http://www.nelson.com/econmacro1e.

Bank notes images used with the permission of the Bank of Canada.

© Jim Barber/Shutterstock.com

Contents

3 Economic Decision Makers 37

4 Demand, Supply, and Markets 54

© David R. Frazier Photolibrary, Inc./Alamy

Part 2
FUNDAMENTALS
OF MACROECONOMICS 79

6 Tracking the Canadian Economy 96

Stephen C. Host/The Canadian Press

7 Unemployment and Inflation 113

8 Productivity and Growth 132

9 Aggregate Expenditure and Aggregate Demand 148

10 Aggregate Supply 168

Masterfile RF

© Brand X Pictures/Jupiterimages/Getty Images

Part 3
FISCAL AND MONETARY POLICY 183

11 Fiscal Policy 183

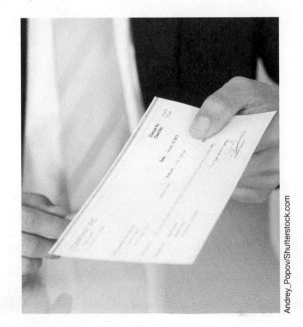

Andrey_Popov/Shutterstock.com

12 Money and the Financial System 201

13 Banking and the Money Supply 215

14 Monetary Theory and Policy in an Open Economy 230

Part 4
INTERNATIONAL ECONOMICS 261

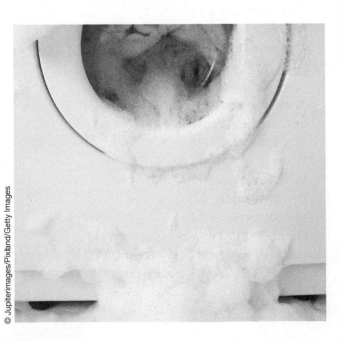

© Jupiterimages/Pixland/Getty Images

© payphoto/iStock.com; Bank notes images used with the permission of the Bank of Canada.

ONLINE

To access online chapters, go to http://www.nelson
.com/econmacro1e.

17 International Trade 1

The Canadian Press Images–Mario Beauregard

18 Economic Development 1

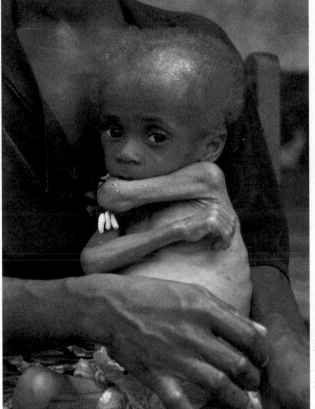

© Jenny Matthews/Alamy

ONLINE

Case Studies

1

The Art and Science of Economic Analysis

LEARNING OUTCOMES

LO1	Explain the economic problem of scarce resources and unlimited wants
LO2	Describe the forces that shape economic choices
LO3	Explain how economists use the scientific method
LO4	Identify some pitfalls of economic analysis
LO5	Describe several reasons to study economics

> ## In what way are people who pound on vending machines relying on theory?

Why are comic-strip and TV characters like Foxtrot, the Simpsons, and the Family Guy missing a finger on each hand? Why do the kids on South Park have hands that look like mittens? And where is Dilbert's mouth? In what way are people who pound on vending machines relying on theory? Why is a good theory like a California Closet? What's the big idea with economics? These and other questions are answered in this chapter, which introduces the art and science of economic analysis.

You have been reading and hearing about economic issues for years—unemployment, inflation, poverty, recessions, federal deficits, tuition, airfares, wage rates, stock prices, computer prices, gas prices. When explanations of such issues go into any depth, your eyes may glaze over and you may tune out, the same way you do when a weather forecaster tries to provide an in-depth analysis of high-pressure fronts colliding with moisture carried in from the coast.

What many people fail to realize is that economics is livelier than the dry accounts offered by the news media. Economics is about making choices, and you make economic choices every day—choices about whether to get a part-time job or focus on your studies, live in a dorm or off campus, take a course in accounting or one in history, get married or stay single, pack a lunch or buy a sandwich. You already know much more about economics than you realize. You bring to the subject a rich personal experience, an experience that will be tapped throughout the book to reinforce your understanding of the basic ideas.

LO 1 The Economic Problem: Scarce Resources, Unlimited Wants

Would you like a new car, a nicer home, better meals, more free time, a more interesting social life, more spending money, more leisure, more sleep? Who wouldn't? But even if you can satisfy some of these desires, others keep popping up. *The problem is that, although your wants, or desires, are virtually unlimited, the resources available to satisfy these wants are scarce.* A resource is *scarce* when it is not freely available—that is, when its price exceeds zero. Because resources are scarce, you must choose from among your many wants, and whenever you choose, you must forgo satisfying some other wants. The problem of scarce resources but unlimited wants exists to a greater or lesser extent for each of the 7 billion people on earth. Everybody—cab driver, farmer, brain surgeon, dictator, shepherd, student, politician—faces the problem. For example, a cab driver uses time and other scarce resources, such as the taxi, knowledge of the city, driving skills, and gasoline, to earn income. That income, in turn, buys housing, groceries, clothing, trips to Disney World, and thousands of other goods and services that help satisfy some of the driver's unlimited wants. **Economics** examines how people use their scarce resources to satisfy their unlimited wants. A broader definition put forth in 1890 by the father of modern economic theory, British economist Alfred Marshall, of Cambridge University, is this: "Political Economy or Economics is a study of mankind in the ordinary business of life. It examines that part of individual and social action which is most closely connected with the attainment and with the use of material requisites of well-being." Let's pick apart the scarcity-related definition, beginning with resources, then goods and services, and finally focus on the heart of the matter—economic choice, which arises from scarcity.

Resources

Resources are the inputs, or factors of production, used to produce the goods and services that people want. *Goods and services are scarce because resources are scarce.* Resources sort into four broad categories: labour, capital, natural resources, and entrepreneurial ability. **Labour** is human effort, both physical and mental. Labour includes the effort of the cab driver and the brain surgeon. Labour itself comes from a more fundamental resource: *time*. Without time we can accomplish nothing. We allocate our time to alternative uses: we can *sell* our time as labour, or we can *spend* our time doing other things, like sleeping, eating, studying, playing sports, going online, attending class, watching TV, or just relaxing with friends. But labour time also has a very important additional component, which is how hard and how smart we work or how hard and smart we play and engage in leisure activities.

Capital includes all human creations used to produce goods and services. Economists often distinguish between physical capital and human capital. *Physical capital* consists of factories, tools, machines, computers, buildings, airports, highways, and other human creations used to produce goods and services. Physical capital includes the cab driver's taxi, the surgeon's scalpel, and the building where your economics class meets (or, if you are taking

© imac/Alamy

this course online, your computer and online connectors). *Human capital* consists of the knowledge and skill people acquire to increase their productivity, such as the cab driver's knowledge of city streets, the surgeon's knowledge of human anatomy, and your knowledge of economics.

Natural resources include all *gifts of nature*, such as bodies of water, trees, oil reserves, minerals, even animals. Natural resources can be divided into renewable resources and exhaustible resources. A *renewable resource* can be drawn on indefinitely if used conservatively. Thus, timber is a renewable resource if felled trees are replaced to regrow a steady supply. The air and rivers are renewable resources if they are allowed sufficient time to cleanse themselves of any pollutants. More generally, biological resources like fish, game, livestock, forests, rivers, groundwater, grasslands, and soil are renewable if managed properly. An *exhaustible resource*—such as oil or coal—does not renew itself and so is available in a limited amount. Once burned, each barrel of oil or tonne of coal is gone forever. The world's oil and coal deposits are exhaustible.

A special kind of human skill called **entrepreneurial ability** is the talent required to dream up a new product or find a better way to produce an existing one. This special skill comes from an entrepreneur. An **entrepreneur** is a profit-seeking decision maker who starts with an idea, organizes an enterprise to bring that idea to life, and then assumes the risk of operation. An entrepreneur pays resource owners for the opportunity to employ their resources in the firm. Every firm in the world today, such as Ford, Microsoft, Google, and Tim Hortons, began as an idea in the mind of an entrepreneur.

Resource owners are paid **wages** for their labour, **interest** for the use of their capital, and **rent** for the use of their natural resources. Entrepreneurial ability is rewarded by **profit**, which equals the *revenue* from items sold minus the *cost* of the resources employed to make those items. The word *profit* comes from the

economics the study of how people use their scarce resources to satisfy their unlimited wants

resources the inputs, or factors of production, used to produce the goods and services that people want; resources consist of labour, capital, natural resources, and entrepreneurial ability

labour the time and physical and mental effort used to produce goods and services

capital the buildings, equipment, and human skills used to produce goods and services

natural resources all gifts of nature used to produce goods and services; includes renewable and exhaustible resources

entrepreneurial ability the imagination required to develop a new product or process, the skill needed to organize production, and the willingness to take the risk of profit or loss

entrepreneur a profit-seeking decision maker who starts with an idea, organizes an enterprise to bring that idea to life, and assumes the risk of the operation

wages payment to resource owners for their labour

interest payment to resource owners for the use of their capital

rent payment to resource owners for the use of their natural resources

profit reward for entrepreneurial ability; sales revenue minus resource cost

Latin *proficere*, which means "to benefit." The entrepreneur benefits from what's left over after paying other resource suppliers. Sometimes the entrepreneur suffers a loss. Resource earnings are usually based on the *time* these resources are employed. Resource payments therefore have a time dimension, as in a wage of $10 *per hour,* interest of 6 percent *per year,* rent of $600 *per month,* or profit of $10,000 *per year.*

There's no such thing as a free napkin.

© Randy Faris/Corbis

Goods and Services

Resources are combined in a variety of ways to produce goods and services. A farmer, a tractor, 50 hectares of land, seeds, and fertilizer combine to grow the good: corn. One hundred musicians, musical instruments, chairs, a conductor, a musical score, and a music hall combine to produce the service: Beethoven's *Fifth Symphony*. Corn is a **good** because it is something you can see, feel, and touch; it requires scarce resources to produce; and it satisfies human wants. The book you are now holding, the chair you are sitting in, the clothes you are wearing, and your next meal are all goods. The performance of the *Fifth Symphony* is a **service** because it is intangible, yet it uses scarce resources to satisfy human wants. Lectures, movies, concerts, phone service, broadband connections, yoga lessons, dry cleaning, and haircuts are all services.

Because goods and services are produced using scarce resources, they are themselves scarce. *A good or service is scarce if the amount people desire exceeds the amount available at a zero price.* Because we cannot have all the goods and services we would like, we must continually choose among them. We must choose among more pleasant living quarters, better meals, nicer clothes, more reliable transportation, faster computers, and so on. Making choices in a world of **scarcity** means we must pass up some goods and services. But not everything is scarce. In fact some things we would prefer to have less of. For example, we would prefer to have less garbage, less spam email, and less pollution. Things we want none of even at a zero price are called *bads,* the opposite of goods.

A few goods and services seem *free* because the amount available at a zero price exceeds the amount people want. For example, air and seawater often seem free because we can breathe all the air we want and have all the seawater we can haul away. Yet, despite the old saying "The best things in life are free," most goods and services are scarce, not free, and even those that appear to be free come with strings attached. For example, clean air and clean seawater have become scarce. *Goods and services that are truly free are not the subject matter of economics. Without scarcity, there would be no economic problem and no need for prices.*

Sometimes we mistakenly think of certain goods as free because they involve no apparent cost to us. Napkins seem to be free at Tim Hortons. Nobody stops you from taking a fistful. Supplying napkins, however, costs the company millions each year and prices reflect that cost. Some restaurants make special efforts to keep napkin use down—such as packing them tightly into the dispenser or making you ask for them.

You may have heard the expression "There is no such thing as a free lunch." There is no free lunch because all goods and services involve a cost to someone. The lunch may seem free to you, but it draws scarce resources away from the production of other goods and services, and whoever provides a free lunch often expects something in return. A Russian proverb makes a similar point but with a bit more bite: "The only place you find free cheese is in a mousetrap." Albert Einstein once observed, "Sometimes one pays the most for things one gets for nothing."

Economic Decision Makers

There are four types of decision makers in the economy: households, firms, governments, and the rest of the world. Their interaction determines how an economy's resources are allocated. *Households* play the starring role. As consumers, households demand the goods and services produced. As resource owners, households supply labour, capital, natural resources, and entrepreneurial ability to firms, governments, and the rest of the world. *Firms, governments,* and *the rest of the world* demand the resources that households supply and then use these resources to supply the goods and services that households demand. The rest of the world includes foreign households, foreign firms, and foreign governments that supply resources and products to Canadian markets and demand resources and products from Canadian markets.

Markets are the means by which buyers and sellers carry out exchange. By bringing together the two sides of exchange, markets determine price, quantity, and quality. Markets are often physical places, such as supermarkets, department stores, shopping malls, or yard sales. But markets also include other mechanisms by which buyers and sellers communicate, such as classified ads, radio and television ads, telephones, bulletin boards, online sites, and face-to-face bargaining. These market mechanisms provide information about the quantity, quality, and price of products offered for sale. Goods and services are bought and sold in **product markets**. Resources are bought and sold in **resource markets**. The most important resource market is the labour, or job, market. Think about your own experience looking for a job, and you'll already have some idea of that market.

A Simple Circular-Flow Model

Now that you have learned a bit about economic decision makers, consider how they interact. Such a picture is conveyed by the **circular-flow model**, which describes the flow of resources, products, income, and revenue among economic decision makers. The simple circular-flow model focuses on the primary interaction in a market economy—that between households and firms. Exhibit 1 shows households on the left and firms on the right; please take a look.

Households supply labour, capital, natural resources, and entrepreneurial ability to firms through resource markets, shown in the lower portion of the exhibit. In return, households demand goods and services from firms through product markets, shown on the upper portion of the exhibit. Viewed from the business end, firms demand labour, capital, natural resources, and entrepreneurial ability from households through resource markets, and firms supply goods and services to households through product markets.

The flows of resources and products are supported by the flows of income and expenditure—that is, by the flow of money. So let's add money. The demand and supply of resources come together in resource

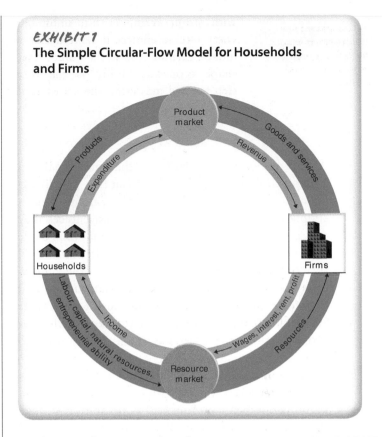

EXHIBIT 1

The Simple Circular-Flow Model for Households and Firms

markets to determine what firms pay for resources. These resource prices—wages, interest, rent, and profit—flow as *income* to households. The demand and supply of products come together in product markets to determine what households pay for goods and services. These product prices of goods and services flow as *revenue* to firms. Resources and products flow in one direction—in this case, counterclockwise—and the corresponding payments flow in the other direction—clockwise. What goes around comes around. Take a little time now to trace the logic of the circular flows.

market a set of arrangements by which buyers and sellers carry out exchange at mutually agreeable terms

product market a market in which a good or service is bought and sold

resource market a market in which a resource is bought and sold

circular-flow model a diagram that traces the flow of resources, products, income, and revenue among economic decision makers

LO 2 What Forces Shape Our Economic Decisions?

An economy results as millions of individuals attempt to satisfy their unlimited wants. Because their choices lie at the heart of the economic problem—coping with scarce resources but unlimited wants—these choices deserve a closer look. Learning about the forces that shape economic choice is the first step toward mastering the art of economic analysis.

Rational Self-Interest

A key economic assumption is that individuals, in making choices, rationally select what they perceive to be in their best interests. By *rational*, economists mean simply that people try to make the best choices they can, given the available time and information. People may not know with certainty which alternative will turn out to be the best. They simply select the alternatives they *expect* will yield the most satisfaction and happiness. In general, **rational self-interest** means that each individual tries to maximize the expected benefit achieved with a given cost or to minimize the expected cost of achieving a given benefit.

Rational self-interest should not be viewed as blind materialism, pure selfishness, or greed. We all know people who are tuned to radio station WIIFM (What's In It For Me?). For most of us, however, self-interest often includes the welfare of our family, our friends, and perhaps the poor of the world. Even so, our concern for others is influenced by the personal cost of that concern. We may readily volunteer to drive a friend to the airport on Saturday afternoon but are less likely to offer a ride if the plane leaves at 6:00 A.M. When we donate clothes to an organization such as Goodwill Industries, they are more likely to be old and worn than brand new. People tend to give more to charities when their contributions are tax deductible and when contributions garner social approval in the community (as when contributor names are made public or when big donors get buildings named after them). TV stations are more likely to donate airtime for public-service announcements during the dead of night than during prime time (in

fact, 80 percent of such announcements air between 11:00 P.M. and 7:00 A.M.[1]). In Asia some people burn money to soothe the passage of a departed loved one. But they burn fake money, not real money. The notion of self-interest does not rule out concern for others; it simply means that concern for others is influenced by the same economic forces that affect other economic choices. *The lower the personal cost of helping others, the more help we offer.* We don't like to think that our behaviour reflects our self-interest, but it often does. As Jane Austen wrote in *Pride and Prejudice*, "I have been a selfish being all my life, in practice, though not in principle."

Choice Requires Time and Information

Rational choice takes time and requires information, but time and information are scarce and therefore valuable. If you have any doubts about the time and information needed to make choices, talk to someone who recently purchased a home, a car, or a personal computer. Talk to a corporate official trying to decide whether to introduce a new product, sell online, build a new factory, or buy another firm. Or think back to your own experience in choosing a university. You probably talked to friends, relatives, teachers, and guidance counsellors. You likely used school calendars, university guides, and websites. You may have visited some campuses to meet the admissions staff and anyone else willing to talk. The decision took time and money, and it probably involved aggravation and anxiety.

Because information is costly to acquire, we are often willing to pay others to gather and digest it for us. University guidebooks, stock analysts, real estate agents, career counsellors, restaurant critics, movie reviewers,

© Yuliyan Velchev/Shutterstock

---

[1] Sally Goll Beatty, "Media and Agencies Brawl Over Do-Good Advertising," *Wall Street Journal*, 29 September 1997.

specialized websites, and *Consumer Reports* magazine attest to our willingness to pay for information that improves our choices. As we'll see next, *rational decision makers continue to acquire information as long as the additional benefit expected from that information exceeds the additional cost of gathering it.*

Economic Analysis Is Often Marginal Analysis

Economic choice usually involves some adjustment to the existing situation, or status quo. Amazon.com must decide whether to add an additional line of products. The school superintendent must decide whether to hire another teacher. Your favourite jeans are on sale, and you must decide whether to buy another pair. You are wondering whether to carry an extra course next term. You just finished lunch and are deciding whether to order dessert.

Economic choice is often based on a comparison of the *expected marginal benefit* and the *expected marginal cost* of the action under consideration. **Marginal** means incremental, additional, or extra. Marginal refers to a change in an economic variable, a change in the status quo. *A rational decision maker changes the status quo if the expected marginal benefit from the change exceeds the expected marginal cost.* For example, Amazon.com compares the marginal benefit expected from adding a new line of products (the additional sales revenue) with the marginal cost (the additional cost of the resources required). Likewise, you compare the marginal benefit you expect from eating dessert (the additional pleasure or satisfaction) with its marginal cost (the additional money, time, and calories).

Typically, the change under consideration is small, but a marginal choice can involve a major economic adjustment, as in the decision to quit school and find a job. For a firm, a marginal choice might mean building a plant in Mexico or even filing for bankruptcy. By focusing on the effect of a marginal adjustment to the status quo, the economist is able to cut the analysis of economic choice down to a manageable size. Rather than confront a bewildering economic reality head-on, the economist begins with a marginal choice to see how this choice affects a particular market and shapes the economic system as a whole. Incidentally, to the noneconomist, *marginal* usually means relatively inferior, as in "a movie of marginal quality." Forget that meaning for this course and instead think of *marginal* as meaning incremental, additional, or extra.

Microeconomics and Macroeconomics

Although you have made thousands of economic choices, you probably seldom think about your own economic behaviour. For example, why are you reading this book right now rather than doing something else? **Microeconomics** is the study of your economic behaviour and the economic behaviour of others who make choices about such matters as how much to study and how much to party, how much to borrow and how much to save, what to buy and what to sell. Microeconomics examines individual economic choices and how markets coordinate the choices of various decision makers. Microeconomics explains how price and quantity are determined in individual markets—the market for breakfast cereal, sports equipment, or used cars, for instance.

You have probably given little thought to what influences your own economic choices. You have likely given even less thought to how your choices link up with those made by millions of others in the Canadian economy to determine economy-wide measures such as total production, employment, and economic growth. **Macroeconomics** studies the performance of the economy as a whole. Whereas microeconomics studies the individual pieces of the economic puzzle, as reflected in particular markets, macroeconomics puts all the pieces together to focus on the big picture.

The national economy usually grows over time, but along the way it sometimes stumbles, experiencing *recessions* in economic activity, as reflected by a decline in production, employment, and other aggregate measures. **Economic fluctuations** are the rise and fall of economic activity relative to the long-term growth trend of the economy. These fluctuations, or *business cycles,* vary in length and intensity, but they usually involve the entire nation and often other nations too. For example, the Canadian economy now produces more than five times as much as it did in 1960 (this is the growth trend), despite experiencing four recessions since then.

To Review: The art of economic analysis focuses on how people use their scarce resources in an attempt to satisfy their unlimited wants. Rational self-interest guides individual choice. Choice requires

marginal incremental, additional, or extra; used to describe a change in an economic variable

microeconomics the study of the economic behaviour in particular markets, such as that for computers or skilled and unskilled labour

macroeconomics the study of the economic behaviour of entire economies, as measured, for example, by total production and employment

economic fluctuations the rise and fall of economic activity relative to the long-term growth trend of the economy; also called business cycles

Siri Stafford/Getty Images

A good theory can act like a closet organizer for your mind, helping you understand a messy and confusing world.

economic theory (economic model) a simplification of reality used to make predictions about cause and effect in the real world

time and information and involves a comparison of the expected marginal benefit and the expected marginal cost of alternative actions. Microeconomics looks at the individual pieces of the economic puzzle; macroeconomics fits the pieces together to form the big picture.

LO 3 Economics and the Scientific Method

Economists use scientific analysis to develop theories, or models, that help explain economic behaviour. An **economic theory**, or **economic model**, is a simplification of economic reality that *is used to make predictions about the real world*. A theory, or model, such as the circular-flow model, captures the important elements of the problem under study but need not spell out every detail and interrelation. In fact, adding more details may make a theory more unwieldy and, therefore, less useful. For example, a wristwatch is a model that tells time, but a watch festooned with extra features is harder to read at a glance and is therefore less useful as a time-telling model. The world is so complex that we must simplify it to make sense of things. Store mannequins simplify the human form (some even lack arms and heads). Comic strips and cartoons simplify characters—leaving out fingers or a mouth, for instance. You might think of economic theory as a stripped-down, or streamlined, version of economic reality.

A good theory helps us understand a messy and confusing world. Lacking a theory of how things work, our thinking can become cluttered with facts, one piled on another, as in a messy closet. You could think of a good theory as a closet organizer for the mind. A good theory offers a helpful guide to sorting, saving, and understanding information.

The Role of Theory

Most people don't understand the role of theory. Perhaps you have heard "Oh, that's fine in theory, but in practice it's another matter." The implication is that the theory in question provides little aid in practical matters. People who say this fail to realize that they are merely substituting their own theory for a theory they either do not believe or do not understand. They are really saying, "I have my own theory that works better."

All of us employ theories, however poorly defined or understood. Someone who pounds on the Pepsi machine that just ate a quarter has a crude theory about how that machine works. One version of that theory might be "The quarter drops through a series of *whatchamacallits*, but sometimes it gets stuck. *If* I pound on the machine, *then* I can free up the quarter and send it on its way." Evidently, this theory is widespread enough that people continue to pound on machines that fail to perform (a real problem for the vending machine industry and one reason newer machines are fronted with glass). Yet if you were to ask these mad pounders to explain their "theory" about how the machine works, they would look at you as if you were crazy.

The Scientific Method

To study economic problems, economists employ a process of theoretical investigation called the *scientific method,* which consists of four steps, as outlined in Exhibit 2.

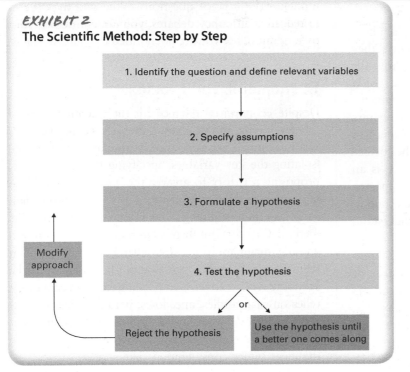

EXHIBIT 2
The Scientific Method: Step by Step

1. Identify the question and define relevant variables

↓

2. Specify assumptions

↓

3. Formulate a hypothesis

↓

4. Test the hypothesis

or

Reject the hypothesis → Modify approach

Use the hypothesis until a better one comes along

variables such as consumer income, the average temperature, or the price of Coke.

We also make assumptions about how people behave; these are called **behavioural assumptions**. The primary behavioural assumption is rational self-interest. Earlier we assumed that each decision maker pursues self-interest rationally and makes choices accordingly. Rationality implies that each consumer buys the products expected to maximize his or her level of satisfaction. Rationality also implies that each firm supplies the products expected to maximize the firm's profit. These kinds of assumptions are called behavioural assumptions because they specify how we expect economic decision makers to behave—what makes them tick, so to speak.

Step Three: Formulate a Hypothesis The third step in the scientific method is to formulate a **hypothesis**, which is a theory about how key variables relate to each other. For example, one hypothesis holds that if the price of Pepsi goes up, other things constant, then the quantity purchased declines. The hypothesis becomes a prediction of what happens to the quantity purchased if the price increases. *The purpose of this hypothesis, like that of any theory, is to help make predictions about cause and effect in the real world.*

Step One: Identify the Question and Define Relevant Variables The scientific method begins with curiosity: someone wants to answer a question. Thus, the first step is to identify the economic question and define the variables relevant to a solution. For example, the question might be "What is the relationship between the price of Pepsi and the quantity of Pepsi purchased?" In this case, the relevant variables are price and quantity. A **variable** is a measure that can take on different values at different times. The variables of concern become the elements of the theory, so they must be selected with care.

Step Two: Specify Assumptions The second step is to specify the assumptions under which the theory is to apply. One major category of assumptions is the **other-things-constant assumption**—in Latin, the *ceteris paribus* assumption. The idea is to identify the variables of interest and then focus exclusively on the relationships among them, assuming that nothing else important changes—that other things remain constant. Again, suppose we are interested in how the price of Pepsi influences the amount purchased. To isolate the relation between these two variables, we assume that there are no changes in other relevant

Step Four: Test the Hypothesis In the fourth step, by comparing its predictions with evidence, we test the validity of a hypothesis. To test a hypothesis, we must focus on the variables in question, while carefully controlling for other effects assumed not to change. The test leads us either to (1) reject the hypothesis, or theory, if it predicts worse than the best alternative theory or (2) use the hypothesis, or theory, until a better one comes along. If we reject the hypothesis, we can go back and modify our approach in light of the results. Please spend a moment now reviewing the steps of the scientific method in Exhibit 2.

variable a measure, such as price or quantity, that can take on different values at different times

other-things-constant assumption the assumption, when focusing on the relation among key economic variables, that other variables remain unchanged; in Latin, *ceteris paribus*

behavioural assumption an assumption that describes the expected behaviour of economic decision makers, what motivates them

hypothesis a theory about how key variables relate

Normative Versus Positive

Economists usually try to explain how the economy works. Sometimes they concern themselves not with how the economy *does* work but how it *should* work. Compare these two statements: "The Canadian unemployment rate is 6.9 percent." and "The Canadian unemployment rate should be lower." The first, called a **positive economic statement**, is an assertion about economic reality that can be supported or rejected by reference to the facts. Positive economics, like physics or biology, attempts to understand the world around us. The second, called a **normative economic statement**, reflects an opinion. And an opinion is merely that—it cannot be shown to be true or false by reference to the facts. Positive statements concern what is; normative statements concern what, in someone's opinion, *should be*. Positive statements need not necessarily be true, but they must be subject to verification or refutation by reference to the facts. Theories are expressed as positive statements such as "If the price of Pepsi increases, then the quantity demanded decreases."

Most of the disagreement among economists involves normative debates—such as the appropriate role of government—rather than statements of positive analysis. To be sure, many theoretical issues remain unresolved, but economists generally agree on most fundamental theoretical principles—that is, about positive economic analysis. For example, in a survey of 464 U.S. economists, only 6.5 percent disagreed with the statement "A ceiling on rents reduces the quantity and quality of housing available." This happens to be a positive statement because it can be tested against the evidence and shown to be consistent or inconsistent with the evidence. In contrast, there was much less agreement on normative statements such as "The distribution of income in the United States should be more equal." Half the economists surveyed "generally agreed," a quarter "generally disagreed," and a quarter "agreed with provisos."[2]

Normative statements, or value judgments, have a place in a policy debate such as the proper role of government, provided that statements of opinion are distinguished from statements of fact. Opinions often influence the type of questions asked and hypotheses tested. In such policy debates, you are entitled to your own opinion, but you are not entitled to your own facts.

Economists Tell Stories

Despite economists' reliance on the scientific method for developing and evaluating theories, economic analysis is as much art as science. Formulating a question, isolating the key variables, specifying the assumptions, proposing a theory to answer the question, and devising a way to test the predictions all involve more than simply an understanding of economics and the scientific method. Carrying out these steps requires good intuition and the imagination of a storyteller. Economists explain their theories by telling stories about how they think the economy works. To tell a compelling story, an economist relies on case studies, anecdotes, parables, the personal experience of the listener, and supporting data. Throughout this book, you'll hear stories that bring you closer to the ideas under consideration. The stories, such as the one about the Pepsi machine, breathe life into economic theory and help you personalize abstract ideas.

Predicting Average Behaviour

The goal of an economic theory is to predict the impact of an economic event on economic choices and, in turn, the effect of these choices on particular markets or on the economy as a whole. Does this mean that economists try to predict the behaviour of particular consumers or producers? Not necessarily, because a specific individual may behave in an unpredictable way. But the unpredictable actions of numerous individuals often cancel one another out, so the *average behaviour* of groups can be predicted more accurately. For example, if the federal government cuts personal income taxes, certain households may decide to save the entire tax cut. On average, however, household spending increases. Likewise, if Pizza Pizza cuts the price of large pizzas, the manager can better predict how much sales will increase than how a specific customer coming through the door will respond. *The random actions of individuals tend to offset one another, so the average behaviour of a large group can be predicted more accurately than the behaviour of a particular individual.* Consequently, economists tend to focus on the average, or typical, behaviour of people in groups—for example, as average taxpayers or average large pizza consumers—rather than on the behaviour of a specific individual.

[2] Richard M. Alston et al., "Is There a Consensus Among Economists in the 1990s?" *American Economic Review,* 82 (May 1992): 203–209, Table 1.

LO 4   Some Pitfalls of Faulty Economic Analysis

Economic analysis, like other forms of scientific inquiry, is subject to common mistakes in reasoning that can lead to faulty conclusions. Here are three sources of confusion.

The Fallacy That Association Is Causation

In the past two decades, the number of physicians specializing in cancer treatment increased sharply. At the same time, the incidence of some cancers increased. Can we conclude that physicians cause cancer? No. To assume that event A caused event B simply because the two are associated in time is to commit the **association-is-causation fallacy**, a common error. The fact that one event precedes another or that the two events occur simultaneously does not necessarily mean that one causes the other. Remember: association is not necessarily causation.

The Fallacy of Composition

Perhaps you have been to a rock concert where everyone stands to get a better view. At some concerts, most people even stand on their chairs. But even standing on chairs does not improve the view if others do the same, unless you are quite tall. Likewise, arriving early to buy game tickets does not work if many have the same idea. These are examples of the **fallacy of composition**, which is an erroneous belief that what is true for the individual, or the part, is also true for the group, or the whole.

The Mistake of Ignoring the Secondary Effects

In many cities, public officials have imposed rent controls on apartments. The primary effect of this policy, the effect policymakers focus on, is to keep rents from rising. Over time, however, fewer new apartments get built because renting them becomes less profitable. Moreover, existing rental units deteriorate because owners have plenty of customers anyway. Thus, the quantity and quality of housing may decline as a result of what appears to be a reasonable measure to keep rents from rising. The mistake was to ignore the **secondary effects**, or the unintended consequences, of the policy. Economic actions have secondary effects that often turn out to be more important than the primary effects. Secondary effects may develop more slowly and may not be immediately obvious, but good economic analysis tries to anticipate them and take them into account.

> **association-is-causation fallacy** the incorrect idea that if two variables are associated in time, one must necessarily cause the other
>
> **fallacy of composition** the incorrect belief that what is true for the individual, or part, must necessarily be true for the group, or the whole
>
> **secondary effects** unintended consequences of economic actions that may develop slowly over time as people react to events

LO 5   Why Study Economics?

If economists are so smart, why aren't they rich? Well, some are, earning over $25,000 per appearance on the lecture circuit. Others top $2 million a year as consultants and expert witnesses.[3] Economists have been appointed to senior civil service positions within the government, including finance, human resources and skills development, environment, and international trade, and to head the Bank of Canada. Economics is the only social science and the only business discipline for which the prestigious Nobel Prize is awarded,[4] and pronouncements by economists are reported in the media daily. *The Economist,* a widely respected news weekly from London, has argued that economic ideas

[3] As reported by George Anders, "An Economist's Courtroom Bonanza," *Wall Street Journal,* 19 March 2007.
[4] The prize awarded is technically "a category of the Nobel Prize" and is actually named the Sveriges Riksbank Prize in Economic Sciences in Memory of Alfred Nobel.

James Whitaker/Getty Images

have influenced policy "to a degree that would make other social scientists drool."[5]

The economics profession thrives because its models usually do a better job of making economic sense out of a confusing world than do alternative approaches. Most economists are not wealthy, nor is personal wealth the goal of the discipline. Many individuals become economists because economics provides tools to help better understand and even improve our complex and often confusing world. In a similar

vein, not all doctors are healthy (some even smoke), not all carpenters live in perfectly built homes, not all marriage counsellors are happily married, and not all child psychologists have well-adjusted children. Still, those who study economics do reap financial rewards.

Among university graduates, all kinds of factors affect earnings, such as general ability, effort, occupation, university attended, university major, and highest degree earned. The Canadian Labour Market and Skills Researcher Network looked at the average wages of undergraduate degree holders in 50 different university majors during 2005. The top 22 majors measured by average hourly wage are shown in Exhibit 3. The

[5] "The Puzzling Failure of Economics," *Economist*, 23 August 1997, p. 11.

EXHIBIT 3
Average Annual Pay and Unemployment Rates by University Major

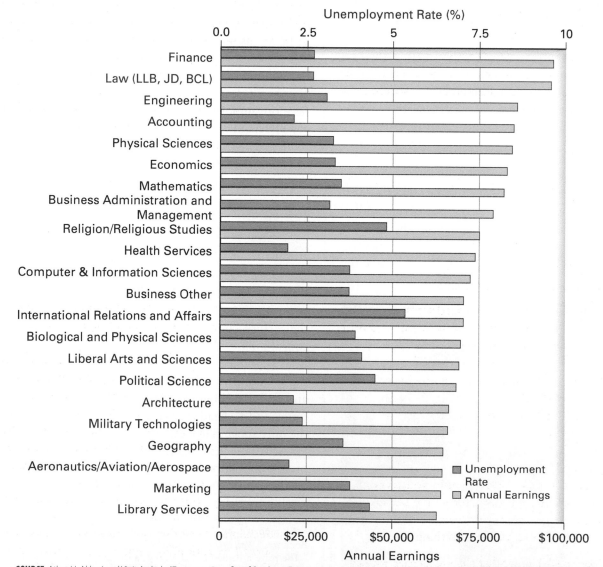

SOURCE: Ather H. Akbari and Yigit Aydede, "Economic Benefits of Studying Economics in Canada: A Comparison of Wages of Economics Majors with those in Other Disciplines Circa 2005," *Canadian Labour Market and Skills Researcher Network Working Paper No. 109*, February 2013.

table includes full-time workers with a postsecondary degree earned in Canada who are between the ages of 25 and 55, as reported in the 2006 Census. Note that economics ranks sixth highest, with annual average earnings of more than $83,000.

The red bars show the unemployment rates for each of the majors with the highest hourly wage. The university major with the lowest unemployment rate, at 1.94 percent, is health services, followed closely by architecture and accounting. The national unemployment rate at the time was 6.8 percent—all of the top 22 fields had unemployment rates lower than the average. Note that the majors ranked toward the top of the list, both in salary and unemployment rates, tend to be more quantitative and analytical. The selection of a relatively more challenging major such as economics may send a favourable signal to future employers.

Final Word

This textbook describes how economic factors affect individual choices and how all these choices come together to shape the economic system. Economics is not the whole story, and economic factors are not always the most important. But economic considerations have important and predictable effects on individual choices, and these choices affect the way we live.

Sure, economics is a challenging discipline, but it is also an exciting and rewarding one. The good news is that you already know a lot about economics. To use this knowledge, however, you must cultivate the art and science of economic analysis. You must be able to simplify the world to formulate questions, isolate the relevant variables, and then tell a persuasive story about how these variables relate.

An economic relation can be expressed in words, represented as a table of quantities, described by a mathematical equation, or illustrated as a graph. The appendix to this chapter introduces graphs. You may find this unnecessary. If you are already familiar with relations among variables, slopes, tangents, and the like, you can probably just browse. But if you have little recent experience with graphs, you might benefit from a more careful reading with pencil and paper in hand.

The next chapter introduces key tools of economic analysis. Subsequent chapters use these tools to explore economic problems and to explain economic behaviour that may otherwise seem puzzling. You must walk before you can run, however, and in the next chapter, you take your first wobbly steps.

CHAPTER PROBLEMS

LO1 Explain the economic problem of scarce resources and unlimited wants

1.1. *(Definition of Economics)* What determines whether or not a resource is scarce? Why is the concept of scarcity important to the definition of economics?

1.2. *(Definition of Economics)* Identify each of the following as a resource, an economic actor, or a good or service.
   a. A stay-at-home parent
   b. A computer
   c. Oil
   d. A hamburger

1.3. *(Scarce Resources)* How would you respond to the remark that clean water is free because you can simply get a glass or even a jug from your home tap without paying anything?

LO2 Describe the forces that shape economic choices

2.1. *(Rational Self-Interest)* Discuss the impact of rational self-interest on each of the following decisions:

   a. Whether to attend college full time or enter the workforce full time
   b. Whether to buy a new textbook or a used one
   c. Whether to attend a local college or an out-of-town college

2.2. *(Rational Self-Interest)* If behaviour is governed by rational self-interest, why do people make charitable contributions of time and money?

2.3. *(Marginal Analysis)* The owner of a small pizzeria is deciding whether to increase the radius of its delivery area by two kilometres. What considerations must be taken into account if such a decision is to increase profitability?

2.4. *(Time and Information)* It is often costly to obtain the information necessary to make good decisions. Yet your own interests can be best served by rationally weighing all options available to you. This requires informed decision making. Does this mean that making uninformed decisions is irrational? How do you determine how much information is the right amount?

2.5. *(Time)* A vacuum cleaner costs $600 and a high-quality broom costs only $5. Why would most people purchase the more expensive vacuum cleaner to do their home cleaning?

2.6. *(Information)* You want to purchase a car. You, like most people, probably don't want to spend too much time searching for information. You certainly don't want to check out all the dealers. You might simply do an intensive search of one or two. How can you reconcile such normal behaviour with rational behaviour? (Hint: think of the costs of information.)

LO3   Explain how economists use the scientific method

3.1. *(Role of Theory)* What good is economic theory if it can't predict the behaviour of a specific individual?

3.2. *(Normative versus Positive)* Are the following statements normative or positive?
   a. If the government wants to raise the price level it should increase the money supply.
   b. Corporate taxes in Canada are too high.
   c. Employment insurance programs cause the unemployment rate to rise.

3.3. *(Role of Theory)* Some economists argue that economic theory should be based on realistic behavioural assumptions. Why might realism of assumptions improve the capacity of theory to both predict and explain economic outcomes?

3.4. *(Normative versus Positive)* Determine whether each of the following statements is normative or positive:
   a. The Canadian unemployment rate fell from 8.3 percent in October 2009 to 6.5 percent in October 2014.
   b. The inflation rate in Canada is too high.
   c. The Canadian government should increase the minimum wage.

   d. Canadian restrictions in the dairy industry dramatically increase the cost of milk to Canadian consumers.

LO4   Identify some pitfalls of economic analysis

4.1. *(Pitfalls of Economic Analysis)* Review the discussion of pitfalls in economic thinking in this chapter. Then identify the fallacy, or mistake in thinking, in each of the following statements:
   a. Raising taxes always increases government revenues.
   b. Whenever there is a recession, imports decrease. Therefore, to stop a recession, we should increase imports.
   c. Raising the tariff on imported steel helps the Canadian steel industry. Therefore, the entire economy is helped.

4.2. *(Association Versus Causation)* Suppose I observe that communities with lots of doctors tend to have relatively high rates of illness. I conclude that doctors cause illness. What's wrong with this reasoning?

4.3. *(Secondary Effects)* Cigarette smuggling often increases when taxes on cigarettes are raised. Should the government eliminate cigarette taxes?

4.4. *(Pitfalls of Economic Analysis)* Prior to the financial crisis of 2008, most economists maintained the economy was doing quite well, booming in fact. Discuss what was missing in this type of analysis. If an economy is currently booming, does this necessarily mean that the economy is doing quite well?

LO5   Describe several reasons to study economics

5.1. *(Studying Economics)* According to the text, economics majors on average make more money than most other majors and have more job opportunities. Are these the primary motivations one might have for studying economics? What are your motivations for studying economics?

CASE STUDY

A Yen for Vending Machines

Japan faces a steady drop in the number of working-age people. Here are three reasons why: (1) Japan's birth rate has dropped to a record low, (2) Japan allows little immigration, and (3) Japan's population is aging. As a result, unemployment has usually been lower in Japan than in other countries. For example, Japan's unemployment rate in 2011, at 4.5 percent, was only about 60 percent of Canada's (7.5 percent), and half that of the United States and Europe. Because labour is relatively scarce in Japan, it is relatively costly. To sell products, Japanese retailers rely more on physical capital, particularly vending machines, which obviously eliminate the need for sales clerks.

Japan has more vending machines per capita than any other country on the planet—twice as many as the United States, 7 times as many as in Canada, and nearly 10 times as many as Europe. And vending machines in Japan sell a wider range of products than elsewhere, including beer, sake, whisky, rice, fresh eggs, beef, vegetables, pizza, entire meals, fried foods, fresh flowers, clothes, toilet paper, fishing supplies including bait, video games, software, ebooks, toys, DVDs, cellphone recharging, and even X-rated comic books. Japan's vending machines are also more sophisticated. Newer models come with video monitors and touch-pad screens. Wireless chips alert vendors when supplies run low. Some cigarette and liquor machines have artificial vision and are reportedly better at estimating age than are nightclub bouncers. Sanyo makes a giant machine that sells up to 200 different items at three different temperatures. Some cold-drink dispensers automatically raise prices in hot weather. Thousands of machines allow cellphone users to pay by pressing a few buttons on their phones.

As noted earlier, it is common practice in Canada to shake down vending machines that malfunction. Such abuse increases the probability the machines will fail again, leading to a cycle of abuse. Vending machines in Japan are less abused, in part because they are more sophisticated and more reliable and in part because the Japanese generally have greater respect for private property and, consequently, a lower crime rate (for example, Japan's theft rate is about half the U.S. rate).

Forty percent of all soft-drink sales in Japan are through vending machines, compared to only 12 percent of U.S. sales. Japanese sales per machine are double the U.S. rate. Research shows that most Japanese consumers prefer an anonymous machine to a salesperson. This sociological and cultural factor helps explain the relative abundance of vending machines in Japan. Despite that abundance, more growth is forecast, spurred on by a shrinking labour pool, technological innovations, and wide acceptance of machines there.

SOURCES: "Machines That Can See," *The Economist*, 5 March 2009; Hiroko Tabuchi, "Beef Bowl Economics," *New York Times*, 30 January 2010; and Trends in Japan at http://web-japan.org/trends/lifestyle/lif060720.html. For a photo gallery of vending machines in Japan, Type 'Japan vending machines' in your favourite search engine to find some interesting examples.

QUESTIONS

1. Do vending machines conserve on any resources other than labour? Does your answer offer any additional insight into the widespread use of vending machines in Japan?
2. Suppose you had the choice of purchasing identically priced lunches from a vending machine or at a cafeteria. Which would you choose? Why?

APPENDIX

Understanding Graphs

Take out a pencil and a blank piece of paper. Go ahead. Put a point in the middle of the paper. This is your point

of departure, called the **origin**. With your pencil at the origin, draw a straight line off to the right. This line is called the **horizontal axis**. The value of the variable

origin on a graph depicting two-dimensional space, the zero point

horizontal axis line on a graph that begins at the origin and goes to the right and left; sometimes called the *x* axis

x measured along the horizontal axis increases as you move to the right of the origin. Now mark off this line from 0 to 20, in increments of 5 units each. Returning to the origin, draw another line, this one straight north. This line is called the **vertical axis**. The value of the variable *y* measured along the vertical axis increases as you move north of the origin. Mark off this line from 0 to 20, in increments of 5 units each.

Within the space framed by the two axes, you can plot possible combinations of the variables measured along each axis. Each point identifies a value measured along the horizontal, or *x*, axis *and* a value measured along the vertical, or *y*, axis. For example, place point *a* in your graph to reflect the combination where *x* equals 5 units and *y* equals 15 units. Likewise, place point *b* in your graph to reflect 10 units of *x* and 5 units of *y*. Now compare your results with points shown in Exhibit 4.

A **graph** is a picture showing how variables relate, and a picture can be worth a thousand words. Take a look at Exhibit 5, which shows the Canadian annual unemployment rate since 1921. The year is measured along the horizontal axis and the unemployment rate is measured as a percentage along the

vertical axis line on a graph that begins at the origin and goes up and down; sometimes called the *y* axis

graph a picture showing how variables relate in two-dimensional space; one variable is measured along the horizontal axis and the other along the vertical axis

dependent variable a variable whose value depends on that of the independent variable

independent variable a variable whose value determines that of the dependent variable

EXHIBIT 5
Canadian Unemployment Rate Since 1921

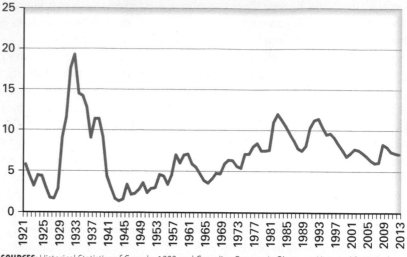

SOURCES: Historical Statistics of Canada, 1983 and Canadian Economic Observer: *Historical Statistical Supplement*, 2011. Copyright © Minister of Industry, 2011.

vertical axis. Exhibit 5 is a *time-series graph*, which shows the value of a variable, in this case the percent of the labour force unemployed, over time. If you had to describe the information presented in Exhibit 5 in words, the explanation could take many words. The picture shows not only how one year compares to the next but also how one decade compares to another and how the unemployment rate trends over time. The sharply higher unemployment rate during the Great Depression of the 1930s is unmistakable. *Graphs convey information in a compact and efficient way.*

This appendix shows how graphs express a variety of possible relations among variables. Most graphs of interest in this book reflect the relationship between two economic variables, such as the unemployment rate and the year, the price of a product and the quantity demanded, or the price of production and the quantity supplied. Because we focus on just two variables at a time, we usually assume that other relevant variables remain constant.

One variable often depends on another. The time it takes you to drive home depends on your average speed. Your weight depends on how much you eat. The amount of Pepsi you buy depends on the price. A *functional relation* exists between two variables when the value of one variable *depends* on the value of another variable. The value of the **dependent variable** depends on the value of the **independent variable**. We can write a *general* functional form or a *specific* functional form. In a general form, a function simply states that one independent variable is a function of one or more independent variables. A specific functional form would show us exactly how

EXHIBIT 4
Basics of a Graph

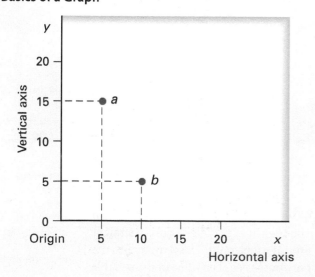

the variables are related. If we let Q^d stand for quantity demanded, P stand for price, and Y stand for income, a general functional form such as this one

$$Q^d = f(P, Y)$$

says that the quantity demanded is a function of the price and income. A specific functional form would look like this:

$$Q^d = 200 - 0.75P + 0.4Y$$

Now we know exactly how the variables are related to one another.

The task of the economist is to isolate economic relations and determine the direction of causality, if any. Recall that one of the pitfalls of economic thinking is the erroneous belief that association is causation. We cannot conclude that, simply because two events relate in time, one causes the other. There may be no relation between the two events.

Drawing Graphs

Let's begin with a simple relation. Suppose you are planning to drive across the country and want to figure out how far you will travel each day. You plan to average 80 kilometres per hour. Possible combinations of driving time and distance travelled per day appear in Exhibit 6. One column lists the hours driven per day, and the next column lists the number of kilometres travelled per day, assuming an average speed of 80 kilometres per hour. The distance travelled, the *dependent* variable, depends on the number of hours driven, the *independent* variable. Combinations of hours driven and distance travelled are shown as *a, b, c, d,*

and *e*. Each combination is represented by a point in Exhibit 7. For example, point *a* shows that if you drive for 1 hour, you travel 80 kilometres. Point *b* indicates that if you drive for 2 hours, you travel 160 kilometres. By connecting the points, or possible combinations, we create a line running upward and to the right. This makes sense, because the longer you drive, the farther you travel. Assumed constant along this line is your average speed of 80 kilometres per hour.

Types of relations between variables include the following:

1. As one variable increases, the other increases—as in Exhibit 7; this is called a **positive**, or **direct**, **relation** between the variables.
2. As one variable increases, the other decreases; this is called a **negative**, or **inverse**, **relation**.
3. As one variable increases, the other remains unchanged; the two variables are said to be *independent,* or *unrelated.*

One of the advantages of graphs is that they easily convey the relation between variables. We do not need to examine the particular combinations of numbers; we need only focus on the shape of the curve.

The Slopes of Straight Lines

A more precise way to describe the shape of a curve is to measure its slope. The **slope of a line** indicates

EXHIBIT 6
Schedule Relating Distance Travelled to Hours Driven

	Hours Driven per Day	Distance Travelled per Day (kilometres)
a	1	80
b	2	160
c	3	240
d	4	320
e	5	400

© Image Source/Getty Images

EXHIBIT 7
Graph Relating Distance Travelled to Hours Driven

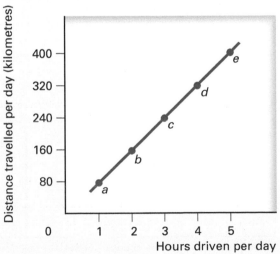

how much the vertical variable changes for a given increase in the horizontal variable. Specifically, the slope between any two points along any straight line is the vertical change between these two points divided by the horizontal increase, or

$$\text{Slope} = \frac{\text{Change in the vertical distance}}{\text{Increase in the horizontal distance}}$$

Each of the four panels in Exhibit 8 indicates a vertical change, given a 10-unit increase in the horizontal variable. In panel (a), the vertical distance increases by 5 units when the horizontal distance increases by 10 units. The slope of the line is therefore $5 \div 10$, or 0.5. Notice that the slope in this case is a positive number because the relation between the two variables is positive, or direct. This slope indicates that for every 1-unit increase in the horizontal variable, the vertical variable increases by 0.5 units. The slope, incidentally, does not imply causality; the increase in the horizontal variable does not necessarily *cause* the increase in the vertical variable. The slope simply measures the relation between an increase in the horizontal variable and the associated change in the vertical variable.

In panel (b) of Exhibit 8, the vertical distance declines by 7 units when the horizontal distance increases by 10 units, so the slope equals $-7 \div 10$, or -0.7. The slope in this case is a negative number because the two variables have a negative, or inverse, relation. In panel (c), the vertical variable remains unchanged as the horizontal variable increases by 10, so the slope equals $0 \div 10$, or 0. These two variables are not related. Finally, in panel (d), the vertical variable can take on any value, although the horizontal variable remains unchanged. Again, the two variables are not related. In this case, any change in the vertical measure, for example a 10-unit change, is divided by 0, because the horizontal value does not change. Any change divided by 0 is mathematically undefined, but as the line tilts toward vertical, its slope gets incredibly large. For practical purposes, we will assume that the slope of this line is not undefined but infinitely large.

The Slope, Units of Measurement, and Marginal Analysis

The mathematical value of the slope depends on the units measured on the graph. For example, suppose copper tubing costs $1 a decimetre. Graphs depicting the relation between total cost and quantity purchased are shown in Exhibit 9. In panel (a), the total cost increases by $1 for each 1-decimetre increase in the amount of tubing purchased. Thus, the slope equals $1 \div 1$, or 1. If the cost per decimetre remains the same but units are measured not in *decimetres* but in *metres*, the relation between total cost and quantity purchased is as depicted in panel (b). Now total cost increases by $10 for each 1-metre increase in output, so the slope equals $10 \div 1$, or 10. Because different units are used to measure the copper tubing, the two panels reflect different slopes, even though the cost is $1 per decimetre in each panel. Keep in mind that *the slope depends in part on the units of measurement.*

Economic analysis usually involves *marginal analysis,* such as the marginal cost of one more unit of output. The slope is a convenient device for measuring marginal effects because it reflects the change in total cost, measured along the vertical axis, for each 1-unit change in output, measured along the horizontal axis. For example, in panel (a) of Exhibit 9, the marginal cost of another

EXHIBIT 8
Alternative Slopes for Straight Lines

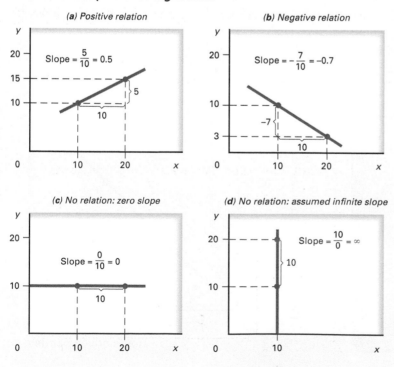

(a) Positive relation

$\text{Slope} = \frac{5}{10} = 0.5$

(b) Negative relation

$\text{Slope} = -\frac{7}{10} = -0.7$

(c) No relation: zero slope

$\text{Slope} = \frac{0}{10} = 0$

(d) No relation: assumed infinite slope

$\text{Slope} = \frac{10}{0} = \infty$

EXHIBIT 9
Slope Depends on the Unit of Measure

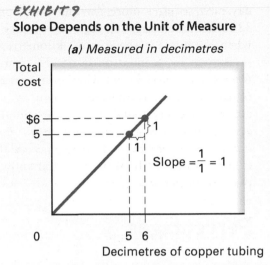

(a) Measured in decimetres

Decimetres of copper tubing

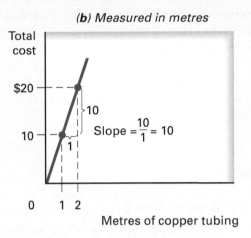

(b) Measured in metres

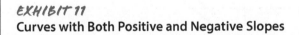

Metres of copper tubing

decimetre of copper tubing is $1, which also equals the slope of the line. In panel (b), the marginal cost of another *metre* of tubing is $10, which again is the slope of that line. Because of its applicability to marginal analysis, the slope has special relevance in economics.

The Slopes of Curved Lines

The slope of a straight line is the same everywhere along the line, but the slope of a curved line differs along the curve, as shown in Exhibit 10. To find the slope of a curved line at a particular point, draw a straight line that just touches the curve at that point but does not cut or cross the curve. Such a line is called a tangent to the curve at that point. The slope of the **tangent** gives the slope of the curve at that point. Look at line *A*, which is tangent to the curve at point *a*. As the horizontal value increases from 0 to 10, the vertical value drops along *A* from 40 to 0.

Thus, the vertical change divided by the horizontal change equals $-40 \div 10$, or -4, which is the slope of the curve at point *a*. This slope is negative because the vertical value decreases as the horizontal value increases. Line *B*, a line tangent to the curve at point *b*, has the slope $-10 \div 30$, or -0.33. As you can see, the curve depicted in Exhibit 10 gets flatter as the horizontal variable increases, so the value of its slope approaches zero.

Other curves, of course, will reflect different slopes as well as different changes in the slope along the curve. Downward-sloping curves have negative slopes, and upward-sloping curves, positive slopes. Sometimes curves, such as those in Exhibit 11, are more complex, having both positive and negative ranges, depending on the horizontal value. In the hill-shaped curve, for small values of *x*, there is a positive relation between *x* and *y*, so the slope is positive. As the value of *x* increases, however, the slope declines

> **tangent** a straight line that touches a curve at a point but does not cut or cross the curve; used to measure the slope of a curve at a point

EXHIBIT 10
Slopes at Different Points on a Curved Line

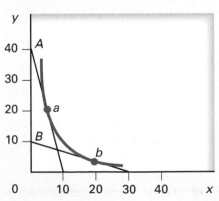

EXHIBIT 11
Curves with Both Positive and Negative Slopes

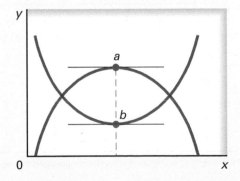

and eventually becomes negative. We can divide the curve into two segments: (1) the segment between the origin and point *a*, where the slope is positive; and (2) the segment of the curve to the right of point *a*, where the slope is negative. The slope of the curve at point *a* is 0. The U-shaped curve in Exhibit 11 represents the opposite relation: *x* and *y* are negatively related until point *b* is reached; thereafter, they are positively related. The slope equals 0 at point *b*.

Line Shifts

Let's go back to the example of your cross-country trip, where we were trying to determine how many kilometres you would travel per day. Recall that we measured hours driven per day on the horizontal axis and kilometres travelled per day on the vertical axis, assuming an average speed of 80 kilometres per hour. That same relation is shown as line *T* in Exhibit 12. What happens if the average speed is 60 kilometres per hour? The entire relation between hours driven and distance travelled would change, as shown by the shift to the right of line *T* to *T'*. With a slower average speed, any distance travelled per

EXHIBIT 12
Shift of Line Relating Distance Travelled to Hours Driven

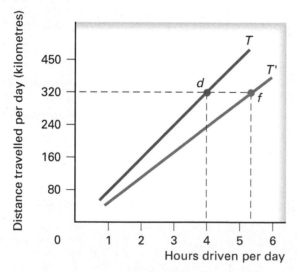

day now requires more driving time. For example, 320 kilometres travelled requires 4 hours of driving when the average speed is 80 kilometres per hour (as shown by point *d* on curve *T'*), but 320 kilometres takes 5.33 hours when your speed averages 60 kilometres per hour (as shown by point *f* on curve *T'*). Thus, *a change in the assumption about average speed changes the relationship between the two variables observed.* This changed relationship is expressed by a shift of the line that shows how the two variables relate.

Percentages

Students often confuse the terms "percent change" with "percentage point change." The way to calculate percent change is

$$\text{Percent change} = \frac{\text{Final value} - \text{initial value}}{\text{Initial value}} \times 100$$

If I have $200 in my bank account at the beginning of the year and $220 in the account at the end of the year, what is the percent change in my bank balance?

$$\text{Percent change} = \frac{220 - 200}{200} \times 100 = 10\%$$

When we are considering the percent change in dollars or physical quantities such as litres or cups of coffee, the calculation is straightforward. The confusion comes when we are talking about changes in a percentage. Let's look at a simple example. Suppose you score 70 percent on your first economics mid-term exam and 80 percent on your second mid-term exam. That is an improvement of 10 percentage points (80 − 70). If we want to know the percent change, we need to do the calculation as stated above:

$$\frac{80 - 70}{70} \times 100 = 14.3\%$$

So your grade improved 14.3 percent or 10 percentage points.

That ends our once-over of graphs. Return to this appendix when you need a review.

2

Economic Tools and Economic Systems

LEARNING OUTCOMES

LO1 Describe the impact of differing opportunities on choice

LO2 Explain how comparative advantage, specialization, and exchange affect economic outcomes (output)

LO3 Outline how economies function as production systems

LO4 Describe different economic systems and the decision-making rules that define them

" Why is there no sense crying over spilt milk? "

Why are you reading this book right now rather than doing something else? What is your postsecondary education costing you? Why will you eventually major in one subject rather than continue to take courses in different ones? Why is fast food so fast? Why is there no sense crying over spilt milk?

These and other questions are addressed in this chapter, which introduces some tools of economic analysis—some tools of the trade. Chapter 1 introduced the idea that scarcity forces us to make choices, but the chapter said little about how to make economic choices. This chapter develops a framework for evaluating economic alternatives. First, we consider the cost involved in selecting one alternative over others. Next, we develop tools to explore the choices available to individuals and to the economy as a whole. Finally, we introduce the ideas of absolute advantage and comparative advantage, which are essential in understanding specialization and trade both within and between countries.

LO 1 Choice and Opportunity Cost

Think about a choice you just made: the decision to begin reading this chapter right now rather than use your time to study for another course, play sports, watch TV, go online, get some sleep, hang with friends, or do something else. Suppose it's late and your best alternative to reading right now is getting some sleep. The cost of reading is passing up the opportunity of sleep. Because of scarcity, whenever you make a choice, you must pass up another opportunity; you must incur an *opportunity cost*.

Opportunity Cost

What do we mean when we talk about the cost of something? Isn't it what we must give up—must forgo—to get that thing? The **opportunity cost** of the chosen item or activity is *the value of the best alternative that is forgone*. You can think of opportunity cost as the *opportunity lost*. Sometimes opportunity cost can be measured in terms of money, although, as we shall see, money is usually only part of opportunity cost.

How many times have you heard people say they did something because they "had nothing better to do"? They actually mean they had nothing else going on. Yet, according to the idea of opportunity cost, people *always* do what they do because they have nothing better to do. The choice selected seems, at the time, preferable to any other possible alternative. You are reading this chapter right now because you have nothing better to do. In fact, you are attending college or university for the same reason: it appears more attractive than your best alternative.

> **opportunity cost**
> the value of the best alternative forgone when an item or activity is chosen

Opportunity Cost Is Subjective

Like beauty, opportunity cost is in the eye of the beholder. It is subjective. Only the individual making the choice can identify the most attractive alternative. But the chooser seldom knows the actual value of what was passed up, because that alternative is "the road not taken." If you give up an evening of pizza and conversation with friends to work on a research paper, you will never know exactly what you gave up. You know only what you *expected*. Evidently, you expected the benefit of working on that paper to exceed the benefit of the best alternative. (Incidentally, focusing on the best alternative forgone makes all other alternatives irrelevant.)

Calculating Opportunity Cost Requires Time and Information Economists assume that people rationally choose the most valued alternative. This does not mean you exhaustively assess the value of all possibilities. You assess alternatives as long as the expected marginal benefit of gathering more information about your options exceeds the expected marginal cost (even if you are not aware of making such conscious calculations). In other words, you do the best you can for yourself, given all the constraints that you face.

Because learning about alternatives is costly and time consuming, some choices are based on limited or even wrong information. Indeed, some choices may turn out badly (you went for a picnic but it rained; the movie you rented stunk; the stock you bought tanked). Regret about lost opportunities is captured in the common expression "coulda, woulda, shoulda." At the time you made the selection, however, you thought you were making the best use of all your scarce resources, including the time required to gather and evaluate information about your choices.

Time: The Ultimate Constraint The Sultan of Brunei is among the richest people on earth, worth billions based on huge oil revenues that flow into his tiny country. He and his royal family (which has ruled since 1405) live in a palace with 1,788 rooms, 257 bathrooms, and a throne room the size of a football field. The family owns hundreds of cars, including dozens of Rolls-Royces; he can drive any of these or pilot one of his seven planes, including the 747 with gold-plated furniture. Supported by such wealth, the Sultan would appear to have overcome the economic problem of scarcity. Though he can buy just about whatever he wants, he lacks the time to enjoy his stuff. If he pursues one activity, he cannot at the same time do something else. Each activity involves an opportunity cost. Consequently, the Sultan must choose from among the competing uses of his scarcest resource, time. Although your alternatives are less exotic, you too face a time constraint, especially as the university term winds down.

> **sunk cost** a cost that has already been incurred, cannot be recovered, and thus should be irrelevant for present and future economic decisions

Opportunity Cost Varies with Circumstance Opportunity cost depends on your alternatives. This is why you are more likely to study on a Tuesday night than on a Saturday night. The opportunity cost of studying is lower on a Tuesday night, because your alternatives are less attractive than on a Saturday night, when more is going on. Suppose you go to a movie on Saturday night. Your opportunity cost is the value of your best alternative forgone, which might be watching a hockey game. For some of you, studying on Saturday night may rank well down the list of possibilities—perhaps ahead of reorganizing your closet but behind doing your laundry.

Opportunity cost is subjective, but in some cases, money paid for goods and services is a reasonable approximation. For example, the opportunity cost of the new video game you bought is the benefit from spending that $70 on the best forgone alternative. The money measure may leave out some important elements, however, particularly the value of the time involved. For example, watching the latest hit movie costs you not only the $10 admission price but also the time needed to get there, watch the movie, and return home.

Sunk Cost and Choice

Suppose you have just finished grocery shopping and are wheeling your cart toward the checkout counters. How do you decide which line to join? Easy. You pick the one with the shortest expected wait. Suppose that line barely moves for 10 minutes, when you notice that a cashier has opened a new line and invites you to check out. Do you switch to the open cashier, or do you think, "Since I've already spent 10 minutes in this line, I'm staying put"? The 10 minutes you waited represents a **sunk cost**, which is a cost that has already been incurred and cannot be recovered, regardless of what you do next. You should ignore sunk costs in making economic choices. Hence, you should switch. *Economic decision makers should consider only those costs that are affected by the choice. Sunk costs have already been incurred and are not affected by the choice, so they are irrelevant.* Likewise, you should walk out on a bad movie, even if you spent $10 to

© 13/Garry Wade/Ocean/Corbis

carpets (granted, in reality you may not fold laundry or vacuum carpets, but this example will help you understand some important principles). You often have friends over who leave crumbs from their snacks all over the house. You both prefer to live in a somewhat tidy house and to wear T-shirts that do not look like they spent the entire week crumpled in a laundry basket. Let's say it takes 10 minutes to vacuum one room. Your roommate is a slow poke and takes about half an hour, or three times as long, to vacuum one room. But your roommate is a talented folder and can fold a T-shirt in 2 minutes flat. You take more than twice as long, 5 minutes, to fold one T-shirt.

BEAUTYofLIFE/Shutterstock

Suppose you both decide to spend half an hour each working on the two chores. You manage to fold six T-shirts and vacuum three rooms. Your roommate vacuums one room and folds fifteen T-shirts. Thus, if you each divide your time evenly, the combined output is four vacuumed rooms and 21 folded T-shirts.

The Law of Comparative Advantage

Before long, you each realize that total output would increase if you did all the vacuuming and your roommate did all the folding. In the hour available for these tasks, you vacuum six rooms, almost your entire house, and your roommate folds 30 T-shirts. As a result of specialization, total output increases by two rooms and nine T-shirts! You strike a deal to exchange your vacuuming for your roommate's folding, so you each end up with a tidier house and 15 folded T-shirts. Thus, *each of you is better off as a result of specialization and exchange.* By specializing in the task that you each do better, you rely on the **law of comparative advantage**, which states that the individual with the lower opportunity cost of producing a particular output should specialize in that output. You face a lower opportunity cost of vacuuming than does your roommate, because in the time it takes you to vacuum one room, you could fold 2 T-shirts whereas your roommate could fold 15 T-shirts in the time it takes your roommate to vacuum one room. And if you face a lower opportunity cost of vacuuming, your

law of comparative advantage the individual, firm, region, or country with the lowest opportunity cost of producing a particular good should specialize in that good

get in. Your $10 is gone, and sitting through that stinker only makes you worse off. The irrelevance of sunk costs is underscored by proverbs such as "Don't throw good money after bad," "Let bygones be bygones," and "There's no sense crying over spilt milk." The milk has already spilled, so whatever you do now cannot change that. But sometimes we don't ignore sunk costs because of psychological pain incurred in admitting we might have made a wrong decision in the first place or in the hope that things will turn out all right if we just stick with it.

Now that you have some idea about opportunity cost, let's see how it helps solve the economic problem.

LO 2 Comparative Advantage, Specialization, and Exchange

Suppose you live in an off-campus rental house. You and your roommate have such tight schedules that you each can spare only about an hour a week for mundane tasks like folding laundry and vacuuming

roommate must face a lower opportunity cost of folding (you can't have a lower opportunity cost of both activities).

Absolute Advantage Versus Comparative Advantage

The gains from specialization and exchange so far are obvious. A more interesting case is if you are faster at both tasks. Suppose the example changes only in one respect: Your roommate takes six minutes to fold a T-shirt compared with your five minutes. You now have an *absolute advantage* in both tasks, meaning each task takes you less time than it does your roommate. More generally, having an **absolute advantage** means making something using fewer resources than other producers require.

Does your absolute advantage in both activities mean specialization is no longer a good idea? Recall that the law of comparative advantage states that the individual with *the lower opportunity cost* of producing a particular good should specialize in that good. You still take 10 minutes to vacuum a room and 5 minutes to fold a T-shirt, so your opportunity cost of vacuuming the room remains at two folded T-shirts. Your roommate takes a half-hour to vacuum a room and 6 minutes to fold a T-shirt, so your roommate could fold five T-shirts in the time it takes to vacuum a room. Your opportunity cost of vacuuming a room is folding two T-shirts; for your roommate, it's folding five T-shirts. *Because your opportunity cost of vacuuming is lower than your roommate's, you still have a comparative advantage in vacuuming.* Consequently, your roommate must have a comparative advantage in folding. Therefore, you should do all the vacuuming and your roommate, all the folding. Although you have an absolute advantage in both tasks, your **comparative advantage** calls for specializing in the task for which you have the lower opportunity cost—in this case, vacuuming.

If neither of you specialized, you could vacuum three rooms and fold six T-shirts in an hour. Your roommate could vacuum one room and fold five T-shirts. Your combined output would be four rooms and eleven T-shirts. Now suppose your roommate completely specializes in his comparative advantage product, folding T-shirts and you partially specialize, by spending 45 minutes vacuuming and 15 minutes folding. Total output is now 4.5 vacuumed rooms and 13 folded T-shirts. Thus, specialization increases total output by half a room and two T-shirts. Even though

you are better at both tasks than your roommate, you are comparatively better at vacuuming. Put another way, your roommate, although worse at both tasks, is not quite as bad at folding as at vacuuming.

Don't think that this is just common sense. Common sense would lead you to do your own vacuuming and folding, because you are better at both. *Absolute advantage focuses on who uses the fewest resources, but comparative advantage focuses on what else those resources could produce—that is, on the opportunity cost of those resources.* Comparative advantage is the better guide to who should do what.

The law of comparative advantage applies not only to individuals but also to firms, regions of a country, and entire nations. Individuals, firms, regions, or countries with the lowest opportunity cost of producing a particular good should specialize in producing that good. Because of such factors as climate, workforce skills, natural resources, and capital stock, certain parts of the country and certain parts of the world have a comparative advantage in producing particular goods. From Alberta and Saskatchewan wheat to Prince Edward Island potatoes, from software in India to hardware in Taiwan—*resources are allocated most efficiently across the country and around the world when production and trade conform to the law of comparative advantage.* For a more detailed numerical example of comparative advantage, see Chapter 18.

Specialization and Exchange

In the previous example, you and your roommate specialized and then exchanged output. No money was involved. In other words, you engaged in **barter**, where products are traded directly for other products. Barter works best in simple economies with little specialization and few traded goods. But for economies with greater specialization, *money* facilitates exchange. Money—coins, bills, cheques, and debit cards—is a *medium of exchange* because it is the one thing that everyone accepts in return for goods and services. By using money as opposed to bartering, you save scarce resources that can be best used elsewhere. You no longer have to find someone who wants exactly what you've produced—also referred

absolute advantage the ability to make something using fewer resources than other producers use

comparative advantage the ability to make something at a lower opportunity cost than other producers face

barter the direct exchange of one product for another without using money

CHAPTER 2: ECONOMIC TOOLS AND ECONOMIC SYSTEMS

to as the double coincidence of wants. They just need cash or a debit card.

Because of specialization and comparative advantage, most people consume little of what they produce and produce little of what they consume. Each individual specializes, then exchanges that product for money, which in turn is exchanged for other products. Did you make anything you are wearing? Probably not. Think about the degree of specialization that went into your cotton shirt. A farmer in a warm climate grew the cotton and sold it to someone who spun it into thread, who sold it to someone who wove it into fabric, who sold it to someone who sewed the shirt, who sold it to a wholesaler, who sold it to a retailer, who sold it to you. Many specialists in the chain of production created that shirt.

Evidence of specialization is all around us. Shops at the mall specialize in products as diverse as luggage and lingerie. Restaurants range from subs to sushi. Or quickly scan Monster.ca, where you will find thousands of specializations. Without moving a muscle, you can observe the division of labour within a single industry by watching the credits roll at the end of a movie. The credits list scores of specialists—such as gaffer (lighting electrician) and assistant location scout. As an extreme example, more than 3,000 specialists helped create the movie *Avatar*.[1] Even a typical TV drama, such as *Game of Thrones* or *CSI: Miami*, requires hundreds of specialists.

Some specialties may seem odd. For example, professional mourners in Taiwan are sometimes hired by grieving families to scream, wail, and otherwise demonstrate the deep grief befitting a proper funeral. The sharp degree of specialization is perhaps most obvious online, where the pool of potential customers is so vast that individual websites become finely focused. For example, you can find sites specializing in musical bowls, tongue studs, toe rings, brass knuckles, mouth harps, ferret toys, and cat bandannas—just to name a few of the hundreds of thousands of specialty sites. You won't find such precise specialization at the mall. Adam Smith said

the degree of specialization is limited by the extent of the market. Online sellers draw on the broadest customer base in the world to find a market niche.

Division of Labour and Gains from Specialization

Picture a visit to McDonald's: "Let's see, I'll have a Big Mac, an order of fries, and a chocolate shake." Less than a minute later your order is ready. It would take you much longer to make a homemade version of this meal. Why is the McDonald's meal faster, cheaper, and—for some people—tastier than one you could make yourself? Why is fast food so fast? McDonald's takes advantage of the gains resulting from the **division of labour**. Each worker, rather than preparing an entire meal, specializes in separate tasks. This division of labour allows the group to produce much more.

How is this increase in productivity possible? First, the manager can assign tasks according to *individual preferences and abilities*—that is, according to the law of comparative advantage. The worker with the friendly smile and pleasant personality can handle the customers up front; the one with the strong back but few social graces can handle the heavy lifting out back. Second, a worker who performs the same task again and again gets better at it (experience is a good teacher). The worker filling orders at the drive-through, for example, learns to deal with special problems that arise. As another example, consider the experience gained by someone screening bags at airport security. Experience helps the screener distinguish the harmful from the harmless. Third, specialization means no time is lost moving from one task to another. Finally, and perhaps most importantly, the **specialization of labour** allows for the introduction of more sophisticated production techniques—techniques that would not make sense on a smaller scale. For example, McDonald's large shake machine would be impractical in the home. *Specialized machines make each worker more productive.*

To summarize: The specialization of labour (a) takes advantage of individual preferences and natural abilities, (b) allows workers to develop more

division of labour breaking down the production of a good into separate tasks

specialization of labour focusing work effort on a particular product or a single task

[1] As reported in Hendrik Hertzberg, "And the Oscar Goes To," *The New Yorker*, 15 & 22 February 2010.

experience at a particular task, (c) reduces the need to shift between different tasks, and (d) permits the introduction of labour-saving machinery. Specialization and the division of labour occur not only among individuals but also among firms, regions, and indeed entire countries. The cotton shirt mentioned earlier might involve growing cotton in one country, turning it into cloth in another, making the shirt in a third, and selling it in a fourth.

We should also acknowledge the downside of specialization. Doing the same thing all day can become tedious. Consider, for example, the assembly-line worker whose sole task is to tighten a particular bolt. Such a monotonous job could drive that worker bonkers or lead to repetitive motion injury. Thus, the gains from dividing production into individual tasks must be weighed against any problems caused by assigning workers to repetitive, tedious, and potentially harmful jobs. Fortunately, many routine tasks, particularly on assembly lines, can be turned over to robots.

LO 3 The Economy's Production Possibilities

The focus to this point has been on how individuals choose to use their scarce resources to satisfy their unlimited wants or, more specifically, how they specialize based on comparative advantage. This emphasis on the individual has been appropriate because the economy is shaped by the choices of individual decision makers, whether they are consumers, producers, or public officials. Just as resources are scarce for the individual, they are also scarce for the economy as a whole (no fallacy of composition here). An economy has millions of different resources that can be combined in all kinds of ways to produce millions of different goods and services. This section steps back from the immense complexity of the real economy to develop another simple model, which explores the economy's production options.

Efficiency and the Production Possibilities Frontier, or PPF

Let's develop a model to get some idea of how much an economy can produce with the resources available.

What are the economy's production capabilities? Here are the model's assumptions:

1. To simplify matters, output is limited to just two broad classes of products: consumer goods and capital goods.

2. The focus is on production during a given period—in this case, a year.

3. The economy's resources are fixed in both quantity and quality during that period.

4. Society's knowledge about how these resources combine to produce output—that is, the available *technology*—does not change during the year.

5. Also assumed fixed during the period are the "rules of the game" that facilitate production and exchange. These include such things as the legal system, property rights, labour rights, gender rights, tax laws, patent laws, and the manners, customs, and conventions of the market.

The point of these simplifying assumptions is to freeze in time the economy's resources, technology, and rules of the game so we can focus on the economy's production options. Otherwise, the production possibilities of the economy would be a moving target.

Given the resources, technology, and rules of the game available in the economy, the **production possibilities frontier**, or **PPF**, identifies possible combinations of the two types of goods that can be produced when all available resources are employed efficiently. *Resources are employed efficiently when there is no change that could increase the production of one good without decreasing the production of the other good.* **Efficiency** involves getting the most from available resources.

The economy's PPF for consumer goods and capital goods is shown by the curve *AF* in Exhibit 1. Point *A* identifies the amount produced per year if all the economy's resources are used efficiently to produce consumer goods. Point *F* identifies the amount produced per year if all the economy's resources are used efficiently to produce capital goods. Points along the curve between *A* and *F* identify possible combinations of the two goods that can be produced when all the economy's resources are used efficiently.

Inefficient and Unattainable Production

Points inside the PPF, such as *I* in Exhibit 1, identify combinations that do not employ resources efficiently.

production possibilities frontier (PPF) a curve showing alternative combinations of goods that can be produced when available resources are used efficiently; a boundary line between inefficient and unattainable combinations

efficiency the condition that exists when there is no way resources can be reallocated to increase the production of one good without decreasing the production of another; getting the most from available resources

EXHIBIT 1
The Economy's Production Possibilities Frontier

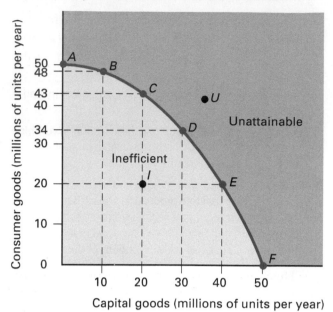

Note that *C* yields more consumer goods and no fewer capital goods than *I*. And *E* yields more capital goods and no fewer consumer goods than *I*. Indeed, any point along the PPF between *C* and *E,* such as *D,* yields both more consumer goods and more capital goods than *I*. Hence, combination *I* is *inefficient*. By using resources more efficiently, the economy can produce more of at least one good without reducing the production of the other good. Points outside the PPF, such as *U* in Exhibit 1, identify *unattainable* combinations, given the availability of resources, technology, and rules of the game. Thus, *the PPF not only shows efficient combinations of production but also serves as the boundary between inefficient combinations inside the frontier and unattainable combinations outside the frontier.*

law of increasing opportunity cost
to produce more of one good, a successively larger amount of the other good must be sacrificed

economic growth
an increase in the economy's ability to produce goods and services; reflected by an outward shift of the economy's production possibilities frontier

The Shape of the Production Possibilities Frontier

Any movement along the PPF involves producing less of one good to produce more of the other. Movements down along the curve indicate that the opportunity cost of more capital goods is fewer consumer goods. For example, moving from point *A* to point *B increases* capital production from none to 10 million units but *reduces* consumer units from 50 million to 48 million. Increasing capital goods to 10 million reduces consumer goods only a little. Capital production initially employs resources (such as heavy machinery used to build factories) that add few consumer units but are quite productive in making capital.

As shown by the dashed lines in Exhibit 1, each additional 10 million units of capital produced reduce consumer goods by successively larger amounts. The resources used to produce more capital are increasingly better suited to producing consumer goods. *The opportunity cost of making more capital goods increases, because resources in the economy are not all perfectly adaptable to the production of both types of goods.* The shape of the production possibilities frontier reflects the **law of increasing opportunity cost**. If the economy uses all resources efficiently, the law of increasing opportunity cost states that each additional increment of one good requires the economy to sacrifice successively larger and larger increments of the other good.

The PPF derives its bowed-out shape from the law of increasing opportunity cost. For example, whereas the first 10 million units of capital have an opportunity cost of only 2 million consumer units, the final 10 million units of capital—that is, the increase from *E* to *F*—have an opportunity cost of 20 million consumer units. Notice that the slope of the PPF shows the opportunity cost of an increment of capital. As the economy moves down the curve, the curve becomes steeper, reflecting the higher opportunity cost of capital goods in terms of forgone consumer goods. The law of increasing opportunity cost also applies when shifting from capital goods to consumer goods. Incidentally, if resources were perfectly adaptable to the production of both consumer goods and capital goods, the PPF would be a straight line, reflecting a constant opportunity cost along the PPF.

What Can Shift the Production Possibilities Frontier?

Any production possibilities frontier assumes the economy's resources, technology, and rules of the game are fixed during the period under consideration. Over time, however, the PPF may shift if resources, technology, or the rules of the game change. **Economic growth** is an expansion in the economy's production possibilities as reflected by an outward shift of the PPF.

Changes in Resource Availability If people decide to work longer hours, the PPF shifts outward, as shown in panel (a) of Exhibit 2. An increase in the size or health of the labour force, improvements to gender rights (increasing female education and labour force participation), an increase in the skills of the labour force, or an increase in the availability of other resources, such as new oil discoveries, also shifts the PPF outward, as did the invention of money, which released scarce resources to produce more output. In contrast, a decrease of resources shifts the PPF inward, as depicted in panel (b). For example, in 1990 Iraq invaded Kuwait, setting oil fields ablaze and destroying much of Kuwait's physical capital.

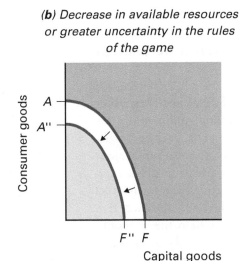

Disasters cause an inward shift or retraction of the PPF.

In West Africa, the encroaching sands of the Sahara destroy thousands of square kilometres of farmland each year. And in northwest China, a rising tide of wind-blown sand has claimed grasslands, lakes, and forests, and swallowed entire villages, forcing tens of thousands of people to flee. And in 2011, record spring flooding in Saskatchewan ruined structures, forced people out of their homes, and hindered river cargo.

The new PPFs in panels (a) and (b) appear to be parallel to the original ones, indicating that the resources that changed could produce both capital goods and consumer goods. For example, an increase in electrical power can enhance the production of both, as shown in panel (a). If a resource such as farmland benefits just consumer goods, then increased availability or productivity of that resource shifts the PPF more along the consumer goods axis, as shown in panel (c). Panel (d) shows the effect of an increase in a resource such as construction equipment that is suited only to capital goods.

EXHIBIT 2
Shifts of the Economy's Production Possibilities Frontier

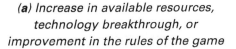

(a) Increase in available resources, technology breakthrough, or improvement in the rules of the game

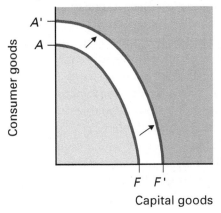

(b) Decrease in available resources or greater uncertainty in the rules of the game

(c) Change in resources, technology, or rules that benefit consumer goods

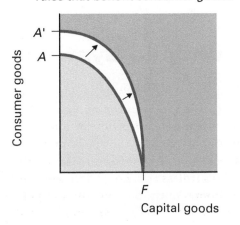

(d) Change in resources, technology, or rules that benefit capital goods

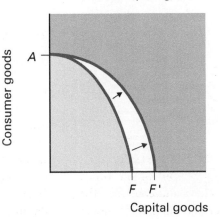

CHAPTER 2: ECONOMIC TOOLS AND ECONOMIC SYSTEMS

Increases in the Capital Stock An economy's PPF depends in part on the stock of human and physical capital. The more capital an economy produces one period, the more output can be produced the next period. Thus, producing more capital goods this period (for example, more machines in the case of physical capital or more education in the case of human capital) shifts the economy's entire PPF outward the next period.

Technological Change A technological discovery that employs resources more efficiently could shift the economy's PPF outward. Some discoveries enhance the production of both consumer goods and capital goods, as shown in panel (a) of Exhibit 2. For example, the Internet has increased each firm's ability to find available resources. A technological discovery that benefits consumer goods only, such as more disease-resistant crops, is reflected by a rotation outward of the PPF along the consumer goods axis, as shown in panel (c). Note that point *F* remains unchanged because the breakthrough does not affect the production of capital goods. Panel (d) shows a technological advance in the production of capital goods, such as better software for designing heavy machinery.

Improvements in the Rules of the Game The *rules of the game* are the formal and informal institutions that support the economy—the laws, customs, manners, conventions, and other institutional underpinnings that encourage people to pursue productive activity. A more stable political environment and more reliable property rights increase the incentive to work and to invest, and thus help the economy grow. For example, people have more incentive to work if taxes claim less of their paycheques. People have more incentive to invest if they are confident that their investment will not be appropriated by government, stolen by thieves, destroyed by civil unrest, or blown up by terrorists. Improvements in the rules of the game shift the economy's PPF outward. On the other hand, greater uncertainty about the rules of the game reduces the economy's productive capacity as reflected by an inward shift of the PPF.

What We Learn from the PPF

The PPF demonstrates several ideas introduced so far. The first is *efficiency*: the PPF describes efficient combinations of output, given the economy's resources, technology, and rules of the game. The second idea is *scarcity*: given the resources, technology, and rules of the game, the economy can produce only so much output per period. The PPF slopes downward, because more of one good means less of the other good, thus demonstrating *opportunity cost*. The PPF's bowed-out shape reflects the *law of increasing opportunity cost*, which arises because some resources are not perfectly adaptable to the production of each type of good. And a shift outward in the PPF reflects *economic growth*.

Finally, because society must somehow select a specific combination of output—a single point— along the PPF, the PPF also underscores the need for *choice*. Selecting a particular combination determines not only consumer goods available this period, but also the capital stock available next period. One thing the PPF does not tell us is which combination to choose. The PPF tells us only about the costs, not the benefits, of the two goods. To make a selection, we need to know about both costs *and* benefits. How society goes about choosing a particular combination depends on the nature of the economic system, as you will see next.

LO 4 Economic Systems

Each point along the economy's production possibilities frontier is an efficient combination of outputs. Whether the economy produces efficiently and how the economy selects the most preferred combination depends on the decision-making rules employed. But regardless of how decisions are made, each economy must answer three fundamental questions.

Good rules make for a productive and fair game.

Three Questions Every Economic System Must Answer

What goods and services are to be produced? How are they to be produced? And for whom are they to be produced? An **economic system** is the set of mechanisms and institutions that resolve the *what, how,* and *for whom* questions. Some criteria used to distinguish among economic systems are (1) who owns the resources, (2) what decision-making process is used to allocate resources and products, and (3) what types of incentives guide economic decision makers.

What Goods and Services Are to Be Produced? Most of us take for granted the incredible number of choices that go into deciding what gets produced—everything from which new kitchen appliances are introduced, which roads get built, to which of the 10,000 movie scripts purchased by U.S. studios each year get to be among the 500 movies made.[2] Although different economies resolve these and millions of other questions using different decision-making rules and mechanisms, all economies must somehow make such choices.

How Are Goods and Services to Be Produced? The economic system must determine how output gets produced. Which resources should be used, and how should they be combined to make stuff? How much labour should be used and at what skill levels? What kinds of machines should be used? What new technology should be incorporated into the latest video games? Should the office complex be built in the city or closer to the highway? Millions of individual decisions determine which

[2] As reported in Ian Parker, "The Real McKee," *New Yorker*, 20 October 2003.

"Of the 10,000 movie scripts Hollywood studios buy each year, only 500 get made into movies."

resources are employed and how these resources are combined.

For Whom Are Goods and Services to Be Produced? Who will actually consume the goods and services produced? The economic system must determine how to allocate the fruits of production among the population. Should everyone receive equal shares? Should the weak and the sick get more? Should those willing to wait in line get more? Should goods be allocated according to height? Religion? Age? Strength? Political connections? The value of resources supplied? The question "For whom are goods and services to be produced?" is often referred to as the *distribution question.*

Although the three economic questions were discussed separately, they are closely related. The answer to one depends on the answers to the others. For example, an economy that distributes goods and services uniformly to all will, no doubt, answer the what-will-be-produced question differently than an economy that somehow allows more personal choice. As we have seen, laws about resource ownership and the role of government determine the "rules of the game"—the set of conditions that shape individual incentives and constraints. Along a spectrum ranging from the freest to the most regimented types of economic systems, *pure capitalism* would be at one end and the *pure command system* at the other.

Pure Capitalism

Under **pure capitalism**, the rules of the game include the private ownership of resources and the market distribution of products. Owners have *property rights* to the use of their resources and are therefore free to supply those resources to the highest bidder. **Private property rights** allow individual owners to use resources or to charge others for their use. Any income derived from supplying labour, capital, natural resources, or entrepreneurial ability goes to the individual resource owners. Producers are free to make and sell whatever they think will be profitable. Consumers are free to buy whatever goods they can afford. All this voluntary buying and selling is coordinated by unrestricted markets, where buyers and sellers make their intentions known. Market prices guide resources to their most productive use and channel goods and services to the consumers who value them the most.

economic system the set of mechanisms and institutions that resolve the what, how, and for whom questions

pure capitalism an economic system characterized by the private ownership of resources and the use of prices to coordinate economic activity in unregulated markets

private property rights an owner's right to use, rent, or sell resources or property

Under pure capitalism, markets answer the what, how, and for whom questions. That's why capitalism is also referred to as a *market system.* Markets transmit information about relative scarcity, provide individual incentives, and distribute income among resource suppliers. No individual or small group coordinates these activities. Rather, it is the voluntary choices of many buyers and sellers responding only to their individual incentives and constraints that direct resources and products to those who value them the most.

According to Adam Smith (1723–1790), market forces allocate resources as if by an "invisible hand"— an unseen force that harnesses the pursuit of self-interest to direct resources where they earn the greatest reward. According to Smith, *although each individual pursues his or her self-interest, the "invisible hand" of market forces promotes the general welfare.* Capitalism is sometimes called *laissez-faire;* translated from the French, this phrase means "to let do," or to let people do as they choose without government intervention. Thus, under capitalism, voluntary choices based on rational self-interest are made in unrestricted markets to answer the questions what, how, and for whom. But even for Adam Smith, government was required to set and enforce appropriate rules of the game and correct some market failures for "pure" capitalism to work.

As we will see in later chapters, pure capitalism has its flaws. The most notable market failures are these:

1 No central authority protects property rights, enforces contracts, and otherwise ensures that the rules of the game are followed.

2 People with no resources to sell could starve.

3 Unequal bargaining power can result in some individuals earning very low incomes, well below their productive potential—a point made by Adam Smith.

4 Some producers may try to monopolize markets by eliminating the competition.

5 The production or consumption of some goods involves side effects that can harm or benefit people not involved in the market transaction.

6 Private firms have no incentive to produce so-called *public goods,* such as national defence, because private firms cannot prevent nonpayers from enjoying the benefits of public goods.

Because of these limitations, countries have modified pure capitalism to allow some role for government. Canada is among the most market-oriented economies in the world today. According to the Heritage Foundation and the *Wall Street Journal,* Canada ranked sixth in the world for economic freedom, ahead of the United States, which was ranked twelfth.[3] Be this as it may, even in countries like Canada and the United States government plays a highly significant role in the economy in setting and enforcing the rules of the game and in purchasing goods and services.

Pure Command System

In a **pure command system**, resources are directed and production is coordinated not by market forces but by the "command," or central plan, of government. In theory at least, instead of private property, there is public, or *communal,* ownership of property. That's why central planning is sometimes called *communism.* Government planners, as representatives of all the people, answer the three questions through *central plans* spelling out how much steel, how many cars, and how much housing to produce. They also decide how to produce these goods and who gets them.

In theory, the pure command system incorporates individual choices into collective choices, which, in turn, are reflected in the central plans. In fact, command economies often have names that focus on collective choice, such as the People's Republic of China and the Democratic People's Republic of Korea (North Korea). In practice, the pure command system also has flaws, most notably these:

1 Running an economy is so complicated that some resources are used inefficiently.

[3] "2015 Index of Economic Freedom," The Heritage Foundation, www.heritage.org/index.

Common ownership can sometimes lead to common neglect.

2 Because nobody in particular owns resources, each person has less incentive to employ them in their highest-valued use, so some resources are wasted.

3 Central plans may reflect more the preferences of central planners than those of society.

4 Because government is responsible for all production, the variety of products tends to be more limited than in a capitalist economy.

Because of these limitations, countries have modified the pure command system to allow a role for markets. North Korea is perhaps the most centrally planned economy in the world today.

Mixed and Transitional Economies

No country on earth exemplifies either type of economic system in its pure form. Economic systems have grown more alike over time, with the role of government increasing in capitalist economies and the role of markets increasing in command economies. Canada represents a **mixed system**, with government directly accounting for about one-quarter of all economic activity. What's more, Canadian governments at all levels regulate the private sector in a variety of ways. For example, local zoning boards determine lot sizes, home sizes, and the types of industries allowed. Federal and provincial bodies regulate workplace safety, environmental quality, competitive fairness, food and drug quality, and many other activities.

Although both ends of the spectrum have moved toward the centre, capitalism has gained the most converts in recent decades. Perhaps the benefits of markets are no better illustrated than when a country, as a result of war or political upheaval, became divided by ideology into a capitalist economy and a command economy, such as with Taiwan and China or South Korea and North Korea. In each case, the economies began with similar human and physical resources, but once they went their separate ways, economic growth diverged sharply, with the capitalist economies outperforming the command economies. For example, Taiwan's production per capita in 2010 was nearly five times that of China's, and South Korea's production per capita was almost 17 times that of North Korea's.

Consider an example from American history. When the pilgrims first established Plymouth Colony in 1620, they tried communal ownership of the land. That turned out badly. Crops were neglected and food shortages developed. After three years of near starvation, the system was changed so that each family was assigned a plot of land and granted the fruits of that plot. Yields increased sharply. The pilgrims learned that people take better care of what they own individually; common ownership can sometimes lead to common neglect.

Recognizing the incentive power of property rights and markets, some of the most die-hard central planners are now allowing a role for markets. For example, about one-fifth of the world's population lives in China, which grows more market oriented each day, even going so far as to give private property constitutional protection on a par with state property. In a poll of Chinese citizens, 74 percent agreed that "the free enterprise system is the best system on which to base the future of the world." Among Americans polled, 71 percent agreed with that statement.[4] Two decades ago, the former Soviet Union dissolved into 15 independent republics; most converted state-owned enterprises into private firms. From Moscow to Beijing, from Hungary to Mongolia, the transition to mixed economies now underway in former command economies will shape the world for decades to come.

> **mixed system** an economic system characterized by the private ownership of some resources and the public ownership of other resources; some markets are regulated by government

Economies Based on Custom or Religion

Finally, some economic systems are moulded largely by custom or religion. For example, caste systems in India and elsewhere restrict occupational choices. Charging interest is banned under Islamic law. Family relations also play significant roles in organizing and coordinating economic activity. Even in Canada, some occupations are still dominated by women, others by men, largely because of tradition and how men and women are raised in their families and communities. Your own pattern of consumption and choice of occupation may be influenced by some of these considerations.

Final Word

Although economies can answer the three economic questions in a variety of ways, this book focuses primarily on the mixed market system, such as exists in Canada. This type of economy blends *private choice*, guided by the price system in competitive markets, with *public choice*, guided by democracy in political markets. The study of mixed market systems grows more relevant as former command economies try to develop markets. The next chapter focuses on the economic actors in a mixed economy and explains why and how government gets into the act.

[4] As reported in "Capitalism, Comrade!", *Wall Street Journal*, 18 January 2006.

CHAPTER PROBLEMS

LO1 Describe the impact of differing opportunities on choice

1.1. *(Sunk Cost and Choice)* Suppose you go to a restaurant and buy an expensive meal. Halfway through, despite feeling quite full, you decide to clean your plate. After all, you think, you paid for the meal, so you are going to eat all of it. What's wrong with this thinking?

1.2. *(Opportunity Cost)* You can spend spring break either at home working for $80 per day for five days or go to Florida for the week. If you stay home, your expenses will total about $100. If you go to Florida, the airfare, hotel, food, and miscellaneous expenses will total about $700. What's your opportunity cost of going to Florida?

1.3. *(Opportunity Cost)* Let's say that you simply love to work—it's not just about the money you earn. Given this assumption, what would be the opportunity cost of not working? How would this assumption affect simply using monetary values to measure opportunity cost?

1.4. *(Opportunity Cost)* Determine whether each of the following statements is true, false, or uncertain. Explain your answers:
   a. The opportunity cost of an activity is the total value of all the alternatives passed up.
   b. Opportunity cost is an objective measure of cost.
   c. When making choices, people carefully gather all available information about the costs and benefits of alternative choices.
   d. A decision maker seldom knows the actual value of a forgone alternative and therefore must make decisions based on expected values.

LO2 Explain how comparative advantage, specialization, and exchange affect economic outcomes (output)

2.1. *(Absolute and Comparative Advantage)* You have the following information concerning the production of wheat and cloth in Canada and the United Kingdom:

Labour Hours Required to Produce One Unit

	United Kingdom	Canada
Wheat	2	1
Cloth	6	5

   a. What is the opportunity cost of producing a unit of wheat in the United Kingdom? In Canada?
   b. Which country has an absolute advantage in producing wheat? In producing cloth?
   c. Which country has a comparative advantage in producing wheat? In producing cloth?
   d. Which country should specialize in producing wheat? In producing cloth?

2.2. *(Specialization)* Provide some examples of specialized markets or retail outlets. What makes the Web so conducive to specialization?

2.3. *(Specialization)* Explain how the specialization of labour can lead to increased productivity.

2.4. *(Specialization)* If specialization yields increased productivity, why do some people do various household tasks on their own as opposed to hiring specialists to do these jobs?

LO3 Outline how economies function as production systems

3.1. *(Shape of the PPF)* Suppose a production possibilities frontier includes the following combinations:

Cars	Washing Machines
0	1,000
100	600
200	0

   a. Graph the PPF, assuming that it has no curved segments.
   b. What is the cost of producing an additional car when 50 cars are being produced?
   c. What is the cost of producing an additional car when 150 cars are being produced?
   d. What is the cost of producing an additional washing machine when 50 cars are being produced? When 150 cars are being produced?
   e. What do your answers tell you about opportunity costs?

3.2. *(Production Possibilities)* Suppose an economy uses two resources (labour and capital) to produce two goods (wheat and cloth). Capital is relatively more useful in producing cloth, and labour is relatively more useful in producing wheat. If the supply of capital falls by 10 percent and the supply of labour increases by 10 percent, how will the PPF for wheat and cloth change?

3.3. (*Production Possibilities*) There's no reason why a production possibilities frontier could not be used to represent the situation facing an individual. Imagine your own PPF. Right now—today—you have certain resources—your time, your skills, perhaps some capital. And you can produce various outputs. Suppose you can produce combinations of two outputs, call them studying and partying.
   a. Draw your PPF for studying and partying. Be sure to label the axes of the diagram appropriately. Label the points where the PPF intersects the axes, as well as several other points along the frontier.
   b. Explain what it would mean for you to move upward and to the left along your personal PPF. What kinds of adjustments would you have to make in your life to make such a movement along the frontier?
   c. Under what circumstances would your personal PPF shift outward? Do you think the shift would be a "parallel" one? Why, or why not?
3.4. (*Shifting Production Possibilities*) Determine whether each of the following would cause the economy's PPF to shift inward, outward, or not at all:
   a. An increase in average length of annual vacations
   b. An increase in immigration
   c. A decrease in the average retirement age
   d. The migration of skilled workers to other countries
3.5. (*Production Possibilities*) Under what conditions would an economy be operating inside its PPF? On its PPF? Outside its PPF? Which of these three are possible and why?
3.6. (*Shifting Production Possibilities*) We have one economy where people save a larger percentage of their income than in another. Both economies start off with the same level of per capita income. If both economies invest their savings, how would this affect the production possibility curves and why?

LO4 Describe different economic systems and the decision-making rules that define them

4.1. (*Economic Systems*) Canada is best described as having a mixed economy. What are some elements of command in Canada? What are some market elements? What are some traditional elements?
4.2. (*Economic Systems*) Why would you expect mixed economies such as Canada's to perform better than pure exchange or pure command economies? For example, Canada performs much better than more free market New Zealand. Why is this the case?

CASE STUDY

The Opportunity Cost of University

What is your opportunity cost of attending university full time this year? What was the best alternative you gave up? If you held a full-time job, you have some idea of the income you gave up to attend university. Suppose you expected to earn $20,000 a year, after taxes, from a full-time job. As a full-time university student, you plan to work part time during the academic year and full time during the summer, earning a total of $10,000 after taxes (about 40 percent of university students hold jobs during the academic year). Thus, by attending university this year, you gave up after-tax earnings of $10,000 (= $20,000 − $10,000).

There is also the direct cost of university itself. Suppose you are paying $7,500 this year for tuition, fees, and books at university. The opportunity cost of paying for tuition, fees, and books is what you and your family could otherwise have purchased with that money.

How about room and board? Expenses for room and board are not necessarily an opportunity cost because, even if you were not attending university, you would still need to live somewhere and eat something, though these could cost more in university. Likewise, whether or not you attended university, you would still buy goods such as CDs, clothes, and toiletries, and services such as laundry, haircuts, and mobile service.

Your spending for such products is not an opportunity cost of attending university but the personal cost that arises regardless of what you do. So for simplicity, assume that room, board, and personal expenses are the same whether or not you attend university. The forgone earnings of $10,000 plus the $7,500 for tuition, fees, and books yield an opportunity cost of $17,500 this year. Scholarships, but not loans, would reduce your opportunity cost (why not loans?).

This analysis assumes that other things remain constant. But if, in your view, attending university is more of a pain than you expected your next best alternative to be, then the opportunity cost of attending university is even higher. In other words, if you are one of those people who find university difficult, often boring, and in most ways more unpleasant than a full-time job, then the money cost understates your opportunity cost, because your best alternative offers a more enjoyable quality of life. If, on the other hand, you believe the wild and crazy life of a university student is more enjoyable than a full-time job would be, then the dollar figures overstate your opportunity cost, because your next best alternative involves a less satisfying quality of life.

Apparently, you view university as a wise investment in your future, even though it's costly and perhaps even painful. University graduates on average earn about twice as much per year as high school graduates, a difference that exceeds $1 million over a lifetime. These pay gains from university encourage a growing fraction of university students to pile up debts to finance their education.

Canadian university students in 2013 were expecting to graduate with an average debt of over $26,000. Still, postsecondary education is not for everyone. Some find the opportunity cost too high. For example, Bill Gates and Paul Allen dropped out of college to cofound Microsoft (both are now among the richest people on earth). Tiger Woods, once an economics major at Stanford, dropped out after two years to earn a fortune in professional golf. And Paula Creamer, who skipped college to play golf, won her first $1 million sooner than any other LPGA player in tour history. High school basketball players who believed they were ready for the pros, such as Kobe Bryant and LeBron James, also skipped college (now players can't enter the pros until reaching 19 years of age and out of high school at least a year), as do most tennis pros. Many actors even dropped out of high school to follow their dreams, including Jim Carrey, Russell Crowe, Tom Cruise, Johnny Depp, Robert DeNiro, Cameron Diaz, Colin Farrell, Nicole Kidman, Jude Law, Lindsay Lohan, Demi Moore, Keanu Reeves, Kiefer Sutherland, Hilary Swank, Charlize Theron, and Kate Winslet. However, you usually don't hear of all those high school and university students who dropout to pursue their dreams in sports and business and end up being either impoverished or earning incomes well below what they would have earned had they remained in school.

SOURCES: Elyse Ashburn, "Why Do Students Drop Out? Because They Must Work at Jobs Too," *Chronicle of Higher Education*, 9 December 2009; Mary Pilon, "The $550,000 Student-Loan Burden," *Wall Street Journal*, 13 February 2010; "The World's Billionaires," *Forbes*, 11 March 2010; "College Board Connect to College Success" at http://www.collegeboard.com/; Joseph Berger and Andrew Parkin, "The Value of a Degree: Education, Employment and Earnings in Canada"; and "BMO 2013 Student Survey: Canadian Students Relying Less on Family to Finance Higher Education."

QUESTION

1. During the Vietnam War, colleges and universities in the United States were overflowing with students. Was this bumper crop of students caused by a greater than expected return on a college education or by a change in the opportunity cost of attending college? Explain.

Economic Decision Makers

LEARNING OUTCOMES

LO1 Explain the role of the household in an economic system

LO2 Identify the different types of firms and describe their roles in the economy

LO3 Outline the ways governments affect their economies

LO4 Outline the international influences on an economy

> ## If we live in the age of specialization, then why haven't specialists taken over all production?

If we live in the age of specialization, then why haven't specialists taken over all production? For example, why do most of us still do our own laundry and perform dozens of other tasks for ourselves? In what sense has some production moved from the household to the firm and then back to the household? If the "invisible hand" of competitive markets is so efficient, why does government get into the act? Answers to these and other questions are addressed in this chapter, which discusses the four economic decision makers: households, firms, governments, and the rest of the world.

To develop a better feel for how the economy works, you must get more acquainted with the key players. You already know more about them than you may realize. You grew up in a household. You have dealt with firms all your life, from Sony to Subway to Tim Hortons. You know much about governments—for example, in the form of taxes and public schools. And you have a growing awareness of the rest of the world gained from online sites, imports, foreign travel, and so on. This chapter draws on your abundant personal experience with economic decision makers to consider their makeup and goals.

LO 1 The Household

Households play the starring role in a market economy. Their demand for goods and services determines what gets produced. And their supply of labour, capital, natural resources, and entrepreneurial ability produces that output. As demanders of goods and services and suppliers of resources, households make all kinds of choices, such as what to buy, how much to save, where to live, and where to work. Although a household usually consists of several individuals, as a simplifying assumption, we will view each household as acting like a single decision maker. In reality, household decisions are made through discussion, debate, and argument among the various members of the household unit. Household members once built their own homes, made their own clothes and furniture, grew their own food, and amused themselves with books, games, and hobbies. Over time, however, the efficiency arising from comparative advantage resulted in a greater specialization among resource suppliers. This section takes a look at households and firms, beginning with their evolution.

The Evolution of the Household

In earlier times, when the economy was primarily agricultural, a farm household was largely self-sufficient. Each family member often specialized in a specific farm task—cooking meals, making clothes, tending livestock, planting crops, and so on. These early households produced what they consumed and consumed what they produced. With the introduction of new seed varieties, better fertilizers, and labour-saving machinery, farm productivity increased sharply. Fewer farmers were needed to grow enough food to feed a nation. At the same time, the growth of urban factories increased the demand for factory labour. As a result, many workers moved from farms to cities, where they became more specialized but less self-sufficient.

Households evolved in other ways. For example, in 1976, only about 39 percent of women with children under the age of 16 worked outside the home. Since then, higher levels of education among women and a growing demand for their labour increased women's earnings, thus raising their opportunity cost of working in the home. This higher opportunity cost contributed to their growing labour force participation. Today about 73 percent of women with children under 16 are employed.

The rise of two-earner households has affected the family as an economic unit. Households produce less for themselves and demand more from the market. For example, child-care services and fast-food restaurants have displaced some household production. The rise in two-earner families has reduced specialization within the household—a central feature of the farm family. Nonetheless, some production still occurs in the home, as we'll explore later.

Households Maximize Utility

There are more than 12 million Canadian households. All those who live together under one roof are considered part of the same household. What exactly do households attempt to accomplish in making decisions? Economists assume that people try to maximize their level of satisfaction, sense of well-being, happiness, and overall welfare. In short, households attempt to maximize **utility**. Households, like other economic decision makers, are viewed as rational, meaning that they try to act in their best interests and do not deliberately try to make themselves less happy. Utility maximization depends on each household's subjective goals, not on some objective standard. For example, some households maintain neat homes with well-groomed lawns; others pay little attention to their homes and use their lawns as junkyards.

Seventy-three percent of women with children under 16 are in the labour force.

Households as Resource Suppliers

utility the satisfaction received from consumption; sense of well-being

Households use their limited resources—labour, capital, natural resources, and entrepreneurial ability—in an attempt to satisfy their unlimited wants. They can use these resources to produce goods and services in their homes. For example, they can cook, wash, sew, dust, iron, sweep, vacuum, mop, mow, paint, and fix a leaky faucet. They can also sell these resources in the resource market and use the income to buy goods and services in the product market. The most valuable resource sold by most households is labour.

Panel (a) of Exhibit 1 shows the sources of personal income received by Canadian households in 2010, when personal income totalled $1.3 trillion. As you can see, 66 percent of personal income came from wages and salaries. A distant second was transfer payments (to be discussed next), at 15 percent of personal income, followed by interest and investment income at 10 percent, and proprietors' income at 8 percent. *Proprietors* are people who work for themselves rather than for employers; farmers, plumbers, and doctors are often self-employed.

Proprietors' income should also be considered a form of labour income. *Over two-thirds of personal income in Canada comes from labour earnings rather than from the ownership of other resources such as capital or natural resources.*

Because of a limited education, disability, discrimination, poor health, the time demands of caring for

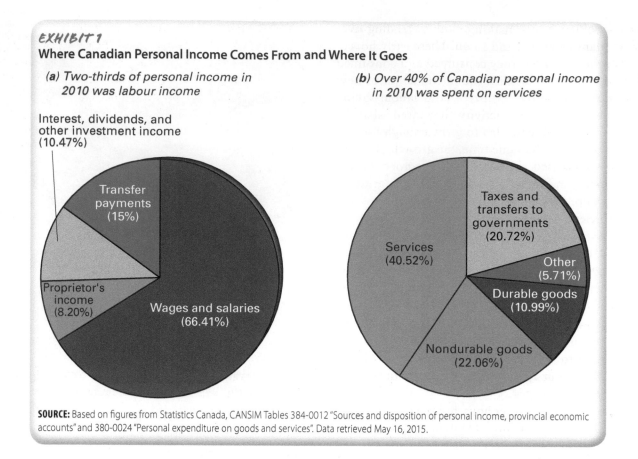

EXHIBIT 1

Where Canadian Personal Income Comes From and Where It Goes

(a) Two-thirds of personal income in 2010 was labour income

Interest, dividends, and other investment income (10.47%)

Transfer payments (15%)

Proprietor's income (8.20%)

Wages and salaries (66.41%)

(b) Over 40% of Canadian personal income in 2010 was spent on services

Services (40.52%)

Taxes and transfers to governments (20.72%)

Other (5.71%)

Durable goods (10.99%)

Nondurable goods (22.06%)

SOURCE: Based on figures from Statistics Canada, CANSIM Tables 384-0012 "Sources and disposition of personal income, provincial economic accounts" and 380-0024 "Personal expenditure on goods and services". Data retrieved May 16, 2015.

transfer payments
benefits given to individuals as outright grants from the government

small children, or just bad luck, some households have few resources that are valued in the market. Society has made the political decision that individuals in such circumstances should receive short-term public assistance. Consequently, the government gives some households **transfer payments**, which are outright grants. Transfer payments in Canada include Old Age Security, employment insurance, social assistance, Canada Pension Plan, and Quebec Pension Plan.

Households as Demanders of Goods and Services

What happens to personal income once it comes into the household? Most goes to personal consumption, which sorts into three broad spending categories: (1) *durable goods*—that is, goods expected to last three or more years—such as an automobile or a refrigerator; (2) *nondurable goods,* such as food, clothing, and gasoline; and (3) *services,* such as haircuts, air travel, and medical care. As you can see from panel (b) of Exhibit 1, spending on durable goods in 2010 claimed

11 percent of Canadian personal income; nondurables, 22 percent; and services, 40.5 percent. Taxes and transfers to the government claimed 21 percent, and all other categories, including savings, claimed just 6 percent. So about two-fifths of all personal income went for services—the fastest-growing sector, because many services, such as child care, are shifting from do-it-yourself home production to market purchases.

LO 2 The Firm

As noted above, household members once built their own homes, made their own clothes and furniture, grew their own food, and amused themselves with books, games, and hobbies. Over time, however, the efficiency arising from comparative advantage resulted in a greater specialization among resource suppliers. This section takes a look at firms, beginning with their evolution.

The Evolution of the Firm

Specialization and comparative advantage explain why households are no longer self-sufficient. But why is a firm the natural result? For example, rather than make a woollen sweater from scratch, couldn't a consumer take advantage of specialization by negotiating with someone who produced the wool, another who spun the wool into yarn, and a third who knit the yarn into a sweater? Here's the problem with that model: if the consumer had to visit each of these specialists and reach an agreement, the resulting *transaction costs* could easily erase the gains from specialization. Instead of visiting and bargaining with each specialist, the consumer can pay someone to do the bargaining—an entrepreneur, who hires all the resources necessary to make the sweater. *An entrepreneur, by contracting for many sweaters rather than just one, is able to reduce the transaction costs per sweater.*

For about 200 years, profit-seeking entrepreneurs relied on "putting out" raw material, like wool and cotton, to rural households that turned it into finished products, like woollen goods made from yarn. The system developed in the British Isles, where workers' cottages served as tiny factories, especially during winter months, when farming chores were few (so the opportunity cost was low). This approach, which came to be known as the *cottage industry system,* still exists in some parts of the world. You might think of this system as partway between household self-sufficiency and the modern firm.

As the British economy expanded in the 18th century, entrepreneurs began organizing the stages of production under one roof. Technological developments, such as water power and later steam power, increased the productivity of each worker and helped shift employment from rural areas to urban factories. *Work, therefore, became organized in large, centrally powered factories that (1) promoted a more efficient division of labour, (2) allowed for the direct supervision of production, (3) reduced transportation costs, (4) facilitated the introduction and development of improved technology and (5) facilitated the use of machines far bigger than anything used in the home.* The development of large-scale factory production, known

as the **Industrial Revolution**, began in Great Britain around 1750 and spread to the rest of Europe, North America, parts of South America, Australia, and New Zealand. Production, then, evolved from self-sufficient rural households to the cottage industry system, where specialized production occurred in the household, to production in a firm. Today, entrepreneurs combine resources in firms such as factories, mills, offices, stores, and restaurants. **Firms** are economic units formed by profit-seeking entrepreneurs who combine labour, capital, and natural resources to produce goods and services. Just as we assume that households try to maximize utility, we assume that firms try to *maximize profit.* Profit, the entrepreneur's reward, equals sales revenue minus the cost of production, including the opportunity cost of the entrepreneur's time.

Types of Firms

There are more than 1.3 million "employer businesses" in Canada. An employer business is a business with at least one employee. Over half of the employer businesses in Canada have between one and four employees. Firms are organized in one of three ways: as a sole proprietorship, as a partnership, or as a corporation.

Sole Proprietorships The simplest form of business organization is the **sole proprietorship**, a single-owner firm. Examples are self-employed plumbers, farmers, and dentists. Most sole proprietorships consist of just the self-employed proprietor—there are no hired employees. To organize a sole proprietorship, the owner simply opens for business by, for example, taking out a classified ad announcing availability for plumbing services or whatever. The owner is in complete control. But he or she faces unlimited liability and could lose everything, including a home and other personal assets, to settle business debts or other claims against the business. Also, because the sole proprietor has no partners or other investors, raising enough money to get the business

© Photos.com/Jupiterimages/Thinkstock

Industrial Revolution development of large-scale factory production that began in Great Britain around 1750 and spread to the rest of Europe, North America, Australia, and New Zealand

firms economic units formed by profit-seeking entrepreneurs who employ resources to produce goods and services for sale

sole proprietorship a firm with a single owner who has the right to all profits but who also bears unlimited liability for the firm's losses and debts

up and running and keep it going can be a challenge. One final disadvantage is that a sole proprietorship usually goes out of business when the proprietor dies or leaves the business.

Partnerships A more complicated form of business is the **partnership**, which involves two or more individuals who agree to combine their funds and efforts in return for a share of any profit or loss. Law, accounting, and medical partnerships typify this business form. Partners have strength in numbers and often find it easier than sole proprietors to raise enough funds to get the business going. But partners may not always agree. Also, each partner usually faces unlimited liability for any debts or claims against the partnership, so one partner could lose everything because of another's mistake. Finally, the death or departure of one partner can disrupt the firm's continuity and require a complete reorganization.

Corporations By far the most influential form of business is the corporation. A **corporation** is a legal entity established through articles of incorporation. Shares of stock confer corporate ownership, thereby entitling shareholders to a claim on any profit. A major advantage of the corporate form is that many investors—hundreds, thousands, even millions—can pool their funds, so incorporating represents the easiest way to amass large sums to finance the business. Also, shareholders' liability for any loss is limited to the value of their shares, meaning shareholders enjoy *limited liability*. A final advantage of this form of organization is that the corporation has a life apart from its owners. The corporation survives even if ownership changes hands, and it can be taxed, sued, and even charged with a crime as if it were a person.

The corporate form has some disadvantages as well. A shareholder's ability to influence corporate policy is limited to voting for a board of directors, which oversees the operation of the firm. Each share of stock usually carries with it one vote. The typical shareholder of a large corporation owns only a tiny fraction of the shares and thus has little say. Whereas the income from sole proprietorships and partnerships is taxed only once, corporate income gets whacked twice—first as corporate profits and second as shareholder income, either as corporate dividends or as realized capital gains. A *realized capital gain* is any increase in the market price of a share that occurs between the time the share is purchased and the time it is sold.

Cooperatives

A **cooperative**, or "co-op" for short, is a group of people who cooperate by pooling their resources to buy and sell more efficiently than they could independently. Cooperatives try to minimize costs and operate with limited liability of members. Many cooperatives don't attempt to maximize profits in the narrow sense of the term, although they always attempt to cover their costs. Often, instead, they deliberately charge lower prices or provide better services to their members. The government grants most cooperatives tax-exempt status. There are three types: consumer, producer, and worker cooperatives. The first two are by far the most important with regard to output produced and employment.

Consumer Cooperatives A *consumer cooperative* is a retail business owned and operated by some or all of its customers in order to reduce costs. Some cooperatives require members to pay an annual fee and others require them to work a certain number of hours each year. Members sometimes pay lower prices than other customers or may share in any revenues that exceed costs. In Canada, consumer cooperatives operate credit unions, electric-power facilities, oil refineries, apartment buildings, and grocery stores, among other businesses.

Producer Cooperatives In a *producer cooperative*, producers join forces to buy supplies and equipment and to market their output. Each producer's objective is to reduce costs and increase profits. Federal legislation allows farmers to cooperate without violating antitrust laws. Firms in other industries could not do this legally. Farmers pool their funds to purchase machinery and supplies, provide storage and processing facilities, and transport products to market. An example of a producer cooperative is the UFA, originally established as the United Farmers of Alberta Co-operative Limited and founded in 1909. It currently has over 120,000 members and operates businesses in agriculture, oil refining, and construction.

Worker Cooperatives A worker cooperative is owned by the workers. Workers share all profits and losses and make all decisions, often by delegating day-to-day decision making to managers and a board of directors. But the worker-owners have the ultimate say. These cooperatives attempt to be economically efficient and competitive, while serving the needs of their members and community. This might result in sacrificing short-term economic gain for longer-term benefit. In Canada, worker cooperatives are represented by the Canadian Worker Co-operative Federation.

Not-for-Profit Organizations

So far, you have learned about organizations that try to maximize profits or, in the case of cooperatives, to minimize costs. Some organizations have neither as a goal. **Not-for-profit organizations** engage in charitable, educational, humanitarian, cultural, professional, and other activities, often with a social purpose. Any revenue exceeding cost is plowed back into the organization. Government agencies do not have profit as a goal either, but governments are not included in this definition of not-for-profit organizations.

Like businesses, not-for-profit organizations evolved to help people accomplish their goals. Examples are nonprofit hospitals, private schools, religious organizations, activist groups such as Greenpeace, soup kitchens, orchestras, and professional organizations. There are about 80,000 not-for-profit organizations registered with the Canada Revenue Agency.

North Bay Fishermen's Co-op Ltd. exports seafood to the Pacific Rim, Europe, and North America.

© Alex Segre/Alamy

But even not-for-profit organizations must somehow pay the bills. Revenue typically includes some combination of voluntary contributions and service charges, such as college tuition and hospital charges. In Canada, not-for-profit organizations are usually exempt from taxes.

> **not-for-profit organizations** groups that do not pursue profit as a goal; they engage in charitable, educational, humanitarian, cultural, professional, or other activities, often with a social purpose

Why Does Household Production Still Exist?

If firms are so efficient at reducing transaction and production costs, why don't they make everything? Why do households still perform some tasks, such as cooking and cleaning? *If a household's opportunity cost of performing a task is below the market price, then the household usually performs that task.* People with a lower opportunity cost of time do more for themselves. For example, janitors are more likely to mow their lawns than are physicians. Let's look at some reasons for household production.

No Skills or Special Resources Are Required Some activities require so few skills or special resources that householders find it cheaper to do the jobs themselves. Sweeping the kitchen floor requires only a broom and some time so it's usually performed by household members. Sanding a wooden floor, however, involves special machinery and expertise, so this service is usually left to professionals. Similarly, although you wouldn't hire someone to brush your teeth, dental work is not for amateurs. *Households usually perform domestic chores that demand neither expertise nor special machinery.*

Household Production Avoids Taxes Suppose you are deciding whether to pay someone $3,000 to paint your house or do it yourself. If the income tax rate is one-third, you must earn $4,500 before taxes to have the $3,000 after taxes to pay for the job. And the painter who charges you $3,000 nets only $2,000 after paying $1,000 in taxes. Thus, you must earn $4,500 so that the painter can take home $2,000. If you paint the house yourself, no taxes are involved. The tax-free nature of do-it-yourself activity favours household production over market transactions.

Household Production Reduces Transaction Costs Getting estimates, hiring a contractor, negotiating terms, and monitoring job performance all take time

Do it yourself, or pay someone to do it for you?

household tasks. Also, new technologies such as Blu-ray players, DVRs, HDTVs, broadband downloads, and computer games enhance home entertainment. Indeed, microchip-based technologies have shifted some production from the firm back to the household.

<table>
<tr><td>LO 3</td><td></td></tr>
</table>

LO 3 The Government

You might think that production by households and firms could satisfy all consumer wants. Why must yet another economic decision maker get into the act? After all, governments play some role in every nation on earth.

The Role of Government

Sometimes the unrestrained operation of markets yields undesirable results. Too many of some goods and too few of other goods get produced. This section discusses the sources of **market failure** and how society's overall welfare may be improved through government intervention in the market.

Establishing and Enforcing the Rules of the Game Market efficiency depends on people like you using your resources to maximize your utility. But what if you were repeatedly robbed of your paycheque on your way home from work? Or what if, after you worked two weeks in a new job, your boss called you a sucker and said you wouldn't get paid? Why bother working? The market system would break down if you could not safeguard your private property or if you could not enforce contracts. Governments safeguard private property through police protection and enforce contracts through a judicial system. More generally, governments try to make sure that market participants abide by the rules of the game. These rules are established through government laws and regulations and also through the customs and conventions of the marketplace.

Promoting Competition Although the "invisible hand" of competition usually promotes an efficient allocation of resources, some firms try to

market failure a condition that arises when the unregulated operation of markets yields socially undesirable results

and require information. Doing the job yourself reduces these transaction costs. Household production also allows for more personal control over the final product than is usually available through the market. For example, some people prefer home cooking, because they can prepare home-cooked meals to individual tastes.

Technological Advances Increase Household Productivity Technological breakthroughs are not confined to market production. Vacuum cleaners, washers and dryers, dishwashers, microwave ovens, and other modern appliances reduce the time and often the skill required to perform

avoid competition through *collusion*, which is an agreement among firms to divide the market and fix the price. Or an individual firm may try to eliminate the competition by using unfair business practices. For example, to drive out local competitors, a large firm may temporarily sell at a price below cost. Government antitrust laws try to promote competition by prohibiting collusion and other anticompetitive practices.

Regulating Natural Monopolies Competition usually keeps the product price below the price charged by a **monopoly**, a sole supplier to the market. In rare instances, however, a monopoly can produce and sell the product for less than could competing firms. For example, electricity is delivered more efficiently by a single firm that wires the community than by competing firms each stringing its own wires. When it is cheaper for one firm to serve the market than for two or more firms to do so, that one firm is called a **natural monopoly**. Since a natural monopoly faces no competition, it maximizes profit by charging a higher price than would be optimal from society's point of view. A lower price and greater output would improve social welfare. Therefore, the government usually regulates a natural monopoly, forcing it to lower its price and increase output.

Providing Public Goods So far this book has been talking about private goods, which have two important features. First, private goods are *rival* in consumption, meaning that the amount consumed by one person is unavailable for others to consume. For example, when you and some friends share a pizza, each slice they eat is one less available for you. Second, the supplier of a private good can easily exclude those who fail to pay. Only paying customers get pizza. Thus, private goods are said to be *excludable*. So **private goods**, such as pizza, are both rival in consumption and excludable. In contrast, **public goods** are *nonrival* in consumption. For example, your family's benefit from a safer neighbourhood does not reduce your neighbour's benefit. What's more, once produced, public goods are available to all. Suppliers cannot easily prevent consumption by those who fail to pay. For example, reducing terrorism is *nonexcludable*. It benefits all in the community, regardless of who pays to reduce terrorism and who doesn't. Because public goods are *nonrival* and *nonexcludable*, private firms cannot sell them profitably. The government, however, has the authority

to enforce tax collections for public goods. Thus, the government sometimes provides public goods and funds them with taxes.

Dealing with Externalities Market prices reflect the private costs and private benefits of producers and consumers. But sometimes production or consumption imposes costs or benefits on third parties—on those who are neither suppliers nor demanders in a market transaction. For example, a paper mill fouls the air breathed by nearby residents, but the price of paper usually fails to reflect such costs. Because these pollution costs are outside, or external to, the market, they are called *externalities*. An **externality** is a cost or a benefit that falls on a third party. A negative externality imposes an external cost, such as factory pollution, auto emissions, or traffic congestion. A positive externality confers an external benefit, such as getting a good education, getting inoculated against a disease (thus reducing the possibility of infecting others), or driving carefully. Because market prices usually do not reflect externalities, governments often use taxes, subsidies, and regulations to align private and public benefits and costs. For example, a polluting factory may face taxes and regulations aimed at curbing that pollution. And because more educated people can read road signs and have options that pay better than crime, governments try to encourage education with free public schools, with subsidized higher education, and by keeping people in school until their 16th birthday.

A More Equal Distribution of Income As mentioned earlier, some people, because of poor education, mental or physical disabilities, bad luck, or perhaps the need to care for small children, are unable to support themselves and their families. Because resource markets do not guarantee even a minimum level of income, transfer payments reflect society's willingness to provide a basic standard of living to all households. Most Canadians agree that government should redistribute some income to the poor (note the normative nature of this statement). Opinions differ about who should receive benefits, how much

monopoly a sole supplier of a product with no close substitutes

natural monopoly one firm that can supply the entire market at a lower per-unit cost than could two or more firms

private good a good, such as pizza, that is both rival in consumption and excludable

public good a good that, once produced, is available for all to consume, regardless of who pays and who doesn't; such a good is nonrival and nonexcludable, such as a safer community

externality a cost or a benefit that affects neither the buyer nor seller, but instead affects people not involved in the market transaction

fiscal policy the use of government purchases, transfer payments, taxes, and borrowing to influence economy-wide variables such as inflation, employment, and economic growth

monetary policy regulation of the money supply to influence economy-wide variables such as inflation, employment, and economic growth

they should get, what form benefits should take, and how long benefits should last.

Full Employment, Price Stability, and Economic Growth Perhaps the most important responsibility of government is fostering a healthy economy, which benefits just about everyone. The government—through its ability to tax, to spend, and to control the money supply—attempts to promote full employment, price stability, and economic growth. Pursuing these objectives by taxing and spending is called **fiscal policy**. Pursuing them by regulating the money supply is called **monetary policy**. Macroeconomics examines both policies.

Government's Structure and Objectives

Canada is a constitutional monarchy with a parliamentary system of government. The *federal system* of government in Canada means that responsibilities are shared across levels of government. Provincial governments grant some powers to local governments and surrender some powers to the national, or federal, government. As the system has evolved, the federal government has primary responsibility for national security, economic stability, and market competition. Provincial governments are responsible for education, health, welfare, and transportation. Local governments provide primary and secondary education with aid from the provinces, plus police and fire protection. Here are some distinguishing features of government.

Difficulty in Defining Government Objectives We assume that households try to maximize utility and firms try to maximize profit, but what about governments—or, more specifically, what about government decision makers? What do they try to maximize? One problem is that our federal system consists of not one but many governments—more than 4,000 separate jurisdictions in all, made up of 1 nation, 10 provinces, 3 territories, 4,208 municipalities, and more than 250 school boards. For example, at the same time as Health Canada required health warnings on cigarette packages, Agriculture Canada pursued

policies to benefit tobacco growers. Within the federal government alone there are three distinct branches: executive, legislative, and judicial. Given this thicket of jurisdictions, branches, and bureaus, one useful theory of government behaviour is that elected officials try to maximize the number of votes they get in the next election. So let's assume that elected officials are vote maximizers. In this theory, vote maximization guides the decisions of elected officials who, in turn, oversee government employees.

Voluntary Exchange Versus Coercion Market exchange relies on the voluntary behaviour of buyers and sellers. Don't like tofu? No problem—don't buy any. But in political markets, the situation is different. Any voting rule except unanimous consent must involve some government coercion. Public choices are enforced by the police power of the state. Those who don't pay their taxes could go to jail, even though they may object to some programs those taxes support.

No Market Prices Another distinguishing feature of governments is that public output is usually offered at either a zero price or at some price below the cost of providing it. If you attend a public college or university in Canada, your tuition covers only a fraction of the cost of providing your education. Because the revenue side of the government budget is usually separate from the expenditure side, there is no necessary link between the cost of a program and the benefit. In the private sector, the expected marginal benefit of

The Canadian Press Images/Nathalie Madore

a product is at least as great as marginal cost; otherwise, nobody would buy it.

The Size and Growth of Government

One way to track the impact of government over time is by measuring government outlays relative to the Canadian *gross domestic product*, or *GDP*, which is the total value of all final goods and services produced in Canada. In 1929, the year the Great Depression began, all government outlays, mostly by provincial and local governments, totalled about 15 percent of GDP. At the time, the federal government played a minor role.

By 2010, the Great Depression, World War II, and a change in macroeconomic thinking had boosted the share of government outlays in Canada to 44 percent of GDP. In comparison, government outlays relative to GDP were 41 percent in Japan, 47 percent in Germany, 51 percent in Italy, 51 percent in the United Kingdom, and 56 percent in France. Government outlays by the 28 largest industrial economies averaged 45 percent of GDP in 2010.[1] Thus, government outlays in Canada relative to GDP are slightly below that of most other advanced economies.

Let's look briefly at the composition of federal outlays. Since 1961, defence spending had declined from over 20 percent of federal outlays to approximately 7 percent by 2011, as shown in Exhibit 2. Redistribution—family and child benefits, Employment Insurance, Old Age Security— had increased from about half of federal outlays in 1961 to two-thirds by 2011.

Sources of Government Revenue

Taxes provide the bulk of revenue at all levels of government. The federal government relies primarily on individual income tax, provincial governments rely on income and sales taxes,

[1] The Organization of Economic Cooperation and Development, *OECD Economic Outlook*, 88 (November 2010), Annex Table 25.

and local governments rely on property tax. Other revenue sources are user charges, such as health and drug insurance premiums, and borrowing. For additional revenue, some provinces also act as monopolies in certain markets, such as for lottery tickets and liquor.

Exhibit 3 focuses on the composition of federal revenue since 1961. The share made up by individual income tax has risen from about one-third in 1961

EXHIBIT 2

Redistribution Has Grown and Defence Has Declined as Share of Federal Outlays Since 1961

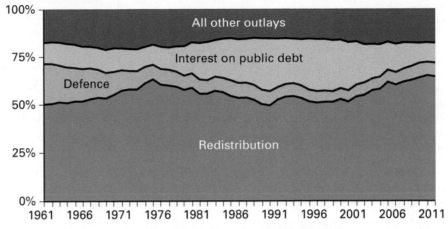

SOURCE: Computed based on figures from Statistics Canada, CANSIM Table 380-0034 "Income and expenditure sub-sector accounts, federal government, quarterly (dollars x 1,000,000)"

EXHIBIT 3

Individual Income Taxes Have Grown as a Share of Federal Revenue since 1961

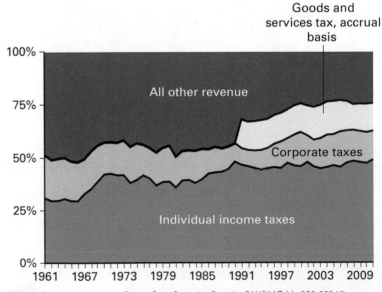

SOURCE: Computed based on figures from Statistics Canada, CANSIM Table 380-0034 "Income and expenditure sub-sector accounts, federal government, quarterly (dollars x 1,000,000)"

ability-to-pay tax principle those with a greater ability to pay, such as those earning higher incomes or those owning more property, should pay more taxes

benefits-received tax principle those who get more benefits from the government program should pay more taxes

tax incidence the distribution of tax burden among taxpayers; indicates who ultimately pays the tax

proportional taxation the tax as a percentage of income remains constant as income increases; also called a flat tax

progressive taxation the tax as a percentage of income increases as income increases

marginal tax rate the percentage of each additional dollar of income that goes to the tax

to one-half in 2011. The goods and services tax (GST—a federal sales tax) was introduced in 1991 and now provides 13 percent of government revenue. Corporate taxes accounted for one-fifth of federal government revenue in 1961, falling to a low of 7.6 percent in 1992, and have now settled at around 13 percent. Less than one-quarter of the government's revenue now comes from all other sources combined.

Tax Principles and Tax Incidence

The structure of a tax is often justified on the basis of one of two general principles. First, a tax could relate to the individual's ability to pay, so those with a greater ability pay more taxes. Income or property taxes often rely on this **ability-to-pay tax principle**.

Alternatively, the **benefits-received tax principle** relates taxes to the benefits taxpayers receive from the government activity funded by the tax. For example, the tax on gasoline funds highway construction and maintenance, thereby linking tax payment to road use, since those who drive more pay more gas taxes.

Tax incidence indicates who actually bears the burden of the tax. One way to evaluate tax incidence is by measuring the tax as a percentage of income. Under **proportional taxation**, taxpayers at all income levels pay the same percentage of their income in taxes. A proportional income tax is also called a flat tax, since the tax as a percentage of income remains constant, or flat, as income increases. Note that under proportional taxation, although taxes remain constant as a percentage of income, the dollar amount of taxes increases proportionately as income increases.

Under **progressive taxation**, the percentage of income paid in taxes increases as income increases. The **marginal tax rate** indicates the percentage of each additional dollar of income that goes to taxes. Because

In Egypt, property tax is not assessed until a building is completed.

high marginal rates reduce the after-tax return from working or investing, high marginal rates can reduce people's incentives to work and invest. The four marginal rates applied to the Canadian federal personal income tax range from 15% to 29%; they have remained fairly constant for over a decade.

Finally, under **regressive taxation**, the percentage of income paid in taxes decreases as income increases, so the marginal tax rate declines as income increases. Canada Pension Plan and Employment Insurance contributions are regressive, because they impose a flat rate up to a certain level of income, above which the marginal rate drops to zero. For example, Canada Pension Plan contributions were levied on the first $53,600 of workers' pay in 2015 at a rate of 4.95 percent.

Taxes often do more than fund public programs. Some taxes discourage certain activity. For example, a pollution tax can help clean the air. A tax on gasoline can encourage people to work at home, carpool, or use public transportation. Some taxes have unintended consequences. For example, in Egypt a property tax is not imposed until a building is complete. To avoid such taxes, builders never finish the job; multistorey dwellings are usually missing the top floor. As another example of how poorly designed taxes can distort the allocation of resources, property taxes in Amsterdam and Vietnam were originally based on the width of the building. As a result, buildings in those places are extremely narrow.

This discussion of revenue sources brings to a close, for now, our examination of the role of government in the Canadian economy. Government has a pervasive influence on the economy, and its role is discussed throughout the book.

LO 4 The Rest of the World

So far, the focus has been on institutions within Canada—that is, on *domestic* households, firms, and governments. This focus is appropriate because our primary objective is to understand the workings of the Canadian economy. But the rest of the world affects what Canadian households consume and what Canadian firms produce. For example, Japan and China supply all kinds of manufactured goods to Canada, thereby affecting Canadian prices, wages, and profits. Likewise, political events in the Persian Gulf or North Africa can affect what Canadians pay for oil. Foreign decision makers, therefore, influence the Canadian economy—what we produce and what we consume. The *rest of the world* consists of the households, firms, and governments in the other 200 or so sovereign nations throughout the world.

International Trade

In the previous chapter, you learned about comparative advantage and the gains from specialization. These gains explain why householders stopped doing everything for themselves and began to specialize. International trade arises for the same reasons. *International trade occurs because the opportunity cost of producing specific goods differs across countries.* Canadians import raw materials like crude oil, bauxite (aluminum ore), and coffee beans, and finished goods like cameras, gaming consoles, and cut diamonds. Canadian producers export sophisticated products like automobiles and aircraft, as well as agricultural products like wheat, corn, and soybeans. International trade occurs because the opportunity cost of producing specific goods differs across countries.

Trade between Canada and the rest of the world has increased in recent decades. In 1961, Canadian exports and imports were both roughly 15 percent of gross domestic product. Now Canadian exports represent about one-third of GDP and imports are 45 percent of GDP. The United States is by far Canada's largest trading partner, with the majority of its exports and imports being American-related. The European Union is a far distant second, followed by China.

The **merchandise trade balance** equals the value of exported goods minus the value of imported goods. Goods in this case are distinguished from services, which show up in another trade account. For the past 50 years, Canada has exported more goods than it has imported in most of those years. The merchandise trade surplus is offset by a deficit in one or more of the other *balance-of-payments* accounts. A nation's **balance of payments** is the record of all economic transactions between its residents and residents of the rest of the world.

regressive taxation the tax as a percentage of income decreases as income increases

merchandise trade balance the value during a given period of a country's exported goods minus the value of its imported goods

balance of payments a record of all economic transactions during a given period between residents of one country and residents of the rest of the world

Exchange Rates

foreign exchange foreign money needed to carry out international transactions

tariff a tax on imports

quota a legal limit on the quantity of a particular product that can be imported or exported

The lack of a common currency complicates trade between countries. How many Canadian dollars buy a Porsche? A Canadian buyer cares only about the dollar cost; the German carmaker cares only about the *euros* received (the common currency of 19 European countries). To facilitate trade funded by different currencies, a market for foreign exchange has developed. **Foreign exchange** is foreign currency needed to carry out international transactions. The supply and demand for foreign exchange comes together in *foreign exchange markets* to determine the exchange rate. The *exchange rate* measures the price of one currency in terms of another. For example, the exchange rate between the euro and the Canadian dollar might indicate that one euro exchanges for $1.20. At that exchange rate, a Porsche selling for €100,000 costs $120,000. The exchange rate affects the prices of imports and exports and thus helps shape the flow of foreign trade.

© wen mingming/Shutterstock.com

Trade Restrictions

Despite clear gains from international specialization and exchange, nearly all nations restrict trade to some extent. These restrictions can take the form of (1) **tariffs**, which are taxes on imports; (2) **quotas**, which are limits on the quantity of a particular good that can be imported or exported; and (3) other trade restrictions. If specialization according to comparative advantage is so beneficial, why do most countries restrict trade? Restrictions benefit certain domestic producers that lobby their governments for these benefits. For example, U.S. growers of sugarcane have benefited from legislation restricting imports, thereby raising U.S. sugar prices. These higher prices hurt domestic consumers, but consumers are usually unaware of this harm. In 2002, Kraft Foods Inc. moved production of its famous Life Savers candy from Michigan to Montreal. Why? Canadian food processors can purchase sugar on the world market at much lower prices than U.S. companies must pay. The loss of American jobs in food-processing industries (such as candy and breakfast cereal) can be directly tied to the protection of the U.S. sugar industry. Trade restrictions, especially where inefficient firms are concerned, interfere with the free flow of products across borders and tend to hurt the overall economy.

Final Word

This chapter examined the four economic decision makers: households, firms, governments, and the rest of the world. Domestic households are by far the most important, for they supply resources and demand goods and services.

If you were to stop reading right now, you would already know more economics than most people. But to understand market economies, you must learn how markets work. The next chapter introduces demand and supply.

CHAPTER PROBLEMS

LO1 Explain the role of the household in an economic system

1.1. *(Evolution of the Household)* Determine whether each of the following would increase or decrease the opportunity costs for mothers who choose not to work outside the home. Explain your answers.

a. Higher levels of education for women
b. Higher unemployment rates for women

c. Higher average pay levels for women

d. Lower demand for labour in industries that traditionally employ large numbers of women

1.2. *(Household Production)* Many households supplement their food budget by cultivating small vegetable gardens. Explain how each of the following might influence this kind of household production:

a. Both husband and wife are professionals who earn high salaries.

b. The household is located in a city rather than in a rural area.

c. The household is located in a region where there is a high sales tax on food.

d. The household is located in a region that has a high property tax rate.

1.3. *(Household Production)* What factors does a householder consider when deciding whether to produce a good or service at home or buy it in the marketplace?

1.4. *(Objectives of the Economic Decision Makers)* In economic analysis, what are the assumed objectives of households, firms, and the government?

1.5. *(Evolution of the Household)* Discuss why a much larger percentage of women work in the labour market in Sweden, Norway, and Denmark, where high-quality daycare is quite inexpensive as compared to Canada, where high-quality daycare can be quite expensive.

1.6. *(Household Production)* Why might lower-income families rely on their kids to do a significant amount of household work whereas in relatively wealthy households much of this type of work is contracted out?

LO2 Identify the different types of firms and describe their roles in the economy

2.1. *(Corporations)* How did the institution of the firm get a boost from the advent of the Industrial Revolution? What type of business organization existed before this?

2.2. *(Sole Proprietorships)* What are the disadvantages of the sole proprietorship form of business?

2.3. *(Cooperatives)* How do cooperatives differ from typical businesses?

2.4. *(Evolution of the Firm)* Explain how production after the Industrial Revolution differed from production under the cottage industry system.

2.5. *(Cooperatives)* What are the key differences between consumer, producer, and labour-owned cooperatives? See the following for important bits of information: http://ica.coop/en/what-co-operative.

2.6. *(Evolution of the Firm)* Why did the firm develop, as opposed to individuals producing all that they require for themselves?

2.7. *(Not-For-Profit)* Discuss the key differences between not-for-profit and for-profit firms. What role does the not-for-profit firm play in market economies?

LO3 Outline the ways governments affect their economies

3.1. *(Government)* Complete each of the following sentences:

a. When the private operation of a market leads to overproduction or underproduction of some good, this is known as a(n) _____.

b. Goods that are nonrival and nonexcludable are known as _____.

c. _____ are cash or in-kind benefits given to individuals as outright grants from the government.

d. A(n) _____ confers an external benefit on third parties that are not directly involved in the market transaction.

e. _____ refers to the government's pursuit of full employment and price stability through variations in taxes and government spending.

3.2. *(Tax Rates)* Suppose taxes are related to income as follows:

Income	Taxes
$1,000	$200
$2,000	$350
$3,000	$450

a. What percentage of income is paid in taxes at each level?

b. Is the tax rate progressive, proportional, or regressive?

c. What is the marginal tax rate on the first $1,000 of income? The second $1,000? The third $1,000?

3.3. *(Government Revenue)* What are the sources of government revenue in Canada? Which types of taxes are most important at each level of government? Which two taxes provide the most revenue to the federal government?

3.4. *(Government Spending)* Describe the key changes in government spending that have occurred in Canada from 1961 to 2011.

3.5. *(Externalities)* Suppose there is an external cost, or negative externality, associated with production of a certain good. What's wrong with letting the market determine how much of this good will be produced?

3.6. *(Government Spending)* Explain how and why government spending has increased over the past 50 years among developed economies. Discuss how this increase has affected these economies' capacity to grow and to influence the overall well-being of their population.

3.7. *(Tax Rates)* Define regressive tax rates. Define progressive tax rates and compare the two types of rates. Provide examples of progressive and regressive tax rates in Canada.

3.8. *(Role of Government)* Discuss the importance of government—including some of its key roles—to a well-functioning market economy.

LO4 Outline the international influences on an economy

4.1. *(International Trade)* Why does international trade occur? What does it mean to run a surplus in the merchandise trade balance?

4.2. *(International Trade)* Distinguish between a tariff and a quota. Who benefits from and who is harmed by such restrictions on imports?

4.3. *(International Trade)* Why would having a single world currency make trade easier?

4.4. *(International Trade)* Many critics of international trade argue for restrictions to trade as this would protect the poor and disadvantaged in society. Evaluate this argument.

4.5. *(International Trade)* Define exchange rate. If the Canadian exchange rate depreciates relative to the American, how does this affect Canada's ability to export goods and services? What effect would the appreciation of the Canadian exchange rate have on Canada's ability to export goods and services?

CASE STUDY

User-Generated Products

In a market economy, new products and processes are usually developed by profit-seeking entrepreneurs, but sometimes sheer curiosity and the challenge of solving problems lead to new and better ways of doing things. For example, loose communities of computer programmers have been collaborating for decades. By the early 1990s, they formed a grassroots movement known as "open source," which was fuelled by the Internet. In 1991, Linus Torvalds, a student at the University of Helsinki in Finland, wrote the core for what became known as the Linux operating system. He posted his program online and invited anyone to tinker with the coding. Word spread, and computer aficionados around the world began spending their free time making Linux better.

Other software has developed in the open-source arena. For example, from the University of Illinois came Web server software named Apache, and Swedish researchers developed database software called MySQL. The *Free Software Directory* lists more than 5,000 free software packages. The term *free* refers not only to the dollar cost of the software, which is zero, but to what you can do with the software—you can examine it, modify it, and redistribute it to anyone. Free user-generated software now includes the most widely used Web server (Apache), the second most popular desktop operating system (Linux), the Web browser Firefox, and the office suite OpenOffice.

Other user-generated products include some familiar names—Wikipedia, MySpace, Facebook, and YouTube. Wikipedia is a free online encyclopedia written and edited by volunteers. The idea is that collaboration over time will improve content much the way that open-source software has evolved. Wikipedia claims to be one of the most visited online sites. Founder Jimmy Wales says he spent half a million dollars getting Wikipedia going, but now the project relies on volunteers and donations.

MySpace and Facebook are social networking sites that allow users to post personal profiles, blogs, photos, music, videos, and more. So the main attraction of the sites is material provided by users. The companies simply provide the software and hardware framework to support the network. MySpace, founded in July 2003, was sold in July 2005 for about $330 million. Facebook was started by a college sophomore in 2004; the company had 500 million users by 2010 and an estimated market value of $10 billion.

YouTube is an online video site that allows users to post their own videos and to view those posted by others. Searching is easy. For example, "comparative advantage" turned up more than 150 videos, including "Econ Concepts in 60 Seconds." When sold to Google in 2006, YouTube had only 67 employees and no profit. Still, because visitors were viewing more than 100 million videos a day, all those eyeballs offered tremendous advertising potential. Google paid $1.7 billion for a company with no profit.

Finally, Twitter is a social networking and microblogging service that allows users to send and receive "tweets," which are messages limited to 140 characters. Delivery can be online via the Twitter website, by cellphones, or by using other applications. The company had about 100 million users in 2010, but projected 1 billion users by 2013.

User-generated products are not new. Radio call-in shows have been making money off callers for decades. But the Internet has increased opportunities for users to create new products and to improve existing products. Most of the users are just having fun. The more users involved, the more attractive that product is to each user. That's why networking and video sites try to dominate their markets.

SOURCES: Jaron Lanier, *You Are Not a Gadget* (Knopf, 2010); "A World of Connections," *The Economist*, 5 February 2010; and Jessica Vascellaro, "Facebook CEO in No Rush to 'Friend' Wall Street," *Wall Street Journal*, 3 March 2010. The Free Software Directory is found at http://directory.fsf.org/.

QUESTION

1. Why are users willing to help create certain products even though few, if any, users are paid for their efforts?

4

Demand, Supply, and Markets

LEARNING OUTCOMES

LO1 Explain how the law of demand affects market activity

LO2 Explain how the law of supply affects market activity

LO3 Describe the interaction between demand and supply and the resulting market equilibrium

LO4 Describe how market equilibrium adjusts to shifting demand and supply

LO5 Explain how markets react during periods of disequilibrium

© Andres Rodriguez/Alamy

> **Why does it cost Canadians more to move themselves from East to West than from West to East?**

Why does it cost Canadians more to move themselves from East to West than from West to East? Why do TV ads cost more during the Super Bowl ($4.0 million for 30 seconds in 2014) than during *Nick at Nite* reruns? Why do Whistler, B.C. hotels charge more in February than in August? Why do basketball pros earn more than hockey pros? Why do economics majors earn more than many other majors? Answers to these and most economic questions boil down to the workings of demand and supply—the subject of this chapter.

This chapter introduces demand and supply and shows how they interact in competitive markets. *Demand and supply are among the most fundamental and the most powerful of all economic tools.* Indeed, some believe that if you program a computer to answer "demand and supply" to every economic question, you could put many economists out of work. An understanding of the two ideas will take you far in mastering the art and science of economic analysis. This chapter uses more graphs, so you may need to review the Chapter 1 appendix as a refresher.

LO 1 Demand

How many six packs of Pepsi will people buy each month at a price of $4? (Use Coke as the example, if that fits better with your taste). What if the price is $3? What if it's $5? The answers reveal the relationship between the price of a six pack and the quantity of Pepsi demanded. Such a relationship is called the *demand* for Pepsi. **Demand** indicates the quantity consumers are both *willing and able* to buy at each possible price during a given time period, other things constant. Because demand pertains to a specific period—a day, a week, a month—think of demand as the *amounts purchased per period* at each possible price. Also, notice the emphasis on *willing and able*. You may be *able* to buy a new Harley-Davidson Sportster Forty-Eight for $13,000 because you can afford one, but you may not be *willing* to buy one if motorcycles don't interest you. Or you might be willing to purchase proper food and clothing for your kids, but you may not be able to.

Sometimes it helps to think of the demand relationship in reverse—what is the largest price consumers are *willing and able* to pay to receive a particular quantity, other things constant? This is known as the **willingness-to-pay (WTP)**.

demand a relation between the price of a good and the quantity that consumers are willing and able to buy per period, other things constant

willingness-to-pay (WTP) a relation between the quantity of a good and the largest amount that consumers are willing and able to pay per period, other things constant

The Law of Demand

In 1962, Sam Walton opened his first store in Rogers, Arkansas, with a sign that read: "Wal-Mart Discount City. We sell for less." Walmart now sells more than any other retailer in the world because prices there are among the lowest around. As a consumer, you understand why people buy more at a lower price. Sell for less, and the world will beat a path to your door. Walmart, for example, sells on average over 20,000 pairs of shoes *an hour*. The inverse relationship between the price and the quantity demanded, other things constant, is known as the **law of demand**. Thus, the higher the price, the smaller the quantity demanded; the lower the price, the greater the quantity demanded.

Demand, Wants, and Needs Consumer demand and consumer wants are not the same. As we have seen, wants are unlimited. You may want a new Mercedes-Benz SL Roadster, but the $123,000 price tag is likely beyond your budget (that is, the quantity you demand at that price is zero). Nor is demand the same as need. You may need a new muffler for your car, but a price of $300 is just too high for you right now. If, however, the price drops enough—say, to $200—then you become both willing and able to buy one.

The Substitution Effect of a Price Change What explains the law of demand? Why, for example, is more demanded at a lower price? The explanation begins with unlimited wants confronting scarce resources. Many goods and services could satisfy particular wants. For example, you can satisfy your hunger with pizza, burgers, falafel, or hundreds of other foods. Similarly, you can satisfy your desire for warmth in the winter with warm clothing, a home-heating system, a trip to Hawaii, or in many other ways. Clearly, some alternatives have more appeal than others (vacationing in Hawaii is more fun than a sweater). In a world without scarcity, everything would be free, so you would always choose the most attractive alternative. Scarcity, however, is a reality, and the degree of scarcity of one good relative to another helps determine each good's relative price.

Notice that the definition of *demand* includes the other-things-constant assumption. Among the "other things" assumed to remain constant are the prices of other goods. For example, if the price of pizza declines while other prices remain constant, pizza becomes relatively cheaper. Consumers are more *willing* to purchase pizza when its relative price falls; they substitute pizza for other goods. This principle is called the **substitution effect of a price change**. On the other hand, an increase in the price of pizza, other things constant, increases the opportunity cost of pizza—that is, the amount of other goods you must give up to buy pizza. This higher opportunity cost causes consumers to substitute other goods for the now higher-priced pizza, thus reducing their quantity of pizza demanded. Remember that *it is the change in the relative price—the price of one good relative to the prices of other goods—that causes the substitution effect*. If all prices changed by the same percentage, there would be no change in relative prices and no substitution effect.

The Income Effect of a Price Change A fall in the price of a good increases the quantity demanded for a second reason. Suppose you earn $30 a week from a part-time job. **Money income** is simply the number of dollars received per period, in this case, $30 per week. Suppose you spend all that on pizza, buying three a week at $10 each. What if the price drops to $6? At the lower price, you can now afford five pizzas a week. Your money income remains at $30 per week, but the decrease in the price has increased your **real income**—that is, your income measured in terms of what it can buy. The price reduction, other things constant, increases the purchasing power of your income, thereby increasing your ability to buy pizza. The quantity of pizza you demand will likely increase because of this **income effect of a price change**. You may not increase your quantity demanded to five pizzas, but you could. If you decide to purchase four pizzas a week when the price drops to $6, you would still have $6 remaining to buy other stuff. Thus, the income effect of a lower price increases your real income and thereby increases your ability to purchase all goods, making you better off. The income effect is reflected in Walmart's slogan, which trumpets low prices: "Save money. Live better." Because of the income effect, consumers typically increase their quantity demanded when the price declines.

Conversely, an increase in the price of a good, other things constant, reduces real income, thereby reducing your *ability* to purchase all goods. Because of the income effect, consumers typically reduce their quantity demanded when the price increases. Again, note that money income, not real income, is assumed to remain constant along a demand curve. A change in price changes your real income, so real income varies along a demand curve. The lower the price, the greater your real income.

The Demand Schedule and Demand Curve

Demand can be expressed as a *demand schedule* or as a *demand curve*. Panel (a) of Exhibit 1 shows a hypothetical demand schedule for pizza. In describing demand, we must specify the units measured and the period considered. In our example, the unit is a 12-inch regular pizza and the period is a week. The schedule lists possible prices, along with the quantity demanded at each price. At a price of $15, for example, consumers demand 4 million pizzas per week. As you can see, the lower the price, other things constant, the greater the quantity demanded. Consumers substitute pizza for other foods. And as the price falls, real income increases, causing consumers to increase the quantity of pizza they demand. If the price drops as low as $3, consumers demand 16 million per week.

EXHIBIT 1
The Demand Schedule and Demand Curve for Pizza

(a) Demand schedule

	Price per Pizza	Quantity Demanded per Week (millions)
a	$15	4
b	12	7
c	9	10
d	6	13
e	3	16

(b) Demand curve

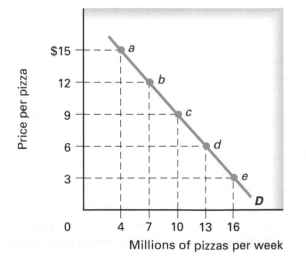

The demand schedule in panel (a) appears as a **demand curve** in panel (b), with price measured on the vertical axis and the quantity demanded per week on the horizontal axis. Each price-quantity combination listed in the demand schedule in the left panel becomes a point in the right panel. Point *a,* for example, indicates that if the price is $15, consumers demand 4 million pizzas per week. Connecting the points forms the demand curve for pizza, labelled *D.* (By the way, some demand curves are straight lines, some are curved lines, and some are even jagged lines, but they all are called demand *curves.*)

A demand curve slopes downward, reflecting the *law of demand*: price and quantity demanded are inversely related, other things constant. Besides money income, also assumed constant along the demand curve are the prices of other goods. Thus, along the demand curve for pizza, the price of pizza changes *relative to the prices of other goods*. The demand curve shows the effect of a change in the *relative price* of pizza—that is, relative to other prices, which do not change.

Take care to distinguish between *demand* and *quantity demanded*. The *demand* for pizza is not a specific amount, but rather the *entire relationship* between price and quantity demanded—represented by the demand schedule or the demand curve. An individual point on the demand curve indicates the **quantity demanded** at

demand curve a curve showing the relation between the price of a good and the quantity consumers are willing and able to buy per period, other things constant; sometimes known as the willingness-to-pay (WTP) curve

quantity demanded the amount of a good consumers are willing and able to buy per period at a particular price, as reflected by a point on a demand curve

a particular price. For example, at a price of $12, the quantity demanded is 7 million pizzas per week. If the price drops from $12 to, say, $9, this is shown in Exhibit 1 by *a movement along the demand curve*—in this case from point *b* to point *c*. Any movement along a demand curve reflects a *change in quantity demanded,* not a change in demand.

The law of demand applies to the millions of products sold in grocery stores, department stores, clothing stores, drugstores, bookstores, other retailers, travel agencies, and restaurants, as well as through mail-order catalogues, online sites, stock markets, job markets, flea markets, and all other markets. The law of demand applies even to choices that seem more personal than economic, such as whether to own a pet. For example, after New York City passed an anti-dog-litter law, law-abiding owners had to follow their dogs around the city with scoopers, plastic bags—whatever would do the job. Because the law in effect raised the personal cost of owning a dog, the quantity of dogs demanded decreased. Some dogs were abandoned, increasing strays in the city. The number of dogs left at animal shelters doubled. The law of demand predicts this inverse relation between cost, or price, and quantity demanded.

It is useful to distinguish between **individual demand**, which is the demand of an individual consumer, and **market demand**, which is the sum of the individual demands of all consumers in the market. In most markets, there are many consumers, sometimes millions. Unless otherwise noted, when we talk about demand, we are referring to market demand, as shown in Exhibit 1.

Willingness-to-Pay and Consumer Value

If the demand curve is understood as a willingness-to-pay (WTP) curve, then you can think of the value you (or the market) receive(s) from consuming a particular quantity of a good or service—the **consumer value**. The consumer value generated by the consumption of a good is the WTP summed over the number of units consumed. Suppose you were willing to pay at most $40 for one haircut in a month, $8 for a second, and $0.50 for a third. If you consumed two haircuts in a month (ignore the cost for now), you realize a consumer value of $48 (i.e., $40 + $8).

EXHIBIT 2

Consumer Value from Consuming 7 Million Pizzas in One Week

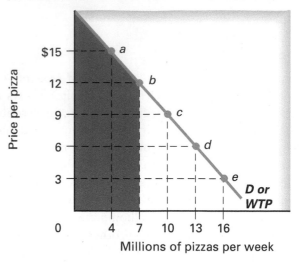

The same idea can be applied to our pizza demand in Exhibit 2. This is the same market identified in Exhibit 1 with the lines extended to meet the axes. Suppose in a week, 7 million pizzas were consumed in this market. The consumer value in this case is represented by the area under the WTP (demand) curve, up to 7. This is identified in red in Exhibit 2. As you can imagine, the consumer value would increase if more pizzas were consumed each week, and would fall if pizza consumption declined.

Shifts of the Demand Curve

A demand curve isolates the relation between the price of a good and quantity demanded when other factors that could affect demand remain unchanged. What are those other factors, and how do changes in them affect demand? Variables that can affect market demand are (1) the money income of consumers, (2) prices of other goods, (3) consumer expectations, (4) the number or composition of consumers in the market, and (5) consumer tastes. How do changes in each affect demand?

Changes in Consumer Income

Exhibit 3 shows the market demand curve *D* for pizza. This demand curve assumes a given level of money income. Suppose consumer income increases. Some consumers are then willing and able to buy more pizza at each price, so market demand increases. The demand curve shifts to the right from *D* to *D'*. For example, at a price of $12, the amount of pizza demanded increases

EXHIBIT 3

An Increase in the Market Demand for Pizza

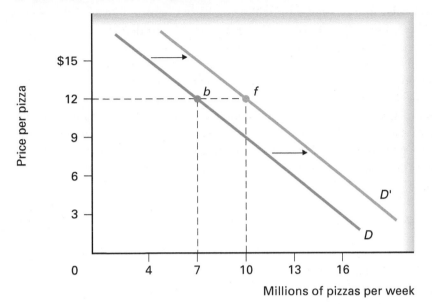

from 7 million to 10 million per week, as indicated by the movement from point *b* on demand curve *D* to point *f* on demand curve *D′*. In short, *an increase in demand—that is, a rightward shift of the demand curve—means that consumers are willing and able to buy more pizza at each price.*

Goods are classified into two broad categories, depending on how consumers respond to changes in money income. The demand for a **normal good** increases as money income increases. Because pizza is a normal good, its demand curve shifts rightward when money income increases. Most goods are normal. In contrast, demand for an **inferior good** actually decreases as money income increases, so the demand curve shifts leftward. Examples of inferior goods are bologna or peanut butter sandwiches, used furniture, and used clothes. As money income increases, consumers tend to switch from these inferior goods to normal goods (such as roast beef or cheese sandwiches, new furniture, and new clothes).

Changes in the Prices of Other Goods

Again, the prices of other goods are assumed to remain constant along a given demand curve. Now let's bring these other prices into play. Consumers have various ways of trying to satisfy any particular want. Consumers choose among substitutes based on relative prices.

For example, pizza and tacos are substitutes, though not perfect ones. An increase in the price of tacos, other things constant, reduces the quantity of tacos demanded along a given taco demand curve. An increase in the price of tacos also increases the demand for pizza, shifting the demand curve for pizza to the right. Two goods are considered **substitutes** if an increase in the price of one shifts the demand for the other rightward and, conversely, if a decrease in the price of one shifts demand for the other leftward.

Goods used in combination are called **complements**. Examples are Coke and pizza, computer software and hardware, and airline tickets and rental cars. Two goods are considered complements if an increase in the price of one decreases the demand for the other, shifting that demand curve leftward. For example, an increase in the price of pizza shifts the demand curve for Coke leftward. But most pairs of goods selected at random are *unrelated*—for example, pizza and housing, or milk and gasoline. Still, an increase in the price of an unrelated good reduces the consumers' real income and can reduce the demand for pizza and other goods. For example, a sharp increase in housing prices reduces the amount of income remaining for other goods, such as pizza.

Changes in Consumer Expectations

Another factor assumed constant along a given demand curve is consumer expectations about factors that influence demand, such as incomes or prices. A change in consumers' *income expectations* can shift the demand curve. For example, a consumer who learns about a pay raise might increase demand well before the raise takes effect. A third-year university student who lands that first real job may buy a new car even before graduation. Likewise, a change in consumers' *price expectations* can shift the demand curve. For example, if you expect

normal good a good, such as new clothes, for which demand increases, or shifts rightward, as consumer income rises

inferior good a good, such as used clothes, for which demand decreases, or shifts leftward, as consumer income rises

substitutes goods, such as Coke and Pepsi, that relate in such a way that an increase in the price of one shifts the demand for the other rightward

complements goods, such as milk and cookies, that relate in such a way that an increase in the price of one shifts the demand for the other leftward

the price of pizza to jump next week, you may buy an extra one today for the freezer, shifting this week's demand for pizza rightward. Or if consumers come to believe that home prices will climb next year, some will increase their demand for housing now, shifting this year's demand for housing rightward. On the other hand, if housing prices are expected to fall next year, some consumers will postpone purchases, thereby shifting this year's housing demand leftward.

Changes in the Number or Composition of Consumers

As mentioned earlier, the market demand curve is the sum of the individual demand curves of all consumers in the market. If the number of consumers changes, the demand curve will shift. For example, if the population grows, the demand curve for pizza will shift rightward. Even if total population remains unchanged, demand could shift with a change in the composition of the population. For example, an increase over time in the teenage population could shift pizza demand rightward. A baby boom would shift rightward the demand for car seats and baby food.

Changes in Consumer Tastes

Do you like anchovies on your pizza? Are you into tattoos and body piercings? Is music to your ears more likely to be rock, country, hip-hop, reggae, jazz, funk, gospel, or classical? Choices in food, body art, music, books, movies—indeed, all consumer choices—are influenced by consumer tastes. **Tastes** are nothing more than your likes and dislikes as a consumer. What determines tastes? Your desires for food when hungry and drink when thirsty are largely biological. So too is your desire for comfort, rest, shelter, friendship, love, status, personal safety, and a pleasant environment. Your family background affects some of your tastes—your taste in food, for example, has been shaped by years of home cooking. Other influences include the surrounding culture, peer pressure, and religious convictions. So economists can say a little about the origin of tastes, but they claim no special expertise in understanding how tastes develop and change over time. Economists recognize, however, that tastes have an important impact on demand. For example, although pizza is popular, some people just don't like it and those who are lactose intolerant can't stomach the cheese topping. Thus, most people like pizza but some don't.

In our analysis of consumer demand, *we will assume that tastes are given and are relatively stable.* Tastes are assumed to remain constant along a given demand curve. A change in the tastes for a particular good would shift that good's demand curve. For example, a discovery that the tomato sauce and cheese combination on pizza promotes overall health could change consumer tastes, shifting the demand curve for pizza to the right. But because a change in tastes is so difficult to isolate from other economic changes, we should be reluctant to attribute a shift of the demand curve to a change in tastes. Many economists tend to rule out other possible reasons for a shift of the demand curve before accepting a change in tastes as the explanation. Nevertheless, changes in tastes can be quite important, often influenced by advertisements, product information, and the purchases of friends and enemies.

That wraps up our look at changes in demand. Before we turn to supply, you should remember the distinction between a **movement along a given demand curve** and a **shift of a demand curve**. A change in *price,* other things constant, causes a *movement along an existing demand curve,* changing the quantity demanded. A change in one of the determinants of demand other than price causes a *shift of the whole demand curve,* changing demand.

LO2 Supply

Just as demand is a relation between price and quantity demanded, supply is a relation between price and quantity supplied. **Supply** indicates how much producers are *willing and able* to offer for sale per period at each possible price, other things constant. The **law of supply** states that the quantity supplied is usually directly related to its price, other things constant. Thus, the lower the price, the smaller the quantity supplied; the higher the price, the greater the quantity supplied.

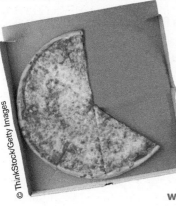

Sometimes it helps to think of the supply relationship in reverse—what is the lowest price producers are *willing and able* to receive to sell a particular quantity, other things constant? This is known as the **willingness-to-sell (WTS)**.

The Supply Schedule and Supply Curve

Exhibit 4 presents the market *supply schedule* and market **supply curve** *S* for pizza. Both show the quantities supplied per week at various possible prices by the thousands of pizza makers in the economy. As you can see, price and quantity supplied are directly, or positively, related. Producers offer more at a higher price than at a lower price, so the supply curve slopes upward.

There are two reasons why producers offer more for sale when the price rises. First, as the price increases, other things constant, a producer becomes more *willing* to supply the good. Prices act as signals to existing and potential suppliers about the rewards for producing various goods. A higher pizza price attracts resources from lower-valued uses. *A higher price makes producers more willing and more able to increase quantity supplied.*

Higher prices also increase the producer's *ability* to supply the good. The law of increasing opportunity cost, as noted in Chapter 2, states that the opportunity cost of producing more of a particular good rises as output increases—that is, the *marginal cost* of production increases as output increases. Because producers face a higher marginal cost for additional output, they need to get a higher price for that output to be *able* to increase the quantity supplied. *A higher price makes producers more able to increase quantity supplied.* As a case in point, a higher price for gasoline increases oil companies' ability to extract oil from oil sands, to drill deeper, and to

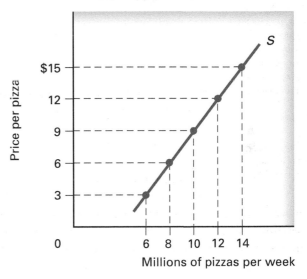

EXHIBIT 4
The Supply Schedule and Supply Curve for Pizza

(a) *Supply schedule*

Price per Pizza	Quantity Supplied per Week (millions)
$15	14
12	12
9	10
6	8
3	6

(b) *Supply curve*

explore in less accessible areas, such as the frozen tundra above the Arctic Circle. For example, at a market price of $50 per barrel, extracting oil from oil sands is unprofitable, but at a price of $100 per barrel, producers are able to supply millions of barrels per month.

On the other hand, a lower price makes production less attractive. Suppliers are less *willing* to produce at a lower price as resources are attracted to higher-valued uses. Suppliers are also less *able* to produce at levels with high marginal costs, which means a reduction in the quantity supplied. For example, a mining company "reacted quickly to steep copper price declines in

willingness-to-sell (WTS) a relation between the quantity of a good and the least amount that producers are willing and able to receive in order to sell per period, other things constant

supply curve a curve showing the relation between price of a good and the quantity producers are willing and able to sell per period other things constant; sometimes known as the willingness-to-sell (WTS) curve

2008 by curbing production at its North American sites and implementing layoffs at its mines and corporate headquarters."[1]

As with demand, we distinguish between *supply* and *quantity supplied*. *Supply* is the entire relationship between prices and quantities supplied, as reflected by the supply schedule or supply curve. **Quantity supplied** refers to a particular amount offered for sale at a particular price, as reflected by a point on a given supply curve. We also distinguish between **individual supply**, the supply of an individual producer, and **market supply**, the sum of individual supplies of all producers in the market. Unless otherwise noted, the term *supply* refers to market supply.

Willingness-to-Sell and Operational Cost

If you think of the supply curve as a willingness-to-sell (WTS) curve, then you can think of the costs you (or the market) incur(s) from producing a particular quantity of a good or service—the **operational cost**. The operational cost of producing a particular quantity is the WTS summed over the number of units produced. (Technically it is the sum of the marginal costs or equivalently the variable costs of production.) Suppose you were willing to sell your first available hour of your day for $1.25 because you weren't doing much other than playing video games anyway. Your second hour might be worth $4.15 because you are then cutting into study time, and your third might be worth $10.00 because you are now cutting into hours you could work at your part-time job. (Notice how we haven't dealt with fixed costs like the cost of your education, but rather just your variable costs.) If you provide three hours of your time, you incur an operational cost of $15.40 (i.e., $1.25 + $4.15 + $10.00).

The same idea can be expressed in our pizza supply in Exhibit 5. This is the same market identified in Exhibit 4 with the curve extended to meet the vertical axis. Suppose that in one week, 8 million pizzas were produced in this market. The operational cost in this case is represented by the area under the WTS (supply

[1] Andrew Johnson, "Freeport Outsourcing Will Cut 60 Valley Jobs," *Arizona Republic*, 23 February 2010.

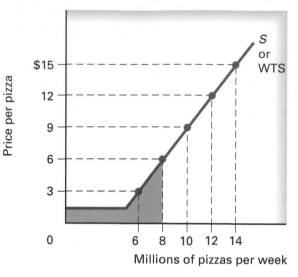

EXHIBIT 5

Operational Cost from Producing 8 Million Pizzas in One Week

curve), up to 8. This is identified in blue in Exhibit 5. As you can imagine, the operational costs for a given quantity increase if production increases and decreases when production costs decrease.

Shifts of the Supply Curve

The supply curve isolates the relation between the price of a good (Pizza) and the quantity supplied, other things constant. Assumed constant along a supply curve are the determinants of supply other than the price of the good (Pizza): (1) the state of technology, (2) the prices of resources, (3) the prices of other goods, (4) producer expectations, and (5) the number of producers in the market. Let's see how a change in each affects the supply curve.

Changes in Technology

Recall from Chapter 2 that the state of technology represents the economy's knowledge about how to combine resources efficiently. Along a given supply curve, technology is assumed to remain unchanged. If a better technology is discovered, production costs will fall and suppliers will be more willing and able to supply the good at each price. For example, new techniques helped Marathon Oil cut drilling time for a new well from 56 days in 2006 to only 24 days in 2009, thereby shifting Marathon's supply curve rightward.[2] Suppose a new, high-tech oven that costs the same as existing

[2] Ben Casselman, "Oil Industry Boom—in North Dakota," *Wall Street Journal*, 26 February 2010.

EXHIBIT 6
An Increase in the Supply of Pizza

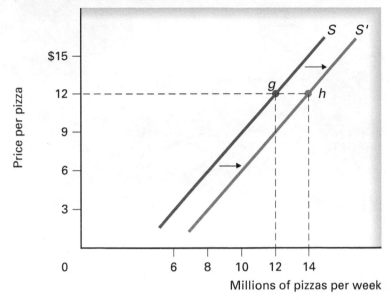

© ThinkStock/Getty Images

instead. A drop in the price of one of these other goods, with the price of pizza unchanged, makes pizza production more attractive. For example, if the price of Italian bread declines, some bread makers become pizza makers so the supply of pizza increases, shifting the supply curve of pizza rightward as in Exhibit 6. On the other hand, if the price of Italian bread increases, supplying pizza becomes relatively less attractive compared to supplying Italian bread. As resources shift from pizza to bread, the supply of pizza decreases, or shifts to the left.

> **movement along a supply curve** change in quantity supplied resulting from a change in the price of the good, other things constant
>
> **shift of a supply curve** movement of a supply curve left or right resulting from a change in one of the determinants of supply other than the price of the good

ovens bakes pizza in half the time. Such a breakthrough would shift the market supply curve rightward, as from *S* to *S'* in Exhibit 6, where more is supplied at each possible price. At a price of $12, the amount supplied increases from 12 million to 14 million pizzas, as shown in Exhibit 6 by the movement from point *g* to point *h*. In short, *an increase in supply—that is, a rightward shift of the supply curve—means that producers are willing and able to sell more pizza at each price.*

Changes in the Prices of Resources

The prices of resources employed to make the good affect the cost of production and therefore the supply of the good. A reduction in the price of mozzarella cheese reduces the cost of making pizza, so producers are more willing and better able to supply it and the supply curve for pizza shifts rightward, as shown in Exhibit 6. On the other hand, an increase in the price of a resource reduces supply, meaning a shift of the supply curve leftward.

Changes in the Prices of Other Goods

Nearly all resources have alternative uses. The labour, building, machinery, ingredients, and knowledge needed to run a pizza business could produce other goods

Changes in Producer Expectations

Changes in producer expectations can shift the supply curve. For example, a pizza maker expecting higher pizza prices in the future may expand his or her pizzeria now, thereby shifting the supply of pizza rightward. When a good can be easily stored (crude oil, for example, can be left in the ground), expecting higher prices in the future might prompt some producers to *reduce* their current supply while awaiting the higher price. Thus, an expectation of higher prices in the future could either increase or decrease current supply, depending on the good. More generally, any change affecting future profitability, such as a change in business taxes, could shift the supply curve now.

Changes in the Number of Producers

Because market supply sums the amounts supplied at each price by all producers, market supply depends on the number of producers in the market. If that number increases, supply will increase, shifting supply to the right. If the number of producers decreases, supply will decrease, shifting supply to the left.

Finally, note again the distinction between a **movement along a supply curve** and a **shift of a supply curve**. A change in *price*, other things constant, causes *a movement along a supply curve,* changing the quantity supplied. A change in one of the determinants of supply other than price causes a *shift of a supply curve,* changing supply.

You are now ready to bring demand and supply together.

LO 3 Demand, Supply, and Market Equilibrium

© Charles Zachritz/Shutterstock.com

Demanders and suppliers have different views of price. Demanders pay the price and suppliers receive it. Thus, a higher price is bad news for consumers but good news for producers. As the price rises, consumers reduce their quantity demanded along the demand curve and producers increase their quantity supplied along the supply curve. How is this conflict between producers and consumers resolved?

Markets

Markets sort out differences between demanders and suppliers. A *market,* as you know from Chapter 1, includes all the arrangements used to buy and sell a particular good or service. Markets reduce **transaction costs**—the costs of time and information required for exchange. For example, suppose you are looking for a summer job. One approach might be to go from employer to employer looking for openings. But this could have you running around for days or weeks. A more efficient strategy would be to pick up a copy of the local newspaper or go online and look for openings. Classified ads and websites, which are elements of the job market, reduce the transaction costs of bringing workers and employers together.

The coordination that occurs through markets takes place not because of some central plan but because of Adam Smith's "invisible hand." For example, the auto dealers in your community tend to locate together, usually on the outskirts of town, where land is cheaper. The dealers congregate not because they all took an economics course or because they like one another's company but because grouped together they become a more attractive destination for car buyers. A dealer who makes the mistake of locating away from the others misses out on a lot of business. Similarly, stores locate together so that more shoppers will be drawn by the call of the mall. Whether it's Orlando theme parks, Broadway theatres, or Las Vegas casinos, suppliers congregate to attract demanders. Some groupings can be quite specialized. For example, shops in Hong Kong that sell dress mannequins cluster along Austin Road. And diamond merchants in New York City congregate within a few blocks.

transaction costs the costs of time and information required to carry out market exchange

surplus at a given price, the amount by which quantity supplied exceeds quantity demanded; a surplus usually forces the price down

shortage at a given price, the amount by which quantity demanded exceeds quantity supplied; a shortage usually forces the price up

Market Equilibrium

To see how a market works, let's bring together market demand and market supply. Exhibit 7 shows the market for pizza, using schedules in panel (a) and curves in panel (b). Suppose the price initially is $12. At that price, producers supply 12 million pizzas per week, but consumers demand only 7 million, resulting in an *excess quantity supplied,* or a **surplus**, of 5 million pizzas per week. Suppliers don't like getting stuck with unsold pizzas. Their desire to eliminate the surplus puts downward pressure on the price, as shown by the arrow pointing down in the graph. As the price falls, producers reduce their quantity supplied and consumers increase their quantity demanded. The price continues to fall as long as quantity supplied exceeds quantity demanded.

Alternatively, suppose the price initially is $6. You can see from Exhibit 7 that at that price consumers demand 13 million pizzas but producers supply only 8 million, resulting in an *excess quantity demanded,* or a **shortage**, of 5 million pizzas per week. Producers quickly notice they have sold out and those customers still demanding pizzas are grumbling. Profit-maximizing producers and frustrated consumers create market pressure for a higher price, as shown by the arrow pointing up in the graph. As the price rises, producers increase their quantity supplied and consumers

EXHIBIT 7
Equilibrium in the Pizza Market

(a) Market schedules

Price per Pizza	Millions of Pizzas per Week			
	Quantity Demanded	Quantity Supplied	Surplus or Shortage	Effect on Price
$15	4	14	Surplus of 10	Falls
12	7	12	Surplus of 5	Falls
9	10	10	Equilibrium	Remains the same
6	13	8	Shortage of 5	Rises
3	16	6	Shortage of 10	Rises

(b) Market curves

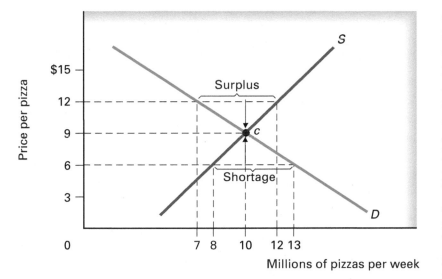

equilibrium the condition that exists in a market when the plans of buyers match those of sellers, so quantity demanded equals quantity supplied and the market clears

and quantity, the market *clears*. Because there is no shortage or surplus, there is no pressure for the price to change. The demand and supply curves form an "x" at the intersection. The equilibrium point is found where "x" marks the spot.

A market finds equilibrium through the independent actions of thousands, or even millions, of buyers and sellers. In one sense, the market is personal because each consumer and each producer make a personal decision about how much to buy or sell at a given price. In another sense, the market is impersonal because it requires no conscious communication or coordination among consumers or producers. The price does all the talking. *Impersonal market forces synchronize the personal and independent decisions of many individual buyers and sellers to achieve equilibrium price and quantity.* Prices reflect relative scarcity. For example, to rent a 26-foot truck one way from Toronto to Edmonton, U-Haul recently charged $4,298. Its one-way charge for that same truck from Edmonton to Toronto was just $2,088. Why the difference? Far more people wanted to move from Toronto to Edmonton than vice versa, so U-Haul had to pay its own employees to drive the empty trucks back from Alberta. Rental rates reflected that extra cost.

reduce their quantity demanded. The price continues to rise as long as quantity demanded exceeds quantity supplied.

Thus, *a surplus creates downward pressure on the price, and a shortage creates upward pressure.* As long as quantity demanded differs from quantity supplied, this difference forces a price change. Note that a shortage or a surplus depends on the price. There is no such thing as a general shortage or a general surplus, only a shortage or a surplus at a particular price.

A market reaches equilibrium when the quantity demanded equals quantity supplied at one price. In **equilibrium**, the independent plans of buyers and sellers exactly match, so market forces exert no pressure for change. In Exhibit 7, the demand and supply curves intersect at the *equilibrium point,* identified as point *c.* The *equilibrium price* is $9 per pizza, and the *equilibrium quantity* is 10 million per week. At that price

© Arthur Gebuys/Alamy

Efficiency

Economists think of efficiency in many ways, but one way to define **economic efficiency** is the degree to which all mutually beneficial exchanges of a good take place. Ideally the market should produce all units of a good for which the willingness-to-pay exceeds the willingness-to-sell. Why? Because every time a unit is produced and consumed for which WTP exceeds WTS, extra value is created in the market. For instance, if you are willing to pay $40 to get a haircut that takes 30 minutes and a stylist has a willingness-to-sell her 30 minutes of labour for say $6, then society gains when the customer gets a haircut that the stylist produces. By getting this haircut, the consumer value increases by $40 while the operational cost to the stylist is $6 resulting in a gain of $34 (i.e., $40-$6). Both sides will gain if they can agree on a price that is no bigger than $40 and no less than $6. (We'll deal with the division of this gain below.)

In Exhibit 8 we consider our pizza market from the willingness-to-pay and willingness-to-sell perspective. In panel (a) notice that at the equilibrium, where the quantity is 10 million pizzas per week, $WTP_{10} = WTS_{10}$. For quantities less than this, say at 7 million pizzas per week, $WTP_7 > WTS_7$, meaning that producing additional pizza

EXHIBIT 8
Equilibrium and Efficiency in the Pizza Market

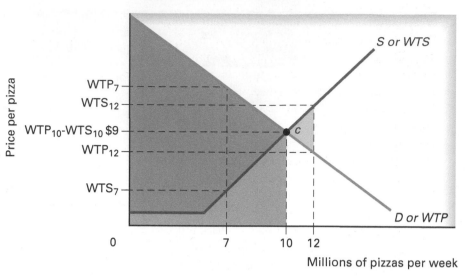

(a) Total Surplus at Equilibrium

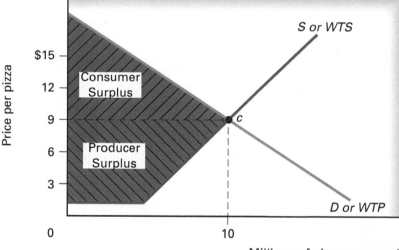

(b) Consumer and Producer Surplus at Equilibrium

generates more additional consumer value than additional operational cost. Indeed, for all quantities less than 10 million, the WTP > WTS and consumer value exceeds operational cost. Somewhat confusingly, the value generated when a good for which the WTP exceeds the WTS is exchanged is called the surplus. If we sum the surpluses across all units exchanged, then we call this the **total surplus**.

As seen in panel (a) the total surplus is the area between the demand curve and the supply curve up to the number of units exchanged. Notice that for a quantity of 7 million pizzas per week, the total surplus would be the area between the demand and supply curves up to 7 on the horizontal axis. Also notice that total surplus increases all the way up to 10 million pizzas per week. Why not produce more pizzas, say 12 million per week? While it is true that additional pizzas generate consumer value, the operational cost of producing these pizzas exceeds the value they generate. When 12 million pizzas are consumed, the total surplus realized up to 10 million pizzas is actually reduced by the green shaded area.

At the market equilibrium, and nowhere else, total surplus is maximized. Consequently, economists say the market equilibrium is **efficient** because the

economic efficiency the degree to which all mutually beneficial exchanges of a good take place

total surplus the sum of the difference between the consumer value and the operational cost over all units exchanged; the area between the demand and supply curves up to the number of units exchanged

efficient a market equilibrium is said to be efficient because it maximizes total surplus

largest possible total surplus is realized. The market equilibrium also performs another service—it determines a price at which exchange takes place. Recall that the equilibrium price in the pizza market is $9 per pizza, which ensures that 10 million pizzas are sold each week as shown in panel (b). The portion of the total surplus that the consumer realizes is the entire area beneath the demand curve up to the quantity exchanged—the consumer value—less the amount paid to realize this consumer value. Simply put, the **consumer surplus** is the area beneath the demand curve and above the price paid up to the number of units exchanged. Similarly, the **producer surplus** is the amount by which the price received exceeds the operational cost summed over all units exchanged. It is the area above the supply curve but beneath the price received up to the number of units exchanged.

It is simple to see that the consumer surplus and the producer surplus in panel (b) add up to the total surplus in panel (a). A market that achieves equilibrium determines the quantity that maximizes total surplus and sets a price that divides—though not necessarily equally—this total surplus between consumers and producers. This is pretty amazing.

![LO 4] **Changes in Equilibrium**

Equilibrium occurs when the intentions of demanders and suppliers exactly match. Once a market reaches equilibrium, that price and quantity prevail until something happens to demand or supply. A change in any determinant of demand or supply usually changes equilibrium price and quantity in a predictable way, as you'll see.

Shifts of the Demand Curve

In Exhibit 9, demand curve D and supply curve S intersect at point c to yield the initial equilibrium price of $9 and the initial equilibrium quantity of 10 million

EXHIBIT 9
Effects of an Increase in Demand

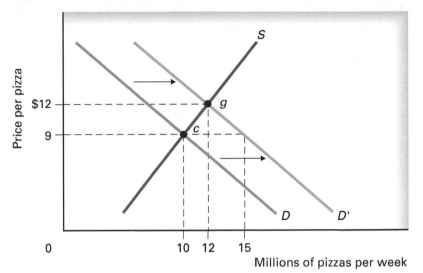

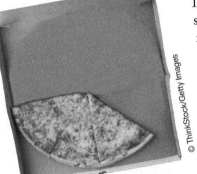

12-inch regular pizzas per week. Now suppose that one of the determinants of demand changes in a way that increases demand, shifting the demand curve to the right from D to D'. Any of the following could shift the demand for pizza rightward: (1) an increase in the money income of consumers (because pizza is a normal good); (2) an increase in the price of a substitute, such as tacos, or a decrease in the price of a complement, such as Coke; (3) a change in consumer expectations that causes people to demand more pizzas now; (4) a growth in the number of pizza consumers; or (5) a change in consumer tastes—based, for example, on a discovery that the tomato sauce on pizza has antioxidant properties that improve overall health.

After the demand curve shifts rightward to D' in Exhibit 9, the amount demanded at the initial price of $9 is 15 million pizzas, which exceeds the amount supplied of 10 million by 5 million pizzas. This shortage puts upward pressure on the price. As the price increases, the quantity demanded decreases along the new demand curve D', and the quantity supplied increases along the existing supply curve S until the two quantities are equal once again at equilibrium point g. The new equilibrium price is $12, and the

consumer surplus
the remainder once the price paid is subtracted from the consumer value realized; the area beneath the demand curve and above the price paid up to the number of units exchanged

producer surplus
the remainder once the operational cost realized is subtracted from the price received; the area above the supply curve but beneath the price received up to the number of units exchanged

new equilibrium quantity is 12 million pizzas per week. Thus, given an upward-sloping supply curve, an increase in demand increases both equilibrium price and quantity. A decrease in demand would lower both equilibrium price and quantity. These results can be summarized as follows: *Given an upward-sloping supply curve, a rightward shift of the demand curve increases both equilibrium price and quantity and a leftward shift decreases both equilibrium price and quantity.*

Shifts of the Supply Curve

Let's now consider shifts of the supply curve. In Exhibit 10, as before, we begin with demand curve *D* and supply curve *S* intersecting at point *c* to yield an equilibrium price of $9 and an equilibrium quantity of 10 million pizzas per week. Suppose one of the determinants of supply changes, increasing supply from *S* to *S'*. Changes that could shift the supply curve rightward include (1) a technological breakthrough in pizza ovens; (2) a reduction in the price of a resource such as mozzarella cheese; (3) a decline in the price of another good such as Italian bread; (4) a change in expectations that encourages pizza makers to expand production now; or (5) an increase in the number of pizzerias.

After the supply curve shifts rightward in Exhibit 10, the amount supplied at the initial price of $9 increases from 10 million to 15 million, so producers now supply 5 million more pizzas than consumers demand. This surplus forces the price down. As the price falls, the quantity supplied declines along the new supply curve and the quantity demanded increases along the existing demand curve until a new equilibrium point *d* is established. The new equilibrium price is $6, and the new equilibrium quantity is 13 million pizzas per week. In short, an increase in supply reduces the price and increases the quantity. On the other hand, a decrease in supply increases the price but decreases the quantity. Thus, *given a downward-sloping demand curve, a rightward shift of the supply curve decreases price but increases quantity, and a leftward shift increases price but decreases quantity.*

EXHIBIT 10
Effects of an Increase in Supply

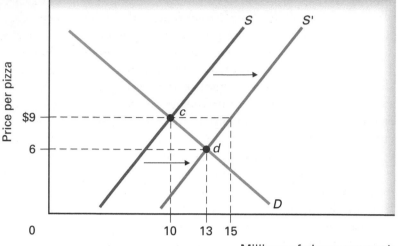

Millions of pizzas per week

Simultaneous Shifts of Demand and Supply Curves

As long as only one curve shifts, we can say for sure how equilibrium price and quantity will change. If both curves shift, however, the outcome is less obvious. For example, suppose both demand and supply increase, or shift rightward, as in Exhibit 11. Note that in panel (a), demand shifts more than supply, and in panel (b), supply shifts more than demand. In both panels, equilibrium quantity increases. The change in equilibrium price, however, depends on which curve shifts more. If demand shifts more, as in panel (a), equilibrium price increases. For example, between 1995 and 2005, the demand for housing increased more than the supply, so both price and quantity increased. But

EXHIBIT 11
Indeterminate Effect of an Increase in Both Demand and Supply

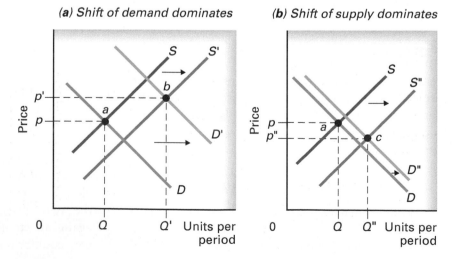

(a) Shift of demand dominates   *(b) Shift of supply dominates*

if supply shifts more, as in panel (b), equilibrium price decreases. For example, in the past decade, the supply of personal computers has increased more than the demand, so price has decreased and quantity increased.

Conversely, if both demand and supply decrease, or shift leftward, equilibrium quantity decreases. But, again, we cannot say what will happen to equilibrium price unless we examine relative shifts. (You can use Exhibit 11 to consider decreases in demand and supply by viewing D' and S' as the initial curves.) If demand shifts more, the price will fall. If supply shifts more, the price will rise.

If demand and supply shift in opposite directions, we can say what will happen to equilibrium price. Equilibrium price will increase if demand increases and supply decreases. Equilibrium price will decrease if demand decreases and supply increases. Without reference to particular shifts, however, we cannot say what will happen to equilibrium quantity.

These results are no doubt confusing, but Exhibit 12 summarizes the four possible combinations of changes. Using Exhibit 12 as a reference, please take the time right now to work through some changes in demand and supply to develop a feel for the results.

The Market for Professional Basketball Look at Exhibit 13, which shows the market for NBA players, with demand and supply in 1980 as D_{1980} and S_{1980}. The intersection of these two curves generated an average pay in 1980 of $170,000, or $0.17 million, for the 300 or so players in the league. Since 1980, the talent pool expanded somewhat, shifting the supply curve a bit rightward from S_{1980} to S_{2010} (almost by definition, the supply of the top few hundred players in the world is limited). But demand exploded from D_{1980} to D_{2010}. With supply relatively fixed, the greater demand boosted average pay for NBA players to $4.9 million by 2010 for the 450 or so players in the league. Such pay attracts younger and younger players. NBA players are now the highest-paid team athletes in North America—earning at least double that of professionals in baseball, football, and hockey.

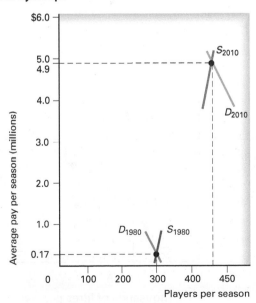

But rare talent alone does not command high pay. Top rodeo riders, top bowlers, and top women basketball players also possess rare talent, but the demand for their talent is

EXHIBIT 12
Effects of Shifts of Both Demand and Supply

EXHIBIT 12
Effects of Shifts of Both Demand and Supply

	Change in demand	
	Demand increases	**Demand decreases**
Supply increases	Equilibrium price change is indeterminate.	Equilibrium price falls.
	Equilibrium quantity increases.	Equilibrium quantity change is indeterminate.
Supply decreases	Equilibrium price rises.	Equilibrium price change is indeterminate.
	Equilibrium quantity change is indeterminate.	Equilibrium quantity decreases.

EXHIBIT 13
NBA Pay Leaps

(Graph: vertical axis "Average pay per season (millions)" with values $0.17, 1.0, 2.0, 3.0, 4.0, 4.9, 5.0, $6.0; horizontal axis "Players per season" with values 0, 100, 200, 300, 400, 450. Curves D_{1980}, S_{1980} intersect at 300 players, $0.17 million; curves S_{2010}, D_{2010} intersect at 450 players, $4.9 million.)

not sufficient to support pay anywhere near NBA levels. Some sports aren't even popular enough to support professional leagues.

LO5 Disequilibrium

A surplus exerts downward pressure on the price, and a shortage exerts upward pressure. Markets, however, don't always reach equilibrium quickly. During the time required to adjust, the market is said to be in disequilibrium. **Disequilibrium** is usually temporary as the market gropes for equilibrium. But sometimes, often as a result of government intervention, disequilibrium can last a while, perhaps decades, as we will see next.

Price Floors

A **price floor** is a *minimum* selling price set by government. Only if a price floor is above the equilibrium price is it binding, affecting market outcomes. For example, governments often regulate some agriculture prices, setting a price floor, in an attempt to ensure farmers a higher and more stable income than they would otherwise earn. Setting agricultural floors is common practice across the world with a few exceptions, such as Australia and New Zealand. Panel (a) of Exhibit 14 shows the effect of a $2.50 per litre price floor for milk. At that price, farmers supply 24 million litres per week, but consumers demand only 14 million litres, yielding a surplus of 10 million litres. This surplus milk will pile up on store shelves, eventually souring. To take it off

EXHIBIT 14
Price Floors and Price Ceilings

(a) Price floor for milk

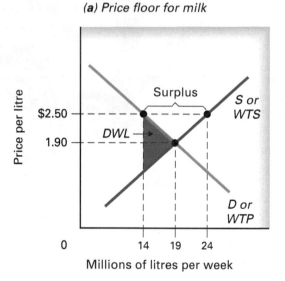

(b) Price ceiling for rent

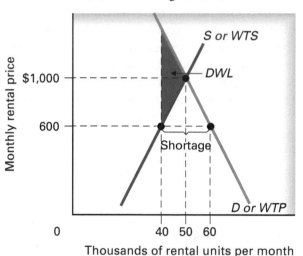

(c) Milk quota

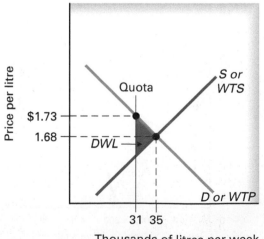

(d) A per-unit (excise) tax

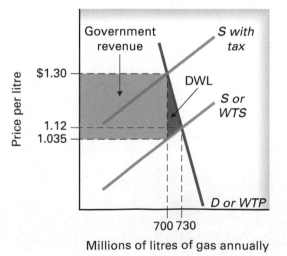

the market, the government usually agrees to buy the surplus milk. In general, governments, worldwide, spend billions buying and storing surplus agricultural products. Often governments dump (sell at well below market equilibrium price) or donate such artificially created agricultural surpluses to low-income economies, undermining the ability of local farmers to produce foodstuffs. Price floors distort markets and reduce economic welfare. Canadians, for example, pay about three times more for their milk than Americans because of the effective price floor established for Canadian dairy producers (in Canada this is largely achieved through quota; see below).

In addition to generating a surplus of 10 million litres of milk, notice that at the price floor, the WTP > WTS (the demand curve is above the supply curve). At the lower market-clearing price of $1.90, firms would never have produced so much milk. However, at $1.90, demand for milk is 19 million litres, or 5 million litres of milk greater than it is at the higher government-ordained price floor. In other words, the price floor prevents consumers from purchasing the amount of milk that they'd purchase at the lower market-clearing price. And farmers are induced to produce more than they would at the lower unregulated price. The value of these unmade but mutually beneficial exchanges is called the **deadweight loss (DWL)**. In panel (a), the DWL is the triangle formed between demand and supply from the 14 million litres of milk consumed under the price floor to the 19 million litres that would have been consumed at the equilibrium.

Note: To have an impact, a price floor must be set *above* the equilibrium price. A price floor set at or below the equilibrium price wouldn't matter since the market sets the equilibrium price. Price floors distort the market and reduce economic welfare because at a price floor the quantity demanded is less than the quantity supplied and the exchanged quantity is less than the equilibrium quantity.

disequilibrium the condition that exists in a market when the plans of buyers do not match those of sellers; a temporary mismatch between quantity supplied and quantity demanded as the market seeks equilibrium

price floor a minimum legal price below which a product cannot be sold; to have an impact, a price floor must be set above the equilibrium price

deadweight loss (DWL) the value of mutually beneficial trades that go unmade because of market interference; the area between the demand and supply curves and between the quantity exchanged under a particular policy and the equilibrium quantity

Price Ceilings

price ceiling a maximum legal price above which a product cannot be sold; to have an impact, a price ceiling must be set below the equilibrium price

Sometimes public officials try to keep a price below the equilibrium level by setting a **price ceiling**, or a *maximum* selling price. Concern about the rising cost of rental housing in some Canadian cities prompted city officials to impose rent ceilings. Panel (b) of Exhibit 14 depicts the demand and supply of rental housing. The vertical axis shows monthly rent, and the horizontal axis shows the quantity of rental units. The equilibrium, or market-clearing, rent is $1,000 per month, and the equilibrium quantity is 50,000 housing units. Suppose city officials set a maximum rent of $600 per month. At that ceiling price, 60,000 rental units are demanded, but only 40,000 supplied, resulting in a housing shortage of 20,000 units. Because of the price ceiling, the rental price no longer rations housing to those who value it the most. Other devices emerge to ration housing, such as long waiting lists, personal connections, and the willingness to make under-the-table payments, such as "key fees," "finder's fees," high security deposits, and the like.

Even if the price ceiling price is "enhanced" with extra fees, the exchanged quantity of 40,000 units is less than the equilibrium quantity of 50,000 and the WTP > WTS. In other words, at the price ceiling, some otherwise mutually beneficial trades do not get made, and once again we see a deadweight loss.

To have an impact, a price ceiling must be set *below* the equilibrium price. A price ceiling set at or above the equilibrium level wouldn't matter since the market sets the equilibrium price. Price ceilings distort the market and reduce economic welfare because at a price ceiling the quantity supplied is less than the quantity demanded and the exchanged quantity is less than the equilibrium quantity.

Quotas

Sometimes governments and institutions manage the quantity available to the market in order to prevent low prices. Examples are agricultural or fish quotas or even import quotas on foreign-produced automobiles. In this latter case, the price of foreign vehicles is driven up, allowing domestic production to be more price-competitive. Moreover, there is no worry of how to deal with excess supply. Suppose the market for milk in Prince Edward Island would typically reach equilibrium at $1.68 per litre in the stores with 35,000 litres sold provincially per week. The government could set a quota of 31,000 litres per week, driving prices up to $1.73 per litre as shown in panel (c) of Exhibit 14, thus permitting dairies to pay a higher price to dairy farmers.

Once again, WTP > WTS at the quota quantity of 31,000 litres per week, which necessarily means some mutually beneficial exchanges do not take place. And again we see an inefficiency expressed as a deadweight loss.

Per-Unit Taxes

Governments also sometimes tax certain goods and services. Taxes on goods and services come in many forms, the two most common being sales taxes—a percentage of the price paid for a good—and per-unit taxes—a fixed tax per unit. Let's consider the latter. In all provinces and territories, governments charge a per-litre tax on gasoline consumption. In Newfoundland and Labrador, the per-unit tax is $0.165 per litre. The federal government also charges a $0.10 per-litre tax on gasoline consumption. How does this tax affect the market for gasoline?

Panel (d) of Exhibit 14 is an example of the gasoline market both with and without a per-unit tax of $0.265 per litre. Suppose at the market equilibrium without the tax, the price of a litre of gas was $1.12 with annual province-wide sales of 730 million litres. With a tax imposed, gasoline retailers want to receive the original price plus the extra tax; the willingness-to-sell curve (the supply curve) would shift upwards by $0.265. But just because the retailers would like to receive the extra money does not mean that they will get it. Indeed, as long as the demand for gasoline has a slope that is anything other than perfectly vertical, retailers can pass on only some of the gas tax because consumers respond to the higher prices by reducing some of their gasoline consumption. After the tax is imposed, consumers reduce their consumption to 700 million litres. The price consumers pay at the pumps increases to $1.30 per litre while the amount the seller keeps drops to $1.035 because for each litre of gas they sell, the government collects $0.265 in taxes. The government's annual tax revenue is $185.5 million (i.e., $0.265 × 700 million) of which $115.5 million goes to the government of Newfoundland and Labrador (recall the provincial rate is only $0.165 per litre). This revenue is marked in panel (d).

Notice that at the after-tax quantity of 700 million, the quantity is less than the equilibrium quantity of 730 million. Moreover, at 700 million the WTP > WTS (i.e., the gap between the price the consumer pays and the amount the retailer actually keeps). In other words, with a per-unit tax, some otherwise mutually beneficial trades do not get made and once again we see a deadweight loss. This example is examined more closely as a Case Study in Chapter 5.

Some Caveats

The results we have derived above critically depend upon there being a perfectly competitive market (see Chapter 8) but they are often reasonable approximations to the real world. It is also important to note that government intervention is not the only source of market disequilibrium. And good government and governance are required for markets to work effectively, efficiently, and competitively. And, this requires tax revenue. Sometimes, when new products are introduced or when demand suddenly changes, it takes a while to reach equilibrium. For example, popular toys, best-selling books, and chart-busting CDs sometimes sell out. On the other hand, some new products attract few customers and pile up unsold on store shelves, awaiting a "clearance sale."

Final Word

Demand and supply are the building blocks of a market economy. Although a market usually involves the interaction of many buyers and sellers, few markets are consciously designed. Just as the law of gravity works whether or not we understand Newton's principles, market forces operate whether or not participants understand demand and supply. These forces arise naturally, much the way car dealers cluster on the outskirts of town to attract more customers.

Markets have their critics. Some observers may be troubled, for example, that an NHL star like Sidney Crosby earns a salary that could pay for more than 350 new schoolteachers, or that corporate executives, such as the head of Goldman Sachs, a financial firm, earns enough to pay for 1,000 new schoolteachers, or that Canadian consumers spend almost $9 billion on their pets. On your next trip to the supermarket, notice how much shelf space goes to pet products—often an entire aisle. PetSmart, a chain store, sells over 12,000 different pet items. Veterinarians offer cancer treatment, cataract removal, root canals, even acupuncture.

In a market economy, consumers are kings and queens. Consumer sovereignty rules, deciding what gets produced. Those who don't like the market outcome usually look to government for a solution through price ceilings and price floors, regulations, income redistribution, and public finance more generally.

CHAPTER PROBLEMS

LO1 Explain how the law of demand affects market activity

1.1. *(Shifting Demand)* List all the factors that shift the demand curve. Consider the market for hockey skates. Give a specific example for each of the shift factors listed, and state whether the demand curve would increase (shift out to the right) or decrease (shift in to the left).

1.2. *(Substitutes and Complements)* For each of the following pair of goods, determine whether the goods are substitutes, complements, or unrelated:
   a. Peanut butter and jelly
   b. Private and public transportation
   c. Coke and Pepsi
   d. Alarm clocks and automobiles
   e. Golf clubs and golf balls

LO2 Explain how the law of supply affects market activity

2.1. *(Supply)* What is the law of supply? Give an example of how you have observed the law of supply at work. What is the relationship between the law of supply and the supply curve?

2.2. *(Shifts in Supply)* Explain whether or not the following increase, decrease, or have no impact on the supply curve for hamburgers.
   a. Workers in meat-processing plants form a country-wide union.
   b. More corn is used in the production of ethanol.
   c. The price of hot dogs falls.
   d. The price of hamburgers falls.

LO3 Describe the interaction between demand and supply and the resulting market equilibrium

3.1. *(Demand and Supply)* How do you think each of the following would affect the world price of oil? (Use demand and supply analysis.)
   a. Tax credits are offered for expenditures on home insulation.
   b. The Keystone XL oil pipeline is completed.
   c. Oil is discovered in the Arctic Ocean.
   d. Sport utility vehicles and minivans regain popularity.
   e. The use of nuclear power declines.

3.2. *(Demand and Supply)* What happens to the equilibrium price and quantity of ice cream in response to each of the following? Explain your answers.
   a. The price of dairy cow fodder increases.
   b. The price of beef decreases.
   c. Concerns arise about the fat content of ice cream. Simultaneously, the price of sugar (used to produce ice cream) increases.

3.3. *(Shifting Demand and Supply)* Using demand and supply curves, show the effect of each of the following on the market for cigarettes:
   a. A cure for lung cancer is found.
   b. The price of cigars increases.
   c. Wages increase substantially in regions that grow tobacco.
   d. A fertilizer that increases the yield per hectare of tobacco is discovered.
   e. There is a sharp increase in the price of matches, lighters, and lighter fluid.
   f. More municipalities pass laws restricting smoking in restaurants and public places.

LO4 Describe how market equilibrium adjusts to shifting demand and supply

4.1. *(Equilibrium)* "If a price is not an equilibrium price, there is a tendency for it to move to its equilibrium level. Regardless of whether the price is too high or too low to begin with, the adjustment process will increase the quantity of the good purchased." Explain, using a demand and supply diagram.

4.2. *(Equilibrium)* Assume the market for corn is depicted as in the table that appears below.
   a. Complete the table below.
   b. What market pressure occurs when quantity demanded exceeds quantity supplied? Explain.
   c. What market pressure occurs when quantity supplied exceeds quantity demanded? Explain.
   d. What is the equilibrium price?
   e. What could change the equilibrium price?
   f. At each price in the first column of the table below, how much is sold?

4.3. *(Market Equilibrium)* Determine whether each of the following statements is true, false, or uncertain. Then briefly explain each answer.
   a. In equilibrium, all sellers can find buyers.
   b. In equilibrium, there is no pressure on the market to produce or consume more than is being sold.
   c. At prices above equilibrium, the quantity exchanged exceeds the quantity demanded.
   d. At prices below equilibrium, the quantity exchanged is equal to the quantity supplied.

4.4. *(Changes in Equilibrium)* What are the effects on the equilibrium price and quantity of steel if the wages of steelworkers rise and, simultaneously, the price of aluminum rises?

LO5 Explain how markets react during periods of disequilibrium

5.1. *(Price Floor)* There is considerable interest in whether agricultural price floors contribute to surplus production. Draw a demand and supply diagram for the milk market, and discuss the effects of a price floor. Who is helped and who is hurt by price floors in the milk market and, more generally, in the market for foodstuffs?

Price per Bushel	Quantity Demanded (millions of bushels)	Quantity Supplied (millions of bushels)	Surplus/ Shortage	Will Price Rise or Fall?
$1.80	320	200	_____	_____
2.00	300	230	_____	_____
2.20	270	270	_____	_____
2.40	230	300	_____	_____
2.60	200	330	_____	_____
2.80	180	350	_____	_____

CASE STUDY

The Market for Professional Basketball

Toward the end of the 1970s, the NBA seemed on the brink of collapse. Attendance had sunk to little more than half the capacity. Some teams were nearly bankrupt. Championship games didn't even merit prime-time television coverage. But in the 1980s, three superstars turned things around. Michael Jordan, Larry Bird, and Magic Johnson created millions of fans and breathed new life into the sagging league. New generations of stars, such as Dwayne Wade, Kevin Durant, and LeBron James, continue to fuel interest.

Since 1980 the league has expanded from 22 to 30 teams and game attendance has more than doubled. More importantly, league revenue from broadcast rights jumped about *50-fold* from $19 million per year during the 1978–1982 contract to $930 million per year in the current contract, which runs to 2016. Popularity also increased around the world as international players, such as Yao Ming of China and Dirk Nowitzki of Germany, joined the league (basketball is now the most widely played team sport in China). NBA rosters now include more than 80 international players. The NBA formed marketing alliances with global companies such as Coca-Cola and McDonald's, and league playoffs are televised in more than 200 countries in 45 languages to a potential market of 3 billion people.

What's the key resource in the production of NBA games? Talented players. Exhibit 15 shows the market for NBA players, with demand and supply in 1980 as D_{1980} and S_{1980}. The intersection of these two curves generated an average pay in 1980 of $170,000, or $0.17 million, for the 300 or so players in the league. Since 1980, the talent pool expanded somewhat, so the supply curve in 2010 was more like S_{2010} (almost by definition, the supply of the top few hundred players in the world is limited). But demand exploded from D_{1980} to D_{2010}. With supply relatively fixed, the greater demand boosted average pay to $4.9 million by 2010 for the 450 or so players in the league. Such pay attracts younger and younger players. Stars who entered the NBA right out of high school include Kobe Bryant, Kevin Garnett, and LeBron James. (After nine players entered the NBA draft right out of high school in 2005, the league, to stem the flow, required draft candidates to be at least 19 years old and out of high school for one year. So talented players started turning pro after their first year of college; in 2008, for example, 12 college freshmen

©RUBBERBALL/Getty Images

Because the supply of the world's top few hundred basketball players is relatively fixed by definition, the big jump in the demand for such talent caused average league pay to explode. Average pay increased from $170,000 in 1980 to $4,900,000 in 2010. Because the number of teams in the NBA increased, the number of players in the league grew from about 300 to about 450.

were drafted, including five of the top seven picks.)

But rare talent alone does not command high pay. Top rodeo riders, top bowlers, and top women basketball players also possess rare talent, but the demand for their talent is not sufficient to support pay anywhere near NBA levels. NBA players earn nearly 100 times more than WNBA players. For example, Diana Taurasi, a great college player, earned only $40,800 in her first pro season. Some sports aren't even popular enough to support professional leagues.

NBA players are now the highest-paid team athletes in North America—earning at least double that of professionals in baseball, football, and hockey. Both demand *and* supply determine average pay. But the NBA is not without its problems. In 2010 NBA players received 57 percent of all team revenue. Some team owners say they have been losing money, so they want to cut the share of revenue going to players. To cut costs, some teams, such as the Detroit Pistons, have traded their highest-paid players.

EXHIBIT 15

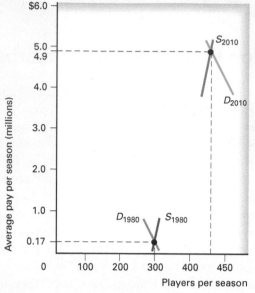

SOURCES: Howard Beck, "Falk Says NBA and Players Headed for Trouble," *New York Times*, 13 February 2010; Jonathan Abrams, "NBA's Shrinking Salary Cap Could Shake Up 2010 Free Agency," *New York Times*, 8 July 2010; and U.S. Census Bureau, *Statistical Abstract of the United States: 2010* at http://www.census.gov/compendia/statab/.

QUESTION

1. Average salaries in the top four North American sports leagues are NBA, $5.15 million; MLB, $3.2 million; NHL, $2.4 million; and NFL, $1.9 million. What demand and supply factors might contribute to this discrepancy?

APPENDIX

An Algebraic Approach to Demand, Supply, and Equilibrium

Functional Forms

From the outset it is important to note that the linear functions used in this appendix are simply approximations. It is very unlikely that either demand or supply is linear in nature. Solving for the solution in a non-linear case is essentially the same, just more complex. The example below is a hypothetical market for bananas in a medium-sized city.

Demand

Suppose that the weekly demand for bananas can be described by the function $P = 9.50 - 3Q$, where P is expressed in $/kg and Q is measured in thousands of kilograms per week. You might interpret the relationship this way. Until the price of bananas drops below $9.50/kg, no one will buy bananas. Thereafter, in order to get consumers to buy an additional 1,000 kilograms (i.e., Q increases by 1), the price must drop by $3.

The "=" in the function might be thought of as passive; it is a statement about what holds true for this example.

Supply

Suppose that the weekly supply for bananas can be described by the function $P = 0.50 + 0.60Q$, where P and Q are in the units mentioned earlier. In this case, suppliers are unwilling to supply bananas if they sell for below \$0.50/kg. Thereafter, in order to sell an additional 1,000 kilograms (i.e., Q increases by 1), the price suppliers receive must increase by \$0.60. Again, the passive "=" is used.

Equilibrium

A perfectly competitive market equilibrium exists when there is *one price at which the quantity demanded equals the quantity supplied*. Here it is helpful to create the active "=." While the passive "=" is a definitional statement describing how price and quantity are related in the case of either demand or supply, the active "=" reflects the fact that we, as economists, are applying a theory to this situation—demand and supply for a good or service exist independently but we believe that the system is driven to equilibrium. At the equilibrium, the price in the demand function is the same as the price in the supply function. So (actively) setting them equal results in:

$$9.50 - 3Q = 0.50 + 0.60Q$$

This relationship can be altered as long as it is kept in balance. What is done to the left side must also be done to the right. Let's collect the Q variables on the right. Our first step is to remove the Q term on the left,

$$9.50 - \cancel{3Q + 3Q} = 0.50 + 0.60Q + 3Q$$
$$\rightarrow 9.50 = 0.50 + 3.60Q$$

Likewise the 0.50 on the right can be removed,

$$9.50 - 0.50 = \cancel{0.50 - 0.50} + 3.60Q \rightarrow 9.00 = 3.60Q$$

We now know what $3.60Q$ is equal to, but we'd like to know what Q is equal to. To get there, we must divide both sides by 3.60.

$$9.00 \div 3.60 = \cancel{3.60}Q \div \cancel{3.60} \rightarrow 2.5 = Q$$

In other words, the equilibrium quantity is $2.5 \times 1,000 = 2,500$ kg/week.

The equilibrium price can be found by substituting the equilibrium quantity into either the demand or supply equation. For instance, if we substitute into the demand function we get $9.50 - 3(2.5) = 2.00$. Likewise, we get $0.50 + 0.60(2.5) = 2.00$ through substitution into the supply function. Consequently, the equilibrium price is \$2.00/kg.

Measuring Consumer and Producer Surplus

Both the consumer and producer surplus have been defined in the text. The consumer surplus is the area beneath the demand curve but above the price paid up to the number of units exchanged. It forms a triangle in this case. A triangle is simply half of a rectangle, so the area of a triangle is simply ½ × base × height. Thus, in the case of our banana market, $CS = ½ \times (\$9.50 - \$2.00) \times (2.5 - 0) = ½ \times 7.50 \times 2.5 = \$9.375$ thousand per week (or \$9,375 per week).

The producer surplus is the area above the supply curve but beneath the price the seller receives up to the number of units exchanged. In this case the $PS = ½ \times (\$2.00 - \$0.50) \times (2.5 - 0) = \$1.875$ thousand per week (or \$1,875 per week).

Disequilibrium (These are advanced topics)

Algebra also provides an easy way to look at cases of disequilibrium. Suppose the government imposes a *price floor* of \$3.00/kg to support banana growers. We can solve for the quantity demanded:

$$3.00 = 9.50 - 3Q \rightarrow \text{(subtract 9.50 from both sides)} \rightarrow -6.50 = -3Q \rightarrow \text{(divide both sides by } -3) \rightarrow Q^D = 2.167$$

We can also solve for the quantity supplied:

$$3.00 = 0.50 + 0.60Q \rightarrow \text{(subtract 0.50 from both sides)} \rightarrow 2.50 = 0.6Q \rightarrow \text{(divide both sides by 0.60)} \rightarrow Q^S = 4.167$$

As expected, a price floor leads to an excess of supply ($Q^S > Q^D$) but now we can calculate it to be a surplus of 2,000 kg/week (i.e., $4.167 - 2.167$). Sellers supply more than people want to buy at \$3/kg. Notice that while a higher price is paid for bananas, fewer bananas are now exchanged—2,167 kg/week instead of 2,500 kg/week at the equilibrium.

Suppose instead that the government imposes a *price ceiling* of \$1.00/kg to encourage banana consumption. (Now we'll skip steps.) The quantity demanded at \$1/kg is $1.00 = 9.50 - 3Q \rightarrow Q^D = 2.83$, while the quantity supplied is $1.00 = 0.50 + 0.60Q \rightarrow Q^S = 0.83$. As expected, a price ceiling leads to an excess of demand ($Q^D > Q^S$) and we calculate that to be a shortage of 2,000 kg/week (i.e., $0.83 - 2.83$). Moreover, while it is true that consumers would like to consume more bananas under this policy, there are now fewer bananas actually exchanged—830 kg/week now instead of 2,500 kg/week at the equilibrium.

What if the government is instead worried about foreign competition in the domestic fruit market and they decide to limit banana imports through a quota? Suppose they permit no more than 1,500 kg/week of bananas to be sold (notice this is less than the equilibrium value of 2.5). When quantity is fixed at 1.5, buyers are willing to pay up to $P^D = 9.50 - 3(1.5) = \$5$/kg while sellers would be willing to sell them for as little as $P^S = 0.50 + 0.6(1.5) = \$1.40$/kg. There's a strong potential here to get to the higher price, which means that the sellers receive $3.60 over their minimum willingness to sell 1,500 kg/week. The government could let foreign banana growers receive the higher price (an arrangement called *voluntary export restraint*) or they could do a favour to banana importers in the domestic economy who can buy at the low price internationally and then sell at the higher price domestically.

Finally, suppose the government wants to raise revenues through a special banana tax of $0.10/kg which they will collect from sellers (this is known as an excise tax or a per-unit tax). From the sellers' point of view, they must now get an additional $0.10/kg beyond their original willingness-to-sell. We can handle this simply by adjusting our supply curve. The taxed price (P^t) must be the original price (P) plus the tax:

$$P^t = P + t = 0.50 + 0.60Q + 0.10 = 0.60 + 0.60Q$$

In other words, the supply curve is raised by exactly the amount of the tax. What is the after-tax equilibrium? Setting the demand equal to the new supply curve, we get

$$9.50 - 3Q = 0.60 + 0.60Q \rightarrow Q = 8.90 \div 3.60 = 2.472$$

or 2,472 kg/week. The price the consumer pays and the seller receives at the cash register is $2.08/kg, but once the sellers hand over the tax to the government, they get to keep $1.98/kg (i.e., $2.08 − $0.10). The government revenue from this tax is equal to the tax rate ($0.10/kg) times the quantity sold (2,472 kg/week) or $247.20/week.

Problems

1. Solve for the equilibrium price and quantity in the following situations:
   a. Demand: $P = 50 - 2Q$ and Supply: $P = 5 + 3Q$
   b. Demand: $P = 155 - 1.5Q$ and Supply: $P = 15 + 2.5Q$
   c. Demand: $P = 209 - 1.75Q$ and Supply: $P = 17 + 3.3Q$
2. Suppose the weekly demand and supply for bananas is the same as in this appendix (Demand: $P = 9.50 - 3Q$ and Supply: $P = 0.50 + 0.60Q$).

   a. As practice, solve for the equilibrium quantity and price.
   b. Suppose we are not at the equilibrium price. Instead, the government wants to keep the price at $1.50 to encourage consumption. Calculate the quantity demanded and the quantity supplied of bananas. Is there a shortage or surplus of bananas in this market? What is the size of the surplus or shortage?
   c. Does the government's plan succeed in encouraging banana consumption?
3. Suppose the demand and supply for some product can be described by Demand: $P = a - bQ$ and Supply: $P = c + dQ$, where a, b, c, and d are greater than zero.
   a. Can you think of any reason why it makes sense that we add the following restriction: $a > c$?
   b. Solve for the equilibrium quantity and price. *If you can do this, you have now solved for all possible solutions to perfectly competitive markets described by linear demand and supply functions.*
4. Suppose demand for some product can be described by Demand: $P = 55 - 2Q$ while supply is fixed at $Q = 10$. What is the equilibrium quantity and price in this case?
5. Using the banana example in this appendix, suppose the tax on bananas was $0.15/kg instead of $0.10.
   a. Without calculating, estimate the effects of this tax. Will the new exchange price be higher or lower? How about the price kept by sellers? What about the quantity? What about the government revenue?
   b. Calculate the new price paid by consumers, the price kept by sellers, the quantity of bananas sold, and the new government revenue. Compare your answers to the expectations you formed in (a) above.
   c. Draw a diagram of the market before any tax and label the equilibrium. Then add to your diagram the new supply curve with the $0.15/kg tax in place and indicate the price paid by consumers, the amount kept by producers, and the new quantity exchanged. Clearly indicate the consumer surplus, the producer surplus, the government revenue, and the deadweight loss.
   d. Calculate the deadweight loss, as defined in the main text, of the tax. (*This is a bit more challenging, but it is similar to the calculation of consumer and producer surplus; recall how to calculate the area of a triangle.*)

5

Introduction to Macroeconomics

LEARNING OUTCOMES

LO1 Discuss macroeconomics and the national economy

LO2 Discuss economic fluctuations and growth

LO3 Explain aggregate demand and aggregate supply

LO4 Describe the history of the Canadian economy

> ## Which has more impact on your standard of living, the economy's short-term ups and downs or its long-term growth trend?

What's the big idea with macroeconomics? Why is its focus the national economy? How do we measure the economy's performance over time? Which has more impact on your standard of living, the economy's short-term ups and downs or its long-term growth trend? What's the difference between demand-side economics and supply-side economics? How has the economic role of government evolved during the past century? Answers to these and related questions are provided in this chapter, which introduces macroeconomics. Macroeconomics looks at the big picture—not the demand for iPhones but the demand for everything produced in the economy; not the price of gasoline but the average price of all goods and services produced in the economy; not consumption by the Martinez household but consumption by all households; not investment by Google but investment by all firms in the economy.

Macroeconomists develop and test theories about how the economy as a whole works—theories that can help predict the impact of economic policies and events. Macroeconomists are concerned not only with what determines such big-picture indicators as production, employment, and the price level but also with understanding how and why they change over time. Macroeconomists are especially interested in what makes an economy grow, because a growing economy creates more jobs and more goods and services—in short, more growth means a rising standard of living. What determines the economy's ability to use resources productively, to adapt, to grow? This chapter begins exploring such questions.

LO 1   The National Economy

Macroeconomics concerns the overall performance of the *economy*. The term **economy** describes the structure of economic life, or economic activity, in a community, a region, a country, a group of countries, or the world. We could talk about the Ontario economy, the Canadian economy, the North American economy, or the world economy. We measure an economy's size in different ways, such as the amount produced, the number of people working, or their total income. The most common yardstick is *gross product,* which measures the market value of final goods and services produced in a particular geographical region during a given period, usually one year.

economy the structure of economic activity in a community, a region, a country, a group of countries, or the world

gross domestic product (GDP) the market value of all final goods and services produced in the nation during a particular period, usually a year

If the focus is the Ontario economy, we consider the *gross provincial product.* If the focus is the Canadian economy, we consider the **gross domestic product,** or **GDP,** which measures the market value of all final goods and services produced in Canada during a given period, usually

WE CAN USE THE GROSS DOMESTIC PRODUCT TO COMPARE DIFFERENT ECONOMIES AT THE SAME TIME OR TO TRACK THE SAME ECONOMY OVER TIME.

The United States and Canada usually allow people and goods to move more freely within their borders than across their borders.

a year. GDP adds up production of the economy's incredible variety of goods and services, from trail bikes to pedicures. We can use the gross domestic product to compare different economies at the same time or to track the same economy over time. We could also consider the **gross world product**, which measures the value of all final goods and services produced in the world during a given period, usually a year. But the focus of macroeconomics is usually the national economy.

What's Special about the National Economy?

The national economy deserves special attention. Here's why. If you were to drive from one province to another within Canada, you would hardly notice any crossing. But if, instead, you were to drive south into the United States, you would be stopped at the border, asked for identification, and possibly searched. You would become quite aware of crossing an international border. Like most

countries, Canada and the United States usually allow people and goods to move more freely *within* their borders than *across* their borders.

The differences between Canada and the United States are far greater than the differences between Ontario and Manitoba. For example, each country has its own standard of living and currency, its own culture and language, its own communication and transportation systems, its own system of government, and its own "rules of the game"—that is, its own laws, regulations, customs, manners, and ways of doing business, both within and across its borders.

Macroeconomics typically focuses on the performance of the national economy, including how the national economy interacts with other national economies around the world. The world economy is made up of about 200 sovereign nations, ranging from tiny Liechtenstein, with only 35,000 people, to China, with 1.4 billion people. These numbers offer snapshots, but the economy is a motion picture, a work in progress—too complex to capture in snapshots. This is why we use theoretical models to focus on key relationships.

> **gross world product** the market value of all final goods and services produced in the world during a given period, usually a year

flow variable a measure of something over an interval of time, such as your income per week

stock variable a measure of something at a particular point in time, such as the amount of money you have with you right now

To help you get your mind around the economy, let's begin with a simple analogy.

The Human Body and the Canadian Economy

Consider the similarities and differences between the human body and the economy. The body consists of millions of cells, each performing particular functions yet each linked to the entire body. Similarly, the Canadian economy is composed of millions of decision makers, each acting with some independence yet each connected with the economy as a whole. The economy, like the body, is continually renewing itself, with new households, new businesses, a changing cast of public officials, and new foreign competitors and customers. Blood circulates throughout the body, facilitating the exchange of oxygen and vital nutrients among cells. Similarly, *money* circulates throughout the economy, facilitating the exchange of resources and products among individual economic units. In fact, blood and money are each called a *medium of exchange*. In Chapter 1 we saw that the movement of money, products, and resources throughout the economy follows a *circular flow,* as does the movement of blood, oxygen, and nutrients throughout the body.

Flow and Stock Variables Just as the same blood recirculates as a medium of exchange in the body, the same dollars recirculate as a medium of exchange in the economy to finance transactions. The dollars you spend on bagels are spent by the baker on butter and then spent by the dairy farmer on work boots. Dollars *flow* through the economy. To measure a flow, we use a **flow variable**, which is an amount per unit of time, such as your average spending per week or your heartbeats per minute. In contrast, a **stock variable** is an amount measured at a particular point in time, such as the amount of money you have with you right now or your weight this morning.

Testing New Theories Physicians and other natural scientists test their theories using controlled experiments. Macroeconomists, however, have no laboratories and little ability to run economy-wide experiments of any kind. Granted, they can study different economies around the world, but

each economy is unique, so comparisons are tricky. Controlled experiments also provide the natural scientists with something seldom available to economists—the chance, or serendipitous, discovery (such as penicillin). Macroeconomists studying the Canadian economy have only one patient, so they can't introduce particular policies in a variety of alternative settings. You can't squeeze economies into a test tube. Cries of "Eureka!" are seldom heard from macroeconomists.

Knowledge and Performance

Throughout history, little was known about the human body, yet many people still enjoyed good health. For example, the fact that blood circulates in the body was not established until 1638; it took scientists another 150 years to figure out why. Similarly, over the millennia, various complex economies developed and flourished, although at the time there was little understanding about how an economy worked.

The economy is much like the body: as long as it functions smoothly, policymakers need not understand how it works. But if a problem develops—severe unemployment, high inflation, or sluggish growth, for example—we must know how a healthy economy works before we can consider whether anything can be done about it. We need not know every detail of the economy, just as we need not know every detail of the body. But we must understand essential relationships among key variables. For example, does the economy work well on its own, or does it often perform poorly? If it performs poorly, are there remedies? Can we be sure that a proposed remedy would not do more harm than good? When doctors didn't understand how the human body worked, their attempted "cures" were often worse than the diseases. Much of the history of medicine describes misguided efforts to deal with maladies. Even today, medical care is based on less scientific evidence than you might think. According to one study, only one in seven medical interventions is supported by reliable scientific evidence.[1] For example, acetaminophen (e.g., Tylenol) is a popular pain reliever, but nobody really knows how it works. According to an old saying, "Nature heals and the doctor collects the fee." Or as Voltaire

---

[1] As reported by Sherwin Nuland, "Medical Fads: Bran, Midwives and Leeches," *New York Times*, 25 June 1995.

wrote, "The art of medicine consists of amusing the patient while nature cures the disease."

Likewise, policymakers may adopt the wrong prescription because of a flawed theory about how the economy works. At one time, for example, a nation's economic vitality was thought to spring from the stock of precious metals accumulated in the public treasury. This theory spawned a policy called **mercantilism**, which held that, as a way of accumulating gold and silver, a nation should try to export more than it imports. To achieve this, nations restricted imports by such barriers as tariffs and quotas. But these restrictions led to retaliations by other countries, reducing international trade and the gains from specialization. Another flawed economic theory prompted U.S. president Herbert Hoover to introduce a major tax *increase* during the Great Depression. Economists have since learned that such a policy does more harm than good. Debates about the effectiveness of government policies were widespread as officials reacted to the crushing U.S. recession of 2007–2009.

We turn now to the performance of the Canadian economy.

LO 2 Economic Fluctuations and Growth

The Canadian economy and other industrial market economies historically have experienced alternating periods of expansion and contraction in economic activity. As noted in Chapter 1, *economic fluctuations* are the rise and fall of economic activity relative to the long-term growth trend of the economy. These fluctuations, or *business cycles,* vary in length and intensity, yet some features appear common to all. The ups and downs usually involve the entire nation and often many other economies around the world, and they affect nearly all dimensions of economic activity, not just production and employment.

Canadian Economic Fluctuations

Perhaps the easiest way to understand the business cycle is to examine its components. During the 1920s and 1930s, Wesley C. Mitchell, director of the U.S. National Bureau of Economic Research (NBER), analyzed business cycles, noting that the economy has two phases: *expansions* and *contractions.* During an **expansion**, the economy grows as reflected by rising output, employment, income, and other aggregate measures. During a **contraction**, the economy declines as reflected by falling output, employment, income, and other aggregate measures. Prior to World War II, a contraction might be so sharp as to be called a **depression**, which is a severe and prolonged reduction in the nation's economic activity as occurred during the 1930s. A milder contraction is called a **recession**, which is a period of decline in economic activity lasting more than a few months, as reflected by falling output, employment, income, and other aggregate measures. The Canadian economy experienced both recessions and depressions before World War II. Since then, there have been recessions but no depressions, so things have improved.

Despite these ups and downs, the Canadian economy has grown dramatically over the long term. Although economic activity is measured in a variety of ways, if we had to settle on a single indicator, output best captures what's going on. Output is measured by real GDP, the value of final goods and services after stripping away changes due to **inflation**, which is an increase in the economy's average price level. Production increased because of (1) increases in the amount and quality of resources, especially labour and capital; (2) better technology; and (3) improvements in the *rules of the game* that facilitate production and exchange, such as property rights, patent laws, the legal system, and market practices.

Exhibit 1 shows the long-term growth trend in economic activity as an upward-sloping straight line. Economic fluctuations reflect movements around this growth trend. A contraction begins after the previous expansion has reached a *peak,* or high point, and continues until the economy reaches a *trough,* or low point. The period between a peak and trough is a *contraction,* and the period between a trough and subsequent peak is an *expansion*. Note that

mercantilism the incorrect theory that a nation's economic objective should be to accumulate precious metals in the public treasury; this theory prompted trade barriers to cut imports, but trading partners retaliated, reducing trade and the gains from specialization

expansion a period during which the economy grows as reflected by rising output, employment, income, and other aggregate measures

contraction a period during which the economy declines as reflected by falling output, employment, income, and other aggregate measures

depression a severe and prolonged reduction in economic activity as occurred during the 1930s

recession a period of decline in economic activity lasting more than a few months, as reflected by falling output, employment, income, and other aggregate measures

inflation an increase in the economy's average price level

EXHIBIT 1
Hypothetical Business Cycles

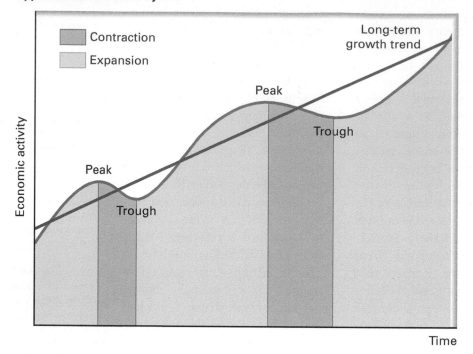

expansions last longer than contractions, but the length of the full cycle varies.

Exhibit 2 shows annual percentage changes in real GDP since 1949. Years of declining real GDP are shown as negative. Growth since 1949 has averaged 3.6 percent a year.

The intensity of economic fluctuations varies across regions. A recession hits hardest those regions that produce capital goods, such as heavy machinery, and durable goods, such as appliances, furniture, and automobiles. The demand for these goods falls more during hard times than does the demand for other goods and services, such as breakfast cereal, gasoline, and haircuts.

EXHIBIT 2
Annual Percentage Change in Canadian Real GDP since 1949

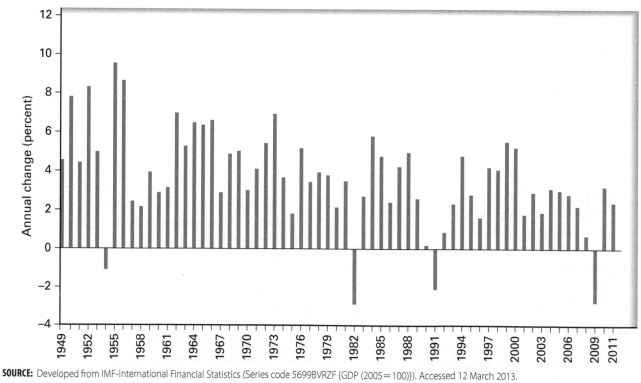

SOURCE: Developed from IMF-International Financial Statistics (Series code 5699BVRZF {GDP (2005 = 100)}). Accessed 12 March 2013.

BECAUSE OF SEASONAL FLUCTUATIONS AND RANDOM DISTURBANCES, THE ECONOMY DOES NOT MOVE SMOOTHLY THROUGH PHASES OF THE BUSINESS CYCLE.

Because of seasonal fluctuations and random disturbances, the economy does not move smoothly through phases of the business cycle. Economists can't always distinguish a temporary drop in economic activity from the beginning of a downturn. A drop in economic activity may result from a temporary slowdown, such as a snowstorm or a poor growing season. Turning points—peaks and troughs—are thus identified by Statistics Canada only after the fact. Because a recession means economic activity declines for more than a few months (two quarters, or six months, is sometimes used as a rule of thumb), and because the official announcement that a recession has begun is not made until months after that, we sometimes don't know for sure when a recession has started until a year later. Likewise, a recession's end is sometimes not announced until a year or more after it's over.

As noted, fluctuations usually involve the entire nation. Indeed, major economies around the world often move together. For example, the Great Depression was a worldwide calamity. The unemployment rate in Germany reached 34 percent, which helped bring Adolf Hitler to power. Recession also spanned most of the globe as a result of the financial crisis of 2008. The following section compares the year-to-year output changes in Canada with those in two other major economies, the United States and the United Kingdom, during the past three decades.

The Global Economy Though business cycles are not perfectly synchronized across countries, a link is usually apparent. Consider the experience of three leading economies—Canada, the United States, and the United Kingdom. Exhibit 3 shows for each economy the year-to-year percentage change in real GDP since 1978. Again, *real* means that the effects of inflation have been erased, so remaining changes reflect *real* changes in the total amount of goods and services produced each year.

By examining the annual changes in each economy, you can see the similarities. For example, all three economies went into recession in the early 1980s, grew well for the rest of the decade, entered another recession in 1991, recovered for the rest of the decade, then slowed down in 2001. The economies picked up steam in 2004, but the global financial crisis of 2008 caused sharply lower output by 2009.

When linkage across economies occurs, a slump in other major economies could worsen a recession in Canada and vice versa. For example, the financial crisis of 2008 affected economies around the world, increasing unemployment and cutting production. Trouble in seemingly minor economies, such as Greece, can spill over and drag other economies down with them. But economic strength overseas can give the Canadian economy a lift.

Economic Indicators

Certain events foreshadow a turning point in economic activity. Months before a recession is fully under way, changes in leading economic indicators point to the coming storm. In the early stages of a recession, business slows down, orders for machinery

CHAPTER 5: INTRODUCTION TO MACROECONOMICS

EXHIBIT 3

Canada, U.S., and U.K. Annual Growth Rates

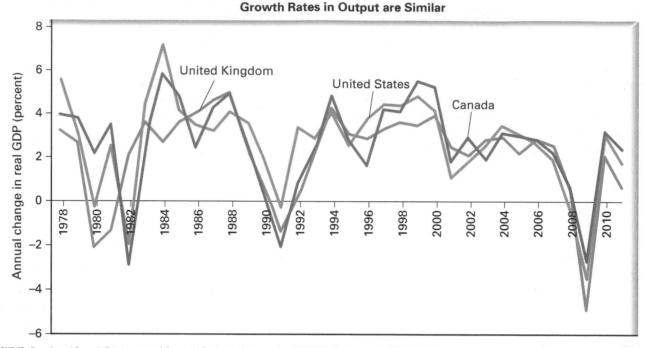

Growth Rates in Output are Similar

SOURCE: Developed from IMF-International Financial Statistics (Series code 15699BVRZF). Accessed 12 March 2013.

---

leading economic indicators variables that predict, or lead to, a recession or recovery; examples are consumer confidence, stock market prices, business investment, and big-ticket purchases, such as automobiles and homes

coincident economic indicators variables that reflect peaks and troughs in economic activity; examples are employment, personal income, and industrial production

lagging economic indicators variables that follow, or trail, changes in overall economic activity; examples are the interest rate and the average duration of unemployment

and computers slip, and the stock market, anticipating lower profits, turns down. Consumer confidence in the economy also begins to sag, so households spend less, especially on big-ticket items like homes and automobiles. Unsold goods start piling up. All these signs are called **leading economic indicators** because they usually predict, or *lead to,* a downturn. Likewise, upturns in leading indicators point to an economic recovery. But leading indicators cannot predict precisely *when* a turning point will occur, or even *whether* one will occur. Sometimes leading indicators sound a false alarm.

Some economic indicators measure what's going on in the economy right now. **Coincident economic indicators** are those measures that reflect expansions, contractions, peaks, and troughs as they occur. Coincident indicators include total employment, personal income, and industrial production. And some economic indicators measure what has already happened. **Lagging economic indicators** follow, or trail, changes

in overall economic activity. Lagging indicators, which look at the economy through the rear-view mirror, include interest rates, the unemployment rate, and how long people remain unemployed.

Our introduction to business cycles has been largely mechanical, focusing on the history and measurement of these fluctuations. We have not discussed why economies fluctuate, in part because such a discussion requires firmer footing in macroeconomic theory and in part because the causes remain in dispute. In the next section, we begin to build a macroeconomic framework by introducing a key model of analysis.

LO 3 Aggregate Demand and Aggregate Supply

The economy is so complex that we need to simplify matters, or to abstract from the millions of relationships to isolate the important ones. We must step back from all the individual economic transactions to survey the resulting mosaic.

Aggregate Output and the Price Level

Let's begin with something you already know. Picture a pizza. Now picture food more generally. Food, of course, includes not just pizza but thousands of other items. Although food is more general than pizza, you probably have no difficulty picturing food. Now make the leap from food to all goods and services produced in the economy—food, housing, clothing, entertainment, transportation, healthcare, and so on. Economists call this **aggregate output**. Because *aggregate* means total, aggregate output is the total amount of goods and services produced in the economy during a given period. Because output is measured per period, it's a flow measure. The best measure of aggregate output is *real GDP*, which you'll soon learn more about.

Just as we can talk about the demand for pizza, or the demand for food, we can talk about the demand for aggregate output. **Aggregate demand** is the relationship between the average price of aggregate output in the economy and the quantity of aggregate output demanded. The average price of aggregate output is called the economy's **price level**. You are more familiar than you may think with these aggregate measures. Headlines refer to the growth of aggregate output—as in "Growth Slows in Second Quarter." News accounts also report on changes in the "cost of living," reflecting movements in the economy's price level—as in "Prices Jump in June."

In a later chapter, you learn how the economy's price level is computed. All you need to know now is that the price level in any year is an *index number*, or a reference number, comparing average prices that year with average prices in some base, or reference, year. If we say that the price level is higher, we mean compared with where it was. In Chapter 4, we talked about the price of a particular product, such as pizza, *relative to the prices of other products*. Now we talk about the *average price* of all goods and services produced in the economy *relative to the price level in some base year*.

The price level in the *base year* is standardized to a benchmark value of 100, and price levels in other years are expressed relative to the base-year price level. For example, in 2012, the Canadian price level, or price index, was 109.6, indicating that the price level that year was 9.6 percent higher than its value of 100 in the base year of 2007.

The price level, or price index, is used not only to compare prices over time but also to compare real aggregate output over time. Economists use the *price index* to eliminate year-to-year changes in GDP due solely to changes in the price level. What's left is the change in real output—the change in the amount of goods and services produced. After adjusting GDP for price level changes, we end up with what is called the **real gross domestic product**, or **real GDP**. So the price index (1) shows how the economy's price level changes over time and (2) is used to figure out real GDP each year. You'll get a better idea of these two roles as we discuss the Canadian economy.

Aggregate Demand Curve

In Chapter 4, you learned about the demand for a particular product, such as pizza. Now let's talk about the demand for our composite measure of output—aggregate output, or real GDP. The **aggregate demand curve** shows the relationship between the price level in the economy and real GDP demanded, other things constant. Exhibit 4 shows a hypothetical aggregate demand curve, *AD*.

aggregate output a composite measure of all final goods and services produced in an economy during a given period; real GDP

aggregate demand the relationship between the economy's price level and aggregate output demanded, with other things constant

price level a composite measure reflecting the prices of all goods and services in the economy relative to prices in a base year

real gross domestic product (real GDP) the economy's aggregate output measured in dollars of constant purchasing power

aggregate demand curve a curve representing the relationship between the economy's price level and real GDP demanded per period, with other things constant

EXHIBIT 4
Aggregate Demand Curve

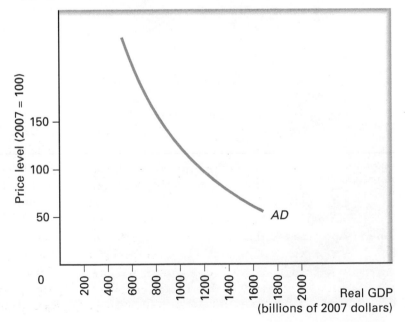

AGGREGATE DEMAND SUMS DEMANDS OF THE FOUR ECONOMIC DECISION MAKERS.

aggregate supply curve a curve representing the relationship between the economy's price level and real GDP supplied per period, with other things constant

The vertical axis measures an index of the economy's price level relative to a 2007 base-year price level of 100. The horizontal axis shows real GDP, which measures output in dollars of constant purchasing power (here we use 2007 prices).

The aggregate demand curve in Exhibit 4 reflects an inverse relationship between the price level in the economy and real GDP demanded. Aggregate demand sums demands of the four economic decision makers: households, firms, governments, and the rest of the world. As the price level increases, other things constant, households demand less housing and furniture, firms demand fewer trucks and tools, governments demand less computer software and military hardware, and the rest of the world demands less Canadian grain and Canadian aircraft.

© Davo Blair/Alamy

The reasons behind this inverse relationship get a closer look in later chapters, but here's a quick summary. Real GDP demanded depends in part on household *wealth*. Some wealth is usually held in bank accounts and in currency. An increase in the price level, other things constant, decreases the purchasing power of bank accounts and currency. Households are therefore poorer when the price level increases, so the quantity of real GDP they demand decreases. Conversely, a reduction in the price level increases the purchasing power of bank accounts and currency. Because households are richer as the price level decreases, the quantity of real GDP they demand increases.

Factors held constant along a given aggregate demand curve include the price levels in other countries as well as the exchange rates between the Canadian dollar and foreign currencies. When the Canadian price level increases, Canadian products become more expensive relative to foreign products. Consequently, households, firms, and governments both here and abroad decrease the quantity of Canadian products demanded. On the other hand, a lower Canadian price level makes Canadian products cheaper relative to foreign products, so the quantity of Canadian products demanded increases.

Consider the demand for a particular product versus aggregate demand. If the price of a particular product, such as pizza, increases, quantity demanded declines in part because pizza becomes more costly compared to substitutes. If the economy's price level increases, the quantity of Canadian real GDP demanded declines in part because Canadian products become more costly compared to foreign products.

Aggregate Supply Curve

The **aggregate supply curve** shows how much Canadian producers are willing and able to supply at each price level, other things constant. How does quantity supplied respond to changes in the price level? The upward-sloping aggregate supply curve, *AS*, in Exhibit 5 shows a positive relationship between the price level and the quantity of real GDP supplied. Assumed constant along an aggregate supply curve are (1) resource prices, (2) the state of technology, and (3) the rules of the game that provide production

EXHIBIT 5
Aggregate Demand and Aggregate Supply in 2012

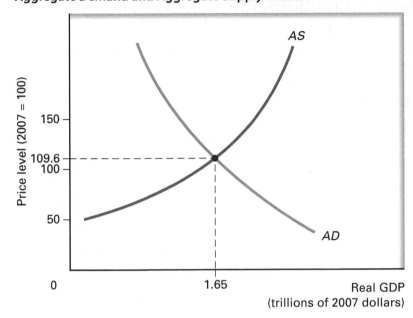

incentives, such as patents and business practices. With regard to resource prices, wage rates are typically assumed to be constant along the aggregate supply curve. With wages constant, firms find a higher price level more profitable, so they increase real GDP supplied. *As long as the prices firms receive for their products rise faster than their cost of production, firms find it profitable to expand output, so real GDP supplied varies directly with the economy's price level.*

Equilibrium

The aggregate demand curve intersects the aggregate supply curve to determine the equilibrium levels of price and real GDP in the economy. Exhibit 5 is a rough depiction of aggregate demand and aggregate supply in 2012. Equilibrium real GDP that year was about $1.65 trillion (measured in dollars of 2007 purchasing power). The equilibrium price level was 109.6 (compared with a price level of 100 in the base year of 2007). At any other price level, quantity demanded would not match quantity supplied.

Incidentally, although employment is not measured directly along the horizontal axis, firms usually must hire more workers to produce more output. So higher levels of real GDP can be beneficial because (1) more goods and services become available in the economy, and (2) more people are usually employed. Perhaps the best way to understand aggregate demand and aggregate supply is to apply these tools to the

Canadian economy. The following section simplifies Canada's economic history to review changes in the price and output levels over time.

LO 4 Brief History of the Canadian Economy

The history of the Canadian economy can be divided roughly into four economic eras: (1) the Great Depression and before, (2) after the Great Depression to the early 1980s, (3) from the early 1980s to 2007, and (4) the recession of 2008–2009 and beyond. The first era suffered from recessions and depressions, culminating in the Great Depression of the 1930s. These depressions were often accompanied by a falling price level. The second era was one of generally strong economic growth, with only moderate increases in the price level. The third era saw both high unemployment

KEYNES PROPOSED THAT THE GOVERNMENT JOLT THE ECONOMY OUT OF ITS DEPRESSION BY INCREASING AGGREGATE DEMAND.

and high inflation at the same time in the early 1980s, a troubling combination, and afterwards the economy grew with only moderate increases in price level. And the fourth era brought us the worst global recession since the Great Depression.

1. The Great Depression and Before

Before World War II, the Canadian economy alternated between hard times and prosperity. The National Policy, introduced in 1879 to protect Canadian manufacturers, called for high tariffs on imported manufactured items, mainly from the United States. In the years following implementation of the National Policy, Canada saw its manufacturing base develop, an economic boom, and an increased price level. In October 1929, the stock market crash began what became one of the deepest and longest economic contractions in history, the Great Depression of the 1930s.

In terms of aggregate demand and aggregate supply, the Great Depression can be viewed as a shift to the left of the aggregate demand curve, as shown in Exhibit 6. AD_{1929} is the aggregate demand curve in 1929, before the onset of the depression. The price level was 36.3 (relative to a 1971 base-year price level of 100). By 1933, aggregate demand shifted leftward, decreasing to AD_{1933}. Real GDP fell from 16.9 billion in 1929 to 11.8 billion in 1933 and price

levels also fell from 36.3 to 29.6. Why did aggregate demand decline? Though economists still debate the exact causes, most agree that the stock market crash of 1929 was the trigger. From there, grim business expectations cut investment, consumer spending fell, banks failed, and world trade was severely restricted by high tariffs. All this contributed to a large decline in aggregate demand. The aggregate supply curve probably also shifted somewhat during this period, but the drop in aggregate demand was the dominant force.

Because of the decline in aggregate demand, both the price level and real GDP dropped. Real GDP fell 30 percent, from $16.9 billion in 1929 to $11.8 billion in 1933, and the price level fell 18.5 percent, from 36.3 to 29.6. As real GDP declined, unemployment soared from only 3 percent of the labour force in 1929 to 24 percent at the depth of the depression in 1933.

Before the Great Depression, macroeconomic policy was based primarily on the *laissez-faire* philosophy of Adam Smith. Smith, you may recall, argued in his famous book, *The Wealth of Nations*, that if people are allowed to pursue their self-interest in free markets, resources would be guided as if by an "invisible hand" to produce the most efficient and most valued level of aggregate output. Although the Canadian economy suffered many sharp contractions even before the Great Depression, most economists of the day viewed these as a natural phase of the economy—unfortunate for those who lost jobs and savings but ultimately therapeutic and *self-correcting*.

2. The Age of Keynes: After the Great Depression to the Early 1980s

The Great Depression was so deep that it stimulated new thinking about how the economy worked (or didn't work). In 1936, John Maynard Keynes (1883–1946) published *The General Theory of Employment, Interest, and Money*, the most famous economics book of the 20th century. In it, he argued that aggregate demand was inherently unstable, in part

EXHIBIT 6

The Decrease in Aggregate Demand from 1929 to 1933

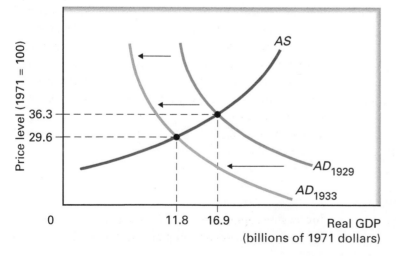

because investment decisions were often guided by the unpredictable "animal spirits" of business expectations. If businesses grew pessimistic about the economy, they would invest less, which would reduce aggregate demand, output, and employment. Keynes saw no natural market forces operating to ensure that the economy, even if allowed a reasonable time to adjust, would get output and employment growing again.

Keynes proposed that the government jolt the economy out of its depression by increasing aggregate demand. He recommended an expansionary fiscal policy to help offset contractions. The government could achieve this stimulus either directly by increasing its own spending, or indirectly by cutting taxes to stimulate consumption and investment. But either action would likely create a federal budget deficit. A **federal budget deficit** is a flow variable that measures, for a particular period, the amount by which federal outlays exceed federal revenues.

To understand what Keynes had in mind, imagine federal budget policies that would increase aggregate demand in Exhibit 6, shifting the aggregate demand curve to the right, back to its original position. Such a shift would raise real GDP, which would increase employment. According to the Keynesian prescription, the miracle drug of fiscal policy—changes in government spending and taxes—could compensate for what he viewed as the instability of private sector spending, especially investment. If demand in the private sector declined, Keynes said the government should pick up the slack. We can think of the Keynesian approach as **demand-side economics** because it focused on how changes in aggregate demand might promote full employment. Keynes argued that government stimulus could shock the economy out of its depression. Once investment returned to normal levels, and the economy started growing on its own, the government's shock treatment would no longer be necessary.

The outbreak of World War II boosted employment to fight for the country and to make tanks, ships, aircraft, and the like. Federal government spending increased and the explosion of output and sharp drop in unemployment seemed to confirm the powerful role government spending could play in the economy. The increase in government spending, with no significant increase in tax rates, created large federal deficits during the war.

The economy seemed to prosper during the 1950s largely without added stimulus from fiscal policy. The 1960s, however, proved to be the *golden age of Keynesian economics,* a period when fiscal policymakers thought they could "fine-tune" the economy for top performance—just as a mechanic fine-tunes a race car. During the early 1960s, nearly all advanced economies around the world enjoyed low unemployment and healthy growth with only modest inflation.

From 1974 to 1975 and in 1980, however, the business cycle returned, though the recessions were short and mild in Canada compared with the United States. Worse yet, the problems of recession were compounded by higher inflation, which increased during the recession of 1981–1982. Prior to that, high inflation was limited primarily to periods of expansion—that is, to boom times. Confidence in demand-side policies was shaken, and the expression "fine-tuning" dropped from the economic vocabulary. What ended the golden age of Keynesian economics? The Organization of Petroleum Exporting Countries (OPEC) cut its supply of oil to the world in 1973, and oil prices jumped. This policy resulted in **stagflation**, meaning a *stag*nation, or a contraction, in the economy's aggregate output and in*flation*, or increase, in the economy's price level.

Stagflation hit again six years later, stoked again by more OPEC cutbacks. Between 1981 and 1982, real GDP declined but the price level increased. The OPEC action reduced aggregate supply, shown in Exhibit 7 by the leftward shift of the aggregate supply curve from AS_{1981} to AS_{1982}. Real GDP declined by 3.1 percent between 1981 and 1982. During the same period, the price level jumped by 8.8 percent. Macroeconomics has not been the same since. Because stagflation was on the supply side, not on the demand side, the demand-management prescriptions of Keynes seemed ineffective. Increasing aggregate demand might reduce unemployment but would worsen inflation.

3. Early 1980s to 2007

Increasing aggregate supply seemed an appropriate way to combat stagflation, for such a move

federal budget deficit a flow variable measuring the amount by which federal government outlays exceed federal government revenues in a particular period, usually a year

demand-side economics macroeconomic policy that focuses on shifting the aggregate demand curve as a way of promoting full employment and price stability

stagflation a contraction, or stagnation, of a nation's output accompanied by inflation in the price level

EXHIBIT 7
Stagflation from 1981 to 1982

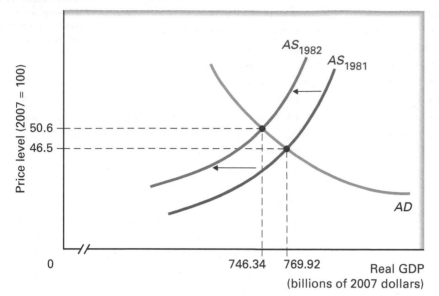

booming stock market to increase tax revenue enough to yield a federal budget surplus by the end of the 1996 fiscal year and every fiscal year after that to the 2008 recession.

4. The Recession of 2008–2009 and Beyond

The 2008–2009 recession in Canada was precipitated by declining home prices and rising foreclosures in the United States, as more borrowers failed to make their mortgage payments. With home prices falling, fewer were getting built, meaning fewer jobs in residential construction, furnishings, and other industries that rely on the housing sector.

Fears about the effect of rising home foreclosures on the banking system fed into a full-scale global financial panic in September 2008, triggered by the collapse of Lehman Brothers, a Wall Street investment bank. Banks grew reluctant to lend, so credit dried up—a major problem for an economy that relies a lot on credit. Businesses cut investments sharply. Consumers cut their spending in the face of sliding home prices, mounting job losses, and a collapsing stock market. You could picture all this as a leftward shift of the aggregate demand curve.

After the collapse of Lehman Brothers and the freezing up of financial flows around the world, policymakers around the world were emboldened to

supply-side economics

macroeconomic policy that focuses on a rightward shift of the aggregate supply curve through tax cuts or other changes to increase production incentives

would both lower the price level and increase output and employment. Attention thus turned from aggregate demand to aggregate supply. A key idea behind **supply-side economics** was that the federal government, by lowering tax rates, would increase after-tax wages, which would provide incentives to increase the supply of labour and other resources. According to advocates of the supply-side approach, the resulting increase in aggregate supply would achieve the happy result of expanding real GDP and reducing the price level. You can get the idea behind supply-side economics in Exhibit 7 by picturing the aggregate supply curve as shifting back to the right from AS_{1982} to AS_{1981}. Such a move would increase real GDP while lowering the price level. But this was easier said than done.

Once the recession ended in late 1982, the economy began to grow, and this growth continued for the rest of the decade until the recession in 1990–1992, which was brought on by the first war in the Persian Gulf and the introduction of the GST. But robust economic growth during the remainder of the 1990s boosted employment and real GDP. The expanding economy combined with a

enact some extraordinary measures to shore up confidence in financial institutions, open up the flow of credit, and stimulate consumer spending.

The decline in Canada was less pronounced than in the United States and other major industrialized countries as the Canadian financial system was relatively less exposed to the subprime housing market in the United States. The economy began to stabilize in mid-2009 in response to policy measures in Canada and abroad. The recovery was quicker and more complete in Canada, the only country in the G7 in which real GDP and employment have returned to prerecession levels.

Final Word

Since 1929, the average education of workers has increased. Other resources, especially capital, also rose sharply. What's more, the level of technology has improved steadily, thanks to breakthroughs such as the personal computer and the Internet. The availability of more and higher-quality human capital and physical capital increased the productivity of each worker.

Real GDP is important, but the best measure of the average standard of living is an economy's real GDP per capita, which tells us how much an economy produces on average per resident.

Because macroeconomists have no test subjects and cannot rely on luck, they hone their craft by developing models of the economy and then searching for evidence to support or reject these models. In this sense, macroeconomics is retrospective, always looking at recent developments for hints about which model works best. The macroeconomist is like a traveller who can see only the road behind and must find the way ahead using a collection of poorly drawn maps. The traveller must continually check each map (or model) against the landmarks to see whether one map is more consistent with the terrain than the others. Each new batch of information about the economy causes macroeconomists to shuffle through their "maps" to check their models.

Macroeconomics often emphasizes what can go wrong with the economy. Sagging output, high unemployment, and rising inflation capture much of the attention, and we'll examine those problems in the next two chapters. But perhaps the most important performance measure is economic growth, and we'll devote a chapter to that after you learn more about real GDP, unemployment, and inflation.

> **real GDP per capita** real GDP divided by the population; the best measure of an economy's standard of living

CHAPTER PROBLEMS

LO1 Discuss macroeconomics and the national economy

1.1. *(The National Economy)* Why do economists pay more attention to national economies (for example, the U.S. or Canadian economies) than to state or provincial economies (such as California or Ontario)?

1.2. *(The Human Body and the Canadian Economy)* Based on your own experiences, extend the list of analogies between the human body and the economy as outlined in this chapter. Then determine which variables in your list are stocks and which are flows.

1.3. *(Flow and Stock Variables)* How is a flow variable different from a stock variable? In each case state whether it's a flow or stock variable.

Wages
Wealth
Inflation
Unemployment

LO2 Discuss economic fluctuations and growth

2.1. *(Economic Fluctuations)* Describe the various components of fluctuations in economic activity over time. Because economic activity fluctuates, how is long-term growth possible?

2.2. *(Global Economy)* Explain why a link between business cycles across countries is usually apparent.

2.3. *(Economic Indicators)* What are economic indicators and how do they reflect the state of the economy?

LO3 Explain aggregate demand and aggregate supply

3.1. *(Aggregate Demand and Supply)* Review the information on demand and supply curves in Chapter 4. How do the aggregate demand and aggregate supply curves presented below differ from the market curves of Chapter 4?

Aggregate Demand and Aggregate Supply in 2012

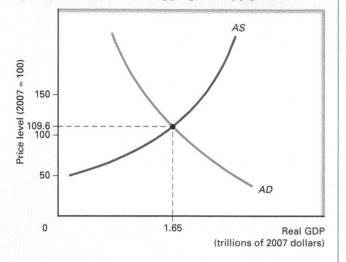

3.2. *(Aggregate Demand and Supply)* Determine whether each of the following would cause a shift of the aggregate demand curve, a shift of the

aggregate supply curve, neither, or both. Which curve shifts, and in which direction? What happens to aggregate output and the price level in each case?
   a. The price level changes.
   b. Consumer confidence declines.
   c. The supply of resources increases.
   d. The wage rate increases.

3.3. *(Aggregate Demand and Supply)* Why does a decrease of the aggregate demand curve result in less employment, given an aggregate supply curve?

LO4 Describe a brief history of the Canadian economy

4.1. *(Supply-Side Economics)* Use an aggregate demand/aggregate supply diagram to show the effect of a cut in income tax rates on the aggregate supply curve. What might happen if such a tax cut also shifted the aggregate demand curve?

4.2. *(Demand-Side Economics)* If demand in the private sector declined, Keynes said the government should pick up the slack. What are the implications of such an intervention on federal budgets?

4.3. *(Recession of 2008–2009)* How did the recession of 2008–2009 affect the economy?

CASE STUDY

The Global Economy

Years ago what happened in other economies was not that important to North Americans. But now many resources flow freely across borders. Technology has also spread around the globe. Though business cycles are not perfectly synchronized across countries, a link is often apparent. Consider the experience of three leading economies—Canada, the United States, and the United Kingdom. Exhibit 3 on page 86 shows for each economy the year-to-year percentage change in real GDP since 1978. Again, *real* means that the effects of inflation have been erased, so remaining changes reflect *real* changes in the total amount of goods and services produced each year.

   If you spend a little time following the annual changes in each economy, you can see the similarities. For example, all three economies went into recession in the early 1980s, grew well for the rest of the decade, entered another recession in 1991, recovered for the rest of the decade, then slowed down in 2001. The economies picked up steam 2004, but the global financial crisis of 2008 caused sharply lower output by 2009. When linkage across economies occurs, a slump in other major economies could worsen a recession in Canada and vice versa. For example, the financial crisis of 2008 affected economies around the world, increasing unemployment and cutting production. Trouble in seemingly minor economies, such as Greece, can spill over and drag other economies down with them. But economic strength overseas can give the Canadian economy a lift.

Though economic fluctuations are not perfectly synchronized across major economies, a link is usually apparent. For example, the United States' and the United Kingdom's real GDPs changed from year to year by roughly similar percentages during the past quarter century.

SOURCE: Developed from IMF-International Financial Statistics (Series code 15699BVRZF). Accessed 12 March 2013.

QUESTION

1. How are economic fluctuations linked among national economies? Could a recession in the United States trigger a recession in Canada?

6

Tracking the Canadian Economy

LEARNING OUTCOMES

LO1 Explain the gross domestic product

LO2 Discuss the circular flow of income and expenditure

LO3 Assess the limitations of national income accounting

LO4 Explain how to account for price changes

> # How do we keep track of one of the world's largest economies?

How do we keep track of one of the world's largest economies? What's gross about the gross domestic product? What's domestic about it? If you make yourself a tuna sandwich, how much does your effort add to the gross domestic product? Because prices change over time, how can we compare the economy's production in one year with that in other years? Answers to these and other questions are addressed in this chapter, which introduces an economic scorecard for a $1.4-trillion Canadian economy. That scorecard is the national income accounting system, which reduces a huge network of economic activity to a few aggregate measures.

As you will see, aggregate output is measured either by the spending on that output or by the income derived from producing it. We examine each approach and learn why they are equivalent. The major components and important equalities built into the national income accounts are offered here as another way of understanding how the economy works—not as a foreign language to be mastered before the next exam. The emphasis is more on economic intuition than on accounting precision. The body of the chapter provides the background you need for later chapters.

LO 1 The Product of a Nation

How do we measure the economy's performance? During much of the 17th and 18th centuries, when the dominant economic policy was mercantilism, many thought that economic prosperity was best measured by the *stock* of precious metals a nation accumulated in the public treasury. Mercantilism led to restrictions on international trade, with the unintended consequence of reducing the gains from comparative advantage. In the latter half of the 18th century, François Quesnay became the first to measure economic activity as a *flow*. In 1758 he published his *Tableau Économique*, which described the *circular flow* of output and income through different sectors of the economy. His insight was likely inspired by his knowledge of blood's circular flow in the body—Quesnay was court physician to King Louis XV of France.

Rough measures of national income were developed in England two centuries ago, but detailed calculations built up from microeconomic data were refined in the United States during the Great Depression. The resulting *national income accounting system* organized huge quantities of data collected from a variety of sources. These data were summarized, assembled into a coherent framework, and reported by the U.S. federal government. The U.S. national income accounts are the most widely copied and most highly regarded in the world and earned their developer, Simon Kuznets, the Nobel Prize in 1971 for "giving quantitative precision to economic entities." In Canada, the National

Income and Expenditure Accounts are similar to the U.S. accounts and are reported each quarter by Statistics Canada.

National Income Accounts

How do the national income accounts keep track of the economy's incredible variety of goods and services, such as hiking boots and Pilates classes? The *gross domestic product,* or GDP, measures the market value of all final goods and services produced during a year by resources located in Canada, regardless of who owns the resources. For example, GDP includes production in Canada by foreign firms, such as a Ford plant in Ontario, but excludes foreign production by Canadian firms, such as a Bombardier plant in the United States.

The national income accounts are based on the simple fact that *one person's spending is another person's income.* GDP can be measured either by total spending on Canadian production or by total income received from that production. The **expenditure approach** adds up spending on all final goods and services produced during the year. The **income approach** adds up earnings during the year by those who produce all that output. In the *double-entry bookkeeping system* used to track the economy, spending on aggregate output is recorded on one side of the ledger and income from producing that aggregate output is recorded on the other side.

Stephen C. Host/The Canadian Press

Gross domestic product includes only **final goods and services,** which are goods and services sold to the final, or end, user. A toothbrush, a pair of contact lenses, and a bus ride are examples of final goods and services. Whether a sale is to the final user depends on who buys the product. When you buy chicken for dinner, that's reflected in GDP. When KFC buys chicken, however, that's not counted in GDP because KFC is not the final consumer. Only after the chicken is cooked and sold by KFC is the transaction counted in GDP.

Intermediate goods and services are those purchased for additional processing and resale, like KFC's chicken. This change may be imperceptible, as when a grocer buys canned goods to restock shelves. Or the intermediate goods can be dramatically altered, as when a painter transforms a $100 canvas and $30 in oils into a work of art that sells for $5,000. Sales of intermediate goods and services are excluded from GDP to avoid the problem of **double counting,** which is counting an item's value more than once. For example, suppose the grocer buys a can of tuna for $1.00 and sells it for $1.50. If GDP counted both the intermediate transaction of $1.00 and the final transaction of $1.50, the recorded value of $2.50 would exceed its final value by $1.00. Hence, GDP counts only the market value of the final sale. As another example, in a recent year George Weston Limited paid $24.4 billion for products it sold for $32.4 billion (George Weston Limited is the parent company of Loblaws, one of Canada's largest grocery store chains). If GDP counted both the intermediate transactions and final transactions, the company's impact on GDP would be $24.4 billion too high. GDP also ignores most of the secondhand value of used goods, such as existing homes, used cars, and used textbooks. These goods were counted in GDP when they were produced. But just as the services provided by the grocer and by Loblaws are captured in GDP, so are the services provided by real estate agents, used-car dealers, and used-book sellers.

GDP Based on the Expenditure Approach

As noted already, one way to measure GDP is to add up spending on all final goods and services produced in the economy during the year. The easiest way to understand the spending approach is to sort aggregate expenditure into its components: consumption, investment, government purchases, and net exports. **Consumption,** or more specifically, *personal* *expenditure on consumer goods and services,* consists of purchases of final goods and services by households during the year. Consumption is the largest spending category, averaging 60 percent of Canadian GDP during this past decade. Along with *services* like dry cleaning, haircuts, and air travel, consumption includes *nondurable goods* like soap and soup, *semi-durable goods* like clothing and bed sheets, and *durable goods* like furniture and kitchen appliances. Nondurable goods are consumed only once or within the span of one year. Durable goods are expected to last considerably more than one year based on normal use. Semi-durable goods fall somewhere between the two extremes—they may last longer than a year but will not last as long as a car or washing machine.

Investment consists of spending on new capital goods and on net additions to inventories. Statistics Canada includes investment spending in two separate categories of the national accounts, *business gross fixed capital formation* and *business investment in inventories*. The most important investment is **physical capital**, such as new buildings and new machinery. Investment also includes new **residential construction**. Although it fluctuates from year to year, investment averaged 20 percent of Canadian GDP this past decade. More generally, investment consists of spending on current production that is not used for current consumption. A net increase to inventories also counts as investment because it represents current production not used for current consumption. **Inventories** are stocks of goods in process, such as computer parts, and stocks of finished goods, such as new computers awaiting sale. Inventories help manufacturers cope with unexpected changes in the supply of their resources or in the demand for their products.

Although investment includes purchasing a new residence, it excludes purchases of *existing* buildings and machines and purchases of financial assets, such as stocks and bonds. Existing buildings and machines were counted in GDP when they were produced. Stocks and bonds are not investments themselves but simply indications of ownership.

Government purchases include government spending for goods and services—whether it's clearing snowy roads or clearing court dockets, buying library books or paying librarians. Government purchases averaged 23 percent of Canadian GDP during the past decade. In the national accounts, government spending is included in the following categories: government current expenditure on goods and services, government gross fixed capital formation, and government inventories. Government purchases, and therefore GDP, exclude transfer payments, such as Canada Pension Plan benefits, welfare benefits, and Employment Insurance. Such payments are not true purchases by the government or true earnings by the recipients.

The final spending component, net exports, reflects international trade in goods and services. Goods include physical items such as bananas and HDTVs (stuff you can load on a ship). Services include intangible items, such as European tours and online customer service from India. Foreign purchases of Canadian goods and services are counted as part of Canadian GDP. But Canadian purchases of foreign goods and services are subtracted from Canadian GDP. **Net exports** equal the value of Canadian exports of goods and services minus the value of Canadian imports of goods and services. From 1993 to 2004, Canadian exports exceeded imports, meaning Canadian net exports were positive. Since 2005, however, net exports have been negative, averaging negative 6 percent of GDP.

With the expenditure approach, the nation's **aggregate expenditure** sums consumption, *C;* investment, *I;* government purchases, *G;* and net exports, *NX,* which is the value of

---

investment the purchase of new plants, new equipment, new buildings, and new residences, plus net additions to inventories

physical capital manufactured items used to produce goods and services; includes new plants and new equipment

residential construction building new homes or dwelling places

inventories producers' stocks of finished and in-process goods

government purchases spending for goods and services by all levels of government; government outlays minus transfer payments

net exports the value of a country's exports minus the value of its imports

aggregate expenditure total spending on final goods and services in an economy during a given period, usually a year

CHAPTER 6: TRACKING THE CANADIAN ECONOMY

THE VALUE ADDED AT EACH STAGE EQUALS THE INCOME EARNED BY THOSE WHO SUPPLY RESOURCES AT THAT STAGE.

aggregate income all earnings of resource suppliers in an economy during a given period, usually a year

value added at each stage of production, the selling price of a product minus the cost of intermediate goods purchased from other firms

exports, X, minus the value of imports, IM, or $(X - IM)$. Summing these yields aggregate expenditure, or GDP:

$$C + I + G + (X - IM)$$
$$= \text{Aggregate expenditure}$$
$$= \text{GDP}$$

GDP Based on the Income Approach

The expenditure approach sums, or aggregates, spending on production. The income approach sums, or aggregates, income arising from that production. Again, double-entry bookkeeping ensures that the value of aggregate output equals the aggregate income paid for resources used to produce that output: the wages, interest, rent, and profit arising from production. The price of a Coffee Crisp reflects the income earned by resource suppliers along the way. **Aggregate income** equals the sum of all the income earned by resource suppliers in the economy. Thus, we can say that

$$\text{Aggregate expenditure} = \text{GDP}$$
$$= \text{Aggregate income}$$

A product usually goes through several stages involving different firms on its way to the consumer. A wooden desk, for example, starts as raw timber, which is typically cut by one firm, milled by another, made into a desk by a third, and retailed by a fourth. We avoid double counting either by including only the market value of the desk when sold to the final user or by *summing the value added at each stage of production*. The **value added** by each firm equals that firm's selling price minus payments for inputs from other firms. The value added at each stage equals the income earned by those who supply resources at that stage. *The value added at all stages sums to the market value of the final good, and the value added for all final goods sums to GDP based on the income approach.*

$C + I + G + (X - IM)$
$= \text{Aggregate expenditure}$
$= \text{GDP}$

For example, suppose you buy a wooden desk for $200. This final market value gets added directly into GDP. Consider the history of that desk. Suppose the tree that gave its life for your studies was cut into a log and sold to a miller for $20, who converted the log to lumber that sold for $50 to a desk maker, who made the desk and sold it for $120 to a retailer, who sold it to you for $200.

Column (1) of Exhibit 1 lists the selling price at each stage of production. If all these transactions were added up, the sum of $390 would exceed the $200 market value of the desk. To avoid double counting, we include only the value added at each stage, listed in column (3) as the difference between the purchase price and the selling price at that stage. Again, *the value added at each stage equals the income earned by those who supply their resources at that stage.* For example, the $80 in value added by the retailer consists of income to resource suppliers at that stage, from the salesperson to the janitor who cleans the showroom to the trucker who provides "free delivery" of your desk. The value added at all stages totals $200, which is both the final market value of the desk and the total income earned by all resource suppliers along the way.

To reinforce your understanding of the equality of income and spending, let's return to something introduced in the first chapter, the circular-flow model.

EXHIBIT 1
Computing Value Added for a New Desk

Stage of Production	(1) Sale Value	(2) Cost of Intermediate Goods	(3) Value Added (3) = (1) = (2)
Logger	$20	_____	$20
Miller	$50	$20	$30
Manufacturer	$120	$50	$70
Retailer	$200	$120	$80
		Market value of final good	$200

LO 2 Circular Flow of Income and Expenditure

The model in Exhibit 2 outlines the circular flow of income and spending in the economy for not only households and firms, as was the case in Chapter 1, but governments and the rest of the world. The main stream flows clockwise around the circle, first as income from firms to households (in the lower half of the circle), and then as spending from households back to firms (in the upper half of the circle). For each flow of money, there is an equal and opposite flow of products or resources. Here we follow the money.

Income Half of the Circular Flow

To develop a circular flow of income and spending, we must make some simplifying assumptions. Specifically, by assuming that physical capital does not wear out (i.e., no capital depreciation) and that firms pay out all profits to firm owners (i.e., firms retain no earnings), we can say that *GDP equals aggregate income.* The circular flow is a continuous process, but the logic of the model is clearest if we begin at juncture (1) in Exhibit 2, where Canadian firms make production decisions. After all, production must occur before output can be sold and income earned. As Henry Ford explained, "It is not the employer who pays the wages—the employer only handles the money. It is the product that pays wages." Households supply their labour, capital, natural resources, and entrepreneurial ability to make products that sell to pay wages, interest, rent, and profit. Production of aggregate output, or GDP, gives rise to an equal amount of aggregate income.

Thus at juncture (1), aggregate output equals aggregate income. But not all that income is available to spend. At juncture (2), governments collect taxes. Some of these tax dollars return as transfer payments to the income stream at juncture (3). By subtracting taxes and adding transfers, we transform aggregate income into **disposable income, DI**, which flows to households at juncture (4). Disposable income is take-home pay, which households can spend or save.

The bottom half of this circular flow is the *income half* because it focuses on the income arising from production. Aggregate income is the total income from producing GDP, and disposable income is the income remaining after taxes are subtracted and transfers added. To simplify the discussion, we define **net taxes, NT**, as taxes minus transfer payments. So *disposable income equals GDP minus net*

disposable income (DI) the income households have available to spend or to save after paying taxes and receiving transfer payments

net taxes (NT) taxes minus transfer payments

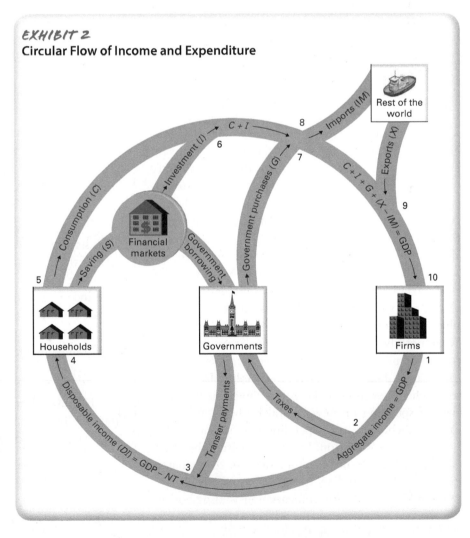

EXHIBIT 2
Circular Flow of Income and Expenditure

taxes. Put another way, we can say that aggregate income equals disposable income plus net taxes:

$$GDP = \text{Aggregate income} = DI + NT$$

At juncture (4), firms have produced output and have paid resource suppliers; governments have collected taxes and made transfer payments. With the resulting disposable income in hand, households now decide how much to spend and how much to save. Because firms have already produced the output and have paid resource suppliers, firms wait to see how much consumers want to spend. Any unsold production gets added to firm inventories.

Expenditure Half of the Circular Flow

Disposable income splits at juncture (5). Part is spent on consumption, C, and the rest is saved, S. Thus,

$$DI = C + S$$

Consumption remains in the circular flow and is the biggest aggregate expenditure, about 60 percent of the total. Household saving flows to **financial markets**, which consist of banks and other financial institutions that link savers to borrowers. For simplicity, Exhibit 2 shows households as the only savers, though governments, firms, and the rest of the world could save as well (for example, savers from the United States finance Canadian borrowers). The primary borrowers are firms and governments, but households borrow too, particularly for new homes, and the rest of the world also borrows. In reality, financial markets should be connected to all four economic decision makers, but we have simplified the flows to keep the model from looking like a plate of spaghetti.

In our simplified model, firms pay resource suppliers an amount equal to the entire value of output. With nothing left for investment, firms must borrow to finance purchases of physical capital plus any increases in their inventories. Households also borrow to purchase new homes. Therefore, investment, I, consists of spending on new capital by firms, including inventory changes, plus spending on residential construction. Investment enters the circular flow at juncture (6), so aggregate spending at that point totals C + I.

Governments must also borrow whenever they incur deficits, that is, whenever their total *outlays*—transfer payments plus purchases of goods and services—exceed their revenues. Government purchases of goods and services, represented by G, enter the spending stream in the upper half of the circular flow at juncture (7). Remember that G *excludes* transfer payments, which already entered the stream as income at juncture (3).

Some spending by households, firms, and governments goes for imports. Because spending on imports flows to foreign producers, spending on imports, IM, leaks from the circular flow at juncture (8). But the rest of the world buys Canadian products, so foreign spending on Canadian exports, X, enters the spending flow at juncture (9).

Net exports, the impact of the *rest of the world* on aggregate expenditure, equal exports minus imports, $X - IM$, which can be positive, negative, or zero. In recent years, net exports have been negative.

The upper half of the circular flow, the *expenditure half*, tracks the four components of aggregate expenditure: consumption, C; investment, I; government purchases, G; and net exports, $X - IM$. Aggregate expenditure flows into firms at juncture (10). Aggregate expenditure equals the market value of aggregate output, or GDP. In short,

$$C + I + G + (X - IM) = \text{Aggregate expenditure} = GDP$$

Leakages Equal Injections

Let's step back now to view the big picture. In the upper half of the circular flow, aggregate expenditure is total spending on Canadian output. In the lower half, aggregate income is the income arising from that spending. This is the first accounting identity. Aggregate expenditure (spending by each sector) equals aggregate income (disposable income plus net taxes), or

$$C + I + G + (X - IM) = DI + NT$$

Because disposable income equals consumption plus saving, we can substitute C + S for DI in the above equation to yield

$$C + I + G + (X - IM) = C + S + NT$$

After subtracting C from both sides and adding M to both sides, the equation reduces to

$$I + G + X = S + NT + IM$$

financial markets
banks and other financial institutions that facilitate the flow of funds from savers to borrowers

GDP = Aggregate income = DI + NT

The labour of working mothers is reflected in the GDP; the labour of those who stay home is not.

Monkey Business Images/Shutterstock

Note that **injections** into the main stream occur at various points around the circular flow. Investment, I, government purchases, G, and exports, X, are *injections* of spending into the circular flow. At the same time, some of the circular flow leaks from the main stream. Saving, S, net taxes, NT, and imports, IM, are **leakages** from the circular flow. As you can see from the equation, *injections into the circular flow equal leakages from the flow.* This injections-leakages equality demonstrates a second accounting identity based on double-entry bookkeeping.

LO 3 Limitations of National Income Accounting

Imagine the difficulty of developing an accounting system that must capture such a complex and dynamic economy. In the interest of clarity and simplicity,

certain features get neglected. In this section, we examine some limitations of the national income accounting system, beginning with production not captured by GDP.

Some Production Is Not Included in GDP

With some minor exceptions, GDP includes only those products that are sold in markets. This ignores all do-it-yourself production—child care, meal preparation, house cleaning, family laundry, and home maintenance and repair. Thus an economy in which householders are largely self-sufficient has a lower GDP than an otherwise similar economy in which households specialize and sell products to one another. As recently as 1976, more than 60 percent of Canadian mothers with small children remained at home caring for the family, but all this care added not one cent to GDP. Today most mothers with small children are in the workforce, where their labour gets counted in GDP. Meals, child care, and the like are now often

injection any spending other than by households or any income other than from resource earnings; includes investment, government purchases, exports, and transfer payments

leakage any diversion of income from the domestic spending stream; includes saving, taxes, and imports

THE GROSS DOMESTIC PRODUCT FAILS TO CAPTURE CHANGES IN THE AVAILABILITY OF LEISURE TIME.

purchased in markets and thus get reflected in GDP. In less developed economies, more economic activity is do-it-yourself.

GDP also ignores off-the-books production. The term **underground economy** describes market activity that goes unreported because either it's illegal or because people want to evade taxes on otherwise legal activity. Although there is no official measure of the underground economy, most economists agree that it is substantial. Statistics Canada estimates that in 2008 the Canadian underground economy was at most $36 billion, which represents less than 3 percent of GDP.

For some economic activity, income must be *imputed*, or assigned a value, because market exchange does not occur. For example, included in GDP is an *imputed rental income* from home ownership, even though no rent is actually paid or received. Also included in GDP is an imputed dollar amount for (1) wages paid *in kind*, such as employers' payments for employees' medical insurance, and (2) food produced by farm families for their own consumption. *GDP therefore includes some economic production that does not involve market exchange.*

Leisure, Quality, and Variety

The average Canadian workweek is much shorter now than it was a century ago, so people work less to produce today's output. People also retire earlier and live longer after retirement. As a result of a shorter workweek and earlier retirement, more leisure is available. But leisure is not reflected in GDP because it is not directly bought and sold in a market. The quality and variety of products available have also improved on average over the years because of technological advances and greater competition. For example, the magazine *Consumer Reports* finds a consistent improvement in the quality of the automobile over time. Yet most of these improvements are not reflected in GDP. Recording systems, computers, tires, running shoes, cellphones, and hundreds of other products have got better over the years. Also, new products are being introduced all the time, such as smartphones, e-readers, and energy drinks. *The gross domestic product fails to capture changes in the availability of leisure time and often fails to reflect changes in the quality of products or in the availability of new products.*

What's Gross about Gross Domestic Product?

In the course of producing GDP, some capital wears out, such as the delivery truck that finally dies, and some capital becomes obsolete, such as an aging computer that can't run the latest software. A new truck that logs 100,000 kilometres its first year has been subject to wear and tear and therefore has a diminished value as a resource. A truer picture of the *net* production that actually occurs during a year is found by subtracting this capital *depreciation* from GDP. **Depreciation** measures the value of the capital stock that is used up or becomes obsolete in the production process. Gross domestic product is called "gross" because it fails to take into account depreciation. **Net domestic product** equals gross domestic product minus depreciation, the capital stock used up in the production process.

We now have two measures of investment. *Gross investment* is the value of all investment during a year and is used in computing GDP. *Net investment* equals gross investment minus depreciation. The economy's production possibilities depend on what happens to net investment. If net investment is positive—that is, if gross investment exceeds depreciation—the economy's capital stock increases, so its contribution to output increases as well. If net investment is zero, the capital stock remains constant, as does its contribution to output. And if net investment is negative, the capital stock declines, as does its contribution to output.

As the names imply, *gross* domestic product reflects gross investment and *net* domestic product reflects net investment. But estimating depreciation involves some guesswork. For example, what is the appropriate measure of depreciation for the roller coasters at Canada's Wonderland, the metal display shelves at Walmart, or the runways at Vancouver International Airport?

GDP Does Not Reflect All Costs

Some production and consumption degrades the quality of our environment. Trucks and automobiles pump pollution into the atmosphere, which may contribute to climate change. Housing developments displace scenic open space and forests. Paper mills foul the lungs and burn the eyes. Oil spills foul the coastline. These negative externalities—costs that fall on those not directly involved in the transactions—are mostly ignored in GDP calculations, even though they diminish the quality of life now and in the future. To the extent that growth in GDP generates negative externalities, a rising GDP may not be as attractive as it would first appear.

Although the national income accounts reflect the depreciation of buildings, machinery, vehicles, and other manufactured capital, this accounting ignores the depletion of natural resources, such as standing timber, oil reserves, fish stocks, and soil fertility. So national income accounts reflect depreciation of the physical capital stock but not the natural capital stock. For example, intensive farming may raise productivity and boost GDP temporarily, but this depletes soil fertility. Worse still, some production may speed the extinction of certain plants and animals. Statistics Canada has developed the Canadian System of Environmental and Resource Accounts (CSERA), trying to register the impact of production on air pollution, water pollution, soil depletion, and the loss of other natural resources.

GDP and Economic Welfare

In computing GDP, the market price of output is the measure of its value. Therefore, each dollar spent on alcohol or cigarettes is counted in GDP the same as each dollar spent on baby formula or fitness programs. Positive economic analysis tries to avoid making value judgments about *how* people spend their money. Because GDP, as a number, provides no information about its composition, some economists question whether GDP is the best measure of the nation's economic welfare. Another measure, published by the

United Nations, is the Human Development Index. This is discussed in the following section.

GDP and the Human Development Index GDP estimates have been refined for decades and are arguably the most complex data aggregation effort in the world. But they have their limits and their critics. One criticism is that GDP leaves out much of what's going on in a nation. Since 1990 the United Nations has computed the Human Development Index, or HDI, as a more complete measure of well-being.

The HDI has three components, one to measure economic well-being, one to measure education, and another to measure health. The education component includes the average number of years of schooling for a 25-year-old and also the expected number of years of schooling for a child entering school. Health is measured by life expectancy at birth and, economic well-being is measured by gross national product, or GNP, per person. Gross national product is similar to GDP, except that instead of including all goods and services produced within a country, it includes all goods and services produced by a country's resources, regardless of where the production occurs. So when BlackBerry produces cellphone components in South Korea, that production is part of South Korea's GDP and Canada's GNP.

These three factors, health, education, and economic well-being, are combined to create a number between 0 and 1. In 2013 Norway had the highest

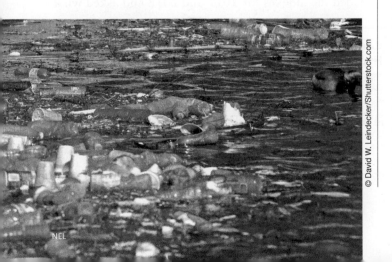

nominal GDP GDP based on prices prevailing at the time of production

base year the year with which other years are compared when constructing an index; the index equals 100 in the base year

price index a number that shows the average price of products; changes in a price index over time show changes in the economy's average price level

HDI with a score of 0.944 and Niger had the lowest HDI at 0.337. Canada ranked eighth (0.902) and the United States ranked fifth (0.914). If we look instead at GDP per capita, a measure of only income and output, Norway is second, Canada twelfth, and the United States tenth.

The HDI is an example of a measure of well-being, but it is not the only one. The Economist Intelligence Unit considers the HDI when it computes its "most liveable city" index each year. The measure is reported at the city level rather than the country level, and it includes factors such as traffic congestion and crime. In 2012, three of the top ten "most liveable cities" were in Canada and five were in Australia.[1]

Despite the limitations of official GDP estimates, GDP offers a useful snapshot of the Canadian economy at a point in time. Inflation, however, clouds comparability over time. In the next section, we discuss how to adjust GDP for changes in the economy's price level.

LO 4 Accounting for Price Changes

As noted earlier, the national income accounts are based on the market values of final goods and services produced in a particular year. Initially, gross domestic product measures the value of output in *nominal dollars*—that is, in the dollar values at the time production occurs. When GDP is based on nominal dollars, the national income accounts measure the *nominal value* of national output. Thus, **nominal GDP** is based on the prices prevailing when production takes place. National income accounts based on nominal dollars allow for comparisons among income or expenditure components in a particular year. Because the economy's average price level changes over time, however, nominal-dollar comparisons across years can be misleading. For example, between 1981 and 1982, nominal GDP increased by about 5 percent. That sounds fine, but the economy's average price level rose more than 5 percent. So the growth in

nominal GDP came entirely from inflation. Real GDP, or GDP measured in terms of the goods and services produced, in fact declined. If nominal GDP increases in a given year, part of this increase may simply reflect inflation—pure hot air. To make meaningful comparisons of GDP across years, we must take out the hot air, or *deflate* nominal GDP. We focus on *real* changes in production by eliminating changes due solely to inflation.

Price Indexes

To compare the price level over time, let's first establish a point of reference, a base year to which prices in other years can be compared. An *index number* compares the value of some variable in a particular year to its value in a base year, or reference year. Think about the simplest of index numbers. Suppose bread is the only good produced in an economy. As a reference point, let's look at its price in some specific year. The year selected is called the **base year**; prices in other years are expressed relative to the base-year price.

Suppose the base year is 2010, when a loaf of bread in our simple economy sold for $1.25. Let's say the price of bread increased to $1.30 in 2011 and to $1.40 in 2012. We construct a **price index** by dividing each year's price by the price in the base year and then multiplying by 100, as shown in Exhibit 3. For 2010, the base year, we divide the base price of bread by itself, $1.25 ÷ $1.25, or 1, so the price index in 2010 equals 1 × 100 = 100. *The price index in the base period is always 100.* The price index in 2011 is $1.30 ÷ $1.25, or 1.04, which when multiplied by 100 equals 104. In 2012, the index is $1.40 ÷ $1.25, or 1.12, which when multiplied by 100 equals 112. Thus, the index is 4 percent higher in 2011 than in the base year and 12 percent higher in 2012 than in the base year. The price index permits comparisons across years. For example, what if you were provided the indexes for 2011 and 2012 and asked what

---

[1] A.B. "Australian Gold," *Economist*, 14 August 2012.

EXHIBIT 3

Hypothetical Example of a Price Index (base year = 2010)

Year	(1) Price of Bread in Current Year	(2) Price of Bread in Base Year	(3) Price Index (3) = [(1) ÷ (2)] × 100
2010	$1.25	$1.25	100
2011	1.30	1.25	104
2012	1.40	1.25	112

THE CPI CALCULATIONS OVERESTIMATE THE TRUE EXTENT OF INFLATION EXPERIENCED BY THE TYPICAL HOUSEHOLD.

happened to the price level between the two years? By dividing the 2012 price index by the 2011 price index, 112 ÷ 104, you find that the price level rose 7.7 percent.

This section has shown how to develop a price index assuming we already know the price level each year. Determining the price level is a bit more involved, as we'll now see.

Consumer Price Index

The price index most familiar to you is the **consumer price index**, or **CPI**, which measures changes over time in the cost of buying a "market basket" of goods and services purchased by a typical family. For simplicity, suppose a typical family's market basket for the year includes 365 packages of Twinkies, 2,000 litres of heating oil, and 12 months of cable TV. Prices in the base year are listed in column (2) of Exhibit 4. The total cost of each product in the base year is found by multiplying price by quantity, as shown in column (3). The cost of the market basket in the base year is shown at the bottom of column (3) to be $3,256.55.

Prices in the current year are listed in column (4). Notice that not all prices changed by the same percentage since the base year. The price of fuel oil increased by 50 percent, but the price of Twinkies declined. The cost of that same basket in the current year is $4,139.75, shown as the sum of column (5).

To compute the consumer price index for the current year, we simply divide the cost in the current year by the cost of that same basket in the base year, $4,139.75 ÷ $3,256.55, and then multiply by 100. This yields a price index of 127.1. We could say that between the base period and the current year, the "cost of living" increased by about 27 percent, although not all prices increased by the same percentage.

Statistics Canada collects over 875,000 price quotes each year in estimating the CPI. Most price quotes are obtained by individual visits to retail locations. The frequency of obtaining price quotes depends on the nature of the good or service in question. University tuition prices are obtained once per year. The prices of food items are obtained every month. The quantities used currently to calculate the CPI in Canada are from 2009. In reality, each household consumes a unique market basket, so we could theoretically develop about 12 million CPIs—one for each household.

Problems with the CPI

There is no perfect way to measure changes in the price level. As we have already seen, the quality and variety of some products are improving all the time, so some price increases may be as much a reflection of improved quality as of inflation. Thus there is a *quality bias* in the CPI, because

© Jupiterimages/Getty Images

EXHIBIT 4
Hypothetical Market Basket Used to Develop the Consumer Price Index

Product	(1) Quantity in Market Basket	(2) Prices in Base Year	(3) Cost of Basket in Base Year (3) = (1) × (2)	(4) Prices in Current Year	(5) Cost of Basket in Current Year (5) = (1) × (4)
Twinkies	365 packages	$1.47/package	$536.55	$1.15	$419.75
Fuel Oil	2,000 litres	$1.00/litre	2000.00	$1.50	3,000.00
Cable TV	12 months	$60.00/month	720.00	$60.00	720.00
			$3256.55		$4139.75

GDP price index
a comprehensive inflation measure of all goods and services included in the gross domestic product

it assumes that the quality of the market basket remains relatively constant over time. *To the extent that the CPI ignores quality improvements, it overstates the true extent of inflation.* Those who come up with the CPI each month try to make some quality adjustments.

But the CPI tends to overstate inflation for another reason. Recall that the CPI holds constant over time the kind and amount of goods and services in the typical market basket. Because not all items in the market basket experience the same rate of price change, relative prices change over time. A rational household would respond to changes in relative prices by buying less of the more expensive products and more of the cheaper products. The CPI allows for some substitution within narrow categories (for example, shoppers in Toronto can switch among choices of ground beef based on price), but consumers can't easily switch across categories because the point of the CPI is to look at price changes over time for a given market basket. Because the CPI holds the market basket constant for long periods, the CPI is slow to incorporate consumer responses to changes in relative prices. *The CPI calculations overestimate the true extent of inflation experienced by the typical household.* The CPI has also failed to keep up with the consumer shift toward discount stores such as Walmart, Canadian Tire, and Home Depot. Government statisticians consider goods sold by discounters as different from goods sold by regular retailers. Hence the discounter's lower price does not necessarily translate into a reduction in the cost of living, but simply as a different consumer purchase decision.

Finally, the CPI overstates inflation because it includes an item in the market basket only after the product becomes widely used. By that time, the major price drops have already taken place. For example, the first portable video recorder and camera, the Ampex VR-3000 Backpack, weighed over 18 kilograms and sold for $65,000. Now for about $200 you can buy a high-definition video camera that fits in your pocket. The CPI captured little of the major price drops. The same is true for all kinds of new products, such as the cellphone, which began as big as a brick and priced north of $1,000. Only after the price of cellphones fell far enough for wide adoption did they make the CPI basket.

Experts conclude the CPI has overestimated inflation by 0.2 percent to 0.6 percent per year, meaning that if the CPI is reported as 2 percent, it may actually be as low as 1.4 percent. This problem is of more than academic concern because changes in the CPI determine changes in tax brackets and in an array of payments, such as wage agreements that include a cost-of-living adjustment, Canada Pension Plan benefits, welfare benefits, and even child support payments. Even if the overstatement is only 0.2 percent, a correction would save the federal government $72 million per year in Old Age Security payments alone.

Overstating the CPI also distorts other measures, such as wages, that use the CPI to adjust for inflation. For example, based on the official CPI, the average real wage in the Canadian economy rose by a total of about 11 percent in the past 15 years. But if the CPI overstated inflation by only 0.2 percent per year, then the average real wage actually increased by about 29 percent. Statistics Canada is working on the "CPI Enhancement Initiative" to address the problem of overstating the actual inflation rate.

The GDP Price Index

A price index is a weighted sum of various prices. Whereas the CPI focuses on just a sample of consumer purchases, a more complex and more comprehensive price index, the **GDP price index**, measures the average price of all goods and services produced in the economy. To calculate the GDP price index, we use the formula

$$\text{GDP price index} = \frac{\text{Nominal GDP} \times 100}{\text{Real GDP}}$$

where nominal GDP is the dollar value of GDP in a particular year measured in prices of that same year, and real GDP is the dollar value of GDP in a particular year measured in base-year prices. The

The Home Depot's lower prices do not necessarily mean a reduction in the cost of living.

challenge is finding real GDP in a particular year. Any measure of real GDP is constructed as the weighted sum of thousands of different goods and services produced in the economy. The question is what weights, or prices, to use. Prior to 2001, Statistics Canada used prices for a particular base year (most recently 1992) to estimate real GDP. In this case, the quantity of each output in a particular year was valued by using the 1992 price of each output. So real GDP in, say, 1996 was the sum of 1996 output valued at 1992 prices.

Moving from Fixed Weights to Chain Weights

Estimating real GDP by using prices from a base year yields an accurate measure of real GDP as long as the year in question is close to the base year. But Statistics Canada used prices that prevailed in 1992 to value production from 1926 to 2000. In 2003, Statistics Canada switched from a fixed-price weighting system to a **chain-weighted system**, using a complicated process that changes price weights from year to year. All you need to know is that the chain-weighted real GDP adjusts the weights more or less continuously from year to year, reducing the bias caused by a fixed-price weighting system.

Even though the chain-type index adjusts the weights from year to year, any index, by definition, must still use some year as an anchor, or reference point—that is, any index must answer the question "Compared to what?" To provide such a reference point, Statistics Canada measures Canadian real GDP and its components in *chained (2002) dollars*. Exhibit 5 presents nominal-dollar estimates of GDP as well as chained (2002) dollar estimates of real GDP. The blue line indicates nominal-dollar GDP since 1961. The red line indicates real GDP since 1961, or GDP measured in chained (2002) dollars. The two lines intersect

EXHIBIT 5

Canadian Gross Domestic Product in Nominal Dollars and Chained (2002) Dollars

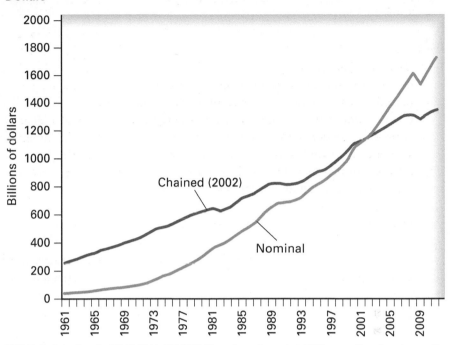

SOURCE: Statistics Canada, CANSIM Table 380-0017, "Gross domestic product (GDP), expenditure-based, annual." Data retrieved 17 July 2012.

in 2002, because that's when real GDP equalled nominal GDP. Nominal GDP is below real GDP in years prior to 2002 because real GDP is based on chained (2002) prices, which on average are higher than prices prior to 2002. Nominal GDP reflects growth in real GDP and in the price level. Chained-dollar GDP reflects growth only in real GDP. So nominal-dollar GDP grows faster than chained-dollar GDP.

chain-weighted system an inflation measure that adjusts the weights from year to year in calculating a price index, thereby reducing the bias caused by a fixed-price weighting system

Final Word

This chapter discussed how GDP is measured and how it's adjusted for changes in the price level over time. The national income accounts have limitations, but they offer a reasonably accurate picture of the economy at a point in time as well as year-to-year movements in the economy. Subsequent chapters will refer to the distinction between real and nominal values.

© dwori/Shutterstock.com

CHAPTER PROBLEMS

LO1 Explain the gross domestic product

1.1. *(Income Approach to GDP)* How does the income approach to measuring GDP differ from the expenditure approach? Explain the meaning of *value added* and its importance in the income approach. Consider the following data for the selling price at each stage in the production of a 2-kilogram bag of flour sold by your local grocer. Calculate the final market value of the flour.

Stage of Production	Sale Price
Farmer	$0.30
Miller	$0.50
Wholesaler	$1.00
Grocer	$1.50

1.2. *(Expenditure Approach to GDP)* Given the following annual information about a hypothetical country, answer questions a through d.

	Billions of Dollars
Personal consumption expenditures	200
Personal taxes	50
Exports	30
Depreciation	10
Government purchases	50
Gross private domestic investment	40
Imports	40
Government transfer payments	20

a. What is the value of GDP?
b. What is the value of net domestic product?
c. What is the value of net investment?
d. What is the value of net exports?

1.3. *(Investment)* Given the following annual data, answer questions a through c.

	Billions of Dollars
New residential construction	500
Purchases of existing homes	250
Sales value of newly issued stocks and bonds	600
New physical capital	800

Depreciation	200
Household purchases of new furniture	50
Net change in firms' inventories	100
Production of new intermediate goods	700

a. What is the value of gross private domestic investment?
b. What is the value of net investment?
c. Are any intermediate goods included in the measure of gross investment?

LO2 Discuss the circular flow of income and expenditure

2.1. *(Leakages and Injections)* What are the leakages from and injections into the circular flow? How are leakages and injections related in the circular flow?

LO3 Assess the limitations of national income accounting

3.1. *(Limitations of National Income Accounting)* Explain why each of the following should be taken into account when GDP data are used to compare the "level of well-being" in different countries:
a. Population levels
b. The distribution of income
c. The amount of production that takes place outside of markets
d. The length of the average work week
e. The level of environmental pollution

3.2. *(Limitations of National Income Accounting)* Other than child care, what are some tasks that households in the past would complete themselves, but now they pay others to do for them?

LO4 Explain how to account for price changes

4.1. *(Consumer Price Index)* Calculate a new consumer price index for the data in the following exhibit. Calculate the current year's cost of the market basket and the value of the current year's price index. What is this year's percent change in the price level compared to the base year?

Good or Service	Quantity in Market Basket	Prices in Base Year	Cost of Basket in Base Year	Prices in Current Year	Cost of Basket in Current Year
Twinkies	365 packages	$1.47/package	536.55	$.95/package	
Fuel Oil	2,000 litres	$1.00/litre	2000.00	$1.25/litre	
Cable TV	12 months	$60.00/month	720.00	$40.00/month	
			3256.55		

4.2. *(Consumer Price Index)* Given the following data, what was the value of the consumer price index in the base year? Calculate the annual rate of consumer price inflation in 2013 in each of the following situations:

a. The CPI equals 200 in 2012 and 240 in 2013.
b. The CPI equals 150 in 2012 and 175 in 2013.
c. The CPI equals 325 in 2012 and 340 in 2013.
d. The CPI equals 325 in 2012 and 315 in 2013.

CASE STUDY

The Economy and the Environment

The national accounts do a pretty good job tracking the economy by summing up all transactions involving final goods and services produced in the economy during a given year. Beginning in the early 1990s, Statistics Canada developed the Canadian System of Environmental and Resource Accounts (CSERA), to quantify the monetary and physical use of Canada's natural resources.

The first component in the CSERA is the value of natural assets in Canada's national balance sheet, which shows Canada's assets and liabilities attributed to businesses, governments, and individuals. Prior to the quantification of these assets by the CSERA, such natural assets were not included—in theory, a country could deplete all of its natural resources, and this would never show up in its overall economic position as illustrated in its balance sheet. The assets included fall into four categories: sub-soil assets, such as iron ore and oil, land, water, and "non-cultivated biological resources." "Non-cultivated" resources are things that grow that are not farmed by people, such as timber and wildlife.

Additionally, the CSERA computes "Material and Energy Flow Accounts," which measure flows of natural resources and waste during a given period. Any economic activity that results in environmental degradation would therefore be captured in these accounts. The third area covered by the CSERA is an explicit accounting of spending to protect the environment, divided among governments, businesses, and households.

By tracking the flow of expenditures on environmental protection, and the waste that results from economic production, it should be possible to calculate a "green" measure of gross or net domestic product. Another purpose of estimating and tracking these quantities over time is to ensure that countries are following a sustainable economic growth path. Sustainability means producing enough during a year that the country's assets are not being depleted to provide for current consumption. Without a formal accounting of environmental impacts, it is impossible to tell whether our current economic growth path is sustainable.

Other countries also track their environment and resource use with formal accounting methods. Pioneers in this field are Norway, which began in the 1970s, Finland, Germany, Australia, the Netherlands, Denmark, Sweden, and France. Missing from this list is the United States, the world's largest economy, and other key polluting countries such as India, Russia, and China. The United Nations oversees work on the System of Environmental-Economic Accounting, a system that lays out agreed-on rules, concepts, definitions, and so forth. The UN uses it to encourage countries to adopt methods that allow for international comparisons, similar to the national accounts systems already in widespread use to track GDP.

SOURCES: Reuters, "Who Are the World's Biggest Polluters?"; Statistics Canada, "Concepts, Sources, and Methods of the Environmental and Resource Accounts," 2006; United Nations Statistics Division, "Environmental-Economic Accounts," http://unstats.un.org/unsd/envaccounting/default.asp.

QUESTION

1. What are the three components in the Canadian System of Environmental and Resource Accounts? Why is it important to measure these quantities?

Unemployment and Inflation

LEARNING OUTCOMES

LO1 Discuss the effects of unemployment on the economy

LO2 Discuss the effects of inflation on the economy

> # " What type of unemployment might be healthy for the economy? "

Who among the following would be counted as unemployed: a college student who is not working, a bank teller displaced by an automatic teller machine, Kristen Stewart between movies, or NHL goalie Carey Price in the off-season? What type of unemployment might be healthy for the economy? What's so bad about inflation? Why is anticipated inflation less of a problem than unanticipated inflation? These and other questions are answered in this chapter, where we explore two macroeconomic problems: unemployment and inflation.

To be sure, unemployment and inflation are not the only problems an economy could face. Sluggish growth and widespread poverty are others. But low unemployment and low inflation go a long way toward reducing other economic problems. Although unemployment and inflation are often related, each is introduced separately. The causes of each and the relationship between the two will become clearer as you learn more about how the economy works.

This chapter shows that not all unemployment or all inflation harms the economy. Even in a healthy economy, a certain amount of unemployment reflects the voluntary choices of workers and employers seeking their best options. And low inflation that is fully anticipated creates fewer distortions than does unanticipated inflation.

LO 1 Unemployment

"They scampered about looking for work.... They swarmed on the highways. The movement changed them; the highways, the camps along the road, the fear of hunger and the hunger itself, changed them. The children without dinner changed them, the endless moving changed them."[1] There is no question, as John Steinbeck writes in *The Grapes of Wrath*, a novel set in the Great Depression, that a long stretch of unemployment profoundly affects the jobless and their families. The most obvious loss is a steady paycheque, but the unemployed often lose self-esteem and part of their identity as well. Losing a job often means losing the social connections to co-workers. According to psychologists, when assessing stressful events, the loss of a good job ranks only slightly below a divorce or the death of a loved one. Moreover, unemployment appears to be linked to a greater incidence of crime and to a variety of afflictions, including heart disease, suicide, and clinical depression.[2] No matter how often

---

[1] John Steinbeck, *The Grapes of Wrath* (Viking, 1939): 293.
[2] For a study linking a higher incidence of suicides to recessions, see Christopher Ruhm, "Are Recessions Good for Your Health," *The Quarterly Journal of Economics*, 115 (May 2000): 617–650. Clinical depression is also higher among the unemployed, as demonstrated in Frederick Zimmerman and Wayne Katon, "Socioeconomic Status, Depression Disparities, and Financial Strain: What Lies Behind the Income-Depression Relationship," *Health Economics*, 14 (December 2004): 1197–1215.

WHEN THOSE WHO ARE WILLING AND ABLE TO WORK CAN'T FIND JOBS, THEIR LABOUR IS LOST FOREVER.

Pixsooz/Shutterstock.com

people complain about their jobs, they rely on those same jobs not only for their livelihood but for part of their personal identity. When strangers meet, one of the first questions asked is "What do you do for a living?" Alfred Marshall wrote that your job is often the main object of your thoughts and intellectual development.

In addition to the personal costs, unemployment imposes a cost on the economy as a whole because fewer goods and services are produced. When those who are willing and able to work can't find jobs, their labour is lost forever. *This lost output coupled with the economic and psychological cost of unemployment on the individual and the family are the true costs of unemployment.* As we begin our analysis, keep in mind that the national unemployment rate reflects millions of individuals with their own stories. As U.S. president Harry Truman once remarked, "It's a recession when your neighbor loses his job; it's a depression when you lose your own." For some lucky people, unemployment is a brief vacation between jobs. For some others, a long stretch can have a lasting effect on family stability, economic welfare, self-esteem, and personal identity.

Measuring Unemployment

The unemployment rate is the most widely reported measure of the nation's economic health. What does the unemployment rate measure? What are the sources of unemployment? How has unemployment changed over time? These are some of the questions explored in this section. Let's first see how to measure unemployment.

We begin with the Canadian *civilian noninstitutional adult population,* which consists of all civilians 15 years of age and older, except those in prison, in mental facilities, or in homes for the aged. The adjective *civilian* means the definition excludes those in the military. From here on, references to the *adult population* mean the civilian noninstitutional adult population. The **labour force** consists of the people in the adult population who are either working or looking for work. *Those who want a job but can't find one are unemployed.* Statistics Canada interviews 54,000 households monthly (which translates into about 100,000 individuals) and counts people as unemployed if they have no job but want one and have looked for work at least once during the preceding four weeks. Thus the college student, the displaced bank teller, Kristen Stewart, and Carey Price would all be counted as unemployed if they want a job and looked for work in the previous month. The **unemployment rate** measures the percentage of those in the labour force who are unemployed. Hence the unemployment rate, which is reported monthly, equals the number unemployed—that is, people without jobs who are looking for work—divided by the number in the labour force.

Only a fraction of adults who are not working are considered unemployed. The others may have retired, are students, are caring for children at home, or simply don't want to work. Others may be unable to work because of long-term illness or disability. Some may have become so discouraged by a long, unfruitful job search that they have given up in frustration. These **discouraged workers** have, in effect, dropped out of the labour force, so they are not counted as unemployed. Finally, some of those working part time would prefer to work full time, yet all part-timers are counted as employed. A "full-time" job means 30 or more hours of paid labour per week. Because the official unemployment rate does not include discouraged workers and counts all part-time workers as employed, it may underestimate the true extent of unemployment in the economy. Later we consider some reasons why the unemployment rate may exaggerate the true extent of unemployment.

labour force those 15 years of age and older who are either working or looking for work

unemployment rate the number unemployed as a percentage of the labour force

discouraged workers those who drop out of the labour force in frustration because they can't find work

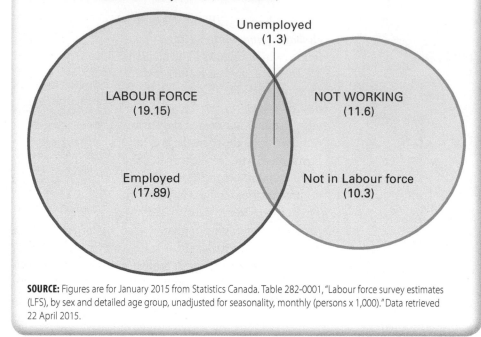

EXHIBIT 1

The Adult Population—the Employed, the Unemployed, and Those Not in the Labour Force: January 2015 (in millions)

Unemployed
(1.3)

LABOUR FORCE
(19.15)

NOT WORKING
(11.6)

Employed
(17.89)

Not in Labour force
(10.3)

SOURCE: Figures are for January 2015 from Statistics Canada. Table 282-0001, "Labour force survey estimates (LFS), by sex and detailed age group, unadjusted for seasonality, monthly (persons x 1,000)." Data retrieved 22 April 2015.

---

labour force participation rate
the labour force as a percentage of the adult population

These definitions are illustrated in Exhibit 1, where circles represent the various groups, and the number (in millions) of individuals in each category and subcategory is shown in parentheses. The circle on the left depicts the entire Canadian labour force in January 2015, including both employed and unemployed people. The circle on the right represents those in the adult population who, for whatever reason, are not working. These two circles combined show the adult population. The overlapping area identifies the number of *unemployed* workers—that is, people in the labour force who are not working. The unemployment rate is found by dividing the number unemployed by the number in the labour force. In January 2015, 1.3 million people were unemployed in a labour force of 18.9 million, yielding an unemployment rate of 6.9 percent.

Labour Force Participation Rate

The productive capability of any economy depends in part on the proportion of adults in the labour force, measured as the *labour force participation rate*. In Exhibit 1, the Canadian adult population

equals those in the labour force (18.9 million) plus those not in the labour force (10.3 million)—a total of 29.2 million people. The **labour force participation rate** therefore equals the number in the labour force divided by the adult population, or 64.7 percent (=18.9 million/29.2 million). So, on average, about two out of three adults are in the labour force. The labour force participation rate increased from 61 percent in 1976 to 67 percent in 1989, and has remained relatively steady since then.

One striking development since World War II has been the convergence in the labour force participation rates of men and women. From 1951 to today, adult women have increased their participation in the labour force from 25 percent to 62 percent. Over the same period, the labour force participation rate among men has fallen from 84 percent to 72 percent, primarily because of earlier retirement. The participation rate is slightly higher for native-born Canadians than landed immigrants (68 percent compared to 62 percent). Finally, the participation rate climbs with education—from 47 percent for those without a high school diploma to 79 percent among those with a university degree.

Unemployment over Time

Exhibit 2 shows the Canadian unemployment rate since 1921. As you can see, rates rise during contractions and fall during expansions. Note that the rate trended upward, reaching a high of 12% in 1983. For the past 30 years, the unemployment rate has been trending downward overall, with one period of relatively high unemployment during the recession of the early 1990s. In 2007, the unemployment rate reached 6.1%, the lowest in almost 40 years. The world-wide recession in 2008 caused the Canadian unemployment rate to rise by two percentage points, before gradually falling again.

EXHIBIT 2
The Canadian Unemployment Rate since 1921

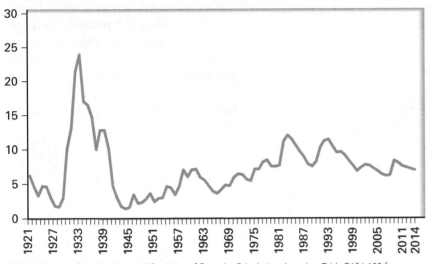

SOURCE: Statistics Canada. *Historical Statistics of Canada.* Calculations based on Table D124-133 for 1921–1975. Cansim Table 282-0087 for 1976 to 2014.

Unemployment among Various Groups

The unemployment rate says nothing about who is unemployed or for how long. The overall rate masks wide differences in the labour force based on education, immigrant status, gender, and age. For example, when the Canadian unemployment rate in January 2015 was 6.6 percent, the rate among workers 25 years of age or older who were high school dropouts was 11.2 percent and only 4.3 percent for someone in the same age group with a university degree. So education provides some insurance against unemployment. Unemployment also differs based on immigrant status; the rate was 6.4 percent among native-born Canadians and 10.7 percent among recent immigrants. Finally, the unemployment rate was 5.8 percent among males 25 and older, 5.2 percent among females 25 and older, and 12.8 percent among workers 15 to 24 years of age. Why is the unemployment rate among young workers so much higher than other workers? Young workers enter the labour force with little education or job experience, so they take unskilled jobs and are the first laid off if the economy slows down (last hired,

first fired). These workers also move in and out of the labour force more frequently as they juggle school demands. Even those who have left school often shop around more than workers 25 and older, quitting one job in search of a better one.

Unemployment rates for different groups since 1976 appear in Exhibit 3. Panel (a) shows the rates for workers 15 to 24 compared with workers 25 to 54, while panel (b) shows the gender gap. Periods of recession are shaded pink. As you can see, rates are higher among younger workers than older workers. The gender story is interesting. Prior to 1990, the unemployment rate was usually, though not always, higher for women. However, since 1990, the unemployment rate has been uniformly lower for women than for men. During recessions, rates climbed for all groups. There are two noticeable highs for the unemployment rate, in 1983 and again in 1992. Unemployment rates continued on a downward trend from 1992 until the 2008 recession. Exhibit 3A shows that the unemployment rate among young workers was nearly double that among older workers.

Unemployment Rates for Various Groups

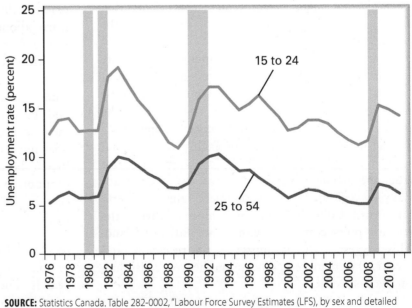

SOURCE: Statistics Canada. Table 282-0002, "Labour Force Survey Estimates (LFS), by sex and detailed age group, annual (persons unless otherwise noted)." Accessed 24 August 2012.

Unemployment Rates During the 2008 Recession and Recovery (index 2008 = 6.1%)

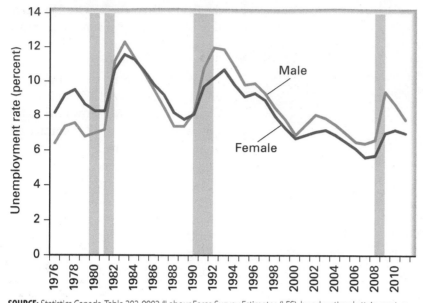

SOURCE: Statistics Canada. Table 282-0003. "Labour Force Survey Estimates (LFS), by educational attainment, sex and age group, unadjusted for seasonality, monthly (persons unless otherwise noted)". Accessed 22 April 2014.

Unemployment Varies across Occupations and Regions

frictional unemployment unemployment that occurs because job seekers and employers need time to find each other

seasonal unemployment unemployment caused by seasonal changes in the demand for certain kinds of labour

The unemployment rate varies by occupation. Professional and technical workers experience lower unemployment rates than blue-collar workers. Construction workers at times face high rates because that occupation is both seasonal and subject to wide swings over the business cycle.

Partly because certain occupations dominate labour markets in certain regions, unemployment rates also vary by region. We can see this by looking at unemployment rates across provinces during the recent worldwide recession and recovery. Suppose we set the unemployment rates for each province equal to the national average for 2008 (we know this is not true; the actual unemployment rate varies substantially by region). The unemployment rates in Alberta and British Columbia grew much more relative to the starting point compared with Prince Edward Island. This suggests that the impact of the recession (and recovery) were more significant on the west coast than on the east coast.

Exhibit 4 shows unemployment rates for 33 major metropolitan areas in January 2015. As you can see

Windsor had the highest unemployment rate, at 9.4 percent. This was more than triple the rate for the city with the lowest rate, Kelowna, at 2.8 percent. The point is that *the national unemployment rate masks differences across the country and even across an individual province.* Still, most cities in Exhibit 4 had rates between 6.0 percent and 8.0 percent.

Sources of Unemployment

Pick up any metropolitan newspaper and thumb through the classifieds. The help-wanted section may include thousands of jobs, from accountants to X-ray technicians. Online job sites such as Monster.ca list thousands of openings. Why, when millions are unemployed, are so many jobs available? To understand this, we must think about all the reasons why people are unemployed. They may be looking for a first job, or they may be reentering the labour force after an absence. They may have quit or been fired from their last job.

More generally, there are four sources of unemployment: frictional, seasonal, structural, and cyclical.

Frictional Unemployment Just as employers do not always hire the first applicant who comes through the door, job seekers do not always accept the first offer. Both employers and job seekers need time to explore the job market. Employers need time to learn about the talent available, and job seekers need time to learn about employment opportunities. The time required to bring together employers and job seekers is the source of **frictional unemployment**. Although unemployment often creates economic and psychological hardships, not all unemployment is necessarily bad. Frictional unemployment does not usually last long, and it results in a better match between workers and jobs, so the entire economy works more efficiently. Policymakers and economists are not that concerned about frictional unemployment.

Seasonal Unemployment Unemployment caused by seasonal changes in labour demand during the year is called **seasonal unemployment**. During cold winter months, demand for farm hands, lifeguards, landscapers, and construction workers shrinks, as it

EXHIBIT 4
Unemployment Rates across Canadian Metropolitan Areas

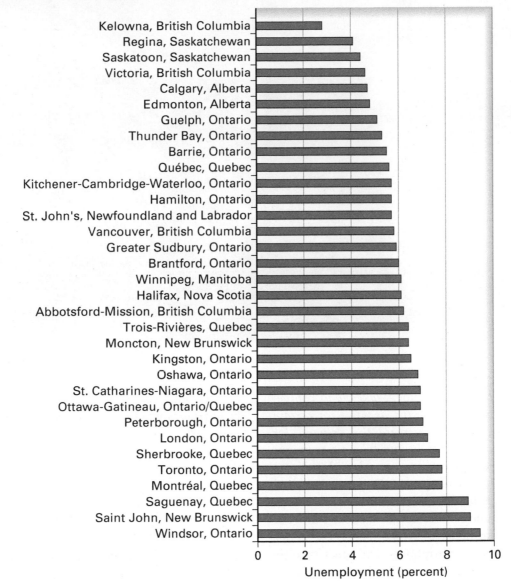

SOURCE: Based on figures for January 2015 from Table 282-0135 Statistics Canada.

does for dozens of other seasonal occupations. Likewise, tourism in winter destinations such as Whistler, B.C., melts in the heat of summer. The Christmas season increases the demand for sales clerks, postal workers, and Santa Clauses. Those in seasonal jobs realize their jobs disappear in the off-season. Some even choose seasonal occupations to complement their lifestyles or academic schedules. To eliminate seasonal unemployment, we would have to outlaw winter and abolish Christmas. Monthly employment data are *seasonally adjusted* to smooth out the unemployment bulges that result from seasonal

factors. Policymakers and economists are not that concerned about seasonal unemployment.

Structural Unemployment A third reason why job vacancies and unemployment coexist is that unemployed workers often do not have the skills in demand or do not live where their skills are demanded. Unemployment arising from a mismatch of skills or geographic location is called **structural unemployment**. *Structural unemployment occurs because changes in*

structural unemployment
unemployment because (1) the skills demanded by employers do not match those of the unemployed, or (2) the unemployed do not live where the jobs are

© Gary He/AP Photo

cyclical unemployment unemployment that fluctuates with the business cycle, increasing during contractions and decreasing during expansions

tastes, technology, taxes, and competition reduce the demand for certain skills and increase the demand for other skills. In our dynamic economy, some workers are stuck with skills no longer demanded. Golf carts replaced caddies, ATMs replaced bank tellers, and office technology is replacing clerical staff. For example, because of email, voice mail, PCs, PDAs, tablets, BlackBerrys, smartphones, and other wireless devices, the number of secretaries, typists, and administrative assistants in Canada has fallen over the past two decades. Structural unemployment may also arise from a change in tastes and preferences. For example, because Canadians smoke less, some tobacco farmers had to look for other work. And because Canadians buy fewer newspapers, employment in that industry has declined.

Whereas most frictional unemployment is short term and voluntary, structural unemployment poses more of a problem because workers must either develop the skills demanded in the local job market or look elsewhere. Moving is not easy. Most people prefer to remain near friends and relatives. Those laid off from good jobs hang around in hopes of getting rehired. Married couples with one spouse still employed may not want to give up that job to look

for two jobs elsewhere. Finally, available jobs may be in regions where the living cost is much higher. So those structurally unemployed often stay put. Some federal retraining programs aim to reduce structural unemployment.

Cyclical Unemployment As output declines during recessions, firms reduce their demand for nearly all resources, including labour. **Cyclical unemployment** increases during recessions and decreases during expansions. Between 1932 and 1933, when unemployment averaged about 22 percent, there was clearly much cyclical unemployment. Between 1942 and 1945, when unemployment averaged less than 2 percent, there was no cyclical unemployment. Cyclical unemployment means the economy is operating inside its production possibilities frontier. Government policies that stimulate aggregate demand aim to reduce cyclical unemployment.

Duration of Unemployment

A given unemployment rate tells us little about how long people have been unemployed. In January 2015, with the unemployment rate at 6.6 percent, the average duration of unemployment was 21 weeks. Some people were unemployed longer than others: 36 percent were unemployed less than 5 weeks; 27 percent

5 to 13 weeks; 16 percent 14 to 26 weeks; 6 percent 27 to 51 weeks; and 12 percent 52 weeks or longer.* Those out of work for a year or more are called the **long-term unemployed** and are of special concern to policymakers.

The Meaning of Full Employment

In a dynamic economy such as ours, changes in product demand and in technology continually alter the supply and demand for particular types of labour. Thus even in a healthy economy, there is some frictional, structural, and seasonal unemployment. The economy is viewed as operating at *full employment* if there is no cyclical unemployment. The amount of unemployment without the cyclical unemployment is called the "natural rate" of unemployment. When economists talk about "full employment," they do not mean zero unemployment but low unemployment. In Canada, the natural rate of unemployment is likely between 6 and 7 percent. Even when the economy is at **full employment**, there is some frictional, structural, and seasonal unemployment.

Unemployment Compensation

As noted at the outset, unemployment often involves an economic and psychological hardship. For a variety of reasons, however, the burden of unemployment on the individual and the family may not be as severe today as it was during the Great Depression. Today, many households have two or more workers in the labour force, so if one loses a job, another may still have one. *Having more than one family member in the labour force cushions the shock of unemployment.*

Moreover, unlike the experience during the Great Depression, most who lose their jobs now collect **unemployment benefits**—cash transfers to those who have lost their jobs and are actively seeking employment. In response to the Great Depression, Parliament passed the Unemployment Insurance Act in 1940, which provided unemployment insurance financed in part by a tax on employers and employees, and in part by the federal government. The program was renamed Employment Insurance (EI) in 1996. Currently, recipients of EI benefits receive 55 percent of average insured earnings, up to a maximum of $524 per week for a maximum of 45 weeks.

Because these benefits reduce the opportunity cost of remaining unemployed, they may reduce the incentives to find work. For example, if faced with a choice of washing dishes for $350 per week or collecting $250 per week in unemployment benefits, which would you choose? Evidence suggests that those collecting unemployment benefits remain out of work weeks longer than those without benefits. Many leave the labour force once their benefits are exhausted.[3] So although employment insurance provides a safety net, it may reduce the urgency of finding work, thereby increasing unemployment. On the plus side, because beneficiaries need not take the first job that comes along, employment insurance allows for a higher quality job search. As a result of a higher quality search, there is a better match between job skills and job requirements, and this promotes economic efficiency.

[3] See David Card, Raj Chetty, and Andrea Weber, "Cash-On-Hand and Competing Models of Intertemporal Behavior: New Evidence from the Labor Market," *Quarterly Journal of Economics*, 122 (November 2007): 1511–1560.

long-term unemployed those out of work for 52 weeks or longer
full employment employment level when there is no cyclical unemployment
unemployment benefits cash transfers to those who lose their jobs and actively seek employment

Having more than one family member in the labour force cushions the shock of unemployment.

*For 3 percent of unemployed persons, the duration of unemployment is unknown.

International Comparisons of Unemployment

How do Canadian unemployment rates compare with those around the world? Exhibit 5 shows rates since 1984 for Canada, the United States, Japan, and the average of four major European economies (France, Germany, Italy, and the United Kingdom). Over the past two decades and prior to the recent recession, unemployment trended down in Europe and Canada, trended up in Japan, and was variable in the United States. At the beginning of the period, Canada had the highest rate among the four economies. By the end of 2013, Canada's unemployment rate was below Europe's and the United States' in the aftermath of the global recession and the European debt crisis. While higher than at the beginning of this period, the Japanese unemployment rate is substantially lower than the other three.

The unemployment rates in Europe and Canada were similar over the past three decades, averaging 8.8 percent in Europe and 8.6 percent in Canada. The U.S. average rate was 6.4 percent. Why have rates averaged lower in the United States? The ratio of unemployment benefits to average pay is lower in the United States. In some European countries, unemployment benefits last longer, sometimes years. So those collecting unemployment benefits have less incentive to find work. What's more, government regulations have made European employers more reluctant to hire new workers because firing them is difficult.

Historically, unemployment has been low in Japan because many firms there offered job security for life. Thus some employees who do little or no work are still carried on company payrolls. Both labour laws and social norms limit layoffs in Japan. Unemployment has increased there since the early 1990s because more firms went bankrupt.

Problems with Official Unemployment Figures

Official unemployment statistics are not problem free. Not counting discouraged workers and others marginally attached to the labour force as unemployed understates unemployment. Official employment data also ignore the problem of **underemployment**, which arises because people are counted as employed even if they can find only part-time work or are vastly overqualified for their jobs, as when someone with a Ph.D. in literature can find only a clerk's position. Counting overqualified and part-time workers as employed tends to understate the actual amount of unemployment.

On the other hand, because unemployment insurance benefits and most welfare programs require recipients to seek work, some people may go through the motions of looking for a job just to qualify for

EXHIBIT 5
International Comparison of Unemployment Rates

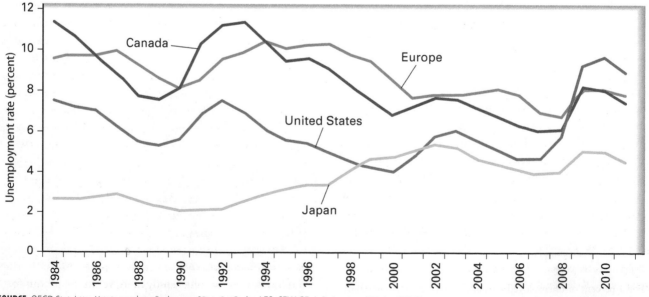

SOURCE: OECD Stat. http://stats.oecd.org/Index.aspx?DataSetCode=LFS_SEXAGE_I_R. Accessed 28 April 2015.

these benefits. If they do not in fact want a job, counting them as unemployed overstates actual unemployment. Likewise, some people who would prefer to work part time can find only full-time jobs, and some forced to work overtime and weekends would prefer to work less. To the extent that people must work more than they would prefer, the official unemployment rate overstates the actual rate. Finally, people in the underground economy may not admit they have jobs because they are breaking the law. For example, someone working off the books or someone selling illegal drugs would not admit to being employed.

However, because discouraged workers and others marginally attached to the labour force aren't counted as unemployed and because underemployed workers are counted as employed, most experts agree that official Canadian unemployment figures tend to underestimate unemployment. Still, the size of this underestimation may not be huge, even in the wake of a recession. Despite these qualifications and limitations, the Canadian unemployment rate is a useful measure of trends across demographic groups, across regions, and over time.

We turn next to inflation.

LO 2 Inflation

As noted already, *inflation* is a sustained increase in the economy's average price level, and we have already discussed inflation in different contexts. If the price level bounces around—moving up one month, falling back the next month—any particular increase in the price level would not necessarily be called inflation in a meaningful sense. We typically measure inflation on an annual basis. The annual *inflation rate* is the percentage increase in the average price level from one year to the next. For example, between January 2014 and January 2015, the Canadian *consumer price index* increased 1.0 percent. Extremely high inflation is called **hyperinflation**. A sustained *decrease* in the average price level is called **deflation**, as occurred in Canada during the Great Depression. Japan, Hong Kong, and Taiwan have also experienced deflation in recent years. And a reduction in the rate of inflation is called **disinflation**, as occurred in Canada in the early 1980s and early 1990s.

In this section, we first consider two sources of inflation. Then we examine the extent and consequences of inflation in Canada and around the world.

In Zimbabwe by 2009, hyperinflation made the local $100-billion note worth only Canadian pennies.

Two Sources of Inflation

Inflation is a sustained increase in the economy's price level; it results from an increase in aggregate demand, a decrease in aggregate supply, or both. Panel (a) of Exhibit 6 shows that an increase in aggregate demand raises the economy's price level from P to P'. In such cases, a shift to the right of the aggregate demand curve *pulls up* the price level. Inflation resulting from increases in aggregate demand is called **demand-pull inflation**. To generate continuous demand-pull inflation, the aggregate demand curve would have to keep shifting out along a given aggregate supply curve. Rising Canadian inflation during the late 1960s came from demand-pull inflation, when exports, particularly to the United States, and domestic consumption boosted aggregate demand.

Alternatively, inflation can arise from reductions in aggregate supply, as shown in panel (b) of Exhibit 6, where a leftward shift of the aggregate supply curve raises the price level. For example, OPEC price hikes reduced aggregate supply during 1974 and 1975, thereby raising the price level in the economy. Inflation stemming from decreases in aggregate supply is called **cost-push inflation**, suggesting that increases in the cost of production *push up* the price level. Prices increase and real GDP decreases, a combination identified earlier as *stagflation*. Again, to generate sustained and continuous cost-push inflation, the aggregate supply curve would have to keep shifting left along a given aggregate demand curve.

hyperinflation a very high rate of inflation

deflation a sustained decrease in the price level

disinflation a reduction in the rate of inflation

demand-pull inflation a sustained rise in the price level caused by a rightward shift of the aggregate demand curve

cost-push inflation a sustained rise in the price level caused by a leftward shift of the aggregate supply curve

INFLATION ERODES CONFIDENCE IN THE VALUE OF THE DOLLAR OVER THE LONG TERM.

EXHIBIT 6
Inflation Caused by Shifts of Aggregate Demand and Aggregate Supply Curves

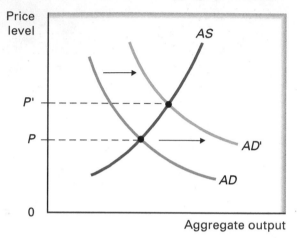

(a) Demand-pull inflation: inflation caused by an increase of aggregate demand

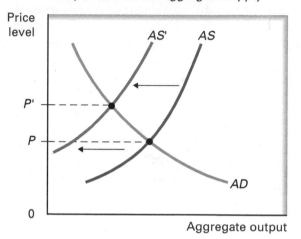

(b) Cost-push inflation: inflation caused by a decrease of aggregate supply

A Historical Look at Inflation and the Price Level

The consumer price index is the inflation measure you most often encounter, so it gets the most attention here. As you learned in the previous chapter, the *consumer price index*, or *CPI*, measures the cost of a market basket of consumer goods and services over time. Exhibit 7 shows prices in Canada since 1915, using the consumer price index. Panel (a) shows the price *level*, measured by an index relative to the base period of 2002. As you can see, the price level was lower in 1940 than in 1920. Since 1940, however, it has risen steadily, especially during the 1970s.

People are concerned less about the price level and more about year-to-year changes in that level. The lower panel shows the annual *rate of change* in the consumer price index (CPI), or the annual rate of *inflation* or *deflation*. The 1970s was not the only period of high inflation. Inflation exceeded 10 percent from 1917 to 1920 and in 1948—periods associated with world wars. Prior to the 1950s, high inflation was war related and was usually followed by deflation. Such an inflation-deflation cycle stretches back over the past two centuries. So fluctuations in the price level are nothing new. But prior to World War II, years of inflation and deflation balanced out over

the long run. Therefore, people had good reason to believe the dollar would retain its purchasing power over the long term. Since the end of World War II, however, the CPI has increased by an average of 4 percent per year. That may not sound like much, but it translates into more than a twelvefold increase in the consumer price index since 1946. *Inflation erodes confidence in the value of the dollar over the long term.*

Anticipated Versus Unanticipated Inflation

What is the effect of inflation on the economy? *Unanticipated inflation* creates more problems than *anticipated inflation*. To the extent that inflation is higher or lower than anticipated, it arbitrarily creates winners and losers. For example, suppose inflation is expected to be 3 percent next year, and you and your employer agree to a 4 percent increase in your nominal, or money, wage. You both expect your *real* wage—that is, your wage measured in dollars of constant purchasing power—to increase by 1 percent. If inflation turns out to be 3 percent, as expected, you and your employer are both satisfied. If inflation turns out to be 5 percent, your real wage will fall by 1 percent, so you are a loser and your employer a winner. If inflation turns out to be only 1 percent, your real

EXHIBIT 7

Consumer Price Index Since 1915

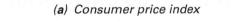

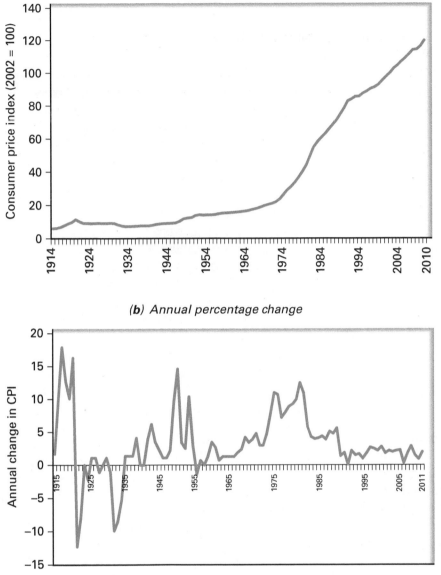

(a) Consumer price index

(b) Annual percentage change

SOURCE: Statistics Canada. Table 326-0021. "Consumer Price Index (CPI), 2009 basket, annual (2002 = 100 unless otherwise noted)." Accessed 28 April 2015.

The Transaction Costs of Variable Inflation

During long periods of price stability, people correctly believe they can predict future prices and can therefore plan accordingly. If inflation changes unexpectedly, however, the future is cloudier, so planning gets harder. Uncertainty about inflation undermines money's ability to link the present with the future. Canadian firms dealing with the rest of the world face an added burden. They must not only anticipate Canadian inflation, they must also guess how the value of the dollar will change relative to foreign currencies. Inflation uncertainty and the resulting exchange-rate uncertainty complicate international transactions. In this more uncertain environment, managers must shift attention from production decisions to anticipating the effects of inflation and exchange-rate changes on the firm's finances. Market transactions, particularly long-term contracts, become more complicated as inflation becomes more unpredictable. Some economists believe that the high and variable Canadian inflation during the 1970s and early 1980s cut economic growth during those periods.

Inflation Obscures Relative Price Changes

Even with no inflation, some prices would increase and some would decrease, reflecting normal activity in particular markets. For example, since the mid-1980s the Canadian price level has doubled, yet the prices of flat-screen TVs, computers, long-distance phone service, and many other products have declined sharply. Because the prices of various goods change by different amounts, *relative prices* change. Consider price changes over a longer period. On June 29, 1912, the *Globe and Mail* advertised building lots for sale in Brantford, Ontario, with the price ranging from $100 to $375. The same newspaper advertised diamond earrings for sale at a well-known Toronto jewellery store for between

wage increased by 3 percent, so you are a winner and your employer a loser.

More generally, if inflation is higher than expected, the losers are those who agreed to sell at a price that anticipated lower inflation and the winners are those who agreed to pay that price. If inflation is lower than expected, the situation is reversed: the losers are those who agreed to pay a price that anticipated higher inflation, and the winners are those who agreed to sell at that price. *The arbitrary gains and losses arising from unanticipated inflation is one reason inflation is so unpopular.* Inflation just doesn't seem fair.

$75 and $300. It is hard to imagine diamond earrings selling for the same price as land today. Whereas the economy's price level describes the exchange rate between a market basket and *money*, relative prices describe the exchange rate among goods—that is, how much one good costs compared to another.

Inflation does not necessarily cause a change in relative prices, but it can obscure that change. During periods of volatile inflation, there is greater uncertainty about the price of one good relative to another— that is, about relative prices. But relative price changes are important signals for allocating the economy's resources efficiently. If all prices moved together, suppliers could link the selling prices of their goods to the overall inflation rate. Because prices usually do not move in unison, however, tying a particular product's price to the overall inflation rate may result in a price that is too high or too low based on market conditions. The same is true of agreements to link wages with inflation. If the price of an employer's product grows more slowly than the rate of inflation in the economy, the employer may be hard-pressed to increase wages by the rate of inflation. Consider the problem confronting oil refiners who signed labour contracts agreeing to pay their workers cost-of-living wage increases. In some years, those employers had to increase wages at a time when the price of oil was falling like a rock.

Inflation across Metropolitan Areas

Inflation rates differ across cities and regions in Canada. Statistics Canada tracks separate CPIs for each of 16 Canadian metropolitan areas. The average annual inflation rate presented in Exhibit 8 is based on these CPIs from 2010 to 2014. Annual inflation in those years averaged from a low of 1.0 percent in Victoria to a high of 2.3 percent in St. John's. Most cities averaged between 1.6 percent and 2.1 percent. In the United States, much of the regional differences in inflation is attributable to a difference in housing prices across cities. In Canada,

EXHIBIT 8

Average Annual Inflation from 2010 to 2014 across Canadian Metropolitan Areas

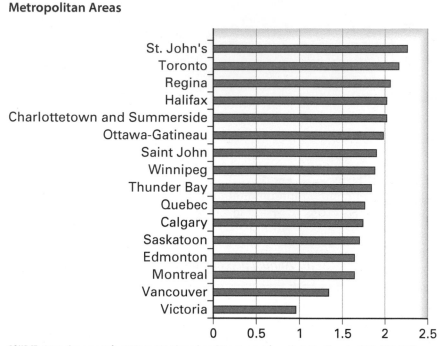

SOURCE: Annual averages for 2010 to 2014 based on CPI estimates from Statistics Canada. Table 326-0021. "Consumer Price Index (CPI), annual (2002 = 100 unless otherwise noted)." Accessed 28 April 2015.

there is no clear relationship between housing prices and inflation rates. Vancouver and Toronto share the honours for highest housing prices, and yet inflation is almost twice as high in Toronto. There also does not appear to be a regional influence. Measured by inflation, the top five cities are spread across the country.

International Comparisons of Inflation

Exhibit 9 shows annual inflation based on the CPI for the past three decades in Canada, the United States, Japan, and Europe, represented here as the average of four major nations (France, Germany, Italy, and the United Kingdom). All four economies show a similar trend, with declining inflation, or disinflation, during the first half of the 1980s, rising inflation during the second half of the 1980s to a peak in the early 1990s, and then another trend lower. The overall trend since 1980 has been toward lower inflation. Inflation rates in Europe and the United States were similar to those in Canada. Rates in Japan were consistently lower, even dipping into deflation in recent years. In the United States and Japan, the price level declined in 2009 due to slack demand from the global recession.

EXHIBIT 9

Inflation Rates in Major Economies Have Trended Lower over the Past Three Decades

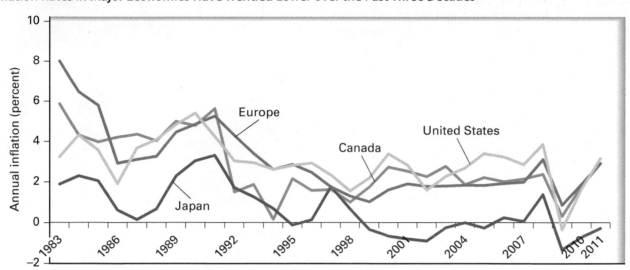

SOURCE: Developed from CPI inflation reported in OECD Statistics Directorate. Downloaded 6 December 2012. Figures for Europe are the averages for France, Germany, Italy, and the United Kingdom.

Rates rebounded somewhat in 2010 as the economies recovered. Inflation since 1980 averaged 2.7 percent in Canada, 3.0 percent in Europe and the United States, and 0.6 percent in Japan.

The quantity and quality of data going into the price index varies across countries. Governments in less developed countries sample fewer products and measure prices only in the capital city. Whereas hundreds of items are sampled to determine the Canadian consumer price index, as few as 30 might be sampled in some developing countries.

Inflation and Interest Rates

No discussion of inflation would be complete without some mention of the interest rate. **Interest** is the dollar amount paid by borrowers to lenders. Lenders must be rewarded for forgoing present consumption, and borrowers are willing to pay a premium to spend now. The **interest rate** is the amount paid per year as a percentage of the amount borrowed. For example, an interest rate of 5 percent means $5 per year on a $100 loan. The greater the interest rate, other things constant, the greater the reward for lending money. The amount people are willing to lend, called *loanable funds*, increases as the interest rate rises, other things constant. The supply curve for loanable funds therefore slopes upward, as indicated by curve *S* in Exhibit 10.

These funds are demanded by households, firms, and governments to finance homes, buildings, machinery, postsecondary education, and other major purchases. The lower the interest rate, other things constant,

the cheaper the cost of borrowing. So the quantity of loanable funds demanded increases as the interest rate decreases, other things constant. That is, the interest rate and the quantity of loanable funds demanded are inversely related. The demand curve therefore slopes downward, as indicated by curve *D* in Exhibit 10. The downward-sloping demand curve and the upward-sloping supply curve intersect to yield the equilibrium nominal rate of interest, *i*.

The **nominal interest rate** measures interest in terms of the current dollars paid. The nominal rate

> **interest** the dollar amount paid by borrowers to lenders
>
> **interest rate** Interest per year as a percentage of the amount loaned
>
> **nominal interest rate** the interest rate expressed in dollars of current value (that is, not adjusted for inflation) as a percentage of the amount loaned; the interest rate specified on the loan agreement

EXHIBIT 10
The Market for Loanable Funds

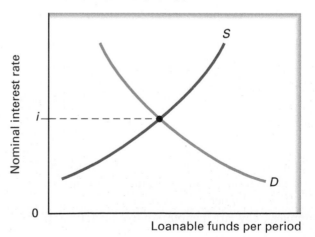

real interest rate
the interest rate expressed in dollars of constant purchasing power as a percentage of the amount loaned; the nominal interest rate minus the inflation rate

is the one that appears on the loan agreement; it is the rate discussed in the news media and is often of political significance. The **real interest rate** equals the nominal rate minus the inflation rate:

Real interest rate = Nominal interest rate
− Inflation rate

For example, if the nominal interest rate is 5 percent and the inflation rate is 3 percent, the real interest rate is 2 percent. With no inflation, the nominal rate and the real rate would be identical. But with inflation, the nominal rate exceeds the real rate. If inflation is unexpectedly high—higher, for example, than the nominal rate—then the real interest rate would be negative. In this case, the nominal interest earned for lending money would not even cover the loss of spending power caused by inflation. Lenders would lose purchasing power. This is why lenders and borrowers are concerned more about the real rate than the nominal rate. The real interest rate, however, is known only after the fact—that is, only after inflation actually occurs.

Because the future is uncertain, lenders and borrowers must form expectations about inflation, and they base their willingness to lend and borrow on these expectations. The higher the *expected* inflation, the higher the nominal rate of interest that lenders require and that borrowers are willing to pay. Lenders and borrowers base their decisions on the *expected* real interest rate, which equals the nominal rate minus the expected inflation rate.

Although the discussion has implied that there is only one market rate of interest, there are many rates. Rates differ depending on such factors as the duration of the loan, tax treatment of interest, and the risk the loan will not be repaid.

Why Is Inflation Unpopular?

Whenever the price level increases, spending must increase just to buy the same amount of goods and services. If you think of inflation only in terms of spending, you consider only the problem of paying those higher prices. But if you think of inflation in terms of the higher money income that results, you see that higher prices mean higher receipts for resource suppliers, including higher wages for workers. When viewed from the income side, inflation is not so bad.

If every higher price is received by some resource supplier, why are people so troubled by inflation?

gvictoria/Shutterstock

People view their higher incomes as well-deserved rewards for their labour, but they see inflation as a penalty that unjustly robs them of purchasing power. Most people do not stop to realize that unless they are producing more with each hour of labour, higher wages *must* result in higher prices. Prices and wages are simply two sides of the same coin. To the extent that nominal wages on average keep up with inflation, workers retain their purchasing power.

Although inflation affects everyone to some extent, it hits hardest those whose incomes are fixed in nominal terms. For example, pensions are often fixed dollar amounts and are eroded by inflation. And retirees who rely on fixed nominal interest income also see their incomes shrunk by inflation. But the benefits paid by the Canadian government, Old Age Security, and Canada Pension Plan are adjusted for changes in the CPI.

To Review: Anticipated inflation is less of a problem than unanticipated inflation. Unanticipated inflation arbitrarily redistributes income and wealth from one group to another, reduces the ability to make long-term plans, and forces people to focus more on money and prices. The more unpredictable inflation becomes, the harder it is to negotiate long-term contracts. Productivity suffers because people must spend more time coping with inflation, leaving less time for production.

Final Word

This chapter has focused on unemployment and inflation. Although we have discussed them separately, they are related in ways that will unfold in later chapters.

Politicians sometimes add the unemployment rate to the inflation rate to come up with what they refer to as the "misery index." In 1982, for example, an unemployment rate of 11.1 percent combined with a CPI increase of 10.9 percent yields a misery index of 22. Successful efforts by the Bank of Canada to reduce inflation beginning in the late 1980s have had an impact. The inflation rate has been below 3 percent since 1991 and the misery index has been below 10 for most of the past 15 years, rising to 10.4 in 2011 as a result of the recent recession.

CHAPTER PROBLEMS

LO1 Discuss the effects of unemployment on the economy

1.1. *(Measuring Unemployment)* Determine the impact on each of the following if 2 million formerly unemployed workers decide to return to school full time and stop looking for work:
   a. The labour force participation rate
   b. The size of the labour force
   c. The unemployment rate

1.2. *(Measuring Unemployment)* Suppose that the Canadian noninstitutional adult population is 23 million and the labour force participation rate is 67 percent.
   What would be the size of the Canadian labour force?
   If 8.5 million adults are not working, what is the unemployment rate?

1.3. *(Types of Unemployment)* Determine whether each of the following would be considered frictional, structural, seasonal, or cyclical unemployment:
   a. A UPS employee who was hired for the Christmas season is laid off after Christmas.
   b. A worker who is laid off due to reduced aggregate demand in the economy.
   c. A worker in a DVD rental store becomes unemployed as video-on-demand cable service becomes more popular.
   d. A new college graduate is looking for employment.

1.4. *(Unemployment Compensation)* What are the costs and benefits, in terms of economic efficiency, for having unemployment compensation?

LO2 Discuss the effects of inflation on the economy

2.1. *(Inflation)* Here are some recent data on the Canadian consumer price index:

Year	CPI	Year	CPI	Year	CPI
1992	140.3	1998	163.0	2004	188.9
1993	144.5	1999	166.6	2005	195.3
1994	148.2	2000	172.2	2006	201.6
1995	152.4	2001	177.1	2007	207.3
1996	156.9	2002	179.9	2008	215.3
1997	160.5	2003	184.0	2009	214.5

Compute the inflation rate for each year from 1993 to 2009 and determine which years were years of inflation. In which years did deflation occur? In which years did disinflation occur? Was there hyperinflation in any year?

2.2. *(Unanticipated Inflation)* William bought his first house in 1971. His mortgage term was for ten years, at a nominal interest rate of 5.3 percent. William's friend, Mary, bought her first house in 1981. Her mortgage term was also for ten years, but her nominal interest rate was 14.8 percent.
   The following table shows the inflation rate for Canada for the 20-year period beginning in 1971. Which friend, William or Mary, was made better off during the time of their mortgage? Which friend was made worse off? Why? Which bank was better off, the one loaning to William or the one loaning to Mary?

1971	3	1981	12.5
1972	4.8	1982	10.9
1973	7.8	1983	5.8
1974	11	1984	4.3
1975	10.7	1985	4
1976	7.2	1986	4.1
1977	8	1987	4.4
1978	8.9	1988	3.9
1979	9.3	1989	5.1
1980	10	1990	4.8

2.3. *(Sources of Inflation)* Using the concepts of aggregate supply and aggregate demand, explain why inflation usually accelerates during wartime.

2.4. *(Inflation and Interest Rates)* Using a demand-supply diagram for loanable funds (like Exhibit 10), show what happens to the nominal interest rate and the equilibrium quantity of loans when both borrowers and lenders increase their estimates of the expected inflation rate from 5 percent to 10 percent.

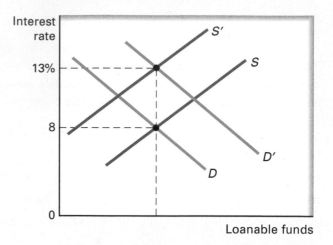

CASE STUDY

Hyperinflation in Zimbabwe

In the troubled nation of Zimbabwe in southern Africa, the Zimbabwean dollar was once worth about two Canadian dollars. But the collapse of the economy in the early 2000s severely devalued the Zimbabwean dollar. The government tried paying its bills by printing huge amounts of money, and the result was inflation on an epic scale—hyperinflation. Consider this: The price level at the end of 2008 was *150 million times* higher than at the beginning of that year. To put that in perspective, with such inflation in Canada, a litre of gasoline that sold for $1.40 at the beginning of the year would cost $210 million by year-end. Jeans that sold for $25 would cost $3.8 billion at year-end. With the value of the Zimbabwean dollar cheapening by the hour, nobody wanted to hold any for long. Those fortunate enough to have jobs in this wreck of an economy wanted to get paid at least daily; they then immediately spent their pay before prices climbed more.

With such wild inflation, everyone, including merchants, had trouble keeping up with prices. Different price increases among sellers of the same product encouraged buyers to shop around more. Even though the government was printing money at an astounding rate, the huge spike in prices meant that it took mountains of cash to buy anything, an amount both difficult to round up and onerous to carry. For months, the maximum amount people could withdraw daily from their bank had the purchasing power of about one Canadian dollar. Because carrying enough money for even small purchases became physically impossible, currency in Zimbabwe was issued in ever higher denominations, with the highest being a $100-trillion note; that's $100,000,000,000,000. In addition to issuing these higher denominations, the central bank issued an entirely new series of notes three times, each a huge multiple of the previous one, while doing away with the old series. For example, the new Zimbabwean dollar issued in February 2009 exchanged for 1 trillion of the dollars it replaced. Larger denominations and new series of notes facilitated transactions but fed inflation, which raged all the more.

Many merchants would accept only stable currencies such as the U.S. dollar or the South African rand and would rather barter than accept Zimbabwean currency. No question, the country had all kinds of other problems, but hyperinflation made everything worse. For example, Zimbabwe's GDP plunged 75 percent between 2006 and 2009, and the unemployment rate reached 90 percent.

As a way out of the mess, by mid-2009 the government allowed all transactions to be conducted in foreign currencies, something that was already happening. The local currency, already worthless (a $100-trillion note was worth only U.S. pennies), mostly disappeared. Thus Zimbabwe is now under what it calls a "multiple currency system." There are currently currencies from eight different countries circulating legally. Price inflation has been below 10 percent since 2009 under the multiple currency system. Although Zimbabwe ended its inflation nightmare, hyperinflation is usually flaring up somewhere in the world, as yet another country looks to print money as a "free lunch" solution to budget problems. For example, inflation in Venezuela reached 40 percent in 2013.

SOURCES: "Zimbabwe: Reaching Rock Bottom," *The Economist*, 8 December 2008; Douglas Rogers, "Zimbabwe's Accidental Triumph," *New York Times*, 14 April 2010; Zimbabwe's Federal Reserve Bank at http://www.rbz.co.zw/; "Zimbabwe's Multi-currency Confusion," http://www.bbc.com/news/world -africa-26034078. This case study also drew on Brian Hungwe's visit to Zimbabwe in September 2008.

QUESTION

1. In countries such as Zimbabwe, which had problems with high inflation, the increased use of another country's currency (such as the U.S. dollar or South African rand) became common. Why do you suppose this occurred?

8

Productivity and Growth

LEARNING OUTCOMES

LO1 Explain the theory of productivity and growth

LO2 Describe productivity and growth in practice

LO3 Discuss other issues of technology and growth

> # Why is the long-term growth rate more important than short-term fluctuations in economic activity?

Why is the standard of living so much higher in some countries than in others? How does an economy increase its living standard? Why is the long-term growth rate more important than short-term fluctuations in economic activity? What's labour productivity and why is Canadian productivity so much lower than productivity in the United States? What's been the impact of computers and the Internet on labour productivity? Answers to these and other questions are addressed in this chapter, which focuses on arguably the most important criteria for judging an economy's performance—productivity and growth.

The single most important determinant of a nation's standard of living in the long run is the productivity of its resources. Even seemingly low growth in productivity, if sustained for years, can have a substantial effect on the average living standard—that is, on the average availability of goods and services per capita. Growing productivity is therefore critical to a rising standard of living.

Economic growth is a complicated process, one that even experts do not yet fully understand. Since before Adam Smith inquired into the sources of countries' wealth in the *Wealth of Nations*, economists have puzzled over what makes some economies prosper while others founder. Because a market economy is not the product of conscious design, it does not reveal its secrets readily, nor can it be easily manipulated in pursuit of growth. We can't simply push here and pull there to achieve the desired result. Changing the economy is not like remodelling a home by knocking out a wall to expand the kitchen. Because we have no clear blueprint of the economy, we cannot make changes to specifications.

Still, there is much economists do know. In this chapter, we first develop a few simple models to examine productivity and growth. Then we use these models to help explain why some nations are rich and some poor. Canadian performance gets special attention, particularly compared with other major economies around the world. We close with some controversies of technology and growth.

LO1 Theory of Productivity and Growth

Just prior to Confederation, 40 percent of the Canadian workforce was in farming. If we include labourers and lumbermen, the number rises to 66 percent. Many of these workers toiled from sunrise to sunset for a wage that bought just the bare necessities. People had little intellectual stimulation and little contact with the outside world. Farm life in the 1830s was difficult: "The basic diet in winter was monotonous: pea soup and pork, potatoes and bread, and perhaps some preserved fruit while supplies lasted through the long winter.... The trick to survival, physical and financial, was to be self-sufficient."[1]

[1] C. Gray, *Sisters in the Wilderness* (Viking, 1999), p. 107.

Over the past two centuries, there has been an incredible increase in the Canadian *standard of living* as measured by the amount of goods and services available on average per person. An economy's standard of living grows over the long run because of (1) increases in the amount and quality of resources, especially labour and capital, (2) better technology, and (3) improvements in the *rules of the game* that facilitate production and exchange, such as tax laws, property rights, patent laws, the legal system, and the manners, customs, and conventions of the market. Perhaps the easiest way to introduce economic growth is by beginning with something you have already read about, the production possibilities frontier.

Growth and the Production Possibilities Frontier

The *production possibilities frontier*, or *PPF*, first introduced in Chapter 2, shows what the economy can produce if available resources are used efficiently. Let's briefly review the assumptions made in developing the frontier shown in Exhibit 1. During the period under consideration, usually a year, the quantity of resources in the economy and the level of technology are assumed to be fixed. Also assumed fixed during the period are the rules of the game that facilitate production and exchange. We classify all production into two broad categories—in this case, consumer goods and capital goods. Capital goods are used to produce other goods. For example, the

economy can bake pizzas and make pizza ovens. Pizzas are consumer goods, and ovens are capital goods.

When resources are employed efficiently, the production possibilities frontier *CI* in each panel of Exhibit 1 shows the possible combinations of consumer goods and capital goods that can be produced in a given year. Point *C* depicts the quantity of consumer goods produced if all the economy's resources are employed efficiently to produce them. Point *I* depicts the same for capital goods. Points inside the frontier are inefficient combinations, and points outside the frontier are unattainable combinations, given the resources, technology, and rules of the game. The production possibilities frontier is bowed out because resources are not perfectly adaptable to the production of both goods; some resources are specialized.

Economic growth is shown by an outward shift of the production possibilities frontier, as reflected in each panel of Exhibit 1. What can cause growth? An increase in resources, such as a growth in the labour supply or in the capital stock, shifts the frontier outward. Labour supply can increase either because of population growth or because the existing population works more. The capital stock increases if the economy produces more capital this year. The more capital produced this year, the more the economy grows, as reflected by an outward shift of the production frontier.

Breakthroughs in technology also shift out the frontier by making more efficient use of resources. Technological change often improves the quality of capital, but it can enhance the productivity of any resource. And technological change can free up resources for other uses. For example, the development of synthetic dyes in the 19th century freed up millions of acres of agricultural land that had been growing dye crops such as madder (red) and indigo (blue). The development of fibre-optic cable and cellular technology freed up the world's largest stock of copper in the form of existing telephone wires strung on poles across the nation.

Finally, any improvement in the rules of the game that nurtures production and exchange promotes growth and expands the frontier.

EXHIBIT 1

Economic Growth Shown by Shifts Outward of the Production Possibilities Frontier

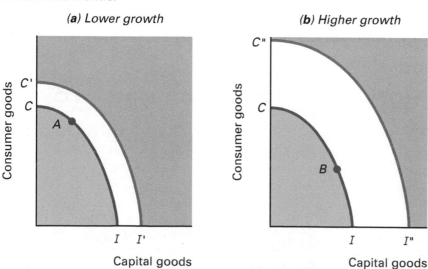

(a) Lower growth   *(b)* Higher growth

For example, the economy can grow as a result of improved patent laws that encourage more inventions[2] or legal reforms that reduce transaction costs. Thus *the economy grows because of a greater availability of resources, an improvement in the quality of resources, technological change that makes better use of resources, or improvements in the rules of the game that enhance production.*

The amount of capital produced this year shapes the PPF next year. For example, in panel (a) of Exhibit 1, the economy has chosen point *A* from possible points along *CI*. The capital produced this year shifts the PPF out to *C'I'* next year. But if more capital goods are produced this year, as reflected by point *B* in panel (b), the PPF shifts farther out next year, to *C"I"*.

An economy that produces more capital this year is said to *invest* more in capital. As you can see, to invest more, people must give up some consumer goods this year. Thus the opportunity cost of more capital goods this year is fewer consumer goods. More generally, we can say that people must *save* more now—that is, forgo some current consumption—to invest in capital. *Investment cannot occur without saving.* Economies that save more can invest more, as we'll see later. But let's get back to production.

What Is Productivity?

Production *is a process that transforms resources into goods and services.* Resources coupled with technology produce output. Productivity measures how efficiently resources are employed. In simplest terms, the greater the productivity, the more can be produced from a given amount of resources, and the farther out the production possibilities frontier. Economies that use resources more efficiently create a higher standard of living, meaning that more goods and services are produced per capita.

Productivity is defined as the ratio of total output to a specific measure of input. Productivity usually reflects an average, expressing total output divided by the amount of a particular kind of resource employed to produce that output. For example, **labour productivity** is the output per unit of labour and measures total output divided by the hours of labour employed to produce that output.

[2] For evidence of how the greater protection of intellectual property stimulates technological change, see Sunil Kanwar and Robert Evenson, "Does Intellectual Property Protection Spur Technological Change?" *Oxford Economic Papers*, 55 (April 2003): 235–264.

We can talk about the productivity of any resource, such as labour, capital, or natural resources. When agriculture accounted for most output in the economy, land productivity, such as bushels of grain per hectare, was a key measure of economic welfare. Where soil was rocky and barren, people were poorer than where soil was fertile and fruitful. Even today, soil productivity determines the standard of living in some economies. Industrialization and trade, however, have liberated many from dependence on soil fertility. Today, some of the world's most productive economies have little land or have land of poor fertility. For example, Japan has only about 2 percent as much land per capita as Russia, but Japan's GDP per capita is more than double Russia's.

Labour Productivity

Labour is the resource most commonly used to measure productivity. Why labour? First, labour accounts for most production cost—about 60 percent on average. Second, labour is more easily measured than other inputs, whether we speak of hours per week or full-time workers per year. Statistics about employment and hours worked are more readily available and more reliable than those about other resources.

But the resource most responsible for increasing labour productivity is capital. As introduced in Chapter 1, the two broad categories are human capital and physical capital. *Human capital* is the accumulated knowledge, skill, and experience of the labour force. As workers acquire more human capital, their productivity and their incomes grow. That's why surgeons earn more than butchers and accountants earn more than file clerks. You are reading this book right now to enhance your human capital. *Physical capital* includes the machines, buildings, roads, airports, communication networks, and other human creations used to produce goods and services. Think about digging a ditch with bare hands versus using a shovel. Now switch the shovel for a backhoe. More physical capital obviously makes diggers more productive. Or consider picking oranges with bare hands versus using a picking machine that combs the trees with steel bristles. In less than 15 minutes the machine can pick 18 tonnes of oranges from

production a process that transforms resources into goods and services

productivity the ratio of a specific measure of output, such as real GDP, to a specific measure of input, such as labour; in this case productivity measures real GDP per hour of labour

labour productivity output per unit of labour; measured as real GDP divided by the hours of labour employed to produce that output

per-worker production function the relationship between the amount of capital per worker in the economy and average output per worker

capital deepening an increase in the amount of capital per worker; one source of rising labour productivity

100 trees, catch the fruit, and drop it into storage carts. Without the machine, that would take four workers all day.[3] The operator of the picking machine is at least 128 times more productive than an orange picker using hands only.

In poorer countries, labour is cheap and capital dear, so producers substitute labour for capital. For example, in India a beverage truck makes its rounds festooned with workers so as to minimize the time the truck, the valuable resource, spends at each stop. In Canada, where labour is more costly (compared with capital), the truck makes its rounds with just the driver. As another example, in Haiti, the poorest country in the western hemisphere, a ferry service could not afford to build a dock, so it hired workers to carry passengers through the water to and from the ferry on their shoulders.[4]

As an economy accumulates more capital per worker, labour productivity increases and the standard of living grows. The most productive combination of all is human capital combined with physical capital. For example, one certified public accountant with a computer and specialized software can sort out a company's finances more quickly and more accurately than could a thousand high school–educated file clerks using just pencils and paper.

Per-Worker Production Function

We can express the relationship between the amount of capital per worker and the output per worker as an economy's **per-worker production function**. Exhibit 2 shows the amount of capital per worker, measured along the horizontal axis, and average output per worker, or labour productivity, measured along the vertical axis, other things constant—including the amount of labour, the level of technology, and rules of the game. Any point on the production function, *PF*, shows the average output per worker on the vertical axis for each level of capital per

[3] Eduardo Porter, "In Florida Groves, Cheap Labor Means Machines," *New York Times*, 22 March 2004.
[4] This example was noted by Tyler Cowen, "The Ricardo Effect in Haiti," 23 February 2004, http://www. marginalrevolution.com.

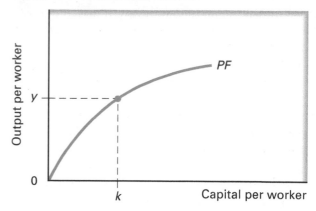

EXHIBIT 2
Per-Worker Production Function

worker on the horizontal axis. For example, with *k* units of capital per worker, the average output per worker in the economy is *y*. The curve slopes upward from left to right because an increase in capital per worker helps each worker produce more output. For example, bigger trucks make truck drivers more productive.

An increase in the amount of capital per worker is called **capital deepening** and is one source of rising productivity. *Capital deepening contributes to labour productivity and economic growth.* As the quantity of capital per worker increases, output per worker increases but at a diminishing rate, as reflected by the shape of the per-worker production function. The diminishing slope of this curve reflects the *law of diminishing marginal returns from capital*, which says that beyond some level of capital per worker, increases in capital add less and less to output per worker. For example, increasing the size of trucks beyond some point has diminishing returns as trucks become too large to negotiate some public roads. Thus, given the amount of labour, the level of technology, and the rules of the game, additional gains from more capital per worker eventually diminish and could turn negative.

Technological Change

Held constant along a per-worker production function is the level of technology in the economy.

© bhathaway/Shutterstock

Technological change usually improves the *quality* of capital and represents another source of increased productivity. For example, a tractor is more productive than a horse-drawn plow, a word processor more productive than a typewriter, and an Excel spreadsheet more productive than pencil and paper. Better technology is reflected in Exhibit 3 by an upward rotation in the per-worker production function from *PF* to *PF'*. As a result of a technological breakthrough, more is produced at each level of capital per worker. For example, if there are *k* units of capital per worker, a major breakthrough in technology increases the output per worker in the economy from *y* to *y'*.

Simon Kuznets, who won a Nobel Prize in part for his analysis of economic growth, claimed that technological change and the ability to apply such breakthroughs to all aspects of production are the driving forces behind economic growth in market economies. Kuznets argued that changes in the *quantities* of labour and capital account for only one-tenth of the increase in economic growth. Nine-tenths came from improvements in the *quality* of these inputs. As technological breakthroughs become *embodied* in new capital, resources are combined more efficiently, increasing total output. *From the wheel to the assembly line robot, capital embodies the fruits of discovery and drives economic growth.*

Thus two kinds of changes in capital improve worker productivity: (1) an increase in the *quantity* of capital per worker, as reflected by a movement along the per-worker production function, and (2) an improvement in the *quality* of capital per worker, as reflected by technological change that rotates the curve upward. More capital per worker and better capital per worker result in more output per worker, which, over time, translates into more output per capita, meaning a higher standard of living.

© David R. Frazier Photolibrary, Inc./Alamy

> **rules of the game**
> the formal and informal institutions that promote economic activity; the laws, customs, manners, conventions, and other institutional elements that determine transaction costs and thereby affect people's incentive to undertake production and exchange

Rules of the Game

Perhaps the most elusive ingredients for productivity and growth are the **rules of the game**, the formal and informal institutions that promote economic activity: the laws, customs, manners, conventions, and other institutional elements that encourage people to undertake productive activity. A stable political environment and system of well-defined property rights are important. Less investment occurs if potential investors believe their capital could be seized by the government, stolen by thieves, destroyed by civil unrest, or blown up by terrorists. For example, countries whose colonizers established strong property rights hundreds of years ago have, on average, much higher incomes today than countries whose colonizers did not.[5] Improvements in the rules of the game could result in more output

[5] Daron Acemoglu, Simon Johnson, and James A. Robinson, "The Colonial Origins of Comparative Development: An Empirical Investigation," *The American Economic Review*, 91 (December 2001): 1369–1401.

EXHIBIT 3

Impact of a Technological Breakthrough on the Per-Worker Production Function

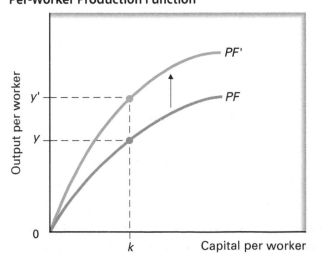

© James Steidl/Shutterstock

industrial market countries economically advanced capitalist countries of Western Europe, North America, Australia, New Zealand, and Japan, plus the newly industrialized Asian economies of Taiwan, South Korea, Hong Kong, and Singapore

developing countries countries with a low living standard because of less human and physical capital per worker

for each level of capital per worker, thus reflected by a rotation up in the per-worker production function as shown in Exhibit 3.

We tend to think that laws are the backbone of market exchange, but we should not underestimate the role of manners, customs, and conventions. According to the 18th-century British philosopher Edmund Burke, "Manners are of more importance than law…. The law touches us but here and there and now and then. Manners are what vex or soothe, corrupt or purify, exalt or debase, barbarize or refine us, by a constant, steady, uniform and insensible operation like that of the air we breathe in."[6] The Russian proverb "Custom is stronger than law" makes a similar point.

Simply put, a more stable political climate could benefit productivity just like a technological improvement. Conversely, events that foster instability can harm an economy's productivity and rotate the per-worker production function downward. The terrorist attack on the World Trade Center and Pentagon was such a destabilizing event. According to Albert Abadie, a Harvard economist, the attack affected "the spinal cord of any favorable business environment"—the ability of business and workers "to meet and communicate effectively without incurring risks."[7] The 9/11 attacks increased the vacancy rates of tall buildings even in cities besides New York, such as Chicago's Sears Tower, making that capital less productive.[8] As other examples, a greater threat to airport security adds to the time and cost of flying. Shops in countries plagued by suicide bombers must hire security guards to deter such horror, and this increases the cost of doing business.

Now that you have some idea about the theory of productivity and growth, let's look at them in practice, beginning with the vast difference in performance among economies around the world. Then we turn to Canada.

[6] Edmund Burke, *Letters to Parliament*, 2nd ed. (London, 1796): 105.
[7] As quoted in Greg Ip and John McKinnon, "Economy Likely Won't See Gain from War against Terrorism," *Wall Street Journal*, 25 September 2001.
[8] Alberto Abadie and Sofia Dermisi, "Is Terrorism Eroding Agglomeration Economies in Central Business Districts? Lessons from the Office Real Estate Market in Downtown Chicago," *Journal of Urban Economics*, 64 (September 2008): 451–463.

LO 2 Productivity and Growth in Practice

Differences in the standard of living among countries are vast. To give you some idea, per capita output in Canada is over 100 times that of the world's poorest countries. Poor countries are poor because they experience low labour productivity. We can sort the world's economies into two broad groups. **Industrial market countries**, or *developed countries*, make up about 16 percent of the world's population. They consist of the economically advanced capitalist countries of Western Europe, North America, Australia, New Zealand, and Japan, plus the newly industrialized Asian countries of Taiwan, South Korea, Hong Kong, and Singapore. Industrial market countries were usually the first to experience long-term economic growth during the 19th century and today have the world's highest standard of living based on abundant human and physical capital. Industrial market countries produce nearly three-quarters of the world's output. The rest of the world, the remaining 84 percent of the world's population, consists of **developing countries**, which have a lower standard of living because they have less human and physical capital. Many workers in developing countries are farmers. Because farming methods there are primitive, labour productivity is low and most people barely subsist, much like Canadians two centuries ago.

Education and Economic Development

Another important source of productivity is human capital—the skill, experience, and education of workers.

If knowledge is lacking, other resources may not be used efficiently. *Education makes workers aware of the latest production techniques and more receptive to new approaches and methods.* Exhibit 4 shows the percentage of the population ages 25 to 64 who have at least a degree beyond high school. Figures are presented for Canada and six other industrial market economies, together called the *Group of Seven*, or *G-7* (sometimes Russia is added to form the G-8, but Russia is not yet an industrial market economy and has a per capita income less than half of any G-7 country). In 1999, 39 percent of the Canadian adult population had at least a degree beyond high school, the highest of the G-7 countries. The Canadian percentage grew to 53 by 2012 (the latest year for which data are available). If we consider younger adults, Canada has an even larger percentage—57 percent of those 25 to 34 have a post-secondary degree or diploma. Of developed countries, only one other is higher than Canada—South Korea, at 66 percent.

Not shown in Exhibit 4 are developing countries, which have far lower education levels. For example, while the literacy rate exceeds 95 percent in industrial market economies, more than half the adults in the world's poorest countries can't read or write.

Canadian Labour Productivity

What has been the record of labour productivity in Canada? Exhibit 5 shows growth in real output per work hour for the past 50 years.

Productivity fell during the 1970s, a decline common across the OECD countries. One of the compelling reasons put forth for this decline was the sharp rise in oil prices caused by the formation of OPEC, as discussed in Chapter 5. However, since oil prices started falling in the 1980s, we would expect to see productivity rise again if oil prices were the driving factor behind the productivity decline. In the United States, productivity began to rise during the 1990s and increased further in the early 2000s. In Canada, there was a slight improvement in the 1990s followed by another decline, as seen in Exhibit 5.

Economists and policymakers in Canada have been trying to explain this divergence—Canada's productivity seems low compared to many other OECD countries. In 2013, researchers found a possible explanation—it may be that the numbers produced by Statistics Canada have been significantly underestimating productivity in Canada.

Exhibit 6 shows "multifactor productivity" in the United States compared with the same measure of productivity in Canada, both as calculated by Statistics Canada and by researchers W. Erwin Diewert and

Tom Wang/Shutterstock:

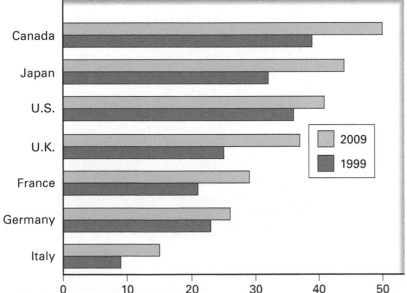

EXHIBIT 4
Percent of Adult Population with at Least a Post-High School Degree: 1999 and 2012

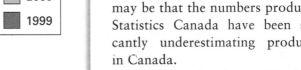

Legend: 2009, 1999

Categories: Canada, Japan, U.S., U.K., France, Germany, Italy

Axis: 0, 10, 20, 30, 40, 50

SOURCE: Based on figures in *Education at a Glance: 2014*, OECD at http://www.oecd.org.

THE CUMULATIVE POWER OF PRODUCTIVITY GROWTH IS WHY ECONOMISTS PAY SO MUCH ATTENTION TO LONG-TERM GROWTH.

EXHIBIT 5
Canadian Labour Productivity from 1961 to 2007

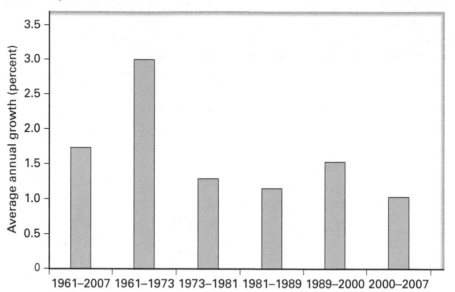

SOURCE: Adapted from Andrew Sharpe, Jean-Francois Arsenault and Peter Harrison, *"Why Have Real Wages Lagged Labour Productivity Growth in Canada?" International Productivity Monitor,* 17 (October 2008): 16–27.

Emily Yu.[9] Multifactor productivity (MFP) is a measure of output per unit of combined inputs—in this case, capital (K), labour (L), energy (E), materials (M),

EXHIBIT 6
Productivity in Canada and the United States: MFP Growth in the Canadian and U.S. Business Sector, Comparison between Diewert and Yu, Statistics Canada, and the Bureau of Labor Statistics, 1961–2011

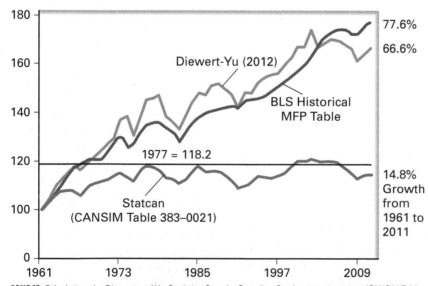

SOURCE: Calculations by Diewert and Yu; Statistics Canada, Canadian Productivity Accounts (CANSIM Table 383-0021), and Bureau of Labor Statistics, 1961-2011.

and services (S), or (KLEMS) for short. The productivity numbers as calculated by Diewert and Yu appear comparable to productivity estimates for the United States. It will be interesting to see how this debate unfolds in the coming few years.

Output per Capita

As noted earlier, the best measure of an economy's standard of living is output per capita. *Output per capita*, or GDP divided by the population, indicates how much an economy produces on average per resident. Exhibit 7 presents real GDP per capita for Canada since 1962. Notice the general upward trend, interrupted by four recessions, indicated by the pink bars. Real GDP per capita more than doubled for an average annual growth rate of 2.0 percent.

[9] W. E. Diewert and E. Yu, "New Estimates of Real Income and Multifactor Productivity Growth for the Canadian Business Sector, 1961–2011," *International Productivity Monitor,* Number 24, Fall 2012, pp. 27–48.

© Nati Harnik/AP Photo

International Comparisons

How does Canadian output per capita compare with that of other industrial countries? Exhibit 8 compares GDP per capita in 2010 for Canada and the six other leading industrial nations. Local currencies have been converted to U.S. dollars of 2010 purchasing power for ease of comparison. With nominal GDP per capita of $39,500 in 2010, Canada was second only to the United States, which was 20 percent higher at $47,400.

Exhibit 8 looks at the *level* of output per capita. What about the *growth* in output per capita? Exhibit 9 shows growth in real GDP per capita from 1979 to 2008. With an average growth of 1.6 percent per year, Canada is tied for fourth place (with Germany)

among the seven major economies. The United Kingdom ranked first, thanks in part to Prime Minister Margaret Thatcher, who converted some crusty government enterprises into dynamic for-profit firms. Industries she privatized during the 1980s include coal, iron and steel, gas, electricity, railways, trucking, airlines, telecommunications, and the water supply. She also cut income tax rates.

To Review: Canadian labour productivity growth has averaged 2.0 percent per year since 1962. Productivity growth slowed between 1974 and 1982. It appeared that Canadian productivity growth rates did not rebound as they did in other OECD countries. However, this assertion has been recently contested with new calculation methods. Whether or not productivity rates in Canada have remained low, our per capita GDP was the second highest in leading industrial nations.

LO3 Other Issues of Technology and Growth

In this section we consider some other issues of technology and growth, beginning with the question of whether technological change creates unemployment.

Does Technological Change Lead to Unemployment?

Because technological change usually reduces the labour needed to produce a given amount of output, some observers fear technological change increases unemployment. True, technological change can create dislocations as displaced workers try to find jobs elsewhere. But technological change can also create new products and job opportunities and make existing products more affordable. For example, the assembly line cut the cost of automobiles, making them more affordable for the average household. This increased the quantity of automobiles demanded, boosting production and employment. Even in industries

EXHIBIT 7

Canadian Real GDP per Capita since 1962

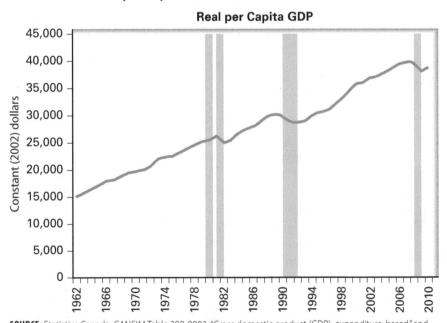

Real per Capita GDP

y-axis: Constant (2002) dollars — 0; 5,000; 10,000; 15,000; 20,000; 25,000; 30,000; 35,000; 40,000; 45,000

x-axis: 1962, 1966, 1970, 1974, 1978, 1982, 1986, 1990, 1994, 1998, 2002, 2006, 2010

SOURCE: Statistics Canada. CANSIM Table 380-0002, "Gross domestic product (GDP), expenditure-based," and Table 383-0027, "Natural resources, the terms of trade, and real income growth in Canada; real income estimates, annual"; extracted July 19, 2015.

CHAPTER 8: PRODUCTIVITY AND GROWTH

EXHIBIT 8

Canadian GDP per Capita in 2010 Compared with Other Major Economies

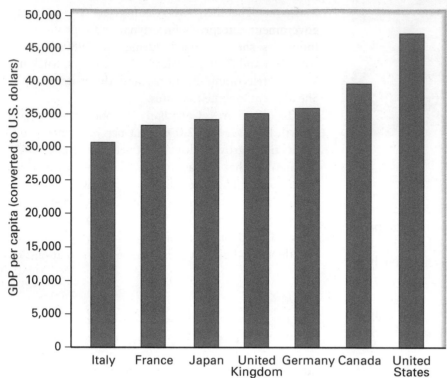

SOURCE: Based on 2010 dollar estimates from OECD at http://www.oecd.org/ and *The World Factbook*: at https://www.cia.gov/library/publications/the-world-factbook/index.html. Estimates have been adjusted across countries using the purchasing power of the local currency in 2010.

where machines displace some workers, those who keep their jobs become more productive, so they earn more. And *because human wants are unlimited, displaced workers usually find jobs producing other goods and services demanded in a growing economy.*

EXHIBIT 9

Canadian Real GDP per Capita Growth Average Compared with Other Major Economies between 1979 and 2009

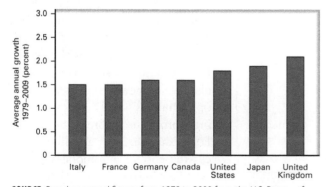

SOURCE: Based on annual figures from 1979 to 2009 from the U.S. Bureau of Labor Statistics ftp://ftp.bls.gov/pub/special.requests/ForeignLabor/flsgdp.txt. Figures were converted into U.S. dollars based on the purchasing power of local currency. The German growth rate prior to 1991, is for West Germany. For the latest data, go to http://www.stats.bls.gov/fls/.

If technological change causes unemployment, then we should see a clear positive relationship between the unemployment rate and the productivity growth rate. Looking at the last two periods in Exhibit 5, the productivity growth rate went from 1.5 percent to 1.0 percent, while the average unemployment rates for the same periods were 9.2 percent and 7.0 percent. And if technological change causes unemployment, then unemployment rates should be lower in economies where the latest technology has not yet been adopted, such as in developing countries. But unemployment is much worse there, and those fortunate enough to find work earn little because they are not very productive.

Again, there is no question that technological change sometimes creates job dislocations and hardships in the short run, as workers scramble to adjust to a changing world. Some workers with specialized skills made obsolete by technology may be unable to find jobs that pay as well as the ones they lost. These dislocations are one price of progress. Over time, however, most displaced workers find other jobs, often in new industries created by technological change.

Research and Development

As noted several times already, a prime contributor to labour productivity growth has been an improvement in the quality of human and physical capital. Human capital has benefited from better education and more job training. Better technology embodied in physical capital has also helped labour productivity. For example, because of extensive investments in cellular transmission, new satellites, and fibre-optic technology, labour productivity in the telecommunications industry has increased by an average of 5.5 percent per year during the past three decades.

Improvements in technology arise from scientific discovery, which is the fruit of research. We

BASIC RESEARCH YIELDS A HIGHER RETURN TO SOCIETY AS A WHOLE THAN DOES APPLIED RESEARCH.

can distinguish between basic research and applied research. **Basic research**, the search for knowledge without regard to how that knowledge will be used, is a first step toward technological advancement. With regard to economic growth, however, scientific discoveries are meaningless until they are implemented, which requires applied research. **Applied research** seeks to answer particular questions or to apply scientific discoveries to the development of specific products. Because technological breakthroughs may or may not have commercial possibilities, the payoff is less immediate with basic research than with applied research. *Yet basic research yields a higher return to society as a whole than does applied research.*

Because technological change is the fruit of research and development (R&D), investment in R&D improves productivity through technological discovery. One way to track R&D spending is to measure it relative to gross domestic product, or GDP. Exhibit 10 shows R&D spending as a share of GDP for Canada and the six other major economies for the 1980s, 1990s, and 2008. Overall R&D spending in Canada has fallen, with R&D spending by government and nonprofits remaining fairly stable, but R&D spending by businesses declining substantially. Business R&D is more likely to target applied research and innovations. R&D spending by governments and nonprofits, such as universities, may generate basic knowledge that has applications in the long run (for example, the Internet sprang from R&D spending on national defence in the United States).

Industrial Policy

Policymakers have debated whether government should become more involved in shaping an economy's technological future. One concern is that technologies of the future will require huge sums to develop, sums that an individual firm cannot easily raise and put at risk. Another concern is that some technological breakthroughs spill over to other firms and other industries, but the firm that develops the breakthrough may not be in a position to reap benefits from these spillover effects, so individual firms may underinvest in such research. One possible solution is more government involvement in economic planning.

Industrial policy is the idea that government, using taxes, subsidies, regulations, and coordination of the private sector, could help nurture the industries and technologies of the future to give domestic industries an advantage over foreign competitors. The idea is to secure a leading role for domestic industry in the world economy. One example of European industrial policy is Airbus Industrie, a four-nation aircraft consortium. With an estimated $20 billion in government aid, the aircraft maker has become Boeing's main rival. When Airbus seeks aircraft orders around the world, it can draw on government backing to promise favourable terms, such as landing rights at key European airports and an easing of regulatory constraints. In Canada, Bombardier has received substantial subsidies from both federal and provincial governments over the years.

But skeptics wonder whether the government should be trusted to identify emerging technologies and to pick the industry clusters that will lead the way. Critics of industrial policy believe that markets allocate scarce resources better than governments do. For example, European governments' costly attempt to develop the supersonic transport Concorde never became cost efficient. Airbus has also run into financial difficulties, and sponsoring governments have tried to distance themselves from the company.

> **basic research** the search for knowledge without regard to how that knowledge will be used
>
> **applied research** research that seeks answers to particular questions or to apply scientific discoveries to develop specific products
>
> **industrial policy** the view that government—using taxes, subsidies, and regulations—should nurture the industries and technologies of the future, thereby giving these domestic industries an advantage over foreign competition

© Reuters/Boeing/Landov

EXHIBIT 10

R&D Spending as a Percentage of GDP for Major Economies in the 1980s, 1990s, and 2008

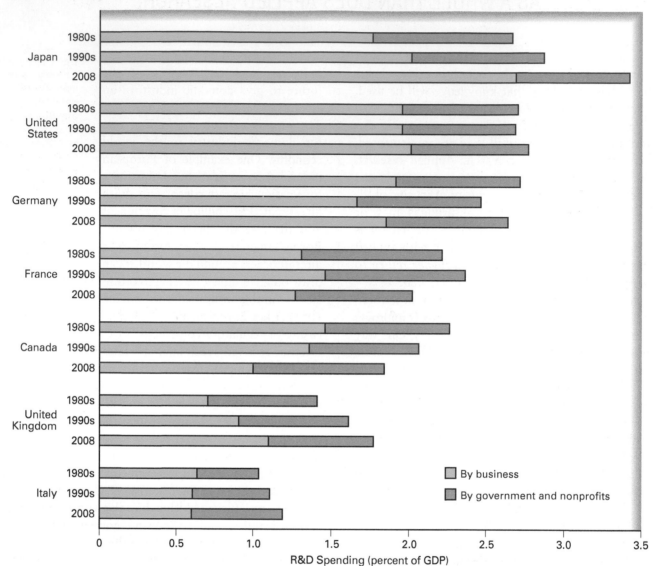

SOURCE: Based on estimates developed by the OECD at www.oecd.org.

convergence a theory predicting that the standard of living in economies around the world will grow more similar over time, with poorer countries eventually catching up with richer ones

Economists, among others, wonder if the government should be in the business of picking "winners and losers" in industries or particular firms. Most industrial policy is focused on the manufacturing industry. In Canada, this can create tension between the central provinces of Ontario and Quebec, and the rest of the country, which has historically relied more heavily on natural resource extraction and processing. There is also concern that an industrial policy might evolve into a government giveaway program. Rather than going to the most promising technologies, the money and the competitive advantages would go to

the politically connected. Critics also wonder how wise it is to sponsor corporate research when beneficiaries may share their expertise with foreign companies or even build factories abroad. Most economists would prefer to let Microsoft, Telus, BlackBerry, or some start-up bet their own money on the important technologies of the future.

Do Economies Converge?

If given enough time, will poor countries eventually catch up with rich ones? The **convergence** theory argues that developing countries can grow faster than advanced ones and should eventually close the gap.

WHEREAS TECHNOLOGY IS INDEED PORTABLE, THE KNOWLEDGE, SKILL, AND TRAINING NEEDED TO TAKE ADVANTAGE OF THAT TECHNOLOGY ARE NOT.

Here's why: it is easier to copy existing technology than to develop new ones. Countries that are technologically backward can grow faster by adopting existing technology. But economies already using the latest technology must come up with a steady stream of breakthroughs to grow faster.

What's the evidence on convergence? Some poor countries have begun to catch up with richer ones. For example, the newly industrialized Asian economies of Hong Kong, Singapore, South Korea, and Taiwan, by adopting the latest technology and investing in human resources, are closing the gap with the world leaders. Real output per capita in South Korea has grown three times faster than the average for the seven major economies. These *Asian Tigers* have graduated from developing economies to industrial market economies. But these are the exceptions. According to research by the World Bank, among the nations made up of the poorest third of the world's population, consumption per capita has grown only about 1.0 percent per year over the past two decades compared with a 2.5 percent growth in the rest of the world, so the standard of living in the poorest third of the world has grown somewhat in absolute terms but has fallen further behind in relative terms. Worse yet, a billion people seem trapped in poor economies that are going nowhere.

One reason per capita consumption has grown so slowly in the poorest economies is that birth rates there are double those in richer countries, so poor economies must produce still more just to keep up with a growing population. Another reason why convergence has not begun, particularly for the poorest third of the world, is the vast difference in the quality of human capital across countries. Whereas technology is indeed portable, the knowledge, skill, and training needed to take advantage of that technology are not. Countries with a high level of human capital can make up for other shortcomings. For example, much of the capital stock in Japan and Germany was destroyed during World War II. But the two countries retained enough of their well-educated and highly skilled labour force to rejoin elite industrial market economies in little more than a generation. But some countries, such as those in parts of Africa, simply lack the human capital needed to identify and absorb

new technology. As noted already, such poor economies tend to have low education levels and low literacy rates. What's more, some countries lack the stable macroeconomic environment and the established institutions needed to nurture economic growth. Many developing countries have serious deficiencies in their infrastructures, lacking, for example, the reliable source of electricity to power new technologies. For example, in Northern Nigeria, near the Sahara, 90 percent of the villages have no electricity. Some of the poorest nations have been ravaged by civil war for years. And simply communicating can be challenging in some developing countries. In Nigeria, for example, more than 400 languages are spoken by 250 distinct ethnic groups. (To learn more about the challenges facing the poorest nations, read the final chapter of this book, entitled "Economic Development.")

Final Word

Productivity and growth depend on the supply and quality of resources, the level of technology, and the rules of the game that nurture production and exchange. These elements tend to be correlated with one another. An economy with an unskilled and poorly educated workforce usually is deficient in physical capital, in technology, and in the institutional support that promotes production and exchange. Similarly, an economy with a high-quality workforce likely excels in the other sources of productivity and growth.

We should distinguish between an economy's standard of living, as measured by output per capita, and improvements in that standard of living, as measured by the growth in output per capita. Growth in output per capita can occur when labour productivity increases or when the number of workers in the economy grows faster than the population. *In the long run, productivity growth and the growth in workers relative to the growth in population will determine whether Canada continues to enjoy one of the world's highest standards of living.*

CHAPTER PROBLEMS

LO1 Explain the theory of productivity and growth

1.1. *(Growth and the PPF)* Use the production possibilities frontier (PPF) to demonstrate economic growth.
   a. With consumption goods on one axis and capital goods on the other, show how the combination of goods selected this period affects the PPF in the next period.
   b. Extend this comparison by choosing a different point on this period's PPF and determining whether that combination leads to more or less growth over the next period.

1.2. *(Shifts in the PPF)* Terrorist attacks foster instability and may affect productivity over the short and long term. Do you think the September 11, 2001, terrorist attacks on the World Trade Center and the Pentagon affected short- and/or long-term productivity in the United States? Explain your response and show any movements in the PPF.

1.3. *(Per-worker Production Function)* Within the next 20 years, 3D printers may revolutionize the way goods are manufactured. Draw a per-worker production function and explain what will happen to that production function as more and more firms adopt this new technology.

LO2 Describe productivity and growth in practice

2.1. *(Long-Term Productivity Growth)* Suppose that two nations start out in 2012 with identical levels of output per work hour—say, $100 per hour. In the first nation, labour productivity grows by 1 percent per year. In the second, it grows by 2 percent per year. Use a calculator or a spreadsheet to determine how much

output per hour each nation will be producing 20 years later, assuming that labour productivity growth rates do not change. Then determine how much each will be producing per hour 100 years later. What do your results tell you about the effects of small differences in productivity growth rates?

2.2. *(Education and Economic Growth)* Consider two developing countries that are exactly alike with one exception—in country A, girls are not allowed to attend school or university, and in country B, girls can get an education. What do you expect would be true about economic growth in both countries?

LO3 Discuss other issues of technology and growth

3.1. *(Technological Change and Unemployment)* What are some examples, other than those given in the chapter, of technological change that has caused unemployment? And what are some examples of new technologies that have created jobs? How do you think you might measure the net impact of technological change on overall employment and GDP in Canada?

3.2. *(Industrial Policy)* In 2014, Chrysler asked the Ontario and Canadian governments for $700 million to support expansion of their manufacturing facilities in Ontario. Chrysler later withdrew its request due to public pressure. How do you think the following individuals would respond to the idea of government funds to support this type of investment:
   a. An auto worker in Windsor, Ontario
   b. A wheat farmer in Alberta
   c. An economist

CASE STUDY

Income and Happiness

Gross domestic product is a useful measure of both output and income, but how does that relate to the well-being of a country's citizens? As a first approximation, it would seem that a country with higher incomes can afford to spend more on its citizens' education and healthcare. This is why we often see a strong correlation between GDP and other measures of well-being such as literacy, life expecancy, and low rates of infant mortality. However, there are limits to this link between income and happiness. Eighteenth-century philosopher and social reformer Jeremy Bentham argued that government policy should promote the greatest happiness for the greatest number of people.

Many people today apparently agree. In recent polls, 77 percent of Australians and 81 percent of Britons believed that a government's prime objective should be promoting the greatest happiness rather than the greatest wealth. The United Nations sponsored an international conference called "Happiness and Public Policy." Thailand now compiles a monthly Gross Domestic Happiness Index. Even China has joined in the fun, reporting a happiness index based on polling results about living conditions, income, the environment, social welfare, and employment. Australia, Canada, Germany, and the United Kingdom are also developing indexes of happiness or well-being.

Researchers at the University of Waterloo first published the Canadian Index of Wellbeing in 2011. They found that from 1994 to 2010, Canadian GDP increased by 28.9 percent while the index of well-being increased by just 5.7 percent. The index does include a measure of the standard of living but also takes into account health, the environment, education, time use, democratic engagement, leisure, and culture.

Economists have long shied away from asking people how they feel, preferring instead to observe their behaviour. But more now see some value in asking questions. In the most extensive of polls, the Gallup organization asked people in 130 countries "How satisfied are you with your life, on a scale of zero to ten?" The results are not surprising. Most people in the high-income areas, such as the United States, Europe, and Japan, said they are happy. Most people in the poor areas, especially in Africa, said they are not. Also, within a given country, income and happiness are positively related. After evaluating all the results of the Gallup world poll, Angus Deaton of Princeton concluded: "The very strong global relationship between per capita GDP and life satisfaction suggests that on average people have a good idea of how income, or the lack of it, affects their lives."

So these results are no surprise. What does puzzle economists is that other surveys conducted in the United States suggest that people on average do not seem any happier over time even though each generation became richer than the last. The proportion of Americans who say they are happy has stayed about the same despite 60 years of economic growth.

The United States is unusual in that regard. Surveys in Europe and Japan do find an increase in happiness with increases in income over time. It may be the problem of "keeping up with the Joneses" at work here. Individuals gain pleasure by comparing themselves to other people. When the entire distribution becomes richer, overall happiness does not change because most people's positions in the rankings do not change. However, when an individual moves up in the ranking by attaining a higher income, they are, indeed, happier. Research into the links between happiness and income continues to grow.

SOURCES: Jon Gertner, "The Rise and Fall of the GDP," *New York Times*, 10 May 2010; Daniel Gilbert, *Stumbling on Happiness* (New York: Knopf, 2006); Guglielmo Caporale et al., "Income and Happiness Across Europe: Do Reference Values Matter?" *Journal of Economic Psychology*, 30 (February 2009): 42–51; Angus Deaton, "Income, Health, and Well-Being Around the World: Evidence from the Gallup World Poll," *Journal of Economic Perspectives*, 22 (Spring 2008): 53–72; Betsey Stevenson and Justin Wolfers, "The Paradox of Declining Female Happiness," *American Economic Journal: Economic Policy*, 1 (August 2009): 190–225; and https://uwaterloo.ca/canadian-index-wellbeing/.

QUESTION

1. How would you explain the finding that people in high-income economies seem happier than people in low-income economies, but, over time, people in high-income economies do not seem to be happier even though their country grows richer?

9

Aggregate Expenditure and Aggregate Demand

LEARNING OUTCOMES

LO1 Explain the role of consumption

LO2 Analyze the effects of investment, government purchases, and net exports

LO3 Explain how total spending in the economy changes with income

LO4 Discuss how the simple spending multiplier accounts for changes in spending plans

LO5 Describe the aggregate demand curve

> ## When driving through a neighbourhood new to you, how can you guess the income of the residents?

When driving through a neighbourhood new to you, how can you guess the income of the residents? How would your spending change if your summer job pays more than you expected? What's the most predictable and useful relationship in macroeconomics? Why are consumer confidence and business confidence in the economy so important? Answers to these and other questions are addressed in this chapter, which focuses on the makeup of aggregate expenditure. Consumption is the most important expenditure, accounting for about two-thirds of all spending. In this chapter, we also examine investment, government purchases, and net exports. We discuss how each relates to income in the economy. Then we combine these spending components to derive the aggregate demand curve. On the text's website, Appendix A shows what happens when imports increase with income, and Appendix B develops the algebra behind all this. In the next chapter, we develop the aggregate supply curve and see how the two curves interact to determine the economy's equilibrium levels of price and output.

LO 1 Consumption

What if a college friend invites you home for the weekend? On your first visit, you would get some idea of the family's standard of living. Is their house a mansion, a dump, or in between? Do they drive a new BMW or take the bus? The simple fact is that consumption tends to reflect income. Although some people can temporarily live beyond their means and others still have the first nickel they ever earned, in general, consumption depends on income.

A key decision in the circular-flow model developed three chapters back was how much households spent and how much they saved. Consumption depends primarily on income. Although this relationship seems obvious, the link between consumption and income is fundamental to understanding how the economy works. Let's look at this link in the Canadian economy over time.

A First Look at Consumption and Income

Exhibit 1 shows the relationship between disposable income and consumption in Canada from 1981 to 2013. Consumption is measured along the vertical axis and disposable income along the horizontal axis. Notice that each axis measures the same units: billions of 2007 chained dollars. Each year is depicted by a blue point that reflects two flow values: disposable income and consumption. For example, the combination for 2000, identified by the red point, shows that when disposable income (measured along the horizontal axis) was $605 billion, consumption (measured along the vertical axis) was $584 billion.

In 2013, consumption was about 95 percent of disposable income. As you can see, there is a clear and direct relationship between consumption and disposable income. You need little imagination to see that by connecting the dots in Exhibit 1, you could trace a line relating consumption to income. This relationship has special significance in macroeconomics.

The Consumption Function

Exhibit 1 shows that the link between consumption and income is quite stable. Based on their disposable income, households decide how much to consume and how much to save. So consumption depends on disposable income. *Consumption is the dependent variable and disposable income, the independent variable.* Because consumption depends on income, we say that consumption

consumption function the relationship in the economy between consumption and income, other things constant

marginal propensity to consume (MPC) the fraction of a change in income that is spent on consumption; the change in consumption divided by the change in income that caused it

is a *function* of income. Exhibit 2 presents a hypothetical **consumption function**, which shows that consumption increases with disposable income, assuming other determinants of consumption remain constant. Again, both consumption and disposable income are in real terms, or in inflation-adjusted dollars. Notice that this hypothetical consumption function reflects the historical relationship between consumption and income shown in Exhibit 1.

Marginal Propensity to Consume

In Chapter 1, you learned that economic analysis focuses on activity at the margin. For example, what happens to consumption if income changes by a certain amount? Suppose Canadian households receive another billion dollars in disposable income. Some is spent on consumption, and the rest is saved. The fraction of the additional income that is spent is called the marginal propensity to consume. More precisely, the **marginal propensity to consume**, or **MPC**, equals the change in consumption divided by the change in income.

For example, if Canadian income increases from $1,800 billion to $1,850 billion, consumption increases by $40 billion and saving by $10 billion. The marginal propensity to consume equals the change in consumption divided by the change in income. In this case, the change in consumption is $40 billion and the change in income is $50 billion, so the marginal propensity to consume is 40 ÷ 50, or 4 ÷ 5.

EXHIBIT 1
Canadian Consumption and Disposable Income, 1981–2013

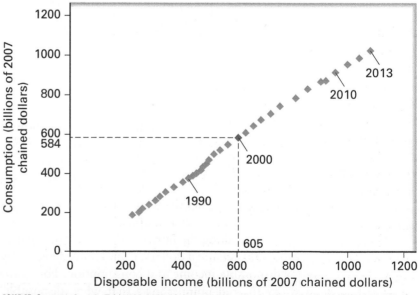

SOURCE: Statistics Canada. Table 380-0072, "Current and capital accounts - Households, quarterly (dollars unless otherwise noted)" (accessed: May 23, 2015).

EXHIBIT 2
The Consumption Function

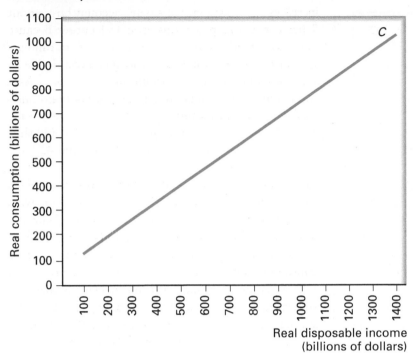

SOURCE: Statistics Canada. Table 380-0072, "Current and capital accounts - Households, quarterly (dollars unless otherwise noted)" (accessed: May 23, 2015).

increase in income. Because the slope of any straight line is constant everywhere along the line, the MPC for any linear, or straight-line, consumption function is constant at all incomes. We assume here for convenience that the consumption function is a straight line, though it need not be.

Non-income Determinants of Consumption

Along a given consumption function, consumer spending depends on disposable income in the economy, other things constant. Now we look at the factors that are held constant and how changes in them could shift the entire consumption function up or down.

Net Wealth and Consumption Given the economy's income, an important influence on consumption is each household's **net wealth**—that is, the value of all assets that each household owns minus any liabilities, or debts. Net wealth is a *stock* variable. Consumption and income are *flow* variables. Your family's assets may include a home, automobiles, bank accounts, corporate stock, and cash. Your family's liabilities, or debts, may include a mortgage, car loans, student loans, credit card balances, and the like.

net wealth the value of all assets minus liabilities

MPC and the Slope of the Consumption Function

You may recall from the appendix to Chapter 1 that the slope of a straight line is the vertical distance between any two points divided by the horizontal distance between those same two points. Consider, for example, the slope between points *a* and *b* on the consumption function in Exhibit 3, where the delta symbol (Δ) means "change in." The horizontal distance between these points shows the change in disposable income, denoted as Δ*DI*—in this case, $50 billion. The vertical distance shows the change in consumption, denoted as Δ*C*—in this case, $40 billion. The slope equals the vertical distance divided by the horizontal distance, or 40 ÷ 50, which equals the marginal propensity to consume of 4 ÷ 5.

Thus, the marginal propensity to consume is measured graphically by the slope of the consumption function. After all, the slope is nothing more than the increase in consumption divided by the

EXHIBIT 3
Marginal Propensity to Consume

Consumption function

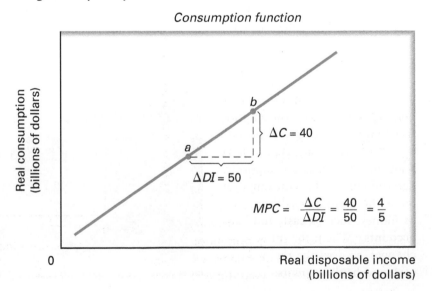

$$MPC = \frac{\Delta C}{\Delta DI} = \frac{40}{50} = \frac{4}{5}$$

EXHIBIT 4
Shifts of the Consumption Function

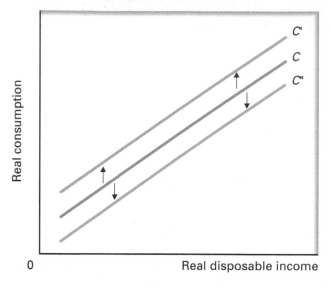

Net wealth is assumed to be constant along a given consumption function. A decrease in net wealth would make consumers less inclined to spend and more inclined to save at each income level. To see why, suppose prices rise sharply on the stock market. Shareholders are richer than they were, so they spend more. This increase in consumption spending can be seen by the upward shift of the consumption function in Exhibit 4 from C to C'.

Again, it is a change in net wealth, not a change in disposable income, that shifts the consumption function. A change in disposable income, other things constant, means a movement along a given consumption function, not a shift of that function. Be mindful of the difference between a movement along the consumption function, which results from a change in income, and a shift of the consumption function, which results from a change in one of the non-income determinants of consumption, such as net wealth.

The Price Level Another variable that affects the consumption function is the price level prevailing in the economy. As we have seen, net wealth is an important determinant of consumption. Some household wealth is held as money, such as cash and bank accounts. When the price level changes, so does the real value of cash and bank accounts.

For example, suppose your wealth consists of a $20,000 bank account. If the economy's price level increases by 5 percent, your bank account buys about 5 percent less in real terms. You feel poorer because you are poorer. To rebuild the real value of your money holdings to some desired comfort level, you decide to spend less and save more. *An increase in the price level reduces the purchasing power of money holdings, causing households to consume less and save more at each income level.* So the consumption function would shift downward from C to C'', as shown in Exhibit 4.

The Interest Rate Interest is the reward savers earn for deferring consumption and the cost borrowers pay for current spending power. When graphing the consumption function, we assume a given interest rate in the economy. If the interest rate increases, other things constant, savers or lenders are rewarded more, and borrowers are charged more. The higher the interest rate, the less is spent on those items typically purchased on credit, such as cars. Thus, at a higher interest rate, households save more, borrow less, and spend less. Greater saving at each income level means less consumption. Simply put, *a higher interest rate, other things constant, shifts the consumption function downward.* Conversely, *a lower interest rate, other things constant, shifts the consumption function upward.*

Expectations Expectations influence economic behaviour in a variety of ways. For example, suppose you land a good job that starts after graduation. Your consumption probably jumps long before the job actually begins because you expect an increase in your income. You might buy a car, for example. On the other hand, a worker who gets a layoff notice to take effect at the end of the year likely reduces consumption

How would your spending change if you were expecting an increase in income?

© FUSE/Getty Images

FIRMS BUY NEW CAPITAL GOODS ONLY IF THEY EXPECT THE INVESTMENT TO YIELD A HIGHER RETURN THAN OTHER POSSIBLE USES OF THEIR FUNDS.

immediately, well before the actual layoff. More generally, if people grow more concerned about their job security, they reduce consumption at each income level.

A change in expectations about price levels or interest rates also affects consumption. For example, a change that leads householders to expect higher car prices or higher interest rates in the future prompts some to buy a new car now. On the other hand, a change leading householders to expect lower car prices or lower interest rates in the future causes some to defer a car purchase. Thus expectations affect spending, and a change in expectations can shift the consumption function. This is why economic forecasters monitor consumer confidence so closely.

To Review: Keep in mind the distinction between *a movement along a given consumption function,* which results from a change in income, and a *shift of the consumption function,* which results from a change in one of the factors assumed to remain constant along the consumption function.

The Life-Cycle Hypothesis Do people with high incomes save a larger fraction of their incomes than those with low incomes? Both theory and evidence suggest they do. The easier it is to make ends meet, the more income is left over to save. Does it follow from this that richer economies save more than poorer ones—that economies save a larger fraction of total disposable income as they grow? You might think so, but evidence suggests that the *fraction of disposable income saved in an economy seems to stay constant as the economy grows.*

So how can it be that richer people save more than poorer people, yet richer countries do not necessarily save more than poorer ones? According to the **life-cycle model of consumption and saving,** young people tend to borrow to finance education and home purchases. In middle age, people pay off debts and save more. In old age, they draw down their savings, or dissave. Some still have substantial wealth at death, because they are not sure when death will occur and because some parents want to bequeath wealth to their children. And some people die in debt. But on average, net savings over a person's lifetime tend to be small. The life-cycle hypothesis suggests that the saving rate for an economy as a whole depends on, among other things, the relative number of savers and dissavers in the population.

But a problem with the life-cycle hypothesis is that the elderly do not seem to draw down their assets as much as the theory predicts. One reason is to leave bequests to children. Another is that the elderly seem concerned about covering unpredictable expenses such as those arising from divorce, health problems, or living much longer than expected. Because of such uncertainty, many elderly spend less and save more than the life-cycle theory predicts. Researchers have found that those elderly who have not experienced a divorce or health problems build their net wealth well into old age.

We turn next to the other components of aggregate expenditure—investment, government spending, and net exports. Keep in mind that our initial goal is to understand the relationship between total spending and income.

LO 2 Investment, Government Spending, and Net Exports

The remaining components of aggregate expenditure are investment, government spending, and net exports. Investment consists of spending on (1) new factories, office buildings, malls, and equipment, such as computers; (2) new housing; and (3) net increases to inventories. People invest now in the expectation of a future return. Because the return is in the future, a would-be investor must estimate how much a particular investment will yield this year, next year, the year after, and in all years during the productive life of the investment. *Firms buy new capital goods only if they expect this investment to yield a higher return than other possible uses of their funds.* Government spending includes spending on goods and services (*not* transfer payments) by all three levels of government: federal, provincial, and municipal. The rest of

> **life-cycle model of consumption and saving** young people borrow, middle-agers pay off debts and save, and older people draw down their savings; on average, net savings over a lifetime is usually little or nothing

the world affects aggregate expenditure through imports and exports and has a growing influence on the Canadian economy.

Investment Demand Curve

The market interest rate is the opportunity cost of investing in capital. More is invested when the opportunity cost of borrowing is lower, other things constant. A downward-sloping investment demand curve for the entire economy can be derived, with some qualifications, from a horizontal summation of each firm's downward-sloping investment demand curves. The economy's *investment demand curve* is depicted as *D* in Exhibit 5, which shows the inverse relationship between the quantity of investment demanded and the market interest rate, other things—including business expectations—held constant. For example, in Exhibit 5, when the market rate is 8 percent, the quantity of investment demanded is $100 billion. If the interest rate rises to 10 percent, investment declines to $90 billion, and if the rate falls to 6 percent, investment increases to $110 billion. Assumed constant along the investment demand curve are business expectations about the economy. If firms grow more optimistic

about profit prospects, the demand for investment increases, so the investment demand curve shifts to the right.

Investment and Disposable Income

To integrate the discussion of investment with our earlier analysis of consumption, we need to know if and how investment varies with income in the economy. Whereas we were able to present evidence relating consumption to income over time, the link between investment and income is weaker. Investment in a particular year shows little relation to income that year. *Investment depends more on interest rates and on business expectations than on the prevailing income level.* One reason investment is less related to income is that some investments, such as a new power plant, take years to build. And investment, once in place, is expected to last for years, sometimes decades. The investment decision is thus said to be *forward looking*, based more on expected profit than on current income.

So how does the amount firms plan to invest relate to income? The simplest **investment function** assumes that *investment* is unrelated to disposable income. Investment is assumed to be **autonomous** with respect to disposable income. For example, suppose that, given current business expectations and a market interest rate of 8 percent, firms plan to invest $100 billion per year, regardless of the economy's income level. Exhibit 6 measures disposable income on the horizontal axis and investment on the vertical axis. Investment of $100 billion is shown by the flat investment function, *I*. As you can see, along *I*, investment does not vary even though disposable income does.

Non-income Determinants of Investment

The investment function isolates the relationship between income in the economy and *investment*—the amount firms plan to invest, other things constant. We have already introduced two determinants that are assumed to be constant: the interest rate and business expectations. Now let's look at how changes in each factor would affect investment.

Market Interest Rate Exhibit 5 shows that if the market interest rate is 8 percent, investment is $100 billion. This investment is also shown as *I* in

EXHIBIT 5
Investment Demand Curve for the Economy

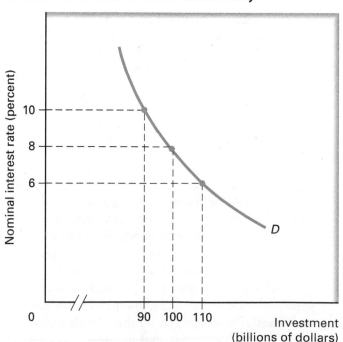

EXHIBIT 6

Investment Function

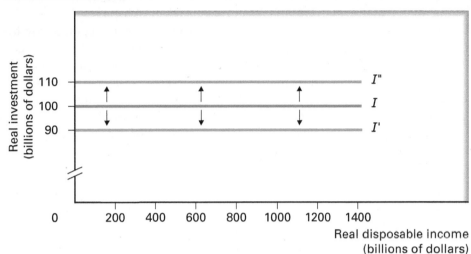

Government Purchase Function

The **government purchase function** relates government purchases to income in the economy, other things constant. Decisions about government purchases are largely under the control of public officials, such as the decision to build a highway, boost military spending, or hire more teachers. These spending decisions do not depend directly on income in the economy. We therefore assume that *government*

> **government purchase function**
> the relationship between government purchases and the economy's income, other things constant

Exhibit 6. If the interest rate increases because of, say, a change in the nation's monetary policy, the cost of borrowing increases, which increases the opportunity cost of investment. For example, if the interest rate increases from 8 percent to 10 percent, investment drops from $100 billion to $90 billion. This decrease is reflected in Exhibit 6 by a shift of the investment function from *I* down to *I'*. Conversely, if the market interest rate decreases because of, say, a change in the nation's monetary policy, the cost of borrowing decreases, which reduces the opportunity cost of investment. For example, a drop in the rate of interest from 8 percent to 6 percent, other things remaining constant, reduces the cost of borrowing and increases investment from $100 billion to $110 billion, as reflected by the upward shift of the investment function from *I* to *I''*. Notice that the shifts in Exhibit 6 match interest rate movements along the investment demand curve in Exhibit 5.

Business Expectations Investment depends primarily on business expectations, or on what Keynes called the "animal spirits" of business. Suppose investment initially is $100 billion, as depicted by *I* in Exhibit 6. If firms now become more pessimistic about their profit prospects, perhaps expecting the worst, as in 2008 during the global financial crisis, investment decreases at every income, as reflected in Exhibit 6 by a shift of the investment function from *I* down to *I'*. On the other hand, if profit expectations become rosier, as they did in 2010, firms become more willing to invest, thereby increasing the investment function from *I* up to *I''*. *Examples of factors that could affect business expectations, and thus investment plans,*

net export function the relationship between net exports and the economy's income, other things constant

purchases are autonomous, or independent of income. Such a function would relate to income as a flat line similar to the investment function shown in Exhibit 6. An increase in government purchases would result in an upward shift of the government purchase function. And a decrease in government purchases would result in a downward shift of the government purchase function.

Net Taxes

As noted earlier, government purchases represent only one of the two components of government outlays; the other is *transfer payments,* such as for Canada Pension Plan, welfare benefits, and employment insurance. Transfer payments are outright grants from governments to households and are thus not considered part of aggregate expenditure. Transfer payments vary inversely with income—as income increases, transfer payments decline.

To fund government outlays, governments impose taxes. Taxes vary directly with income; as income increases, so do taxes. *Net taxes* equal taxes minus transfers. Taxes tend to increase with income but transfers tend to decrease with income. However, for

simplicity, let's assume that net taxes do not vary with income. Thus we assume for now that *net taxes* are *autonomous*, or independent of income.

Net taxes affect aggregate spending indirectly by changing disposable income, which in turn changes consumption. We saw from the discussion of circular flow that by subtracting net taxes, we transform real GDP into *disposable income*. Disposable income is take-home pay—the income households can spend or save. We examine the impact of net taxes in the next few chapters.

Net Exports

How do imports and exports relate to the economy's income? When incomes rise, Canadians spend more on all normal goods, including imports. Higher incomes lead to more spending on American cars, French wine, Chinese toys, European vacations, and thousands of other foreign goods and services. Likewise, when residents of foreign countries have higher income, they purchase more of everything, including Canadian exports.

The **net export function** shows the relationship between net exports and Canadian income, other things constant. Because our exports are insensitive to Canadian income but our imports tend to increase

Government purchases as a percent of GDP declined from 22 percent during the 1960s to an average of 18 percent in the past decade due primarily to decreases in defence spending.

with income, *net exports*, which equal the value of exports minus the value of imports, tend to decline as Canadian incomes increase. However, for simplicity, we assume that net exports are *autonomous*, or independent of income.

If exports exceed imports, net exports are positive; if imports exceed exports, net exports are negative; and if exports equal imports, net exports are zero. As with government spending, the net export function would be a horizontal line similar to the investment function in Exhibit 6. Factors assumed constant along the net export function include the Canadian price level, price levels in other countries, interest rates here and abroad, foreign income levels, and the exchange rate between the dollar and foreign currencies. Any one of these factors that causes net exports to increase would cause the net export function to shift up. A non-income factor that causes net exports to decrease would shift the net export function down.

LO 3 Aggregate Expenditure and Income

In the first section of this chapter, the big idea was that consumption depends on income, a link that is the most stable in all of macroeconomics. Next, we build on that connection to learn how total spending in the economy changes with income. If we try to confront the economy head-on, it soon becomes a bewildering maze, which is why we make progress by starting with simple models. We continue to assume, as we did in developing the circular-flow model, that there is no capital depreciation and no business saving. Thus we can say that *each dollar of spending translates directly into a dollar of income.*

© Eye Ubiquitous/Alamy

Therefore, gross domestic product, or GDP, equals aggregate income.

The Components of Aggregate Expenditure

When income increases, consumption increases. As we have already learned, the marginal propensity to consume indicates the fraction of each additional dollar of income that is spent on consumption. For example, if the marginal propensity to consume is 4 ÷ 5 (four-fifths), spending increases by $4 for every $5 increase in income. The consumption function shows how much consumption increases with income.

For simplicity, we continue to assume that the other spending components do not vary with income; thus investment, government purchases, and net exports are autonomous, or independent of the economy's income level. Specifically, we'll assume that investment and government purchases each equals $100 billion for the year in question and net exports are a negative $40 billion. We'll also assume that government purchases equal net taxes, so the government budget is balanced. We first want to see how a balanced budget works before we consider the effects of budget deficits or surpluses.

If we stack up the consumption function, the investment function, the government purchase function, and the net export function, we get the aggregate expenditure line presented in Exhibit 7 as $C + I + G + (X - IM)$. Real GDP is measured on the horizontal axis, and aggregate expenditure is measured on the vertical axis. The **aggregate expenditure line** shows how much households, firms, governments, and the rest of the world plan to spend on Canadian output at each level of real GDP, or real income. Again, the only spending component that varies with real GDP is consumption. Since only consumption varies with income, the slope of the aggregate expenditure line equals the marginal propensity to consume.

Real GDP Demanded

Let's begin developing the aggregate demand curve by asking how much aggregate output would be demanded at a given price level. By finding the quantity demanded at a given price level, we'll end up identifying a single point on the aggregate demand curve. We begin by considering the relationship between aggregate spending in the economy and aggregate income. To get us started, suppose that the price level in the

aggregate expenditure line a relationship tracing, for a given price level, spending at each level of income, or real GDP; the total of $C + I + G + (X + IM)$ at each level of income, or real GDP

EXHIBIT 7
Deriving the Real GDP Demanded for a Given Price Level

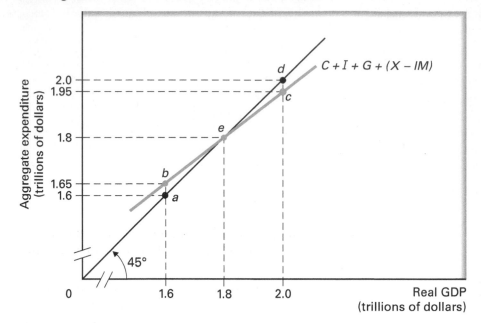

given price level of 110, the quantity of real GDP demanded equals $1.8 trillion.

What if Spending Exceeds Real GDP?

To find the real GDP demanded at the given price level, consider what happens if real GDP is initially less than $1.8 trillion. As you can see from Exhibit 7, when real GDP is less than $1.8 trillion, the aggregate expenditure line is above the 45-degree line, indicating that spending exceeds the amount produced (give this a little thought). For example, if real GDP is $1.6 trillion, spending is $1.65 trillion, as indicated by point *b* on the aggregate expenditure line, so spending exceeds output by $50 billion. When the amount people want to spend exceeds the amount produced, something has to give. Ordinarily what gives is the price, but remember that we are seeking the real GDP demanded for a given price level, so the price level is assumed to remain constant, at least for now. What gives in this model are *inventories*. Unplanned reductions in inventories cover the $50 billion shortfall in output. Because firms can't draw down inventories indefinitely, *inventory reductions* prompt firms to produce more output. That increases employment and consumer income, leading to more spending. As long as spending exceeds output, firms increase production to make up the difference. This process of more output, more income, and more spending continues until spending equals real GDP, an equality achieved at point *e* in Exhibit 7.

When output reaches $1.8 trillion, spending exactly matches output, so no unintended inventory adjustments occur. More importantly, when output reaches $1.8 trillion, the amount people want to spend equals the amount produced and equals the total income generated by that production. Earlier we assumed a price level of 110. Therefore, $1.8 trillion is the real GDP demanded at that price level.

What if Real GDP Exceeds Spending?

To reinforce the logic of the model, consider what happens when the amount produced exceeds the amount people want to spend. Notice in Exhibit 7 that, to the

income-expenditure model a relationship that shows how much people plan to spend at each income level; this model identifies, for a given price level, where the amount people plan to spend equals the amount produced in the economy

economy is 110, or 10 percent higher than in the base-year price level. We want to find out how much is spent at various levels of real income, or real GDP. By *real* GDP, we mean GDP measured in terms of real goods and services produced. Exhibit 7 combines the relationships introduced earlier in this chapter—consumption, saving, investment, government purchases, net taxes, and net exports.

Real GDP, measured along the horizontal axis in Exhibit 7, can be viewed in two ways—as the value of *aggregate output* and as the *aggregate income* generated by that output. Because real GDP or aggregate income is measured on the horizontal axis, and aggregate expenditure is measured on the vertical axis, this graph is often called the **income-expenditure model**. To gain perspective on the relationship between income and expenditure, we use a handy analytical tool: the 45-degree ray from the origin. The special feature of this line is that any point along it is the same distance from each axis. Thus the 45-degree line identifies all points where spending equals real GDP. *Aggregate output demanded at a given price level occurs where aggregate expenditure, measured along the vertical axis, equals real GDP, measured along the horizontal axis.* In Exhibit 7, this occurs at point *e*, where the aggregate expenditure line intersects the 45-degree line. At point *e*, the amount people spend equals the amount produced. We conclude that, at the

REAL GDP CAN BE THOUGHT OF AS BOTH THE VALUE OF PRODUCTION AND THE INCOME ARISING FROM THAT PRODUCTION.

right of point *e*, spending falls short of production. For example, suppose real GDP is $2 trillion. Spending, as indicated by point *c* on the aggregate expenditure line, is $50 billion less than real GDP, indicated by point *d* on the 45-degree line. Because real GDP exceeds spending, unsold goods accumulate. This swells inventories by $50 billion more than firms planned on. Rather than allow inventories to pile up indefinitely, firms cut production, which reduces employment and income. *Unplanned inventory buildups* cause firms to cut production until the amount they produce equals aggregate spending, which occurs, again, where real GDP is $1.8 trillion. Given the price level, real GDP demanded is found where the amount people spend equals the amount produced. *For a given price level, there is only one point along the aggregate expenditure line at which spending equals real GDP.*

We have now discussed the forces that determine real GDP demanded for a given price level. In the next section, we examine changes that can alter spending plans.

LO 4 The Simple Spending Multiplier

We just used the aggregate expenditure line to find real GDP demanded for a particular price level. In this section, we continue to assume that the price level stays the same as we trace the effects of other changes that could affect spending plans. Like a stone thrown into a still pond, the effects of any change in spending ripple through the economy, generating changes in aggregate output that exceed the initial change in spending.

An Increase in Spending

We begin at point *e* in Exhibit 8, where spending equals real GDP at $1.8 trillion. Now let's consider the effect of an increase in one of the components of spending.

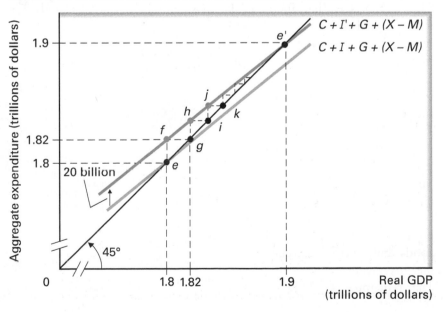

Suppose that firms become more optimistic about profit prospects and decide to increase their investment from $100 billion to $120 billion per year at each level of real GDP. Exhibit 8 reflects this change by an upward shift of the aggregate expenditure line by $20 billion, from C + I + G + (X − M) to C + I' + G + (X − M).

What happens to real GDP demanded? An instinctive response is to say that real GDP demanded increases by $20 billion as well. In this case, however, instinct is a poor guide. As you can see, the new spending line intersects the 45-degree line at point *e'*, where real GDP demanded is $1.9 trillion. How can

EXHIBIT 8
Effect of an Increase in Investment on Real GDP Demanded

a $20 billion increase in spending increase real GDP demanded by $100 billion? What's going on?

The idea of the circular flow is central to an understanding of the adjustment process. As noted earlier, real GDP can be thought of as both the value of production and the income arising from that production. Recall that production yields income, which generates spending. We can think of each trip around the circular flow as a "round" of income and spending.

Round One An upward shift of the aggregate expenditure line means that, at the initial real GDP of $1.8 trillion, spending now exceeds output by $20 billion. This is shown in Exhibit 8 as the distance between points *e* and point *f*. Initially, firms match this increased investment spending by an unplanned reduction in inventories. John Deere, for example, satisfies the increased demand for tractors by drawing down tractor inventories. But reduced inventories prompt firms to expand production by $20 billion, as shown by the movement from point *f* to point *g*. This generates $20 billion more income. The movement from point *e* to point *g* shows the first round in the multiplier process. The income-generating process does not stop there, however, because those who earn this additional income spend some of it and save the rest, leading to round two of spending and income.

Round Two Given a marginal propensity to consume of 0.8, those who earn the additional $20 billion spend $16 billion on toasters, backpacks, gasoline, restaurant meals, and thousands of other goods and services. They save the other $4 billion. The move from point *g* to point *h* in Exhibit 8 shows this $16 billion spending increase. Firms respond by increasing their output by $16 billion, shown by the movement from point *h* to point *i*. Thus the $20 billion in new income increases real GDP by $16 billion during round two.

Round Three and Beyond We know that four-fifths of the $16 billion earned during round two gets spent during round three and one-fifth gets saved. Thus $12.8 billion is spent during round three on still more goods and services, as reflected by the movement from point *i* to point *j*. The remaining $3.2 billion gets saved. The added spending causes firms to increase output by $12.8 billion, as shown by the movement from point *j* to point *k*. Round three's additional production generated $12.8 billion more income, which sets up subsequent rounds of spending, output, and income. *As long as spending exceeds output, production increases, thereby creating more income, which generates still more spending.*

Exhibit 9 summarizes the multiplier process, showing the first three rounds, round 10, and the cumulative effect of all rounds. The new spending from each round is shown in the second column, and the accumulation of new spending appears in the third column. For example, the cumulative new spending as of the third round totals $48.8 billion—the sum of the first three rounds of spending ($20 billion + $16 billion + $12.8 billion). The new saving from each round appears in the fourth column, and the accumulation of new saving appears in the final column. All this develops with the price level assumed to remain unchanged.

Using the Simple Spending Multiplier

In our model, consumers spend four-fifths of the change in income each round, with each fresh round equal to the change in spending from the previous round times the marginal propensity to consume, or the MPC. This goes on round after round, leaving less and less to fuel more spending and income. At some point, the new rounds of income and spending become so small that they disappear and the process stops. The question is, by how much does total spending increase? We can get some idea of the total by working through a limited number of rounds. For example, as shown in Exhibit 9, total

EXHIBIT 9

Tracking the Rounds of Spending Following a $20-Billion Increase in Investment (billions of dollars)

Round	New Spending This Round	Cumulative New Spending	New Saving This Round	Cumulative New Saving
1	20	20	—	—
2	16	36	4	4
3	12.8	48.8	3.2	7.2
⋮	⋮	⋮	⋮	⋮
10	2.68	89.26	0.67	17.32
⋮	⋮	⋮	⋮	⋮
∞	0	100	0	20

new spending after 10 rounds sums to $89.3 billion. But calculating the exact total for all rounds would require us to work through an infinite number of rounds—an impossible task.

Fortunately, we can borrow a shortcut from mathematicians, who have shown that the sum of an infinite number of rounds, each of which is MPC times the previous round, equals $1/(1 − MPC)$ times the initial change. Translated, the cumulative spending change equals $1/(1 − MPC)$, which, in our example, was $1 ÷ 0.2$, or 5, times the initial increase in spending, which was $20 billion. In short, the increase in investment eventually boosts real GDP demanded by 5 times $20 billion, or $100 billion—and again, all this happens with the price level assumed to remain unchanged.

$$\text{Simple spending multiplier} = \frac{1}{1 − MPC}$$

The **simple spending multiplier** is the factor by which real GDP demanded changes for a given initial change in spending.

The simple spending multiplier provides a shortcut to the total change in real GDP demanded. This multiplier depends on the MPC. The larger the MPC, the larger the simple spending multiplier. That makes sense—the more people spend from each dollar of fresh income, the more total spending increases. For example, if the MPC was 0.9 instead of 0.8, the denominator of the multiplier formula would equal 1.0 minus 0.9, or 0.1, so the multiplier would be $1 ÷ 0.1$, or 10. With an MPC of 0.9, a $20-billion investment increase would boost real GDP demanded by $200 billion. On the other hand, an MPC of 0.75 would yield a denominator of 0.25 and a multiplier of 4. So a $20-billion investment increase would raise real GDP demanded by $80 billion.

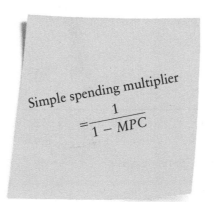

Simple spending multiplier $= \dfrac{1}{1 − MPC}$

Let's return to Exhibit 8. The $20-billion rise in autonomous investment raised real GDP demanded from $1.8 trillion to $1.9 trillion. Note that real GDP demanded would have increased by the same amount if consumers had decided to spend $20 billion more at each income level—that is, if the consumption function, rather than the investment function, had shifted up by $20 billion. Real GDP demanded likewise would have increased if government purchases or net exports increased $20 billion. *The change in aggregate output demanded depends on how much the aggregate expenditure line shifts, not on which spending component causes the shift.*

In our example, investment increased by $20 billion in the year in question. *If this greater investment is not sustained the following year, real GDP demanded would fall back*. For example, if investment returns to its initial level, other things constant, real GDP demanded would return to $1.8 trillion.

simple spending multiplier the ratio of a change in real GDP demanded to the initial change in spending that brought it about; the numerical value of the simple spending multiplier is $1/(1 − MPC)$; called "simple" because only consumption varies with income

LO 5 The Aggregate Demand Curve

In this chapter, we have used the aggregate expenditure line to find real GDP demanded *for a given price level*. But what happens if the price level changes? As you will see, for each price level, there is a unique aggregate expenditure line, which yields a unique real GDP demanded. By altering the price level, we find a different real GDP demanded. By pairing a price level with the real GDP demanded at that price level, we can derive the aggregate demand curve.

A Higher Price Level

What is the effect of a higher price level on spending and, in turn, on real GDP demanded? Recall that consumers hold many assets that are fixed in dollar terms, such as currency and bank accounts. A higher price level decreases the real value of these money holdings. This cuts consumer wealth, making people less willing to spend at each income level. For reasons that will be explained in a later chapter, a higher price level also tends to increase the market interest rate, and a higher interest rate reduces investment. Finally, a higher Canadian price level, other things constant, means that foreign goods become relatively cheaper for Canadian consumers, and Canadian goods become more expensive abroad. So imports rise and exports fall, decreasing net exports. Therefore, *a higher price level reduces consumption, investment, and net exports, which all reduce aggregate spending.* This decrease in spending reduces real GDP demanded.

THE AGGREGATE EXPENDITURE LINE AND THE AGGREGATE DEMAND CURVE PRESENT REAL OUTPUT FROM DIFFERENT PERSPECTIVES.

Exhibit 10 represents two different ways of expressing the effects of a change in the price level on real GDP demanded. Panel (a) offers the income-expenditure model, and panel (b) offers the aggregate demand curve, showing the inverse relationship between the price level and real GDP demanded. The idea is to find the real GDP demanded for a given price level in panel (a), and then show that price-quantity combination as a point on the aggregate demand curve in panel (b). The two panels measure real GDP on the horizontal axes. At the initial price level of 110 in panel (a), the aggregate expenditure line, now denoted simply as *AE*, intersects the 45-degree line at point *e* to yield real GDP demanded of $1.8 trillion. Panel (b) shows more directly the link between real GDP demanded and the price level. As you can see, when the price level is 110, real GDP demanded is $1.8 trillion. This combination is identified by point *e* on the aggregate demand curve.

What if the price level increases from 110 to, say, 120? As you've just learned, an increase in the price level reduces consumption, investment, and net exports. This reduction in spending is reflected in panel (a) by a downward shift of the aggregate expenditure line from *AE* to *AE'*. As a result, real GDP demanded declines from $1.8 trillion to $1.7 trillion. Panel (b) shows that an increase in the price level from 110 to 120 decreases real GDP demanded from $1.8 trillion to $1.7 trillion, as reflected by the movement from point *e* to point *e'*.

A Lower Price Level

The opposite occurs if the price level falls. At a lower price level, the value of bank accounts, currency, and other money holdings increases. Consumers on average are wealthier and thus spend more at each income level. A lower price level also tends to decrease

EXHIBIT 10
Changing the Price Level to Find the Aggregate Demand Curve

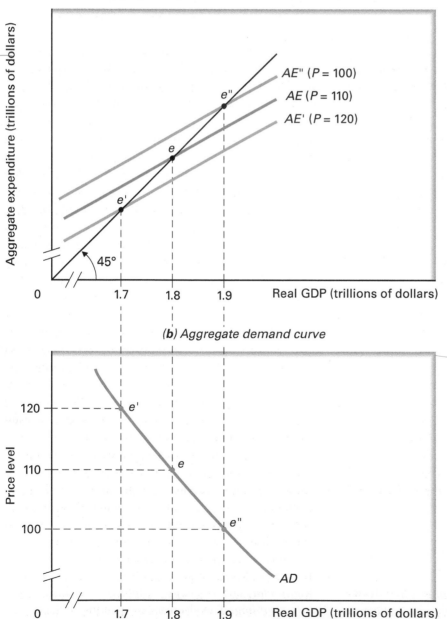

(a) Aggregate expenditure lines for different price levels

(b) Aggregate demand curve

PART 2: FUNDAMENTALS OF MACROECONOMICS

NEL

© WU KAIXIANG/Xinhua/Landov

the market interest rate, which increases investment. Finally, a lower Canadian price level, other things constant, makes Canadian products cheaper abroad and foreign products relatively more expensive here, so exports increase and imports decrease. *Because of a decline in the price level, consumption, investment, and net exports increase at each income level.*

Refer again to Exhibit 10 and suppose the price level declines from 110 to, say, 100. This increases spending at each income level, as reflected by an upward shift of the spending line from *AE* to *AE″* in panel (a). An increase in spending increases real GDP demanded from $1.8 trillion to $1.9 trillion, as indicated by the intersection of the top aggregate expenditure line with the 45-degree line at point *e″*. This same price decrease can be viewed more directly in panel (b). As you can see, when the price level decreases to 100, real GDP demanded increases to $1.9 trillion.

The aggregate expenditure line and the aggregate demand curve present real output from different perspectives. The aggregate expenditure line shows, for a given price level, how spending relates to income, or the amount produced in the economy. Real GDP demanded is found where spending equals income, or the amount produced. The aggregate demand curve shows, for various price levels, the quantities of real GDP demanded.

The Multiplier and Shifts of Aggregate Demand

Now that you have some idea how changes in the price level shift the aggregate expenditure line to generate

the aggregate demand curve, let's reverse course and return to the situation where the price level is assumed to remain constant. What we want to do now is trace through the effects of a shift of a spending component on aggregate demand, assuming the price level does not change. For example, suppose that a jump in business confidence spurs a $20 billion increase in investment at each real GDP level. Each panel of Exhibit 11 shows a different way of expressing the effects of an increase in spending on real GDP demanded, assuming the price level remains unchanged. Panel (a) presents the income-expenditure model and panel (b), the aggregate demand model. Again, the two panels measure real GDP on the horizontal axes. At a price level of 110 in panel (a), the aggregate expenditure line, $C + I + G + (X - M)$, intersects the 45-degree line at point *e* to yield $1.8 trillion in real GDP demanded. Panel (b) shows more directly the link between real GDP demanded and the price level. As you can see, when the price level is 110, real GDP demanded is $1.8 trillion, identified as point *e* on the aggregate demand curve.

Exhibit 11 shows how a shift of the aggregate expenditure line relates to a shift of the aggregate demand curve, given a constant price level. In panel (a), a $20 billion increase in investment shifts the aggregate expenditure line up by $20 billion. Because of the multiplier effect, real GDP demanded climbs from $1.8 trillion to $1.9 trillion. Panel (b) shows the effect of the increase in spending on the aggregate demand curve, which shifts to the right, from *AD* to *AD′*. At the prevailing price level of 110, real GDP demanded increases from $1.8 trillion to $1.9 trillion as a result of the $20 billion increase in investment.

Our discussion of the simple spending multiplier exaggerates the actual effect we might expect. For one thing, we have assumed that the price level remains constant. As we shall see in the next chapter, incorporating aggregate supply into the analysis reduces the multiplier because of the resulting price change. Moreover, as income increases, there are leakages from the circular flow in addition to saving, such as higher income taxes and additional imports; these leakages reduce the multiplier. Finally, although we

EXHIBIT 11

A Shift of the Aggregate Expenditure Line That Shifts the Aggregate Demand Curve

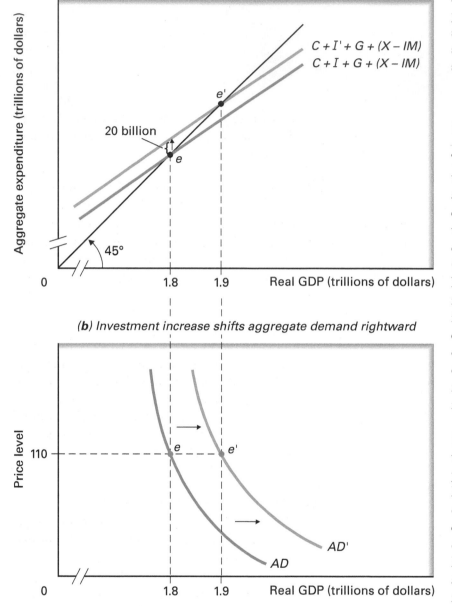

(a) Investment increase shifts up the aggregate expenditure line

(b) Investment increase shifts aggregate demand rightward

expenditure line, changing real GDP demanded. Changes in the price level and consequent changes in real GDP demanded generate points along an aggregate demand curve. But at a given price level, changes in spending plans, such as changes in investment, consumption, or government purchases, shift the aggregate demand curve.

Final Word

This chapter has focused, first, on the relationship between spending and income. We considered the four components of aggregate expenditure: consumption, investment, government purchases, and net exports. Consumption increases with income. Investment relates more to interest rates and business expectations than it does to income. Government purchases also tend to be autonomous, or independent of income. And net exports are assumed to be affected more by such factors as the exchange rate than by Canadian income.

Three ideas central to this topic are (1) certain forces determine the quantity of real GDP demanded at a given price level, (2) changes in the price level change the quantity of real GDP demanded and these price-quantity combinations generate the aggregate demand curve, and (3) at a given price level, changes in spending plans shift the aggregate demand curve. The simple multiplier provides a crude but exaggerated idea of how a change in spending plans affects real GDP demanded.

have presented the process in a timeless framework, the spending multiplier takes time to work through rounds—perhaps a year or more.

To Review: For a given price level, the aggregate expenditure line relates spending plans to income, or real GDP. Real GDP demanded is found where the amount people plan to spend equals the amount produced. A change in the price level shifts the aggregate

The chapter also focused on aggregate spending. A simplifying assumption used throughout was that imports do not vary with income. Appendix A on the text's website adds more realism by considering what happens when imports increase with income. Because spending on imports leak from the circular flow, this more realistic approach reduces the spending multiplier.

So far, we have derived real GDP demanded using intuition, examples, and graphs. With the various approaches, we find that for each price level there is a specific quantity of real GDP demanded, other things constant. Appendix B, also on the text's website, uses algebra to show the same results.

CHAPTER PROBLEMS

LO1 Explain the role of consumption

1.1. *(Consumption)* Use the following data to answer the questions below.

Real Disposable Income (billions)	Consumption Expenditures (billions)	Saving (billions)
$100	$150	$____
200	200	____
300	250	____
400	300	____

a. Graph the consumption function, with consumption spending on the vertical axis and disposable income on the horizontal axis.
b. If the consumption function is a straight line, what is its slope?
c. Fill in the saving column at each level of income. If the saving function is a straight line, what is its slope?

LO2 Analyze the effects of investment, government purchases, and net exports

2.1. *(Investment)* Why would the following investment expenditures increase as the interest rate declines?
a. Purchases of a new plant and equipment
b. Construction of new housing
c. Increase of inventories

2.2. *(Government Spending)* How do changes in disposable income affect government purchases and the government purchase function? How do changes in net taxes affect the consumption function?

LO3 Explain how total spending in the economy changes with income

3.1. *(Aggregate Expenditure)* What are the components of aggregate expenditure? Which components vary with changes in the level of real GDP? What determines the slope of the aggregate expenditure line?

LO4 Discuss how the simple spending multiplier accounts for changes in spending plans

4.1. *(Simple Spending Multiplier)* For each of the following values for the MPC, determine the size of the simple spending multiplier and the total change in real GDP demanded following a $10-billion decrease in spending:
a. MPC = 0.9
b. MPC = 0.75
c. MPC = 0.6

4.2. *(Simple Spending Multiplier)* Suppose that the MPC = 0.8 and that $2 trillion of real GDP is currently being demanded. The government wants to increase real GDP demanded to $2.4 trillion at the given price level. By how much would it have to increase government spending to achieve this goal?

LO5 Describe the aggregate demand curve

5.1. *(Shifts in Aggregate Demand)* Assume the simple spending multiplier equals 10. Determine the size and direction of any changes in the aggregate expenditure line, real GDP demanded, and the aggregate demand curve for each of the following changes in spending:
a. Spending rises by $8 billion at each income level.
b. Spending falls by $5 billion at each income level.
c. Spending rises by $20 billion at each income level.

CASE STUDY

Economic Effects of Terrorism

Economists analyze the impact of various shocks to aggregate demand and supply. Terrorist attacks are sometimes used as an example of just such a shock. But is there really an impact on the economy? And how long would such an impact last? The largest terror attack in North America happened on September 11, 2001, when two airplanes slammed into the World Trade Center in New York City. Fears about flying, coupled with the airport delays from added security, reduced the demand for air travel. For short flights, it became quicker and easier to drive than to fly. Two weeks after the attacks, airlines were operating only 75 percent of their flights, and these flights were only 30 percent full instead of the usual 75 percent full. Airlines requested federal support, saying they would go bankrupt otherwise. The U.S. Congress quickly approved a $15-billion aid package of loans and grants.

Despite the promise of federal aid, American airlines laid off 85,000 workers, or about 20 percent of their workforce. Flight reductions meant that as many as 900 aircraft would be parked indefinitely, so investment in new planes collapsed. Boeing, the major supplier of new planes and America's leading exporter, announced layoffs of 30,000 workers. This triggered layoffs among suppliers of aircraft parts, such as jet engines and electronic components. For example, Rockwell Collins, an electronics supplier, said 15 percent of its workforce would lose jobs. Other suppliers in the airline service chain also cut jobs. Sky Chef, a major airline caterer, laid off 4,800 of its 16,000 employees.

Airports began rethinking their investment plans. Half the major U.S. airports said they were reevaluating capital improvement plans to see if these investments made sense in this new environment. Honolulu airport, for example, suspended plans to add extra gates and renovate its overseas terminals.

Within three weeks after the attacks, job cuts announced in the industry exceeded 150,000. These were part of only the first round of reduced consumption and investment. In an expanding economy, job losses in one sector can be made up by job expansions in other sectors. But the U.S. economy was already in a recession at the time of the attack, having lost about a million jobs between March 2001 and September 2001. People who lost jobs or who feared for their jobs reduced their demand for housing, clothing, entertainment, restaurant meals, and other goods and services. The terrorist attacks also shook consumer confidence. Within 10 days following the attacks, the number of people filing for unemployment benefits jumped to a nine-year high. Again, these early job losses could be viewed as just part of the first round of reduced aggregate expenditure. The second round would occur when people who lost jobs or who feared they would lose their jobs started spending less. The U.S. economy continued to shed jobs for nearly two years after the attacks, losing about 2 million more jobs. Researchers estimate that business interruptions resulting from the attacks cost the U.S. economy a little over $100 billion, or about 1 percent of GDP.

The attacks also had an impact on cross-border trade between Canada and the United States. Tighter security measures led to longer wait times at the border and, thus, higher costs. Exports to the United States fell by more than imports to Canada, which is what one would expect as goods and people entering the United States were subjected to more scrutiny than prior to the attacks. The impact on trade lasted at least until 2004, with some minor impacts still felt as late as 2008. This reduction in trade has an impact both on Canadians (lower profits for Canadian companies, and possibly job losses in some industries) and on Americans (higher prices for goods produced with parts imported from Canada).

Early studies of terrorism and the economy found, not surprisingly, that decreases in consumption, investment, and net exports result from terrorist attacks. Israel, as a long-time target for terror attacks, has been the focus of many, but not all, such studies. Using monthly data from Israel from 1985 to 2003, one group of reserachers found that terror attacks cause significant and lasting negative shifts to aggregate supply as well as aggregate demand.

Sources: Adam Z. Rose et al., "The Economic Impacts of the September 11 Terrorist Attacks: A Computable General Equilibrium Analysis," *Peace Economics, Peace Science and Public Policy*, 15 (Issue 2, 2009), Berkeley Electronic Press at http://www.bepress.com/peps/vol15/iss2/; Will Pinkston, "Airports Reconsider Expansion Plans as Future of Air Travel Gets Murkier," *Wall Street Journal*, 27 September 2001; Luke Timmerman, "Boeing Warns Bad May Get Worse," *Seattle Times*, 21 September 2001; U.S. Department of Labor at http://www.bls.gov/ and the Federal Aviation Administration at http://www.faa.gov/; Steven Globerman et al., "The Effects of 9/11 on Canadian-U.S. Trade: An Update through 2008," *Metropolitan Policy Program, Brookings Institution*, July 2009; Denis Larocque et al., "Macroeconomic Effects of Terrorist Shocks in Israel," CIRPEE Working Paper, September 2008.

QUESTION

1. How do events such as the World Trade Center and Pentagon attacks described in the case study "Economic Effects of Terrorism" affect the aggregate expenditure line and the aggregate demand curve? Explain fully.

10

Aggregate Supply

LEARNING OUTCOMES

LO1 Explain how aggregate supply operates in the short run

LO2 Discuss short-run aggregate supply in relation to the long run

LO3 Analyze shifts of the aggregate supply curve

> ## If the economy is already operating at full employment, how can it produce more?

What is your normal capacity for academic work, and when do you exceed that effort? If the economy is already operating at full employment, how can it produce more? What valuable piece of information do employers and workers lack when they negotiate wages? Why do employers and workers fail to agree on pay cuts that could save jobs? How might a long stretch of high unemployment reduce the economy's ability to produce in the future? These and other questions are answered in this chapter, which develops the aggregate supply curve in the short run and in the long run.

Up to this point, we have focused on aggregate demand. We have not yet examined aggregate supply in any detail, a much debated topic. The debate involves the shape of the aggregate supply curve and the reasons for that shape. This chapter develops a single, coherent approach to aggregate supply. Although the focus continues to be on economic aggregates, you should keep in mind that aggregate supply reflects billions of production decisions made by millions of individual resource suppliers and firms in the economy. Each firm operates in its own little world, dealing with its own suppliers and customers, and keeping a watchful eye on existing and potential competitors. Yet each firm recognizes that success also depends on the performance of the economy as a whole. The theory of aggregate supply described here must be consistent with both the microeconomic behaviour of individual suppliers and the macroeconomic behaviour of the economy.

LO1 Aggregate Supply in the Short Run

Aggregate supply is the relationship between the economy's price level and the amount of output firms are willing and able to supply, with other things constant. Assumed constant along a given aggregate supply curve are resource prices, the state of technology, and the set of formal and informal institutions that structure production incentives, such as the system of property rights, patent laws, tax systems, respect for laws, and the customs and conventions of the marketplace. The greater the supply of resources, the better the technology, and the more effective the production incentives provided by the economic institutions, the greater the aggregate supply. Let's begin with the key resource—labour.

Labour and Aggregate Supply

Labour is the most important resource, accounting for about 60 percent of production cost. The supply of labour in an economy depends on the size and abilities of the adult population and their preferences for work versus leisure. Along a given labour supply curve—that is, for a given adult population with given abilities and preferences for work

nominal wage the wage measured in dollars of the year in question; the dollar amount on a paycheque

real wage the wage measured in dollars of constant purchasing power; the wage measured in terms of the quantity of goods and services it buys

potential output the economy's maximum sustainable output, given the supply of resources, technology, and rules of the game; the output level when there are no surprises about the price level

and leisure—the quantity of labour supplied depends on the wage. The higher the wage, other things constant, the more labour supplied.

So far, so good. But things start getting complicated once we recognize that the purchasing power of any given nominal wage depends on the economy's price level. *The higher the price level, the less any given money wage purchases, so the less attractive that wage is to workers.* Consider wages and the price level over time. Suppose a worker in 1970 was offered a job paying $20,000 per year. That salary may not impress you today, but its real purchasing power back then would exceed $80,000 in today's dollars. Because the price level matters, we must distinguish between the **nominal wage**, or money wage, which measures the wage in dollars of the year in question (such as 1970), and the **real wage**, which measures the wage in constant dollars—that is, dollars measured by the goods and services they buy. A higher real wage means workers can buy more goods and services.

Both workers and employers care more about the real wage than about the nominal wage. The problem is that nobody knows for sure how the price level will change during the life of the wage agreement, so labour contracts must be negotiated in terms of nominal wages, not real wages. Some resource prices, such as wages set by long-term contracts, remain in force for extended periods, often for two or

© Brand X Pictures/Jupiterimages/Getty Images

Preferences for work and leisure influence the labour supply curve.

three years. Workers as well as other resource suppliers must therefore negotiate based on the *expected* price level.

Even where there are no explicit labour contracts, there is often an implicit agreement that the wage, once negotiated, will not change for a while. For example, in many firms the standard practice is to revise wages annually. So wage agreements may be either *explicit* (based on a labour contract) or *implicit* (based on labour market practices). These explicit and implicit agreements are difficult to renegotiate while still in effect, even if the price level in the economy turns out to be higher or lower than expected.

Potential Output and the Natural Rate of Unemployment

Here's how resource owners and firms negotiate resource price agreements for a particular period, say, a year. Firms and resource suppliers expect a certain price level to prevail in the economy during the year. You could think of this as the *consensus* view for the upcoming year. Based on consensus expectations, firms and resource suppliers reach agreements on resource prices, such as wages. For example, firms and workers may expect the price level to increase 3 percent next year, so they agree on a nominal wage increase of 4 percent, which would increase the real wage by 1 percent. If these price-level expectations are realized, the agreed-on nominal wage translates into the expected real wage, so everyone is satisfied with the way things work out—after all, that's what they willingly negotiated. When the actual price level turns out as expected, we call the result the economy's potential output. *Potential output is the amount produced when there are no surprises about the price level.* So, at the agreed-on real wage, workers are supplying the quantity of labour they want and firms are hiring the quantity of labour they want. Both sides are content with the outcome.

We can think of **potential output** as the economy's maximum sustainable output, given the supply of resources, the state of technology, and the formal and informal production incentives offered by the rules of the game. Potential output is also referred to by other terms, including the *natural rate of output* and the *full-employment rate of output.*

The unemployment rate that occurs when the economy produces its potential GDP is called the

natural rate of unemployment. That rate prevails when cyclical unemployment is zero. When the economy produces its potential output, the number of job openings equals the number of people unemployed for frictional, structural, and seasonal reasons. Widely accepted estimates of the natural rate of unemployment range from about 6 percent to about 8 percent of the labour force.

Potential output provides a reference point, an anchor, for the analysis in this chapter. *When the price-level expectations of both workers and firms are fulfilled, the economy produces its potential output.* Complications arise, however, when the actual price level differs from expectations, as we'll see next.

Actual Price Level Is Higher Than Expected

As you know, each firm's goal is to maximize profit. Profit equals total revenue minus total cost. Suppose workers and firms reach a wage agreement. What if the economy's price level turns out to be higher than expected? What happens *in the short run* to real GDP supplied? The **short run** in macroeconomics is a period during which some resource prices remain fixed by explicit or implicit agreements. Does output in the short run exceed the economy's potential, fall short of that potential, or equal that potential?

Because the prices of many resources are fixed for the duration of contracts, firms welcome a higher than expected price level. After all, the selling prices of their products, on average, are higher than expected, while the costs of at least some of the resources they employ remain constant. *A price level that is higher than expected results in a higher profit per unit, so firms have a profit incentive in the short run to increase production beyond the economy's potential level.*

At first it might appear odd to talk about producing beyond the economy's potential, but remember that potential output means not zero unemployment but the natural rate of unemployment. Even in an economy producing its potential output, there is some unemployed labour and some unused production capacity. If you think of potential GDP as the economy's *normal capacity*, you get a better idea of how production can temporarily exceed that capacity. For example, during World War II, Canada pulled out all the stops to contribute to the war effort. Factories operated around the clock. Overtime was common. The unemployment rate dropped below 2 percent—well under its natural rate. People worked longer and harder for the war effort than they normally would have.

Think about your own study habits. During most of the term, you display your normal capacity for academic work. As the end of the term draws near, however, you may shift into high gear, finishing term papers, studying late into the night for final exams, and generally running yourself ragged trying to pull things together. During those final frenzied days of the term, you study beyond your normal capacity, beyond the schedule you follow on a regular or sustained basis. We often observe workers exceeding their normal capacity for short bursts: fireworks technicians around Canada Day, accountants during tax time, farmers during harvest time, and elected officials toward the end of a campaign or legislative session. Similarly, firms and their workers are able, *in the short run*, to push output beyond the economy's potential. But that higher rate of output is not normal and not sustainable.

natural rate of unemployment the unemployment rate when the economy produces its potential output

short run in macroeconomics, a period during which some resource prices, especially those for labour, are fixed by explicit or implicit agreements

Why Costs Rise When Output Exceeds Potential

The economy is flexible enough to expand output beyond potential GDP, but as output expands, the cost of additional output increases. Although many workers are bound by contracts, wage agreements may require overtime pay for extra hours or weekends. As the economy expands and the unemployment rate declines, additional workers are harder to find. Retirees, homemakers, and students may require extra pay to draw them into the labour force. If few additional workers are available or if workers require additional pay for overtime, the nominal cost of labour increases as output expands in the short run, even though most wages remain fixed by implicit or explicit agreements.

As production increases, the demand for non-labour resources increases as well, so the prices of those resources in markets where prices are flexible—such as the market for oil—will increase, reflecting their greater scarcity. Also, as production increases, firms use their machines and trucks more intensively, so equipment wears out faster and is more prone to breakdowns. Thus the nominal cost per unit of output rises when production is pushed beyond the economy's potential output. But *because some resource prices are fixed by contracts, the economy's price level rises faster than the per-unit production cost, so firms still find it profitable to increase the quantity supplied.*

When the economy's actual price level exceeds the expected price level, the real value of an agreed-on nominal wage declines. We might ask why workers would be willing to increase the quantity of labour they supply when the price level is higher than expected. One answer is that labour agreements require workers to do so, at least until workers have a chance to renegotiate.

In summary: If the price level is higher than expected, firms have a profit incentive to increase the quantity of goods and services supplied. At higher rates of output, however, the per-unit cost of additional output increases. Firms expand output as long as the revenue from additional production exceeds the cost of that production.

An Actual Price Level Lower Than Expected

We have learned that if the price level is greater than expected, firms expand output in the short run, but

as they do, the marginal cost of production increases. Now let's look at the effects of a price level that turns out to be lower than expected. Again, suppose that firms and resource suppliers have reached an agreement based on an expected price level. If the price level turns out to be lower than expected, firms find production less profitable. The prices firms receive for their output are on average lower than they expected, yet many of their production costs, such as nominal wages, do not fall.

Because production is less profitable when prices are lower than expected, firms reduce their quantity supplied, so the economy's output is below its potential. As a result, some workers are laid off, some work fewer hours, and unemployment exceeds the natural rate. Not only is less labour employed, but machines go unused, delivery trucks sit idle, and entire plants may shut down—for example, automakers sometimes halt production for weeks.

Just as some costs increase in the short run when output is pushed beyond the economy's potential, some costs decline when output falls below that potential. As resources become unemployed, resource prices decline in markets where prices are flexible.

To Review: If the economy's price level turns out to be higher than expected, firms maximize profit by increasing the quantity supplied beyond the economy's potential output. As output expands, the per-unit cost of additional production increases, but firms expand production as long as prices rise more than costs. If the economy's price level turns out to be lower than expected, firms produce less than the economy's potential output because prices fall more than costs. All of this is a long way of saying that *there is a direct relationship in the short run between the actual price level and real GDP supplied.*

The Short-Run Aggregate Supply Curve

What we have been describing so far traces out the **short-run aggregate supply (SRAS) curve**, which shows the relationship between the actual price level and real GDP supplied, other things constant. Again, the *short run* in this context is the period during which some resource prices, especially those for labour, are fixed by implicit or explicit agreements. For simplicity, we can think of the short run as the duration of labour contracts, which are based on the expected price level.

Suppose the expected price level is 110. The short-run aggregate supply curve in Exhibit 1, $SRAS_{110}$, is based on that expected price level (hence the subscript 110). If the price level turns out as expected, producers supply the economy's *potential output*, which in Exhibit 1 is $1.8 trillion. Although not shown in the exhibit, the aggregate demand curve would intersect the aggregate supply curve at point *a*. If the economy produces its potential output, unemployment is at the *natural rate*. Nobody is surprised, and all are content with the outcome. There is no tendency to move away from point *a* even if workers and firms could renegotiate wages.

In Exhibit 1, output levels that fall short of the economy's potential are shaded red, and output levels that exceed the economy's potential are shaded blue. The slope of the short-run aggregate supply curve depends on how sharply the marginal cost of production rises as real GDP expands. If costs increase modestly as output expands, the supply curve is relatively flat. If these costs increase sharply as output expands, the supply curve is relatively steep. Much of the controversy about the short-run aggregate supply curve involves its shape. Shapes range from flat to steep. Notice that the short-run aggregate supply curve becomes steeper as output increases, because some resources become scarcer and thus more costly as output increases.

short-run aggregate supply (SRAS) curve a curve that shows a direct relationship between the actual price level and real GDP supplied in the short run, other things constant, including the expected price level

LO 2 From the Short Run to the Long Run

This section begins with the price level exceeding expectations in the short run to see what happens in the long run. The long run is long enough that firms and resource suppliers can renegotiate all agreements based on knowledge of the actual price level. *So in the long run, there are no surprises about the price level.*

Closing an Expansionary Gap

Let's begin our look at the long-run adjustment in Exhibit 2 with an expected price level of 110. The short-run aggregate supply curve for that expected price level is $SRAS_{110}$. Given this short-run aggregate supply curve, the equilibrium price level and real GDP depend on the aggregate demand curve. The actual price level would equal the expected price level only if the aggregate demand curve intersects the aggregate supply curve at point *a*—that is, where the short-run quantity equals potential output. Point *a* reflects potential output of

EXHIBIT 1

Short-Run Aggregate Supply Curve

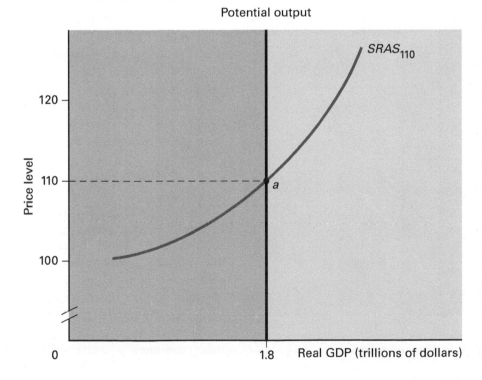

$1.8 trillion and a price level of 110, which is the expected price level.

But what if aggregate demand turns out to be greater than expected, such as *AD*, which intersects the short-run aggregate supply curve $SRAS_{110}$ at point *b*. Point *b* is the **short-run equilibrium**, reflecting a price level of 115 and a real GDP of $1.85 trillion. The actual price level in the short run is higher than expected, and output exceeds the economy's potential of $1.8 trillion.

The amount by which short-run output exceeds the economy's potential is called an **expansionary gap**. In Exhibit 2, that gap is the short-run output of $1.85 trillion minus potential output of $1.8 trillion, or $50 billion. When real GDP exceeds its potential, the unemployment rate is less than its natural rate. Employees are working overtime, machines are being pushed to their limits, and farmers are sandwiching extra crops between usual plantings. Remember

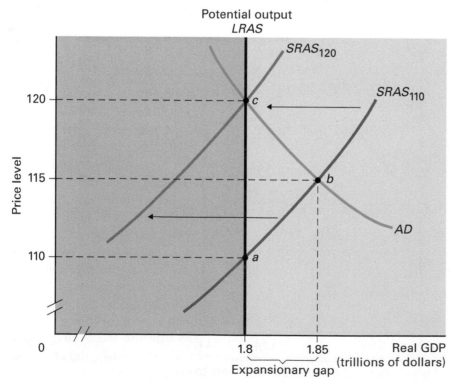

© Chris Batson/Alamy

Production exceeding the economy's potential creates inflationary pressure, which causes the short-run aggregate supply curve to shift to the left, reducing output, increasing the price level, and closing the expansionary gap.

MIND THE GAP

that the nominal wage was negotiated based on an expected price level of 110; because the actual price level is higher, that nominal wage translates into a lower-than-expected real wage. As we will see, output exceeding the economy's potential creates inflationary pressure. *The more that short-run output exceeds the economy's potential, the larger the expansionary gap and the greater the upward pressure on the price level.*

What happens in the long run? The **long run** is a period during which firms and resource suppliers know about market conditions, particularly aggregate demand and the actual price level, and have the time to renegotiate resource payments based on that knowledge. Because the higher-than-expected price level cuts the real value of the nominal wage originally agreed to, workers try to negotiate a higher nominal wage at their earliest opportunity. Workers and other resource suppliers negotiate higher nominal payments, raising production costs for firms, so the short-run aggregate supply curve shifts leftward, resulting in cost-push inflation. In the long run, the expansionary gap causes the short-run aggregate supply curve to shift leftward to $SRAS_{120}$, which results in an expected price level of 120. Notice that the short-run aggregate supply curve shifts until the equilibrium output equals the economy's potential output.

EXHIBIT 2
Long-Run Adjustment When the Price Level Exceeds Expectations

ACTUAL OUTPUT CAN EXCEED THE ECONOMY'S POTENTIAL IN THE SHORT RUN BUT NOT IN THE LONG RUN.

Actual output can exceed the economy's potential in the short run but not in the long run.

As shown in Exhibit 2, the expansionary gap is closed by long-run market forces that shift the short-run aggregate supply curve from $SRAS_{110}$ left to $SRAS_{120}$. Whereas $SRAS_{110}$ was based on resource contracts reflecting an expected price level of 110, $SRAS_{120}$ is based on resource contracts reflecting an expected price level of 120. At point *c* the expected price level and the actual price level are identical, so the economy is not only in short-run equilibrium but it's also in **long-run equilibrium**. Consider all the equalities that hold at point *c*: (1) the expected price level equals the actual price level; (2) the quantity supplied in the short run equals potential output, which also equals the quantity supplied in the long run; and (3) the quantity supplied equals the quantity demanded. Looked at another way, *long-run equilibrium occurs where the aggregate demand curve intersects the vertical line drawn at potential output.* Point *c* continues to be the equilibrium point unless there is some change in aggregate demand or in aggregate supply.

Note that the situation at point *c* is no different *in real terms* from what had been expected at point *a*. At both points, firms supply the economy's potential output of $1.8 trillion. The same amounts of labour and other resources are employed, and although the price level, the nominal wage, and other nominal resource payments are higher at point *c*, the real wage and the real return to other resources are the same as they would have been at point *a*. For example, suppose the nominal wage averaged $22 per hour when the expected price level was 110. If the expected price level increased from 110 to 120, an increase of 9.1 percent, the nominal wage would also increase by that same percentage to an average of $24 per hour, leaving the real wage unchanged. With no change in real wages between points *a* and *c*, firms demand

enough labour and workers supply enough labour to produce $1.8 trillion in real GDP.

Thus if the price level turns out to be higher than expected, the short-run response is to increase quantity supplied. But production exceeding the economy's potential creates inflationary pressure. In the long run this causes the short-run aggregate supply curve to shift to the left, reducing output, increasing the price level, and closing the expansionary gap.

If an increase in the price level is predicted accurately year after year, firms and resource suppliers would build these expectations into their long-term agreements. The price level would move up each year by the expected amount, but the economy's output would remain at potential GDP, thereby skipping the round trip beyond the economy's potential and back.

Closing a Recessionary Gap

Let's begin again with an expected price level of 110 as presented in Exhibit 3, where blue shading indicates

long-run equilibrium the price level and real GDP that occurs when (1) the actual price level equals the expected price level, (2) real GDP supplied equals potential output, and (3) real GDP supplied equals real GDP demanded

EXHIBIT 3

Long-Run Adjustment When the Price Level Is Below Expectations

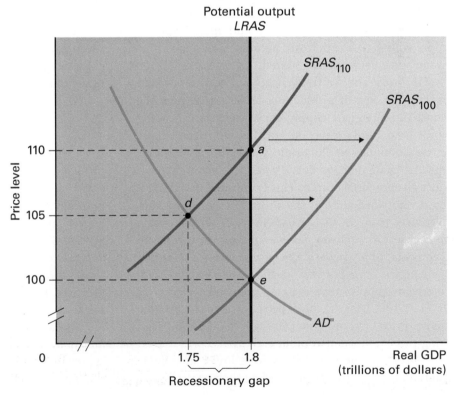

output exceeding potential and red shading indicates output below potential. If the price level turned out as expected, the resulting equilibrium combination would occur at *a*, which would be both a short-run and a long-run equilibrium. Suppose this time that the aggregate demand curve intersects the short-run aggregate supply curve to the left of potential output, yielding a price level below that expected. The intersection of the aggregate demand curve, AD', with $SRAS_{110}$ yields the short-run equilibrium at point *d*, where the price level is below expectations and production is less than the economy's potential. The amount by which actual output falls short of potential GDP is called a **recessionary gap**. In this case, the recessionary gap is $50 billion, and unemployment exceeds its natural rate.

Because the price level is less than expected, the nominal wage, which was based on the expected price level, translates into a higher real wage in the short run. What happens in the long run? With the price level lower than expected, employers are no longer willing to pay as high a nominal wage. And with the unemployment rate higher than the natural rate, more workers are competing for jobs, putting downward pressure on the nominal wage. If the price level and the nominal wage are flexible enough, the combination of a lower price level and a pool of unemployed workers competing for jobs should make workers more willing to accept lower nominal wages next time wage agreements are negotiated.

If firms and workers negotiate lower nominal wages, the cost of production decreases, shifting the short-run aggregate supply curve rightward, leading to deflation and greater output. The short-run supply curve continues to shift rightward until it intersects the aggregate demand curve where the economy produces its potential output. This is reflected in Exhibit 3 by a rightward shift of the short-run aggregate supply curve from $SRAS_{110}$ to $SRAS_{100}$. *If the price level and nominal wage are flexible enough, the short-run aggregate supply curve shifts rightward until the economy produces its potential output.* The new short-run aggregate supply curve is based on an expected price level of 100. Because the expected price level and the actual price level are now identical, the economy is in long-run equilibrium at point *e*.

Although the nominal wage is lower at point *e* than that originally agreed to when the expected price level was 110, the real wage is the same at point *e* as it was at point *a*. Because the real wage is the same, the amount of labour that workers supply is the same and real output is the same. All that has changed between points *a* and *e* are nominal measures—the price level, the nominal wage, and other nominal resource prices.

We conclude that when incorrect expectations cause firms and resource suppliers to overestimate the actual price level, output in the short run falls short of the economy's potential. As long as wages and prices are flexible enough, however, firms and workers should be able to renegotiate wage agreements based on a lower expected price level. The negotiated drop in the nominal wage shifts the short-run aggregate supply curve to the right until the economy once again produces its potential output. If wages and prices are not flexible, they will not adjust quickly to a recessionary gap, so shifts of the short-run aggregate supply curve may be slow to move the economy to its potential output. The economy can therefore get stuck at an output and employment level below its potential.

We are now in a position to provide an additional interpretation of the red- and blue-shaded areas of our exhibits. If a short-run equilibrium occurs in the blue-shaded area, that is, to the right of potential output, then market forces in the long run increase nominal resource costs, shifting the short-run aggregate supply to the left. If a short-run equilibrium occurs in the red-shaded area, then market forces in the long run reduce nominal resource costs, shifting the short-run aggregate supply curve to the right. Closing an expansionary gap involves inflation and closing a recessionary gap involves deflation.

Tracing Potential Output

If wages and prices are flexible enough, the economy produces its potential output in the long run, as indicated in Exhibit 4 by the vertical line drawn at the economy's potential GDP of $1.8 trillion. This vertical line is called the economy's **long-run aggregate supply (LRAS) curve**. *The long-run aggregate supply curve depends on the supply of resources in the economy, the level of technology, and the production incentives provided by the formal and informal institutions of the economic system.*

In Exhibit 4, the initial price level of 110 is determined by the intersection of *AD* with the long-run aggregate supply curve. If the aggregate demand curve shifts out to AD', then in the long run, the equilibrium

AN INCREASE IN AGGREGATE DEMAND USUALLY CLOSES A RECESSIONARY GAP AS THE ECONOMY PULLS OUT OF ITS FUNK.

EXHIBIT 4
EXHIBIT 4
Long-Run Aggregate Supply Curve

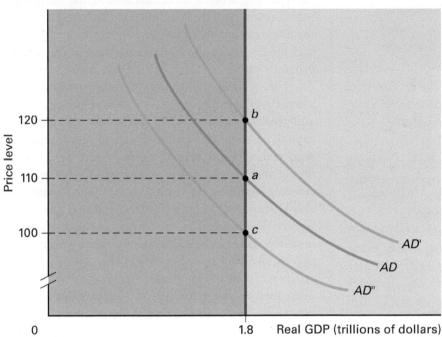

Potential output *LRAS*

varied from year to year but typically has returned to what would be viewed as a natural rate of unemployment—again, estimates range from 6 percent to 8 percent.

An *expansionary* gap creates a labour shortage that eventually results in a higher nominal wage and a higher price level. But a *recessionary* gap does not necessarily generate enough downward pressure to lower the nominal wage. Studies indicate that nominal wages are slow to adjust to high unemployment. Nominal wages do not adjust downward as quickly or as substantially as they adjust upward, and the downward response that does occur tends to be slow and modest. Consequently, we say that nominal wages tend to be "sticky" in the downward direction.[1] *Because nominal wages fall slowly, if at all, the supply-side adjustments needed to close a recessionary gap may take so long as to seem ineffective.* What, in fact, usually closes a recessionary gap is an increase in aggregate demand as the economy pulls out of its funk.

Although the nominal wage seldom falls, an actual decline in the nominal wage is not necessary to close a recessionary gap. All that's needed is a fall in the real wage. And *the real wage falls if the prices increase more than nominal wages.* For example, if the price level increases by 4 percent and the nominal wage increases by 3 percent, the real wage falls by 1 percent. If the real wage falls enough, firms demand enough additional labour to produce the economy's potential output. More generally, total compensation falls if employers cut back on employee benefits such as health insurance.

price level increases to 120 but equilibrium output remains at $1.8 trillion, the economy's potential GDP. Conversely, a decline in aggregate demand from *AD* to *AD''*, in the long run, leads only to a fall in the price level from 110 to 100, with no change in output. Note that these long-run movements are more like tendencies than smooth and timely adjustments. It may take a long time for resource prices to adjust, particularly when the economy faces a recessionary gap. But as long as wages and prices are flexible, the economy's potential GDP is consistent with any price level. *In the long run, equilibrium output equals long-run aggregate supply, which is also potential output. The equilibrium price level depends on the aggregate demand curve.*

Wage Flexibility and Employment

What evidence is there that a vertical line drawn at the economy's potential GDP depicts the long-run aggregate supply curve? Except during the Great Depression, unemployment over the past century has

[1] For evidence on sticky wages, see Alessandro Barattieri et al., "Some Evidence on the Importance of Sticky Wages," NBER Working Paper 16130 (June 2010).

Coordination Failure

When actual output falls short of potential output, the output gap is negative and the economy suffers a recessionary gap. As long as unemployment exceeds its natural rate, the economy suffers a recessionary gap.

Recessionary gaps can thus be viewed as resulting from a **coordination failure**, in which workers, who produce goods and services, and employers, who provide jobs, fail to reach an agreement that seems possible and that all would prefer. For more on coordination failure, wage flexibility, and output gaps, read the online case at www.nelson.com/econmacro1e.

coordination failure a situation in which workers and employers fail to achieve an outcome that all would prefer

supply shocks unexpected events that affect aggregate supply, sometimes only temporarily

To Review: When the actual price level differs from the expected price level, output in the short run departs from the economy's potential. In the long run, however, market forces shift the short-run aggregate supply curve until the economy once again produces its potential output. Thus surprises about the price level change real GDP in the short run but not in the long run. Shifts of the aggregate demand curve change the price level but do not affect potential output, or long-run aggregate supply.

LO 3 Shifts of the Aggregate Supply Curve

In this section, we consider factors other than changes in the expected price level that may affect aggregate supply. We begin by distinguishing between long-term trends in aggregate supply and **supply shocks**, which are unexpected events that affect aggregate supply, sometimes only temporarily.

Aggregate Supply Increases

The economy's potential output is based on the willingness and ability of households to supply resources to firms, the level of technology, and the institutional underpinnings of the economic system. Any change in these factors could affect the economy's potential output. Changes in the economy's potential output over

time were introduced in Chapter 8, which focused on Canadian productivity and growth. The supply of labour may change over time because of a change in the size, composition, or quality of the labour force or a change in preferences for labour versus leisure. For example, the Canadian labour force has more than tripled since 1946 as a result of population growth and a growing labour force participation rate, especially among women with children. At the same time, job training, education, and on-the-job experience increased the quality of labour. Increases in the quantity and the quality of the labour force have increased the economy's potential GDP, or long-run aggregate supply.

The quantity and quality of other resources also change over time. The capital stock—machines, buildings, and trucks—increases when gross investment exceeds capital depreciation. And the capital stock improves with technological breakthroughs. Even the quantity and quality of land can be increased—for example, by claiming land from the sea, as is done in the Netherlands and Hong Kong, or by revitalizing soil that has lost its fertility. These increases in the quantity and quality of resources increase the economy's potential output.

Finally, institutional changes that define property rights more clearly or make contracts more enforceable, such as the introduction of clearer patent and copyright laws, will increase the incentives to undertake productive activity, thereby increasing potential output. *Changes in the labour force, in the quantity and quality of other resources, and in the institutional arrangements of the economic system tend to occur gradually.* Exhibit 5 depicts a gradual shift of

EXHIBIT 5
Effect of a Gradual Increase in Resources on Aggregate Supply

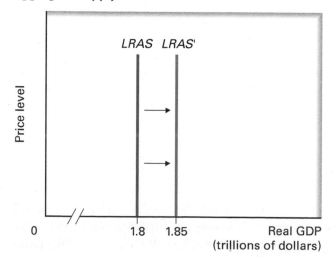

Reclaiming land from the sea increases that economy's potential output, or long-run aggregate supply.

© Mike Clarke/AFP/Getty Images

the economy's potential output from $1.8 trillion to $1.85 trillion. The long-run aggregate supply curve shifts from *LRAS* out to *LRAS'*.

In contrast to the gradual, or long-run, changes that often occur in the supply of resources, *supply shocks* are unexpected events that change aggregate supply, sometimes only temporarily. **Beneficial supply shocks** increase aggregate supply; examples are (1) abundant harvests that increase the food supply, (2) discoveries of natural resources, such as oil in Alberta or the North Sea, (3) technological breakthroughs that allow firms to combine resources more efficiently, such as faster computers or the Internet, and (4) sudden changes in the economic system that promote more production, such as tax cuts that stimulate production incentives or stricter limits on frivolous product liability suits.

Exhibit 6 shows the effect of a beneficial supply shock from a technological breakthrough. The beneficial supply shock shown here shifts the short-run and long-run aggregate supply curves rightward. Along the aggregate demand curve, *AD*, the equilibrium combination of price and output moves from point *a* to point *b*. *For a given aggregate demand curve, the happy outcome of a beneficial supply shock is an increase in output and a decrease in the price level.* The new equilibrium at point *b* is a short-run and a long-run equilibrium in the sense that there is no tendency to move from that point

as long as whatever caused the beneficial effect continues, and a technological discovery usually has a lasting effect. Likewise, substantial new oil discoveries usually benefit the economy for a long time. On the other hand, an unusually favourable growing season won't last. When a normal growing season returns, the

beneficial supply shocks unexpected events that increase aggregate supply, sometimes only temporarily

EXHIBIT 6

Effects of a Beneficial Supply Shock on Aggregate Supply

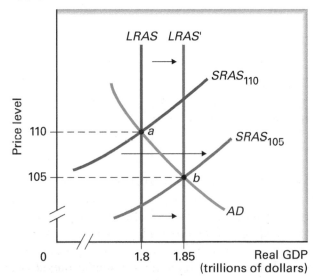
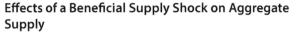

adverse supply shocks unexpected events that reduce aggregate supply, sometimes only temporarily

hysteresis the theory that the natural rate of unemployment depends in part on the recent history of unemployment; high unemployment rates increase the natural rate of unemployment

short-run and long-run aggregate supply curves return to their original equilibrium position—back to point *a* in Exhibit 6.

Decreases in Aggregate Supply

Adverse supply shocks are sudden, unexpected events that reduce aggregate supply, sometimes only temporarily. For example, a drought could reduce the supply of a variety of resources, such as food, building materials, and water-powered electricity. An overthrow of a government could destabilize the economy. Or terrorist attacks could shake the institutional underpinnings of the economy, as occurred in the United States, England, and Spain. Such attacks add to the cost of doing business—such as airline screening and building security.

An adverse supply shock is depicted as a leftward shift of both the short-run and long-run aggregate supply curves, as shown in Exhibit 7, moving the equilibrium combination from point *a* to point *c* and reducing potential output from $1.8 trillion to $1.75 trillion. As mentioned earlier, the combination of reduced output and a higher price level is often referred to as stagflation. Canada encountered stagflation during the 1970s, when the economy was rocked by a series of adverse supply shocks, such as crop failures around the globe and the oil price

hikes by OPEC in 1974 and 1979. If the effect of the adverse supply shock is temporary, such as a poor growing season, the aggregate supply curve returns to its original position once things return to normal. But some economists question an economy's ability to bounce back.

For example, for most of the 20th century unemployment in Western Europe was low, seldom even reaching as high as 4 percent. That changed when the worldwide recession of the mid-1970s caused unemployment to rise. But well after the recession, unemployment continued to climb in continental Europe, topping 10 percent during the 1990s, and 8 percent to 10 percent in 2009. Some observers claim that the natural rate of unemployment has increased in these countries.

Economists have borrowed a term from physics, **hysteresis** (pronounced *his-ter-eé-sis*), to argue that the natural rate of unemployment depends in part on the recent history of unemployment. *The longer the actual unemployment rate remains above what had been the natural rate, the more the natural rate itself increases.* No consensus exists regarding the validity of hysteresis. The theory seems to be less relevant in Canada and the United States, where unemployment fell from 10–11 percent in 1982 to 6.0 percent and 4.5 percent, respectively, in 2007. There is some speculation that the natural rate of unemployment in Canada has been slightly higher since the 2008 recession, but we will need a few more years of data before we can be certain. An alternative explanation for high unemployment in continental Europe is that legislation introduced there in the 1970s made it more difficult to lay off workers so firms grew reluctant to hire more workers.

Final Word

This chapter explains why the aggregate supply curve slopes upward in the short run and is vertical at the economy's potential output in the long run. Firms and resource suppliers negotiate contracts based on the economy's expected price level, which depends on expectations about aggregate demand. Unexpected changes in the price level can move output in the short run away from its potential level. But if firms and resource suppliers fully adjust to price surprises, the economy in the long run moves toward its potential output. Potential output is the anchor for analyzing aggregate supply in the short run and long run.

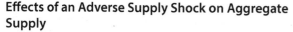

EXHIBIT 7

Effects of an Adverse Supply Shock on Aggregate Supply

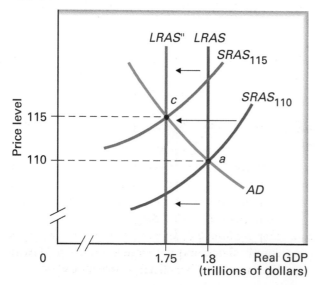

CHAPTER PROBLEMS

LO1 Explain how aggregate supply operates in the short run

1.1. *(Natural Rate of Unemployment)* What is the relationship between potential output and the natural rate of unemployment?
  a. If the economy currently has a frictional unemployment rate of 2 percent, structural unemployment of 2 percent, seasonal unemployment of 0.5 percent, and cyclical unemployment of 2 percent, what is the natural rate of unemployment? Where is the economy operating relative to its potential GDP?
  b. What happens to the natural rate of unemployment and potential GDP if cyclical unemployment rises to 3 percent with other types of unemployment unchanged from part (a)?
  c. What happens to the natural rate of unemployment and potential GDP if structural unemployment falls to 1.5 percent with other types of unemployment unchanged from part (a)?

1.2. *(Real Wages)* In Exhibit 2 in this chapter, how does the real wage rate at point c compare with the real wage rate at point a? How do nominal wage rates compare at those two points? Explain your answers.

LO2 Discuss short-run aggregate supply in relation to the long run

2.1. *(Expansionary and Recessionary Gaps)* Answer questions (a) through (f) on the basis of the following graph:
  a. If the actual price level exceeds the expected price level reflected in long-term contracts, real GDP equals _____ and the actual price level equals _____ in the short run.
  b. The situation described in part (a) results in a(n) _____ gap equal to _____.
  c. If the actual price level is lower than the expected price level reflected in long-term contracts, real GDP equals _____ and the actual price level equals _____ in the short run.

d. The situation described in part (c) results in a(n) _____ gap equal to _____.
  e. If the actual price level equals the expected price level reflected in long-term contracts, real GDP equals _____ and the actual price level equals _____ in the short run.
  f. The situation described in part (e) results in _____ gap equal to _____.

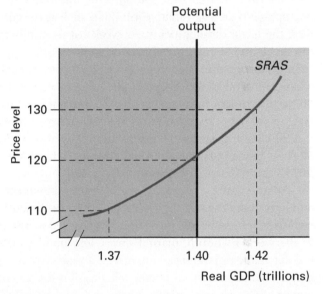

2.2. *(Long-Run Adjustment)* The ability of the economy to eliminate any imbalance between actual and potential output is sometimes called self-correction. Using an aggregate supply and aggregate demand diagram, show why this self-correction process involves only temporary periods of inflation or deflation.

LO3 Analyze shifts of the aggregate supply curve

3.1. *(Changes in Aggregate Supply)* List three factors that can change the economy's potential output. What is the impact of shifts of the aggregate demand curve on potential output? Illustrate your answers with a diagram.

3.2. *(Supply Shocks)* Give an example of an adverse supply shock and illustrate graphically. Now do the same for a beneficial supply shock.

CASE STUDY

Why Has Unemployment Been So High in Europe?

Between World War II and the mid-1970s, unemployment in Western Europe was low. From 1960 to 1974, for example, the unemployment rate in France never got as high as 4 percent. The worldwide recession of the mid-1970s, however, jacked up unemployment rates. But unemployment continued to climb in continental Europe long after the recession ended, topping 10 percent during the 1990s, and was still 8 percent to 9 percent in 2007, even before the recession (once the recession set in, rates returned to 10 percent in 2009). Some observers claim that the natural rate of unemployment has increased in these countries.

Some economists have borrowed a term from physics, hysteresis (pronounced *his-ter-eé-sis*), to argue that the natural rate of unemployment depends in part on the recent history of unemployment. *The longer the actual unemployment rate remains above what had been the natural rate, the more the natural rate itself increases.* For example, those unemployed can lose valuable job skills, such as the computer programmer who loses touch with the latest developments. As weeks of unemployment stretch into months and years, the shock and stigma may diminish, so the work ethic weakens. What's more, some European countries offer generous unemployment benefits indefinitely, reducing the hardship of unemployment. On average, unemployment benefits in Western Europe replace 60 to 80 percent of lost pay versus about 50 percent in Canada. Some Europeans have collected benefits *for more than a decade*. Unemployment benefits in Belgium have no time limit.

Still, no consensus exists regarding the validity of hysteresis. The theory has been less relevant in Canada and the United States, where unemployment fell from 10–11 percent in 1982 to 6.0 and 4.5, respectively, in 2007.

An alternative explanation for high unemployment in continental Europe is that legislation introduced there in the 1970s made it more difficult to lay off workers. In most European countries, job dismissals must be approved by worker councils, which consider such factors as the worker's health, marital status, and number of dependants. Severance pay has also become mandatory and can amount to a year's pay or more. With layoffs difficult and costly, hiring became almost an irreversible decision for an employer, so firms have become reluctant to add workers, particularly untested workers with little experience. Also, high minimum wages throughout Europe, high payroll taxes, and an expanded list of workers' rights have increased labour costs. For example, in Sweden, parents are guaranteed between them a total of 16 months' paid leave after the birth of a child, and the mother has the right to work no more than six hours a day until the child reaches elementary school. In Austria, mothers are guaranteed two years of paid leave after a birth plus job protection. Swedish workers are also guaranteed at least five weeks of vacation a year; French workers get at least six weeks.

Regardless of the explanation, the result has been high unemployment in continental Europe during normal times, particularly among young workers.

SOURCES: Francine Fontaine and Jagadeesh Sivadasan, "Do Labor Market Rigidities Have Microeconomic Effects? Evidence from within the Firm," *American Economic Journal: Applied Economics*, 1 (April 2009): 88–129; Rafael Lalive and Josef Zweimüller, "How Does Parental Leave Affect Fertility and Return to Work?" *The Quarterly Journal of Economics*, 124 (August 2009): 1363–1402; "The Trap: The Curse of Long-Term Unemployment Will Bedevil the Economy," *The Economist*, 14 January 2010; Katrin Bennhold, "In Sweden, Men Can Have It All," *New York Times*, 9 June 2010; and *OECD Economic Outlook*, 87 (May 2010).

QUESTION

1. European unemployment is a hot topic. Use any Web browser to search for the words "European unemployment." Just by scanning the headlines, see how many possible explanations you can list. How do they compare to the explanations reviewed in the chapter case study?

11

Fiscal Policy

LEARNING OUTCOMES

LO1 Explain the theory of fiscal policy

LO2 Describe how aggregate supply affects fiscal policy

LO3 Discuss the evolution of fiscal policy

LO4 Discuss the fiscal impact of the federal budget and debt

> ## "Why did fiscal policy fall on hard times for a quarter century, and what brought it back to life?"

The Harper government argued that its low tax plan implemented in 2006 benefited Canadian families. U.S. President Barack Obama claimed on February 17, 2010, that "it is largely thanks to the Recovery Act that a second depression is no longer a possibility." The Japanese government cut taxes and increased spending to stimulate its troubled economy. These are examples of **fiscal policy**, which focuses on the effects of taxing and public spending on aggregate economic activity. What is the proper role of fiscal policy in the economy? Can fiscal policy reduce swings in the business cycle? Why did fiscal policy fall on hard times for a quarter century, and what brought it back to life? Does fiscal policy affect aggregate supply? Answers to these and other questions are addressed in this chapter, which examines the theory and practice of fiscal policy.

In this chapter, we first explore the effects of fiscal policy on aggregate demand. Next we bring aggregate supply into the picture. Then we examine the role of fiscal policy in moving the economy to its potential output. Finally, we review Canada's fiscal policy and federal debt. Throughout the chapter, we use simple tax and spending models to explain fiscal policy.

A more complex treatment, along with the algebra behind it, appears in the appendix to this chapter, available on the text's website.

LO 1 Theory of Fiscal Policy

Our macroeconomic model so far has viewed government as passive. But general government expenditure at all levels in Canada totalled more than $740 billion in the last quarter of 2012, making government an important player in the economy. From highway construction to unemployment insurance to income taxes to federal deficits, fiscal policy affects the economy in myriad ways. We now move fiscal policy to centre stage. As introduced in Chapter 3, *fiscal policy* refers to government purchases, transfer payments, taxes, and borrowing as they affect macroeconomic variables such as real GDP, employment, the price level, and economic growth. When economists study fiscal policy, they usually focus on the federal government, although governments at all levels affect the economy.

fiscal policy focuses on the effects of taxing and public spending on aggregate economic activity

automatic stabilizers structural features of government spending and taxation that reduce fluctuations in disposable income, and thus consumption, over the business cycle

Fiscal Policy Tools

The tools of fiscal policy sort into two broad categories: automatic stabilizers and discretionary fiscal policy. **Automatic stabilizers** are revenue and spending programs in the federal budget that automatically adjust with the ups and downs of the economy to stabilize disposable income and, consequently, consumption and real GDP. For example, the federal income tax is an automatic stabilizer because (1) once adopted, it requires no parliamentary action to operate year after year, so it's *automatic*, and (2) it reduces the drop in disposable income during recessions and reduces the jump in disposable income during expansions, so it's a *stabilizer*, a smoother. **Discretionary fiscal policy**, on the other hand, requires the deliberate manipulation of government purchases, transfer payments, and taxes to promote macroeconomic goals like full employment, price stability, and economic growth. U.S. President Obama's 2009 stimulus plan is an example of discretionary fiscal policy. Some discretionary policies are temporary, such as one-time tax cuts or government spending increases to fight a recession. The Harper government's 2009 one-time economic stimulus plan is an example.

Using the income-expenditure framework developed earlier, we initially focus on the demand side to consider the effect of changes in government purchases, transfer payments, and taxes on real GDP demanded. The short story is this: *At any given price level, an increase in government purchases or in transfer payments increases real GDP demanded, and an increase in net taxes decreases real GDP demanded, other things constant.* Next, we see how and why.

Changes in Government Purchases

Let's begin by looking at Exhibit 1, with real GDP demanded of $1.8 trillion, as reflected at point *a*, where the aggregate expenditure line crosses the 45-degree line. Suppose at this equilibrium government purchases and net taxes equalled $100 billion each and do not vary with income—that is, they are autonomous, or independent of income. Because government purchases equal net taxes, the government budget is balanced.

EXHIBIT 1

Effect of a $10-Billion Increase in Government Purchases on Aggregate Expenditure and Real GDP Demanded

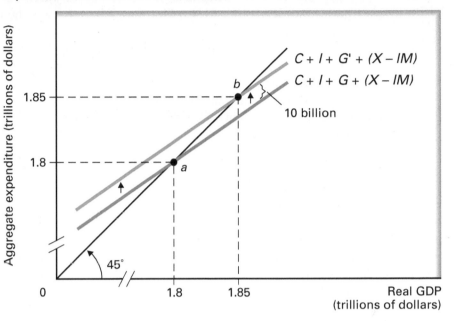

Now suppose federal policymakers, believing that unemployment is too high, decide to stimulate aggregate demand by increasing government purchases by $10 billion. To consider the effect on aggregate demand, let's initially assume that nothing else changes, including the price level and net taxes. This additional spending shifts the aggregate expenditure line up by $10 billion to $C + I + G' + (X - M)$. At real GDP of $1.8 trillion, spending now exceeds output, so production increases. This increase in production increases income, which in turn increases spending, and so it goes through the series of spending rounds.

discretionary fiscal policy the deliberate manipulation of government purchases, taxation, and transfer payments to promote macroeconomic goals, such as full employment, price stability, and economic growth

Adrian Wyld/The Canadian Press

The initial increase of $10 billion in government purchases eventually increases real GDP demanded at the given price level from $1.8 trillion to $1.85 trillion, shown as point *b* in Exhibit 1. Because output demanded increases by $50 billion as a result of an increase of $10 billion in government purchases, the multiplier in our example is equal to 5 (assuming, as in earlier chapters, that the marginal propensity to consume is 0.8). *As long as consumption is the only spending component that varies with income, the multiplier for a change in government purchases, other things constant, equals $1/(1 - MPC)$,* or $1/(1 - 0.8)$ in our example. Thus we can say that for a given price level, and assuming that only consumption varies with income,

Δ means "change in."

$$\Delta \text{ Real GDP demanded} = \Delta G \times \frac{1}{1 - MPC}$$

where, again, the delta symbol (Δ) means "change in." This same multiplier appeared two chapters back, when we discussed shifts of the consumption function, the investment function, and the net exports function.

Changes in Net Taxes

A change in net taxes also affects real GDP demanded, but the effect is less direct. A *decrease* in net taxes, other things constant, *increases* disposable income at each level of real GDP, so consumption increases. In Exhibit 2, we begin again at equilibrium point *a,* with real GDP demanded equal to $1.8 trillion. To stimulate aggregate demand, suppose federal policy makers cut net taxes by $10 billion, other things constant. We continue to assume that net taxes are autonomous—that is, that they do not vary with income. A $10-billion reduction in net taxes could result from a tax cut, an increase in transfer payments, or some combination of the two. The $10-billion decrease in net taxes increases disposable income by $10 billion at each level of real GDP. Because households now have more disposable income, they spend more and save more at each level of real GDP.

Because households save some of the tax cut, consumption increases in the first round of spending by less than the full tax cut. Specifically, *consumption spending at each level of real GDP rises by the decrease in net taxes multiplied by the marginal propensity to consume.* In our example, consumption at each level of real GDP increases by $10 billion times 0.8, or $8 billion. Cutting net taxes by $10 billion causes the aggregate expenditure line to shift up by $8 billion, at all levels of real GDP, as shown in Exhibit 2. This initial increase in spending triggers subsequent rounds of spending, following a now-familiar pattern in the income-expenditure cycle based on the marginal propensities to consume and to save. For example, the $8 billion increase in consumption increases output and income by $8 billion, which in the second round leads to $6.4 billion in consumption and $1.6 billion in saving, and so on through successive rounds. As a result, real GDP demanded eventually increases from $1.8 trillion to $1.84 trillion per year, or by $40 billion.

The effect of a change in net taxes on real GDP demanded equals the resulting shift of the aggregate expenditure line times the simple spending multiplier. Thus we can say that the effect of a change in net taxes is

$$\Delta \text{ Real GDP demanded} = (-MPC \times \Delta NT) \times \frac{1}{1 - MPC}$$

The simple spending multiplier is applied to the shift of the aggregate expenditure line that results from the change in net taxes. This equation can be rearranged as

$$\Delta \text{ Real GDP demanded} = \Delta NT \times \frac{-MPC}{1 - MPC}$$

where $-MPC/(1 - MPC)$ is the **simple tax multiplier,** which can be applied directly to the change in net taxes to yield the change in real GDP demanded at a given price level. This tax multiplier is called *simple* because, by assumption, only

Andrey_Popov/Shutterstock.com

WHAT IF THE ECONOMY PRODUCES LESS THAN ITS POTENTIAL?

EXHIBIT 2
Effect of a $10-Billion Decrease in Net Taxes on Aggregate Expenditure and Real GDP Demanded

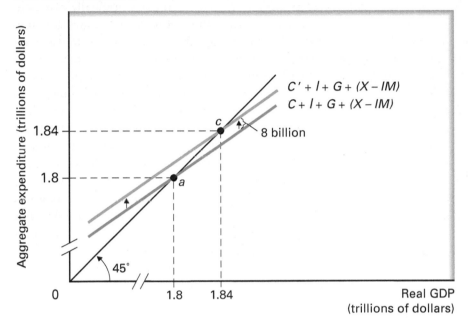

consumption varies with income (taxes do not vary with income). For example, with an MPC of 0.8, the simple tax multiplier equals −4. In our example, a *decrease* of $10 billion in net taxes results in an *increase* in real GDP demanded of $40 billion, assuming a given price level. As another example, an *increase* in net taxes of $20 billion would, other things constant, *decrease* real GDP demanded by $80 billion.

Note two differences between the government purchase multiplier and the simple tax multiplier. First, the government purchase multiplier is positive, so an increase in government purchases leads to an increase in real GDP demanded. The simple tax multiplier is negative, so an increase in net taxes leads to a decrease in real GDP demanded. Second, the multiplier for a given change in government purchases is larger by 1 than the absolute value of the multiplier for an identical change in net taxes. In our example, the government purchase multiplier is 5, while the absolute value of the tax multiplier is 4. This holds because changes in government purchases affect aggregate spending directly—a $10 billion increase in government purchases increases spending in the first round by $10 billion. In contrast, a $10 billion decrease in net taxes increases consumption indirectly

by way of a change in disposable income. Thus, each $10 billion decrease in net taxes increases disposable income by $10 billion, which, given an MPC of 0.8, increases consumption in the first round by $8 billion; people save the other $2 billion. In short, an increase in government purchases has a greater impact on real GDP demanded than does an identical tax cut because some of the tax cut gets saved, so it leaks from the spending flow.

To Review: An increase in government purchases or a decrease in net taxes, other things constant, increases real GDP demanded. Although not shown, the combined effect of changes in government purchases and in net taxes is found by summing their individual effects.

LO2 Including Aggregate Supply

To this point in the chapter, we have focused on the amount of real GDP demanded at a given price level. We are now in a position to bring aggregate supply into the picture. The previous chapter introduced the idea that natural market forces may take a long time to close a recessionary gap. Let's consider the possible effects of using discretionary fiscal policy in such a situation.

Discretionary Fiscal Policy to Close a Recessionary Gap

What if the economy produces less than its potential? Suppose the aggregate demand curve *AD* in Exhibit 3 intersects the aggregate supply curve at point *e,* yielding the short-run output of $1.75 trillion and price level of 105. Output falls short of the economy's potential, opening up a recessionary gap of $50 billion. Unemployment exceeds the natural rate. If markets adjusted naturally to high unemployment,

EXHIBIT 3
Discretionary Fiscal Policy to Close a Recessionary Gap

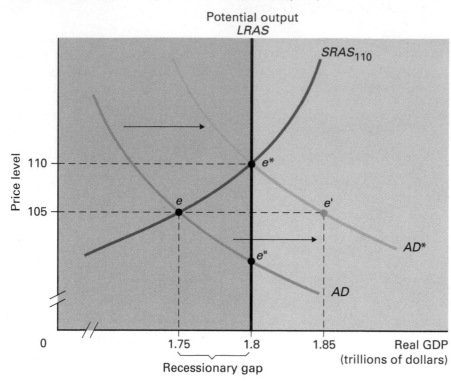

the short-run aggregate supply curve would shift rightward in the long run to achieve equilibrium at the economy's potential output, point e″. History suggests, however, that wages and other resource prices could be slow to respond to a recessionary gap.

Suppose policymakers believe that natural market forces will take too long to return the economy to potential output. They also believe that the appropriate increase in government purchases, decrease in net taxes, or some combination of the two could increase aggregate demand just enough to return the economy to its potential output. A $20-billion increase in government purchases reflects an **expansionary fiscal policy** that increases aggregate demand, as shown in Exhibit 3 by the rightward shift from AD to AD*. If the price level remained at 105, the additional spending would increase the quantity demanded from $1.75 to $1.85 trillion. This increase of $100 billion reflects the simple spending multiplier effect, given a constant price level.

At the original price level of 105, however, excess quantity demanded causes the price level to rise. As the price level rises, real GDP supplied increases, but real GDP demanded decreases along the new aggregate

expansionary fiscal policy an increase in government purchases, decrease in net taxes, or some combination of the two aimed at increasing aggregate demand enough to reduce unemployment and return the economy to its potential output; fiscal policy used to close a recessionary gap

demand curve. The price level rises until quantity demanded equals quantity supplied. In Exhibit 3, the new aggregate demand curve intersects the aggregate supply curve at e*, where the price level is 110, the one originally expected, and output equals potential GDP of $1.8 trillion. Note that *an expansionary fiscal policy aims to close a recessionary gap.*

The intersection at point e* is not only a short-run equilibrium but a long-run equilibrium. If fiscal policymakers are accurate enough (or lucky enough), the appropriate fiscal stimulus can close the recessionary gap and foster a long-run equilibrium at potential GDP. But the increase in output results in a higher price level. What's more, if the federal budget was in balance before the fiscal stimulus, the increase in government spending creates a budget deficit. What if policymakers overshoot the mark and stimulate aggregate demand more than necessary to achieve potential GDP? In the short run, real GDP exceeds potential output. In the long run, the short-run aggregate supply curve shifts back until it intersects the aggregate demand curve at potential output, increasing the price level further but reducing real GDP to $1.8 trillion, the potential output.

Discretionary Fiscal Policy to Close an Expansionary Gap

Suppose output exceeds potential GDP. In Exhibit 4, the aggregate demand curve, AD′, intersects the aggregate supply curve to yield short-run output of $1.85 trillion, an amount exceeding the potential of $1.8 trillion. The economy faces an expansionary gap of $50 billion. Ordinarily, this gap would be closed by a leftward shift of the short-run aggregate supply curve, which would return the economy to potential output but at a higher price level, as shown by point e″.

But the use of discretionary fiscal policy introduces another possibility. By reducing government purchases, increasing net taxes, or employing some combination of the two, the government can implement a

A CONTRACTIONARY FISCAL POLICY AIMS TO CLOSE AN EXPANSIONARY GAP.

EXHIBIT 4
Discretionary Fiscal Policy to Close an Expansionary Gap

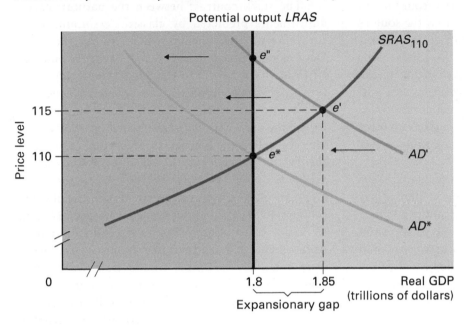

The Multiplier and the Time Horizon

In the short run, the aggregate supply curve slopes upward, so a shift of aggregate demand changes both the price level and the level of output. When aggregate supply gets in the act, we find that the simple multiplier overstates the amount by which output changes. The exact change of equilibrium output in the short run depends on the steepness of the aggregate supply curve, which in turn depends on how sharply production costs increase as output expands. *The steeper the short-run aggregate supply curve, the less impact a given shift of the aggregate demand curve has on real GDP and the more impact it has on the price level, so the smaller the spending multiplier.*

If the economy is already producing its potential, then in the long run, any change in fiscal policy aimed at stimulating demand increases the price level but does not affect output. Thus, *if the economy is already producing its potential, the spending multiplier in the long run is zero.*

contractionary fiscal policy to reduce aggregate demand. This could move the economy to potential output without the resulting inflation. If the policy succeeds, aggregate demand in Exhibit 4 shifts leftward from *AD'* to *AD**, establishing a new equilibrium at point *e**. Again, with just the right reduction in aggregate demand, output falls to $1.8 trillion, the potential GDP. Closing an expansionary gap through fiscal policy rather than through natural market forces results in a lower price level, not a higher one. Increasing net taxes or reducing government purchases also reduces a government deficit or increases a surplus. So a contractionary fiscal policy could reduce inflation and reduce a federal deficit. Note that *a contractionary fiscal policy aims to close an expansionary gap.*

Such precisely calculated expansionary and contractionary fiscal policies are difficult to achieve. Their proper execution assumes that (1) potential output is accurately gauged, (2) the relevant spending multiplier can be predicted accurately, (3) aggregate demand can be shifted by just the right amount, (4) various government entities can somehow coordinate their fiscal efforts, and (5) the shape of the short-run aggregate supply curve is known and remains unaffected by the fiscal policy itself.

LO3 The Evolution of Fiscal Policy

Now that you have some idea of how fiscal policy can work in theory, let's take a look at fiscal policy in practice, beginning with the approach used before the Great Depression.

Prior to the Great Depression

Before the 1930s, discretionary fiscal policy was seldom used to influence the macroeconomy. Public policy

contractionary fiscal policy a decrease in government purchases, increase in net taxes, or some combination of the two aimed at reducing aggregate demand enough to return the economy to potential output without worsening inflation; fiscal policy used to close an expansionary gap

was shaped by the views of **classical economists,** who advocated *laissez-faire,* the belief that free markets were the best way to achieve economic prosperity. Classical economists did not deny that depressions and high unemployment occurred from time to time, but they argued that the sources of such crises lay outside the market system, in the effects of wars, tax increases, poor growing seasons, natural disasters, changing tastes, and the like. Such external shocks could reduce output and employment, but classical economists also believed that natural market forces, such as changes in prices, wages, and interest rates, could correct these problems.

Simply put, classical economists argued that if the economy's price level was too high to sell all that was produced, prices would fall until the quantity supplied equalled the quantity demanded. If wages were too high to employ all who wanted to work, wages would fall until the quantity of labour supplied equalled the quantity demanded. And if the interest rate was too high to invest all that had been saved, interest rates would fall until the amount invested equalled the amount saved.

So the classical approach implied that natural market forces, through flexible prices, wages, and interest rates, would move the economy toward potential GDP. There appeared to be no need for government intervention. What's more, the government, like households, was expected to live within its means. The idea of government running a deficit year after year was considered immoral. Thus before the onset of the Great Depression, most economists believed that discretionary fiscal policy could do more harm than good.

The Great Depression and World War II

Although classical economists acknowledged that capitalistic, market-oriented economies could experience high unemployment from time to time, the depth and duration of the depression strained belief in the economy's ability to heal itself. The Great Depression was marked by four consecutive years of contraction during which unemployment reached 25 percent. Investment plunged and many factories sat idle. With vast unemployed resources, output and income fell well short of the economy's potential.

The stark contrast between the natural market adjustments predicted by classical economists and the years of high unemployment during the Great Depression represented a collision of theory and fact. In 1936, John Maynard Keynes of Cambridge University, England, published *The General Theory of Employment, Interest, and Money,* a book that challenged the classical view and touched off what would later be called the Keynesian revolution. *Keynesian theory and policy were developed in response to the problem of high unemployment during the Great Depression.* Keynes's main quarrel with the classical economists was that prices and wages did not seem to be flexible enough to ensure the full employment of resources. According to Keynes, prices and wages were relatively inflexible in the downward direction—they were "sticky"—so natural market forces would not return the economy to full employment in a timely fashion. Keynes also believed business expectations might at times become so grim that even very low interest rates would not spur firms to invest all that consumers might save.

Two developments in the years following the Great Depression bolstered the use of discretionary

fiscal policy in Canada. The first was the influence of Keynes's *General Theory,* in which he argued that natural forces would not necessarily close a recessionary gap. Keynes thought the economy could get stuck well below its potential, requiring the government to increase aggregate demand to boost output and employment. The second development was the impact of World War II on output and employment. The demands of war greatly increased production and erased cyclical unemployment during the war years, pulling Canada's economy out of its depression.

Prior to the Great Depression, the dominant fiscal policy was a balanced budget. In the wake of Keynes's *General Theory* and World War II, however, policymakers grew more receptive to the idea that fiscal policy could improve economic stability. The objective of fiscal policy was no longer to balance the budget but to promote economic growth, full employment, and price stability even if budget deficits resulted.

Automatic Stabilizers

This chapter has focused mostly on discretionary fiscal policy—conscious decisions by public policymakers to change taxes and government spending to achieve the economy's potential output. Now let's get a clearer picture of automatic stabilizers. *Automatic stabilizers smooth out fluctuations in disposable income over the business cycle by stimulating aggregate demand during recessions and dampening aggregate demand during expansions.* Consider the federal income tax. For simplicity, we have assumed that net taxes are independent of income. In reality, the federal income tax system is progressive, meaning that the fraction of income paid in taxes increases as a taxpayer's income increases. During an economic expansion, employment and incomes rise, moving some taxpayers into higher tax brackets. As a result, taxes claim a growing fraction of income. This slows the growth in disposable income and, hence, slows the growth in consumption. Therefore, the progressive income tax relieves some of the inflationary pressure that might otherwise arise as output increases during an economic expansion. Conversely, when the economy is in recession, output declines, and employment and incomes fall, moving some people into lower tax brackets. As a result, taxes take a smaller bite out of income, so disposable income does not fall as much as GDP. Thus the progressive income tax cushions declines in disposable income, in consumption, and in aggregate demand.

Another automatic stabilizer is unemployment insurance. During economic expansions, the system automatically increases the flow of unemployment insurance taxes from the income stream into the unemployment insurance fund, thereby moderating consumption and aggregate demand. During contractions, unemployment increases and the system reverses itself. Unemployment insurance payments automatically flow from the insurance fund to the unemployed, increasing disposable income and propping up consumption and aggregate demand.

Likewise, welfare payments automatically increase during hard times as more people become eligible. *Because of these automatic stabilizers, GDP fluctuates less than it otherwise would, and disposable income varies proportionately less than does GDP. Because disposable income varies less than GDP does, consumption also fluctuates less than GDP does.*

The progressive income tax, unemployment insurance, and welfare benefits were initially designed not so much as automatic stabilizers but as income redistribution programs. Their roles as automatic stabilizers were secondary effects of the legislation. Automatic stabilizers do not eliminate economic fluctuations, but they do reduce their magnitude. The stronger and more effective the automatic stabilizers are, the less need for discretionary fiscal policy. Because of the greater influence of automatic stabilizers, *the economy is more stable today than it was during the Great Depression and before. Without much fanfare, automatic stabilizers have been quietly doing their work, keeping the economy on a more even keel.*

Stagflation

Discretionary fiscal policy is a demand-management policy; the objective is to increase or decrease aggregate demand to smooth economic fluctuations. But the 1970s brought a different problem—stagflation, the double trouble of higher inflation and higher unemployment resulting from a decrease in aggregate supply. The aggregate supply curve shifted left because of crop failures around the world, sharply

CHAPTER 11: FISCAL POLICY

higher OPEC-driven oil prices, and other adverse supply shocks. Demand-management policies are ill suited to cure stagflation because an increase of aggregate demand would increase inflation, whereas a decrease of aggregate demand would increase unemployment.

Other concerns also caused policymakers and economists to question the effectiveness of discretionary fiscal policy. These concerns included the difficulty of estimating the natural rate of unemployment, the time lags involved in implementing fiscal policy, the distinction between current income and permanent income, and the possible feedback effects of fiscal policy on aggregate supply. We consider each in turn.

Fiscal Policy and the Natural Rate of Unemployment

As we have seen, the unemployment that occurs when the economy is producing its potential GDP is called the *natural rate of unemployment*. Before adopting discretionary policies, public officials must correctly estimate this natural rate. Suppose the economy is producing its potential output of $1.8 trillion, as in Exhibit 5, where the natural rate of unemployment is 6.0 percent. Also suppose that public officials mistakenly believe the natural rate to be 5.0 percent, and they attempt to reduce unemployment and increase real GDP through discretionary fiscal policy. As a result of their policy, the aggregate demand curve shifts to the right, from *AD* to *AD'*. In the short run, this stimulation of aggregate demand expands output to $1.82 trillion and reduces unemployment to 5.0 percent, so the policy appears successful. But stimulating aggregate demand opens up an expansionary gap, which in the long run results in a leftward shift of the short-run aggregate supply curve. This reduction in aggregate supply pushes up prices and reduces real GDP to $1.8 trillion, the economy's potential. Thus policymakers initially believe their plan worked, but pushing production beyond the economy's potential leads only to inflation in the long run.

Let's look at how political considerations could shape fiscal policies.

EXHIBIT 5

When Discretionary Fiscal Policy Overshoots Potential Output

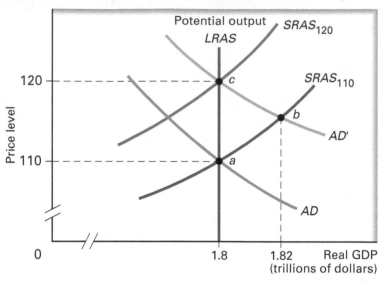

Fiscal Policy and Politics Given the effects of fiscal policy, particularly in the short run, we should not be surprised that elected officials might try to use it to get reelected. The link between economic performance and reelection success has a long history. Ray Fair of Yale University in the United States examined U.S. presidential elections dating back to 1916 and found, not surprisingly, that the state of the economy during the election year affected the outcome.[1] Specifically, Fair found that a declining unemployment rate and strong growth rate in GDP per capita increased election prospects for the incumbent party.

Another Yale economist, William Nordhaus, developed a theory of **political business cycles**, arguing that incumbent presidents, during an election year, use expansionary policies to stimulate the economy, often only temporarily. There is also evidence of a political business cycle of sorts at the municipal level, where, prior to an election, city officials spend more on those items most visible to the electorate, such as city parks. But the evidence to support the theory of political business cycles is not entirely convincing.

Lags in Fiscal Policy

The time required to approve and implement fiscal legislation may hamper its effectiveness and weaken discretionary fiscal policy as a tool of macroeconomic

[1] Ray Fair, *Predicting Presidential Elections and Other Things* (Stanford University Press, 2002).

CHANGING TAX RATES DOES NOT AFFECT CONSUMPTION MUCH IF PEOPLE VIEW THE CHANGE AS ONLY TEMPORARY.

stabilization. Even if a fiscal prescription is appropriate for the economy when proposed, the months and sometimes years required to approve and implement legislation means the medicine could do more harm than good. The policy might kick in only after the economy has already turned itself around. Because a recession is not usually identified until at least six months after it begins, and because recessions may last less than a year, discretionary fiscal policy allows little room for error (more later about timing problems).

© Peter Bowater/Science Source

Discretionary Fiscal Policy and Permanent Income

It was once believed that discretionary fiscal policy could be turned on and off like a water faucet, stimulating or dampening the economy at the right time by just the right amount. Given the marginal propensity to consume, tax changes could increase or decrease disposable income to bring about desired change in consumption. A more recent view suggests that people base their consumption decisions not merely on changes in their current income but on changes in their permanent income.

Permanent income is the income a person expects to receive on average over the long term. Changing tax rates does not affect consumption much if people view the change as only temporary. For example, one-time tax rebates seem to have had little impact on consumption. The stimulative effects of a $117-billion (US) tax-rebate program in early 2008 were disappointing. Surveys showed that only about 20 percent of households spent most of their rebate cheque. Other households saved most of it or paid down debt.[2] The *temporary* nature of the tax cuts meant that consumers faced only a small increase in their permanent income. Because permanent income changed little, consumption changed little. In short, *to the extent that consumers base spending decisions on their permanent income, attempts to fine-tune the economy with temporary tax changes are less effective.*

> **permanent income** income that individuals expect to receive on average over the long term

[2] See Matthew Shapiro and Joel Slemrod, "Did the 2008 Tax Rebates Stimulate Spending," *American Economic Review*, 99 (May 2009): 374–379.

The Feedback Effects of Fiscal Policy on Aggregate Supply

annually balanced budget budget philosophy prior to the Great Depression; aimed at matching annual revenues with outlays, except during times of war

So far we have limited the discussion of fiscal policy to its effect on aggregate demand. Fiscal policy may also affect aggregate supply, although this is usually unintentional. For example, suppose the government increases employment insurance benefits, paid with higher taxes on earnings. If the marginal propensity to consume is the same for both groups, the increased spending by beneficiaries just offsets the reduced spending by workers. There would be no change in aggregate demand and thus no change in equilibrium real GDP, simply a redistribution of disposable income from the employed to the unemployed.

But could the program affect labour supply? Higher employment insurance benefits reduce the opportunity cost of not working, so some job seekers may decide to search at a more leisurely pace. Meanwhile, higher tax rates reduce the opportunity cost of leisure, so some with jobs may decide to work fewer hours. In short, the supply of labour could decrease as a result of higher employment insurance benefits funded by higher taxes on earnings. A decrease in the supply of labour would decrease aggregate supply, reducing the economy's potential GDP.

Both automatic stabilizers, such as employment insurance and the progressive income tax, and discretionary fiscal policies, such as changes in tax rates, may affect individual incentives to work, spend, save, and invest, although these effects are usually unintended consequences. We should keep these secondary effects in mind when we evaluate fiscal policies.

LO 4 The Fiscal Impact of the Federal Budget and Debt

When a provincial or federal government's outlays—government purchases plus cash and in-kind transfer programs—exceed its revenue, the result is a *budget deficit,* a flow measure already introduced. To place provincial and federal deficits in perspective, let's first examine the economic rationale for deficit financing.

The Rationale for Deficits

Deficit financing has been justified for outlays that increase the economy's productivity—capital outlays for investments such as highways, waterways, and dams. The cost of these capital projects should be borne in part by future taxpayers, who will also benefit from these investments. Thus there is some justification for shifting some of the cost of capital projects to future taxpayers. Provincial and municipal governments issue debt to fund capital projects, such as schools and infrastructure. But, as noted already, the federal government does not budget capital projects separately, so there is no explicit link between capital budgets and federal deficits.

Before the Great Depression, federal deficits occurred only during wartime. Because wars often involve great personal hardship, public officials are understandably reluctant to tax citizens much more to finance war-related spending. Deficits during wars were largely self-correcting, however, because military spending dropped after a war, but tax revenue did not.

The Great Depression led John Maynard Keynes to argue that public spending should offset any drop in private spending. As you know by now, Keynes argued that a federal budget deficit would stimulate aggregate demand. As a result of the Great Depression, automatic stabilizers were also introduced, which increased public outlays during recessions and decreased them during expansions. Deficits increase during recessions because tax revenues decline while spending programs such as unemployment insurance benefits and welfare increase. An economic expansion reverses these flows. As the economy picks up, so do personal income and corporate profits, boosting tax revenue. Unemployment insurance compensation and welfare spending decline. Thus federal deficits usually fall during the recovery stage of the business cycle.

Budget Philosophies and Deficits

Several budget philosophies have emerged over the years. Prior to the Great Depression, fiscal policy focused on maintaining an **annually balanced budget**, except during wartime. Because tax revenues rise during expansions and fall during recessions, an annually balanced budget means that spending increases during expansions and declines during recessions. But such a pattern magnifies fluctuations in the business cycle, overheating the economy during expansions and increasing unemployment during recessions.

AS EXPECTATIONS GROW MORE FAVOURABLE, FIRMS BECOME MORE WILLING TO INVEST.

A second budget philosophy calls for a **cyclically balanced budget**, meaning that budget deficits during recessions are covered by budget surpluses during expansions. Fiscal policy dampens swings in the business cycle without increasing the national debt.

A third budget philosophy is **functional finance**, which says that policymakers should be concerned less with balancing the budget annually, or even over the business cycle, and more with ensuring that the economy produces its potential output. If the budgets needed to keep the economy producing its potential involve chronic deficits, so be it. Since the Great Depression, budgets in this country have seldom balanced.

Deficits, Surpluses, Crowding Out, and Crowding In

What effect do federal deficits and surpluses have on interest rates? Recall that interest rates affect investment, a critical component of economic growth. What's more, year-to-year fluctuations in investment are the primary source of shifts in the aggregate demand curve. Let's look at the impact of government deficits and surpluses on investment.

Suppose the federal government increases spending without raising taxes, thereby increasing the budget deficit. How will this affect national saving, interest rates, and investment? An increase in the federal deficit reduces the supply of national saving, leading to higher interest rates. Higher interest rates discourage, or *crowd out*, some private investment, reducing the stimulating effect of the government's deficit. The extent of **crowding out** is a matter of debate. Some economists argue that although government deficits may displace some private sector borrowing, expansionary fiscal policy results in a net increase in aggregate demand, leading to greater output and employment in the short run. Others believe that the crowding out is more extensive, so borrowing from the public in this way results in little or no net increase in aggregate demand and output. Public spending merely substitutes for private spending.

Although crowding out is likely to occur to some degree, there is another possibility. If the economy is operating well below its potential, the additional fiscal stimulus provided by a higher government deficit could encourage some firms to invest more. Recall that an important determinant of investment is business expectations. Government stimulus of a weak economy could put a sunny face on the business outlook. As expectations grow more favourable, firms become more willing to invest. This ability of government deficits to stimulate private investment is sometimes called **crowding in**, to distinguish it from crowding out. Between 1993 and 2011, the Japanese government pursued deficit spending that averaged 6.0 percent relative to GDP as a way of getting that flat economy going, but with only limited success. Unfortunately, the global financial crisis and recession of 2007–2009 reversed those limited gains.

Were you ever unwilling to patronize a restaurant because it was too crowded? You simply did not want to put up with the hassle and long wait and were thus "crowded out." Similarly, high government deficits may "crowd out" some investors by driving up interest rates. On the other hand, did you ever pass up an unfamiliar restaurant because the place seemed dead—it had no customers? Perhaps you wondered why. If you had seen just a few customers, you might have stopped in—you might have been willing to "crowd in." Similarly, businesses may be reluctant to invest in a seemingly lifeless economy. The economic stimulus resulting from deficit spending could encourage some investors to "crowd in."

The Twin Deficits

To finance the huge deficits, the federal government must sell a lot of government IOUs. To get people to buy these securities, the government must offer higher interest rates, other things constant. So funding a higher deficit pushes up the market interest rates, other things constant. With Canadian interest rates higher, foreigners find government securities more attractive. But to buy them, foreigners must first exchange their currencies for dollars. This greater demand for dollars causes the dollar to appreciate relative to foreign

cyclically balanced budget a budget philosophy calling for budget deficits during recessions to be financed by budget surpluses during expansions

functional finance a budget philosophy using fiscal policy to achieve the economy's potential GDP, rather than balancing budgets either annually or over the business cycle

crowding out the displacement of interest-sensitive private investment that occurs when higher government deficits drive up market interest rates

crowding in the potential for government spending to stimulate private investment in an otherwise dead economy

national debt the net accumulation of federal budget deficits

currencies. The rising value of the dollar makes foreign goods cheaper in Canada and Canadian goods more expensive abroad. Thus Canada's imports increase and Canada's exports decrease, so the trade deficit increases.

Higher trade deficits mean that foreigners have dollars left over after they buy all the Canadian goods and services they want. With these accumulated dollars, foreigners buy Canadian assets, including Canadian government securities, and thereby help fund federal deficits. The increase in funds from abroad is both good news and bad news for the Canadian economy. The supply of foreign saving increases investment spending in Canada over what would have occurred in the absence of these funds. Ask people what they think of foreign investment in their town; they will likely say it's great. But foreign funds to some extent simply offset a decline in Canadian saving. Such a pattern could pose problems in the long run. Canada has surrendered a certain amount of control over its economy to foreign investors. And the return on foreign investments in Canada flows abroad.

The Relative Size of the Public Sector

So far, we have focused on the federal budget, but a fuller picture includes provincial and municipal governments as well. For added context, we can look at government budgets over time compared to other major economies. Exhibit 6 shows government outlays at all levels relative to GDP in 10 industrial economies in 1993 and in 2012. Outlays relative to GDP increased in three of the major economies and decreased in seven. The 10-country average remains at 45 percent. Government grew the most in Japan, rising from 35 percent relative to GDP in 1993 to 41 percent in 2012. Two decades of trying to stimulate the Japanese economy swelled the public sector. Government spending shrank the most in Canada, dropping from 52 percent to 42 percent relative to GDP.

Let's now turn our attention to a consequence of federal deficits—a sizable federal debt.

The National Debt

Federal deficits add up. The federal deficit is a flow variable measuring the amount by which outlays exceed revenues in a particular year. The federal debt, or the **national debt**, is a stock variable measuring the net accumulation of past deficits, the amount owed by the federal government. The sections that follow put the national debt in perspective by looking at (1) changes over time and (2) Canada's debt levels compared with those in other countries.

Measuring the National Debt

In talking about the national debt, we should distinguish between the gross debt and debt held by the public. The *gross debt* includes government securities purchased by various federal agencies. Because the federal government owes this debt to itself, analysts often focus instead on *debt held by the public*, which includes government securities held by households, firms, banks (including the Bank of Canada), and foreign entities. As of March 31, 2012, the gross federal debt stood at $867.8 billion, and the debt held by the public stood at $582.2 billion.

One way to measure debt over time is relative to the economy's production and income, or GDP (just as a bank might compare the size of a mortgage to a borrower's income). Exhibit 7 shows federal debt held by the public relative to GDP. The cost of World

EXHIBIT 6
Government Outlays as a Percentage of GDP in 1993 and 2012

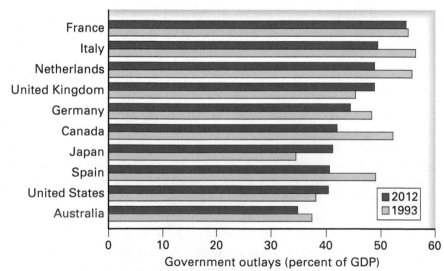

SOURCE: Developed from figures available in *OECD Economic Outlook*, Vol. 89 (May 2011), Annex Table 25. Figures for 2012 are estimates. For the latest data, go to http://www.oecd.org/home/, click on "Statistics," then find the most recent issue of *OECD Economic Outlook*.

EXHIBIT 7
Federal Debt Held by the Public as Percent of GDP

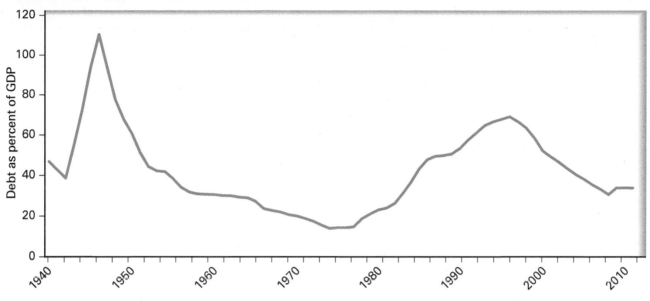

SOURCE: Developed based on Statistics Canada Tables 385-0010, 380-0016 and 380-0039.

War II ballooned the debt from 47 percent relative to GDP in 1940 to 110 percent in 1946. After the war, the economy grew much faster than the debt, so by 1974, debt fell to only 14 percent relative to GDP. But high deficits in the 1980s and early 1990s raised debt to 69 percent relative to GDP by 1996. Budget surpluses from 1997 to 2007 cut debt to 30 percent relative to GDP by 2008. Deficits from the 2007–2009 recession increased federal debt relative to GDP. According to the Department of Finance, debt held by the public relative to GDP by March 31, 2012, was 33.8 percent.

Countries can continue to run deficits as long as the cost of servicing the resulting debt remains manageable. More generally, government could still run a deficit year after year, and the dollar amount of the deficit might even rise. As long as the economy is growing at least as fast as the debt service payments, those deficits should be manageable. Greece had little trouble borrowing until 2010, when the financial community decided the government debt there had become too high and therefore too risky.

International Perspective on Public Debt

Exhibit 7 shows federal debt relative to GDP over time, but how does Canada compare with other major economies around the world? Because different economies have different fiscal structures—for example some rely more on a central government—we should consider the debt at all government levels. Exhibit 8 compares the net government debt in Canada relative to GDP with those of nine other industrial countries. *Net debt* includes outstanding liabilities of federal, provincial or state, and local governments minus government financial assets, such as loans to students and farmers, securities, cash on hand, and foreign exchange on reserve. Net debt for the 10 nations was projected to average 62 percent in 2012 relative to GDP, above the Canadian figure of 35 percent (remember this is for all levels of government, not just the federal level). Australia was the lowest with only 8 percent net debt, and Japan was the highest at 134 percent relative to GDP. Much of Japan's debt was taken on during the "lost decade" of the 1990s as the government borrowed to fund efforts to stimulate the ailing economy. Efforts to recover from the 2011 earthquake and tsunami also had an effect. The United States ranked third among the 10 industrialized nations, up from fifth a decade ago. Thus, although the United States ranks low in public outlays relative to GDP, the country ranks high in public debt relative to GDP. That's because the United States has been running big deficits for decades, and really big ones following the 2007 financial crisis.

EXHIBIT 8

Net Public Debt Relative to GDP for Major Economies in 2012

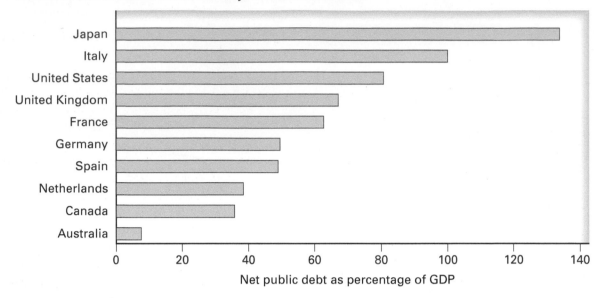

SOURCE: *OECD Economic Outlook*, 89 (May 2011, Annex Table 33. Figures are projections for net debt at all levels of government in 2012. For the latest data, go to http://www.oecd.org/home/, click on "Statistics," then find the latest *OECD Economic Outlook*.

Final Word

John Maynard Keynes introduced the idea that federal deficit spending is an appropriate fiscal policy when private aggregate demand is insufficient to achieve potential output.

This chapter discussed fiscal policy in theory and in practice. It also examined several factors that reduce the size of the spending and taxing multipliers. In the short run, the aggregate supply curve slopes upward, so the impact on equilibrium output of any change in aggregate demand is blunted by a change in the price level. In the long run, aggregate supply is a vertical line, so if the economy is already producing at its potential, the spending multiplier is zero. To the extent that consumers respond primarily to changes in their permanent incomes, temporary changes in taxes affect consumption less, so the tax multiplier is smaller.

In the theory portion of this chapter, we assumed net taxes and net exports would remain unchanged with changes in income. In reality, income taxes increase with income and net exports decrease with income. The appendix, available on the text's website, introduces these more realistic assumptions. The resulting spending multipliers and tax multipliers are smaller than those developed to this point.

Monetary policy is the regulation of the money supply by the Bank of Canada. The next few chapters introduce money and financial institutions, review monetary policy, and discuss the impact of monetary and fiscal policy on economic stability and growth. Once we bring money into the picture, we consider yet another reason why the simple spending multiplier is overstated.

CHAPTER PROBLEMS

LO1   Explain the theory of fiscal policy

1.1. *(Changes in Government Purchases)* Assume that government purchases decrease by $10 billion, with other factors held constant, including the price level. Calculate the change in the level of real GDP demanded for each of the following values of the MPC. Then calculate the change if the government, instead of reducing its purchases, increased autonomous net taxes by $10 billion.

 a. 0.9
 b. 0.8
 c. 0.75
 d. 0.6

1.2. *(Fiscal Multipliers)* Explain the difference between the government purchases multiplier and the net tax multiplier. If the MPC falls, what happens to the tax multiplier?

1.3. *(Changes in Net Taxes)* Using the income-expenditure model, graphically illustrate the impact of a $15-billion drop in government transfer payments on aggregate expenditure if the MPC equals 0.75. Explain why it has this impact. What is the impact on the level of real GDP demanded, assuming the price level remains unchanged?

1.4. *(Multipliers)* Suppose investment, in addition to having an autonomous component, also has a component that varies directly with the level of real GDP. How would this affect the size of the government purchase and net tax multipliers?

LO2 Describe how aggregate supply affects fiscal policy

2.1. *(Fiscal Policy)* Chapter 11 shows that increased government purchases, with taxes held constant, can eliminate a recessionary gap. How could a tax cut achieve the same result? Would the tax cut have to be larger than the increase in government purchases? Why or why not?

2.2. *(Fiscal Policy with an Expansionary Gap)* Using the aggregate demand–aggregate supply model, illustrate an economy with an expansionary gap. If the government is to close the gap by changing government purchases, should it increase or decrease those purchases? In the long run, what happens to the level of real GDP as a result of government intervention? What happens to the price level? Illustrate this on an *AD–AS* diagram, assuming that the government changes its purchases by exactly the amount necessary to close the gap.

LO3 Discuss the evolution of fiscal policy

3.1. *(Evolution of Fiscal Policy)* What did classical economists assume about the flexibility of prices, wages, and interest rates? What did this assumption imply about the self-correcting tendencies

in an economy in recession? What disagreements did Keynes have with classical economists?

LO4 Discuss the fiscal impact of the federal budget and debt

4.1. *(Budget Philosophies)* Explain the differences among an annually balanced budget, a cyclically balanced budget, and functional finance. How does each affect economic fluctuations?

4.2. *(Crowding Out)* Is it possible for federal budget deficits to crowd out investment spending in other countries? How could German or British investment be hurt by large Canadian budget deficits?

4.3. *(The National Debt)* Try the following exercises to better understand how the national debt is related to the government's budget deficit.

 a. Assume that the gross national debt initially is equal to $3 trillion and the federal government then runs a deficit of $300 billion.

  i. What is the new level of gross national debt?

  ii. If 100 percent of the deficit is financed by the sale of securities to federal agencies, what happens to the amount of debt held by the public? What happens to the level of gross debt?

  iii. If GDP increased by 5 percent in the same year that the deficit is run, what happens to gross debt as a percentage of GDP? What happens to the level of debt held by the public as a percentage of GDP?

 b. Now suppose that the gross national debt initially is equal to $2.5 trillion and the federal government then runs a deficit of $100 billion.

  i. What is the new level of gross national debt?

  ii. If 100 percent of this deficit is financed by the sale of securities to the public, what happens to the level of debt held by the public? What happens to the level of gross debt?

  iii. If GDP increases by 6 percent in the same year as the deficit is run, what happens to gross debt as a percentage of GDP? What happens to the level of debt held by the public as a percentage of GDP?

CASE STUDY

Fiscal Policy and Presidential Elections in the United States

After the recession of 1990–1991, the economy was slow to recover. At the time of the 1992 presidential election, the unemployment rate still languished at 7.5 percent, up two percentage points from when President George H. W. Bush took office in 1989. The higher unemployment rate was too much of a hurdle to overcome, and Bush lost his reelection bid to challenger Bill Clinton. Clinton's campaign slogan was "It's the economy, stupid."

The link between economic performance and reelection success has a long history. Ray Fair of Yale University examined presidential elections dating back to 1916 and found, not surprisingly, that the state of the economy during the election year affected the outcome. Specifically, Fair found that a declining unemployment rate and strong growth rate in GDP per capita increased election prospects for the incumbent party. Another Yale economist, William Nordhaus, developed a theory of political business cycles, arguing that incumbent presidents, during an election year, use expansionary policies to stimulate the economy, often only temporarily. For example, evidence suggests that President Nixon used expansionary policies to increase his chances for reelection in 1972, even pressuring the Federal Reserve chairman to pursue an expansionary monetary policy. There is also evidence of a political business cycle of sorts at the municipal level, where, prior to an election, city officials spend more on those items most visible to the electorate, such as city parks.

The evidence to support the theory of political business cycles is not entirely convincing. One problem is that the theory limits presidential motives to reelection, when in fact presidents may have other objectives. For example, the first President Bush, in the election year of 1992, passed up an opportunity to sign a tax cut for the middle class because that measure would also have increased taxes on a much smaller group—upper-income taxpayers.

An alternative to the theory of political business cycles is that Democrats care more about unemployment and less about inflation than do Republicans. This view is supported by evidence indicating that during Democratic administrations, unemployment is more likely to fall and inflation is more likely to rise than during Republican administrations. Republican presidents tend to pursue contractionary policies soon after taking office and are more willing to endure a recession to reduce inflation. The country suffered a recession during the first term of the last six Republican presidents. Democratic presidents tend to pursue expansionary policies to reduce unemployment and are willing to put up with higher inflation to do so. President Barack Obama, for example, pushed through what would turn out to be an $862-billion stimulus package even though it worsened what was already a huge federal deficit.

A final problem with the political-business-cycle theory is that other issues sometimes compete with the economy for voter attention. For example, in the 2004 election, President Bush's handling of the war on terror, especially the war in Iraq, became at least as much of a campaign issue as his handling of the economy.

SOURCES: Linda Veiga and Francisco Veiga, "Political Business Cycles at the Municipal Level," *Public Choice*, 131 (April 2007): 45–64; Burton Abrams, "How Richard Nixon Pressured Arthur Burns: Evidence from the Nixon Tapes," *Journal of Economic Perspectives* (Fall 2006): 177–188; *Economic Report of the President*, February 2010; Ray Fair, *Predicting Presidential Elections and Other Things* (Stanford University Press, 2002); and William Nordhaus, "Alternative Approaches to the Political Business Cycle," *Brookings Papers on Economic Activity*, No. 2 (1989): 1–49.

QUESTION

1. Suppose that fiscal policy changes output faster than it changes the price level. How might such timing play a role in the theory of political business cycles?

Money and the Financial System

LEARNING OUTCOMES

LO1   Discuss the evolution and functions of money

LO2   Financial institutions and the Bank of Canada

> ## " Why is there so much fascination with money? "

Why are you willing to exchange a piece of polymer bearing Sir John A. Macdonald's portrait and the number 10 in each corner for a pepperoni pizza with extra cheese? If Russia can't pay its bills, why don't they simply print more rubles? Why was someone able to cash a cheque written on a clean but frayed pair of underpants? These and other questions are answered in this chapter, which introduces money and banking.

The word *money* comes from the name of the goddess (*Juno Moneta*) in whose temple Rome's money was coined. Money has come to symbolize all personal and business finance. You can read *Money* magazine and the "Money" section of *USA Today*, and visit websites such as money.cnn.com, money.msn.com, and smartmoney.com (a Google search for "money" returned over 3 billion hits).

With money, you can articulate your preferences—after all, money talks. And when it talks, it says a lot, as in "Put your money where your mouth is" and "Show me the money." Money is the grease that lubricates the wheels of market exchange (in fact, an old expression "grease the palm" means to pay someone). Just as grease makes for an easier fit among gears, money reduces the friction—the transaction costs—of exchange. Too little leaves some parts creaking; too much gums up the works.

This chapter is obviously about money. We begin with the evolution of money, tracing its use in broad strokes from primitive economies to our own. Then we turn to developments in Canada.

LO 1   The Evolution and Functions of Money

In the beginning, there was no money. The earliest families were largely self-sufficient. Each produced all it consumed and consumed all it produced, so there was little need for exchange. Without exchange, there was no need for money. When specialization first emerged, as some people went hunting and others took up farming, hunters and farmers had to trade. Thus the specialization of labour resulted in exchange, but the assortment of goods traded was limited enough that people could easily exchange their products directly for other products—a system called *barter*.

Barter and the Double Coincidence of Wants

double coincidence of wants two traders are willing to exchange their products directly

Barter depends on a **double coincidence of wants**, which occurs when one trader is willing to exchange his or her product for something another trader has to offer. If a hunter was willing to exchange hides for a farmer's

ANY COMMODITY THAT ACQUIRES A HIGH DEGREE OF ACCEPTABILITY THROUGHOUT AN ECONOMY BECOMES MONEY.

corn, that was a coincidence. But if the farmer was also willing to exchange corn for the hunter's hides, that was a double coincidence—a *double coincidence of wants.* As long as specialization was limited, to, say, two or three goods, mutually beneficial trades were relatively easy to come by—that is, trade wasn't much of a coincidence. As specialization increased, however, finding the particular goods that each trader wanted became more difficult.

In a barter system, traders must not only discover a double coincidence of wants, they must also agree on an exchange rate. How many bushels of corn should the hunter get for a hide? If only two goods are traded, only one exchange rate needs to be worked out. As the variety of goods traded increases, however, exchange rates multiply. Specialization increased the transaction costs of barter. A huge difference in the values of the units to be exchanged also made barter difficult. For example, a hunter wanting to buy a home that exchanged for 1,000 hides would be hard-pressed finding a home seller needing that many. High transaction costs of barter gave birth to money.

The Earliest Money and Its Functions

Nobody actually recorded the emergence of money. We can only speculate about how it first came into use. Through experience with barter, traders may have found they could always find buyers for certain goods. If a trader could not find a good that he or she desired personally, some other good with a ready market could be accepted instead. So traders began to accept a certain good not for immediate consumption but because that good could be easily traded later. For example, corn might become acceptable because traders knew that it was always in demand. As one good became generally accepted in return for all other goods, that good began to function as **money.** *Any commodity that acquires a high degree of acceptability throughout an economy becomes money.*

Money fulfills three important functions: a *medium of*

© Jim Barber/Shutterstock

exchange, a *unit of account,* and a *store of value.* Let's consider each.

Medium of Exchange Separating the sale of one good from the purchase of another requires an item acceptable to all involved in the transactions. If a society, by luck or by design, can find a commodity that everyone accepts in exchange for whatever is sold, traders can save time, disappointment, and sheer aggravation. Suppose corn takes on this role, a role that clearly goes beyond its role as food. We then call corn a medium of exchange because it is accepted in exchange by all buyers and sellers, whether or not they want corn to eat. A **medium of exchange** is anything that is generally accepted in payment for goods and services. The person who accepts corn in exchange for some product believes corn can be traded later for whatever is desired.

In this example, corn is both a *commodity* and *money,* so we call it **commodity money.** The earliest money was commodity money. Gold and silver have been used as money for at least 4,000 years. Cattle served as money, first for the Greeks, then for the Romans. In fact, the word *pecuniary* (meaning "of or relating to money") comes from the Latin word for cattle, *pecus.* Likewise, the word *fee* comes from the Old English word *feoh,* which also meant cattle. Roman soldiers received part of their pay in salt bricks; the salt portion was called the *salarium,* the origin of the word *salary.* Also used as money were wampum (strings of polished shells) and tobacco in colonial America, furs in colonial Canada, tea pressed into small cakes in Russia, rice in Japan, and palm dates in North Africa. Note that commodity money is a good, not a service; a service is intangible and cannot be held for later exchange.

Unit of Account A commodity such as corn that grows to be widely accepted becomes a **unit of account,** a standard on which prices are based. The price of

> **money** anything that is generally accepted in exchange for goods and services
>
> **medium of exchange** anything that facilitates trade by being generally accepted by all parties in payment for goods or services
>
> **commodity money** anything that serves both as money and as a commodity; money that has intrinsic value such as gold or silver coins
>
> **unit of account** a common unit for measuring the value of each good or service

hides or shoes or pots is measured in bushels of corn. Thus corn serves not only as a medium of exchange; it also becomes a common denominator, a yardstick, for *measuring the value* of each product exchanged in the economy. Rather than having to determine exchange rates among all products, as with a barter economy, people can price everything using a single measure, such as corn. For example, if a pair of shoes sells for 2 bushels of corn and a 5-litre pot sells for 1 bushel of corn, then a pair of shoes has the same value in exchange as two 5-litre pots.

Store of Value Because people do not want to buy something every time they sell something, the purchasing power acquired through a sale must somehow be preserved. Money serves as a **store of value** when it retains purchasing power over time. The better it preserves purchasing power, the better money serves as a store of value, and the more willing people are to hold it. Consider again the distinction between a stock and a flow. Recall that a *stock* is an amount measured at a particular point in time, such as the amount of food in your refrigerator, or the amount of money you have with you right now. In contrast, a *flow* is an amount per unit of time, such as the calories you consume per day, or the income you earn per week. *Money* is a stock and *income* is a flow. Don't confuse money with income. The role of money as a stock is best reflected by money's role as a store of value.

Properties of the Ideal Money

The introduction of commodity money reduced the transaction costs of exchange compared with barter, but commodity money also involves some transaction costs. First, if the commodity money is perishable, as is corn, it must be properly stored or its quality deteriorates; even then, it won't maintain its quality for long. So the ideal money should be *durable*. Second, if the commodity money is bulky, major purchases can become unwieldy. For example, truckloads of corn would be needed to purchase a home selling for 5,000 bushels of corn. So the ideal money should

© Alexandar Iotzov/Shutterstock

be *portable*, or easily carried. Third, some commodity money was not easily divisible into smaller units. For example, when cattle served as money, any price involving a fraction of a cow posed an exchange problem. So the ideal money should be *divisible*.

Fourth, if commodity money like corn is valued equally in exchange, regardless of its quality, people eat the best corn and trade away the rest. As a result, the quality remaining in circulation declines, reducing its acceptability. Sir Thomas Gresham wrote in the 16th century that "bad money drives out good money"; this has come to be known as **Gresham's law**. People tend to trade away inferior money and hoard the best. Over time, the quality of money in circulation becomes less acceptable and, therefore, less useful as a medium of exchange. To avoid this problem, the ideal money should be of *uniform quality*.

Fifth, commodity money usually ties up otherwise valuable resources, so it has a higher opportunity cost than, say, paper money. For example, corn that is used for money cannot at the same time be used for corn on the cob, corn flour, popcorn, corn chips, other food, corn oil, and biofuel. So the ideal money should have *a low opportunity cost*.

If the supply or demand for money fluctuates unpredictably, so will the economy's price level, and this is the final problem with commodity money. For example, if a bumper crop increases the supply of corn, more corn is required to purchase other goods. This we call *inflation*. Likewise, any change in the demand for corn *as food* from, say, the growing popularity of corn chips, would affect the exchange value of corn. Erratic fluctuations in the market for corn limit its usefulness as money, particularly as a unit of account and a store of value. So the ideal money *should maintain a relatively stable value over time*. Money supplied by a responsible issuing authority is likely to retain its value better over time than money whose supply depends on uncontrollable forces of nature such as good or bad growing seasons.

What all this boils down to is that the ideal money is durable, portable, divisible, of uniform quality, has a low opportunity cost, and is relatively stable in value.

EXHIBIT 1
Six Properties of Ideal Money

Quality	Rationale	Good Examples	Bad Examples
1. Durable	Money should not wear out quickly	Coins; sea shells	Strawberries; seafood
2. Portable	Money should be easy to carry, even relatively large sums	Diamonds; paper or polymer money	Lead bars; potatoes
3. Divisible	Market exchange is easier if denominations support a range of possible prices	Honey; paper or polymer money and coins	Cattle; diamonds
4. Uniform Quality	If money is not of uniform quality, people will hoard the best and spend the rest, reducing the quality in circulation	Salt bricks; paper or polymer money; coins	Diamonds
5. Low Opportunity Cost	The fewer resources tied up in creating money, the more available for other uses	Iron coins; paper or polymer money	Gold coins; diamonds
6. Stable Value	People are more willing to accept and hold money if they believe it will keep its value over time	Anything whose supply can be limited by the issuing authority, such as paper or polymer money	Farm crops

These qualities are reinforced in Exhibit 1, which also lists the rationale, good examples, and bad examples. Please spend a minute now reviewing the table. Now consider in the following section how a commodity money emerged where currency was prohibited.

Mackerel Economics in U.S. Federal Prisons Although economic activity is sharply limited, many features of a normal economy are found in prison life. For example, in the absence of any official currency behind bars, cigarettes can serve all three roles of money: medium of exchange, unit of account, and store of value. Cigarettes are of uniform quality, of limited supply, reasonably durable, and individually can support small transactions or, in packs, larger ones. Prices measured in cigarettes are uniform and well known throughout a prison.

Prisoners are not allowed to hold cash. Whatever money sent by relatives or earned from prison jobs goes into commissary accounts that allow inmates to buy items such as snacks and toiletries. In the absence of cash,

to trade among themselves federal prisoners settle on cigarettes as their commodity money (despite official prohibitions against trade of any kind among inmates). Cigarettes served as the informal money until 2004, when smoking was banned in all federal prisons.

Once the ban took effect, the urge to trade created incentives to come up with some other commodity money. Prisoners tried other items sold at the commissary including postage stamps, cans of tuna, and Power Bars, but none of that seemed to catch on. Eventually prisoners settled on cans of mackerel, a bony, oily fish. So inmates informally use "macks"—as the commodity money came to be called—to settle gambling debts, to buy services from other inmates (such as ironing, shoe shining, and cell cleaning), and to buy goods from other inmates (including special foods prepared with items from the commissary and illicit items such as home-brewed "prison hooch"). At those federal prisons where the commissary opens only one day a week, some prisoners fill the void by running minicommissaries out of their lockers.

After wardens banned cans (because they could be refashioned into makeshift knives), the commodity money quickly shifted from cans of mackerel to plastic-and-foil pouches of mackerel. The mack is considered a good stand-in for the dollar because each pouch costs about $1 at the commissary, yet most prisoners, aside from weightlifters seeking extra protein, would rather trade macks than eat them.

Wardens try to discourage the mackerel economy by limiting the amount of food prisoners can stockpile. Those caught using macks as money can lose commissary privileges, can be reassigned to a less desirable cell, or can even spend time in the "hole." Still, market forces are so strong that the mackerel economy survives in many federal prisons.[1]

Coins

The division of commodity money into units was often natural, as in bushels of corn or heads of cattle. When rock salt was used as money, it was cut into uniform bricks. Because salt was usually of consistent quality, a trader had only to count the bricks to determine the amount of money. When silver and gold were used as money, both their quantity and quality were open to question. First, the amount had to be weighed, so transactions required scales. Second, because precious metals could be *debased* with cheaper metals, the quality of the metal had to be determined with each exchange. This was a nuisance.

This quantity and quality control problem was addressed by coining precious metals. *Coinage determined both the quantity and the quality of the metal.* Coins allowed payment by count rather than by weight. A flat surface on which this money was counted came to be called the *counter*, a term still used today. Initially, an image was stamped on only one side of a coin, leaving the other side blank. But people began shaving precious metal from the blank side. To prevent this, images were stamped on both sides. But another problem arose because bits of metal could still be clipped from the coin's edge. To prevent clipping, coins

were bordered with a well-defined rim. If you have a quarter, notice the tiny serrations on the edge. These serrations, throwbacks from the time when these coins were silver, reduced the chances of "getting clipped."

The power to issue coins was vested in the *seignior*, or feudal lord. Counterfeiting was considered an act of treason. If the face value of the coin exceeded the cost of coinage, minting coins was profitable. **Seigniorage** (pronounced "seen'-your-edge") refers to the profit earned by the seignior from coinage. **Token money** is money whose face value exceeds its production cost. Coins and paper money now in circulation in Canada are token money. For example, the 25-cent coin costs the Royal Canadian Mint only about 10 cents to make.

Money and Banking

The word *bank* comes from the Italian word *banca,* meaning "bench," which was a money changer's table. Banking spread from Italy to England, where London goldsmiths offered safekeeping for money and other valuables. The goldsmith gave depositors their money back on request, but because deposits by some tended to offset withdrawals by others, the amount of idle cash, or gold, in the vault changed little over time. Goldsmiths found that they could earn interest by lending from this pool of idle cash.

Goldsmiths offered depositors safekeeping, but visiting the goldsmith to get money to pay for each purchase became a nuisance. For example, a farmer might visit the goldsmith to withdraw enough money to buy a horse. The farmer would then pay the horse trader, who would promptly deposit the receipts with the goldsmith. Thus money took a round trip from goldsmith to farmer to horse trader and back to goldsmith. Because depositors soon grew tired of visiting the goldsmith every time they needed money, they began instructing the goldsmith to pay someone from their account. The payment amounted to moving gold from one stack (the farmer's) to another stack (the horse trader's). *These written instructions to the goldsmith were the first cheques.* **Cheques** have since become official looking, but they need not be, as evidenced in the United States by the actions of a Montana man who paid a speeding fine with instructions written on clean but frayed underpants. The Western Federal Savings and Loan of Missoula honoured the cheque.

[1] Justin Scheck, "Mackerel Economics in Prisons Leads to Appreciation of the Oily Fillets," *The Wall Street Journal*, 2 October 2008.

By combining the ideas of cash loans and cheques, the goldsmith soon discovered how to make loans by cheque. Rather than lend idle cash, the goldsmith could simply create a chequing balance for the borrower. *The goldsmith could extend a loan by creating an account against which the borrower could write cheques. In this way goldsmiths, or banks, were able to create a medium of exchange, or to "create money."* This money, based only on an entry in the goldsmith's ledger, was accepted because of the public's confidence that these claims would be honoured.

The total claims against the goldsmith consisted of claims by people who had deposited their money plus claims by borrowers for whom the goldsmith had created deposits. Because these claims exceeded the value of gold on reserve, this was the beginning of a **fractional reserve banking system**, a system in which bank reserves amounted to just a fraction of total deposits. The *reserve ratio* measured reserves as a percentage of total claims against the goldsmith, or total deposits. For example, if the goldsmith had reserves of $4,000 but deposits of $10,000, the reserve ratio would be 40 percent. The goldsmith was relying on the fact that not everyone would ask for their deposits at the same time.

Representative Money and Fiat Money

Another way a bank could create money was by issuing bank notes. **Bank notes** were pieces of paper promising the bearer specific amounts of gold or silver when the notes were presented to the issuing bank for redemption. In London, goldsmith bankers introduced bank notes about the same time they introduced cheques. *Whereas cheques could be redeemed only if endorsed by the payee, notes could be redeemed by anyone who presented them.* Paper money was often "as good as gold," because the bearer could redeem it for gold. In fact, paper money was more convenient than gold because it was less bulky and more portable. Bank notes that exchanged for a specific commodity, such as gold, were called **representative or commodity-backed money**. The paper money *represented* or was backed by gold in the bank's vault.

The amount of paper money issued by a bank depended on that bank's estimate of the share of notes that would be redeemed. The higher the redemption rate, the fewer notes could be issued based on a given amount of reserves. Initially, these promises to pay were issued by private individuals or banks, but over time, governments took a larger role in printing and circulating notes. Once paper money became widely accepted, it was perhaps inevitable that governments would begin issuing **fiat money**, which derives its status as money from the power of the government, or by *fiat*. Fiat (pronounced "fee at") money is money because the government says so. The word *fiat* is from Latin and means "so be it." Fiat money is not redeemable for anything other than more fiat money; it is not backed by something of intrinsic value. You can think of fiat money as mere paper money. It is acceptable not because it is intrinsically useful or valuable—as is corn or gold—but because the government says it's money. Fiat money is declared **legal tender** by the government, meaning that you have made a valid and legal offer of payment of your debt when you pay with such money. *Gradually, people came to accept fiat money because they believed that others would accept it as well.* The currency issued in Canada and throughout most of the world is fiat money.

A well-regulated system of fiat money is more efficient for an economy than commodity money. Fiat money uses only paper or polymer, but commodity money ties up something intrinsically valuable. Paper or polymer money makes up only part of the money supply. Modern money also includes chequing accounts, which are electronic entries in bank computers.

The Value of Money

Money has grown increasingly more abstract—from a physical commodity, to a piece of paper representing a claim on a physical commodity, to a piece of paper or polymer of no intrinsic value, to an electronic entry representing a claim on a piece of paper of no intrinsic value. So why does money have value? The commodity feature of early money bolstered confidence in its acceptability. Commodities such as corn, tobacco, and gold had value in use even if for some reason they became less acceptable in exchange. When paper money came into use, its acceptability was initially fostered by the promise to redeem it for gold or silver. But because most paper and polymer money throughout the world is now fiat money, there is no promise of redemption. So why can a piece of polymer

fractional reserve banking system bank reserves amount to only a fraction of funds on deposit with the bank

bank notes originally, pieces of paper promising a specific amount of gold or silver to anyone who presented them to issuing banks for redemption; today, Bank of Canada notes are mere polymer money

representative or commodity-backed money bank notes that exchange for a specific commodity, such as gold

fiat money money not redeemable for any commodity; its status as money is conferred initially by government decree but eventually by common experience

legal tender Canadian currency that constitutes a valid and legal offer of payment of debt

PEOPLE ACCEPT THESE PIECES OF POLYMER BECAUSE, THROUGH EXPERIENCE, THEY BELIEVE THAT OTHERS WILL DO THE SAME.

bearing the portrait of Sir John A. Macdonald and the number 10 in each corner be exchanged for a pizza or anything else selling for $10? *People accept these pieces of polymer because, through experience, they believe that others will do the same.* The acceptability of money, which we now take for granted, is based on years of experience with the stability of its value and with the willingness of others to accept it as payment. As we will soon see, when money's value becomes questionable, so does its acceptability.

The *purchasing power* of money is the rate at which it exchanges for goods and services. The higher the price level in the economy, the less can be purchased with each dollar, so the less each dollar is worth. The purchasing power of each dollar over time varies inversely with the economy's price level. As the price level increases, the purchasing power of money falls. To measure the purchasing power of the dollar in a particular year, you first compute the price index for that year and then divide 100 by that price index. For example, relative to the base period of 2002, the consumer price index for 2012 was 121.7. The purchasing power of a dollar was therefore 100/121.7, or $0.82, measured in 2002 dollars. Exhibit 2 shows the steady decline in the purchasing power of the dollar since 1960, when it was worth $6.45 in 2002 dollars.

When Money Performs Poorly

One way to understand the functions of money is to look at instances where money did not perform well. In recent years Zimbabwe has experienced hyperinflation. With prices growing by the hour, money no longer served as a reliable store of value, so workers couldn't wait to exchange their money for goods or for some "hard" currency—that is, a more stable currency. If inflation gets high enough, people no longer accept the nation's money and instead resort to some other means of exchange. On the other hand, if the supply of

EXHIBIT 2

Purchasing Power of $1.00 Measured in 2002 Constant Dollars

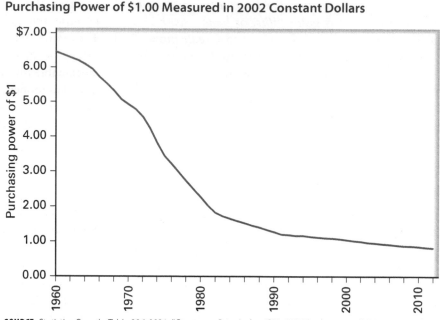

SOURCE: Statistics Canada. Table 326-0021, "Consumer Price Index (CPI), 2009 basket, annual (2002=100 unless otherwise noted)" (assessed: May 7, 2015).

money dries up or if the price system is not allowed to function properly, barter may be the only alternative.

When the official currency fails to serve as a medium of exchange because of price controls or hyperinflation or when hoarding dries up money in circulation, some other means of exchange emerges. But this diverts more resources from production to exchange. A poorly functioning monetary system increases the transaction costs of exchange. *No machine increases the economy's productivity as much as properly functioning money.* Indeed, it seems hard to overstate the value of a reliable monetary system. This is why we pay so much attention to money and banking.

Let's turn now to the development of money and banking in Canada.

LO 2 Financial Institutions and the Bank of Canada

You have already learned about the origin of modern banks: goldsmiths lent money from deposits held for safekeeping. So you already have some idea of how banks work. Recall from the circular-flow model that household saving flows into financial markets, where it is lent to investors. Financial institutions, such as banks, mortgage companies, and finance companies, accumulate funds from savers and lend them to borrowers. Financial institutions, or **financial intermediaries**, earn a profit by "buying low and selling high"—that is, by paying a lower interest rate to savers than they charge borrowers.

Financial Institutions

A wide variety of financial intermediaries respond to the economy's demand for financial services. **Depository institutions**—such as chartered banks, **trust and mortgage loan companies (TMLs)**, and **credit unions and *caisses populaires*** in Quebec **(CUCPs)**—obtain funds primarily by accepting customer *deposits*. Depository institutions play a key role in providing the nation's money supply.

Chartered banks are the oldest, largest, and most diversified of depository institutions. Chartered banks hold most deposits in Canada. Historically, TMLs specialized in making home mortgage loans. CUCPs, which are more numerous but smaller than TMLs, extend loans only to their "members" to finance homes or other major consumer purchases, such as new cars.

Schedule I banks are domestic banks, including the six largest chartered banks: the Royal Bank of Canada, TD Canada Trust, Scotiabank, Bank of Montreal, Canadian Imperial Bank of Commerce, and the National Bank of Canada, which together hold over 90 percent of all banking assets in Canada. The remaining banks are either foreign bank subsidiaries (Schedule II) or branches of foreign banks (Schedule III).

Birth of the Bank of Canada

Before 1850, banks were legislatively chartered in the regions in which they operated. These banks, like the English goldsmiths, issued bank notes. Notes from different banks circulated and most were redeemable for gold. The Free Banking Act of 1850 created a new system of small unit banks. It allowed the creation of banks without a legislative charter, by any group that met the requirements set out in the Free Banking Act.

A depression followed Confederation in the 19th century, and the economy experienced a number of panic "runs" on banks by depositors seeking to withdraw their money. A panic was usually set off by the failure of some prominent financial institution. Fearful customers besieged their banks. Borrowers wanted additional loans and extensions of credit, and depositors wanted their money back. *When many depositors tried to withdraw their money, they found they couldn't do so because each bank held only a fraction of its deposits as cash reserves.* In addition, the Great Depression, which lasted from 1929 to 1933, contributed to changes in Canadian banking policy. In 1934, Parliament passed the Bank of Canada Act, and the newly founded **Bank of Canada** started operations in March 1935.

Nearly all industrialized countries had formed central banks by 1900—such as the Bundesbank in Germany in 1875, the Bank of Japan in 1882, and the Bank of England, which has been around since 1694. The U.S. Federal Reserve System was created in 1913 as the central bank and monetary authority of the United states.

The Functions of the Bank of Canada

The main responsibilities of the Bank of Canada are the promotion of a stable and efficient financial

financial intermediaries institutions such as banks, mortgage companies, and finance companies, that serve as go-betweens, borrowing from people who have saved to make loans to others

depository institutions financial institutions that accept deposits from the public

trust and mortgage loan companies (TMLs) financial institutions that provide trustee functions and specialize in making home mortgage loans

credit unions and *caisses populaires* (CUCPs) depository institutions that extend loans only to their "members"

Bank of Canada the central bank and monetary authority of Canada

© Francis Vachon/Alamy

reserves funds that banks use to satisfy the cash demands of their customers; reserves consist of cash held by banks plus deposits at the Bank of Canada

Governing Council the six-member group that makes decisions about open-market operations; consists of the governor, the senior deputy governor, and four deputy governors

open-market operations purchases and sales of government securities by the Bank of Canada in an effort to influence the money supply

system in Canada, being the sole issuing authority of Canadian bank notes, providing fund-management and banking services for the federal government and for other clients, and conducting monetary policy. Thus the Bank of Canada was authorized to ensure sufficient money and credit in the banking system to support a growing economy. The Bank of Canada has other responsibilities: *to buy and sell government securities, to extend loans to banks, and to keep inflation low, stable, and predictable.*

The Bank of Canada does not deal with the public directly. It may be thought of as a bankers' bank. It holds deposits of banks, just as depository institutions hold deposits of the public, and they extend loans to banks, just as depository institutions extend loans to the public. The Bank of Canada also holds chequing deposits for the Government of Canada.

Reserves are funds that banks have on hand or on deposit with the Bank of Canada to promote banking safety, to facilitate interbank transfers of funds, and to satisfy the cash demands of their customers. Because the bank holds reserves, a cheque written by a depositor at one bank and deposited at another bank can be cleared, much like the goldsmith's moving of gold reserves from the farmer's account to the horse trader's account. The Bank of

Canada is also authorized to lend to banks in need of reserves; the interest rate charged is called the *bank rate.*

Board of Directors The *Board of Directors* of the Bank consists of the governor, the senior deputy governor, the deputy minister of finance, and 12 directors. The governor is appointed by the directors and approved by the prime minister's cabinet for a seven-year term. The board is responsible for setting and implementing the nation's monetary policy. *Monetary policy,* a term introduced in Chapter 3, is the regulation of the economy's money supply and interest rates to promote macroeconomic objectives. *The organization of the Bank of Canada is designed to insulate it from political pressure.* The Bank of Canada has some autonomy in the conduct of monetary policy; it is not responsible to Parliament in the same way as the Department of Finance in the conduct of fiscal policy. However, the Bank of Canada is not completely independent as it consults with the minister of Finance regularly under a system of joint responsibility.

Open Market Operations The Bank's **Governing Council** make decisions about the key tool of monetary policy, **open-market operations**—the buying and selling of government securities that affect both interest rates and the amount of reserves in the banking system (tools of monetary policy are examined in the next chapter). Exhibit 3 shows the organization chart

EXHIBIT 3
Organization Chart of the Bank of Canada

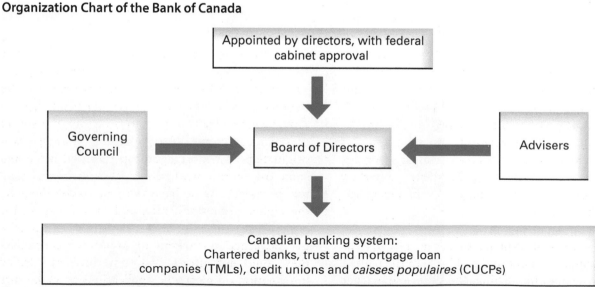

of the Bank of Canada. The Governing Council consists of the governor, who chairs it, the senior deputy governor, and four deputy governors.

Deposit Insurance Panic runs on banks stemmed from fears about the safety of bank deposits. The *Canada Deposit Insurance Corporation (CDIC)* was established in 1967 to insure the first $20,000 of each deposit account in one name. Today the insurance ceiling is $100,000 per depositor per bank. Most banks now purchase CDIC insurance. Other insurance programs take care of the rest. Deposit insurance, by calming fears about the safety of bank deposits, worked wonders to reduce bank runs.

Subprime Mortgages and Mortgage-Backed Securities in the U.S. and the Financial Crisis of 2008

Prior to 2000, only a credit-worthy, or *prime*, borrower could get a home mortgage in the United States. But new statistical techniques and better computers increased a lender's ability to assess the risk of a **subprime mortgage**, which is a mortgage for a borrower with a not-so-good credit rating. Any household with a credit history could be assigned a numerical credit score, and this score could be used to predict how likely that borrower would be to default on mortgage payments. Borrowers more likely to default would pay a higher interest rate to compensate the lender for their higher risk. Hundreds of mortgages could then be bundled together based on credit scores into a **mortgage-backed security**, which represents a claim on the monthly payments made on those mortgages. The idea is that subprime mortgages could be blended with other mortgages in whatever proportion needed to arrive at a particular level of default risk for the security. And a securities-rating agency could look at the mix of mortgages and assign that security an overall credit rating. A higher proportion of subprime loans would result in a higher risk security, but would also yield a higher return for investors. Investors could choose securities based on their tolerance for risk. Mortgage-backed securities opened up new sources of financing for subprime borrowers.

After the U.S. economy recovered from the recession of 2001, subprime mortgages grew in popularity. Fuelled by cash flows coming into the United States from places like China, the subprime market

became a trillion-dollar business by 2007. This development was considered good for America because it gave more households access to mortgage credit. Subprime borrowers might pay higher interest rates than prime borrowers, but at least they could get mortgages. The availability of subprime mortgages turned some renters into homeowners, a group presumably more committed to the community. Indeed, federal regulators pressured financial institutions into lending to groups that before the advent of subprime mortgages had been underserved.

Subprime loans increased the demand for housing, which raised housing prices, which, in turn, fuelled a boom in subprime loans in a reinforcing cycle. As house prices rose, many borrowers saw this as an opportunity to refinance. Based on the rising value of their houses, they would take out a bigger mortgage, use most of that money to pay off the old one, and still have money left over. Of course, monthly mortgage payments would increase too, but rising house prices meant that, in a pinch, the house could always be sold to pay off the mortgage. House prices had been marching higher for at least two decades. Mortgage-backed securities were considered a safe investment offering an attractive return. They were sold around the world. Banks and other financial institutions bought a lot of them. What could go wrong?

Incentive Problems in the U.S. Subprime Mortgage Market

A subprime mortgage typically originated with a mortgage broker (two-thirds originated this way). The mortgage was then sold to an underwriter, who bundled it with other mortgages and sold them as a mortgage-backed security to investors, the source of financing in the deal. Once the mortgage was originated, that mortgage broker earned a fee and soon lost interest in whether the borrower was good for the money. As we have seen, the riskier the loan, the higher the interest rate, and thus the more the broker made on that loan. Brokers had an incentive to encourage borrowers to apply for mortgages they could not afford, and some brokers falsified information on mortgage applications to make sure

subprime mortgage mortgage for a borrower with a not-so-good credit rating

mortgage-backed security a claim on payments made on the many mortgages bundled into this financial instrument

they would get approved. Some borrowers also exaggerated their income if there was no income verification (these became known as "liar's loans"). Making everything worse were lax regulations of mortgage originators, who were not required to tell borrowers whether they could afford the loans.

Meanwhile, banks and other financial institutions were earning attractive fees creating and selling mortgage-backed securities. Underwriters of mortgage-backed securities usually had little incentive to make sure that those who bought the securities would ultimately get paid. Worse yet, the credit-rating agencies that evaluated these securities also had a conflict of interest. They earned their fees by assessing the riskiness of these securities. But underwriters could shop around for the credit-rating agency that offered the highest rating. Thus mortgage-backed securities tended to get better ratings than they deserved—that is, the securities were actually more risky than their credit ratings indicated.

As housing prices rose and the profitability of converting mortgages into securities increased, underlying credit standards fell. Riskier borrowers could get mortgages with little trouble. The size of the mortgage also increased as did the loan-to-value ratio, meaning that instead of borrowing up to 80 percent of a home's value, home buyers could borrow 90 or even 100 percent of its value. And borrowers could often take out a second mortgage to pay for the down payment, so they ended up needing little or no money down to buy a house. In 2001, half of all mortgages required down payments of 20 percent or less; by 2006, at least half required down payments of only 10 percent or less, and a quarter of mortgages had no down payment requirements at all.

Bundling hundreds of mortgages into a single mortgage-backed security made for a complicated investment, and this worsened the incentive problems. Yet as long as home prices rose, everyone was happy—the borrower, the mortgage originator, the banker who underwrote and sold the mortgage-backed security, the credit rater, and the investor who found the yield attractive. But housing prices reached a level that in retrospect had gotten far out of whack with fundamentals of the housing market. After peaking in 2006, housing prices began to fall. Between 2006 and the middle of 2008, U.S. home prices plunged 22 percent on average. With housing prices tumbling, all the corners cut in the mortgage market soon became obvious. Many mortgages slipped "underwater," meaning that borrowers owed more than the house was worth. Such borrowers had an incentive to stop making payments. Many did, and defaults rose sharply, leading to millions of foreclosures.

Mortgage-backed securities quickly turned into "troubled assets." Because nobody wanted them, their value plummeted. Rising home foreclosures fed into a full-scale global financial panic in September 2008. The collapse of the major investment bank Lehman Brothers signalled that other financial institutions could soon follow. Nobody wanted to lend money they might not get back. Credit dried up. Panic spread to consumers, who cut consumption because of falling house prices, mounting job losses, and a collapsing stock market.

Final Word

Money has grown increasingly more abstract over time, moving from commodity money to paper money that represented a claim on some commodity, such as gold, to polymer money with no intrinsic value. As you will see, polymer money constitutes only a fraction of the money supply. Modern money also consists of electronic entries in the banking system's computers. So money has changed from a physical commodity to an electronic entry. Money today does not so much change hands as change electronic accounts.

Money and banking have been intertwined ever since the early goldsmiths offered to hold customers' valuables for safekeeping. Banking has evolved from one of the most staid and regulated industries to one of the most competitive. Deregulation and mergers have increased competition and have expanded the types of bank deposits. Reforms have given the Bank of Canada more uniform control over depository institutions and have given the institutions greater access to the services provided by the Bank of Canada.

Deregulation provided greater freedom not only to prosper but also to fail. Failures of depository institutions create a special problem, however, because these institutions provide the financial underpinning of the nation's money supply, as you will see in the next chapter. There we examine more closely how banks operate and supply the nation's money.

CHAPTER PROBLEMS

LO1 Discuss the evolution and functions of money

1.1. *(Origins of Banking)* Discuss the various ways in which London goldsmiths functioned as early banks.

1.2. *(Functions of Money)* "If an economy had only two goods (both nondurable), there would be no need for money because exchange would always be between those two goods." What important function of money does this statement disregard?

1.3. *(Types of Money)* Complete each of the following sentences:

a. If the face value of a coin exceeds the cost of coinage, the resulting revenue to the issuer of the coin is known as _____.

b. A product that serves both as money and as a commodity is _____.

c. Most coins and polymer money circulating in Canada have face values that exceed the value of the materials from which they are made. Therefore they are forms of _____.

d. If the government declares that creditors must accept a form of money as payment for debts, the money becomes _____.

e. A common unit for measuring the value of every good or service in the economy is known as a(n) _____.

1.4. *(Fiat Money)* Most economists believe that the better fiat money serves as a store of value, the more acceptable it is. What does this statement mean? How could people lose faith in money?

1.5. *(The Value of Money)* When the value of money was based on its gold content, new discoveries of gold were frequently followed by periods of inflation. Explain.

LO2 Financial institutions and the Bank of Canada

2.1. *(Financial Institutions)* What is a depository institution, and what types of depository institutions are found in Canada? How do they act as intermediaries between savers and borrowers? Why do they play this role?

2.2. *(Financial Institutions)* How are Schedule I banks different from Schedule II banks?

2.3. *(Bank of Canada)* What are the main powers and responsibilities of the Bank of Canada?

2.4. *(Subprime Mortgages)* What was the role of subprime mortgages in the financial crisis of 2008?

CASE STUDY

The Hassle of Small Change

Canada phased out the penny in 2013, in part because of rising prices for the metals it's made of—it actually cost 1.6 cents to produce every penny. The government estimated it lost $11 million a year producing and distributing the penny, and that didn't include the costs and frustrations for businesses and consumers that used them in transactions. A 2008 report by the Quebec-based bank Desjardins estimated the penny's existence cost Canada's economy about $150 million in 2006. Canada's big banks alone handled more than 9 billion pennies a year, which cost them $20 million annually to process.

In the United States, about 2.4 billion pennies were minted in 2009, and about 150 billion pennies circulated. That's about 500 pennies per U.S. resident. Most pennies are resting in change jars, drawers, or other gathering places for the lowly coin. Pennies are abandoned in the tiny change bins and donation cans at store counters. Many people won't bother to pick one up on the sidewalk (as evidenced by the number you find there). The penny, like all currency, has over time been robbed of its exchange value by inflation. Pennies can't be used in parking meters, vending machines, or pay telephones, and penny candy is long gone. To avoid the hassle of small change, some restaurants charge prices exactly divisible by 25 cents. That way, pennies, nickels, and dimes aren't needed for any transaction.

Has the penny outlived its usefulness? In the face of rising metal prices, governments that use pennies have some options. First option: mint them from a lower-cost alloy. This would buy some time, but inflation would eventually drive the metallic cost above the exchange value of the coin. Second option: abolish the penny, the option used by Canada. Take it out of circulation. Other countries that have eliminated their smallest coins include Australia, Britain, Finland, Hong Kong, and the Netherlands. New Zealand eliminated its 5-cent coin, as well as its 2-cent and 1-cent coins. The United States abolished the half-cent coin in 1857, at a time when it was worth 8 cents in today's purchasing power.

Third option: decree that the penny is worth 5 cents, the same as a nickel. At the same time, a government could withdraw nickels from circulation. With pennies worth so much more, there would be no incentive to hoard them for their metallic value (a current problem), and it would likely be decades before the metallic value caught up with the exchange value. Rebasing the U.S. penny to 5 cents would create windfall profits for those now hoarding pennies.

If the penny gets so little respect, why did the U.S. Treasury mint 2.4 billion in 2009? As noted, some people are hoarding pennies, waiting for the day when the metallic value exceeds the exchange value. Charities also collect millions from change cans located at check-out counters. And zinc producers lobby heavily to keep the penny around as a major user of the metal. Thus, the penny still has its boosters.

SOURCES: Jean-Pierre Aubry, François Dupuis, and Hendrix Vachon, "100th Anniversary of the Canadian Penny," *Desjardins Economic Studies*, 9 April 2008; Austan Goolsbee, "Now That the Penny Isn't Worth Much, It's Time to Make It Worth 5 Cents," *New York Times*, 1 February 2007; Elizabeth Williamson, "Will Nickel-Free Nickels Make a Dime's Worth of Difference," *Wall Street Journal*, 10 May 2010; and Thomas Sargent and Francois Velde, *The Big Problem of Small Change* (Princeton, NJ: Princeton University Press, 2002).

QUESTION

1. What are three possible solutions to the problem that the U.S. penny now costs more to produce than it's worth in exchange?

Banking and the Money Supply

> ## "How is the Bank of Canada both literally and figuratively a money machine?"

How do banks create money? Why are banks often called National Bank or Canada Bank rather than Benny's Bank or Loadsamoney? How is the Bank of Canada both literally and figuratively a money machine? Why are we so interested in banks, anyway? After all, isn't banking a business like any other, such as dry cleaning, auto washing, or home remodelling? Why not devote a chapter to the home-remodelling business? Answers to these and related questions are provided in this chapter, which examines banking and the money supply.

In this chapter, we take a closer look at the unique role banks play in the economy. Banks are special in macroeconomics because, like the London goldsmith, they can convert a borrower's IOU into money, one key to a healthy economy. Because regulatory reforms have eliminated many of the distinctions between commercial banks and trust and mortgage loan companies, all depository institutions are usually referred to more simply as banks.

We begin by going over the definitions of money, from the narrow to the broad view. Then we look at how banks work and how they create money. We also consider the Bank of Canada in more detail. As you will see, the Bank attempts to control the money supply directly by issuing currency and indirectly by regulating bank reserves.

LO 1 Money Aggregates

When you think of money, what comes to mind is probably currency—dollar notes and coins. But as you learned in the last chapter, dollar notes and coins account for only part of the money supply. In this section, we consider two definitions of money.

Narrow Definition of Money: M1 and M1+

Suppose you have some cash with you right now—dollar notes and coins. These are part of the money supply as narrowly defined. If you were to deposit this cash in your chequing account, you could then write cheques directing your bank to pay someone from your account. **Chequable deposits** are bank deposits that allow the account owner to write cheques to third parties. Chequable deposits are included in the narrow definition of money and can also be tapped with an ATM card or a debit card. Banks hold a variety of chequable deposits. In recent years, financial institutions have developed other kinds of accounts that carry cheque-writing privileges but also earn interest.

chequable deposits bank deposits that allow the account owner to write cheques to third parties; ATM or debit cards can also access these deposits and transmit them electronically

Money aggregates are measures of the money supply defined by the Bank of Canada. The narrow definition, called **M1+**, consists of currency (including coins) held by the nonbanking public, traveller's cheques and chequable deposits at chartered banks, trust and mortgage loans companies (TMLs), and credit unions and caisses populaires (CUCPs). M1, which included currency held by the nonbanking public, traveller's cheques, and chequable deposits at chartered banks (it did not include trust and mortgage loans companies, and credit unions and caisses populaires) was a common definition of money supply until recently. Note that currency in bank vaults is not counted as part of the money supply because it is not being used as a medium of exchange—it's just sitting there out of circulation. But chequable deposits are money because their owners can write cheques or use debit cards to tap them. Chequable deposits are the liabilities of the issuing banks, which stand ready to convert them into cash. But unlike cash, cheques are not legal tender, as signs that say "No cheques!" attest.

Broader Definitions of Money: M2 and M2+

Economists regard currency and chequable deposits as money because each serves as a medium of exchange, a unit of account, and a store of value. Some other financial assets perform the store-of-value function and can be converted into currency or to chequable deposits. Because these are so close to money, they are called near-monies and are included under a broader definition.

Savings deposits earn interest but have no specific maturity date. Banks often allow depositors to shift funds from savings accounts to chequing accounts by phone, ATM card, or online, so distinctions between narrow and broad definitions of money have become blurred. **Time deposits** (also called *certificates of deposit*, or CDs) earn a fixed rate of interest if held for a specified period, ranging from several months to several years. Premature withdrawals are penalized by forfeiture of some interest. Neither savings deposits nor time deposits serve directly as media of

exchange, so they are not included in M1+, the narrow definition of money.

Money market mutual fund accounts are another component of money when defined more broadly. But because of restrictions on the minimum balance, on the number of cheques that can be written per month, and on the minimum amount of each cheque, these accounts are not viewed as money as narrowly defined.

M2 consists of currency (including coins) held by the nonbanking public, traveller's cheques, personal and nonpersonal chequable deposits as well as savings deposits, and personal time deposits held at chartered banks. **M2+** includes M2, plus similar deposits at TMLs and CUCPs, life insurance company individual annuities, personal deposits at government-owned saving institutions, and money market mutual fund accounts. Exhibit 1 shows the size and relative importance of each money aggregate. As you can see, compared to M1+, M2+ is about two times larger. Thus the narrow definition of money is only a fraction of the broader aggregate. But distinctions between M1+ and M2+ become less meaningful as banks allow depositors to transfer funds from one account to another.

money aggregates measures of the economy's money supply

M1+ the narrow measure of the money supply, consisting of currency and coins held by the nonbanking public, traveller's cheques and chequable deposits at chartered banks, trust and mortgage loans companies (TMLs), and credit unions and caisses populaires (CUCPs)

savings deposits deposits that earn interest but have no specific maturity date

time deposits deposits that earn a fixed interest rate if held for the specified period, which can range from several months to several years; also called certificates of deposit

M2 a money aggregate consisting of currency (including coins) held by the nonbanking public and traveller's cheques, personal and nonpersonal chequable deposits as well as savings deposits, and personal time deposits held at chartered banks

M2+ a money aggregate consisting of M2 plus similar deposits at TMLs and CUCPs, life insurance company individual annuities, personal deposits at government-owned saving institutions, and money market mutual fund accounts.

EXHIBIT 1

Measures of Money Supply in Billions of Dollars (September 2013)

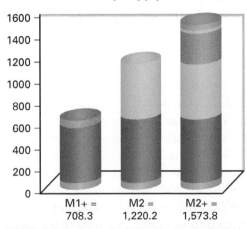

- Personal deposits at government-owned saving institutions ($11.3 billion)
- Life insurance company individual annuities ($42.4 billion)
- Money market mutual funds ($27.1 billion)
- TMLs & CUCPs total deposits ($272.7 billion)
- Savings & time deposits ($581.7 billion)
- TMLs & CUCPs chequable deposits ($69.8 billion)
- Chartered banks chequable deposits ($574.1 billion)
- Currency plus traveller's cheques ($64.4 billion)

M1+ = 708.3   M2 = 1,220.2   M2+ = 1,573.8

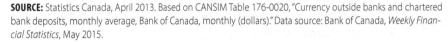

SOURCE: Statistics Canada, April 2013. Based on CANSIM Table 176-0020, "Currency outside banks and chartered bank deposits, monthly average, Bank of Canada, monthly (dollars)." Data source: Bank of Canada, *Weekly Financial Statistics*, May 2015.

The Bank of Canada measures other broader money aggregates such as M2++, which includes M2+ plus Canada Savings Bonds and nonmoney market funds. In general, the broader the measure of money supply, the more it includes other financial assets that perform the store-of-value function and can be converted into currency or to chequable deposits.

Credit Cards and Debit Cards: What's the Difference?

You may be curious about why the narrow definition includes funds accessed by debit cards but not funds accessed by credit cards. After all, most sellers accept credit cards as readily as they accept cash, cheques, or debit cards (online sellers even prefer credit cards), and credit cards finance more than 20 percent of all consumer purchases. Credit cards offer an easy way to get a loan from the card issuer. If you buy an airline ticket with a credit card, the card issuer lends you the money to pay for the ticket. You don't need money until you repay the credit card issuer. The credit card has not eliminated your use of money, merely delayed it.

On the other hand, when you use your debit card, you tap directly into your chequing account, paying with electronic money—part of M1+. Debit cards get their name because they *debit*, or draw down, your chequable account immediately. A **debit card**, also called a cheque card or bank card, combines the functions of an ATM card and a cheque. Debit cards are issued by banks, sometimes jointly with Visa, MasterCard, or other major card issuers. Even though debit cards look like credit cards, and even may bear a name such as Visa, they are not credit cards.

Many people prefer debit cards to cheques because no cheque book is required and payments are made directly and immediately. Transactions using debit cards and other electronic transfers now exceed payments by cheque. Like ATM cards, debit cards and now many credit cards usually require a personal identification number, or PIN, to use. But debit cards have some disadvantages. Whereas a debit card draws down

© FUSE/Getty Images

your chequing account immediately, credit cards provide a grace period between a purchase and required payment. And some people prefer to borrow beyond the grace period—that is, they carry a balance from month to month. Also, because debit cards immediately reduce your chequing account, you can't dispute a bill or withhold payment as you can after using a credit card and you can't stop payment as you can after writing a cheque. Still, debit cards came from nowhere a few years ago and today are used by more than 60 percent of households.

LO2 How Banks Work

Banks attract deposits from savers to lend to borrowers, earning a profit on the difference between the interest paid depositors and the interest charged borrowers. Savers need a safe place for their money, and borrowers need credit; banks try to earn a profit by serving both groups. To inspire depositor confidence, banks usually present an image of trust and assurance with impressive offices, a big safe often visible from the lobby, and names that impress. Banks are more apt to be called Trust Bank, National Bank, or Royal Bank. In contrast, *finance companies* are financial intermediaries that do not get their funds from depositors, so they can choose names aimed more at borrowers—names such as Household Finance or Loan Company. Likewise, mortgage companies do not rely on depositors, so they pick names aimed at home buyers, operating under names such as Home Trust, ClearHome Mortgage Solution, or Mortgagepal.ca.

Banks Are Financial Intermediaries

By bringing together both sides of the money market, banks serve as financial intermediaries or as go-betweens. They gather various amounts from savers and repackage these funds into the amounts demanded by borrowers. Some savers need their money next

debit card cards that tap directly into the depositor's bank account to fund purchases; also called a cheque card, and often doubles as an ATM card

week, some next year, some only after retirement. Likewise, borrowers need credit for different lengths of time. Banks, as intermediaries, offer desirable durations to both groups. In short, *banks reduce the transaction costs of channelling savings to creditworthy borrowers.* Here's how.

Coping with Asymmetric Information Banks, as lenders, try to identify borrowers who are willing to pay interest and are able to repay the loan. But borrowers have more reliable information about their own credit history and financial plans than do lenders. Thus in the market for loans, there is **asymmetric information**—an inequality in what's known by each party to the transaction. Asymmetric information is unequal information. This wouldn't be a problem if borrowers could be trusted to report relevant details to lenders. Some borrowers, however, have an incentive to suppress important information, such as other debts outstanding, a troubled financial history, or plans to use the borrowed money to fund a risky venture. Because of their experience and expertise in evaluating loan applicants, banks can better cope with asymmetric information than could an individual saver. Banks also know more about lending agreements than do individual savers. Thus savers, rather than lending their money directly, are better off depositing their money in banks and letting banks do the lending. *The economy is more efficient because banks develop expertise in evaluating creditworthiness, structuring loans, and enforcing loan contracts.*

Reducing Risk through Diversification By developing a diversified portfolio of assets rather than lending funds to a single borrower, banks reduce the risk to each individual saver. A bank, in effect, lends a tiny fraction of each saver's deposits to each of its many borrowers. If one borrower fails to repay a loan, it hardly affects a large, diversified bank. Certainly such a default does not represent the personal disaster it would if one saver's entire nest egg was loaned directly to that defaulting borrower. But if a number of borrowers stop repaying their loans, as happened with subprime mortgage loans during the recent financial crisis in the United States, then some banks fail.

Starting a Bank

We could consider the operation of any type of depository institution (chartered bank or credit union), but let's focus on chartered banks because they are the most important when measured by total assets. What's more, the operating principles also apply to other depository institutions. Suppose some business leaders in your hometown want to open a chartered bank called Home Bank. To obtain a *charter*, or the right to operate, they must apply to the provisional banking authority in the case of a provisionally regulated bank such as a credit union or to the Office of the Superintendent of Financial Institutions in the case of a federally regulated bank. The chartering agency reviewing the application judges the quality of management, the need for another bank in the region, the proposed bank's funding, and the likely success of the bank.

Suppose the founders plan to invest $500,000 in the bank, and they so indicate on their application for the right to operate. If their application is approved, they incorporate, issuing themselves shares of stock—certificates of ownership. Thus they exchange $500,000 for shares of stock in the bank. These shares are called the *owners' equity*, or the **net worth**, of the bank.

asymmetric information a situation in which one side of the market has more reliable information than the other side

net worth assets minus liabilities; also called owners' equity

© Comstock Images/Getty Images

balance sheet a
financial statement at a given
point in time that shows assets
on one side and liabilities and
net worth on the other side;
because assets must equal
liabilities plus net worth, the
two sides of the statement
must be in balance

asset anything of value that
is owned

liability anything that
is owed to other people or
institutions

desired / required
reserves the dollar
amount of reserves a bank
desires or is obligated by
regulation to hold as cash in
the bank's vault or on account
at the central bank

desired / required
reserve ratio the ratio
of reserves to deposits that
banks desire or are obligated by
regulation to hold

excess reserves
bank reserves exceeding
required or desired reserves

To focus our discussion, we examine the bank's **balance sheet**, presented in Exhibit 2. As the name implies, a balance sheet shows a balance between the two sides of the bank's accounts. The left side lists the bank's assets. An **asset** is any physical property or financial claim owned by the bank. At this early stage, assets include the building and equipment owned by Home Bank. The right side lists the bank's liabilities and net worth. A **liability** is an amount the bank owes. So far the bank owes nothing, so the right side includes only the net worth of $500,000. The two sides of the ledger must always be equal, or in *balance*, which is why it's called a *balance sheet*. So assets must equal liabilities plus net worth:

Assets = Liabilities + Net worth

The bank is now ready for business. Opening day is the bank's lucky day, because the first customer carries in a briefcase full of $100 notes and deposits $1,000,000 into a new chequing account. In accepting this cash, the bank promises to repay the depositor that amount. The deposit therefore is an amount the bank owes—it's a liability of the bank. As a result of this deposit, the bank's assets increase by $1,000,000 in cash and its liabilities increase by $1,000,000 in chequable deposits. Exhibit 3 shows the effects of this transaction on Home Bank's balance sheet. The right side now shows two claims on the bank's assets: claims by the owners, called net worth, and claims by nonowners, called liabilities, which at this point consist of chequable deposits.

Assets = Liabilities + Net worth

EXHIBIT 3
Home Bank's Balance Sheet after $1,000,000 Deposit into Chequing Account

Assets		Liabilities and Net Worth	
Cash	$1,000,000	Chequable deposits	$1,000,000
Building and furniture	500,000	Net worth	500,000
Total	$1,500,000	Total	$1,500,000

Reserve Accounts

Where do we go from here? As mentioned in the previous chapter, banks in many countries are required to hold in reserve a percentage of their chequable deposits. The dollar amount that must be held in reserve is called **required reserves**—chequable deposits multiplied by the required reserve ratio. The **required reserve ratio** dictates the minimum proportion of deposits the bank must hold in reserve. There is no reserve requirement in Canada. However, Canadian chartered banks generally keep a desired reserve of about 2 percent on chequable deposits. Reserves are held either as cash in the bank's vault, which earns the bank no interest; lend to another bank; or kept as deposits at the Bank of Canada. The latter two practices earn small rates of interest.

Home Bank therefore holds $20,000 as reserves, or 2 percent times $1,000,000.

Suppose Home Bank deposits $20,000 in a reserve account with the Bank of Canada. Home Bank's reserves now consist of $20,000 in desired reserves on deposit with the Bank of Canada and $980,000 in **excess reserves** held as cash in the vault. Home Bank earns no interest on cash in its vault. Excess reserves, however, can be used to make loans or to purchase interest-bearing assets, such as government bonds.

Liquidity Versus Profitability

Like the early goldsmiths, modern banks must be prepared to satisfy depositors' requests for funds. A bank loses reserves whenever a depositor withdraws cash, writes a cheque that gets deposited in another bank, or uses a debit card that ultimately shifts deposits to another bank. The bank must be in a position to

EXHIBIT 2
Home Bank's Balance Sheet

Assets		Liabilities and Net Worth	
Building and furniture	$500,000	Net worth	$500,000
Total	$500,000	Total	$500,000

MORE LIQUID ASSETS YIELD LOWER INTEREST RATES THAN LESS LIQUID ASSETS DO.

satisfy all depositor demands, even if many depositors ask for their money at the same time. Required reserves are not meant to be used to meet depositor requests for funds; therefore, banks often hold excess reserves or other assets, such as government bonds, that can be easily liquidated, or converted to cash, to satisfy any unexpected demand for cash. Banks may also want to hold excess reserves in case a valued customer needs immediate credit.

The bank manager must therefore structure the portfolio of assets with an eye toward liquidity but must not forget that survival also depends on profitability. **Liquidity** is the ease with which an asset can be converted into cash without a significant loss of value. *The objectives of liquidity and profitability are at odds.* For example, more liquid assets yield lower interest rates than less liquid assets do. The most liquid asset is cash in the bank's vault, but such reserves earn no interest.

At one extreme, suppose a bank is completely liquid, holding all its assets as cash in its vault. Such a bank would have no difficulty meeting depositors' demands for funds. This bank is playing it safe—too safe. The bank earns no interest and will fail. At the other extreme, suppose a bank uses all its excess reserves to acquire high-yielding but illiquid assets, such as long-term mortgage loans. Such a bank runs into problems whenever withdrawals exceed new deposits. There is a trade-off between liquidity and profitability. The portfolio manager's task is to strike the right balance between liquidity, or safety, and profitability.

Because vault cash earns no interest, banks prefer to hold reserves at the Bank of Canada or lend to other banks in the overnight money market. Any bank short of reserves at the end of the day can borrow from a bank that has excess reserves or from the Bank of Canada. The **overnight money market** provides for day-to-day lending and borrowing among banks.

These funds usually do not leave the Bank of Canada—instead, they shift among accounts. For example, suppose that at the end of the business day, Home Bank has excess reserves of $100,000 on account with the Bank of Canada and wants to lend that amount to another bank that finished the day short $100,000 in reserves. These two banks are brought together in the overnight money market. The interest rate paid on this loan is called the **overnight rate**; this is the rate the Bank of Canada targets as a tool of monetary policy, but more on that later.

Bank notes images used with the permission of the Bank of Canada.

liquidity a measure of the ease with which an asset can be converted into money without a significant loss of value

overnight money market a market for overnight lending and borrowing of reserves among banks; the interbank market for reserves

overnight rate the interest rate charged in the overnight money market; the interest rate banks charge one another for overnight borrowing; the Bank of Canada target interest rate

LO 3 How Banks Create Money

Let's now discuss how the Bank of Canada, Home Bank, and the banking system as a whole can create fiat money. Excess reserves are the raw material the banking system uses to create money. Again, our discussion focuses on chartered banks because they are the largest and most important depository institutions.

Creating Money through Excess Reserves

Suppose Home Bank has already used its $980,000 in excess reserves to make loans and buy government bonds and has no excess reserves left. In fact, let's assume there are no excess reserves in the banking system. With that as a point of departure, let's walk through the money creation process.

Round One To start, suppose the Bank of Canada buys a $1,000 Canada bond from a securities dealer, with the transaction handled by the dealer's bank—Home Bank. The Bank of Canada pays the dealer by crediting Home Bank's reserve account with $1,000, so Home Bank can increase the dealer's chequing account by $1,000. Where does the Bank of Canada get these reserves? It makes them up—creates

George Doyle/Stockbyte/Getty Images

EXHIBIT 4

Changes in Home Bank's Balance Sheet after the Bank of Canada Buys a $1,000 Bond from Securities Dealer

Assets		Liabilities and Net Worth	
Reserves at Bank of Canada	$1,000	Chequable deposits	$1,000

them out of thin air, out of electronic ether! The securities dealer has exchanged one asset, a Canada bond, for another asset, chequable deposits. A Canada bond is not money, but chequable deposits are, so the money supply increases by $1,000 in this first round. Exhibit 4 shows changes in Home Bank's balance sheet as a result of the Bank of Canada's bond purchase. On the assets side, Home Bank's reserves at the Bank of Canada increase by $1,000. On the liabilities side, chequable deposits increase by $1,000. Of the dealer's $1,000 chequable deposit, Home Bank must set aside $20 in desired reserves (based on a 2 percent desired reserve ratio). The remaining $980 becomes excess reserves, which can fuel a further increase in the money supply.

Round Two Suppose Home Bank is your regular bank, and you apply for a $980 loan to help pay student fees. Home Bank approves your loan and increases your chequing account by $980. *Home Bank has converted your promise to repay, your IOU, into a $980-chequable deposit. Because chequable deposits are money, this action increases the money supply by $980.* The money supply has increased by a total of $1,980 to this point—the $1,000 increase in the securities dealer's chequable deposits and now the $980 increase in your chequable deposits. In the process, what had been $980 in Home Bank's excess reserves now back up its loan to you. As shown in Exhibit 5,

Home Bank's loans increase by $980 on the assets side because your IOU becomes the bank's asset. On the bank's liabilities side, chequable deposits increase by $980 because the bank has increased your account by that amount. In short, Home Bank has created $980 in chequable deposits based on your promise to repay the loan.

When you write a $980 cheque for student fees, your college promptly deposits the cheque into its chequing account at Merchants Trust, which increases the college's account by $980, and sends your cheque to the Automated Clearing Settlement System (ACSS) for processing. The ACSS then sends the cheque to Home Bank, which reduces your chequable deposits by $980. The Bank of Canada transfers $980 in reserves from Home Bank's settlement account to Merchants Trust's settlement account. The ACSS and Bank of Canada have thereby "cleared" your cheque by settling the claim that Merchants Trust had on Home Bank. Your $980 in chequable deposits at Home Bank has become your college's $980 in chequable deposits at Merchants Trust. The total increase in the money supply to this point is still $1,980.

Round Three But Merchants Trust now has $980 more in reserves on deposit with the Bank of Canada. After setting aside $19.60 as desired reserves, or 2 percent of your college's chequable deposit increase, the bank has $960.40 in excess reserves. Suppose Merchants Trust lends this $960.40 to an English major starting a new business called "Note This," an online note-taking service for students in large classes. Exhibit 6 shows assets at Merchants Trust are up by $960.40 in loans, and liabilities are up by $960.40 in chequable deposits. At this point, chequable deposits in the banking system, and the money supply in the economy, are up by a total of $2,940.40 (= $1,000 + $980 + $960.40), all

EXHIBIT 5

Changes in Home Bank's Balance Sheet after Lending $900 to You

Assets		Liabilities and Net Worth	
Loans	$980	Chequable deposits	$980

EXHIBIT 6

Changes in Merchants Trust's Balance Sheet after Lending $960.40 to English Major

Assets		Liabilities and Net Worth	
Loans	+$960.40	Chequable deposits	+$960.40

springing from the Bank of Canada's original $1,000 Canada bond purchase.

The $960.40 loan is spent at the college bookstore, which deposits the cheque in its account at Fidelity Bank. Fidelity credits the bookstore's chequable deposits with $960.40 and sends the cheque to the ACSS for clearance. The Bank of Canada reduces Merchants Bank's reserves by $960.40 and increases Fidelity's by the same. Merchants reduces the English major's chequable deposits by $960.40. So chequable deposits are down by $960.40 at Merchants and up by the same amount at Fidelity. Chequable deposits are still up by $2,940.40, as the $960.40 in chequable deposits has simply shifted from Merchants Trust to Fidelity Bank.

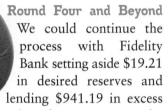

Round Four and Beyond We could continue the process with Fidelity Bank setting aside $19.21 in desired reserves and lending $941.19 in excess reserves, but you get some idea of money creation by now. Notice the pattern of deposits and loans. Each time a bank gets a fresh deposit, 2 percent goes to desired reserves. The rest becomes excess reserves, which fuel new loans or other asset acquisitions. The borrower writes a cheque, which the recipient deposits in a chequing account, thereby generating excess reserves to support still more loans.

To Review: An individual bank can lend no more than its excess reserves. When the borrower spends those funds, reserves at one bank usually fall, but total reserves in the banking system do not. The recipient bank uses most of the new deposit to extend more loans, creating more chequable deposits. The potential expansion of chequable deposits in the banking system therefore equals some multiple of the initial increase in reserves. Note that our example assumes that banks do not allow excess reserves to sit idle, that borrowed funds do not idle in chequing accounts, and that the public does not hold some of the newly created money as cash. If excess reserves remained just that or if borrowed funds idled in chequing accounts, they would not fuel an expansion of the money supply. And if people chose to hold borrowed funds in cash rather than in chequing accounts, that idle cash would not add to reserves in the banking system.

A Summary of the Rounds

Let's review the money creation process: *the initial and most important step is the Bank of Canada's injection of $1,000 in fresh reserves into the banking system.* By buying the bond from the securities dealer, the Bank of Canada immediately increased the money supply by $1,000. Home Bank set aside $20 as desired reserves and lent you its $980 in excess reserves. You paid your college fees, and the $980 ended up in your college's chequable account. This fuelled more money creation, as shown in a series of rounds of Exhibit 7. As you can see, during each round, the increase in chequable deposits (column 1) minus the increase in desired reserves (column 2) equals the potential increase in loans (column 3). Chequable deposits in this example can potentially increase by as much as $50,000.

In our example, money creation results from the Bank of Canada's $1,000 bond purchase from the securities dealer, but excess reserves would also have increased if the Bank of Canada purchased a $1,000 bond from Home Bank, or lent Home Bank $1,000.

What if the Bank of Canada paid the securities dealer in cash? By exchanging Bank of Canada notes, which become part of the money supply in the hands of the public, for a Canada bond, which is not part of the money supply, the Bank of Canada would have increased the money supply by $1,000. Once the securities dealer put this cash into a chequing account—or spent the cash, so the money ended up in someone else's chequing account—the banking system's money creation process would have been off and running.

EXHIBIT 7
Summary of the Money Creation Resulting from the Bank of Canada's Purchase of $1,000 Canada Government Bond

Bank	(1) Increase in Chequable Deposits	(2) Increase in Desired Reserves	(3) Increase in Loans (3) − (1) − (2)
Round 1. Home Bank	$1,000	$20	$980
Round 2. Merchants Trust	980	19.60	960.40
Round 3. Fidelity Bank	960.40	19.21	941.19
All remaining rounds	47,059.60	941.19	46,118.41
Totals	$50,000	$1,000	$49,000

Desired Reserve and Money Expansion

The banking system as a whole eliminates excess reserves by expanding the money supply. With a 2 percent desired reserve, the Bank of Canada's initial injection of $1,000 in fresh reserves could support up to $50,000 in new chequable deposits in the banking system as a whole, *assuming no bank holds excess reserves, borrowed funds don't sit idle, and people don't want to hold more cash.*

The multiple by which the money supply increases as a result of an increase in the banking system's reserves is called the **money multiplier**. The **simple money multiplier** equals the reciprocal of the desired reserve ratio, or 1/r, where r is the reserve ratio. In our example, the reserve ratio was 2 percent, or 0.02, so the reciprocal is 1/0.02, which equals 50. The formula for the multiple expansion of money supply can be written as:

$$\text{Change in the money supply} = \text{Change in fresh reserves} \times 1/r$$

Again, the simple money multiplier assumes that banks hold no excess reserves, that borrowers do not let the funds sit idle, and that people do not want to hold more cash. The higher the desired reserve, the greater the fraction of deposits that is held as reserves, so the smaller the money multiplier. A desired reserve of 20 percent instead of 2 percent would mean each bank sets aside 10 times as much in desired reserves. The simple money multiplier in this case would be 1/0.2, which equals 5. The maximum possible increase in chequable deposits resulting from an initial $1,000 increase in fresh reserves would therefore be $1,000 × 5, or $5,000. *Excess reserves fuel the deposit expansion process, and a higher desired reserve drains this fuel from the banking system, thereby reducing the amount of new money that can be created.*

On the other hand, with a desired reserve of only 1 percent, banks would set aside less for desired reserves, leaving more excess reserves available for loans. The simple money multiplier in that case would be 1/0.01, or 100. With $1,000 in fresh reserves and a 1 percent desired reserve, the banking system could increase the money supply by a maximum of $1,000 × 100, which equals $100,000. Thus the change in the reserve ratio affects the banking system's ability to create money.

In summary, money creation usually begins with the Bank of Canada injecting new reserves into the banking system. An individual bank lends an amount no greater than its excess reserves. The borrower's spending ends up in someone else's chequing account, fuelling additional loans. *The fractional desired reserve is the key to the multiple expansion of chequable deposits.* If each $1 deposit had to be backed by $1 in desired reserves, the money multiplier would be reduced to 1, which is no multiplier at all.

Limitations on Money Expansion

Various leakages from the multiple expansion process reduce the size of the money multiplier, which is why 1/r is called the *simple* money multiplier. You could think of "simple" as meaning maximum. To repeat, our example assumes (1) that banks do not let excess reserves sit idle, (2) that borrowers do something with the money, and (3) that people do not choose to increase their cash holdings. How realistic are these assumptions? With regard to the first, banks have a profit incentive to make loans or buy some higher interest-bearing asset with excess reserves. Granted, banks earn some interest on reserves deposited with the Bank of Canada, but the rate is typically less than could be earned on loans or on most other interest-bearing assets. The second assumption is also easy to defend. Why would people borrow money if they didn't need it for something? The third assumption is trickier. Cash may sometimes be preferable to chequing accounts because cash is more versatile, so people may choose to hold some of the newly created money as cash. To the extent that people prefer to hold idle cash, this drains reserves from the banking system. With less excess reserves, banks are less able to make loans, reducing the money multiplier. Incidentally, for the money multiplier to operate, a particular bank need not use excess reserves in a specific way; it could use them to pay all its employees a Christmas bonus, for that matter. As long as the money ends up as chequable deposits in the banking system, away we go with the money expansion process.

$$\Delta \text{ money supply} = \Delta \text{ fresh reserves} \times 1/r$$

THE BANK OF CANADA'S SALE OF GOVERNMENT BONDS REDUCES BANK RESERVES.

Multiple Contraction of the Money Supply

We have already outlined the money creation process, so the story of how the Bank of Canada can reduce bank reserves, thereby reducing the money supply, can be a brief one. Again, we begin by assuming there are no excess reserves in the system and the desired reserve requirement is 2 percent. Suppose the Bank of Canada *sells* a $1,000 Canada bond to a securities dealer and gets paid with a cheque drawn on the security dealer's account at Home Bank. So the Bank of Canada gets paid by drawing down Home Bank's reserves at the Bank of Canada by $1,000. The Bank of Canada has thereby reduced the money supply by $1,000 in this first round.

Because the dealer's chequing account was reduced by $1,000, Home Bank no longer needs to hold $20 in desired reserves. But Home Bank is still short $980 in desired reserves (remember, when we started, there were no excess reserves in the banking system). To replenish reserves, Home Bank must recall loans (ask for repayment before the due date), or sell some other asset. As the poet Robert Frost wryly observed, "A bank is a place where they lend you an umbrella in fair weather and ask for it back again when it begins to rain." Suppose the bank calls in $980 loaned to a local business, and the loan is repaid with a cheque written against Merchants Bank. When the cheque clears, Home Bank's reserves are up by $980, just

We begin by assuming that there are no excess reserves in the system....

enough to satisfy its desired reserve, but Merchants Bank's reserves and chequable deposits are down by $980. Chequable deposits are now down $1,980 as a result of the Bank of Canada's purchase of a $1,000 bond. Because there were no excess reserves at the outset, the loss of $980 in reserves leaves Merchants $960.40 short of its desired level of reserves, forcing that bank to get more reserves.

And so it goes down the line. The Bank of Canada's sale of government bonds reduces bank reserves, forcing banks to recall loans or to somehow replenish reserves. This reduces chequable deposits each additional round. *The maximum possible effect is to reduce the money supply by the original reduction in bank reserves times the simple money multiplier, which again equals 1 divided by the desired reserve, or 1/r.* In our example, the Bank of Canada's sale of $1,000 in Canada bonds could reduce the money supply by as much as $50,000.

Now that you have some idea how fractional reserve banking works, we are in a position to summarize the Bank of Canada's role in the economy.

LO 4 The Bank of Canada's Tools of Monetary Control

As mentioned in the previous chapter, in its capacity as a bankers' bank, the Bank of Canada clears cheques for, extends loans to, and holds deposits of banks. The Bank of Canada's control over chequable deposits works indirectly through its control over reserves in the banking system. The Bank of Canada's principal tool for controlling reserves, money supply, and interest rates is open-market operations. Other central banks use additional tools such as a reserve requirement, which is the minimum amount of reserves that banks hold against deposits.

Open-Market Operations and the Overnight Interest Rate

The Bank of Canada carries out open-market operations whenever it buys or sells Canada government bonds in the open market. Decisions about open-market operations are made by the Bank's governing council, which meets at eight pre-set dates per year and during emergencies to announce the target for the overnight rate. To increase the money supply, the Bank of Canada buys government bonds. This is called an **open-market purchase**. To reduce the money supply, the Bank of Canada carries out an **open-market sale**. Open-market operations are relatively easy to carry out. They require no change in laws or regulations and can be executed in any amount—large or small—chosen by the Bank of Canada. Their simplicity and ease of use make them the tool of choice for the Bank of Canada.

Through open-market operations, the Bank of Canada influences bank reserves and the overnight rate. Banks that need reserves can borrow excess reserves from other banks, paying the overnight rate. The overnight rate serves as a good indicator of the "tightness" of monetary policy. For example, suppose the Bank of Canada buys bonds in the open market and thereby increases reserves in the banking system. As a result, more banks have excess reserves. Demand for excess reserves in the overnight market falls and supply increases, so the overnight rate—the interest rate for borrowing reserves in this market—declines. We can expect this lower overnight market rate to spread quickly to the economy at large. The excess reserves that have created the lower overnight rate prompt banks to lower short-term and long-term interest rates and this increases the quantity of loans demanded by the public.

Bank of Canada Advances and the Overnight Interest Rate

The **bank rate**—the interest rate the Bank of Canada charges banks that borrow reserves from it—is one-fourth of a percent above the target overnight rate. Thus a Bank of Canada advance is less attractive than borrowing through the overnight funds market, a financial market that allows banks with less than desired reserves to borrow from banks with more reserves than they desire. The interest rate that banks charge for lending funds overnight is called the overnight rate. The Bank of Canada's key policy interest rate is the target overnight rate and its policy is to ensure that the actual overnight rate is within one half of a percent of its target.

An Example of the Bank of Canada's 50-Basis-Point Operating Band for Overnight Interest Rate

1.25%	Bank Rate
1.00%	Target for the Overnight Rate
0.75%	Interest Rate on Deposits

Exhibit 8 shows the relationship between the target for the overnight rate, the bank rate, and the Bank of Canada deposit rate. If the Bank of Canada announces a target for the overnight rate at 1 percent, the bank rate would be 1.25 percent. The bank rate is the rate of interest at which the Bank of Canada is willing to lend any amount to chartered banks; it's the upper limit of the operating band in Exhibit 8. The lower limit of 0.75 percent is the deposit rate, the rate of interest that the Bank of Canada offers to borrow unlimited amounts from chartered banks on their accounts with them. This keeps the actual overnight interest rate within the Bank of Canada's target range—that is, between 1.25 percent and 0.75 percent. It will not be above 1.25 percent because chartered banks would rather borrow from the Bank of Canada at 1.25 percent than at a higher rate from other lenders. Similarly, the actual overnight rate will not be below 0.75 percent because chartered banks would rather lend to the Bank of Canada at 0.75 percent than accept a lower rate from other borrowers.

Chartered banks would increase their lending if the Bank of Canada reduces the target for the overnight rate because the cost of finding themselves with less than desired reserve would be low, causing money supply to increase and vice versa. The Bank of Canada uses the bank rate more as a signal to financial markets about its monetary policy than as a tool for increasing or decreasing the money supply. The bank rate might also be thought of as an emergency tool for injecting liquidity into the banking system in the event of some financial crisis, such as the global credit crisis of 2008. Banks would prefer to borrow reserves from other banks in the overnight funds market rather than borrow reserves directly from the Bank of Canada. The Bank of Canada considers itself as the "lender of last resort."

Reserve Requirements

Many central banks, including the U.S. Federal Reserve, also influence the money supply through reserve requirements, which are regulations regarding the minimum amount of reserves that banks must hold to back up deposits. Reserve requirements determine how much money the banking system can create with each dollar of fresh reserves. If a central bank increases the reserve requirement, then banks have less excess reserves to lend out. This reduces the banking system's ability to create money. On the other hand, a lower reserve requirement increases the banking system's ability to create money. The reserve ratio is the minimum fraction of reserves that banks hold against deposits. Some countries such as Australia, Canada, and the United Kingdom have no reserve requirement. Banks there still hold reserves to deal with everyday cash requirements and can borrow from their central banks if necessary. Canadian chartered banks can hold any desired reserves to maximize their profits, a practice that has been in effect since the Bank of Canada abolished reserve requirements in 1992.

Final Word

Banks play a unique role in the economy because they can transform someone's IOU into a chequable deposit, and a chequable deposit is money. The banking system's ability to expand the money supply depends on the amount of excess reserves in that system. In our example, it was the purchase of a $1,000 Canada bond that started the ball rolling. The Bank of Canada can also increase reserves by lowering the bank rate enough to stimulate bank borrowing from the Bank of Canada (although the Bank of Canada uses changes in the bank rate more to signal its policy than to alter the money supply). And, by reducing the required or desired reserve ratio, a central bank not only instantly creates excess reserves in the banking system but also increases the money multiplier. In practice, central banks rarely change the reserve requirement because of the disruptive effect of such a change on the banking system. Furthermore, the Bank of Canada can alter chartered bank reserves by shifting government deposits between it and chartered banks. *To control the money supply, the Bank of Canada relies primarily on open-market operations.*

Open-market operations can have a direct effect on the money supply, when the Bank of Canada buys bonds from the public. But the Bank also affects the money supply indirectly, as the Bank of Canada's bond purchase increases bank reserves, which then serve as fuel for the money multiplier. In the next chapter, we consider how changes in the money supply affect the economy.

CHAPTER PROBLEMS

LO1 Examine definitions of money aggregates

1.1. *(Monetary Aggregates)* Calculate M1+ and M2 using the following information:

Personal time deposits	$30 billion
Currency and coins held by the nonbanking public	$43 billion
Chequable deposits at chartered banks	$50 billion
Chequable deposits at trust and mortgage loan companies, and credit unions and caisses populaires	$5 billion
Traveller's cheques	$1 billion
Personal savings deposits at chartered banks	$32 billion
Nonpersonal chequable and savings deposits at chartered banks	$63 billion

1.2. *(Credit Cards)* Why are funds accessed by credit cards not considered part of the narrow definition of money?

LO2 Explain how banks work

2.1. *(Reserve Accounts)* Suppose that a bank's customer deposits $4,000 in her chequing account. The desired reserve ratio is 0.25.
   a. What are the desired reserves on this new deposit?
   b. What is the largest loan that the bank can make on the basis of the new deposit?
   c. If the bank chooses to hold reserves of $3,000 on the new deposit, what are the excess reserves on the deposit?

2.2. *(Liquidity versus Profitability)* The objectives of liquidity and profitability are at odds. How does a bank manager structure the portfolio of assets to fulfill the bank's liquidity and profitability objectives?

LO3 Describe how banks create money

3.1. *(Money Creation)* Suppose Bank A, which has a desired reserve of 10 percent, receives a $1,000 deposit from a customer.

a. Assuming that it wishes to hold no excess reserves, determine how much the bank should lend. Show your answer on Bank A's balance sheet.

b. Assuming that the loan shown in Bank A's balance sheet is redeposited in Bank B, show the changes in Bank B's balance sheet if it lends out the maximum possible.

c. Repeat this process for three additional banks: C, D, and E.

d. Using the simple money multiplier, calculate the total change in the money supply resulting from the $1,000 initial deposit.

e. Assume Banks A, B, C, D, and E each wish to hold 5 percent excess reserves. How would holding this level of excess reserves affect the total change in the money supply?

3.2. *(Money Multiplier)* Suppose that the banks lower their desired reserve ratio from 0.10 to 0.05. How does this affect the simple money multiplier, assuming that excess reserves are held to zero and there are no currency leakages? What are the money multipliers for desired reserve ratios of 0.15 and 0.20?

3.3. *(Money Creation)* Show how each of the following would initially affect a bank's assets and liabilities.

a. Someone makes a $10,000 deposit into a chequing account.

b. A bank makes a loan of $1,000 by establishing a chequing account for $1,000.

c. The loan described in part (b) is spent.

d. A bank must write off a loan because the borrower defaults.

3.4. *(Money Creation)* Show how each of the following *initially* affects bank assets, liabilities, and reserves. Do *not* include the results of bank behaviour resulting from the Bank of Canada's action. Assume a desired reserve ratio of 0.05.

a. The Bank of Canada purchases $10 million worth of Canada government bonds from a bank.

b. The Bank of Canada loans $5 million to a bank.

c. The desired reserve ratio rises to 0.10.

LO4 Discuss the Bank of Canada's tools for monetary control

4.1. *(Monetary Control)* Suppose the money supply is currently $50 billion and the Bank of Canada wishes to increase it by $100 billion. Given a desired reserve ratio of 0.25, what should it do?

4.2. *(Overnight Interest Rate)* Explain how the overnight interest rate is used as a monetary policy tool in Canada.

CASE STUDY

Banking for the Poor: Payday Loans

A "payday loan" is a relatively small amount of money—say, $300—borrowed for a short period, usually about two weeks, by lower-income people who have a chequing account, a job, and direct deposit of their paycheque. For example, the borrower writes a postdated cheque for $300 to the payday lender and gets $255 in cash. The lender holds onto the cheque until the next payday, two weeks later, then cashes it, netting $45 on the transaction. Or the borrower can decide to roll over the loan by paying the lender another $45 to hold the cheque for two more weeks. Most borrowers roll over their loans more than once. The implied annual rate of interest is at least 400 percent.

Here are some questions: Do payday loans benefit an underserved population by providing ready access to short-term credit, albeit at a high cost? Or do payday loans trap customers into habitual borrowing at steep interest rates with no way out? Should government regulators protect borrowers from the bad consequences of their own choices? Or would a ban simply force such borrowers into even less attractive options? Some earlier research using geographical differences in regulation across the United States suggested that payday loans, despite their high interest rates, may provide benefits to borrowers and their communities. For example, although this may sound odd, according to one argument, some people may deliberately borrow at such costly rates so they will have more incentive to repay the loan quickly. But more recent research raises some troubling questions about payday loans. For example, Brian Melzer of Northwestern University finds no evidence that having access to payday loans alleviates economic hardship. On the contrary, access to payday lenders leads to more difficulty paying mortgages, rent, and utilities; a greater chance of losing one's home; and an increased tendency to put off needed medical care, dental care, and prescription drug purchases.

Using a database of 145,000 payday loan applicants from a large lender in Texas, Paige Skiba of Vanderbilt and Jeremy Tobacman of the University of Pennsylvania compare payday borrowers with similarly situated applicants who were denied payday loans to determine whether payday borrowing affects the likelihood of bankruptcy. They find that, for first-time applicants with below average credit scores, access to payday loans doubles the chances of filing for bankruptcy during the following two years (compared to first-time applicants with below average credit scores who were denied payday loans). Seemingly small loans cause such a large effect because borrowers are already financially strapped when they begin with a payday loan. In addition, many payday borrowers take out multiple loans, so the interest burden piles up.

Finally, a study by the North Carolina bank commissioner analyzes how families fared after payday lenders were forced from that state in 2006. A survey of payday borrowers found that most knew the dollar cost per $100, but only one in six had any idea about the implied annual percentage rate. Some said they were glad they no longer were tempted by what they viewed as a costly product—easy to get into, but hard to get out of. About three-quarters of the fees collected by payday lenders come from rollovers of existing loans. Many payday lenders offer half-off discounts to new customers.

SOURCES: "North Carolina Consumers After Payday Lending," University of North Carolina, (November 2007); Paige Skiba and Jeremy Tobacman, "Do Payday Loans Cause Bankruptcy?" Unpublished manuscript (November 9, 2009); Ryan Randazzo, "Payday Lender to Close 47 Stores, Leave State," *Arizona Republic*, 12 July 2010; and Brian T. Melzer, "The Real Costs of Credit Access: Evidence from Payday Lending," Northwestern University, (January 3, 2009) at http://www.kellogg.northwestern.edu/faculty/melzer/index.htm.

QUESTION

1. Give one argument in favour of payday loans and one argument against.

14

Monetary Theory and Policy in an Open Economy

LEARNING OUTCOMES

LO1 Describe the relationship between the demand and supply of money

LO2 Explain how changes in the money supply affect aggregate demand in the short run

LO3 Explain how changes in the money supply affect aggregate demand in the long run

LO4 Evaluate targets for monetary policy

"Why do people hold money?"

Why do people maintain chequing accounts and have cash in their pockets, purses, wallets, desk drawers, coffee cans—wherever? In other words, why do people hold money? How does the stock of money in the economy affect your ability to find a job, get a student loan, buy a car, or pay credit card bills? What have economic theory and the historical record taught us about the relationship between the amount of money in the economy and other macroeconomic variables? Answers to these and related questions are addressed in this chapter, which examines monetary theory and policy.

The amount of money in the economy affects you in a variety of ways, but to understand these effects, we must dig a little deeper. So far, we have focused on how banks create money. But a more fundamental question is how money affects the economy, a topic called *monetary theory*. Monetary theory explores the effect of the money supply on the economy's price level, employment, and growth. The Bank of Canada's control over the money supply is called *monetary policy*. In the short run, changes in the money supply affect the economy by working through changes in the interest rate. In the long run, changes in the money supply affect the price level. In this chapter, we consider the theory behind each time frame.

LO 1 The Demand and Supply of Money

Let's begin by reviewing the important distinction between the *stock of money* and the *flow of income*. How much money do you have with you right now? That amount is a *stock*—an amount measured at a point in time. Income, in contrast, is a *flow*—an amount measured per period of time. Income is a measure of how much money you receive per period. Income has no meaning unless the period is specified. You would not know whether to be impressed that a friend earned $400 unless you knew whether this was per month, per week, per day, or per hour.

The **demand for money** is a relationship between the interest rate and how much money people want to hold. Keep in mind that the quantity of money held is a stock measure. It may seem odd at first to be talking about the demand for money. You might think people would demand all the money they could get their hands on. But remember that money, the stock, is not the same as income, the flow. People express their demand for income by selling their labour and other resources. People express their demand for money by holding some of their wealth as money rather than holding other assets that earn more interest.

> **demand for money** the relationship between the interest rate and how much money people want to hold

But we are getting ahead of ourselves. The question is this: Why do people demand money? Why do people have money with them, stash money around the house, and have money in chequing accounts? The most obvious reason people demand money is that money is a convenient medium of exchange. *People demand money to make purchases.*

The Demand for Money

Because barter represents an insignificant portion of exchange in the modern industrialized economy, households, firms, governments, and foreigners need money to conduct their daily transactions. Consumers need money to buy products, and firms need money to buy resources. *Money allows people to carry out economic transactions more easily and more efficiently.* With credit cards, the short-term loan delays the payment of money, but all accounts must eventually be settled with money.

The greater the value of transactions to be financed in a given period, the greater the demand for money. So the more active the economy is—that is, the more goods and services exchanged, reflected by real output—the more money demanded. Obviously an economy with a real GDP of $1.6 trillion needs more money than an economy half that size. Also, the higher the economy's price level, the greater the demand for money. The more things cost on average, the more money is needed to buy them. Shoppers in economies suffering from hyperinflation need mountains of cash.

You demand the money needed to fund your normal spending in the course of the day or week, and you may need money for unexpected expenditures. If you plan to buy lunch tomorrow, you will carry enough money to pay for it. But you may also want to be able to pay for other possible contingencies. For example, you could have car trouble or you could come across a sale on a favourite item. You can use cheques, debit cards, or credit cards, for some of these unexpected purchases, but you still feel safer with some extra cash. You may have a little extra money with you right now for who knows what. Even *you* don't know.

The demand for money is rooted in money's role as a medium of exchange. But as we have seen, money is more than a medium of exchange; it is also a store of value. People save for a new home, for college, for retirement. People can store their purchasing power as money or as some other financial assets, such as corporate and government bonds. When people buy bonds and other financial assets, they are lending their money and are paid interest for doing so.

The demand for any asset is based on the services it provides. The big advantage of money as a store of value is its liquidity: money can be immediately exchanged for whatever is for sale. In contrast, other financial assets, such as corporate or government bonds, must first be *liquidated,* or exchanged for money, which can then be used to buy goods and services. Money, however, has one major disadvantage when compared to other financial assets. Money in the form of currency and traveller's cheques earns no interest, and the rate earned on chequable deposits is well below that earned on other financial assets; in recent years that rate has been close to zero. So holding wealth as money means giving up some interest. For example, suppose a business could earn

3 percent more interest by holding financial assets other than money. The opportunity cost of holding $1 million as money rather than as some other financial asset would amount to $30,000 per year. *The interest forgone is the opportunity cost of holding money.*

Money Demand and Interest Rates

When the market interest rate is low, other things constant, the cost of holding money—the cost of maintaining liquidity—is low, so people hold more of their wealth in the form of money. When the interest rate is high, the cost of holding money is high, so people hold less of their wealth in money and more in other financial assets that pay higher interest. Thus, *other things constant, the quantity of money demanded varies inversely with the market interest rate.*

The money demand curve D_m in Exhibit 1 shows the quantity of money people demand at alternative interest rates, other things constant. Both the quantity of money and the interest rate are in nominal terms. *The money demand curve slopes downward because the lower the interest rate, the lower the opportunity cost of holding money.* Movements along the curve reflect the effects of changes in the interest rate on the quantity of money demanded, other things assumed constant. The quantity of money demanded is inversely related to the price of holding money, which is the interest rate. Assumed constant along the curve are the price level and real GDP. If either increases, the demand for money increases, as reflected by a rightward shift of the money demand curve.

The Supply of Money and the Equilibrium Interest Rate

The supply of money—the stock of money available in the economy at a particular time—is determined primarily by the Bank of Canada through its control over currency and over excess reserves in the banking system. The supply of money S_m is depicted as a vertical line in Exhibit 2. *A vertical supply curve implies that the quantity of money supplied is independent of the interest rate.*

The intersection of the demand for money D_m with the supply of money S_m determines the equilibrium interest rate, i—the interest rate that equates the quantity of money demanded with the quantity supplied. At interest rates above the equilibrium level, the opportunity cost of holding money is higher, so the quantity of money people want to hold is less than the quantity supplied. At interest rates below the equilibrium level, the opportunity cost of holding money is lower, so the quantity of money people want to hold exceeds the quantity supplied.

The Bank of Canada uses open-market operations to achieve its target market interest rate, known as the overnight rate. If the Bank increases the money supply through an open-market purchase of government bonds, the supply curve shifts to the right, as shown by the movement from S_m out to S'_m in Exhibit 2. At interest rate i, the quantity supplied now exceeds the quantity demanded. Because of the increased supply of money, people are *able* to hold more money. But at interest rate i they are *unwilling*

EXHIBIT 1
Demand for Money

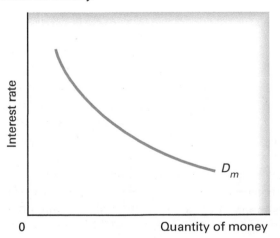

EXHIBIT 2
Effect of an Increase in the Money Supply

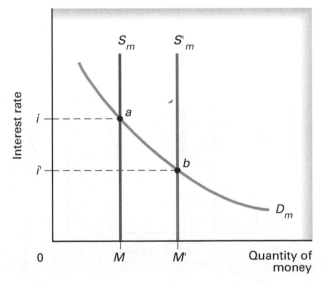

to hold that much. Because people are now holding more of their wealth as money than they would like, they exchange some money for other financial assets, such as bonds. As the demand for bonds increases, bond sellers can pay less interest yet still attract enough buyers. The interest rate falls until the quantity of money demanded just equals the quantity supplied. With the decline in the interest rate to i' in Exhibit 2, the opportunity cost of holding money falls enough that the public is willing to hold the now-larger stock of money. Equilibrium moves from point a to point b. *For a given money demand curve, an increase in the money supply drives down the interest rate, and a decrease in the money supply drives up the interest rate.*

Now that you have some idea how money demand and money supply determine the market interest rate, you are ready to see how money fits into our model of the economy. Specifically, let's see how changes in the money supply affect aggregate demand and equilibrium output.

LO 2 Money and Aggregate Demand in the Short Run

In the short run, money affects the economy through changes in the interest rate. Monetary policy influences the market interest rate, which in turn affects

investment, a component of aggregate demand. Let's work through the chain of causation.

Interest Rates and Investment

Suppose the Bank of Canada believes that the economy is producing less than its potential and decides to stimulate output and employment by increasing the money supply. Recall from the previous chapter that the Bank's primary tool for increasing the money supply is open-market purchases of government securities. The three panels of Exhibit 3 trace the links between changes in the money supply and changes in aggregate demand. We begin with equilibrium interest rate i, which is determined in panel (a) by the intersection of the money demand curve D_m with the money supply curve S_m. Suppose the Bank purchases government bonds and thereby increases the money supply, as shown by a rightward shift of the money supply curve from S_m to S'_m. *After the increase in the supply of money, people are holding more money than they would prefer at interest rate i,* so they try to exchange one form of wealth, money, for other financial assets. Exchanging dollars for financial assets has no direct effect on aggregate demand, but it does reduce the market interest rate.

A decline in the interest rate to i', other things constant, reduces the opportunity cost of financing new plants and equipment, thereby making new investment more profitable. Likewise, a lower interest rate reduces the cost of financing a new house. So a decline in the interest rate increases the amount of investment demanded. Panel (b) shows the demand for

EXHIBIT 3
Effects of an Increase in the Money Supply on Interest Rates, Investment, and Aggregate Demand

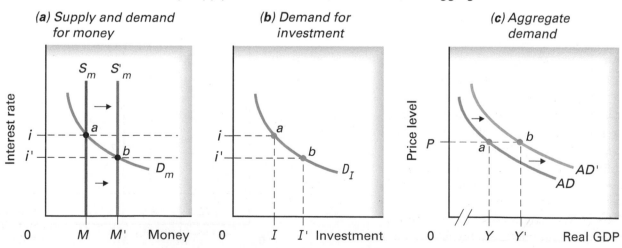

investment D_I first introduced in Chapter 9. When the interest rate falls from i to i', the quantity of investment demanded increases from I to I'.

The spending multiplier magnifies this increase in investment, leading to a greater increase in aggregate demand, reflected in panel (c) by a rightward shift of the aggregate demand curve from AD to AD'. At the given price level P, real GDP increases from Y to Y'. The sequence of events can be summarized as follows:

$$M \uparrow \rightarrow i \downarrow \rightarrow I \uparrow \rightarrow AD \uparrow \rightarrow Y \uparrow$$

An increase in the money supply, M, reduces the interest rate, i. The lower interest rate stimulates investment, I, which increases aggregate demand from AD to AD'. At a given price level, real GDP demanded increases from Y to Y'. The entire sequence is also traced out in each panel by the movement from point a to point b.

Note that the graphs presented here ignore any feedback effects of changes in real GDP on the demand for money. Because the demand for money depends on the level of real GDP, an increase in real GDP would shift the money demand curve to the right in panel (a). If we had shifted the money demand curve, the equilibrium interest rate would still have fallen, but not by as much, so investment and aggregate demand would not have increased by as much. Thus Exhibit 3 is a simplified view, but it still captures the essentials of how changes in the money supply affect the economy.

Now let's consider the effect of a Bank of Canada-orchestrated *increase* in interest rates. In Exhibit 3 such a policy could be traced by moving from point b to point a in each panel, but we dispense with a blow-by-blow discussion of the graphs. Suppose the Bank decides to reduce the money supply to cool down an overheated economy. A decrease in the money supply would increase the interest rate. At the higher interest rate, businesses find it more costly to finance plants and equipment, and households find it more costly to finance new homes. Hence, a higher interest rate reduces the amount invested. The resulting decline in investment is magnified by the spending multiplier, leading to a greater decline in aggregate demand.

As long as the interest rate is sensitive to changes in the money supply, and as long

as investment is sensitive to changes in the interest rate, changes in the money supply affect investment. The extent to which a given change in investment affects aggregate demand depends on the size of the spending multiplier.

Adding the Short-Run Aggregate Supply Curve

Even after tracing the effect of a change in the money supply on aggregate demand, we still have only half the story. To determine the effects of monetary policy on the equilibrium real GDP in the economy, we need the supply side. An aggregate supply curve helps show how a given shift of the aggregate demand curve affects real GDP and the price level. In the short run, the aggregate supply curve slopes upward, so the quantity supplied increases only if the price level increases. *For a given shift of the aggregate demand curve, the steeper the short-run aggregate supply curve, the smaller the increase in real GDP and the larger the increase in the price level.*

Suppose the economy is producing at point a in Exhibit 4, where the aggregate demand curve AD intersects the short-run aggregate supply curve $SRAS_{110}$, yielding a short-run equilibrium output of $\$1.75$ trillion and a price level of 105. As you can see, the actual price level of 105 is below the expected price level of 110, and the short-run equilibrium output of

EXHIBIT 4
Expansionary Monetary Policy to Close a Recessionary Gap

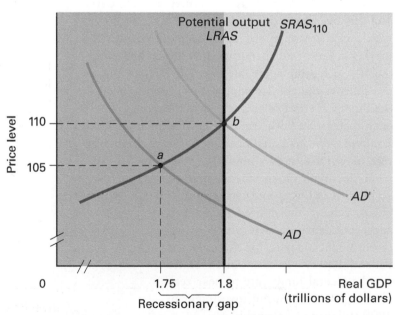

$1.75 trillion is below the economy's potential of $1.8 trillion, yielding a recessionary gap of $50 billion.

At point *a,* real wages are higher than had been negotiated and many people are looking for jobs. The Bank of Canada can wait to see whether the economy recovers on its own. Market forces could cause employers and workers to renegotiate lower nominal wages. This would lower production costs, pushing the short-run aggregate supply curve rightward, thus closing the recessionary gap. But if the Bank officials are impatient with natural market forces, they could try to close the gap using an expansionary monetary policy. For example, during 2007 and 2009, the Bank aggressively cut the target overnight rate from 4.50 percent in December 2007 to 0.25 percent by April 2009 to stimulate aggregate demand. If the Bank lowers that rate by just the right amount, this stimulates investment, thus increasing the aggregate demand curve enough to achieve a new equilibrium at point *b,* where the economy produces its potential output. Given all the connections in the chain of causality between changes in the money supply and changes in equilibrium output, however, it would actually be quite remarkable for the Bank of Canada to execute monetary policy so precisely. If the Bank overshoots the mark and stimulates aggregate demand too much, this would open up an expansionary gap, thus creating inflationary pressure in the economy.

To Review: As long as the money demand curve and the investment demand curve each slopes downward, an increase in the money supply reduces the market interest rate, increasing investment and consequently increasing aggregate demand. And as long as the short-run aggregate supply curve slopes upward, the short-run effect of an increase in the money supply is an increase in both real output and the price level. But here is one final qualification: lowering the interest rate may not always stimulate investment. Economic prospects may become so glum that lower interest rates may fail to achieve the desired increase in aggregate demand. In response to the recent financial crisis, for example, the Federal Reserve in the United States cut the federal funds rate to near zero by the end of 2008, but investment in 2009 still dropped sharply.

$$M \times V = P \times Y$$

$$V = \frac{P \times Y}{M}$$

LO 3 Money and Aggregate Demand in the Long Run

When we looked at the impact of money on the economy in the short run, we found that money influences aggregate demand and equilibrium output through its effect on the interest rate. Here we look at the long-run effects of changes in the money supply on the economy. *The long-run view of money is more direct: if the central bank supplies more money to the economy, sooner or later people spend more. But because the long-run aggregate supply curve is fixed at the economy's potential output, this greater spending simply increases the price level. In short, more money is chasing the same output. Here are the details.*

The Equation of Exchange

Every transaction in the economy involves a two-way swap: the buyer exchanges money for goods and the seller exchanges goods for money. One way of expressing this relationship among key variables in the economy is the **equation of exchange**, first developed by classical economists. Although this equation can be arranged in different ways, depending on the emphasis, the basic version is

$$M \times V = P \times Y$$

where M is the quantity of money in the economy; V is the **velocity of money**, or the average number of times per year each dollar is used to purchase final goods and services; P is the average price level; and Y is real GDP. The equation of exchange says that the quantity of money in circulation, M, multiplied by V, the number of times that money changes hands, equals the average price level, P, times real output, Y. The price level, P, times real output, Y, equals the economy's nominal income and output, or nominal GDP.

By rearranging the equation of exchange, we find that velocity equals nominal GDP divided by the money stock, or

$$V = \frac{P \times Y}{M}$$

For example, nominal GDP in 2012 was $1.82 trillion, and the money stock as measured by M1++ averaged $921 billion. The velocity of money indicates how often each dollar is used on average to pay for final goods and services during the year. So in 2012, velocity was $1.82 trillion divided by $921 billion, or 1.98. Given GDP and the money supply, each dollar in circulation must have been spent 1.98 times on average to pay for final goods and services. There is no other way these market transactions could have occurred. The value of velocity is implied by the values of the other variables. Incidentally, velocity measures spending only on final goods and services—not on intermediate products, secondhand goods, financial assets, or illegal activity, even though such spending also occurs. So velocity underestimates how hard the money supply works during the year.

The equation of exchange says that total spending ($M \times V$) always equals total receipts ($P \times Y$), as was the case in our circular-flow analysis. As described so far, however, the equation of exchange is simply an *identity*—a relationship expressed in such a way that it is true by definition. Another example of an identity would be a relationship equating kilometres per litre to the distance driven divided by the gasoline required.

The Quantity Theory of Money

If velocity is relatively stable over time, or at least predictable, the equation of exchange turns from an identity into a theory—the quantity theory of money. The **quantity theory of money** states that if the velocity of money is stable, or at least predictable, then the equation of exchange can be used to predict the effects of changes in the money supply on *nominal* GDP, $P \times Y$. For example, if M increases by 5 percent and V remains constant, then $P \times Y$, or nominal GDP, must also increase by 5 percent. For a while, some economists believed they could use the equation of exchange to predict nominal output in the short run. Now it's used primarily as a guide in the long run.

So an increase in the money supply results in more spending in

the long run, meaning a higher nominal GDP. How is this increase in $P \times Y$ divided between changes in the price level and changes in real GDP? The answer does not lie in the quantity theory, for that theory is stated only in terms of nominal GDP. The answer lies in the shape of the aggregate supply curve.

The long-run aggregate supply curve is vertical at the economy's potential level of output. With real output, Y, fixed and the velocity of money, V, relatively stable, a change in the stock of money translates directly into a change in the price level. Exhibit 5 shows the effect of an increase in the money supply

> **quantity theory of money** if the velocity of money is stable, or at least predictable, changes in the money supply have predictable effects on nominal GDP

EXHIBIT 5

In the Long Run, an Increase in the Money Supply Results in a Higher Price Level, or Inflation

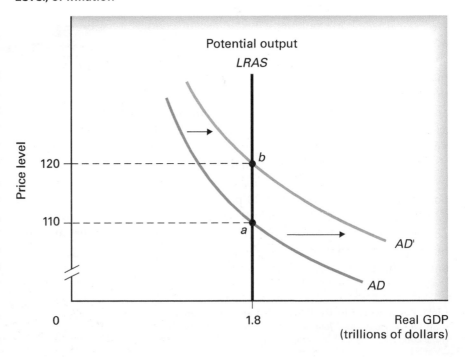

in the long run. An increase in the money supply causes a rightward shift of the aggregate demand curve, which increases the price level but leaves output unchanged at potential GDP. So the economy's potential output level is not affected by changes in the money supply. *In the long run, increases in the money supply, with velocity stable or at least not decreasing, result only in higher prices.* For example, an examination of 73 inflation periods across major economies since 1960 concludes that important triggers to inflation were expansionary monetary policies.[1]

To Review: If velocity is stable, or at least predictable, the quantity theory of money says that changes in the money supply will, in the long run, result in predictable effects on the economy's price level. Velocity's stability and predictability are key to the quantity theory of money. Let's consider some factors that might influence velocity.

What Determines the Velocity of Money?

Velocity depends on the customs and conventions of commerce. In colonial times, money might be tied up in transit for days as a courier on horseback carried a payment from one location to another. Today, the electronic transmission of funds occurs in an instant, so the same stock of money can move around much more quickly to finance many more transactions. *The velocity of money has also increased because of a variety of commercial innovations that facilitate exchange.* For example, a wider use of charge accounts and credit cards has reduced the need for shoppers to carry cash. Likewise, automatic teller machines have made cash more accessible at more times and in more places. What's more, debit cards are used at a growing number of retail outlets, such as grocery stores and drugstores, so people need less "walking around" money.

Another institutional factor that determines velocity is the frequency with which workers get paid. Suppose a worker who earns $52,000 per year gets paid $2,000 every two weeks. Earnings are spent evenly during the two-week period and are gone by the end of the period. In that case, a worker's average money balance during the pay period is $1,000. If a worker

earns the same $52,000 per year but, instead, gets paid $1,000 weekly, the average money balance during the pay period falls to $500. *Thus the more often workers get paid, other things constant, the lower their average money balances, so the more active the money supply and the greater its velocity.* Payment practices change slowly over time, and the effects of these changes on velocity are predictable.

Another factor affecting velocity depends on how stable money is as a store of value. *The better money serves as a store of value, the more money people hold, so the lower its velocity.* For example, the introduction of interest-bearing chequing accounts made money a better store of value, so people were more willing to hold money in chequing accounts and this financial innovation reduced velocity. On the other hand, when inflation increases unexpectedly, money turns out to be a poorer store of value. People become reluctant to hold money and try to exchange it for some asset that retains its value better. This reduction in people's willingness to hold money during periods of high inflation increases the velocity of money. During hyperinflations, workers usually get paid daily, boosting velocity even more. Thus *velocity increases with a rise in the inflation rate, other things constant.* Money becomes a hot potato—nobody wants to hold it for long.

Again, the usefulness of the quantity theory in predicting changes in the price level in the long run hinges on how stable and predictable the velocity of money is over time.

LO 4 Targets for Monetary Policy

In the short run, monetary policy affects the economy largely by influencing the interest rate. In the long run, changes in the money supply affect the price level, though with an uncertain lag. Should monetary authorities focus on the interest rates in the short run or the supply of money in the long run? As we will see, the Bank of Canada lacks the tools to focus on both at the same time.

Contrasting Policies

To demonstrate the effects of different policies, we begin with the money market in equilibrium at point *e* in Exhibit 6. The interest rate is *i* and the money stock

[1] John Boschen and Charles Weise, "What Starts Inflation: Evidence from OECD Countries," *Journal of Money, Credit and Banking*, 35 (June 2003): 323–349.

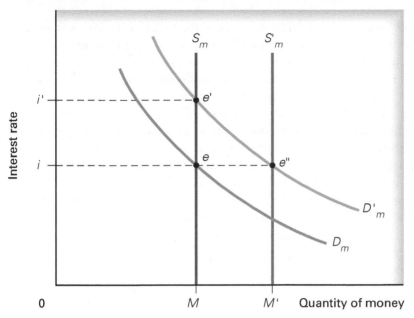

EXHIBIT 6
Targeting Interest Rates Versus Targeting the Money Supply

to keep the interest rate stable. With this latter approach, changes in the money supply would have to offset any changes in the demand for money. This essentially is what the Bank of Canada does when it holds the target overnight rate constant.

Interest rate fluctuations could be harmful if they create undesirable fluctuations in investment. For interest rates to remain stable during economic expansions, the money supply would have to grow at the same rate as the demand for money. Likewise, for interest rates to remain stable during economic contractions, the money supply would have to shrink at the same rate as the demand for money. Hence, for monetary authorities to maintain the interest rate at some specified level, the money supply must increase during economic expansions and decrease during contractions. But an increase in the money supply during an expansion would increase aggregate demand even more, and a decrease in the money supply during a contraction would reduce aggregate demand even more. *Such changes in the money supply would thus tend to worsen fluctuations in economic activity, thereby adding more instability to the economy.* With this in mind, let's review monetary policy over the years.

is M, values the monetary authorities find appropriate. Suppose there is an increase in the demand for money in the economy, perhaps because of an increase in nominal GDP. The money demand curve shifts to the right, from D_m to D'_m.

When confronted with an increase in the demand for money, monetary authorities can choose to do nothing, thereby allowing the interest rate to rise, or they can increase the money supply enough to hold the interest rate constant. If monetary authorities do nothing, the quantity of money in the economy remains at M, but the interest rate rises because the greater demand for money increases the equilibrium combination from point e up to point e'. Alternatively, monetary authorities can try to keep the interest rate at its initial level by increasing the supply of money from S_m to S'_m. *In terms of possible combinations of the money stock and the interest rate, monetary authorities must choose from points lying along the new money demand curve, D'_m.*

A growing economy usually needs a growing money supply to pay for the increase in aggregate output. If monetary authorities maintain a constant growth in the money supply, and if velocity remains stable, the interest rate fluctuates unless the growth in the supply of money each period just happens to match the growth in the demand for money (as in the movement from e to e'' in Exhibit 6). Alternatively, monetary authorities could try to adjust the money supply each period by the amount needed

Monetary Policy Targets

Between World War II and 1975, the Bank of Canada attempted to stabilize interest rates. Stable interest rates were viewed as a prerequisite for an attractive investment environment and, thus, for a stable economy. Milton Friedman, a Nobel Prize winner, argued that this exclusive attention to interest rates made monetary policy a source of instability in the economy because changes in the money supply reinforced fluctuations in the economy. He said that central banks should pay less attention to interest rates and instead should focus on a steady and predictable growth in the money supply. The debate raged during the 1970s, and Friedman won some important converts. Amid growing concern about a rising inflation rate, the Bank of Canada commenced formal targeting of M1 in 1975. Not surprisingly, interest rates became much more volatile.

But the approach never worked the way the Bank of Canada had hoped. The measure of M1 was rarely kept within the Bank's target range for growth following innovations in the financial market and the resulting deposit shifts between bank accounts of various kinds. In 1982, the Bank of Canada formally ended the policy and started paying some attention to interest rates again.

The Bank of Canada is always feeling its way, looking for signs about the direction of the economy. The rapid pace of financial innovations and deregulation during the 1980s made the definition and measurement of the money supply more difficult. Gerald Bouey, who was the Governor of the Bank of Canada in 1983, famously said, "We didn't abandon M1; M1 abandoned us." *No central bank in a major economy now makes significant use of money aggregates to guide policy in the short run. Still, most policymakers also agree that in the long run, changes in the money supply influence the price level and inflation.*

Monetary policy has evolved in many countries toward targeting a low rate of inflation. Inflation-targeting central banks such as the Bank of England and the Reserve Bank of New Zealand target short-term interest rates. When demand is strong, it can push the economy to produce beyond its potential. This tends to raise inflation above the target, so an inflation-targeting central bank would raise interest rates to cool off the economy. When demand is weak and the economy is producing below its potential, inflationary pressures are likely to ease. An inflation-targeting central bank would then lower interest rates to stimulate the economy and absorb economic slack.

The Bank of Canada formally adopted explicit inflation targeting in 1991. The goal of the Bank's inflation-control system is to keep inflation at 2 percent, which is the midpoint of a target band of 1 to 3 percent. The target for the overnight rate, the key short-term interest rate, is announced in January, March, April, May, July, September, October, and December every year.

Also significant is what Bank of Canada officials have to say. For example, they might announce that they are following a problem closely and are prepared to stabilize financial markets as needed. Such reassurance is sometimes all that's required to calm market jitters.

Final Word

This chapter has described two ways of viewing the effects of money on the economy's performance, but we should not overstate the differences. In the model that focuses on the short run, an increase in the money supply means that people are holding more money than they would like at the prevailing interest rate, so they exchange one form of wealth, money, for other financial assets, such as corporate or government bonds. This greater demand for other financial assets has no direct effect on aggregate demand, but it does reduce the interest rate and thereby stimulates investment. The higher investment gets magnified by the spending multiplier, increasing aggregate demand. The effect of this increase in demand on real output and the price level depends on the shape of the short-run aggregate supply curve.

In the model that focuses on the long run, changes in the money supply act more directly on the price level. If velocity is relatively stable or at least predictable, then a change in the money supply has a predictable effect on the price level in the long run. As long as velocity is not declining, an increase in the money supply means that people eventually spend more, increasing aggregate demand. But because long-run aggregate supply is fixed at the economy's potential output, increased aggregate demand leads simply to a higher price level, or to inflation.

CHAPTER PROBLEMS

LO1 Describe the relationship between the demand and supply of money

1.1. *(Money Demand)* Suppose that you never carry cash. Your paycheque of $1,000 per month is deposited directly into your chequing account, and you spend your money at a constant rate so that at the end of each month your chequing account balance is zero.

a. What is your average money balance during the pay period?

b. How would each of the following changes affect your average monthly balance?

i. You are paid $500 twice monthly rather than $1,000 each month.

ii. You are uncertain about your total spending each month.

iii. You spend a lot at the beginning of the month (e.g., for rent) and little at the end of the month.

iv. Your monthly income increases.

LO2 Explain how changes in the money supply affect aggregate demand in the short run

2.1. *(Money and Aggregate Demand)* Would each of the following increase, decrease, or have no impact on the ability of open-market operations to affect aggregate demand? Explain your answer.

a. Investment demand becomes less sensitive to changes in the interest rate.

b. The marginal propensity to consume rises.

c. The money multiplier rises.

d. Banks decide to hold additional excess reserves.

e. The demand for money becomes more sensitive to changes in the interest rate.

2.2. *(Monetary Policy and Aggregate Supply)* Assume that the economy is initially in long-run equilibrium. Using an *AD–AS* diagram, illustrate and explain the short-run and long-run impacts of an increase in the money supply.

2.3. *(Monetary Policy and an Expansionary Gap)* Suppose the Bank of Canada wishes to use monetary policy to close an expansionary gap.

a. Should the Bank increase or decrease the money supply?

b. If the Bank uses open-market operations, should it buy or sell government securities?

c. Determine whether each of the following increases, decreases, or remains unchanged in the short run: the market interest rate, the quantity of money demanded, investment spending, aggregate demand, potential output, the price level, and equilibrium real GDP.

LO3 Explain how changes in the money supply affect aggregate demand in the long run

3.1. *(Equation of Exchange)* Calculate the velocity of money if real GDP is 3,000 units, the average price level is $4 per unit, and the quantity of money in the economy is $1,500. What happens to velocity if the average price level drops to $3 per unit? What happens to velocity if the average price level remains at $4 per unit but the money supply rises to $2,000? What happens to velocity if the average price level falls to $2 per unit, the money supply is $2,000, and real GDP is 4,000 units?

3.2. *(Quantity Theory of Money)* What basic assumption about the velocity of money transforms the equation of exchange into the quantity theory of money? Also:

a. According to the quantity theory, what will happen to nominal GDP if the money supply increases by 5 percent and velocity does not change?

b. What will happen to nominal GDP if, instead, the money supply decreases by 8 percent and velocity does not change?

c. What will happen to nominal GDP if, instead, the money supply increases by 5 percent and velocity decreases by 5 percent?

d. What happens to the price level in the short run in each of these three situations?

3.3. *(Velocity of Money)* What factors affect the velocity of money?

LO4 Evaluate targets for monetary policy

4.1. *(Money Supply Versus Interest Rate Targets)* Assume that the economy's real GDP is growing.

a. What will happen to money demand over time?

b. If the Bank of Canada leaves the money supply unchanged, what will happen to the interest rate over time?

c. If the Bank changes the money supply to match the change in money demand, what will happen to the interest rate over time?

d. What would be the effect of the policy described in part (c) on the economy's stability over the business cycle?

CASE STUDY

The Money Supply and Inflation around the World

If we view economies around the world as evidence, what's the link between inflation and changes in the money supply in the long run? According to the quantity theory, as long as the velocity of money is fairly stable, there should be a positive relation in the long run between the percentage change in the money supply and the percentage change in the price level. Panel (a) of the exhibit below illustrates the relationship between the average annual growth rate in M2 and the average annual inflation rate for the 85 countries over a 10-year period. As you can see, the points fall rather neatly along the trend line, showing a positive relation between money growth and inflation. Because most countries are bunched below an inflation rate of 30 percent, let's break these points out in finer detail in panel (b). Although panel (a) shows a sharper link between money growth and inflation than does panel (b), in both panels countries with higher rates of money growth experience higher rates of inflation.

In panel (a), Argentina, Bolivia, and Israel—countries with inflation of more than 100 percent per year—also experienced annual money growth exceeding 100 percent. Argentina, which had the highest inflation rate over the 10-year period in the sample, at 395 percent per year, also had the highest average annual money growth, at 369 percent. Hyperinflation first appeared about a century ago, and in every case it has been accompanied by rapid growth in the supply of money.

How does hyperinflation end? The central bank must somehow convince the public it is committed to halting the rapid growth in the money supply. The most famous hyperinflation was in Germany between August 1922 and November 1923, when inflation averaged 322 percent *per month*. Inflation was halted when the German government created an independent central bank that issued a new currency convertible into gold. Germany had a similar problem after World War II when currency became nearly useless because Allied victors imposed strict price controls on the country. Experts estimate that the lack of a viable currency cut German output in half. Germany's "economic miracle" of 1948 was due largely to the adoption of a reliable monetary system. Argentina, Bolivia, and Israel all managed to tame the beast of hyperinflation, with inflation under 3 percent by 2000. Residents of all three countries, perhaps mindful of past hyperinflation, still hold lots of U.S. dollars as a store of value.

The exhibit we've been discussing reflects averages from 1980 to 1990, but the relationship holds up if we focus on a more recent decade. From 1992 to 2002, for example, inflation, while generally lower around the world than in the 1980s, was still highest in countries with the highest money growth rates. Brazil, Belarus, Romania, and Russia experienced hyperinflation and also had extremely high rates of money growth. The highest was in Brazil, where the inflation and the money supply each grew an average of about 210 percent per year during the decade. In Venezuela, the money supply increased by 30 percent in 2009 and by July 2010 the annual rate of inflation was

A Decade of Annual Inflation and Money Growth in 85 Countries (average annual percent)

Panel (a) shows that money growth is clearly linked with inflation based on a sample of 85 countries between 1980 and 1990. In each country that experienced hyperinflation, the inflation rate matched the growth in the money supply. Panel (b) offers finer detail for the subset of countries with inflation and money growth below 30 percent. Again, money growth and inflation are positively related in the long run.

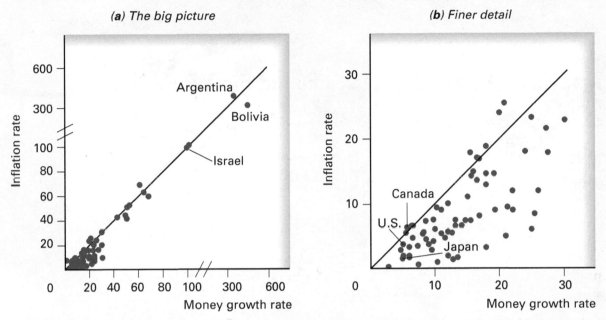

(a) The big picture   *(b) Finer detail*

SOURCE: The World Bank, *World Development Report 1992* (New York: Oxford University Press, 1992), Table 13. Figures are annual averages for 1980 to 1990. p. 242.

33 percent, about the highest in the world at the time. As Nobel prize winner Milton Friedman famously put it, "Inflation is always and everywhere a monetary phenomenon, in the sense that it cannot occur without a more rapid increase in the quantity of money than in output."

SOURCES: *World Development Report* 2010 at http://econ.worldbank.org; Greg Ip, "Taking the Measure of the World's Cash Hoard," *Wall Street Journal*, 3 November 2005; Gerald Dwyer and R. W. Hafer, "Are Money Growth and Inflation Still Related?" *Federal Reserve Bank of Atlanta Economic Review*, (Second Quarter 1999): 32–43; "Economic and Financial Indicators," *The Economist*, 17 July 2010.

QUESTION

1. According to the exhibit above, what is the relationship between the rate of money supply growth and the inflation rate? How does this explain the hyperinflation experienced in some economies?

15

Macro Policy Debate: Active or Passive?

LEARNING OUTCOMES

LO1 Compare an active policy and a passive policy

LO2 Consider the role of expectations

LO3 Discuss policy rules versus discretion

LO4 Explain the Phillips curve

> ## Does the economy work fairly well on its own, or does it require active government intervention?

Does the economy work fairly well on its own, or does it require active government intervention? Does government intervention do more harm than good? If people expect government to intervene if the economy falters, does this expectation affect people's behaviour? Does this expectation affect government's behaviour? What is the relationship between unemployment and inflation in the short run and in the long run? Answers to these and other questions are provided in this chapter, which discusses the appropriate role for government in economic stabilization.

You have studied both fiscal and monetary policy and are now in a position to consider the overall impact of public policy on the Canadian economy. This chapter distinguishes between two general approaches: the active approach and the passive approach. The active approach views the economy as relatively unstable and unable to recover from shocks when they occur. According to the active approach, economic fluctuations arise primarily from the private sector, particularly investment, and natural market forces may not help much or may be too slow once the economy gets off track.

To move the economy to its potential output, the active approach calls for government intervention and discretionary policy. The passive approach, on the other hand, views the economy as relatively stable and able to recover from shocks when they do occur. When the economy derails, natural market forces and automatic stabilizers nudge it back on track in a timely manner. According to the passive approach, not only is active discretionary policy unnecessary, but such activism may also do more harm than good.

In this chapter, we consider the pros and cons of *active* intervention in the economy versus *passive* reliance on natural market forces and automatic stabilizers. We also examine the role that expectations play in stabilization policy. You will learn why unanticipated stabilization policies have more impact on employment and output than do anticipated ones. Finally, the chapter explores the trade-off between unemployment and inflation.

LO 1 Active Policy Versus Passive Policy

According to the *active approach,* discretionary fiscal or monetary policy can reduce the costs of an unstable economy, such as higher unemployment. According to the *passive approach,* discretionary policy may contribute to the instability of the economy and is therefore part of the problem, not part of the solution. The two approaches differ in their assumptions about the effectiveness of natural market forces compared with government intervention.

Closing a Recessionary Gap

Perhaps the best way to describe each approach is by examining a particular macroeconomic problem. Suppose the economy is in short-run equilibrium at point *a* in panel (a) of Exhibit 1, with real gross domestic product (GDP) at $1.75 trillion, which is below the economy's potential of $1.8 trillion. The recessionary gap of $50 billion drives unemployment above its natural rate (the rate when the economy produces potential GDP). This gap could result from lower-than-expected aggregate demand. What should public officials do?

Those who subscribe to the passive approach, as did their classical predecessors, have more faith in the *self-correcting forces* of the economy than do those who favour the active approach. In what sense is the economy self-correcting? According to the passive approach, wages and prices are flexible enough to adjust within a reasonable period to labour shortages or surpluses. High unemployment causes wages to fall, which reduces production costs, which shifts the short-run aggregate supply curve rightward in panel (a) of Exhibit 1. (Money wages need not actually fall; money wage increases need only lag behind price increases, so that real wages fall. Or perhaps nonwage compensation is reduced, such as healthcare benefits.) The short-run aggregate supply curve, within a reasonable period, shifts from $SRAS_{110}$ to $SRAS_{100}$, moving the economy to its potential output at point *b*. *According to the passive approach, the*

economy is stable enough, gravitating in a reasonable time toward potential GDP. Automatic stabilizers also help move the economy toward potential GDP. Consequently, advocates of passive policy see little reason for discretionary policy. The passive approach is to let natural market forces and automatic stabilizers close the recessionary gap. So the prescription of passive policy is to do nothing beyond the automatic stabilizers already built into taxes, transfers, and government purchases.

Advocates of an active approach, on the other hand, believe that prices and wages are not that flexible, particularly in the downward direction. They think that when adverse supply shocks or sagging demand push unemployment above its natural rate, market forces may be too slow to respond. The longer market forces take to reduce unemployment to the natural rate, the greater the output lost and the greater the economic and psychological cost to those unemployed. *Because advocates of an active policy associate a high cost with the passive approach, they favour an active stabilization policy to stimulate aggregate demand.*

A decision by public officials to intervene in the economy to achieve potential output—that is, a decision to use discretionary policy—reflects an active approach. In panel (b) of Exhibit 1, we begin at the same point *a* as in panel (a). At point *a*, short-run equilibrium output is below potential output, so the economy is experiencing a recessionary gap. Through

EXHIBIT 1
Closing a Recessionary Gap

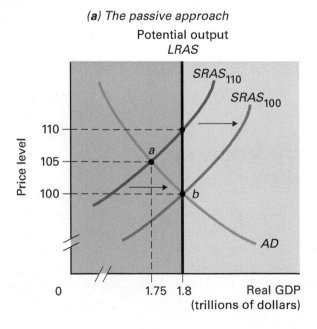

(a) The passive approach

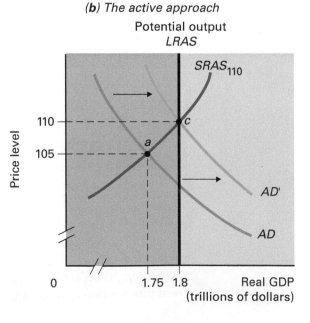

(b) The active approach

discretionary monetary policy, discretionary fiscal policy, or some of both, as occurred in 2008 and 2009, active policy attempts to increase aggregate demand from AD to AD′, moving equilibrium from point a to point c, thus closing the recessionary gap.

In 2008 and 2009, policymakers around the world tried to revive troubled economies using both fiscal and monetary policy. In the United States, President Barack Obama's $862-billion stimulus plan, the largest on record, was approved by Congress in February 2009 and was aimed at counteracting the deep recession triggered by the financial crisis. In Canada, the federal government provided up to $200 billion to improve access to financing for Canadian businesses and households in response to gaps in the credit market. The Federal Reserve and the Bank of Canada had already cut their target interest rates to record lows. These combinations of fiscal and monetary policies were the most coordinated global attempt to boost aggregate demand ever. One possible cost of using discretionary policy to stimulate aggregate demand is an increase in the price level, or inflation. Another cost of fiscal stimulus is to increase a budget deficit or decrease a budget surplus.

Closing an Expansionary Gap

Let's consider the situation in which the short-run equilibrium output exceeds the economy's potential. Suppose the actual price level of 115 exceeds the expected price level of 110, resulting in an expansionary gap of $50 billion, as shown in Exhibit 2. The passive approach argues that natural market forces prompt workers and firms to negotiate higher wages at their next opportunity. These higher nominal wages increase production costs, shifting the short-run supply curve leftward, from $SRAS_{110}$ to $SRAS_{120}$, as shown in panel (a). Consequently, the price level increases and output decreases to the economy's potential. So the natural adjustment process results in a higher price level, or inflation.

An active approach sees discretionary policy as a way to reach potential output without increasing the price level. Advocates of an active policy believe that if aggregate demand can be reduced from AD″ to AD′, as shown in panel (b) of Exhibit 2, then the equilibrium point moves down along the initial aggregate supply curve from d to c. *Although the passive approach relies on natural market forces and automatic stabilizers to close an expansionary gap through a decrease in the short-run aggregate supply curve, the active approach relies on just the right discretionary policy to close the gap through a decrease of the aggregate demand curve.* In the long run, the passive approach results in a higher price level and the active approach results in a lower price level. Thus, the correct discretionary policy can relieve the inflationary pressure associated with an expansionary gap. Whenever the Bank of Canada attempts to cool down an overheated economy by increasing

EXHIBIT 2
Closing an Expansionary Gap

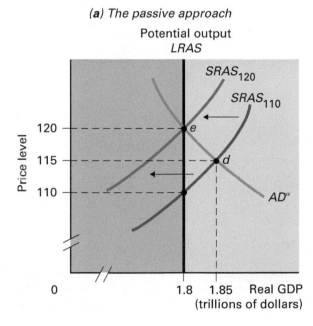

(a) The passive approach

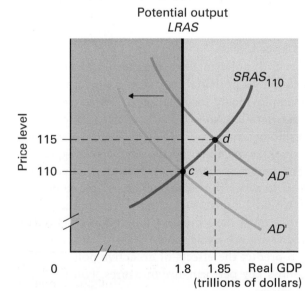

(b) The active approach

© Tony Garcia/SuperStock

recognition lag
the time needed to identify a macroeconomic problem and assess its seriousness

its target for the overnight rate, it employs an active monetary policy to close an expansionary gap. The Bank of Canada tries to orchestrate a so-called *soft landing* to gently slow the rate of growth before that growth triggers unacceptably high inflation.

Problems with Active Policy

The timely adoption and implementation of an active policy is not easy. One problem is identifying the economy's potential output and the natural rate of unemployment. Suppose the natural rate of unemployment is 5 percent, but policymakers mistakenly believe it's 4 percent. As they pursue their elusive goal of 4 percent, they push aggregate output beyond its potential, fuelling higher prices in the long run but with no permanent reduction in unemployment. Recall that when output exceeds the economy's potential, this opens up an expansionary gap, causing a leftward shift of the short-run aggregate supply curve until the economy returns to its potential output at a higher price level.

Even if policymakers can accurately estimate the economy's potential output and the natural rate of unemployment, formulating an effective policy requires detailed knowledge of current and future economic conditions. To craft an effective strategy, policymakers must first be able to forecast aggregate demand and aggregate supply without active intervention. In other words, they must be able to predict what would happen with a passive approach. Second, they must have the tools needed to achieve the desired result relatively quickly. Third, they must be able to predict the effects of an active policy on the economy's key performance measures. Fourth, fiscal

and monetary policymakers must work together, or at least not work at cross-purposes. The government pursues fiscal policy while the Bank of Canada pursues monetary policy; these groups may fail to coordinate their efforts. If an active policy requires coordination, the policy may not work as desired. Fifth, policymakers must be able to implement the appropriate policy, even when this involves short-term political costs. For example, during inflationary times, the optimal policy may call for a tax increase, a reduction in government spending, or a tighter monetary policy—policies that are unpopular because they may increase unemployment. Finally, policymakers must be able to deal with a variety of timing lags. As we see next, these lags complicate the execution of an active policy.

The Problem of Lags

So far, we have ignored the time required to implement policy. That is, we have assumed that the desired policy is selected and implemented instantaneously. We have also assumed that, once implemented, the policy works as advertised—again, in no time. Actually, there may be long, sometimes unpredictable, lags at several stages in the process. These lags reduce the effectiveness and increase the uncertainty of active policies.

First is a **recognition lag**—the time it takes to identify a problem and determine how serious it is. For example, time is required to accumulate evidence that the economy is indeed performing below its potential. Even if initial data look troubling,

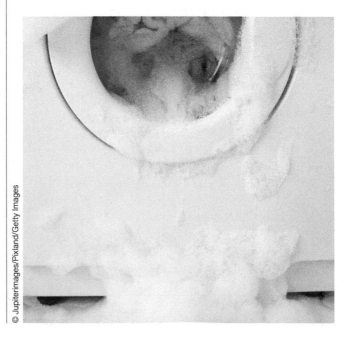

© Jupiterimages/Pixland/Getty Images

data are usually revised later. For example, the government releases three estimates of quarterly GDP growth coming a month apart—an *advanced* estimate, a *preliminary* estimate, and a *final* estimate. What's more, these estimates are often revised years later or even a decade later. Therefore, policymakers sometimes wait for more proof before responding to what may turn out to be a false alarm. Because a recession is not identified as such until more than six months after it begins, a typical recession is nearly over before officially being recognized as a recession.

Even after enough evidence accumulates, policymakers often need time to decide what to do, so there is a **decision-making lag**. In the case of discretionary fiscal policy, the federal government must agree on an appropriate course of action. Fiscal policy usually takes months to develop and approve; it could take more than a year. On the other hand, the Bank of Canada can implement monetary policy more quickly and does not even have to wait for regular meetings. So the decision-making lag is shorter for monetary policy than for fiscal policy.

Once a decision has been made, the new policy must be introduced, which usually involves an **implementation lag**. Again, monetary policy has the advantage: after a policy has been adopted, the Bank of Canada can immediately begin buying or selling bonds to influence bank reserves and thereby change the target for the overnight rate. The implementation lag is longer for fiscal policy. If tax rates change, new tax forms must be printed and distributed advising employers of changes in tax withholding.

Once a policy has been implemented, there is an **effectiveness lag** before the full impact of the policy registers on the economy. With monetary policy, the lag between a change in the target overnight rate and the change in aggregate demand and output can take from months to a year or more. Fiscal policy, once enacted, usually requires three to six months to take effect and between 9 and 18 months to register its full effect. Because of the effectiveness lag, the economy may turn around on its own before the policy registers its full impact. A stimulus package may end up merely adding more inflationary pressure to a recovering economy.

These lags make active policy difficult to execute. The more variable the lags, the harder it is to predict when a particular policy will take hold and what the state of the economy will be at that time. To advocates of passive policy, these lags are reason enough to avoid active discretionary policy. *Advocates of a passive approach argue that an active stabilization policy imposes troubling fluctuations in the price level and real GDP because it often takes hold only after market forces have already returned the economy to its potential output level.*

© Kenneth Summers/Shutterstock.com

Talk in the media about "jump-starting" the economy reflects the active approach, which views the economy as a sputtering machine that can be fixed by an expert mechanic. The passive approach views the economy as more like a supertanker on automatic pilot. The policy question then becomes whether to trust that automatic pilot (the self-correcting tendencies of the economy) or to try to override the mechanism with active discretionary policies.

Comstock/Getty Images

A Review of Policy Perspectives

The active and passive approaches reflect different views about the stability and resiliency of the economy and the ability of government or the Bank of Canada to implement appropriate discretionary policies. As we have seen, advocates of an active approach think that the natural adjustments of wages and prices can be painfully slow, particularly when unemployment is high. Prolonged high

rational expectations a school of thought that argues people form expectations based on all available information, including the likely future actions of government policymakers

unemployment means that much output must be sacrificed, and the unemployed must suffer personal hardship during the slow adjustment period. If high unemployment lasts a long time, labour skills may grow rusty, and some people may drop out of the labour force. Therefore, prolonged unemployment may cause the economy's potential GDP to fall.

Thus active-policy advocates see a high cost of not using discretionary policy. Despite the lags involved, they prefer action—through discretionary fiscal policy, discretionary monetary policy, or some combination of the two—to inaction. Passive-policy advocates, on the other hand, believe that uncertain lags and ignorance about how the economy works undermine active policy. Rather than pursue a misguided activist policy, passivists prefer to sit back and rely on the economy's natural ability to correct itself just using automatic stabilizers.

LO 2 The Role of Expectations

The effectiveness of a particular government policy depends in part on what people expect. As we saw in an earlier chapter, the short-run aggregate supply curve is drawn for a given expected price level reflected in long-term wage contracts. If workers and firms expect continuing inflation, their wage agreements reflect these inflationary expectations. One approach in macroeconomics, called **rational expectations**, argues that people form expectations on the basis of all available information, including information about the probable future actions of policymakers. Thus, aggregate supply depends on what sort of macroeconomic course policymakers are expected to pursue. For example, if people were to observe policymakers using discretionary policy to stimulate aggregate demand every time output falls below potential, people would come to anticipate the effects of this policy on the price level and output.

Robert Lucas, of the University of Chicago, won the 1995 Nobel Prize in Economics for his studies of rational expectations. We consider the role of expectations in the context of monetary policy, but fiscal policy would have a similar effect.

Discretionary Policy and Inflation Expectations

Monetary authorities must testify before parliament regularly to offer an assessment of the economy. As noted in the previous chapter, the Bank of Canada also announces, after each meeting of the Monetary Policy Review Committee, any changes in its interest rate targets and the likely direction, or "bias," of future changes. And Bank of Canada officials often deliver speeches around the country. Those interested in the economy sift through all this material to discover the likely path of monetary policy.

Let's examine the relationship between Bank of Canada policy pronouncements, the Bank's actions, and equilibrium output. Suppose the economy is producing potential output so unemployment is at its natural rate. At the beginning of the year, firms and employees must negotiate wage agreements. While negotiations are under way, the Bank of Canada announces that throughout the year, monetary policy will aim at sustaining potential output while keeping the price level stable. This policy seems appropriate because unemployment is already at the natural rate. Workers and firms understand that the Bank's stable price policy appears optimal under the circumstances because an expansionary monetary policy would lead only to higher inflation in the long run. Until the year is under way and monetary policy is actually implemented, however, the public can't know for sure what the Bank will do.

As long as wage increases do not exceed the growth in labour productivity, the Bank's plan of a stable price level should work. Alternatively, workers could try to negotiate a higher wage growth, but that would ultimately lead to inflation. Suppose workers and firms believe the Bank's pronouncements and reach wage settlements based on a constant price level. If the Bank follows through as

© tobkatrina/Shutterstock

EXHIBIT 3

Short-Run Effects of an Unexpected Expansionary Policy

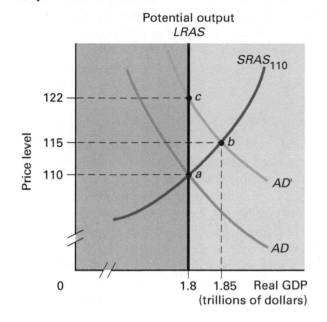

promised, the price level should turn out as expected. Output remains at the economy's potential, and unemployment remains at the natural rate. The situation is depicted in Exhibit 3. The short-run aggregate supply curve, $SRAS_{110}$, is based on wage contracts reflecting an expected price level of 110. If the Bank follows the announced course, the aggregate demand curve will be AD and equilibrium will be at point a, where the price level is as expected and the economy is producing $1.8 trillion, the potential output.

Suppose, however, that after workers and firms have agreed on nominal wages—that is, after the short-run aggregate supply curve has been determined—public officials become dissatisfied with the unemployment rate. Perhaps election-year concerns with unemployment, a false alarm about a recession, or overestimating potential output convince the Bank to act. An expansionary monetary policy increases the aggregate demand curve from AD, the level anticipated by firms and employees, to AD'. This unexpected policy stimulates output and employment in the short run to equilibrium point b. Output increases to $1.85 trillion, and the price level increases to 115. This temporary boost in output and reduction in unemployment may last long enough to help public officials get reelected.

So the price level is now higher than workers expected, and their agreed-on wage buys less in real terms than workers bargained for. At their earliest

opportunity, workers will negotiate higher wages. These higher wage agreements will eventually cause the short-run aggregate supply curve in Exhibit 3 to shift leftward, intersecting AD' at point c, the economy's potential output (to reduce clutter, the shifted short-run aggregate supply curve is not shown). So output once again returns to the economy's potential GDP, but in the process the price level rises to 122.

Thus the unexpected expansionary policy causes a short-run pop in output and employment. But in the long run, the increase in the aggregate demand curve yields only inflation. The **time-inconsistency problem** arises when policymakers have an incentive to announce one policy to shape expectations but then to pursue a different policy once those expectations have been formed and acted on.

Anticipating Policy

Suppose policymakers become alarmed by the high inflation. The next time around, the Bank of Canada once again announces a monetary policy aimed at producing potential output while keeping the price level stable at 122. Based on their previous experience, however, workers and firms have learned that the Bank is willing to accept higher inflation in exchange for a temporary boost in output. Workers may be fooled once by the Bank's actions, but they won't be fooled again. Workers and their employers take the Bank's announcement with a grain of salt. Workers, in particular, do not want to get caught again with their real wages down should the Bank implement a stimulative monetary policy. Workers and firms expect the Bank's actions will increase the price level. The bottom line is that workers and firms negotiate a high wage increase.

In effect, workers and firms are betting the Bank will pursue an expansionary policy regardless of pronouncements to the contrary. The short-run aggregate supply curve reflecting these higher wage agreements is depicted by $SRAS_{132}$ in Exhibit 4, where 132 is the expected price level. Note that AD' would result if the Bank followed its announced policy; that demand curve intersects the potential output line at point c, where the price level is 122. But AD'' is the aggregate demand that workers and firms expect based on an expansionary monetary policy. They have agreed to wage settlements that will produce the economy's potential output if the Bank behaves as *expected,* not

time-inconsistency problem when policymakers have an incentive to announce one policy to influence expectations but then pursue a different policy once those expectations have been formed and acted on

EXHIBIT 4
Short-Run Effects of a More Expansionary Policy Than Announced

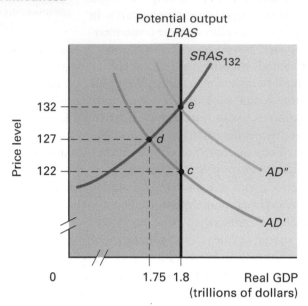

Potential output
LRAS

SRAS$_{132}$

Price level

132 — — — — — — — — *e*

127 — — — — — *d*

122 — — — — *c*   *AD''*

                        AD'

0   1.75 1.8   Real GDP
                      (trillions of dollars)

cold turkey the announcement and execution of tough measures to reduce high inflation

as *announced*. Thus a price level of 132 is based on rational expectations. In effect, workers and firms expect the expansionary monetary policy to shift aggregate demand from *AD'* to *AD''*.

Monetary authorities must now decide whether to stick with their announced plan of a stable price level or follow a more expansionary monetary policy. If they pursue the constant-price-level policy, aggregate demand turns out to be *AD'* and short-run equilibrium occurs at point *d*. Short-run output falls below the economy's potential, resulting in unemployment exceeding the natural rate. If monetary authorities want to keep output at its potential, they have only one alternative—to match public expectations. Monetary authorities will likely pursue an expansionary monetary policy, an action that increases inflation and reinforces public skepticism of policy announcements. This expansionary policy results in an aggregate demand of *AD''*, leading to equilibrium at point *e*, where the price level is 132 and output equals the economy's potential.

Thus, workers and firms enter negotiations realizing that the Bank has an incentive to pursue an expansionary monetary policy. So workers and firms agree to higher wage increases, and the Bank follows with an expansionary policy, one that results in more inflation. Once workers and firms come to expect an expansionary monetary policy and the resulting inflation, such a policy does not spur even a

temporary increase in output beyond the economy's potential. *Economists of the rational expectations school believe that if the economy is already producing its potential, an expansionary policy, if fully anticipated, has no effect on output or employment, not even in the short run. Only unanticipated expansionary policy can temporarily push output beyond its potential.*

Policy Credibility

If the economy was already producing its potential, an unexpected expansionary policy would increase output and employment temporarily. The costs, however, include not only inflation in the long term but also a loss of credibility in Bank of Canada pronouncements the next time around. Is there any way out of this? For the Bank to pursue a policy consistent with a constant price level, its announcements must somehow be *credible*, or believable. Workers and firms must believe that when the time comes to make a hard decision, the Bank will follow through as promised. Perhaps the Bank could offer some sort of guarantee to convince people it will stay the course—for example, the Bank governor could promise to resign if the Bank does not follow the announced policy. Ironically, policymakers are often more credible and therefore more effective if they have some of their discretion taken away. In this case, a hard-and-fast rule could be substituted for a policymaker's discretion. We examine policy rules in the next section.

Consider the problems facing central banks in countries that have experienced hyperinflation. For an anti-inflation policy to succeed at the least possible cost in forgone output, the public must believe central bankers. How can central bankers in an economy ripped by hyperinflation establish credibility? Some economists believe that the most efficient anti-inflation policy is **cold turkey**, which is to announce and execute tough measures to stop inflation, such as halting the growth in the money supply. For example, in 1985, the annual rate of inflation in Bolivia was running at 20,000 percent when the new government announced a stern policy. The restrictive measures worked, and inflation was stopped within a month, with little loss in output. Around the world, credible anti-inflation policies have been successful.[1]

---

[1] For a discussion about how four hyperinflations in the 1920s ended, see Thomas Sargent, "The Ends of Four Big Inflations," *in Inflation: Causes and Consequences*, edited by Robert Hall (University of Chicago Press, 1982): 41–98.

Much depends on the Bank's time horizon. If policymakers take the long view, they will not risk their long-term policy effectiveness for a temporary reduction in unemployment. If the Bank officials realize that their credibility is hard to develop but easy to undermine, they will be reluctant to pursue policies that ultimately just increase inflation.

LO 3 Policy Rules Versus Discretion

Again, the active approach views the economy as unstable and in need of discretionary policy to cut cyclical unemployment when it arises. The passive approach views the economy as stable enough that discretionary policy is not only unnecessary but may actually worsen economic fluctuations. In place of discretionary policy, the passive approach often calls for predetermined rules to guide policymakers. In the context of fiscal policy, these rules take the form of automatic stabilizers, such as employment insurance, a progressive income tax, and transfer payments, all of which aim to dampen economic fluctuations. In the context of monetary policy, passive rules might be the decision to allow the money supply to grow at a predetermined rate, to maintain interest rates at some predetermined level, or to keep inflation below a certain rate. For example, say the European Central Bank announced a rule that it would

ZanyZeus/Shutterstock

not lower its target interest rate if inflation exceeded 2.0 percent a year. Most central banks have committed to achieving low **inflation targets**, usually specifying a particular rate for the next year or two. Advocates of inflation targets say such targets encourage workers, firms, and investors to plan on a low and stable inflation rate. Opponents of inflation targets worry that inflation targeting pays less attention to jobs and economic growth. In this section, we examine the arguments for policy rules versus discretion mostly in the context of monetary policy, the policy focus in recent decades.

Limitations on Discretion

The rationale for the passive approach rather than the use of active discretion arises from different views of

how the economy works. One view holds that *the economy is so complex and economic aggregates interact in such obscure ways and with such varied lags that policymakers cannot comprehend what is going on well enough to pursue an active monetary or fiscal policy.* For example, if the Bank of Canada adopts a discretionary policy that is based on a misreading of the current economy or a poor understanding of the lag structure, the Bank may be lowering the target overnight rate when a more appropriate course would be to leave the rate unchanged or even to raise it. As a case in point, during a meeting of the Federal Open Market Committee in the United States, one member lamented the difficulty of figuring out what was going on with the economy, noting, "As a lesson for the future, I'd like to remind us all that as recently as two meetings ago we couldn't see the strength that was unfolding in the second half [of the year]. . . . It wasn't in our forecast; it wasn't in the other forecasts; and it wasn't in the anecdotal reports. We were standing right on top of it and we couldn't see it. That's just an important lesson to remember going forward."[2]

inflation target
commitment of central bankers to keep inflation below a certain rate for the next year or two

A comparison of economic forecasters and weather forecasters may shed light on the position of those who advocate the passive approach. Suppose you are in charge of the heating and cooling system at a major shopping mall. You realize that weather forecasts are unreliable, particularly in the early spring, when days can be warm or cold. Each day you must guess what the temperature will be and, based on that guess, decide whether to fire up the heater, turn on the air conditioner, or leave them both off. Because the mall is huge, you must start the system long before you know for sure what the weather will be. Once the system is turned on, it can't be turned off until much later in the day.

Suppose you guess the day will be cold, so you turn on the heat. If the day turns out to be cold, your policy is correct and the mall temperature will be just right. But if the day turns out to be warm, the heating system will make the mall unbearable. You

[2] FOMC board member Thomas Melzer, in a transcript of the 22 December 1992 meeting of the Federal Open Market Committee, p. 14. Meeting transcripts are published after a five-year lag and are available at http://www.federalreserve.gov/monetarypolicy/fomc_historical.htm.

would have been better off with nothing. In contrast, if you turn on the air conditioning system expecting a warm day but the day turns out to be cold, the mall will be freezing. The lesson is that if you are unable to predict the weather, you should use neither system. Similarly, if policymakers cannot predict the course of the economy, they should not try to fine-tune monetary or fiscal policy. Complicating the prediction problem is the fact that policy officials are not sure about the lags involved with discretionary policy. The situation is comparable to your not knowing how long the system actually takes to come on once you flip the switch.

This analogy applies only if the cost of doing nothing—using neither heat nor air conditioning—is relatively low. In the early spring, you can assume that there is little risk of weather so cold that water pipes freeze or so hot that walls sweat. A similar assumption in the passive view is that the economy is fairly stable and periods of prolonged unemployment are unlikely. In such an economy, the costs of *not* intervening are relatively low. In contrast, advocates of active policy believe that wide and prolonged swings in the economy (analogous to wide and prolonged swings in the outside temperature) make doing nothing risky.

Rules and Rational Expectations

Another group of economists also advocates the passive approach, but not because they believe the economy is too complex. Proponents of the rational expectations approach, discussed earlier, claim that people have a pretty good idea how the economy works and what to expect from government policymakers. For example, people know enough about monetary policies pursued in the past to forecast, with reasonable accuracy, future policies and their effects on the economy. Some individual forecasts are too high and some too low, but on average, forecasts turn out to be about right. *To the extent that monetary policy is fully anticipated by workers and firms, it has no effect on the level of output; it affects only the price level.* Thus only unexpected changes in policy can bring about short-run changes in output.

In the long run, changes in the money supply affect only inflation, not potential output, so followers of the rational expectations theory believe that the Bank should avoid discretionary monetary policy. Instead, the Bank should follow a predictable monetary rule. A monetary rule would reduce policy surprises and keep output near the natural rate. *Although some economists favour rules over discretion because of ignorance about the lag structure of the economy, rational expectations theorists advocate a predictable rule to avoid surprises, because surprises result in unnecessary departures from potential output.* For example, broad legislation to stimulate the economy and bail out the banks and automakers were said to create uncertainty in the economy about what might be next. And this uncertainty discouraged some firms from hiring and kept some consumers from spending.

Despite support by some economists for explicit rules rather than discretion, central bankers are reluctant to follow hard-and-fast rules about the course of future policy. Discretion has been used more than explicit rules in the United States since the early 1980s, though policy has become more predictable because the Federal Reserve now announces the probable trend of future target rate changes.

The Bank of Canada operates a monetary policy framework to control inflation. It is a rule-based policy, the goal of which is to keep inflation close to the central bank's 2 percent target.

So far, we have looked at active stabilization policy, which focuses on shifts of the aggregate demand curve, and passive stabilization policy, which relies more on natural shifts of the short-run aggregate supply curve. In the final section, we focus on an additional model, the Phillips curve, to shed more light on the relationship between aggregate demand and aggregate supply in the short and long runs.

LO 4 The Phillips Curve

At one time, policymakers thought they faced a long-run trade-off between inflation and unemployment. This view was suggested by the research of New Zealand economist A.W. Phillips, who in 1958 published an article that examined the historical relation between inflation and unemployment in the United Kingdom.[3] Based on about 100 years of evidence, his data traced an inverse relationship between the unemployment rate and the rate of change in nominal wages (serving as a measure of inflation). This relationship implied that the opportunity cost of reducing unemployment was higher inflation, and the opportunity cost of reducing inflation was higher unemployment.

[3] A.W. Phillips, "Relation between Unemployment and the Rate of Change in Money Wage Rates in the United Kingdom, 1861–1957," *Economica*, 25 (November 1958): 283–299.

The Phillips Framework

The possible options with respect to unemployment and inflation are illustrated by the hypothetical **Phillips curve** in Exhibit 5. The unemployment rate is measured along the horizontal axis and the inflation rate along the vertical axis. Let's begin at point *a,* which depicts one possible combination of unemployment and inflation. Fiscal or monetary policy could be used to stimulate output and thereby reduce unemployment, moving the economy from point *a* to point *b.* Notice, however, that the reduction in unemployment comes at the cost of higher inflation. A reduction in unemployment with no change in inflation would be represented by point *c.* But as you can see, this alternative is not available.

Most policymakers of the 1960s came to believe that they faced a stable, long-run trade-off between unemployment and inflation. The Phillips curve was based on an era when inflation was low and the primary disturbances in the economy were shocks to aggregate demand. The effect of changes in aggregate demand can be traced as movements along a given short-run aggregate supply curve. If aggregate demand increases, the price level rises but unemployment falls. If aggregate demand decreases, the price level falls but unemployment rises. With appropriate demand-management policies, policymakers believed they could choose any point along the Phillips curve. The 1970s proved this view wrong in two ways. First, some of the biggest disturbances were adverse *supply* shocks, such as those created by oil embargoes and

worldwide crop failures. These shocks shifted the aggregate supply curve leftward. A reduction of the aggregate supply curve led to both higher inflation *and* higher unemployment. Stagflation was at odds with the Phillips curve. Second, economists learned that when short-run output exceeds potential, an expansionary gap opens. As this gap closes by a leftward shift of the short-run aggregate supply curve, greater inflation *and* higher unemployment result—again, an outcome inconsistent with a Phillips curve.

The increases in both inflation and unemployment caused by a decrease in aggregate supply can be represented by an outcome such as point *d* in Exhibit 5. By the end of the 1970s, increases in both inflation and unemployment suggested either that the Phillips curve had shifted outward or that it no longer described economic reality. The dilemma called for a reexamination of the Phillips curve, and this led to a distinction between the short-run Phillips curve and the long-run Phillips curve.

The Short-Run Phillips Curve

To discuss the underpinnings of the Phillips curve, we must return to the short-run aggregate supply curve. Suppose the price level this year is reflected by a price index of, say, 100, and that people expect prices to be about 3 percent higher next year. So the price level expected next year is 103. Workers and firms therefore negotiate wage contracts based on that expectation. As the short-run aggregate supply curve in Exhibit 6(a) indicates, if *AD* is the aggregate demand curve and the price level is 103, as expected, output equals the economy's potential, shown here to be $1.8 trillion. Recall that when the economy produces its potential, unemployment is at the natural rate.

The short-run relationship between inflation and unemployment is presented in Exhibit 6(b) under the assumption that people expect inflation to be 3 percent. Unemployment is measured along the horizontal axis and inflation along the vertical axis. Panel (a) shows that when inflation is 3 percent, the economy produces its potential. Unemployment is at the natural rate, assumed in panel (b) to be 6 percent. The combination of 3 percent inflation and 6 percent unemployment is reflected by point *a* in panel (b), which corresponds to point *a* in panel (a).

What if aggregate demand turns out to be greater than expected, as indicated by *AD'?* In the short run, the greater demand results in point *b,* with a price level

Phillips curve a curve showing possible combinations of the inflation rate and the unemployment rate

EXHIBIT 5
Hypothetical Phillips Curve

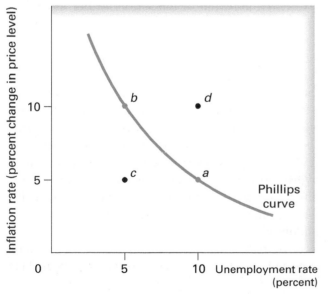

EXHIBIT 6
Aggregate Supply Curves and Phillips Curves in the Short Run and Long Run

(a) Short-run aggregate supply curve

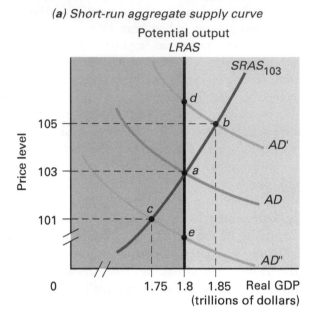

(b) Short-run and long-run Phillips curves

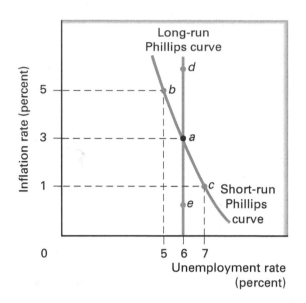

short-run Phillips curve based on an expected inflation rate, a curve that reflects an inverse relationship between the inflation rate and the unemployment rate

of 105 and output of $1.85 trillion. Because the price level exceeds that reflected in wage contracts, inflation also exceeds expectations. Specifically, inflation turns out to be 5 percent, not 3 percent. Because output exceeds potential, unemployment falls below the natural rate to 5 percent. The new combination of unemployment and inflation is depicted by point *b* in panel (b), which corresponds to point *b* in panel (a).

What if aggregate demand turns out to be lower than expected, as indicated by *AD"*? In the short run, the lower demand results in point *c*, where the price level of 101 is less than expected and output of $1.75 trillion is below potential. Inflation of 1 percent is less than the expected 3 percent, and unemployment of 7 percent exceeds the natural rate. This combination is reflected by point *c* in panel (b), which corresponds to point *c* in panel (a).

Note that the short-run aggregate supply curve in panel (a) can be used to develop the inverse relationship between inflation and unemployment shown in panel (b), called a **short-run Phillips curve**. This curve is created by the intersection of alternative aggregate demand curves along a given short-run aggregate supply curve. *The short-run Phillips curve is based on labour contracts that reflect a given expected price level, which implies a given*

expected rate of inflation. The short-run Phillips curve in panel (b) is based on an expected inflation of 3 percent. If inflation turns out as expected, unemployment equals the natural rate. If inflation exceeds expectations, unemployment in the short run falls below the natural rate. If inflation is less than expected, unemployment in the short run exceeds the natural rate.

The Long-Run Phillips Curve

If inflation exceeds expectations, output exceeds the economy's potential in the short run but not in the long run. Labour shortages and shrinking real wages prompt higher wage agreements. The short-run aggregate supply curve shifts leftward until it passes through point *d* in panel (a) of Exhibit 6, returning the economy to its potential output. The unexpectedly higher aggregate demand curve has no lasting effect on output or unemployment. Point *d* corresponds to a higher price level and thus higher inflation. Closing the expansionary gap generates both higher unemployment and higher inflation, a combination depicted by point *d* in panel (b). Note that while points *a*, *b*, and *c* are on the same short-run Phillips curve, point *d* is not.

To trace the long-run effects of a lower-than-expected price level, let's return to point *c* in panel (a), where the actual price level is below the expected level, so output is below its potential. If workers and firms negotiate lower money wages (or if the growth in nominal wages trails inflation), the short-run aggregate supply curve could shift rightward until it passes through point *e*, where the economy returns once again to its potential output. Both inflation and unemployment fall, as reflected by point *e* in panel (b).

Note that points *a*, *d*, and *e* in panel (a) depict long-run equilibrium points; the expected price level equals the actual price level. At those same points in panel (b), expected inflation equals actual inflation, so unemployment equals the natural rate. We can connect points *a*, *d*, and *e* in the right panel to form the **long-run Phillips curve.** *When workers and employers adjust fully to any unexpected change in aggregate demand, the long-run Phillips curve is a vertical line drawn at the economy's natural rate of unemployment.* As long as prices and wages are flexible enough, the rate of unemployment, in the long run, is independent of the rate of inflation. *Thus, according to proponents of this type of analysis, policymakers cannot, in the long run, choose between unemployment and inflation. They can choose only among alternative rates of inflation.*

The Natural Rate Hypothesis

The natural rate of unemployment occurs at the economy's potential output, discussed extensively already. An important idea that emerged from this reexamination of the Phillips curve is the **natural rate hypothesis,** which states that in the long run, the economy tends toward the natural rate of unemployment. This natural rate is largely independent of any *aggregate demand* stimulus provided by monetary or fiscal policy. Policymakers may be able to push output beyond its potential temporarily, but only if the policy surprises the public. The natural rate hypothesis implies that *the policy that results in low inflation is generally the optimal policy in the long run.*

EXHIBIT 7
Short-Run Phillips Curves Since 1967

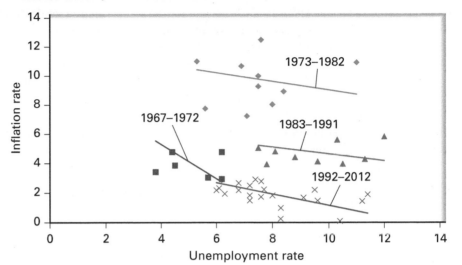

SOURCE: Based on inflation and unemployment data from the Statistics Canada Tables 282-0086, 384-0035 and 326-0021.

Evidence of the Phillips Curve

What has been the actual relationship between unemployment and inflation in Canada? In Exhibit 7, each year since 1967 is represented by a point, with the unemployment rate measured along the horizontal axis and the inflation rate measured along the vertical axis. Superimposed on these points are short-run Phillips curves showing patterns of unemployment and inflation during what turns out to be four distinct periods since 1967. Remember, each short-run Phillips curve is drawn for a given *expected inflation rate.* An increase in inflationary expectations shifts the short-run Phillips curve away from the origin.

A trade-off between unemployment and inflation occurred between 1967 and 1972. Inflation during the period averaged only 3.8 percent, and unemployment averaged 5.1 percent.

The short-run Phillips curve shifted away from the origin for the period from 1973 to 1982 when inflation and unemployment each climbed to an average of 9.6 percent and 7.5 percent respectively. In 1974, sharp increases in oil prices and crop failures around the world reduced aggregate supply, which explains the outward shift of the Phillips curve. After the Bank of Canada reduced inflationary expectations in the early 1980s, the short-run Phillips curve shifted

long-run Phillips curve a vertical line drawn at the economy's natural rate of unemployment that traces equilibrium points that can occur when workers and employers have the time to adjust fully to any unexpected change in aggregate demand

natural rate hypothesis the natural rate of unemployment is largely independent of the stimulus provided by monetary or fiscal policy

inward. Average inflation for 1983 to 1991 fell to 4.8 percent and average unemployment was 9.5 percent. Finally, data for 1992 to 2012 suggest a new, lower short-run Phillips curve, with average inflation of only 1.9 percent and average unemployment of 8.1 percent. Thus the Phillips curve shifted rightward following a 1991 Bank of Canada policy announcement that targeted inflation. Since the 1960s, the Bank of Canada has learned more about how to control inflation, thereby reducing inflation expectations and shifting the Phillips curve rightwards.

Final Word

This chapter examined the implications of active and passive policy. The important question is whether the economy is stable and self-correcting when it gets off track or unstable and in need of active government intervention. Advocates of active policy believe that the Bank of Canada or the federal government or both should reduce economic fluctuations by stimulating aggregate demand when output falls below its potential level and by dampening aggregate demand when output exceeds its potential level. Advocates of active policy argue that government attempts to reduce the ups and downs of the business cycle may not be perfect but are still better than nothing. Some activists also believe that high unemployment may be self-reinforcing because some unemployed workers lose valuable job skills and grow to accept unemployment as a way of life.

Advocates of passive policy, on the other hand, believe that discretionary policy may worsen cyclical swings in the economy, leading to higher inflation in the long run with no permanent increase in potential output and no permanent reduction in the unemployment rate. This group favours passive rules for monetary policy and automatic stabilizers for fiscal policy.

CHAPTER PROBLEMS

LO1 Compare an active policy and a passive policy

1.1. *(Active versus Passive Policy)* Discuss the role each of the following plays in the debate between the active and passive approaches:
   a. The speed of adjustment of the nominal wage
   b. The speed of adjustment of expectations about inflation
   c. The existence of lags in policy creation and implementation
   d. Variability in the natural rate of unemployment over time

1.2. *(Problems with Active Policy)* Use an AD–AS diagram to illustrate and explain the short-run and long-run effects on the economy of the following situation: both the natural rate of unemployment and the actual rate of unemployment are 5 percent. However, the government believes that the natural rate of unemployment is 6 percent and that the economy is overheating. Therefore, it introduces a policy to reduce aggregate demand.

1.3. *(Policy Lags)* What lag in discretionary policy is described in each of the following statements?

Why do long lags make discretionary policy less effective?
   a. The time from when the government determines that the economy is in recession until a tax cut is approved to reduce unemployment
   b. The time from when the money supply is increased until the resulting effect on the economy is felt
   c. The time from the start of a recession until the government identifies the existence and severity of the recession
   d. The time from when the Bank of Canada decides to reduce the money supply until the money supply actually declines

1.4. *(The Problem of Lags)* How does the problem of lags complicate an active stabilization policy to stimulate aggregate demand?

LO2 Consider the role of expectations

2.1. *(Rational Expectations)* Using an AD–AS diagram, illustrate the short-run effects on prices, output, and employment of an increase in the money supply that is correctly anticipated by the public. Assume that the economy is initially at potential output.

2.2. *(Policy Credibility)* An unexpected expansionary policy in an economy producing at its potential would increase output and reduce unemployment temporarily. The costs, however, include inflation and lack of credibility in the central bank's pronouncements the next time around. How can central banks in an economy ripped by hyperinflation establish credibility?

2.3. *(Rational Expectations and Policy)* Suppose that people in an election year believe that public officials are going to pursue expansionary policies to enhance their reelection prospects. How could such expectations put pressure on officials to pursue expansionary policies even if they hadn't planned to?

LO3 Discuss policy rules versus discretion

3.1. *(Rules and Rational Expectations)* Explain this statement: "To the extent that monetary policy is fully anticipated by workers and firms, it has no effect on the level of output; it affects only the price level."

3.2. *(Rationale for Rules)* Some economists call for predetermined rules to guide the actions of government policymakers. What are two contrasting rationales that have been given for such rules?

LO4 Explain the Phillips curve

4.1. *(Short-Run Phillips Curve)* Explain why the short-run Phillips curve is based on labour contracts that reflect a given expected price level.

4.2. *(Long-Run Phillips Curve)* Suppose the economy is at point *d* on the long-run Phillips curve shown in the accompanying graph. If that inflation rate is unacceptably high, how can policymakers get the inflation rate down? Would rational expectations help or hinder their efforts?

Phillips Curves in the Short Run and Long Run

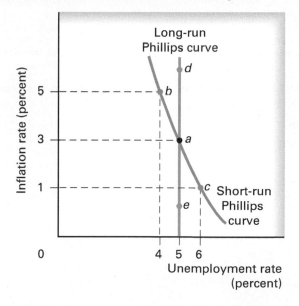

CASE STUDY

Central Bank Independence and Price Stability

Some economists argue that the central bank would do better in the long run if it committed to the single goal of price stability rather than also worry about achieving potential output or reducing unemployment. But to focus on price stability, a central bank should be insulated from political influence, because price stability may involve some painful remedies.

Does central bank independence affect performance? When central banks for 17 advanced industrial countries were ranked from least independent to most independent, inflation during the 15-year span examined turned out to be the lowest in countries with the most independent central banks and highest in countries with the least independent central banks. The least independent banks at the time were in Spain, New Zealand, Australia, and Italy. The most independent central banks were in Germany and Switzerland. Countries with the least independent central banks experienced inflation that averaged four times higher than countries with the most independent central banks. The Canadian and U.S. central banks are considered relatively independent.

The trend around the world is toward greater central bank independence. For example, the Central Bank of New Zealand has adopted a monetary policy of inflation-rate targeting, with price stability as the primary goal. Chile, Colombia, and Argentina—developing countries that suffered hyperinflation—have legislated more central bank independence. The Maastricht agreement, which defined the framework for a single European currency, the euro, identified price stability as the main objective of the new European Central Bank. That bank has a policy of not reducing the interest rate if inflation exceeds 2.0 percent. In fact, the European Central Bank came under criticism recently for not cutting interest rates even though a recession loomed and unemployment topped 8 percent. The Bank of England and Swiss National Bank also have an inflation target of no higher than 2.0 percent. Many central banks have adopted low inflation targets. The Federal Reserve does not have an explicit inflation target, but some Fed watchers claim the Fed has an informal inflation target of 1.5 percent to 2.0 percent.

SOURCES: Natasha Brereton, "U.K. Inflation Eases in May," *Wall Street Journal*, 15 June 2010; Sarah Lynch and Tom Barkley, "Jobless Claims Decline," *Wall Street Journal*, 15 July 2010; Alberto Alesina and Lawrence Summers, "Central Bank Independence and Macroeconomic Performance: Some Comparative Evidence," *Journal of Money, Credit and Banking*, 25 (May 1993): 151–162; Ben Bernanke, "A Perspective on Inflation Targeting: Why It Seems to Work," *Business Economics*, 38 (July 2003): 7–15; Stefano Eusepi and Bruce Preston, "Central Bank Communication and Expectations Stabilization," *American Economic Journal: Macroeconomics*, 2 (July 2010): 235–271; and Ben Bernanke, "Inflation Targeting," *Federal Reserve Bank of St. Louis Review*, 86 (July/August 2004): 165–168. For online links to more than 160 central banks, including all those discussed in this case study, go to http://www.bis.org/cbanks.htm.

QUESTION

1. One source of independence for central banks is the term length for governors. Central banks also have their own sources of income. Does this suggest another source of independence from government?

16

International Finance

LEARNING OUTCOMES

LO1 Explain how the balance of payments works

LO2 Discuss foreign exchange rates and markets

LO3 Define fixed and flexible exchange rates

LO4 Describe the development of the international monetary system

> ## Why does a nation try to influence the value of its currency?

Why does oil price volatility influence the Canadian dollar? Are high trade deficits a worry? What's the official "fudge factor" used to compute the balance of payments? What's meant by a "strong dollar"? Why does a nation try to influence the value of its currency? Answers to these and other questions are explored in this chapter, which focuses on international finance.

If Tim Hortons wants to buy 1,000 espresso machines from the German manufacturer Krups, it will be quoted a price in euros. Suppose the machines cost a total of €1 million (euros). How much is that in dollars? The dollar cost will depend on the exchange rate. When trade takes place across international borders, two currencies are usually involved. Supporting the flows of goods and services are flows of currencies that fund international transactions. The exchange rate between currencies—the price of one in terms of the other—is how the price of a product in one country translates into the price facing a buyer in another country. Cross-border trade therefore depends on the exchange rate. In this chapter we examine the market forces that affect the relative value of one currency in terms of another.

LO 1 Balance of Payments

A country's gross domestic product, or GDP, measures the economy's income and output during a given period. To account for dealings abroad, countries must also keep track of international transactions. A country's *balance of payments*, as introduced in Chapter 3, summarizes all economic transactions during a given period between residents of that country and residents of other countries. *Residents* include people, firms, organizations, and governments.

International Economic Transactions

The balance of payments measures economic transactions between a country and the rest of the world, whether these transactions involve goods and services, real and financial assets, or transfer payments. The balance of payments measures a *flow* of transactions during a particular period, usually a year. Some transactions do not involve actual payments. For example, if TransCanada Corp. ships new equipment to its U.S. subsidiary TC PipeLines LP, no payment is made, yet an economic transaction involving another country has occurred. Similarly, if CARE Canada sends food to Africa, these transactions must be captured in the balance of payments. So remember, although we speak of the *balance of payments,* a more descriptive phrase would be the *balance-of-economic transactions.*

BALANCE-OF-PAYMENTS ACCOUNTS ARE MAINTAINED ACCORDING TO THE PRINCIPLES OF *DOUBLE-ENTRY BOOKKEEPING, WHERE TOTAL CREDITS MUST EQUAL TOTAL DEBITS.*

Balance-of-payments accounts are maintained according to the principles of *double-entry bookkeeping*. Some entries are called *credits,* and others are called *debits.* As you will see, the balance of payments consists of several individual accounts. An individual account may not balance, but a deficit in one or more accounts must be offset by a surplus in the other accounts. Because total credits must equal total debits, there is a *balance* of payments—hence, the name. During a given period, such as a year, the inflow of receipts from the rest of the world, which are entered as credits, must equal the outflow of payments to the rest of the world, which are entered as debits.

The first of two major categories in the balance of payments is the current account. The current account records *current* flows of funds into and out of the country, including imports and exports of goods and services, net income earned by Canadian residents from foreign assets, and net transfer payments from abroad. These are discussed in turn.

The Merchandise Trade Balance

The *merchandise trade balance,* a term introduced in Chapter 3, equals the value of merchandise exports minus the value of merchandise imports. The merchandise account reflects trade in goods, or tangible products (stuff you can put in a box), like French wine, U.S. computers, or Canadian crude oil, and is often referred to simply as the *trade balance.* The value of Canadian merchandise exports is a credit in the Canadian balance-of-payments account because Canadian residents get *paid* for the exported goods. The value of Canadian merchandise imports is a debit in the balance-of-payments account because Canadian residents *pay* foreigners for imported goods.

If merchandise exports exceed merchandise imports, the trade balance is in *surplus.* If merchandise imports exceed merchandise exports, the trade balance is in *deficit.* The merchandise trade balance, which is reported monthly, influences foreign exchange markets, the stock market, and other financial markets. The merchandise trade balance depends on a variety of factors, including the relative strength and competitiveness of the domestic economy compared with other economies and the relative value of the domestic currency compared with other currencies. Strong economies with growing incomes tend to buy more of everything, including imports.

Canada's merchandise trade since 1981 is depicted in Exhibit 1, where exports, the red line, and imports, the blue line, are expressed as a percentage of GDP. Exports exceeded imports from 1981 to 2009, and the resulting trade surplus is the difference between the two. Trade surplus as a percentage of GDP increased from 1 percent in 1991 to a peak of 7.2 percent in 2000. The recession of 2007–2009 slowed exports more than imports, so in 2009 Canada's trade deficit relative to GDP was 0.3 percent, increasing to 0.6 percent in 2010, then falling to 0.4 in 2013.

Exhibit 2 shows Canada's merchandise trade with major economies or regions of the world in 2013. The $43.9-billion trade surplus with the United States was by far the largest, about six times that with the United Kingdom. Canadians bought $314.5 billion worth of goods from the United States in 2013, but Americans bought $358.4 billion worth of Canadian goods. Canada had a trade deficit with the European Union and with the Organisation for Economic Co-operation and Development (OECD). The United States is the world's biggest importer and has a trade surplus with only a few major economies, including Australia, Brazil, and the Netherlands.

EXHIBIT 1
Canada's Merchandise Trade since 1981

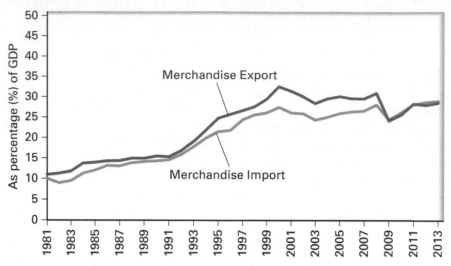

SOURCE: Statistics Canada. CANSIM Table 228-0003 "Merchandise imports and exports, by major groups and principal trading areas for all countries, annual (dollars)" (accessed: March 08, 2015)

balance on goods and services the portion of a country's balance-of-payments account that measures the value of a country's exports of goods and services minus the value of its imports of goods and services

Balance on Goods and Services

The merchandise trade balance focuses on the flow of goods, but services are also traded internationally. *Services* are intangibles, such as transportation, insurance, banking, education, consulting, and tourism. Services are often called "invisibles" because they are not tangible. The value of Canadian service exports, as when an Irish tourist visits Vancouver, is listed as a credit in the Canadian balance-of-payments account because Canadian residents get paid for these services. The value of Canadian service imports, like computer programming outsourced to India, is listed as a debit in the balance-of-payments account because Canadian residents must pay for the imported services.

The **balance on goods and services** is the export value of goods and services minus the import value of goods and services, or *net exports*, a component of GDP.

EXHIBIT 2

Canada's Merchandise Trade in 2013 by Country or Region

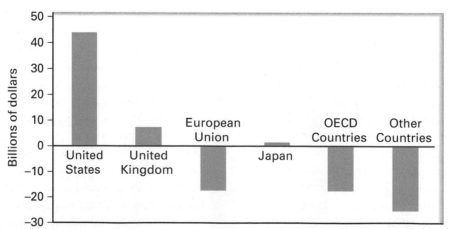

SOURCE: Statistics Canada. CANSIM Table 228-0003 "Merchandise imports and exports, by major groups and principal trading areas for all countries, annual (dollars)" (accessed: March 8, 2015)

THE CURRENT ACCOUNT CAN BE NEGATIVE, REFLECTING A DEFICIT; POSITIVE, REFLECTING A SURPLUS; OR ZERO.

Net Investment Income

Canadian residents earn investment income, such as interest and dividends, from assets owned abroad. This investment income flows to Canada and is a credit in the balance-of-payments account. On the other side, foreigners earn investment income on assets owned in Canada, and this payment flows out of the country. This outflow is a debit in the balance-of-payments account. **Net investment income from abroad** is Canadian investment earnings from foreign assets minus foreigners' earnings from their Canadian assets. From year to year, this figure bounces around between a positive and a negative number. In 2013, net investment income from abroad was negative $23.79 billion.

Unilateral Transfers and the Current Account Balance

Unilateral transfers consist of government transfers to foreign residents, foreign aid, money workers send to family members abroad, personal gifts to friends and relatives abroad, charitable donations, and the like. Money sent out of the country is a debit in the balance-of-payments account. For example, immigrants in Canada often send money to families back home. **Net unilateral transfers abroad** equal the unilateral transfers received from abroad by Canadian residents minus unilateral transfers sent to foreign residents by Canadian residents. In 2013, net unilateral transfers were a negative $2.89 billion, with private transfers accounting for most of that (government grants and transfers made up the rest). Net unilateral transfers abroad averaged about $90 per Canadian resident in 2013.

Canada places few restrictions on money sent out of the country. Other countries, particularly developing countries, strictly limit the amount that may be sent abroad. More generally, many developing countries, such as China, restrict the convertibility of their currency into other currencies.

When we add net unilateral transfers to net exports of goods and services and net income from assets owned abroad, we get the **balance on current account**, which is reported quarterly. Thus, *the current account includes all international transactions in currently produced goods and services, net income*

from foreign assets, and net unilateral transfers. It can be negative, reflecting a current account deficit; positive, reflecting a current account surplus; or zero.

The Financial Account

The current account records international transactions in goods, services, asset income, and unilateral transfers. The **financial account** records international purchases of assets, including financial assets, such as stocks, bonds, and bank balances, and real assets such as land, housing, factories, and other physical assets. For example, Canadian residents purchase foreign securities to earn a higher return and to diversify their portfolios. Money flows out when Canadians buy foreign assets or build factories overseas. Money flows in when foreigners buy Canadian assets or build factories here. The international purchase or sale of assets is recorded in the financial account.

Between 1999 and 2007, Canada ran a financial account deficit, meaning that Canadian residents purchased more foreign assets than foreigners purchased assets from Canada. The net income from these foreign assets improved our current account balance. But in 2008, for the first time in 10 years, foreigners bought more assets in Canada than Canadian residents purchased abroad. Since 2008, foreigners have continued to buy more Canadian assets most years than the other way around, meaning there has usually been a surplus in the financial account.

By the end of 2012, foreigners owned $2.03 trillion in Canadian assets and Canadian residents owned $1.78 trillion in foreign assets. Thus foreigners owned about $250 billion more assets in Canada than Canadian residents owned abroad. This is not as bad as it sounds because foreign purchases of assets in Canada add to Canada's productive capacity and promote employment and labour productivity here. But the income from these assets flows to their foreign owners, not to Canadians, although some of this

net investment income from abroad investment earnings by Canadian residents from their foreign assets minus investment earnings by foreigners from their assets in Canada

net unilateral transfers abroad the unilateral transfers (gifts and grants) received from abroad by Canadian residents minus the unilateral transfers Canadian residents send abroad

balance on current account the portion of the balance-of-payments account that measures that country's balance on goods and services, net investment income from abroad, plus net unilateral transfers abroad

financial account the record of a country's international transactions involving purchases or sales of financial and real assets

THE DEFICIT IN THE CANADIAN CURRENT ACCOUNT IN RECENT YEARS HAS USUALLY BEEN OFFSET BY A FINANCIAL ACCOUNT SURPLUS.

income is reinvested back in Canada. Remember, the investment income from these assets shows up in the current account.

Deficits and Surpluses

Nations, like households, operate under a budget constraint. Spending cannot exceed income plus cash on hand and borrowed funds. We have distinguished between *current* transactions, which include exports, imports, asset income, and unilateral transfers, and *financial* transactions, which reflect purchases of foreign real and financial assets. Any surplus or deficit in one account must be offset by deficits or surpluses in other balance-of-payments accounts.

Exhibit 3 presents Canada's balance-of-payments statement for 2013. All transactions requiring

EXHIBIT 3

Canada Balance of Payments for 2013 (millions of dollars)

Current Account	
1. Merchandise exports	+478,975
2. Merchandise imports	−486,306
3. Merchandise trade balance (1 + 2)	−7,331
4. Service exports	+86,761
5. Service imports	−111,308
6. Goods and services balance (3 + 4 + 5)	−31,878
7. Net investment income from abroad	−23,785
8. Net unilateral transfers	−2,889
9. Current account balance (6 + 7 + 8)	−58,552
Financial Account	
10. Change in Canadian-owned assets abroad	−65,875
11. Change in foreign-owned assets in Canada	+124,203
12. Financial account balance (10 + 11)	+58,328
13. Statistical discrepancy	+244
TOTAL (9 + 12 + 13)	**0.0**

SOURCE: Computed from Statistics Canada CANSIM Tables 376-0001 and 376-0102 (accessed: March 07, 2015)

payments from foreigners to Canadian residents are entered as credits, indicated by a plus sign (+), because they result in an inflow of funds from foreign residents to Canadian residents. All transactions requiring payments to foreigners from Canadian residents are entered as debits, indicated by a minus sign (−), because they result in an outflow of funds from Canadian residents to foreign residents. As you can see, a surplus in the financial account of $58.33 billion was offset by a current account deficit of $58.55 billion. A *statistical discrepancy* is required to balance the payments, and that amounts to $224 million. Think of the statistical discrepancy as the official "fudge factor" that (1) measures the error in the balance of payments and (2) satisfies the double-entry bookkeeping requirement that total debits must equal total credits. *Foreign exchange* is the currency of another country needed to carry out international transactions. A country runs a deficit in its current account when the amount of foreign exchange received from exports, from foreign assets, and from unilateral transfers falls short of the amount needed to pay for imports, pay foreign holders of Canadian assets, and make unilateral transfers. If the current account is in deficit, the necessary foreign exchange must come from a net inflow in the financial account. Such an inflow in the financial account could stem from borrowing from foreigners, selling domestic stocks and bonds to foreigners, selling a potash mine in Saskatchewan or a ski resort in Quebec to foreigners, and so forth.

If a country runs a current account surplus, the foreign exchange received from exports, from foreign assets, and from unilateral transfers from abroad exceeds the amount needed to pay for imports, to pay foreign holders of Canadian assets, and to make unilateral transfers abroad. If the current account is in surplus, this excess foreign exchange results in a net outflow in the financial account through lending abroad, buying foreign stocks and bonds, buying a shoe plant in Italy or a villa on the French Riviera, and so forth.

When all transactions are considered, accounts must balance, though specific accounts usually don't. The statistical discrepancy ensures that, in the aggregate, accounts sum to zero. A deficit in a particular account should not necessarily be viewed as a source of concern, nor should a surplus be a

PART 4: INTERNATIONAL ECONOMICS

source of satisfaction. The deficit in the Canadian current account in recent years has usually been offset by a financial account surplus. As a result, foreigners have been acquiring more claims on Canadian assets.

LO2 Foreign Exchange Rates and Markets

Now that you have some idea about international flows, we can take a closer look at the forces that determine the underlying value of the currencies involved. Let's begin by looking at exchange rates and the market for foreign exchange.

Foreign Exchange

Foreign exchange, recall, is foreign money needed to carry out international transactions. The **exchange rate** is the price measured in one country's currency of buying one unit of another country's currency. Exchange rates are determined by the interaction of the households, firms, private financial institutions, governments, and central banks that buy and sell foreign exchange. The exchange rate fluctuates to equate the quantity of foreign exchange demanded with the quantity supplied. Typically, foreign exchange is made up of bank deposits denominated in the foreign currency. When foreign travel is involved, foreign exchange often consists of foreign paper money.

The foreign exchange market incorporates all the arrangements used to buy and sell foreign exchange. This market is not so much a physical place as a network of telephones and computers connecting financial centres all over the world. Perhaps you have seen pictures of foreign exchange traders in Toronto, New York, Frankfurt, London, or Tokyo in front of computer screens amid a tangle of phone lines. The foreign exchange market is like an all-night diner—it never closes. A trading centre is always open somewhere in the world.

We will consider the market for the euro in terms of the dollar. But first, a little more about the euro. For decades the nations of Western Europe tried to increase their economic cooperation and trade. These countries believed they would be more productive and more competitive with the rest of the world if they acted less like many separate economies and more like the 50 United States or the 10 provinces and three

© Peter Griffin/Alamy

territories that make up Canada, with a single set of trade regulations and a single currency.

In 2002, euro notes and coins entered circulation in the 12 European countries adopting the common currency. The big advantage of a common currency is that Europeans no longer have to change money every time they cross a border or trade with another country in the group.

So the euro is the common currency of the *euro zone,* as the now 19-country region is usually called. The price, or exchange rate, of the euro in terms of the dollar is the number of dollars required to purchase one euro. An increase in the number of dollars needed to purchase a euro indicates weakening, or **depreciation**, of the dollar. A decrease in the number of dollars needed to purchase a euro indicates strengthening, or **appreciation**, of the dollar. Put another way, a decrease in the number of euros needed to purchase a dollar is a depreciation

exchange rate the price measured in one country's currency of purchasing one unit of another country's currency

currency depreciation with respect to the dollar, an increase in the number of dollars needed to purchase one unit of foreign exchange in a flexible rate system

currency appreciation with respect to the dollar, a decrease in the number of dollars needed to purchase one unit of foreign exchange in a flexible rate system

of the dollar, and an increase in the number of euros needed to purchase a dollar is an appreciation of the dollar.

Because the exchange rate is usually a market price, it is determined by demand and supply: the equilibrium price is the one that equates quantity demanded with quantity supplied. To simplify the analysis, suppose that Canada and the euro zone make up the entire world, so the demand and supply for euros in international finance is the demand and supply for foreign exchange from a Canadian perspective.

The Demand for Foreign Exchange

Whenever Canadian residents need euros, they must buy them in the foreign exchange market, which could include your local bank, paying for them with dollars. Exhibit 4 depicts a market for foreign exchange—in this case, euros. The horizontal axis shows the quantity of foreign exchange, measured here in billions of euros per day. The vertical axis shows the price per unit of foreign exchange, measured here in dollars per euro. The demand curve D for foreign exchange shows the inverse relationship between the dollar price of the euro and the quantity of euros demanded, other things assumed constant. Assumed constant along the demand curve are the incomes and preferences of Canadian consumers, expected inflation in Canada and in the euro zone, the euro price of goods in the euro zone, and interest rates in Canada and in the euro zone. Canadian residents have many reasons for

demanding foreign exchange, but in the aggregate, the lower the dollar price of foreign exchange, other things constant, the greater the quantity of foreign exchange demanded.

A drop in the dollar price of foreign exchange, in this case the euro, means that fewer dollars are needed to purchase each euro, so the dollar prices of euro zone products (like German cars, Italian shoes, tickets to the Louvre, and euro zone securities), which list prices in euros, become cheaper. The cheaper it is to buy euros, the lower the dollar price of euro zone products to Canadian residents, so the greater the quantity of euros demanded by Canadian residents, other things constant. For example, a cheap enough euro might persuade you to tour Rome, climb the Austrian Alps, wander the museums of Paris, or crawl the pubs of Dublin.

The Supply of Foreign Exchange

The supply of foreign exchange is generated by the desire of foreign residents to acquire dollars—that is, to exchange euros for dollars. Euro zone residents want dollars to buy Canadian goods and services, acquire Canadian assets, make loans in dollars, or send dollars to their Canadian friends and relatives. Euros are supplied in the foreign exchange market to acquire the dollars people want. An increase in the dollar-per-euro exchange rate, other things constant, makes Canadian products cheaper for foreigners because foreign residents need fewer euros to get the same number of dollars. For example, suppose a piece of computer software sells for $600 in Canada. If the exchange rate is $1.20 per euro, that software costs 500 euros; if the exchange rate is $1.25 per euro, it costs only 480 euros. The quantity of software demanded in the euro zone increases as the dollar-per-euro exchange rate increases, other things constant, so more euros will be supplied on the foreign exchange market to buy dollars.

The positive relationship between the dollar-per-euro exchange rate and the quantity of euros supplied on the foreign exchange market is expressed in Exhibit 4 by the upward-sloping supply curve for foreign exchange (again, euros in our example). The supply curve assumes that other things remain constant, including euro zone incomes and tastes, expectations about

EXHIBIT 4
The Foreign Exchange Market

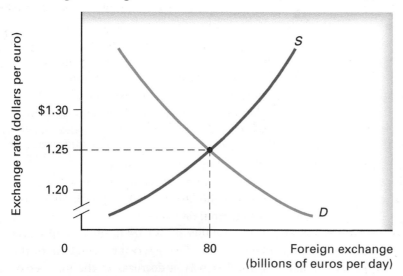

0.629   0.632

inflation in the euro zone and in Canada, and interest rates in the euro zone and in Canada.

Determining the Exchange Rate

Exhibit 4 brings together the demand and supply for foreign exchange to determine the exchange rate. At a rate of $1.25 per euro, the quantity of euros demanded equals the quantity supplied—in our example, 80 billion euros per day. Once achieved, this equilibrium rate will remain constant until a change occurs in one of the factors that affect supply or demand. If the exchange rate is allowed to adjust freely, or to *float*, in response to market forces, the market will clear continually, as the quantities of foreign exchange demanded and supplied are equated.

What if the initial equilibrium is upset by a change in one of the underlying forces that affect demand or supply? For example, suppose higher Canadian incomes increase Canadian demand for all normal goods, including those from the euro zone. This shifts the Canadian demand curve for foreign exchange to the right, as Canadians buy more Italian marble, Dutch chocolate, German machines, Parisian vacations, and euro zone securities.

This increased demand for euros is shown in Exhibit 5 by a rightward shift of the demand curve for foreign exchange. The demand increase from D to D' leads to an increase in the exchange rate per euro from $1.25 to $1.27. Thus the euro increases

If the exchange rate is allowed to adjust freely, or to float, in response to market forces, the market will clear continually, as the quantities of foreign exchange demanded and supplied are equated.

Don Farrall/Photographer's Choice RF/Getty Images

0.637   0.629

in value, or appreciates, while the dollar falls in value, or depreciates. An increase in Canadian income should not affect the euro supply curve, though it does increase the *quantity of euros supplied*. The higher exchange value of the euro prompts those in the euro zone to buy more Canadian products and assets, which are now cheaper in terms of the euro.

To Review: Any increase in the demand for foreign exchange or any decrease in its supply, other things constant, increases the number of dollars required to purchase one unit of foreign exchange, which is a depreciation of the dollar. On the other hand, any decrease in the demand for foreign exchange or any increase in its supply, other things constant, reduces the number of dollars required to purchase one unit of foreign exchange, which is an appreciation of the dollar.

Arbitrageurs and Speculators

Exchange rates between two currencies are nearly identical at any given time in markets around the world. For example, the dollar price of a euro is the same in Toronto, New York, Frankfurt, Tokyo, London, Zurich,

EXHIBIT 5
Effect on the Foreign Exchange Market of an Increased Demand for Euros

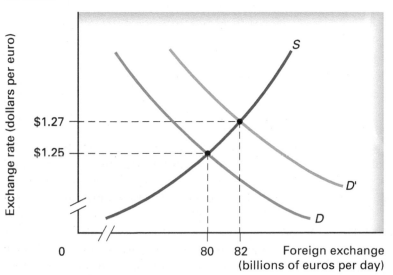

A GIVEN BASKET OF INTERNATIONALLY TRADED GOODS SHOULD SELL FOR ABOUT THE SAME AROUND THE WORLD.

arbitrageur someone who takes advantage of temporary geographic differences in the exchange rate by simultaneously purchasing a currency in one market and selling it in another market

speculator someone who buys or sells foreign exchange in hopes of profiting from fluctuations in the exchange rate over time

purchasing power parity (PPP) theory the idea that the exchange rate between two countries will adjust in the long run to equalize the cost between the countries of a basket of internationally traded goods

Hong Kong, Istanbul, and other financial centres. **Arbitrageurs**—dealers who take advantage of any difference in exchange rates between markets by buying low and selling high—ensure this equality. Their actions help to equalize exchange rates across markets. For example, if one euro costs $1.24 in Toronto but $1.25 in Frankfurt, an arbitrageur could buy, say, $1,000,000 worth of euros in Toronto and at the same time sell them in Frankfurt for $1,008,065, thereby earning $8,065 minus the transaction costs of the trades.

Because an arbitrageur buys and sells simultaneously, little risk is involved. In our example, the arbitrageur increased the demand for euros in Toronto and increased the supply of euros in Frankfurt. These actions increased the dollar price of euros in Toronto and decreased it in Frankfurt, thereby squeezing down the difference in exchange rates. Exchange rates may still change because of market forces, but they tend to change in all markets simultaneously.

The demand and supply of foreign exchange arises from many sources—from importers and exporters, investors in foreign assets, central banks, tourists, arbitrageurs, and speculators. **Speculators** buy or sell foreign exchange in hopes of profiting by trading the currency at a more favourable exchange rate later. By taking risks, speculators aim to profit from market fluctuations—they try to buy low and sell high. In contrast, arbitrageurs take less risk, because they *simultaneously* buy currency in one market and sell it in another.

Finally, people in countries suffering from economic and political turmoil, such as occurred in Russia, Indonesia, the Philippines, and Zimbabwe, may buy *hard* currency such as the U.S. dollar or euro as a hedge against the depreciation and instability of their own currencies. The U.S. dollar has long been accepted as an international medium of exchange. It is also the currency of choice in the world markets for oil and illegal drugs. But the euro eventually may challenge that dominance, in part because the largest euro denomination, the 500 euro note, is worth about six times the largest U.S. denomination, the $100 note. So it would be six times easier to smuggle euro notes than U.S. notes of equal value.

Purchasing Power Parity

As long as trade across borders is unrestricted and as long as exchange rates are allowed to adjust freely, the **purchasing power parity (PPP) theory** predicts that the exchange rate between two currencies will adjust in the long run to reflect price differences between the two currency regions. *A given basket of internationally traded goods should sell for about the same around the world.* Suppose a basket of internationally traded goods that sells for $10,000 in Canada sells for €8,000 in the euro zone. According to the purchasing power parity theory, the equilibrium exchange rate should be $1.25 per euro. If this were not the case—if the exchange rate were, say, $1.20 per euro—then you could exchange $9,600 for €8,000, with which you buy the basket of commodities in the euro zone. You could then sell that basket of goods in Canada for $10,000, yielding you a profit of $400 minus any transaction costs. Selling dollars and buying euros will also drive up the dollar price of euros.

The purchasing power parity theory is more of a long-run predictor than a day-to-day indicator of the relationship between changes in the price level and the exchange rate. For example, a country's currency generally appreciates when inflation is low compared with other countries and depreciates when inflation is high. Likewise, a country's currency generally appreciates when its real interest rates are higher than those in the rest of the world, because foreigners are more willing to buy and hold investments denominated in that high-interest currency. Because of trade barriers, central bank intervention in exchange markets, and the fact that many products are not traded or are not comparable across countries, the purchasing power parity theory usually does not explain exchange rates at a particular point in time that well. For example, if you went shopping in Switzerland tomorrow, you would soon notice a dollar does not buy as much there as it does in Canada.

LO3 Fixed and Flexible Exchange Rates

Flexible Exchange Rates

For the most part, we have been discussing a system of **flexible exchange rates**, which are determined by demand and supply. Flexible, or *floating*, exchange rates adjust continually to the myriad forces that buffet foreign exchange markets. Consider how the exchange rate is linked to the balance-of-payments accounts. Debit entries in the current or financial accounts increase the demand for foreign exchange, resulting in a depreciation of the dollar. Credit entries in these accounts increase the supply of foreign exchange, resulting in an appreciation of the dollar.

Fixed Exchange Rates

When exchange rates are flexible, governments usually have little direct role in foreign exchange markets. But if governments try to set exchange rates, active and ongoing central bank intervention is often necessary to establish and maintain these **fixed exchange rates**. Suppose the European Central Bank selects what it thinks is an appropriate rate of exchange between the dollar and the euro. It attempts to *fix,* or to *peg,* the exchange rate within a narrow band around the particular value selected. If the euro threatens to climb above the maximum acceptable exchange rate, monetary authorities must sell euros and buy dollars, thereby keeping the dollar price of the euro down. Conversely, if the euro threatens to drop below the minimum acceptable exchange rate, monetary authorities must sell dollars and buy euros. This increased demand for the euro will keep its value up relative to the dollar. Through such intervention in the foreign exchange market, monetary authorities try to stabilize the exchange rate, keeping it within the specified band. Many developing countries, including China, have their currencies pegged to a major currency such as the U.S. dollar or a basket of major currencies to try to stabilize the value of their local currencies and provide some degree of certainty in international trade.

If monetary officials must keep selling foreign exchange to keep the value of their domestic currency from falling, they risk running out of foreign exchange reserves. Faced with this threat, the government has several options for eliminating the exchange rate disequilibrium. First, the pegged exchange rate can be increased, meaning that foreign currency costs more in terms of the domestic currency. This is a **devaluation** of the domestic currency. (A decrease in the pegged exchange rate is called a **revaluation**.) Second, the government can reduce the domestic demand for foreign exchange directly by imposing restrictions on imports or on financial outflows. Many developing countries do this. Third, the government can adopt policies to slow the domestic economy, increase interest rates, or reduce inflation relative to that of the country's trading partners, thereby indirectly decreasing the demand for foreign exchange and increasing the supply of foreign exchange. Several Asian economies, such as South Korea and Indonesia, pursued such policies to stabilize their currencies. Finally, the government can allow the disequilibrium to persist and ration the available foreign reserves through some form of foreign exchange control.

This concludes our introduction to the theories of international finance. Let's examine international finance in practice.

LO4 Development of the International Monetary System

From 1879 to 1914, the international financial system operated under a **gold standard**, whereby the major currencies were convertible into gold at a fixed rate. For example, the Canadian colonial dollar, which then aligned with the U.S. currency, could be redeemed for one-twentieth of an ounce of gold. The British pound could be redeemed at the British Exchequer, or treasury, for one-fourth of an ounce of gold. Because each British pound could buy five times as much gold as each dollar, one British pound exchanged for $5.

The gold standard provided a predictable exchange rate, one that did not vary as long as currencies could be redeemed for gold at the announced

---

flexible exchange rates rate determined in foreign exchange markets by the forces of demand and supply without government intervention

fixed exchange rates rate of exchange between currencies pegged within a narrow range and maintained by the central bank's ongoing purchases and sales of currencies

currency devaluation an increase in the official pegged price of foreign exchange in terms of the domestic currency

currency revaluation a reduction in the official pegged price of foreign exchange in terms of the domestic currency

gold standard an arrangement whereby the currencies of most countries are convertible into gold at a fixed rate

rate. But the money supply in each country was determined in part by the flow of gold between countries, so each country's monetary policy was influenced by the supply of gold. A balance-of-payments deficit resulted in a loss of gold, which theoretically caused a country's money supply to shrink. A balance-of-payments surplus resulted in an influx of gold, which theoretically caused a country's money supply to expand. The supply of money throughout the world also depended on the vagaries of gold discoveries. When gold production did not keep pace with the growth in economic activity, the price level dropped, often with the help of an economic downturn, forcing downward adjustment in prices. When gold production exceeded the growth in economic activity, the price level rose. For example, gold discoveries in Alaska and South Africa in the late 1890s expanded the U.S. money supply, leading to inflation.

The Bretton Woods Agreement

During World War I, many countries could no longer convert their currencies into gold, and the gold standard eventually collapsed, disrupting international trade during the 1920s and 1930s. Once an Allied victory in World War II appeared certain, the Allies met in Bretton Woods, New Hampshire, in July 1944 to formulate a new international monetary system. Because the United States had a strong economy and was not ravaged by the war, the dollar was selected as the key reserve currency in the new international monetary system. All exchange rates were fixed in terms of the dollar, and the United States, which held most of the world's gold reserves, stood ready to convert foreign holdings of dollars into gold at a rate of $35 per ounce. Even though the rate that dollars could be exchanged for gold was fixed by the Bretton Woods agreement, *other* countries could adjust *their* exchange rates relative to the U.S. dollar if they found a chronic disequilibrium in their balance of payments—that is, if a country faced a large and persistent deficit or surplus.

The Bretton Woods agreement also created the **International Monetary Fund (IMF)** to set rules for maintaining the international monetary system, to standardize financial reporting for international trade, and to make loans to countries with temporary balance-of-payments problems. Headquartered in Washington, D.C., the IMF has 188 member countries and a staff of about 2,400 drawn from around the world (half the staff members are economists).

The Demise of the Bretton Woods System

During the latter part of the 1960s, inflation increased in the United States more than in other countries. Because of U.S. inflation, the dollar had become *overvalued* at the official exchange rate, meaning that the gold value of the U.S. dollar exceeded the exchange value of the dollar. In 1971, U.S. merchandise imports exceeded merchandise exports for the first time since World War II. Foreigners exchanged dollars for gold. To stem this gold outflow, the United States stopped exchanging gold for U.S. dollars, but this just made the U.S. dollar less attractive. In December 1971, the world's 10 richest countries met in Washington and devalued the dollar by 8 percent. They hoped this devaluation would put the U.S. dollar on firmer footing and would save the "dollar standard." With prices rising at different rates around the world, however, an international monetary system based on fixed exchange rates was doomed.

When the U.S. trade deficit tripled in 1972, it became clear that the U.S. dollar was still overvalued. In early 1973, the U.S. dollar was devalued another 10 percent, but this did not quiet foreign exchange markets. The U.S. dollar, for three

Stockbyte/Getty Images

decades the anchor of the international monetary system, suddenly looked vulnerable, and speculators began betting that the U.S. dollar would fall even more, so they sold U.S. dollars. U.S. dollars were exchanged for German marks because the mark appeared to be the most stable currency. Bundesbank, Germany's central bank, tried to defend the U.S. dollar's official exchange rate by selling marks and buying U.S. dollars. Why didn't Germany want the mark to appreciate? Appreciation would make German goods more expensive abroad and foreign goods cheaper in Germany, thereby reducing German exports and increasing German imports. So the mark's appreciation would reduce German output and employment. But after selling $10 billion worth of marks, the Bundesbank gave up defending the U.S. dollar. As soon as the value of the U.S. dollar was allowed to float against the mark, the Bretton Woods system, already on shaky ground, collapsed.

© Sean Gladwell/Shutterstock.com

The Current System: Managed Float

The Bretton Woods system has been replaced by a **managed float system**, which combines features of a freely floating exchange rate with sporadic intervention by central banks as a way of moderating exchange rate fluctuations among the world's major currencies. Most small countries, particularly developing countries, still peg their currencies to one of the major currencies (such as the U.S. dollar) or to a "basket" of major currencies. What's more, in developing countries, private international borrowing and lending are severely restricted; some governments allow residents to purchase foreign exchange only for certain purposes. In some countries, different exchange rates apply to different categories of transactions.

Critics of flexible exchange rates argue that they are inflationary, because they free monetary authorities to pursue expansionary policies, and flexible exchange rates have often been volatile. This volatility creates uncertainty and risk for importers and exporters, increasing the transaction costs of international trade. Furthermore, exchange rate volatility can lead to wrenching changes in the competitiveness of a country's export sector. These changes cause swings in employment, resulting in louder calls for import restrictions.

Policymakers are always on the lookout for a system that will perform better than the current managed float system, with its fluctuating currency values. *Their ideal is a system that will foster international trade, lower inflation, and promote a more stable world economy.* International finance ministers have acknowledged that the world must find an international standard and establish greater exchange rate stability.

> **managed float system** an exchange rate system that combines features of freely floating rates with sporadic intervention by central banks

Final Word

Canada is very much a part of the world economy, not only as an exporter nation but also as an importer nation. The U.S. dollar remains the unit of transaction in many international settlements, for example, the Organization of the Petroleum Exporting Countries (OPEC) still states oil prices in dollars. However, gyrations of exchange rates have made those involved in international finance wary of putting all their eggs in one basket. The international monetary system is now going through a difficult period as it gropes for a new source of stability four decades after the collapse of the Bretton Woods agreement.

CHAPTER PROBLEMS

LO1 Explain how the balance of payments works

1.1. *(Balance of Payments)* The following are hypothetical data for Canada's balance of payments. Use the data to calculate each of the following:
   a. Merchandise trade balance
   b. Balance on goods and services
   c. Balance on current account
   d. Financial account balance
   e. Statistical discrepancy

	Billions of Dollars
Merchandise exports	35.0
Merchandise imports	242.5
Service exports	214.5
Service imports	20.0
Net income and net transfers	22.1
Change in Canadian-owned assets abroad	24.5
Change in foreign-owned assets in Canada	10.0

1.2. *(Balance of Payments)* Explain where in Canada's balance of payments an entry would be recorded for each of the following:
   a. A Hong Kong financier buys some Canadian corporate stock.
   b. A Canadian tourist in Paris buys some perfume to take home.
   c. A Japanese company sells machinery to a mining company in Saskatoon.
   d. Canadian farmers make a gift of food to starving children in Ethiopia.
   e. The government sells a bond to a British investor.
   f. A Canadian tourist flies to France on Air France.
   g. A Canadian company sells insurance to a foreign firm.

1.3. *(Balance of Payments)* Suppose Canada ran a surplus in its balance on goods and services by exporting goods and services while importing nothing.
   a. How would such a surplus be offset elsewhere in the balance-of-payments accounts?
   b. If the level of Canadian production does not depend on the balance of goods and services, how would running this surplus affect our *current* standard of living?
   c. What is the relationship between total debits and total credits in the balance on goods and services?
   d. When all international economic transactions are considered, what must be true about the sum of debits and credits?
   e. What is the role of the statistical discrepancy?

1.4. *(Merchandise Trade Balance)* Explain why a Canadian recession that occurs as the rest of the world is expanding will tend to reduce Canada's trade deficit.

LO2 Discuss foreign exchange rates and markets

2.1. *(Determining the Exchange Rate)* Use these data to answer the following questions about the market for British pounds:

Pound Price (in $)	Quantity Demanded (of pounds)	Quantity Supplied (of pounds)
$4.00	£50	£100
3.00	75	75
2.00	100	50

   a. Draw the demand and supply curves for pounds, and determine the equilibrium exchange rate (dollars per pound).
   b. Suppose that the supply of pounds doubles. Draw the new supply curve.
   c. What is the new equilibrium exchange rate?
   d. Has the dollar appreciated or depreciated?
   e. What happens to Canadian imports of British goods?

2.2. *(Arbitrageurs and Speculators)* Explain the difference between arbitrageurs and speculators. How do arbitrageurs help equalize exchange rates across markets?

2.3. *(Purchasing Power Parity)* Explain why the purchasing power parity is more of a long-run predictor than a day-to-day indicator of the relationship between changes in the price level and the exchange rate.

3.1. *(Exchange Rates)* Discuss the differences between a flexible exchange rate and a fixed exchange rate. What measures can the government take to maintain fixed exchange rates?

3.2. *(Exchange Rates)* Explain the difference between the following:
  a. Depreciation and devaluation
  b. Appreciation and revaluation

4.1. *(International Monetary System)* Discuss the evolution of the international monetary system. What led to the demise of the Bretton Wood System?

4.2. *(The Current System: Managed Float)* What is a managed float? What are the disadvantages of freely floating exchange rates that led countries to the managed float system?

CASE STUDY

The Big Mac Index

As you have already learned, the PPP theory predicts that in the long run the exchange rate between two currencies should move toward equalizing the cost in each country of an identical basket of internationally traded goods. A light-hearted test of the theory has been developed by *The Economist* magazine, which compares prices around the world for a "market basket" consisting simply of one McDonald's Big Mac—a product that, though not internationally traded, is essentially the same in more than 100 countries. *The Economist* begins with the price of a Big Mac in the local currency and then converts that price into dollars based on the exchange rate prevailing at the time. A comparison of the dollar price of Big Macs across countries offers a crude test of the PPP theory, which predicts that prices should be roughly equal in the long run.

This chart lists the dollar price of a Big Mac in March 2010, in 22 surveyed countries plus the euro zone average. By comparing the price of a Big Mac in the United

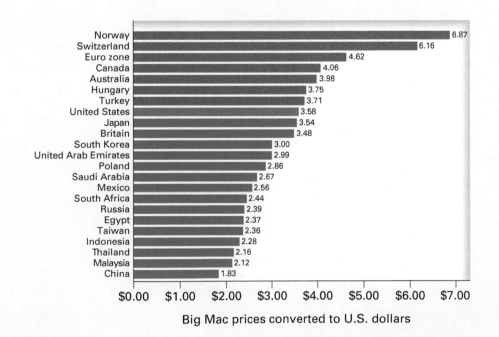

Big Mac prices converted to U.S. dollars

States (shown as the green bar) with prices in other countries, we can derive a crude measure of whether particular currencies, relative to the dollar, are overvalued (red bars) or undervalued (blue bars). For example, because the price of a Big Mac in Norway, at $6.87, was 92 percent higher than the U.S. price of $3.58, the Norwegian krone was the most overvalued relative to the dollar of the countries listed. But Big Macs were cheaper in most of the countries surveyed. The cheapest was in China, where $1.83 was 49 percent below the U.S. price. Hence, the Chinese yuan was the most undervalued relative to the dollar.

Thus Big Mac prices in March 2010 ranged from 92 percent above to 49 percent below the U.S. price. The euro was 29 percent overvalued. The price range lends little support to the PPP theory, but that theory relates only to traded goods. The Big Mac is not traded internationally. Part of the price of a Big Mac must cover rent, which can vary substantially across countries. Taxes and trade barriers, such as tariffs and quotas on beef, may also distort local prices. And wages differ across countries, with a McDonald's worker averaging about $8 an hour in the United States versus more like $1 an hour in China. So there are understandable reasons why Big Mac prices differ across countries. ·

SOURCES: "The Big Mac Index: Exchanging Blows," *The Economist*, 17 March 2010; David Parsley and Shang-Jin Wei, "In Search of a Euro Effect: Big Lessons from a Big Mac Meal?" *Journal of International Money and Finance*, 27 (March 2008): 260–276; Ali Kutan et al., "Toward Solving the PPP Puzzle: Evidence from 113 Countries," *Applied Economics*, 41 (Issue 24, 2009): 3057–3066; and the McDonald's Corporation International Web site at http://www.mcdonalds.com.

QUESTION

1. The Big Mac Index computed by *The Economist* magazine has consistently found the U.S. dollar to be undervalued against some currencies and overvalued against others. This finding seems to call for a rejection of the purchasing power parity theory. Explain why this index may not be a valid test of the theory.

Glossary

ability-to-pay tax principle those with a greater ability to pay, such as those earning higher incomes or those owning more property, should pay more taxes (p. 48)

absolute advantage the ability to make something using fewer resources than other producers use (p. 25)

adverse supply shocks unexpected events that reduce aggregate supply, sometimes only temporarily (p. 180)

aggregate demand the relationship between the economy's price level and aggregate output demanded, with other things constant (p. 87)

aggregate demand curve a curve representing the relationship between the economy's price level and real GDP demanded per period, with other things constant (p. 87)

aggregate expenditure total spending on final goods and services in an economy during a given period, usually a year (p. 99)

aggregate expenditure line a relationship tracing, for a given price level, spending at each level of income, or real GDP; the total of $C + I + G + (X + IM)$ at each level of income, or real GDP (p. 157)

aggregate income all earnings of resource suppliers in an economy during a given period, usually a year (p. 100)

aggregate output a composite measure of all final goods and services produced in an economy during a given period; real GDP (p. 87)

aggregate supply curve a curve representing the relationship between the economy's price level and real GDP supplied per period, with other things constant (p. 88)

annually balanced budget budget philosophy prior to the Great Depression; aimed at matching annual revenues with outlays, except during times of war (p. 194)

applied research research that seeks answers to particular questions or to apply scientific discoveries to develop specific products (p. 143)

arbitrageur someone who takes advantage of temporary geographic differences in the exchange rate by simultaneously purchasing a currency in one market and selling it in another market (p. 270)

asset anything of value that is owned (p. 220)

association-is-causation fallacy the incorrect idea that if two variables are associated in time, one must necessarily cause the other (p. 11)

asymmetric information a situation in which one side of the market has more reliable information than the other side (p. 219)

autarky national self-sufficiency; no economic interaction with foreigners (Online Chapter 17, p. 5)

automatic stabilizers structural features of government spending and taxation that reduce fluctuations in disposable income, and thus consumption, over the business cycle (p. 184)

autonomous a term that means "independent"; for example, autonomous investment is independent of income (p. 154)

balance of payments a record of all economic transactions during a given period between residents of one country and residents of the rest of the world (p. 49)

balance on current account the portion of the balance-of-payments account that measures that country's balance on goods and services, net investment income from abroad, plus net unilateral transfers abroad (p. 265)

balance on goods and services the portion of a country's balance-of-payments account that measures the value of a country's exports of goods and services minus the value of its imports of goods and services (p. 264)

balance sheet a financial statement at a given point in time that shows assets on one side and liabilities and net worth on the other side; because assets must equal liabilities plus net worth, the two sides of the statement must be in balance (p. 220)

bank notes originally, pieces of paper promising a specific amount of gold or silver to anyone who presented them to issuing banks for redemption; today, Bank of Canada notes are mere polymer money (p. 207)

Bank of Canada the central bank and monetary authority of Canada (p. 209)

bank rate the interest rate the Bank of Canada charges banks that borrow reserves from it (p. 226)

barter the direct exchange of one product for another without using money (p. 25)

base year the year with which other years are compared when constructing an index; the index equals 100 in the base year (p. 106)

basic research the search for knowledge without regard to how that knowledge will be used (p. 143)

behavioural assumption   an assumption that describes the expected behaviour of economic decision makers, what motivates them (p. 9)

beneficial supply shocks   unexpected events that increase aggregate supply, sometimes only temporarily (p. 179)

benefits-received tax principle   those who get more benefits from the government program should pay more taxes (p. 48)

capital   the buildings, equipment, and human skills used to produce goods and services (p. 3)

capital deepening   an increase in the amount of capital per worker; one source of rising labour productivity (p. 136)

chain-weighted system   an inflation measure that adjusts the weights from year to year in calculating a price index, thereby reducing the bias caused by a fixed-price weighting system (p. 109)

chequable deposits   bank deposits that allow the account owner to write cheques to third parties; ATM or debit cards can also access these deposits and transmit them electronically (p. 216)

cheque   a written order instructing the bank to pay someone from an amount deposited (p. 206)

circular-flow model   a diagram that traces the flow of resources, products, income, and revenue among economic decision makers (p. 5)

classical economists   a group of 18th- and 19th-century economists who believed that economic downturns corrected themselves through natural market forces; thus they believed the economy was self-correcting and needed no government intervention (p. 190)

coincident economic indicators   variables that reflect peaks and troughs in economic activity as they occur; examples are employment, personal income, and industrial production (p. 86)

cold turkey   the announcement and execution of tough measures to reduce high inflation (p. 252)

commodity money   anything that serves both as money and as a commodity; money that has intrinsic value such as gold or silver coins (p. 203)

comparative advantage   the ability to make something at a lower opportunity cost than other producers face (p. 25)

complements   goods, such as milk and cookies, that relate in such a way that an increase in the price of one shifts the demand for the other leftward (p. 59)

consumer price index, or CPI   a measure of inflation based on the cost of a fixed market basket of goods and services (p. 107)

consumer surplus   the remainder once the price paid is subtracted from the consumer value realized; the area beneath the demand curve and above the price paid up to the number of units exchanged (p. 67)

consumer value   the sum of the willingness-to-pay across the quantity consumed; the area under the WTP curve up to the total quantity consumed; it can be calculated for either an individual or for the market (p. 58)

consumption   household purchases of final goods and services, except for new residences, which count as investment (p. 98)

consumption function   the relationship in the economy between consumption and income, other things constant (p. 150)

contraction   a period during which the economy declines as reflected by falling output, employment, income, and other aggregate measures (p. 83)

contractionary fiscal policy   a decrease in government purchases, increase in net taxes, or some combination of the two aimed at reducing aggregate demand enough to return the economy to potential output without worsening inflation; fiscal policy used to close an expansionary gap (p. 189)

convergence   a theory predicting that the standard of living in economies around the world will grow more similar over time, with poorer countries eventually catching up with richer ones (p. 144)

cooperative   an organization consisting of people who pool their resources to buy and sell more efficiently than they could individually (p. 42)

coordination failure   a situation in which workers and employers fail to achieve an outcome that all would prefer (p. 178)

corporation   a legal entity owned by stockholders whose liability is limited to the value of their stock ownership (p. 42)

cost-push inflation   a sustained rise in the price level caused by a leftward shift of the aggregate supply curve (p. 123)

credit unions and *caisses populaires* (CUCPs)   depository institutions that extend loans only to their "members" (p. 209)

crowding in   the potential for government spending to stimulate private investment in an otherwise dead economy (p. 195)

crowding out   the displacement of interest-sensitive private investment that occurs when higher government deficits drive up market interest rates (p. 195)

currency appreciation   with respect to the dollar, a decrease in the number of dollars needed to purchase one unit of foreign exchange in a flexible rate system (p. 267)

currency depreciation   with respect to the dollar, an increase in the number of dollars needed to purchase one unit of foreign exchange in a flexible rate system (p. 267)

currency devaluation   an increase in the official pegged price of foreign exchange in terms of the domestic currency (p. 271)

currency revaluation a reduction in the official pegged price of foreign exchange in terms of the domestic currency (p. 271)

cyclical unemployment unemployment that fluctuates with the business cycle, increasing during contractions and decreasing during expansions (p. 120)

cyclically balanced budget a budget philosophy calling for budget deficits during recessions to be financed by budget surpluses during expansions (p. 195)

deadweight loss (DWL) the value of mutually beneficial trades that go unmade because of market interference; the area between the demand and supply curves and between the quantity exchanged under a particular policy and the equilibrium quantity (p. 71)

debit card cards that tap directly into the depositor's bank account to fund purchases; also called a cheque card, and often doubles as an ATM card (p. 218)

decision-making lag the time needed to decide what to do once a macroeconomic problem has been identified (p. 249)

deflation a sustained decrease in the price level (p. 123)

demand a relation between the price of a good and the quantity that consumers are willing and able to buy per period, other things constant (p. 55)

demand curve a curve showing the relation between the price of a good and the quantity consumers are willing and able to buy per period, other things constant; sometimes known as the willingness-to-pay (WTP) curve (p. 57)

demand for money the relationship between the interest rate and how much money people want to hold (p. 231)

demand-pull inflation a sustained rise in the price level caused by a rightward shift of the aggregate demand curve (p. 123)

demand-side economics macroeconomic policy that focuses on shifting the aggregate demand curve as a way of promoting full employment and price stability (p. 91)

dependent variable a variable whose value depends on that of the independent variable (p. 16)

depository institutions financial institutions that accept deposits from the public (p. 209)

depreciation the value of capital stock used up to produce GDP or that becomes obsolete during the year (p. 104)

depression a severe and prolonged reduction in economic activity as occurred during the 1930s (p. 83)

desired / required reserve ratio the ratio of reserves to deposits that banks desire or are obligated by regulation to hold (p. 220)

desired / required reserves the dollar amount of reserves a bank desires or is obligated by regulation to hold as cash in the bank's vault or on account at the central bank (p. 220)

developing countries countries with a low living standard because of less human and physical capital per worker (p. 138)

developing countries nations typified by high rates of illiteracy, high unemployment, high fertility rates, and exports of primary products; also known as low-income and middle-income economies (Online Chapter 18, p. 3)

discouraged workers those who drop out of the labour force in frustration because they can't find work (p. 115)

discretionary fiscal policy the deliberate manipulation of government purchases, taxation, and transfer payments to promote macroeconomic goals, such as full employment, price stability, and economic growth (p. 185)

disequilibrium the condition that exists in a market when the plans of buyers do not match those of sellers; a temporary mismatch between quantity supplied and quantity demanded as the market seeks equilibrium (p. 71)

disinflation a reduction in the rate of inflation (p. 123)

disposable income (DI) the income households have available to spend or to save after paying taxes and receiving transfer payments (p. 101)

division of labour breaking down the production of a good into separate tasks (p. 26)

double coincidence of wants two traders are willing to exchange their products directly (p. 202)

double counting the mistake of including both the value of intermediate products and the value of final products in calculating gross domestic product; counting the same production more than once (p. 98)

dumping selling a product abroad for less than charged in the home market or for less than the cost of production (Online Chapter 17, p. 12)

economic efficiency the degree to which all mutually beneficial exchanges of a good take place (p. 66)

economic fluctuations the rise and fall of economic activity relative to the long-term growth trend of the economy; also called business cycles (p. 7)

economic growth an increase in the economy's ability to produce goods and services; reflected by an outward shift of the economy's production possibilities frontier (p. 28)

economic system the set of mechanisms and institutions that resolve the what, how, and for whom questions (p. 31)

economic theory (economic model) a simplification of reality used to make predictions about cause and effect in the real world (p. 8)

economics the study of how people use their scarce resources to satisfy their unlimited wants (p. 3)

economy the structure of economic activity in a community, a region, a country, a group of countries, or the world (p. 80)

effectiveness lag the time needed for changes in monetary or fiscal policy to affect the economy (p. 249)

efficiency the condition that exists when there is no way resources can be reallocated to increase the production of one good without decreasing the production of another; getting the most from available resources (p. 27)

efficient a market equilibrium is said to be efficient because it maximizes total surplus (p. 66)

entrepreneur a profit-seeking decision maker who starts with an idea, organizes an enterprise to bring that idea to life, and assumes the risk of the operation (p. 3)

entrepreneurial ability the imagination required to develop a new product or process, the skill needed to organize production, and the willingness to take the risk of profit or loss (p. 3)

equation of exchange the quantity of money, M, multiplied by its velocity, V, equals nominal GDP, which is the product of the price level, P, and real GDP, Y; or $M \times V = P \times Y$ (p. 236)

equilibrium the condition that exists in a market when the plans of buyers match those of sellers, so quantity demanded equals quantity supplied and the market clears (p. 65)

excess reserves bank reserves exceeding required or desired reserves (p. 220)

exchange rate the price measured in one country's currency of purchasing one unit of another country's currency (p. 267)

expansion a period during which the economy grows as reflected by rising output, employment, income, and other aggregate measures (p. 83)

expansionary fiscal policy an increase in government purchases, decrease in net taxes, or some combination of the two aimed at increasing aggregate demand enough to reduce unemployment and return the economy to its potential output; fiscal policy used to close a recessionary gap (p. 188)

expansionary gap the amount by which actual output in the short run exceeds the economy's potential output (p. 174)

expenditure approach to GDP calculating GDP by adding up spending on all final goods and services produced in the nation during the year (p. 98)

export promotion a development strategy that concentrates on producing for the export market (Online Chapter 18, p. 15)

externality a cost or a benefit that affects neither the buyer nor seller, but instead affects people not involved in the market transaction (p. 45)

fallacy of composition the incorrect belief that what is true for the individual, or part, must necessarily be true for the group, or the whole (p. 11)

federal budget deficit a flow variable measuring the amount by which federal government outlays exceed federal government revenues in a particular period, usually a year (p. 91)

fiat money money not redeemable for any commodity; its status as money is conferred initially by government decree but eventually by common experience (p. 207)

final goods and services goods and services sold to final, or end, users (p. 98)

financial account the record of a country's international transactions involving purchases or sales of financial and real assets (p. 265)

financial intermediaries institutions such as banks, mortgage companies, and finance companies, that serve as go-betweens, borrowing from people who have saved to make loans to others (p. 209)

financial markets banks and other financial institutions that facilitate the flow of funds from savers to borrowers (p. 102)

firms economic units formed by profit-seeking entrepreneurs who employ resources to produce goods and services for sale (p. 41)

fiscal policy focuses on the effects of taxing and public spending on aggregate economic activity (p. 184)

fiscal policy the use of government purchases, transfer payments, taxes, and borrowing to influence economy-wide variables such as inflation, employment, and economic growth (p. 46)

fixed exchange rate rate of exchange between currencies pegged within a narrow range and maintained by the central bank's ongoing purchases and sales of currencies (p. 271)

flexible exchange rate rate determined in foreign exchange markets by the forces of demand and supply without government intervention (p. 271)

flow variable a measure of something over an interval of time, such as your income per week (p. 82)

foreign aid an international transfer made on especially favourable terms for the purpose of promoting economic development (Online Chapter 18, p. 16)

foreign exchange foreign money needed to carry out international transactions (p. 50)

fractional reserve banking system bank reserves amount to only a fraction of funds on deposit with the bank (p. 207)

frictional unemployment unemployment that occurs because job seekers and employers need time to find each other (p. 118)

full employment employment level when there is no cyclical unemployment (p. 121)

functional finance a budget philosophy using fiscal policy to achieve the economy's potential GDP, rather than balancing budgets either annually or over the business cycle (p. 195)

GDP price index a comprehensive inflation measure of all goods and services included in the gross domestic product (p. 108)

General Agreement on Tariffs and Trade (GATT) an international tariff-reduction treaty adopted in 1947 that resulted in a series of negotiated "rounds" aimed at freer trade (Online Chapter 17, p. 12)

gold standard an arrangement whereby the currencies of most countries are convertible into gold at a fixed rate (p. 271)

good a tangible product used to satisfy human wants (p. 4)

Governing Council the six-member group that makes decisions about open-market operations; consists of the governor, the senior deputy governor, and four deputy governors (p. 210)

government purchase function the relationship between government purchases and the economy's income, other things constant (p. 155)

government purchases spending for goods and services by all levels of government; government outlays minus transfer payments (p. 99)

graph a picture showing how variables relate in two-dimensional space; one variable is measured along the horizontal axis and the other along the vertical axis (p. 16)

Gresham's law people tend to trade away inferior money and hoard the best (p. 204)

gross domestic product (GDP) the market value of all final goods and services produced in the nation during a particular period, usually a year (p. 80)

gross world product the market value of all final goods and services produced in the world during a given period, usually a year (p. 81)

horizontal axis line on a graph that begins at the origin and goes to the right and left; sometimes called the x axis (p. 15)

hyperinflation a very high rate of inflation (p. 123)

hypothesis a theory about how key variables relate (p. 9)

hysteresis the theory that the natural rate of unemployment depends in part on the recent history of unemployment; high unemployment rates increase the natural rate of unemployment (p. 180)

implementation lag the time needed to introduce a change in monetary or fiscal policy (p. 249)

import substitution a development strategy that emphasizes domestic manufacturing of products that were imported (Online Chapter 18, p. 15)

income approach to GDP calculating GDP by adding up all earnings from resources used to produce output in the nation during the year (p. 98)

income effect of a price change a fall in the price of a good increases consumers' real income, making consumers more able to purchase goods; for a normal good, the quantity demanded increases (p. 56)

income-expenditure model a relationship that shows how much people plan to spend at each income level; this model identifies, for a given price level, where the amount people plan to spend equals the amount produced in the economy (p. 158)

independent variable a variable whose value determines that of the dependent variable (p. 16)

individual demand the relation between the price of a good and the quantity purchased by an individual consumer per period, other things constant (p. 58)

individual supply the relation between the price of a good and the quantity an individual producer is willing and able to sell per period, other things constant (p. 62)

industrial market countries economically advanced capitalist countries of Western Europe, North America, Australia, New Zealand, and Japan, plus the newly industrialized Asian economies of Taiwan, South Korea, Hong Kong, and Singapore (p. 138; Online Chapter 18, p. 3)

industrial policy the view that government—using taxes, subsidies, and regulations—should nurture the industries and technologies of the future, thereby giving these domestic industries an advantage over foreign competition (p. 143)

Industrial Revolution development of large-scale factory production that began in Great Britain around 1750 and spread to the rest of Europe, North America, Australia, and New Zealand (p. 41)

inferior good a good, such as used clothes, for which demand decreases, or shifts leftward, as consumer income rises (p. 59)

inflation an increase in the economy's average price level (p. 83)

inflation target commitment of central bankers to keep inflation below a certain rate for the next year or two (p. 253)

injection any spending other than by households or any income other than from resource earnings; includes investment, government purchases, exports, and transfer payments (p. 103)

interest payment to resource owners for the use of their capital (p. 3)

interest the dollar amount paid by borrowers to lenders (p. 127)

interest rate interest per year as a percentage of the amount loaned (p. 127)

intermediate goods and services goods and services purchased by firms for further reprocessing and resale (p. 98)

International Monetary Fund (IMF) an international organization that establishes rules for maintaining the international monetary system and provides loans to countries with temporary balance-of-payments problems (p. 272)

inventories producers' stocks of finished and in-process goods (p. 99)

investment the purchase of new plants, new equipment, new buildings, and new residences, plus net additions to inventories (p. 99)

investment function the relationship between the amount businesses plan to invest and the economy's income, other things constant (p. 154)

labour the time and physical and mental effort used to produce goods and services (p. 3)

labour force those 16 years of age and older who are either working or looking for work (p. 115)

labour force participation rate the labour force as a percentage of the adult population (p. 116)

labour productivity output per unit of labour; measured as real GDP divided by the hours of labour employed to produce that output (p. 135)

lagging economic indicators variables that follow, or trail, changes in overall economic activity; examples are the interest rate and the average duration of unemployment (p. 86)

law of comparative advantage the individual, firm, region, or country with the lowest opportunity cost of producing a particular good should specialize in that good (p. 24)

law of demand the quantity of a good that consumers are willing and able to buy per period relates inversely, or negatively, to the price, other things constant (p. 56)

law of increasing opportunity cost to produce more of one good, a successively larger amount of the other good must be sacrificed (p. 28)

law of supply the amount of a good that producers are willing and able to sell per period is usually directly related to its price, other things constant (p. 60)

leading economic indicators variables that predict, or lead to, a recession or recovery; examples are consumer confidence, stock market prices, business investment, and big-ticket purchases, such as automobiles and homes (p. 86)

leakage any diversion of income from the domestic spending stream; includes saving, taxes, and imports (p. 103)

legal tender Canadian currency that constitutes a valid and legal offer of payment of debt (p. 207)

liability anything that is owed to other people or institutions (p. 220)

life-cycle model of consumption and saving young people borrow, middle agers pay off debts and save, and older people draw down their savings; on average, net savings over a lifetime is usually little or nothing (p. 153)

liquidity a measure of the ease with which an asset can be converted into money without a significant loss of value (p. 221)

long run in macroeconomics, a period during which wage contracts and resource price agreements can be renegotiated; there are no surprises about the economy's actual price level (p. 174)

long-run aggregate supply (LRAS) curve depends on the supply of resources in the economy, the level of technology, and the production incentives provided by the formal and informal institutions of the economic system (p. 176)

long-run equilibrium the price level and real GDP that occurs when (1) the actual price level equals the expected price level, (2) real GDP supplied equals potential output, and (3) real GDP supplied equals real GDP demanded (p. 175)

long-run Phillips curve a vertical line drawn at the economy's natural rate of unemployment that traces equilibrium points that can occur when workers and employers have the time to adjust fully to any unexpected change in aggregate demand (p. 257)

long-term unemployed those out of work for 52 weeks or longer (p. 121)

M1+ the narrow measure of the money supply, consisting of currency and coins held by the nonbanking public, traveller's cheques and chequable deposits at chartered banks, trust and mortgage loans companies (TMLs), and credit unions and caisses populaires (CUCPs) (p. 217)

M2 a money aggregate consisting of currency (including coins) held by the nonbanking public and traveller's cheques, personal and nonpersonal chequable deposits as well as savings deposits, and personal time deposits held at chartered banks (p. 217)

M2+ a money aggregate consisting of M2 plus similar deposits at TMLs and CUCPs, life insurance company individual annuities, personal deposits at government-owned saving institutions, and money market mutual fund accounts (p. 217)

macroeconomics the study of the economic behaviour of entire economies, as measured, for example, by total production and employment (p. 7)

managed float system an exchange rate system that combines features of freely floating rates with sporadic intervention by central banks (p. 273)

marginal incremental, additional, or extra; used to describe a change in an economic variable (p. 7)

marginal propensity to consume (MPC) the fraction of a change in income that is spent on consumption; the change in consumption divided by the change in income that caused it (p. 150)

marginal tax rate the percentage of each additional dollar of income that goes to the tax (p. 48)

market a set of arrangements by which buyers and sellers carry out exchange at mutually agreeable terms (p. 5)

market demand   the relation between the price of a good and the quantity purchased by all consumers in the market during a given period, other things constant; sum of the individual demands in the market (p. 58)

market failure   a condition that arises when the unregulated operation of markets yields socially undesirable results (p. 44)

market supply   the relation between the price of a good and the quantity all producers are willing and able to sell per period, other things constant (p. 62)

medium of exchange   anything that facilitates trade by being generally accepted by all parties in payment for goods or services (p. 203)

mercantilism   the incorrect theory that a nation's economic objective should be to accumulate precious metals in the public treasury; this theory prompted trade barriers to cut imports, but trading partners retaliated, reducing trade and the gains from specialization (p. 83)

merchandise trade balance   the value during a given period of a country's exported goods minus the value of its imported goods (p. 49)

microeconomics   the study of the economic behaviour in particular markets, such as that for computers or skilled and unskilled labour (p. 7)

mixed system   an economic system characterized by the private ownership of some resources and the public ownership of other resources; some markets are regulated by government (p. 33)

monetary policy   regulation of the money supply to influence economy-wide variables such as inflation, employment, and economic growth (p. 46)

money   anything that is generally accepted in exchange for goods and services (p. 203)

money aggregates   measures of the economy's money supply (p. 217)

money income   the number of dollars a person receives per period (p. 56)

money multiplier   the multiple by which the money supply changes as a result of a change in fresh reserves in the banking system (p. 224)

monopoly   a sole supplier of a product with no close substitutes (p. 45)

mortgage-backed security   a claim on payments made on the many mortgages bundled into this financial instrument (p. 211)

movement along a demand curve   change in quantity demanded resulting from a change in the price of the good, other things constant (p. 60)

movement along a supply curve   change in quantity supplied resulting from a change in the price of the good, other things constant (p. 63)

national debt   the net accumulation of federal budget deficits (p. 196)

natural monopoly   one firm that can supply the entire market at a lower per-unit cost than could two or more firms (p. 45)

natural rate hypothesis   the natural rate of unemployment is largely independent of the stimulus provided by monetary or fiscal policy (p. 257)

natural rate of unemployment   the unemployment rate when the economy produces its potential output (p. 171)

natural resources   all gifts of nature used to produce goods and services; includes renewable and exhaustible resources (p. 3)

negative relation (inverse relation)   occurs when two variables move in opposite directions; when one increases, the other decreases (p. 17)

net domestic product   gross domestic product minus depreciation (p. 104)

net export function   the relationship between net exports and the economy's income, other things constant (p. 156)

net exports   the value of a country's exports minus the value of its imports (p. 99)

net investment income from abroad   investment earnings by Canadian residents from their foreign assets minus investment earnings by foreigners from their assets in Canada (p. 265)

net taxes (NT)   taxes minus transfer payments (p. 101)

net unilateral transfers abroad   the unilateral transfers (gifts and grants) received from abroad by Canadian residents minus the unilateral transfers Canadian residents send abroad (p. 265)

net wealth   the value of all assets minus liabilities (p. 151)

net worth   assets minus liabilities; also called owners' equity (p. 219)

nominal GDP   GDP based on prices prevailing at the time of production (p. 106)

nominal interest rate   the interest rate expressed in dollars of current value (that is, not adjusted for inflation) as a percentage of the amount loaned; the interest rate specified on the loan agreement (p. 127)

nominal wage   the wage measured in dollars of the year in question; the dollar amount on a paycheque (p. 170)

normal good   a good, such as new clothes, for which demand increases, or shifts rightward, as consumer income rises (p. 59)

normative economic statement   a statement that reflects an opinion, which cannot be proved or disproved by reference to the facts (p. 10)

North American Free Trade Agreement (NAFTA) a free trade agreement established between Canada, Mexico, and the USA in 1994 (Online Chapter 17, p. 13)

not-for-profit organizations groups that do not pursue profit as a goal; they engage in charitable, educational, humanitarian, cultural, professional, or other activities, often with a social purpose (p. 43)

open-market operations purchases and sales of government securities by the Bank of Canada in an effort to influence the money supply (p. 210)

open-market purchase the purchase of Canada government bonds by the Bank of Canada to increase the money supply (p. 226)

open-market sale the sale of Canada government bonds by the Bank of Canada to reduce the money supply (p. 226)

operational cost the sum of the willingness-to-sell across the quantity produced; the area under the WTS curve up to the total quantity produced; it can be calculated for either an individual producer or for the entire market (p. 62)

opportunity cost the value of the best alternative forgone when an item or activity is chosen (p. 22)

origin on a graph depicting two-dimensional space, the zero point (p. 15)

other-things-constant assumption the assumption, when focusing on the relation among key economic variables, that other variables remain unchanged; in Latin, *ceteris paribus* (p. 9)

overnight money market a market for overnight lending and borrowing of reserves among banks; the interbank market for reserves (p. 221)

overnight rate the interest rate charged in the overnight money market; the interest rate banks charge one another for overnight borrowing; the Bank of Canada target interest rate (p. 221)

partnership a firm with multiple owners who share the profits and bear unlimited liability for the firm's losses and debts (p. 42)

per-worker production function the relationship between the amount of capital per worker in the economy and average output per worker (p. 136)

permanent income income that individuals expect to receive on average over the long term (p. 193)

Phillips curve a curve showing possible combinations of the inflation rate and the unemployment rate (p. 255)

physical capital manufactured items used to produce goods and services; includes new plants and new equipment (p. 99)

political business cycles economic fluctuations that occur when discretionary policy is manipulated for political gain (p. 192)

positive economic statement a statement that can be proved or disproved by reference to facts (p. 10)

positive relation (direct relation) occurs when two variables increase or decrease together; the two variables move in the same direction (p. 17)

potential output the economy's maximum sustainable output, given the supply of resources, technology, and rules of the game; the output level when there are no surprises about the price level (p. 170)

price ceiling a maximum legal price above which a product cannot be sold; to have an impact, a price ceiling must be set below the equilibrium price (p. 72)

price floor a minimum legal price below which a product cannot be sold; to have an impact, a price floor must be set above the equilibrium price (p. 71)

price index a number that shows the average price of products; changes in a price index over time show changes in the economy's average price level (p. 106)

price level a composite measure reflecting the prices of all goods and services in the economy relative to prices in a base year (p. 87)

private good a good, such as pizza, that is both rival in consumption and excludable (p. 45)

private property rights an owner's right to use, rent, or sell resources or property (p. 31)

privatization the process of turning government enterprises into private enterprises (Online Chapter 18, p. 13)

producer surplus the remainder once the operational cost realized is subtracted from the price received; the area above the supply curve but beneath the price received up to the number of units exchanged (p. 67)

product market a market in which a good or service is bought and sold (p. 5)

production a process that transforms resources into goods and services (p. 135)

production possibilities frontier (PPF) a curve showing alternative combinations of goods that can be produced when available resources are used efficiently; a boundary line between inefficient and unattainable combinations (p. 27)

productivity the ratio of a specific measure of output, such as real GDP, to a specific measure of input, such as labour; in this case productivity measures real GDP per hour of labour (p. 135)

profit reward for entrepreneurial ability; sales revenue minus resource cost (p. 3)

progressive taxation the tax as a percentage of income increases as income increases (p. 48)

proportional taxation the tax as a percentage of income remains constant as income increases; also called a flat tax (p. 48)

public good a good that, once produced, is available for all to consume, regardless of who pays and who doesn't; such a good is nonrival and nonexcludable, such as a safer community (p. 45)

purchasing power parity (PPP) theory the idea that the exchange rate between two countries will adjust in the long run to equalize the cost between the countries of a basket of internationally traded goods (p. 270)

pure capitalism an economic system characterized by the private ownership of resources and the use of prices to coordinate economic activity in unregulated markets (p. 31)

pure command system an economic system characterized by the public ownership of resources and centralized planning (p. 32)

quantity demanded the amount of a good consumers are willing and able to buy per period at a particular price, as reflected by a point on a demand curve (p. 57)

quantity supplied the amount offered for sale per period at a particular price, as reflected by a point on a given supply curve (p. 62)

quantity theory of money if the velocity of money is stable, or at least predictable, changes in the money supply have predictable effects on nominal GDP (p. 237)

quota a legal limit on the quantity of a particular product that can be imported or exported (p. 50)

rational expectations a school of thought that argues people form expectations based on all available information, including the likely future actions of government policymakers (p. 250)

rational self-interest each individual tries to maximize the expected benefit achieved with a given cost or to minimize the expected cost of achieving a given benefit (p. 6)

real GDP per capita real GDP divided by the population; the best measure of an economy's standard of living (p. 93)

real gross domestic product (real GDP) the economy's aggregate output measured in dollars of constant purchasing power (p. 87)

real income income measured in terms of the goods and services it can buy; real income changes when the price changes (p. 56)

real interest rate the interest rate expressed in dollars of constant purchasing power as a percentage of the amount loaned; the nominal interest rate minus the inflation rate (p. 128)

real wage the wage measured in dollars of constant purchasing power; the wage measured in terms of the quantity of goods and services it buys (p. 170)

recession a period of decline in economic activity lasting more than a few months, as reflected by falling output, employment, income, and other aggregate measures (p. 83)

recessionary gap the amount by which actual output in the short run falls short of the economy's potential output (p. 176)

recognition lag the time needed to identify a macroeconomic problem and assess its seriousness (p. 248)

regressive taxation the tax as a percentage of income decreases as income increases (p. 49)

rent payment to resource owners for the use of their natural resources (p. 3)

representative or commodity-backed money bank notes that exchange for a specific commodity, such as gold (p. 207)

reserves funds that banks use to satisfy the cash demands of their customers; reserves consist of cash held by banks plus deposits at the Bank of Canada (p. 210)

residential construction building new homes or dwelling places (p. 99)

resource market a market in which a resource is bought and sold (p. 5)

resources the inputs, or factors of production, used to produce the goods and services that people want; resources consist of labour, capital, natural resources, and entrepreneurial ability (p. 3)

rules of the game the formal and informal institutions that promote economic activity; the laws, customs, manners, conventions, and other institutional elements that determine transaction costs and thereby affect people's incentive to undertake production and exchange (p. 137)

savings deposits deposits that earn interest but have no specific maturity date (p. 217)

scarcity occurs when the amount people desire exceeds the amount available at a zero price (p. 4)

seasonal unemployment unemployment caused by seasonal changes in the demand for certain kinds of labour (p. 118)

secondary effects unintended consequences of economic actions that may develop slowly over time as people react to events (p. 11)

seigniorage the difference between the face value of money and the cost of supplying it; the "profit" from issuing money (p. 206)

service an activity, or intangible product, used to satisfy human wants (p. 4)

shift of a demand curve movement of a demand curve right or left resulting from a change in one of the determinants of demand other than the price of the good (p. 60)

shift of a supply curve movement of a supply curve left or right resulting from a change in one of the determinants of supply other than the price of the good (p. 63)

short run in macroeconomics, a period during which some resource prices, especially those for labour, are fixed by explicit or implicit agreements (p. 171)

short-run aggregate supply (SRAS) curve a curve that shows a direct relationship between the actual price level and real GDP supplied in the short run, other things constant, including the expected price level (p. 173)

short-run equilibrium the price level and real GDP that result when the aggregate demand curve intersects the short-run aggregate supply curve (p. 174)

short-run Phillips curve based on an expected inflation rate, a curve that reflects an inverse relationship between the inflation rate and the unemployment rate (p. 256)

shortage at a given price, the amount by which quantity demanded exceeds quantity supplied; a shortage usually forces the price up (p. 64)

simple money multiplier   the reciprocal of the desired reserve ratio, or $1/r$; the maximum multiple of fresh reserves by which the money supply can increase (p. 224)

simple spending multiplier   the ratio of a change in real GDP demanded to the initial change in spending that brought it about; the numerical value of the simple spending multiplier is $1/(1 - MPC)$; called "simple" because only consumption varies with income (p. 161)

simple tax multiplier   the ratio of a change in real GDP demanded to the initial change in autonomous net taxes that brought it about; the numerical value of the simple tax multiplier is $-MPC/(1 - MPC)$ (p. 186)

slope of a line   a measure of how much the vertical variable changes for a given increase in the horizontal variable; the vertical change between two points divided by the horizontal increase (p. 17)

social capital   the shared values and trust that promote cooperation in the economy (Online Chapter 18, p. 14)

sole proprietorship   a firm with a single owner who has the right to all profits but who also bears unlimited liability for the firm's losses and debts (p. 41)

specialization of labour   focusing work effort on a particular product or a single task (p. 26)

speculator   someone who buys or sells foreign exchange in hopes of profiting from fluctuations in the exchange rate over time (p. 270)

stagflation   a contraction, or stagnation, of a nation's output accompanied by inflation in the price level (p. 91)

stock variable   a measure of something at a particular point in time, such as the amount of money you have with you right now (p. 82)

store of value   anything that retains its purchasing power over time (p. 204)

structural unemployment   unemployment because (1) the skills demanded by employers do not match those of the unemployed, or (2) the unemployed do not live where the jobs are (p. 119)

subprime mortgage   mortgage for a borrower with a not-so-good credit rating (p. 211)

substitutes   goods, such as Coke and Pepsi, that relate in such a way that an increase in the price of one shifts the demand for the other rightward (p. 59)

substitution effect of a price change   when the price of a good falls, that good becomes cheaper compared to other goods so consumers tend to substitute that good for other goods (p. 56)

sunk cost   a cost that has already been incurred, cannot be recovered, and thus should be irrelevant for present and future economic decisions (p. 23)

supply   a relation between the price of a good and the quantity that producers are willing and able to sell per period, other things constant (p. 60)

supply curve   a curve showing the relation between price of a good and the quantity producers are willing and able to sell per period other things constant; sometimes known as the willingness-to-sell (WTS) curve (p. 61)

supply shocks   unexpected events that affect aggregate supply, sometimes only temporarily (p. 178)

supply-side economics   macroeconomic policy that focuses on a rightward shift of the aggregate supply curve through tax cuts or other changes to increase production incentives (p. 92)

surplus   at a given price, the amount by which quantity supplied exceeds quantity demanded; a surplus usually forces the price down (p. 64)

tangent   a straight line that touches a curve at a point but does not cut or cross the curve; used to measure the slope of a curve at a point (p. 19)

tariff   a tax on imports (p. 50)

tastes   consumer preferences; likes and dislikes in consumption; assumed to remain constant along a given demand curve (p. 60)

tax incidence   the distribution of tax burden among taxpayers; indicates who ultimately pays the tax (p. 48)

terms of trade   how much of one good exchanges for a unit of another good (Online Chapter 17, p. 5)

time deposits   deposits that earn a fixed interest rate if held for the specified period, which can range from several months to several years; also called certificates of deposit (p. 217)

time-inconsistency problem   when policymakers have an incentive to announce one policy to influence expectations but then pursue a different policy once those expectations have been formed and acted on (p. 251)

token money   money whose face value exceeds its cost of production (p. 206)

total surplus   the sum of the difference between the consumer value and the operational cost over all units exchanged; the area between the demand and supply curves up to the number of units exchanged (p. 66)

transaction costs   the costs of time and information required to carry out market exchange (p. 64)

transfer payments   benefits given to individuals as outright grants from the government (p. 40)

trust and mortgage loan companies (TMLs)   financial institutions that provide trustee functions and specialize in making home mortgage loans (p. 209)

underemployment   workers are overqualified for their jobs or work fewer hours than they would prefer (p. 122)

underground economy   market transactions that go unreported either because they are illegal or because people involved want to evade taxes (p. 104)

unemployment benefits   cash transfers to those who lose their jobs and actively seek employment (p. 121)

unemployment rate   the number unemployed as a percentage of the labour force (p. 115)

unit of account   a common unit for measuring the value of each good or service (p. 203)

Uruguay Round   the final multilateral trade negotiation under GATT; this 1994 agreement cut tariffs, formed the World Trade Organization (WTO), and will eventually eliminate quotas (Online Chapter 17, p. 13)

utility   the satisfaction received from consumption; sense of well-being (p. 39)

value added   at each stage of production, the selling price of a product minus the cost of intermediate goods purchased from other firms (p. 100)

variable   a measure, such as price or quantity, that can take on different values at different times (p. 9)

velocity of money   the average number of times per year each dollar is used to purchase final goods and services (p. 236)

vertical axis   line on a graph that begins at the origin and goes up and down; sometimes called the *y* axis (p. 16)

wages   payment to resource owners for their labour (p. 3)

willingness-to-pay (WTP)   a relation between the quantity of a good and the largest amount that consumers are willing and able to pay per period, other things constant (p. 55)

willingness-to-sell (WTS)   a relation between the quantity of a good and the least amount that producers are willing and able to receive in order to sell per period, other things constant (p. 61)

world price   the price at which a good is traded on the world market; determined by the world demand and world supply for the good (Online Chapter 17, p. 9)

World Trade Organization (WTO)   the legal and institutional foundation of the multilateral trading system that succeeded GATT in 1995 (Online Chapter 17, p. 13)

Index

Note: Chapters 17 and 18 can be found online. Index entries on these chapters are denoted by chapter number, hyphen, and page number(s).

Y

Z

1 The Art and Science of Economic Analysis

economics the study of how people use their scarce resources to satisfy their unlimited wants

resources the inputs, or factors of production, used to produce the goods and services that people want; resources consist of labour, capital, natural resources, and entrepreneurial ability

labour the time and physical and mental effort used to produce goods and services

capital the buildings, equipment, and human skills used to produce goods and services

natural resources all gifts of nature used to produce goods and services; includes renewable and exhaustible resources

entrepreneurial ability the imagination required to develop a new product or process, the skill needed to organize production, and the willingness to take the risk of profit or loss

entrepreneur a profit-seeking decision maker who starts with an idea, organizes an enterprise to bring that idea to life, and assumes the risk of the operation

wages payment to resource owners for their labour

interest payment to resource owners for the use of their capital

rent payment to resource owners for the use of their natural resources

profit reward for entrepreneurial ability; sales revenue minus resource cost

good a tangible product used to satisfy human wants

service an activity, or intangible product, used to satisfy human wants

scarcity occurs when the amount people desire exceeds the amount available at a zero price

market a set of arrangements by which buyers and sellers carry out exchange at mutually agreeable terms

product market a market in which a good or service is bought and sold

resource market a market in which a resource is bought and sold

circular-flow model a diagram that traces the flow of resources, products, income, and revenue among economic decision makers

rational self-interest each individual tries to maximize the expected benefit achieved with a given cost or to minimize the expected cost of achieving a given benefit

LO1 **Explain the economic problem of scarce resources and unlimited wants.** The problem is that, although your wants, or desires, are virtually unlimited, the resources available to satisfy these wants are scarce. Because resources are scarce, you must choose from among your many wants, and whenever you choose, you must forgo satisfying some other wants. Without scarcity, there would be no economic problem and no need for prices.

The Simple Circular-Flow Model for Households and Firms

Households earn income by supplying resources to the resource market, as shown in the lower portion of the model. Firms demand these resources to produce goods and services, which they supply to the product market, as shown in the upper portion of the model. Households spend their income to demand these goods and services. This spending flows through the product market as revenue to firms.

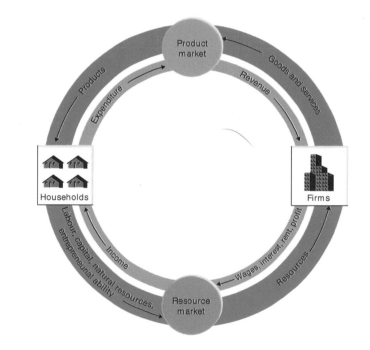

LO2 **Describe the forces that shape economic choices.** An economy results from the choices that millions of individuals make in attempting to satisfy their unlimited wants. A key economic assumption is that individuals, in making choices, rationally select alternatives they perceive to be in their best interests. Economic choice is based on a comparison of the expected marginal benefit and the expected marginal cost of the action under consideration.

LO3 **Explain how economists use the scientific method.** An economic theory is a simplification of economic reality that is used to make predictions about the real world. A theory, or model, captures the important elements of the problem under study but need not spell out every detail and interrelation. You might think of economic theory as a streamlined version of economic reality.

marginal incremental, additional, or extra; used to describe a change in an economic variable

microeconomics the study of the economic behaviour in particular markets, such as that for computers or skilled and unskilled labour

macroeconomics the study of the economic behaviour of entire economies, as measured, for example, by total production and employment

economic fluctuations the rise and fall of economic activity relative to the long-term growth trend of the economy; also called business cycles

economic theory (economic model) a simplification of reality used to make predictions about cause and effect in the real world

variable a measure, such as price or quantity, that can take on different values at different times

other-things-constant assumption the assumption, when focusing on the relation among key economic variables, that other variables remain unchanged; in Latin, *ceteris paribus*

behavioural assumption an assumption that describes the expected behaviour of economic decision makers, what motivates them

hypothesis a theory about how key variables relate

positive economic statement a statement that can be proved or disproved by reference to facts

normative economic statement a statement that reflects an opinion, which cannot be proved or disproved by reference to the facts

association-is-causation fallacy the incorrect idea that if two variables are associated in time, one must necessarily cause the other

fallacy of composition the incorrect belief that what is true for the individual, or part, must necessarily be true for the group, or the whole

secondary effects unintended consequences of economic actions that may develop slowly over time as people react to events

Appendix Terms

origin on a graph depicting two-dimensional space, the zero point

horizontal axis line on a graph that begins at the origin and goes to the right and left; sometimes called the *x* axis

vertical axis line on a graph that begins at the origin and goes up and down; sometimes called the *y* axis

graph a picture showing how variables relate in two-dimensional space; one variable is measured along the horizontal axis and the other along the vertical axis

dependent variable a variable whose value depends on that of the independent variable

The Scientific Method: Step by Step

The steps of the scientific method are designed to develop and test hypotheses about how the world works. The objective is a theory that predicts outcomes more accurately than the best alternative theory. A hypothesis is rejected if it does not predict as accurately as the best alternative. A rejected hypothesis can be modified in light of the test results.

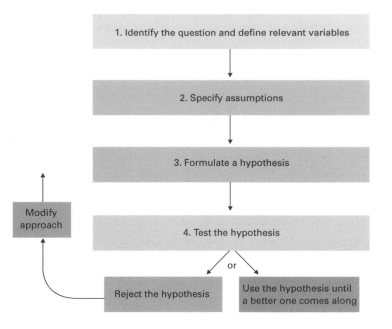

LO4 **Identify some pitfalls of economic analysis.** Economic analysis, like other forms of scientific inquiry, is subject to common mistakes in reasoning that can lead to faulty conclusions. Three sources of confusion are the fallacy that association is causation, the fallacy of composition, and the mistake of ignoring secondary effects.

LO5 **Describe several reasons to study economics.** The economics profession thrives because its models usually do a better job of making economic sense out of a confusing world than do alternative approaches. Studies show that economics majors earn more than most and they have lower unemployment rates than most.

independent variable a variable whose value determines that of the dependent variable

positive relation (direct relation) occurs when two variables increase or decrease together; the two variables move in the same direction

negative relation (inverse relation) occurs when two variables move in opposite directions; when one increases, the other decreases

slope of a line a measure of how much the vertical variable changes for a given increase in the horizontal variable; the vertical change between two points divided by the horizontal increase

tangent a straight line that touches a curve at a point but does not cut or cross the curve; used to measure the slope of a curve at a point

CHAPTER IN REVIEW

2   Economic Tools and Economic Systems

opportunity cost the value of the best alternative forgone when an item or activity is chosen

sunk cost a cost that has already been incurred, cannot be recovered, and thus should be irrelevant for present and future economic decisions

law of comparative advantage the individual, firm, region, or country with the lowest opportunity cost of producing a particular good should specialize in that good

absolute advantage the ability to make something using fewer resources than other producers use

comparative advantage the ability to make something at a lower opportunity cost than other producers face

barter the direct exchange of one product for another without using money

division of labour breaking down the production of a good into separate tasks

specialization of labour focusing work effort on a particular product or a single task

production possibilities frontier (PPF) a curve showing alternative combinations of goods that can be produced when available resources are used efficiently; a boundary line between inefficient and unattainable combinations

efficiency the condition that exists when there is no way resources can be reallocated to increase the production of one good without decreasing the production of another; getting the most from available resources

law of increasing opportunity cost to produce more of one good, a successively larger amount of the other good must be sacrificed

economic growth an increase in the economy's ability to produce goods and services; reflected by an outward shift of the economy's production possibilities frontier

economic system the set of mechanisms and institutions that resolve the what, how, and for whom questions

pure capitalism an economic system characterized by the private ownership of resources and the use of prices to coordinate economic activity in unregulated markets

private property rights an owner's right to use, rent, or sell resources or property

pure command system an economic system characterized by the public ownership of resources and centralized planning

mixed system an economic system characterized by the private ownership of some resources and the public ownership of other resources; some markets are regulated by government

LO1 **Describe the impact of differing opportunities on choice.** Resources are scarce, but human wants are unlimited. Because you cannot satisfy all your wants, you must choose, and whenever you choose, you must forgo some option. Choice involves an opportunity cost. The opportunity cost of the selected option is the value of the best alternative forgone.

LO2 **Explain how comparative advantage, specialization, and exchange affect economic outcomes (output).** The law of comparative advantage says that the individual, firm, region, or country with the lowest opportunity cost of producing a particular good should specialize in that good. Specialization according to the law of comparative advantage promotes the most efficient use of resources. The specialization of labour increases efficiency by (a) taking advantage of individual preferences and natural abilities, (b) allowing each worker to develop expertise and experience at a particular task, (c) reducing the need to shift between different tasks, and (d) allowing for the introduction of more specialized machines and large-scale production techniques.

LO3 **Outline how economies function as production systems.** The production possibilities frontier, or PPF, shows the productive capabilities of an economy when all resources are used efficiently. The frontier's bowed-out shape reflects the law of increasing opportunity cost, which arises because some resources are not perfectly adaptable to the production of different goods. Over time, the frontier can shift in or out as a result of changes in the availability of resources, in technology, or in the rules of the game. The frontier demonstrates several economic concepts, including efficiency, scarcity, opportunity cost, the law of increasing opportunity cost, economic growth, and the need for choice.

The Economy's Production Possibilities Frontier

If the economy uses its available resources and technology efficiently in producing consumer goods and capital goods, that economy is on its production possibilities frontier, *AF*. The PPF is bowed out to reflect the law of increasing opportunity cost: additional units of capital goods require the economy to sacrifice more and more units of consumer goods. Note that more consumer goods must be given up in moving from *E* to *F* than in moving from *A* to *B*, although in each case the gain in capital goods is 10 million units. Points inside the PPF, such as *I*, represent inefficient use of resources. Points outside the PPF, such as *U*, represent unattainable combinations.

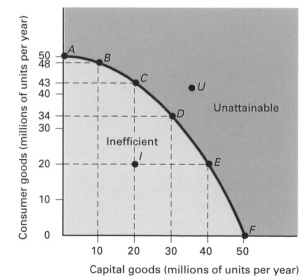

Shifts of the Economy's Production Possibilities Frontier

When the resources available to an economy change, the PPF shifts. If more resources become available or if technology improves, the PPF shifts outward, as in panel (a), indicating that more output can be produced. A decrease in available resources causes the PPF to shift inward, as in panel (b). Panel (c) shows a change affecting consumer goods production. More consumer goods can now be produced at any given level of capital goods. Panel (d) shows a change affecting capital goods production.

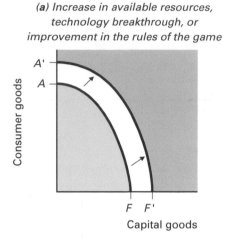

(a) *Increase in available resources, technology breakthrough, or improvement in the rules of the game*

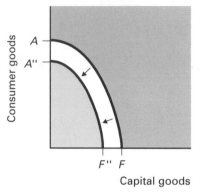

(b) *Decrease in available resources or greater uncertainty in the rules of the game*

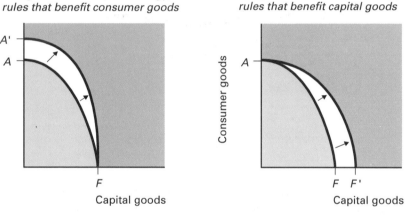

(c) *Change in resources, technology, or rules that benefit consumer goods*

(d) *Change in resources, technology, or rules that benefit capital goods*

LO4
Describe different economic systems and the decision-making rules that define them. All economic systems, regardless of their decision-making processes, must answer three basic questions: What is to be produced? How is it to be produced? And for whom is it to be produced? Economies answer the questions differently, depending on who owns the resources and how economic activity is coordinated. Economies can be directed by market forces, by the central plans of government, or, in most cases, by a mix of the two.

3 Economic Decision Makers

utility the satisfaction received from consumption; sense of well-being

transfer payments benefits given to individuals as outright grants from the government

Industrial Revolution development of large-scale factory production that began in Great Britain around 1750 and spread to the rest of Europe, North America, Australia, and New Zealand

firms economic units formed by profit-seeking entrepreneurs who employ resources to produce goods and services for sale

sole proprietorship a firm with a single owner who has the right to all profits but who also bears unlimited liability for the firm's losses and debts

partnership a firm with multiple owners who share the profits and bear unlimited liability for the firm's losses and debts

corporation a legal entity owned by shareholders whose liability is limited to the value of their stock ownership

cooperative an organization consisting of people who pool their resources to buy and sell more efficiently than they could individually

not-for-profit organizations groups that do not pursue profit as a goal; they engage in charitable, educational, humanitarian, cultural, professional, or other activities, often with a social purpose

market failure a condition that arises when the unregulated operation of markets yields socially undesirable results

monopoly a sole supplier of a product with no close substitutes

natural monopoly one firm that can supply the entire market at a lower per-unit cost than could two or more firms

private good a good, such as pizza, that is both rival in consumption and excludable

public good a good that, once produced, is available for all to consume, regardless of who pays and who doesn't; such a good is nonrival and nonexcludable, such as a safer community

externality a cost or a benefit that affects neither the buyer or seller, but instead affects people not involved in the market transaction

fiscal policy the use of government purchases, transfer payments, taxes, and borrowing to influence economy-wide variables such as inflation, employment, and economic growth

LO1 **Explain the role of a household in an economic system.** Households play the starring role in a market economy. Their demand for goods and services determines what gets produced, and their supplies of labour, capital, natural resources, and entrepreneurial ability produce that output. As demanders of goods and services and suppliers of resources, households make all kinds of choices in an attempt to maximize utility.

Where Canadian Personal Income Comes From and Where It Goes

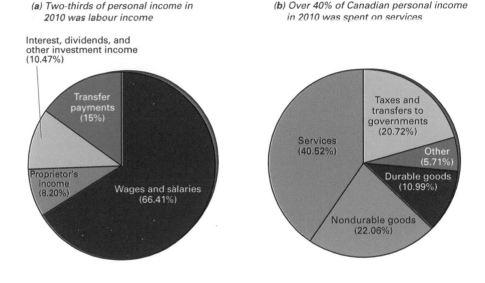

(a) Two-thirds of personal income in 2010 was labour income

Interest, dividends, and other investment income (10.47%)

Transfer payments (15%)

Proprietor's income (8.20%)

Wages and salaries (66.41%)

(b) Over 40% of Canadian personal income in 2010 was spent on services

Taxes and transfers to governments (20.72%)

Services (40.52%)

Other (5.71%)

Durable goods (10.99%)

Nondurable goods (22.06%)

LO2 **Identify the different types of firms and describe their roles in the economy.** Firms are economic units formed by entrepreneurs who combine labour, capital, and natural resources to produce goods and services in an attempt to maximize profit. For-profit firms organize in one of three ways: as a sole proprietorship, as a partnership, or as a corporation. Not-for-profit organizations engage in activities that often have a social purpose, while cooperatives are groups that organize with the goal of minimizing costs.

LO3 **Outline the ways governments affect their economies.** Governments attempt to improve society's overall welfare by intervening in cases of market failure. Beneficial government interventions in markets include establishing and enforcing the rules of the game; promoting competition; regulating natural monopolies; providing public goods; dealing with externalities; more equally distributing income; and pursuing full employment, price stability, and economic growth.

monetary policy regulation of the money supply to influence economy-wide variables such as inflation, employment, and economic growth

ability-to-pay tax principle those with a greater ability to pay, such as those earning higher incomes or those owning more property, should pay more taxes

benefits-received tax principle those who get more benefits from the government program should pay more taxes

tax incidence the distribution of tax burden among taxpayers; indicates who ultimately pays the tax

proportional taxation the tax as a percentage of income remains constant as income increases; also called a flat tax

progressive taxation the tax as a percentage of income increases as income increases

marginal tax rate the percentage of each additional dollar of income that goes to the tax

regressive taxation the tax as a percentage of income decreases as income increases

merchandise trade balance the value during a given period of a country's exported goods minus the value of its imported goods

balance of payments a record of all economic transactions during a given period between residents of one country and residents of the rest of the world

foreign exchange foreign money needed to carry out international transactions

tariff a tax on imports

quota a legal limit on the quantity of a particular product that can be imported or exported

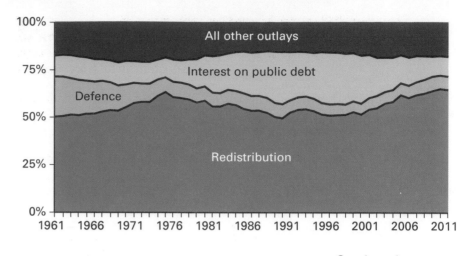

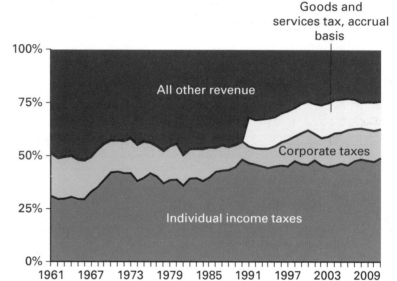

LO4 **Outline the international influences on an economy.** The rest of the world affects what Canadian households consume and what Canadian firms produce. Canadian households and firms are consumers and suppliers of manufactured goods and raw materials from and to foreign economies, and these transactions affect Canadian prices, wages, and profits. International trade, exchange rates, and trade restrictions all affect the Canadian economy.

4 Demand, Supply, and Markets

demand a relation between the price of a good and the quantity that consumers are willing and able to buy per period, other things constant

willingness-to-pay (WTP) a relation between the quantity of a good and the largest amount that consumers are willing and able to pay per period, other things constant

law of demand the quantity of a good that consumers are willing and able to buy per period relates inversely, or negatively, to the price, other things constant

substitution effect of a price change when the price of a good falls, that good becomes cheaper compared to other goods so consumers tend to substitute that good for other goods

money income the number of dollars a person receives per period

real income income measured in terms of the goods and services it can buy; real income changes when the price changes

income effect of a price change a fall in the price of a good increases consumers' real income, making consumers more able to purchase goods; for a normal good, the quantity demanded increases

demand curve a curve showing the relation between the price of a good and the quantity consumers are willing and able to buy per period, other things constant; sometimes known as the willingness-to-pay (WTP) curve

quantity demanded the amount of a good consumers are willing and able to buy per period at a particular price, as reflected by a point on a demand curve

individual demand a relation between the price of a good and the quantity purchased by an individual consumer per period, other things constant

LO1 **Explain how the law of demand affects market activity.** Demand is a relationship between the price of a product and the quantity consumers are willing and able to buy per period, other things constant. According to the law of demand, quantity demanded varies negatively, or inversely, with the price. A demand curve slopes downward because a price decrease makes consumers (a) more willing to substitute this good for other goods and (b) more able to buy the good because the lower price increases real income.

LO2 **Explain how the law of supply affects market activity.** Supply is a relationship between the price of a good and the quantity producers are willing and able to sell per period, other things constant. According to the law of supply, price and quantity supplied are usually positively, or directly, related, so the supply curve typically slopes upward. The supply curve slopes upward because higher prices make producers (a) more willing to supply this good rather than supply other goods that use the same resources and (b) more able to cover the higher marginal cost associated with greater output rates.

The Demand Curve for Pizza

The market demand curve *D* shows the quantity of pizza demanded, at various prices, by all consumers. Price and quantity demanded are inversely related.

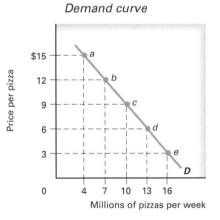

The Supply Curve for Pizza

Market supply curve *S* shows the quantity of pizza supplied, at various prices, by all pizza makers. Price and quantity supplied are directly related.

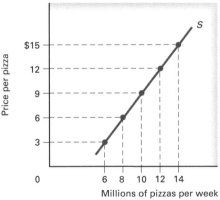

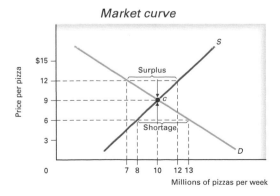

LO3 **Describe the interaction between demand and supply and the resulting market equilibrium.** Demand and supply come together in the market for the good. A market provides information about the price, quantity, and quality of the good. In doing so, a market reduces the transaction costs of exchange—the costs of time and information required for buyers and sellers to make a deal. The interaction of demand and supply guides resources and products to their highest-valued use.

Equilibrium in the Pizza Market

Market equilibrium occurs at the price where quantity demanded equals quantity supplied. This is shown at point *c*. Price pressure occurs at all other points on the curves.

market demand the relation between the price of a good and the quantity purchased by all consumers in the market during a given period, other things constant; sum of the individual demands in the market

consumer value the sum of the willingness-to-pay across the quantity consumed; the area under the WTP curve up to the total quantity consumed; it can be calculated for either an individual or for the market

normal good a good, such as new clothes, for which demand increases, or shifts rightward, as consumer income rises

inferior good a good, such as used clothes, for which demand decreases, or shifts leftward, as consumer income rises

substitutes goods, such as Coke and Pepsi, that relate in such a way that an increase in the price of one shifts the demand for the other rightward

complements goods, such as milk and cookies, that relate in such a way that an increase in the price of one shifts the demand for the other leftward

tastes consumer preferences; likes and dislikes in consumption; assumed to remain constant along a given demand curve

movement along a demand curve change in quantity demanded resulting from a change in the price of the good, other things constant

shift of a demand curve movement of a demand curve right or left resulting from a change in one of the determinants of demand other than the price of the good

supply a relation between the price of a good and the quantity that producers are willing and able to sell per period, other things constant

law of supply the amount of a good that producers are willing and able to sell per period is usually directly related to its price, other things constant

willingness-to-sell (WTS) a relation between the quantity of a good and the least amount that producers are willing and able to receive in order to sell per period, other things constant

supply curve a curve showing the relation between price of a good and the quantity producers are willing and able to sell per period other things constant; sometimes known as the willingness-to-sell (WTS) curve

quantity supplied the amount offered for sale per period at a particular price, as reflected by a point on a given supply curve

individual supply the relation between the price of a good and the quantity an individual producer is willing and able to sell per period, other things constant

market supply the relation between the price of a good and the quantity all producers are willing and able to sell per period, other things constant

operational cost the sum of the willingness-to-sell across the quantity

LO4 Describe how market equilibrium adjusts to shifting demand and supply.

Impersonal market forces reconcile the personal and independent plans of buyers and sellers. Market equilibrium, once established, will continue unless there is a change in a determinant that shapes demand or supply.

Effects of an Increase in Demand

An increase in demand is shown by a shift of the demand curve rightward from D to D'. Both price and quantity are higher following the rightward shift of the demand curve.

Effects of an Increase in Supply

An increase in supply is shown by a shift of the supply curve rightward, from S to S'. At the new equilibrium, quantity is greater and the price is lower than before the increase in supply.

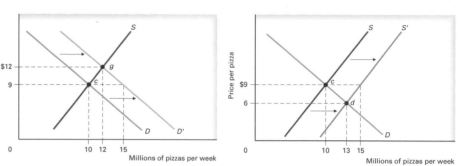

LO5 Explain how markets react during periods of disequilibrium.

Markets can't always achieve equilibrium quickly. Until they do, a period of disequilibrium occurs. Governments often impose price floors or price ceilings to manage the uncomfortable market effects of disequilibrium, like falling income or product surplus.

produced; the area under the WTS curve up to the total quantity produced; it can be calculated for either an individual producer or for the entire market

movement along a supply curve change in quantity supplied resulting from a change in the price of the good, other things constant

shift of a supply curve movement of a supply curve left or right resulting from a change in one of the determinants of supply other than the price of the good

transaction costs the costs of time and information required to carry out market exchange

surplus at a given price, the amount by which quantity supplied exceeds quantity demanded; a surplus usually forces the price down

shortage at a given price, the amount by which quantity demanded exceeds quantity supplied; a shortage usually forces the price up

equilibrium the condition that exists in a market when the plans of buyers match those of sellers, so quantity demanded equals quantity supplied and the market clears

economic efficiency the degree to which all mutually beneficial exchanges of a good take place

total surplus the sum of the difference between the consumer value and the

operational cost over all units exchanged; the area between the demand and supply curves up to the number of units exchanged

efficient a market equilibrium is said to be efficient because it maximizes total surplus

consumer surplus the remainder once the price paid is subtracted from the consumer value realized; the area beneath the demand curve and above the price paid up to the number of units exchanged

producer surplus the remainder once the operational cost realized is subtracted from the price received; the area above the supply curve but beneath the price received up to the number of units exchanged

disequilibrium the condition that exists in a market when the plans of buyers do not match those of sellers; a temporary mismatch between quantity supplied and quantity demanded as the market seeks equilibrium

price floor a minimum legal price below which a product cannot be sold; to have an impact, a price floor must be set above the equilibrium price

deadweight loss (DWL) The value of mutually beneficial trades that go unmade because of market interference; the area between the demand and supply curves and between the quantity exchanged under a particular policy and the equilibrium quantity

price ceiling a maximum legal price above which a product cannot be sold; to have an impact, a price ceiling must be set below the equilibrium price

5   Introduction to Macroeconomics

economy the structure of economic activity in a community, a region, a country, a group of countries, or the world

gross domestic product (GDP) the market value of all final goods and services produced in the nation during a particular period, usually a year

gross world product the market value of all final goods and services produced in the world during a given period, usually a year

flow variable a measure of something over an interval of time, such as your income per week

stock variable a measure of something at a particular point in time, such as the amount of money you have with you right now

mercantilism the incorrect theory that a nation's economic objective should be to accumulate precious metals in the public treasury; this theory prompted trade barriers to cut imports, but trading partners retaliated, reducing trade and the gains from specialization

expansion a period during which the economy grows, as reflected by rising output, employment, income, and other aggregate measures

contraction a period during which the economy declines as reflected by falling output, employment, income, and other aggregate measures

depression a severe and prolonged reduction in economic activity as occurred during the 1930s

recession a period of decline in economic activity lasting more than a few months, as reflected by falling output, employment, income, and other aggregate measures

inflation an increase in the economy's average price level

leading economic indicators variables that predict, or lead to, a recession or recovery; examples are consumer confidence, stock market prices, business investment, and big-ticket purchases, such as automobiles and homes

coincident economic indicators variables that reflect peaks and troughs in economic activity as they occur; examples are employment, personal income, and industrial production

lagging economic indicators variables that follow, or trail, changes in overall economic activity; examples are the interest rate and the average duration of unemployment

LO1 **Discuss macroeconomics and the national economy.** Macroeconomics concerns the overall performance of the national economy. A standard measure of performance is the growth of real gross domestic product, or real GDP, the value of final goods and services produced in the nation during the year.

LO2 **Discuss economic fluctuations and growth.** The economy fluctuates between two phases: periods of expansion and periods of contraction. No two business cycles are the same. The Canadian economy experienced both recessions and depressions before World War II. Since then, there have been recessions but no depressions, so things have improved.

Hypothetical Business Cycles

Business cycles reflect movements of economic activity around a trend line that shows long-term growth. An expansion (shaded in blue) begins when the economy starts to grow and continues until the economy reaches a peak. After an expansion has peaked, a contraction (shaded in pink) begins and continues until the economy reaches a trough.

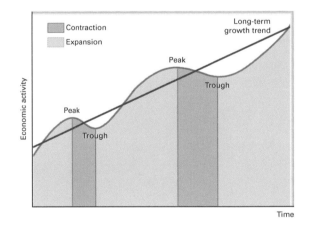

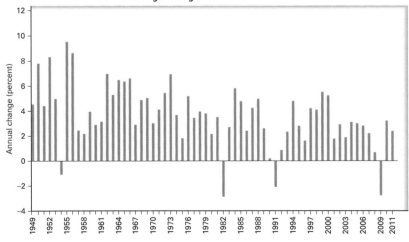

Annual Percentage Change in Canadian Real GDP since 1949

aggregate output a composite measure of all final goods and services produced in an economy during a given period; real GDP

aggregate demand the relationship between the economy's price level and aggregate output demanded, with other things constant

price level a composite measure reflecting the prices of all goods and services in the economy relative to prices in a base year

real gross domestic product (real GDP) the economy's aggregate output measured in dollars of constant purchasing power

aggregate demand curve a curve representing the relationship between the economy's price level and real GDP demanded per period, with other things constant

aggregate supply curve a curve representing the relationship between the economy's price level and real GDP supplied per period, with other things constant

federal budget deficit a flow variable measuring the amount by which federal government outlays exceed federal government revenues in a particular period, usually a year

demand-side economics macroeconomic policy that focuses on shifting the aggregate demand curve as a way of promoting full employment and price stability

stagflation a contraction, or stagnation, of a nation's output accompanied by inflation in the price level

supply-side economics macroeconomic policy that focuses on a rightward shift of the aggregate supply curve through tax cuts or other changes to increase production incentives

real GDP per capita real GDP divided by the population; the best measure of an economy's standard of living

LO3 Explain aggregate demand and aggregate supply.

The aggregate demand curve slopes downward, reflecting a negative, or inverse, relationship between the price level and real GDP demanded. The aggregate supply curve slopes upward, reflecting a positive, or direct, relationship between the price level and real GDP supplied. The intersection of the two curves determines the economy's real GDP and price level.

Aggregate Demand Curve

The quantity of aggregate output demanded is inversely related to the price level, other things constant. This inverse relationship is reflected by the aggregate demand curve *AD*.

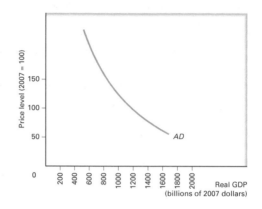

Aggregate Demand and Aggregate Supply in 2012

The total output of the economy and its price level are determined at the intersection of the aggregate demand and aggregate supply curves. This point reflects real GDP and the price level for 2012 using 2007 as the base year.

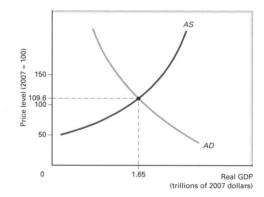

LO4 Describe the history of the Canadian economy.

The Great Depression and earlier depressions prompted John Maynard Keynes to argue that the economy is unstable, largely because business investment is erratic. Keynes did not believe that contractions were self-correcting. His demand-side policies of increased government spending and decreased taxes dominated macroeconomic thinking between World War II and the late 1960s.

During the 1970s, higher oil prices and global crop failures reduced aggregate supply. The result was stagflation, the troublesome combination of declining real GDP and rising inflation. Supply-side tax cuts in the early 1980s were aimed at increasing aggregate supply, thereby increasing output while dampening inflation. Unfortunately, federal spending increased faster than federal tax revenue, resulting in budget deficits that grew into the early 1990s. Tax increases, a slower growth in government spending, and an expanding economy combined with a booming stock market to increase tax revenue enough to yield a federal budget surplus by the end of the 1996 fiscal year and every fiscal year after that to the 2008 recession. The decline in Canada was less pronounced than in the United States and other major industrialized countries as the Canadian financial system was relatively less exposed to the subprime housing market in the United States. The economy began to stabilize in mid-2009 in response to policy measures in Canada and abroad. The recovery was quicker and more complete, with Canada being the only country in the Group of Seven (G7), a group of seven most industrialized countries, in which real GDP and employment have returned to prerecession levels.

6   Tracking the Canadian Economy

expenditure approach to GDP calculating GDP by adding up spending on all final goods and services produced in the nation during the year

income approach to GDP calculating GDP by adding up all earnings from resources used to produce output in the nation during the year

final goods and services goods and services sold to final, or end, users

intermediate goods and services goods and services purchased by firms for further processing and resale

double counting the mistake of including both the value of intermediate products and the value of final products in calculating gross domestic product; counting the same production more than once

consumption household purchases of final goods and services, except for new residences, which count as investment

investment the purchase of new plants, new equipment, new buildings, and new residences, plus net additions to inventories

physical capital manufactured items used to produce goods and services; includes new plants and new equipment

residential construction building new homes or dwelling places

inventories producers' stocks of finished and in-process goods

government purchases spending for goods and services by all levels of government; government outlays minus transfer payments

net exports the value of a country's exports minus the value of its imports

aggregate expenditure total spending on final goods and services in an economy during a given period, usually a year

aggregate income all earnings of resource suppliers in an economy during a given period, usually a year

value added at each stage of production, the selling price of a product minus the cost of intermediate goods purchased from other firms

disposable income (DI) the income households have available to spend or to save after paying taxes and receiving transfer payments

net taxes (NT) taxes minus transfer payments

financial markets banks and other financial institutions that facilitate the flow of funds from savers to borrowers

LO1 **Explain the gross domestic product.** Gross domestic product, or GDP, measures the market value of all final goods and services produced during the year by resources located in Canada, regardless of who owns those resources. The expenditure approach to GDP adds up the market value of all final goods and services produced in the economy during the year. The income approach to GDP adds up all the income generated as a result of that production.

LO2 **Discuss the circular flow of income and expenditure.** The circular-flow model summarizes the flow of income and spending through the economy. Saving, net taxes, and imports leak from the circular flow. These leakages equal the injections into the circular flow from investment, government purchases, and exports.

Circular Flow of Income and Expenditure

The circular-flow model captures important relationships in the economy. The bottom half depicts the income arising from production. At juncture (1), GDP equals aggregate income. Taxes leak from the flow at (2), but transfer payments enter the flow at (3). Taxes minus transfers equals net taxes, NT. Aggregate income minus net taxes equals disposable income, DI, which flows to households at juncture (4). The top half of the model shows the flow of expenditure. At (5), households either spend disposable income or save it. Consumption enters the spending flow directly. Saving leaks from the spending flow into financial markets, where it is channelled to borrowers. At (6), investment enters the spending flow. At (7), government purchases enter the spending flow. At (8), imports leak from the spending flow, and at (9), exports enter the spending flow. Consumption plus investment plus government purchases plus net exports add up to the aggregate expenditure on GDP received by firms at (10).

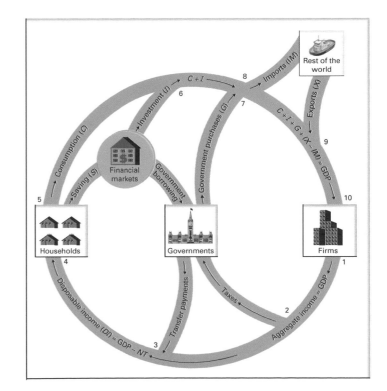

injection any spending other than by households or any income other than from resource earnings; includes investment, government purchases, exports, and transfer payments

leakage any diversion of income from the domestic spending stream; includes saving, taxes, and imports

underground economy market transactions that go unreported either because they are illegal or because people involved want to evade taxes

depreciation the value of capital stock used up to produce GDP or that becomes obsolete during the year

net domestic product gross domestic product minus depreciation

nominal GDP GDP based on prices prevailing at the time of production

base year the year with which other years are compared when constructing an index; the index equals 100 in the base year

price index a number that shows the average price of products; changes in a price index over time show changes in the economy's average price level

consumer price index (CPI) a measure of inflation based on the cost of a fixed market basket of goods and services

GDP price index a comprehensive inflation measure of all goods and services included in the gross domestic product

chain-weighted system an inflation measure that adjusts the weights from year to year in calculating a price index, thereby reducing the bias caused by a fixed-price weighting system

Chapter Equations

Aggregate Expenditure

$$C + I + G + (X - IM) =$$
Aggregate expenditure = GDP
$$C = \text{Consumption}$$
$$I = \text{Investment}$$
$$G = \text{Government}$$
$$\text{purchases}$$
$$(X - IM) = \text{Net exports} =$$
Exports − Imports

Aggregate Income

$$GDP = \text{Aggregate income} =$$
$$DI + NT$$

Disposable Income

$$DI = C + S$$
$$C + I + G + (X - IM) = DI + NT$$
$$C + I + G + (X - IM) =$$
$$C + S + NT$$
$$I + G + X = S + NT + M$$

GDP Price Index

$$\text{GDP Price Index} =$$
$$\frac{\text{Nominal GDP} \times 100}{\text{Real GDP}}$$

LO3 **Assess the limitations of national income accounting.** GDP reflects market production in a given period, usually a year. Most household production and the underground economy are not captured by GDP. Improvements in the quality and variety of products also are often missed in GDP. In other ways GDP may overstate production. GDP fails to subtract for the depreciation of the capital stock or for the depletion of natural resources and fails to account for any negative externalities arising from production.

LO4 **Explain how to account for price changes.** Nominal GDP in a particular year values output based on market prices when the output was produced. To determine real GDP, nominal GDP must be adjusted for price changes. The consumer price index, or CPI, tracks prices for a market basket of goods and services over time. The GDP price index tracks price changes for all output. No adjustment for price changes is perfect, but current approaches offer a reasonably good estimate of real GDP both at a point in time and over time.

Canadian Gross Domestic Product in Nominal Dollars and Chained (2002) Dollars

Real GDP, the red line, shows the value of output measured in chained (2002) dollars. The blue line measures GDP in nominal dollars, of each year shown. The two lines intersect in 2002, when real GDP equalled nominal GDP. Year-to-year changes in nominal-dollar GDP reflect changes in both real GDP and in the price level. Year-to-year changes in chained-dollar GDP reflect changes in real GDP only. Nominal-dollar GDP grows faster than chained-dollar GDP. Prior to 2002, nominal-dollar prices are less than chained-dollar prices, so nominal-dollar GDP is less than chained-dollar GDP.

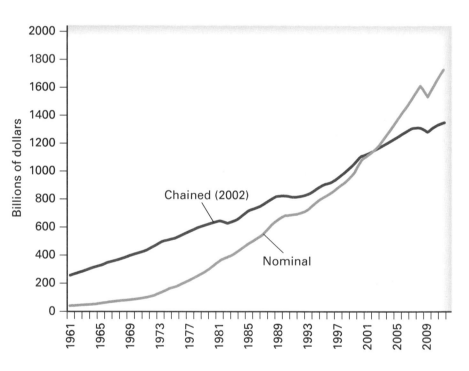

7   Unemployment and Inflation

labour force those 16 years of age and older who are either working or looking for work

unemployment rate the number unemployed as a percentage of the labour force

discouraged workers those who drop out of the labour force in frustration because they can't find work

labour force participation rate the labour force as a percentage of the adult population

frictional unemployment unemployment that occurs because job seekers and employers need time to find each other

seasonal unemployment unemployment caused by seasonal changes in the demand for certain kinds of labour

structural unemployment unemployment because (1) the skills demanded by employers do not match those of the unemployed, or (2) the unemployed do not live where the jobs are

cyclical unemployment unemployment that fluctuates with the business cycle, increasing during contractions and decreasing during expansions

long-term unemployed those out of work for 52 weeks or longer

full employment employment level when there is no cyclical unemployment

unemployment benefits cash transfers to those who lose their jobs and actively seek employment

underemployment workers are overqualified for their jobs or work fewer hours than they would prefer

hyperinflation a very high rate of inflation

deflation a sustained decrease in the price level

disinflation a reduction in the rate of inflation

demand-pull inflation a sustained rise in the price level caused by a rightward shift of the aggregate demand curve

cost-push inflation a sustained rise in the price level caused by a leftward shift of the aggregate supply curve

interest the dollar amount paid by borrowers to lenders

interest rate interest per year as a percentage of the amount loaned

nominal interest rate the interest rate expressed in dollars of current value (that is, not adjusted for inflation) as a percentage of the amount loaned; the interest rate specified on the loan agreement

LO1 **Discuss the effects of unemployment on the economy.** The unemployment rate is the number of people looking for work divided by the number in the labour force. The unemployment rate masks differences among particular groups and across regions. The rate is highest for young workers and those living on the east coast.

There are four sources of unemployment. Frictional unemployment arises because employers and qualified job seekers need time to find one another. Seasonal unemployment stems from the effects of weather and the seasons on certain industries, such as construction and agriculture. Structural unemployment arises because changes in tastes, technology, taxes, and competition reduce the demand for certain skills and increase the demand for other skills. And cyclical unemployment results from fluctuations in economic activity caused by the business cycle. Policymakers and economists are less concerned with frictional and seasonal unemployment. Full employment occurs when cyclical unemployment is zero.

The Adult Population Sums the Employed, the Unemployed, and Those Not in the Labour Force: January 2015 (in millions)

The labour force, depicted by the left circle, consists of those employed plus those unemployed. Those not working, depicted by the right circle, consists of those not in the labour force and those unemployed.

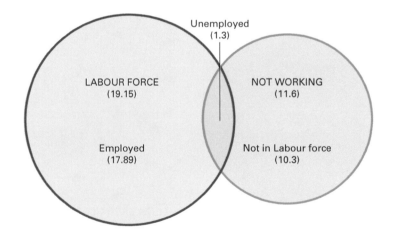

LO2 **Discuss the effects of inflation on the economy.** Inflation is a sustained rise in the average price level. An increase in aggregate demand can cause demand-pull inflation. A decrease in aggregate supply can cause cost-push inflation. Prior to World War II, both inflation and deflation were common, but since then the price level has increased virtually every year.

Anticipated inflation causes fewer distortions in the economy than unanticipated inflation. Unanticipated inflation arbitrarily creates winners and losers and forces people to spend more time and energy coping with the effects of inflation. Because not all prices change by the same amount during inflationary periods, people have trouble keeping track of the changes in relative prices. Unexpected inflation makes long-term planning more difficult and more risky.

The intersection of the demand and supply curves for loanable funds yields the market interest rate. The real interest rate is the nominal interest rate minus the inflation rate. Borrowers and lenders base decisions on the expected real interest rate.

real interest rate the interest rate expressed in dollars of constant purchasing power as a percentage of the amount loaned; the nominal interest rate minus the inflation rate

Chapter Equations

Unemployment Rate

Unemployed ÷ Labour force

Labour Force Participation Rate

Labour force ÷ Adult population

Real Interest Rate

Nominal interest rate − Inflation rate

Inflation Caused by Shifts of Aggregate Demand and Aggregate Supply Curves

Panel (a) illustrates demand-pull inflation. An outward shift of the aggregate demand to *AD'* "pulls" the price level up from *P* to *P'*. Panel (b) shows cost-push inflation. A decrease of aggregate supply to *AS'* "pushes" the price level up from *P* to *P'*.

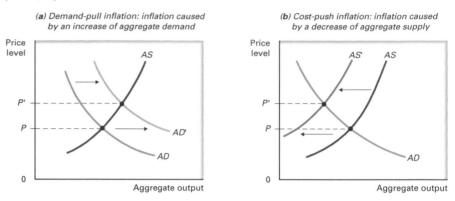

(a) Demand-pull inflation: inflation caused by an increase of aggregate demand

(b) Cost-push inflation: inflation caused by a decrease of aggregate supply

Consumer Price Index Since 1915

Panel (a) shows that, despite fluctuations, the price level, as measured by the consumer price index, was lower in 1940 than in 1920. Since 1940, the price level has risen nearly every year. Panel (b) shows the annual rate of change in the price level. Since 1946, the inflation rate has averaged 4 percent annually.

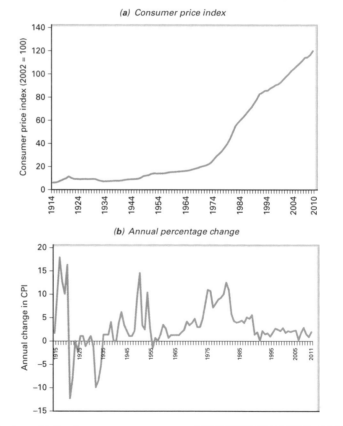

(a) Consumer price index

(b) Annual percentage change

The Market for Loanable Funds

The upward-sloping supply curve, *S*, shows that more loanable funds are supplied at higher interest rates. The downward-sloping demand curve, *D*, shows that the quantity of loanable funds demanded is greater at lower interest rates. The two curves intersect to determine the market interest rate, *i*.

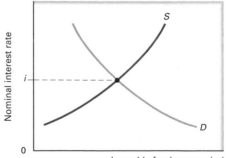

8 Productivity and Growth

production a process that transforms resources into goods and services

productivity the ratio of a specific measure of output, such as real GDP, to a specific measure of input, such as labour; in this case productivity measures real GDP per hour of labour

labour productivity output per unit of labour; measured as real GDP divided by the hours of labour employed to produce that output

per-worker production function the relationship between the amount of capital per worker in the economy and average output per worker

capital deepening an increase in the amount of capital per worker; one source of rising labour productivity

rules of the game the formal and informal institutions that promote economic activity; the laws, customs, manners, conventions, and other institutional elements that determine transaction costs and thereby affect people's incentive to undertake production and exchange

industrial market countries economically advanced capitalist countries of Western Europe, North America, Australia, New Zealand, and Japan, plus the newly industrialized Asian economies of Taiwan, South Korea, Hong Kong, and Singapore

developing countries countries with a low living standard because of less human and physical capital per worker

basic research the search for knowledge without regard to how that knowledge will be used

applied research research that seeks answers to particular questions or to apply scientific discoveries to develop specific products

industrial policy the view that government—using taxes, subsidies, and regulations—should nurture the industries and technologies of the future, thereby giving these domestic industries an advantage over foreign competition

convergence a theory predicting that the standard of living in economics around the world will grow more similar over time, with poorer countries eventually catching up with richer ones

LO1 **Explain the theory of productivity and growth.** If the population is continually increasing, an economy must produce more goods and services simply to maintain its standard of living, as measured by output per capita. If output grows faster than the population, the standard of living rises.

The per-worker production function shows the relationship between the amount of capital per worker in the economy and the output per worker. As capital per worker increases, so does output per worker but at a decreasing rate. Technological change and improvements in the rules of the game shift the per-worker production function upward.

Economic Growth Shown by Shifts Outward of the Production Possibilities Frontier

An economy that produces more capital goods will grow more, as reflected by a shift outward of the production possibilities frontier. More capital goods and fewer consumer goods are produced in panel (b) than in panel (a), so the PPF shifts out more in panel (b).

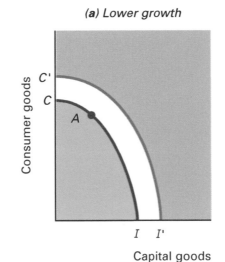

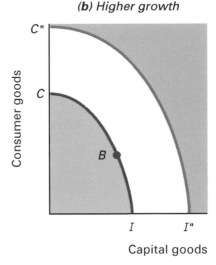

Per-Worker Production Function

The per-worker production function, PF, shows a direct relationship between the amount of capital per worker, k, and the output per worker, y. The bowed shape of PF reflects the law of diminishing marginal returns from capital, which holds that as more capital is added to a given number of workers, output per worker increases but at a diminishing rate and eventually could turn negative.

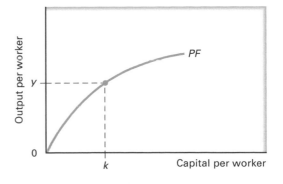

Impact of a Technological Breakthrough on the Per-Worker Production Function

A technological breakthrough increases output per worker at each level of capital per worker. Better technology makes workers more productive. This is shown by a rotation upward in the per-worker production function from *PF* to *PF'*. An improvement in the rules of the game would have a similar effect.

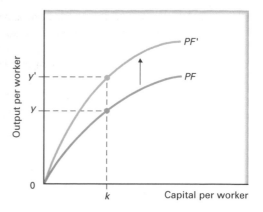

LO2 Describe productivity and growth in practice.
Industrial market countries, or *developed countries*, make up about 16 percent of the world's population, yet they produce nearly three-quarters of the world's output. An important source of productivity is human capital—the skill, experience, and education of workers. In 2012, 57 percent of Canadians aged 25 to 34 had a postsecondary degree or diploma, second highest in the world.

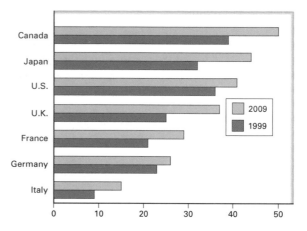

LO3 Discuss other issues of technology and growth.
Technological change sometimes costs jobs in the short run when workers fail to adjust. Over time, however, most displaced workers find other jobs, sometimes in new industries created by technological change. There is no evidence that, in the long run, technological change increases unemployment in the economy.

Some governments use industrial policy in an effort to nurture the industries and technologies of the future, giving domestic industries an advantage over foreign competitors. But critics are wary of the government's ability to pick the winning technologies of the future.

Convergence is a theory predicting that the standards of living around the world will grow more alike, as poorer countries catch up with richer ones. Some Asian countries that had been poor are catching up with the leaders, but many poor countries around the world have failed to close the gap.

Canadian Productivity Is Lower Than in Other Countries

Productivity fell among all Organisation for Economic Co-operation and Development (OECD) countries during the 1970s, but rebounded in most countries since then, although not in Canada. One possible explanation of Canada's lagging productivity numbers is that Statistics Canada has been underestimating productivity here.

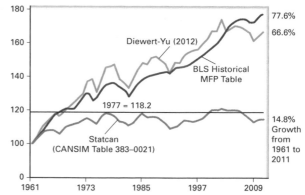

CHAPTER IN REVIEW

9 Aggregate Expenditure and Aggregate Demand

consumption function the relationship in the economy between consumption and income, other things constant

marginal propensity to consume (MPC) the fraction of a change in income that is spent on consumption; the change in consumption divided by the change in income that caused it

net wealth the value of all assets minus liabilities

life-cycle model of consumption and saving young people borrow, middle-agers pay off debts and save, and older people draw down their savings; on average, net savings over a lifetime is usually little or nothing

investment function the relationship between the amount businesses plan to invest and the economy's income, other things constant

autonomous a term that means "independent"; for example, autonomous investment is independent of income

government purchase function the relationship between government purchases and the economy's income, other things constant

net export function the relationship between net exports and the economy's income, other things constant

aggregate expenditure line a relationship tracing, for a given price level, spending at each level of income, or real GDP; the total of $C + I + G + (X - IM)$ at each level of income, or real GDP

income-expenditure model a relationship that shows how much people plan to spend at each income level; this model identifies, for a given price level, where the amount people plan to spend equals the amount produced in the economy

simple spending multiplier the ratio of a change in real GDP demanded to the initial change in spending that brought it about; the numerical value of the simple spending multiplier is $1/(1 - MPC)$; called "simple" because only consumption varies with income

Chapter Equation

Simple Spending Multiplier =

$$\frac{1}{1 - MPC}$$

LO1 **Explain the role of consumption.** The most predictable and most useful relationship in macroeconomics is between consumption and income. The more people have available to spend, the more they spend on consumption, other things constant. The consumption function shows the link between consumption and income in the economy. The slope of the consumption function reflects the marginal propensity to consume, which is the change in consumption divided by the change in income. Increases in net wealth, higher price levels, increases in interest rates, and expectations about future incomes are all factors that can cause consumers to change the amount they want to spend at each income level.

The Consumption Function

The consumption function, C, shows the relationship between consumption and disposable income, other things constant.

Marginal Propensity to Consume

The slope of the consumption function equals the marginal propensity to consume. For the straight-line consumption function the slope is the same at all levels of income and is given by the change in consumption divided by the change in disposable income that causes it. Thus, the marginal propensity to consume equals $\Delta C/\Delta DI$, or $40/50 = 4/5$.

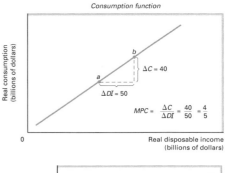

Shifts of the Consumption Function

A downward shift of the consumption function, such as from C to C'', can be caused by a decrease in wealth, an increase in the price level, an unfavourable change in consumer expectations, or an increase in the interest rate. An upward shift, such as from C to C', can be caused by an increase in wealth, a decrease in the price level, a favourable change in expectations, or a decrease in the interest rate.

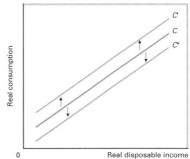

LO2 **Analyze the effects of investment, government purchases, and net exports.** Investment consists of spending on (1) new factories, office buildings, malls, and new equipment, such as computers; (2) new housing; and (3) net increases to inventories. Investment spending depends negatively on the interest rate and positively on business expectations. We assume that there is no relationship between investment spending and income. Decisions about government spending, such as highway construction or hiring new teachers, do not depend directly on income. In our simplest model of aggregate expenditure, we assume that net exports do not depend on income either. In reality, net exports and income are inversely related since an increase in Canadian income leads to an increase in imports and a corresponding decrease in net exports.

LO3 Explain how total spending in the economy changes with income.

The aggregate expenditure line indicates, for a given price level, spending plans at each income level. At a given price level, real GDP demanded is found where the amount that people plan to spend equals the amount produced.

Deriving the Real GDP Demanded for a Given Price Level

Real GDP demanded for a given price level is found where aggregate expenditure equals aggregate output—that is, where spending equals the amount produced, or real GDP. This occurs at point *e*, where the aggregate expenditure line intersects the 45-degree line.

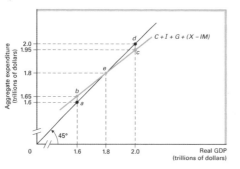

LO4 Discuss how the simple spending multiplier accounts for changes in spending plans.

The spending multiplier indicates the multiple by which a change in the amount people plan to spend changes real GDP demanded. The simple spending multiplier developed in this chapter is $1/(1 - MPC)$. The larger the MPC, the more is spent and the less is saved, so the larger the simple spending multiplier. This multiplier is called "simple" because only consumption changes with changes in income.

Tracking the Rounds of Spending Following a $20-Billion Increase in Investment (billions of dollars)

Round	New Spending This Round	Cumulative New Spending	New Saving This Round	Cumulative New Saving
1	20	20	—	—
2	16	36	4	4
3	12.8	48.8	3.2	7.2
⋮	⋮	⋮	⋮	⋮
10	2.68	89.26	0.67	17.32
⋮	⋮	⋮	⋮	⋮
∞	0	100	0	20

LO5 Describe the aggregate demand curve.

A higher price level causes a downward shift of the aggregate expenditure line, leading to a lower real GDP demanded. A lower price level causes an upward shift of the aggregate expenditure line, increasing real GDP demanded. By tracing the impact of price changes on real GDP demanded, we can derive an aggregate demand curve.

The aggregate expenditure line and the aggregate demand curve portray real output from different perspectives. The aggregate expenditure line shows, for a given price level, how much people plan to spend at each income level. Real GDP demanded is found where spending equals income, or real GDP. The aggregate demand curve shows, for various price levels, the quantities of real GDP demanded. At a given price level, a change in spending plans shifts the aggregate demand curve.

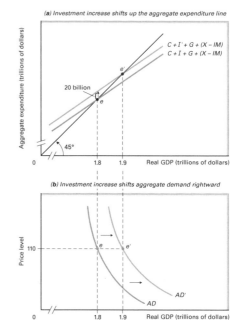

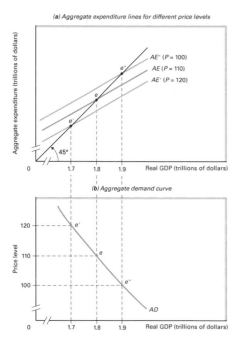

Changing the Price Level to Find the Aggregate Demand Curve

At the initial price level of 110, the aggregate expenditure line is *AE*, which identifies real GDP demanded of $1.8 trillion. This combination of a price level of 110 and a real GDP demanded of $1.8 trillion determines one combination (point *e*) on the aggregate demand curve in panel (b). At the higher price level of 120, the aggregate expenditure line shifts down to *AE′*, and real GDP demanded falls to $1.7 trillion. This price-quantity combination is plotted as point *e′* in panel (b). At the lower price level of 100, the aggregate expenditure line shifts up to *AE″*, which increases real GDP demanded. This combination is plotted as point *e″* in panel (b). Connecting points *e*, *e′*, and *e″* in panel (b) yields the downward-sloping aggregate demand curve, which shows the inverse relation between price and real GDP demanded.

A Shift of the Aggregate Expenditure Line That Shifts the Aggregate Demand Curve

A shift of the aggregate expenditure line at a given price level shifts the aggregate demand curve. In panel (a), an increase in investment of $20 billion, with the price level constant at 110, causes the aggregate expenditure line to increase from $C + I + G + (X − IM)$ to $C + I′ + G (X − IM)$. As a result, real GDP demanded increases from $1.8 trillion to $1.9 trillion. In panel (b), the aggregate demand curve has shifted from *AD* out to *AD′*. At the prevailing price level of 110, real GDP demanded has increased by $0.1 trillion.

10 Aggregate Supply

nominal wage the wage measured in dollars of the year in question; the dollar amount on a paycheque

real wage the wage measured in dollars of constant purchasing power; the wage measured in terms of the quantity of goods and services it buys

potential output the economy's maximum sustainable output, given the supply of resources, technology, and rules of the game; the output level when there are no surprises about the price level

natural rate of unemployment the unemployment rate when the economy produces its potential output

short run in macroeconomics, a period during which some resource prices, especially those for labour, are fixed by explicit or implicit agreements

short-run aggregate supply (SRAS) curve a curve that shows a direct relationship between the actual price level and real GDP supplied in the short run, other things constant, including the expected price level

short-run equilibrium the price level and real GDP that result when the aggregate demand curve intersects the short-run aggregate supply curve

expansionary gap the amount by which actual output in the short run exceeds the economy's potential output

long run in macroeconomics, a period during which wage contracts and resource price agreements can be renegotiated; there are no surprises about the economy's actual price level

long-run equilibrium the price level and real GDP that occurs when (1) the actual price level equals the expected price level, (2) real GDP supplied equals potential output, and (3) real GDP supplied equals real GDP demanded

recessionary gap the amount by which actual output in the short run falls short of the economy's potential output

long-run aggregate supply (LRAS) curve depends on the supply of resources in the economy, the level of technology, and the production incentives provided by the formal and informal institutions of the economic system

coordination failure a situation in which workers and employers fail to achieve an outcome that all would prefer

supply shocks unexpected events that affect aggregate supply, sometimes only temporarily

LO1 Explain how aggregate supply operates in the short run.
The short-run aggregate supply is based on resource demand and supply decisions that reflect the expected price level. If the price level turns out as expected, the economy produces its potential output. If the price level exceeds expectations, short-run output exceeds the economy's potential, creating an expansionary gap. If the price level is below expectations, short-run output falls short of the economy's potential, creating a contractionary gap.

Short-Run Aggregate Supply Curve

The short-run aggregate supply curve is drawn based on a given expected price level, in this case, 110. Point *a* shows that if the actual price level equals the expected price level of 110, producers supply potential output. If the actual price level exceeds 110, firms supply more than potential. If the actual price level is below 110, firms supply less than potential. Output levels that fall short of the economy's potential are shaded red; output levels that exceed the economy's potential are shaded blue.

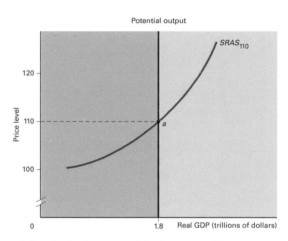

LO2 Discuss short-run aggregate supply in relation to the long run.
Output can exceed the economy's potential in the short run, but in the long run, higher nominal wages will be negotiated at the earliest opportunity. This increases the cost of production, shifting the short-run aggregate supply curve leftward along the aggregate demand curve until the economy produces its potential output.

Long-Run Adjustment When the Price Level Exceeds Expectations

If the expected price level is 110, the short-run aggregate supply curve is $SRAS_{110}$. If the actual price level turns out as expected, the quantity supplied is the potential output of $1.8 trillion. Given the aggregate demand curve shown here, the price level ends up higher than expected, and output exceeds potential, as shown by the short-run equilibrium at point *b*. The amount by which actual output exceeds the economy's potential output is called the expansionary gap. In the long run, price level expectations and nominal wages will be revised upward. Costs will rise and the short-run aggregate supply curve will shift leftward to $SRAS_{120}$. Eventually, the economy will move to long-run equilibrium at point *c*, thus closing the expansionary gap.

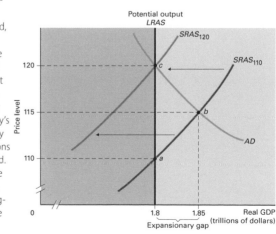

beneficial supply shocks unexpected events that increase aggregate supply, sometimes only temporarily

adverse supply shocks unexpected events that reduce aggregate supply, sometimes only temporarily

hysteresis the theory that the natural rate of unemployment depends in part on the recent history of unemployment; high unemployment rates increase the natural rate of unemployment

Long-Run Aggregate Supply Curve

In the long run, when the actual price level equals the expected price level, the economy produces its potential. In the long run, $1.8 trillion in real GDP will be supplied regardless of the actual price level. As long as wages and prices are flexible, the economy's potential GDP is consistent with any price level. Thus shifts of the aggregate demand curve will, in the long run, not affect potential output. The long-run aggregate supply curve, *LRAS*, is a vertical line at potential GDP.

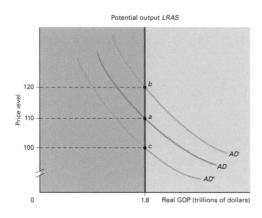

Effect of a Gradual Increase in Resources on Aggregate Supply

A gradual increase in the supply of resources increases the potential GDP—in this case, from $1.8 trillion to $1.85 trillion. The long-run aggregate supply curve shifts to the right.

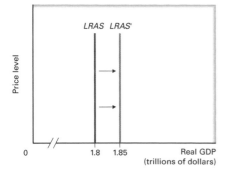

Long-Run Adjustment When the Price Level Is Below Expectations

When the actual price level is below expectations, as indicated by the intersection of the aggregate demand curve *AD″* with the short-run aggregate supply curve *SRAS₁₁₀*, short-run equilibrium occurs at point *d*. Production below the economy's potential opens a recessionary gap. If prices and wages are flexible enough in the long run, nominal wages will be renegotiated lower. As resource costs fall, the short-run aggregate supply curve eventually shifts rightward to *SRAS₁₀₀* and the economy moves to long-run equilibrium at point *e*, with output increasing to the potential level of $1.8 trillion.

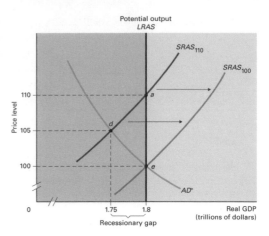

LO3 **Analyze shifts of the aggregate supply curve.** If output in the short run is less than the economy's potential and if wages and prices are flexible enough, lower nominal wages will reduce production costs in the long run. These lower costs shift the short-run aggregate supply curve rightward along the aggregate demand curve until the economy produces its potential output.

Evidence suggests that when output exceeds the economy's potential, nominal wages and the price level increase. But there is less evidence that nominal wages and the price level fall when output is below the economy's potential. Wages appear to be "sticky" in the downward direction. What usually closes a recessionary gap is an increase in aggregate demand.

The long-run aggregate supply curve, or the economy's potential output, depends on the amount and quality of resources available, the state of technology, and formal and informal institutions, such as patent laws and business practices, that shape production incentives. Increases in resource availability, improvements in technology, or institutional changes that provide more attractive production incentives increase aggregate supply and potential output.

Supply shocks are unexpected, often temporary changes in aggregate supply. Beneficial supply shocks increase output, sometimes only temporarily. Adverse supply shocks reduce output and increase the price level, a combination called stagflation. Adverse supply shocks may be temporary.

Effects of a Beneficial Supply Shock on Aggregate Supply

Given the aggregate demand curve, a beneficial supply shock that has a lasting effect, such as a breakthrough in technology, will permanently shift both the short-run aggregate supply curve and the long-run aggregate supply curve, or potential output. A beneficial supply shock lowers the price level and increases output, as reflected by the change in equilibrium from point *a* to point *b*. A temporary beneficial supply shock, such as would result from an unusually favourable growing season, will shift the aggregate supply curves only temporarily. If the next growing season returns to normal, the aggregate supply curves will return to their original equilibrium position at point *a*.

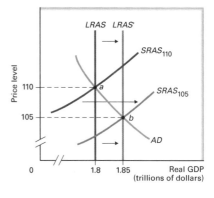

Effects of an Adverse Supply Shock on Aggregate Supply

Given the aggregate demand curve, an adverse supply shock, such as an increased threat of terrorism, shifts the short-run and long-run aggregate supply curves to the left, increasing the price level and reducing real GDP, a movement called stagflation. This change is shown by the move in equilibrium from point *a* to point *c*. If the shock is just temporary, the curves will be temporary.

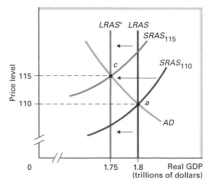

11 Fiscal Policy

fiscal policy focuses on the effects of taxing and public spending on aggregate economic activity

automatic stabilizers structural features of government spending and taxation that reduce fluctuations in disposable income, and thus consumption, over the business cycle

discretionary fiscal policy the deliberate manipulation of government purchases, taxation, and transfer payments to promote macroeconomic goals, such as full employment, price stability, and economic growth

simple tax multiplier the ratio of a change in real GDP demanded to the initial change in autonomous net taxes that brought it about; the numerical value of the simple tax multiplier is $-MPC/(1 - MPC)$

expansionary fiscal policy an increase in government purchases, decrease in net taxes, or some combination of the two aimed at increasing aggregate demand enough to reduce unemployment and return the economy to its potential output; fiscal policy used to close a recessionary gap

contractionary fiscal policy a decrease in government purchases, increase in net taxes, or some combination of the two aimed at reducing aggregate demand enough to return the economy to potential output without worsening inflation; fiscal policy used to close an expansionary gap

classical economists a group of 18th- and 19th-century economists who believed that economic downturns corrected themselves through natural market forces; thus they believed the economy was self-correcting and needed no government intervention

political business cycles economic fluctuations that occur when discretionary policy is manipulated for political gain

permanent income income that individuals expect to receive on average over the long term

annually balanced budget budget philosophy prior to the Great Depression; aimed at matching annual revenues with outlays, except during times of war

cyclically balanced budget a budget philosophy calling for budget deficits during recessions to be financed by budget surpluses during expansions

functional finance a budget philosophy using fiscal policy to achieve the economy's potential GDP, rather than balancing budgets either annually or over the business cycle

LO1 **Explain the theory of fiscal policy.** The tools of fiscal policy are automatic stabilizers and discretionary fiscal measures. Automatic stabilizers, such as the federal income tax, once implemented, operate year after year without parliamentary action. Discretionary fiscal policy results from specific legislation about government spending, taxation, and transfers. If that legislation becomes permanent, then discretionary fiscal policies often become automatic stabilizers.

Effect of a $10-Billion Increase in Government Purchases on Aggregate Expenditure and Real GDP Demanded

As a result of a $10-billion increase in government purchases, the aggregate expenditure line shifts up by $10 billion, increasing the level of real GDP demanded by $50 billion. This model assumes the price level remains unchanged.

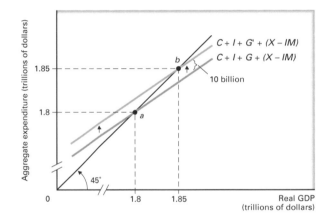

Effect of a $10-Billion Decrease in Net Taxes on Aggregate Expenditure and Real GDP Demanded

As a result of a decrease in net taxes of $10 billion, consumers, who are assumed to have a marginal propensity to consume of 0.8, spend $8 billion more and save $2 billion more at every level of GDP. The consumption function shifts up by $8 billion, as does the aggregate expenditure line. An $8-billion increase of the aggregate expenditure line eventually increases real GDP demanded by $40 billion. Keep in mind that the price level is assumed to remain constant during all this.

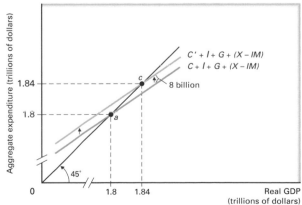

crowding out the displacement of interest-sensitive private investment that occurs when higher government deficits drive up market interest rates

crowding in the potential for government spending to stimulate private investment in an otherwise dead economy

national debt the net accumulation of federal budget deficits

Chapter Equations

Δ Real GDP Demanded

$$\Delta G \times \frac{1}{1 - MPC}$$

Δ Real GDP Demanded

$$(-MPC \times \Delta NT) \times \frac{1}{1-MPC}$$

Δ Real GDP Demanded

$$\Delta NT \times \frac{-MPC}{1 - MPC}$$

LO2 Describe how aggregate supply affects fiscal policy. An expansionary fiscal policy can close a recessionary gap by increasing government purchases, reducing net taxes, or both. Because the short-run aggregate supply curve slopes upward, an increase in aggregate demand raises both output and the price level in the short run. A contractionary fiscal policy can close an expansionary gap by reducing government purchases, increasing net taxes, or both. Fiscal policy that reduces aggregate demand to close an expansionary gap reduces both output and the price level.

Discretionary Fiscal Policy to Close a Recessionary Gap

The aggregate demand curve *AD* and the short-run aggregate supply curve, $SRAS_{110}$, intersect at point *e*. Output falls short of the economy's potential. The resulting contractionary gap is $50 billion. This gap could be closed by discretionary fiscal policy that increases aggregate demand by just the right amount. An increase in government purchases, a decrease in net taxes, or some combination could shift aggregate demand out to AD^*, moving the economy out to its potential output at e^*.

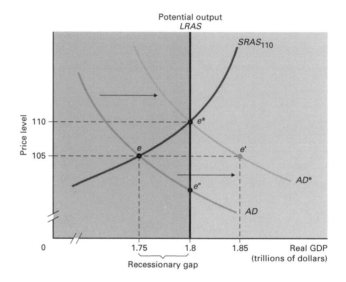

Discretionary Fiscal Policy to Close an Expansionary Gap

The aggregate demand curve *AD'* and the short-run aggregate supply curve, $SRAS_{110}$, intersect at point *e'*, resulting in an expansionary gap of $50 billion. Discretionary fiscal policy aimed at reducing aggregate demand by just the right amount could close this gap without inflation. An increase in net taxes, a decrease in government purchases, or some combination could shift the aggregate demand curve back to AD^* and move the economy back to potential output at point e^*.

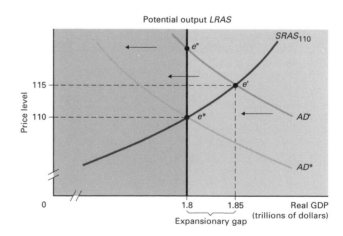

LO3 Discuss the evolution of fiscal policy. Fiscal policy focuses primarily on the demand side, not the supply side. The problems of the 1970s, however, resulted more from a decline of aggregate supply than from a decline of aggregate demand, so demand-side remedies seemed less effective.

The aggregate supply curve shifted left because of crop failures around the world, sharply higher OPEC-driven oil prices, and other adverse supply shocks. Demand-management policies are ill suited to cure stagflation because an increase of aggregate demand would increase inflation, whereas a decrease of aggregate demand would increase unemployment. Other concerns also caused policymakers and economists to question the effectiveness of discretionary fiscal policy. These concerns included the difficulty of estimating the natural rate of unemployment, the time lags involved in implementing fiscal policy, the distinction between current income and permanent income, and the possible feedback effects of fiscal policy on aggregate supply.

When Discretionary Fiscal Policy Overshoots Potential Output

If public officials underestimate the natural rate of unemployment, they may attempt to stimulate aggregate demand even if the economy is already producing its potential output, as at point a. This expansionary policy yields a short-run equilibrium at point b, where the price level and output are higher and unemployment is lower, so the policy appears to succeed. But the resulting expansionary gap will, in the long run, reduce the short-run aggregate supply curve from $SRAS_{110}$ to $SRAS_{120}$, eventually reducing output to its potential level of $1.8 billion while increasing the price level to 120. Thus attempts to increase production beyond potential GDP lead only to inflation in the long run.

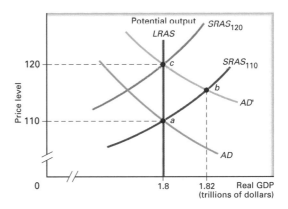

LO4 **Discuss the impact of the federal budget and debt.** Suppose the federal government increases spending without raising taxes, thereby increasing the budget deficit. How will this affect national saving, interest rates, and investment? An increase in the federal deficit reduces the supply of national saving, leading to higher interest rates. Higher interest rates discourage, or *crowd out*, some private investment, reducing the stimulating effect of the government's deficit. The extent of crowding out is a matter of debate. Some economists argue that although government deficits may displace some private sector borrowing, expansionary fiscal policy results in a net increase in aggregate demand, leading to greater output and employment in the short run. Others believe that the crowding out is more extensive, so borrowing from the public in this way results in little or no net increase in aggregate demand and output. Public spending merely substitutes for private spending. Although crowding out is likely to occur to some degree, there is another possibility. If the economy is operating well below its potential, the additional fiscal stimulus provided by a higher government deficit could encourage some firms to invest more. Recall that an important determinant of investment is business expectations. Government stimulus of a weak economy could put a sunny face on the business outlook. As expectations grow more favourable, firms become more willing to invest. This ability of government deficits to stimulate private investment is sometimes called crowding in, to distinguish it from crowding out.

Notes

12 Money and the Financial System

double coincidence of wants two traders are willing to exchange their products directly

money anything that is generally accepted in exchange for goods and services

medium of exchange anything that facilitates trade by being generally accepted by all parties in payment for goods or services

commodity money anything that serves both as money and as a commodity; money that has intrinsic value such as gold or silver coins

unit of account a common unit for measuring the value of each good or service

store of value anything that retains its purchasing power over time

Gresham's Law people tend to trade away inferior money and hoard the best

seigniorage the difference between the face value of money and the cost of supplying it; the "profit" from issuing money

token money money whose face value exceeds its cost of production

cheque a written order instructing the bank to pay someone from an amount deposited

fractional reserve banking system bank reserves amount to only a fraction of funds on deposit with the bank

bank notes originally, pieces of paper promising a specific amount of gold or silver to anyone who presented them to issuing banks for redemption; today, Bank of Canada notes are mere polymer money

representative or commodity-backed money bank notes that exchange for a specific commodity, such as gold

fiat money money not redeemable for any commodity; its status as money is conferred initially by government decree but eventually by common experience

legal tender Canadian currency that constitutes a valid and legal offer of payment of debt

financial intermediaries institutions such as banks, mortgage companies, and finance companies that serve as go-betweens, borrowing from people who have saved to make loans to others

depository institutions financial institutions that accept deposits from the public

LO1 **Discuss the evolution and functions of money.** Barter was the first form of exchange. As specialization grew, it became more difficult to discover the double coincidence of wants that barter required, bringing about the adoption of money. Anything that acquires a high degree of acceptability throughout an economy becomes money. The first monies were commodities, such as gold, then pieces of paper that could be redeemed for such commodities. As paper money became widely accepted, governments introduced fiat money—money by law or by government fiat. People accept fiat money because, through experience, they believe that other people will do so as well.

The value of money depends on what it buys. If money fails to serve as a medium of exchange, traders find other means of exchange. If a monetary system breaks down, more time must be devoted to exchange, leaving less time for production, so efficiency suffers. No machine increases an economy's productivity as much as properly functioning money .

Purchasing Power of $1.00 Measured in 2002 Constant Dollars

An increase in the price level over time reduces what $1.00 buys. The price level has risen every year since 1960, so the purchasing power of $1.00 (measured in 2002 constant dollars) has fallen from $6.45 in 1960 to $0.82 in 2012.

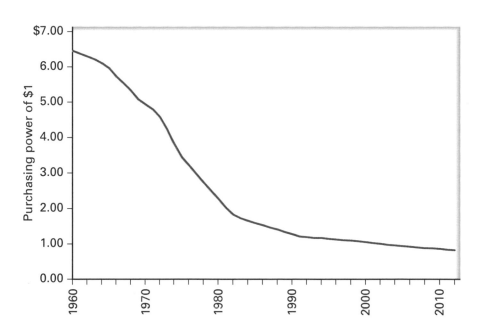

trust and mortgage loan companies (TMLs) financial institutions that provide trustee functions and specialize in making home mortgage loans

credit unions and caisses populaires (CUCPs) depository institutions that extend loans only to their "members"

Bank of Canada the central bank and monetary authority of Canada

reserves funds that banks use to satisfy the cash demands of their customers; reserves consist of cash held by banks plus deposits at the Bank of Canada

Governing Council the six-member group that makes decisions about open-market operations; consists of the governor, the senior deputy governor, and plus four deputy governors

open-market operations purchases and sales of government securities by the Bank of Canada in an effort to influence the money supply

subprime mortgage mortgage for a borrower with a not-so-good credit rating

mortgage-backed security a claim on payments made on the many mortgages bundled into this financial instrument

LO2 Discuss the role of financial institutions and the Bank of Canada.

Financial institutions, or intermediaries, earn a profit by paying a lower interest rate to savers than they charge borrowers. Of these, depository institutions, which obtain funds primarily through customer deposits, can be classified broadly into chartered banks, which hold most deposits in Canada; trust and mortgage loan companies, which specialize in home mortgage loans; and credit unions, which primarily finance loans for members' consumer purchases.

The Bank of Canada was established in 1934 by the Bank of Canada Act to regulate the banking system and issue the nation's currency. The Bank of Canada was authorized to ensure sufficient money and credit in the banking system to support a growing economy. The power to issue bank notes was taken away from chartered banks and turned over to the Bank of Canada. The Bank of Canada was also granted other powers: *to buy and sell government securities, and to extend loans to banks*. The Bank of Canada does not deal with the public directly. It may be thought of as a bankers' bank. It holds deposits of banks, just as depository institutions hold deposits of the public, and it extends loans to banks, just as depository institutions extend loans to the public. The Bank of Canada also holds chequing deposits for the Government of Canada.

Organization Chart of the Bank of Canada

Members of the Board of Directors are appointed by the Board and approved by the federal cabinet.

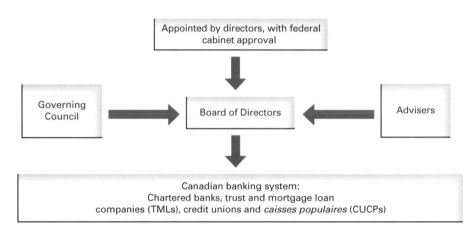

13 Banking and the Money Supply

chequable deposits bank deposits that allow the account owner to write cheques to third parties; ATM or debit cards can also access these deposits and transmit them electronically

money aggregates measures of the economy's money supply

M1+ the narrow measure of the money supply, consisting of currency and coins held by the nonbanking public, traveller's cheques and chequable deposits at chartered banks, trust and mortgage loans companies (TMLs), and credit unions and caisses populaires (CUCPs)

savings deposits deposits that earn interest but have no specific maturity date

time deposits deposits that earn a fixed interest rate if held for the specified period, which can range from several months to several years; also called certificates of deposit

M2 a money aggregate consisting of currency (including coins) held by the nonbanking public and traveller's cheques, personal and nonpersonal chequable deposits as well as savings deposits, and personal time deposits held at chartered banks

M2+ a money aggregate consisting of M2 plus similar deposits at TMLs and CUCPs, life insurance company individual annuities, personal deposits at government-owned saving institutions, and money market mutual fund accounts

debit card a card that taps directly into the depositor's bank account to fund purchases; also called a cheque card, and often doubles as an ATM card

asymmetric information a situation in which one side of the market has more reliable information than the other side

net worth assets minus liabilities; also called owners' equity

balance sheet a financial statement at a given point in time that shows assets on one side and liabilities and net worth on the other side; because assets must equal liabilities plus net worth, the two sides of the statement must be in balance

asset anything of value that is owned

liability anything that is owed to other people or institutions

desired/required reserves the dollar amount of reserves a bank desires or is obligated by regulation to hold as cash in the bank's vault or on account at the central bank

desired/required reserve ratio the ratio of reserves to deposits that banks desire or are obligated by regulation to hold

LO1 **Examine definitions of money aggregates.** The money supply is narrowly defined as M1, which consists of currency held by the nonbanking public plus chequable deposits at chartered banks, trust and mortgage loans companies (TMLs), credit unions and caisses populaires (CUCPs), and traveller's cheques. A broader money aggregate, M2+, includes M2 plus deposits at TMLs and CUCPs, life insurance company individual annuities, personal deposits at government-owned saving institutions, and money market mutual funds.

Measures of the Money Supply in Billions of Dollars (September 2013)

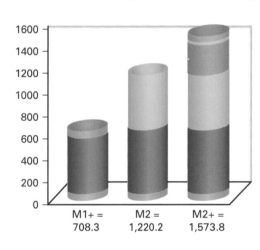

- Personal deposits at government-owned saving institutions ($11.3 billion)
- Life insurance company individual annuities ($42.4 billion)
- Money market mutual funds ($27.1 billion)
- TMLs & CUCPs total deposits ($272.7 billion)
- Savings & time deposits ($581.7 billion)
- TMLs & CUCPs chequable deposits ($69.8 billion)
- Chartered banks chequable deposits ($574.1 billion)
- Currency plus traveller's cheques ($64.4 billion)

M1+ = 708.3 M2 = 1,220.2 M2+ = 1,573.8

LO2 **Explain how banks work.** Banks are unlike other financial intermediaries because they can turn a borrower's IOU into money—they can create money. Banks also evaluate loan applications and diversify portfolios of assets to reduce the risk to any one saver. In acquiring portfolios of assets, banks try to maximize profit while maintaining enough liquidity to satisfy depositors' requests for money. Assets that earn the bank more interest are usually less liquid.

LO3 **Describe how banks create money.** Any single bank can expand the money supply by the amount of its excess reserves. For the banking system as a whole, however, the maximum expansion of the money supply equals a multiple of fresh bank reserves. The simple money multiplier is the reciprocal of the reserve ratio, or $1/r$. This multiplier is reduced to the extent that (a) banks allow excess reserves to remain idle, (b) borrowers sit on their proceeds, and (c) the public withdraws cash from the banking system and holds it.

excess reserves bank reserves exceeding required reserves

liquidity a measure of the ease with which an asset can be converted into money without a significant loss of value

overnight money market a market for overnight lending and borrowing of reserves among banks; the interbank market for reserves

overnight rate the interest rate charged in the overnight money market; the interest rate banks charge one another for overnight borrowing; the Bank of Canada target interest rate

money multiplier the multiple by which the money supply changes as a result of a change in fresh reserves in the banking system

simple money multiplier the reciprocal of the desired reserve ratio, or $1/r$; the maximum multiple of fresh reserves by which the money supply can increase

open-market purchase the purchase of Canada government bonds by the Bank of Canada to increase the money supply

open-market sale the sale of Canada government bonds by the Bank of Canada to reduce the money supply

bank rate the interest rate the Bank of Canada charges banks that borrow reserves from it

LO4 **Discuss the Bank of Canada's tools for monetary control.** The key to changes in the money supply is the Bank of Canada's impact on excess reserves in the banking system. To increase excess reserves and thus increase the money supply, the Bank of Canada can buy Canada government bonds, reduce the bank rate, or shift government deposits from the Bank of Canada to commercial banks. To reduce excess reserves and thus reduce the money supply, the Bank of Canada can sell Canada government bonds, increase the bank rate, or shift government deposits from commercial banks to the Bank of Canada.

Chapter Equations

Assets

Assets = Liabilities + Net worth

Simple Money Multiplier

$$\Delta \text{ money supply} = \Delta \text{ fresh reserves} \times 1/r$$

CHAPTER IN REVIEW

14 Monetary Theory and Policy in an Open Economy

demand for money the relationship between the interest rate and how much money people want to hold

equation of exchange the quantity of money, M, multiplied by its velocity, V, equals nominal GDP, which is the product of the price level, P, and real GDP, Y; or $M \times V = P \times Y$

velocity of money the average number of times per year each dollar is used to purchase final goods and services

quantity theory of money if the velocity of money is stable, or at least predictable, changes in the money supply have predictable effects on nominal GDP

Chapter Equations

Effects of an Increase in the Money Supply

$$M \uparrow \to i \downarrow \to I \uparrow \to AD \uparrow \to Y \uparrow$$

Equation of Exchange

$$M \times V = P \times Y$$

Velocity

$$V = \frac{P \times Y}{M}$$

Total Spending

$$M \times V$$

Total Receipts

$$P \times Y$$

LO1 Describe the relationship between the demand and supply of money. The
opportunity cost of holding money is the higher interest forgone by not holding other financial assets instead. Along a given money demand curve, the quantity of money demanded relates inversely to the interest rate. The demand for money curve shifts rightward as a result of an increase in the price level, an increase in real GDP, or an increase in both.

Demand for Money

The money demand curve, D_m, slopes downward. As the interest rate falls, other things constant, so does the opportunity cost of holding money; the quantity of money demanded increases.

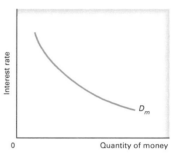

Effect of an Increase in the Money Supply

Because the supply of money is determined by the Bank of Canada, it can be represented by a vertical line. At point a, the intersection of supply of money, S_m, and the demand for money, D_m, determines the market interest rate, i. Following an increase in the money supply to S'_m, the quantity of money supplied exceeds the quantity demanded at the original interest rate, i. People attempt to exchange money for bonds or other financial assets. In doing so, they push down the interest rate to i', where quantity demanded equals the new quantity supplied. This new equilibrium occurs at point b.

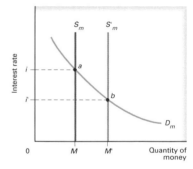

LO2 Explain how changes in the money supply affect aggregate demand in the
short run. The Bank of Canada determines the supply of money, which is assumed to be independent of the interest rate. The intersection of the supply and demand curves for money determines the market interest rate. In the short run, an increase in the supply of money reduces the interest rate, which increases investment. This boosts aggregate demand, which increases real output and the price level.

Effects of an Increase in the Money Supply on Interest Rates, Investment, and Aggregate Demand

In panel (a), an increase in the money supply drives the interest rate down to i'. With the cost of borrowing lower, the amount invested increases from I to I', as shown in panel (b). This sets off the spending multiplier process, so the aggregate output demanded at price level P increases from Y to Y'. The increase is shown by the shift of the aggregate demand curve to the right in panel (c).

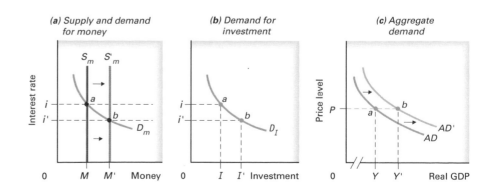

Expansionary Monetary Policy to Close a Recessionary Gap

At point *a*, the economy is producing less than its potential in the short run, resulting in a contractionary gap of $50 billion. If the Bank of Canada increases the money supply by just the right amount, the aggregate demand curve shifts rightward from *AD* to *AD'*. A short-run and long-run equilibrium is established at point *b*, with the price level at 110 and output at the potential level of $1.8 trillion.

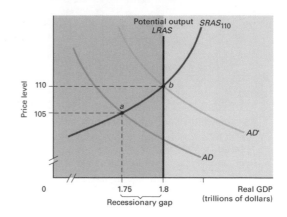

LO3 Explain how changes in the money supply affect aggregate demand in the long run.

The long-run approach focuses on the role of money through the equation of exchange, which states that the quantity of money, M, multiplied by velocity, V, the average number of times each dollar gets spent on final goods and services, equals the price level, P, multiplied by real output, Y. So $M \times V = P \times Y$. Because the aggregate supply curve in the long run is a vertical line at the economy's potential output, a change in the money supply affects the price level but not real output.

In the Long Run, an Increase in the Money Supply Results in a Higher Price Level, or Inflation

The quantity theory of money predicts that if velocity is stable, then an increase in the supply of money in the long run results in a higher price level, or inflation. Because the long-run aggregate supply curve is fixed, increases in the money supply affect only the price level, not real output.

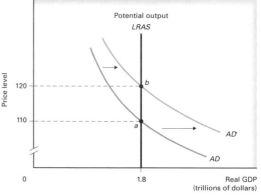

LO4 Evaluate targets for monetary policy.

Between World War II and 1975, the Bank of Canada attempted to stabilize interest rates. Stable interest rates were viewed as a prerequisite for an attractive investment environment and, thus, for a stable economy. During the late 1970s and early 1980s, the Bank paid more attention to growth in money aggregates. To pursue its main goal of inflation targeting, the Bank of Canada adjusts the target overnight rate, raising the rate to prevent higher inflation and lowering the rate to stimulate economic growth.

For a few years, the Bank of Canada focused on changes in the money supply as a target for monetary policy in the short run. Because M1 velocity became so unstable during the 1980s, the Bank terminated the policy in 1982. Since then, the equation of exchange has been considered more of a rough guide linking changes in the money supply to inflation in the long run. The Bank of Canada money aggregates now include M1+, M1++, M2, and M2++.

Targeting Interest Rates Versus Targeting the Money Supply

An increase in the price level or in real GDP, with velocity stable, shifts rightward the money demand curve from D_m to D'_m. If the Bank of Canada holds the money supply at S_m, the interest rate will rise from i (at point e) to i' (at point e'). Alternatively, the Bank of Canada could hold the interest rate constant by increasing the supply of money to S'_m. The Bank of Canada may choose any point along the money demand curve D'_m.

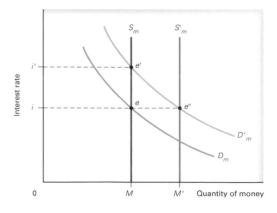

14-2

15 Macro Policy Debate: Active or Passive?

recognition lag the time needed to identify a macroeconomic problem and assess its seriousness

decision-making lag the time needed to decide what to do once a macroeconomic problem has been identified

implementation lag the time needed to introduce a change in monetary or fiscal policy

effectiveness lag the time needed for changes in monetary or fiscal policy to affect the economy

rational expectations a school of thought that argues people form expectations based on all available information, including the likely future actions of government policymakers

time-inconsistency problem when policymakers have an incentive to announce one policy to influence expectations but then pursue a different policy once those expectations have been formed and acted on

cold turkey the announcement and execution of tough measures to reduce high inflation

inflation target commitment of central bankers to keep inflation below a certain rate for the next year or two

Phillips curve a curve showing possible combinations of the inflation rate and the unemployment rate

short-run Phillips curve based on an expected inflation rate, a curve that reflects an inverse relationship between the inflation rate and the unemployment rate

LO1 **Compare an active policy and a passive policy.** Advocates of active policy view the private sector—particularly fluctuations in investment—as the primary source of economic instability in the economy. Activists argue that achieving potential output through natural market forces can be slow and painful, so the Bank of Canada or federal government should stimulate aggregate demand when actual output falls below potential.

Advocates of passive policy argue that the economy has enough natural resiliency to return to potential output within a reasonable period if upset by some shock. They point to the variable and uncertain lags associated with discretionary policy as reason enough to steer clear of active intervention.

Closing a Recessionary Gap

At point *a* in both panels, the economy is in short-run equilibrium, with unemployment exceeding its natural rate. According to the passive approach, shown in panel (a), high unemployment eventually causes wages to fall, reducing the cost of doing business. The decline in costs shifts the short-run aggregate supply curve rightward from $SRAS_{110}$ to $SRAS_{100}$, moving the economy to its potential output at point *b*. In panel (b), the government employs an active approach to shift the aggregate demand curve from *AD* to *AD'*. If the active policy works perfectly, the economy moves to its potential output at point *c*.

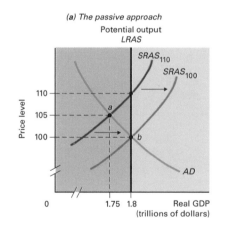

(a) The passive approach

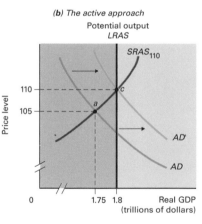

(b) The active approach

Closing an Expansionary Gap

At point *d* in both panels, the economy is in short-run equilibrium, producing $1.85 trillion, which exceeds the economy's potential output. Unemployment is below its natural rate. In the passive approach reflected in panel (a), the government makes no change in policy, so natural market forces eventually bring about a higher negotiated wage, increasing firm costs and shifting the short-run supply curve leftward to $SRAS_{120}$. The new equilibrium at point *e* results in a higher price level and lower output and employment. An active policy reduces aggregate demand, shifting the equilibrium in panel (b) from point *d* to point *c*, thus closing the expansionary gap without increasing the price level.

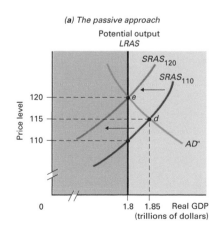

(a) The passive approach

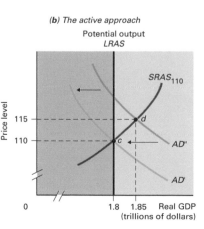

(b) The active approach

long-run Phillips curve a vertical line drawn at the economy's natural rate of unemployment that traces equilibrium points that can occur when workers and employers have the time to adjust fully to any unexpected change in aggregate demand

natural rate hypothesis the natural rate of unemployment is largely independent of the stimulus provided by monetary or fiscal policy

LO2 **Consider the role of expectations.** The theory of rational expectations holds that people form expectations based on all available information, including past behaviour by public officials. According to the rational expectations school, government policies are mostly anticipated by the public, and therefore have less effect than unexpected policies.

LO3 **Discuss policy rules versus discretion.** The active approach views the economy as unstable and in need of discretionary policy to eliminate excess unemployment. The passive approach, however, suggests that discretionary policy is not necessary and may even be harmful. The passive approach suggests that the government should follow clear and predictable policies and avoid discretionary intervention to stimulate or dampen aggregate demand. Passive policies are reflected in automatic fiscal stabilizers and in explicit monetary rules, such as keeping inflation below a certain rate.

LO4 **Explain the Phillips curve.** At one time, public officials thought they faced a stable trade-off between higher unemployment and higher inflation. More recent research suggests that if there is a trade-off, it exists only in the short run, not in the long run. The hypothetical Phillips curve illustrates the relationship between inflation and unemployment. Expansionary fiscal or monetary policies may stimulate output and employment in the short run. But if the economy is already at or near its potential output, these expansionary policies, in the long run, result only in more inflation.

Hypothetical Phillips Curve

The Phillips curve shows an inverse relation between unemployment and inflation. Points *a* and *b* lie on the Phillips curve and represent alternative combinations of inflation and unemployment that are attainable as long as the curve itself does not shift. Points *c* and *d* are off the curve.

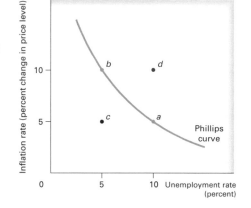

Aggregate Supply Curves and Phillips Curves in the Short Run and Long Run

If people expect a price level of 103, which is 3 percent higher than the current level, and if *AD* turns out to be the aggregate demand curve, then the price level is 103 and output is at its potential.

Point *a* in both panels represents this situation. Unemployment is the natural rate, assumed to be 6 percent in panel (b). If aggregate demand turns out to be greater than expected (*AD'* instead of *AD*), the economy in the short run will be at point *b* in panel (a), where the price level of 105 will exceed expectations and output will exceed its potential. The resulting higher inflation and lower unemployment are shown as point *b* in panel (b). If aggregate demand turns out to be less than expected (*AD'* instead of AD), short-run equilibrium will be at point *c* in panel (a), where the price level of 101 will be lower than expected and output will be short of potential. Lower inflation and higher unemployment are shown as point *c* in panel (b). In panel (b), points *a, b,* and *c* trace a short-run Phillips curve. In the long run, the actual price level equals the expected price level. Output is at the potential level, $1.8 trillion, in panel (a). Unemployment is at the natural rate, 6 percent, in panel (b). Points *a, d,* and *e* depict long-run points in each panel. In panel (a) these points trace potential output, or long-run aggregate supply. In panel (b), these points trace a long-run Phillips curve.

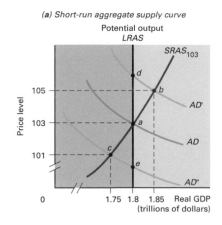

(a) *Short-run aggregate supply curve*

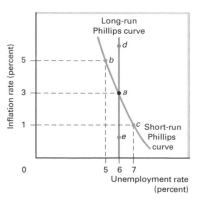

(b) *Short-run and long-run Phillips curves*

16 International Finance

balance on goods and services the portion of a country's balance-of-payments account that measures the value of a country's exports of goods and services minus the value of its imports of goods and services

net investment income from abroad investment earnings by Canadian residents from their foreign assets minus investment earnings by foreigners from their assets in Canada

net unilateral transfers abroad the unilateral transfers (gifts and grants) received from abroad by Canadian residents minus the unilateral transfers Canadian residents send abroad

balance on current account the portion of the balance-of-payments account that measures that country's balance on goods and services, net investment income from abroad, plus net unilateral transfers abroad

financial account the record of a country's international transactions involving purchases or sales of financial and real assets

exchange rate the price measured in one country's currency of purchasing one unit of another country's currency

currency depreciation with respect to the dollar, an increase in the number of dollars needed to purchase one unit of foreign exchange in a flexible rate system

currency appreciation with respect to the dollar, a decrease in the number of dollars needed to purchase one unit of foreign exchange in a flexible rate system

LO1 **Explain how the balance of payments works.** The balance of payments reflects all economic transactions between one country and the rest of the world. The current account measures flows from (a) goods; (b) services, including consulting and tourism; (c) income from holdings of foreign assets; and (d) unilateral transfers, or public and private transfer payments to and from foreign residents. The financial account measures international transactions in real and financial assets.

Canada's Balance of Payments for 2013 (millions of dollars)

Current Account	
1. Merchandise exports	+478,975
2. Merchandise imports	−486,306
3. Merchandise trade balance (1 + 2)	−7,331
4. Service exports	+86,761
5. Service imports	−111,308
6. Goods and services balance (3 + 4 + 5)	−31,878
7. Net investment income from abroad	−23,785
8. Net unilateral transfers	−2,889
9. Current account balance (6 + 7 + 8)	−58,552
Financial Account	
10. Change in Canadian-owned assets abroad	−65,875
11. Change in foreign-owned assets in Canada	+124,203
12. Financial account balance (10 + 11)	+58,328
13. Statistical discrepancy	−224
TOTAL (9 + 12 + 13)	**0.0**

Canada's Merchandise Trade since 1981

Merchandise Export

Merchandise Import

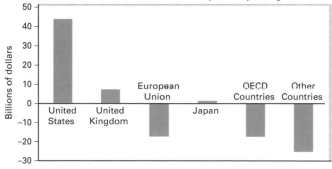

Canada's Merchandise Trade in 2013 by Country or Region

arbitrageur someone who takes advantage of temporary geographic differences in the exchange rate by simultaneously purchasing a currency in one market and selling it in another market

speculator someone who buys or sells foreign exchange in hopes of profiting from fluctuations in the exchange rate over time

purchasing power parity (PPP) theory the idea that the exchange rate between two countries will adjust in the long run to equalize the cost between the countries of a basket of internationally traded goods

flexible exchange rate rate determined in foreign exchange markets by the forces of demand and supply without government intervention

fixed exchange rate rate of exchange between currencies pegged within a narrow range and maintained by the central bank's ongoing purchases and sales of currencies

currency devaluation an increase in the official pegged price of foreign exchange in terms of the domestic currency

currency revaluation a reduction in the official pegged price of foreign exchange in terms of the domestic currency

gold standard an arrangement whereby the currencies of most countries are convertible into gold at a fixed rate

International Monetary Fund (IMF) an international organization that establishes rules for maintaining the international monetary system and makes loans to countries with temporary balance-of-payments problems

managed float system an exchange rate system that combines features of freely floating rates with sporadic intervention by central banks

LO2 Discuss foreign exchange rates and markets.
Under a system of fixed exchange rates, monetary authorities try to stabilize the exchange rate, keeping it between a specified ceiling and floor value. A country may try to hold down the value of its currency, so that exports will be cheaper to foreigners and imports will cost more to domestic consumers. One objective here is to increase domestic production and employment.

The Foreign Exchange Market

The fewer dollars needed to purchase 1 unit of foreign exchange, the lower the price of foreign goods and the greater the quantity of foreign goods demanded. The greater the quantity of foreign goods demanded, the greater the quantity of foreign exchange demanded. Thus the demand curve for foreign exchange slopes downward. An increase in the exchange rate makes Canadian products cheaper for foreigners. The increased demand for Canadian goods implies an increase in the quantity of foreign exchange supplied. The supply curve of foreign exchange slopes upward.

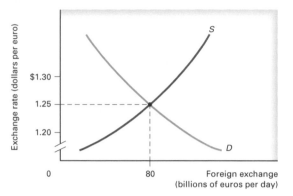

Effect on the Foreign Exchange Market of an Increased Demand for Euros

The intersection of the demand curve for foreign exchange, D, and the supply curve for foreign exchange, S, determines the exchange rate. At an exchange rate of $1.25 per euro, the quantity of euros demanded equals the quantity supplied. An increase in the demand for euros from D to D' increases the exchange rate from $1.25 to $1.27 per euro.

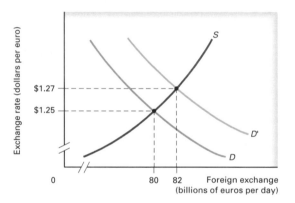

LO3 Define fixed and flexible exchange rates.
Under a system of flexible, or floating, exchange rates, the value of the dollar varies inversely with respect to changes in the demand for foreign exchange and directly with respect to changes in the supply of foreign exchange. If governments, however, try to impose fixed exchange rates, active and ongoing central bank intervention is often necessary to establish and maintain them.

LO4 Describe the development of the international monetary system.
For much of this century, the international monetary system was based on fixed exchange rates. A managed float system has been in effect for the major currencies since the demise of the Bretton Woods system in the early 1970s. Although central banks often try to stabilize exchange rates, fluctuations in rates persist. These fluctuations usually reflect market forces, but they still raise the transaction costs of international trade and finance.

17 International Trade (online)

autarky national self-sufficiency; no economic interaction with foreigners

terms of trade how much of one good exchanges for a unit of another good

world price the price at which a good is traded on the world market; determined by the world demand and world supply for the good

General Agreement on Tariffs and Trade (GATT) an international tariff-reduction treaty adopted in 1947 that resulted in a series of negotiated "rounds" aimed at freer trade; the Uruguay Round created GATT's successor, the World Trade Organization (WTO)

dumping selling a product abroad for less than charged in the home market or for less than the cost of production

Uruguay Round the final multilateral trade negotiation under GATT; this 1994 agreement cut tariffs, formed the World Trade Organization (WTO), and will eventually eliminate quotas

World Trade Organization (WTO) the legal and institutional foundation of the multilateral trading system that succeeded GATT in 1995

North American Free Trade Agreement (NAFTA) a free trade agreement established between Canada, Mexico, and the USA in 1994

LO1 **Describe the gains that trade brings.** The law of comparative advantage says that the individual with the lowest opportunity cost of producing a particular good should specialize in that good. Just as individuals benefit from specialization and exchange, so do states and, indeed, nations. To reap the gains that arise from specialization, countries engage in international trade. Each country specializes in making goods with the lowest opportunity cost. Before countries can trade, however, they must agree on how much of one good exchanges for another (i.e., the terms of trade).

Production Possibilities Frontiers for Canada and Aways without trade (millions of units per day)

Panel (a) shows the Canadian production possibilities frontier; its slope indicates that the opportunity cost of an additional unit of food is 1/2 unit of clothing. Panel (b) shows production possibilities in Aways; an additional unit of food costs 2 units of clothing. Food is produced at a lower opportunity cost in Canada.

Production (and Consumption) Possibility Frontiers with Trade (millions of units per day)

If Aways and Canada can trade at the rate of 1 unit of clothing for 1 unit of food, both can benefit. Consumption possibilities at these terms of trade are shown by the blue lines. Canada was previously producing and consuming C_4. By trading with Aways, it can produce only food and still consume combination C, which has more food and more clothing than C_4. Likewise, Aways can attain preferred combination A by trading its clothing for Canadian food. Both countries are better off as a result of international trade.

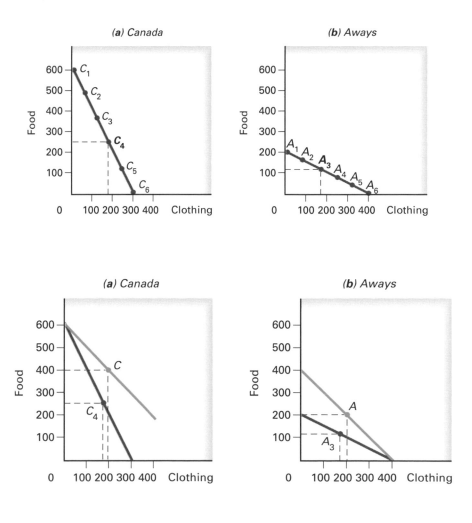

LO2 Discuss the reasons for international specialization.

Countries export products they can produce more cheaply in return for products that are unavailable domestically or are cheaper elsewhere. If production is subject to economies of scale (i.e., if the long-run average cost of production falls as a firm expands its scale of operation), countries can gain from trade if each nation specializes. Consumption patterns differ across countries, and some of this results from differences in tastes, a situation that allows countries to gain from trade.

LO3 Explain trade restrictions and welfare loss. Market

exchange usually generates a surplus, or a bonus, for both consumers and producers. Governments try to regulate surpluses by imposing tariffs (either specific or *ad valorem*) and import quotas, granting export subsidies, or extending low-interest loans to foreign buyers. Loss in Canadian consumer surplus resulting from tariffs is divided three ways: a portion goes to domestic producers; a portion becomes government revenue; and the last portion represents net losses in domestic social welfare. Welfare loss occurs when consumers must pay a higher price for products that could have been imported and sold at a lower price.

Effect of a Tariff

At a world price of $250 per tonne, Canadian consumers demand 32 million tonnes of milk per year, and Canadian producers supply 9 million tonnes per year; the difference is imported. After the imposition of a $300 per tonne tariff, the Canadian price rises to $550 per tonne. Canadian producers increase production to 20 million tonnes, and Canadian consumers cut back to 21 million tonnes. Imports fall to 1 million tonnes. At the higher Canadian price, consumers are worse off; their loss of

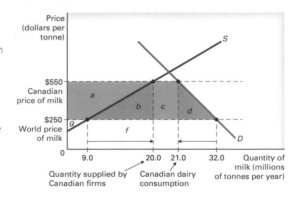

consumer surplus is the sum of areas *a, b, c,* and *d.* Area *a* represents an increase in producer surplus; this area is transferred from consumers to producers. Area *b* reflects the higher marginal cost of domestically producing sugar that could have been produced more cheaply abroad; thus *b* is a net Canadian welfare loss. Area *c* shows government revenue from the tariff. Area *d* reflects the loss of consumer surplus resulting from the drop in consumption. The net welfare loss to the Canadian economy consists of areas *b* and *d.*

Effect of a Quota

In panel (a), *D* is the Canadian demand curve and *S* is the supply curve of Canadian producers. When the government establishes a milk quota of 1 million tonnes per year, the supply curve from both Canadian production and imports becomes horizontal at the world price of $250 per tonne and remains horizontal until the quantity supplied reaches 10 million tonnes. For higher prices, the supply curve equals the horizontal sum of the Canadian supply curve, *S,* and the quota. The new Canadian price, $550 per tonne, is determined by the intersection of the new supply curve, *S′,* with the Canadian demand curve, *D.* Supply curve *S″* is for the non-quota, free-trade supply of milk, most of it being imported. Panel (b) shows the welfare effect of the quota. As a result of the higher Canadian price, consumer surplus is cut by the shaded area. Area *a* represents a transfer from Canadian consumers to Canadian producers. Triangular area *b* reflects a net loss; it represents the amount by which the cost of producing an extra 11 million tonnes of milk in Canada exceeds the cost of buying it from abroad. Rectangular area *c* shows the gain to those who can sell foreign-produced milk at the higher Canadian price instead of the world price. Area *d* also reflects a net loss—a reduction in consumer surplus as consumption falls because of the price increase. Thus, the blue-shaded areas illustrate the loss in consumer surplus that is captured by domestic producers and those who are permitted to fulfill the quota, and the pink-shaded triangles illustrate the net welfare cost of the quota on the Canadian economy.

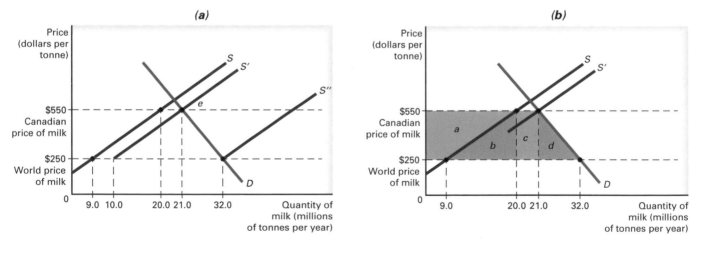

(a)   *(b)*

LO4 List and describe the arguments in favour of trade restrictions.

Arguments used by producer groups to support trade restrictions include promoting national defence, nurturing infant industries, preventing foreign producers from dumping goods in domestic markets, protecting domestic jobs, and allowing declining industries time to wind down and exit the market.

18 Economic Development (online)

developing countries nations typified by high rates of illiteracy, high unemployment, high fertility rates, and exports of primary products; also known as low-income and middle-income economies

industrial market countries economically advanced capitalist countries of Western Europe, North America, Australia, New Zealand, and Japan; also known as developed countries and high-income economies

privatization the process of turning government enterprises into private enterprises

social capital the shared values and trust that promote cooperation in the economy

import substitution a development strategy that emphasizes domestic manufacturing of products that had been imported

export promotion a development strategy that concentrates on producing for the export market

foreign aid an international transfer made on especially favourable terms for the purpose of promoting economic development

LO1 **Describe the worldwide variation in economic vitality.** The most common measure of comparison of standards of living between different countries is output per capita. Developing countries are distinguished by low output per capita, poor health and nutrition, high fertility rates, and poor education.

Share of World Population and Output from High-, Middle-, and Low-Income Economies as of 2009

(a) Share of world population from high-, middle-, and low-income economies

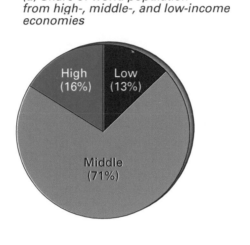

(b) Share of world output from high-, middle-, and low-income economies

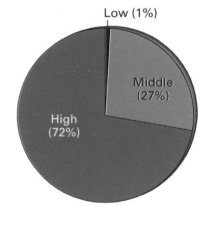

Economic Development Indicators

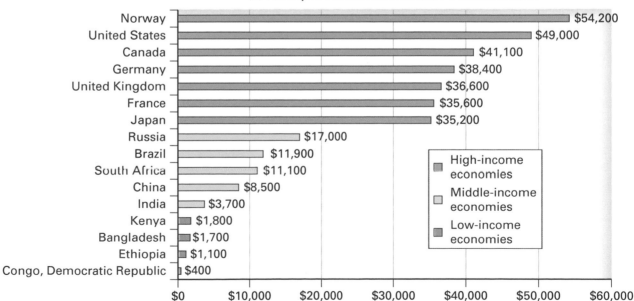

(a) Per-capita income for selected countries in 2011

Country	Per-capita income
Norway	$54,200
United States	$49,000
Canada	$41,100
Germany	$38,400
United Kingdom	$36,600
France	$35,600
Japan	$35,200
Russia	$17,000
Brazil	$11,900
South Africa	$11,100
China	$8,500
India	$3,700
Kenya	$1,800
Bangladesh	$1,700
Ethiopia	$1,100
Congo, Democratic Republic	$400

- High-income economies
- Middle-income economies
- Low-income economies

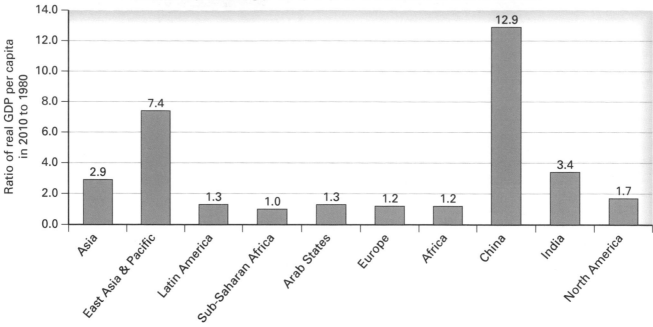

(b) *Ratio of constant dollar or real gross domestic product per capita in 2010 to 1980, measured in purchasing power parity, constant 2005 international dollars*

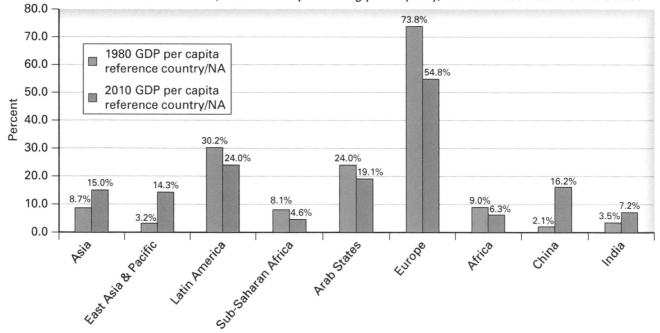

(c) *Ratio of constant dollar or real gross domestic product per capita in reference country to North America in 1980 and 2010, measured in purchasing power parity, constant 2005 international dollars*

(d) *Gap in constant dollar or real gross domestic product per capita between reference country and North America (NA) in 1980 and 2010, measured in purchasing power parity, constant 2005 international dollars*

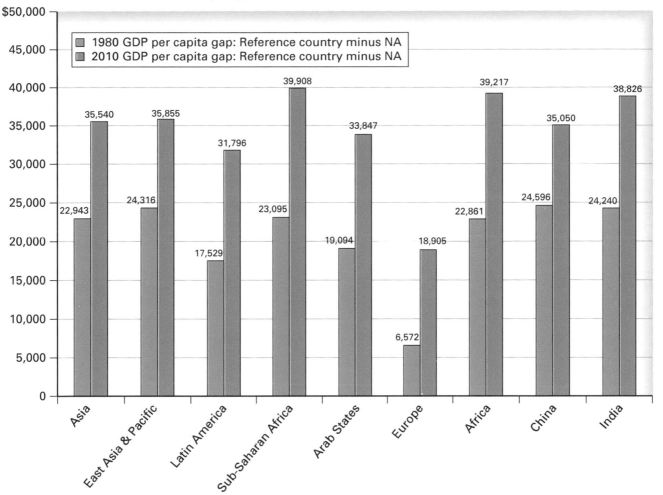

Legend:
- 1980 GDP per capita gap: Reference country minus NA
- 2010 GDP per capita gap: Reference country minus NA

Region	1980	2010
Asia	22,943	35,540
East Asia & Pacific	24,316	35,855
Latin America	17,529	31,796
Sub-Saharan Africa	23,095	39,908
Arab States	19,094	33,847
Europe	6,572	18,905
Africa	22,861	39,217
China	24,596	35,050
India	24,240	38,826

LO2 **Explain why productivity is the key to development.** Labour productivity, measured in terms of output per worker, is by definition low in low-income countries, as it depends on the quality of the labour and other inputs that combine with labour, such as capital and natural resources. The key to a rising standard of living is increased productivity. To foster productivity, developing nations must stimulate investment, support education and training programs, provide sufficient infrastructure, and foster supportive rules of the game.

LO3 **Discuss international trade and development.** Developing countries need to trade with developed countries to acquire the capital and technology that will increase labour productivity. Exports usually generate more than half of the annual flow of foreign exchange in developing countries. Foreign aid and private investment make up the rest. Developing countries often use either import substitution or export promotion strategies to improve production. With import substitution, domestic manufacturers make products that had previously been imported and the government supports them with tariffs and quotas. Export promotion concentrates on producing for the export market. Export promotion has proven generally more successful.

LO4 **Describe the role of foreign aid in economic development.** Foreign aid has been a mixed blessing for most developing countries. In some cases, that aid has helped countries build the roads, bridges, schools, and other capital infrastructure necessary for development. In other cases, foreign aid has simply increased consumption and insulated government from painful but necessary reforms. Worse still, subsidized food from abroad has undermined domestic agriculture, hurting poor farmers.

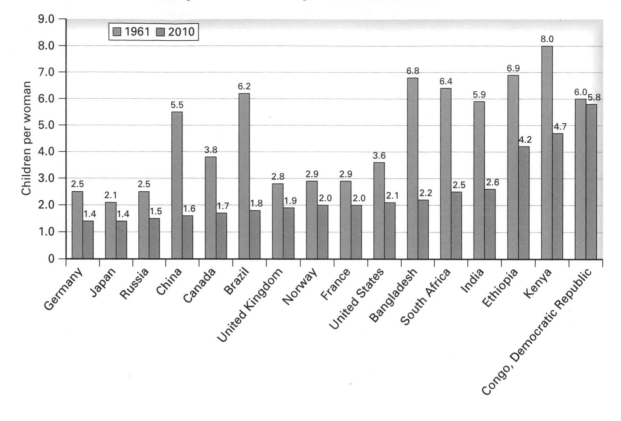

Average Number of Births During a Woman's Lifetime as of 2010

Children per woman

Legend: 1961, 2010

Country	1961	2010
Germany	2.5	1.4
Japan	2.1	1.4
Russia	2.5	1.5
China	5.5	1.6
Canada	3.8	1.7
Brazil	6.2	1.8
United Kingdom	2.8	1.9
Norway	2.9	2.0
France	2.9	2.0
United States	3.6	2.1
Bangladesh	6.8	2.2
South Africa	6.4	2.5
India	5.9	2.6
Ethiopia	6.9	4.2
Kenya	8.0	4.7
Congo, Democratic Republic	6.0	5.8